MANAGEMENT FUNDAMENTALS

Concepts • Applications • Skill Development

Robert N. Lussier, Ph.D.
Springfield College
Springfield, Massachusetts

 South-Western College Publishing
Thomson Learning™

Australia • Canada • Denmark • Japan • Mexico • New Zealand • Philippines
Puerto Rico • Singapore • South Africa • Spain • United Kingdom • United States

Publisher/Team Director:	Dave Shaut
Executive Editor:	John Szilagyi
Developmental Editor:	Leslie Kauffman, Litten Editing and Production
Marketing Manager:	Rob Bloom
Senior Production Editor:	Sharon L. Smith
Production Editor:	Mardell Toomey
Manufacturing Coordinator:	Dana Began Schwartz
Internal Design:	Delgado Design
Cover Design:	A Small Design Studio
Cover Photographer:	© Brad Hood
Photo Researcher:	Cary Benbow
Production House:	nSight, Inc.
Compositor:	Pre-Press Company, Inc.
Printer:	Bawden Printing, Inc.

Library of Congress Cataloging-in-Publication Data
Lussier, Robert N.
   Management Fundamentals/Robert N. Lussier.
     p.   cm.
   Includes bibliographical references and index.
   ISBN 0-324-01337-X (pbk.)
   1. Management.   I. Title.
HD31.L843   1999
658—dc21   99–28301

This book is printed on acid-free paper.

To my wife Marie and our six children:

Jesse, Justin, Danielle, Nicole, Brian, and Renee

Contents in Brief

Contents

PART TWO • PLANNING SKILLS

PART THREE • ORGANIZING SKILLS

PART FOUR • LEADING SKILLS

PART FIVE • CONTROLLING SKILLS

Preface

The world of management has changed and so should how it is taught. Increasing numbers of students want more than just an understanding of the concepts of management. They also want skills they can use in their everyday life at work. It's not enough to learn about management; they want to learn how to *BE* managers. This is why I wrote this book.

Competitive Advantages

I personally developed the total package to have the following competitive advantages:

- The most **"how to manage"** traditional management textbook.
- The most variety (five types) and highest quality **applications** of concepts to develop critical-thinking skills.
- The most variety (four types—55 exercises) and highest quality **skill-development** material to develop skills that can be used on the job.
- The strongest **video** package, including 12 behavior model videos and 9 video cases; more than one per chapter from which to choose.
- The most heavily **referenced** text (957, average of 64 per chapter).
- The most **flexible** package. With all these features, instructors can design the course by selecting the features that meet their needs.
- **Lower price** to students than major competitors.

Integration

Based on my experience teaching management courses for more than 25 years, I created course materials that develop students into managers. As the title of this book implies, it involves a balanced, three-pronged approach to the curriculum:

- a clear understanding of management concepts;
- the application of management concepts for critical thinking in the real world; and
- the development of management skills.

I wrote this text and its supporting ancillary package to support these three distinct but integrated parts. This text follows a management functions approach covering all the traditional concepts and current topics. The applications develop students' critical-thinking skills as they require them to apply specific concepts to their own work experience (part time, summer, or full time), to short situations, and to cases. In addition, this text meets the challenge of the AACSB and SCANS call for skills development. Since I wrote almost every exercise and application in the package, the material is completely integrated to create a seamless experience in the classroom.

Flexibility

Because these three key elements of concepts, applications, and skills are integrated throughout the chapters, you won't find them in broad general sections. However, they are identified clearly and are delineated in some detail for your reference in this preface. Recognizing the diverse needs of students and faculty, they can be used flexibly to fit any classroom. Instructors can create their course by using only features that fit with their objectives.

CONCEPTS

This text covers all key management topics and concepts. It is comprehensive in scope as shown by the detailed learning objectives at the front of each chapter. Each objective is reinforced and identified throughout the chapter. Key terms are placed in the margin to emphasize the vocabulary of management for students.

Systems Integration

Businesses today no longer operate in traditional departments isolated by function. To understand management, students must understand the interrelationships of the various business functions. My text is written from this perspective. The business is shown as a system; managers work within a system of relationships. I focus on viewing the organization as a whole and the interrelationship of its parts. The text emphasizes systems in four ways: (1) the interrelationship of management functions, (2) the interrelationship of the functional areas/departments, (3) systems thinking versus reductionist thinking, and (4) use of traditional systems theory. Figures scattered throughout the text reinforce the integrated learnings through visual appeal.

Current Management Issues

Because this text takes an integrated approach to the subject of management, it is not cluttered with extraneous boxes. Instead, current topics as described by the AACSB, such as globalization, diversity, ethics and social responsibility, quality and TQM, productivity, participative management and teams, and small business, are covered throughout the chapters.

End-of-Chapter Material Reinforcement of Concepts

Each chapter ends with a Chapter Summary and Glossary. The summary reinforces every Learning Objective. The unique glossary aspect of the summary enables the readers to choose the key terms themselves, making it an active glossary. In addition, at least ten Review and Discussion Questions that support and reinforce the key conceptual learnings appear in the chapter.

Test Bank Assessment of Concepts

Over half of the questions in the test bank (print and electronic) assess student knowledge of the managerial concepts taught in the text.

APPLICATIONS

Powerful learning takes place when theory is put within the context of the real world. Using this text, students are challenged to apply the concepts they learn to actual business situations, especially as they have experienced them personally. Students must *think critically* as they apply specific concepts to their own work experience, short situations, and cases.

Opening Case and Internet

At the beginning of each chapter, information about an actual manager and organization is presented. Throughout the chapter, how the manager/organization applies the management concepts is discussed. The student gets a real-world example illustrated extensively throughout the chapter beginning with the opening pages. These cases reflect a mix of large, medium, and small businesses, both for-profit and nonprofit organizations. As appropriate, an Internet address referring students to that company's Web site is provided, allowing students to do further research on the organization. Use of the Internet is optional.

Work Applications

Open-ended questions (approximately ten per chapter) that require the students to explain how the text concepts apply to their own work experience are scattered throughout the chapter. Student experience can be present, past, summer, full-time, or part-time employment. The questions help the students to bridge the gap between theory and their real world.

WORK APPLICATION

1. State the mission of an organization, preferably an organization you work for or have worked for.

APPLYING THE CONCEPT

AC 4–1 Corporate Growth Strategies

Identify each statement by the type of growth strategy it would be making.

a. concentration   d. related diversification
b. forward integration   e. unrelated diversification
c. backward integration

_____ **1.** Sears buys a tool company to make its Craftsman tools.

_____ **2.** General Motors buys the Sea World theme park.

_____ **3.** The Gap opens a new retail store in a mall.

_____ **4.** Lee opens stores to sell its clothes.

_____ **5.** Gateway 2000, a computer manufacturer, manufactures printers.

Applying the Concept

Every chapter contains a series of three to five Applying the Concept boxes that require the student to determine the management concept being illustrated in a specific short example. There are 20 to 25 objective questions per chapter for development of student critical-thinking skills.

End-of-Chapter Case and Internet

Following the review questions, students are presented with another actual manager and organization. The student learns how the manager/organization applies the management concepts from that chapter. Again, the businesses in the cases are large, medium, and small from both the for-profit and nonprofit sectors. Each case is followed by ten multiple-choice questions and open-ended questions. The questions require the student to apply management practices and concepts to the actual organization. As appropriate, an Internet address referring students to that company's Web site is provided, allowing students to do further research on the organization. Use of the Internet is optional.

Appendix: How to Research Case Material Using the Internet

Students familiar and not so familiar with the Internet will find this appendix a practical tool for using the Internet to gain more information about various companies. Whether researching the companies and addresses listed with the text cases or completing other class projects, this short guide shows students how to find the most current information on businesses in our information age.

Businesslink Video Cases

Student learning is enhanced by seeing actual managers tackling real management problems within their workplaces. The Lussier package contains nine video cases provided free to adopters. Each video case centers around the decisions made by managers from the topic of a given chapter. All videos pose critical-thinking questions to be answered by students. BusinessLink Video Cases are integrated at the end of nine chapters. All BusinessLink Video Cases have supporting print material for both instructors and students.

Test Bank (Assessing Application Ability) and Instructor's Manual Reinforcement of Applications

The test bank includes application questions that include true/false and multiple choice questions, learning objectives questions, work application questions, questions similar to "applying the concept" questions, review and discussion questions, and skills questions. The Instructor's Manual contains detailed answers for all of the application features.

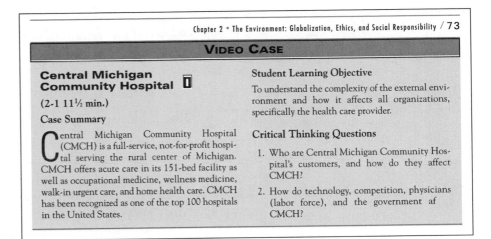

Chapter 2 • The Environment: Globalization, Ethics, and Social Responsibility / 73

VIDEO CASE

Central Michigan Community Hospital

(2-1 11½ min.)

Case Summary

Central Michigan Community Hospital (CMCH) is a full-service, not-for-profit hospital serving the rural center of Michigan. CMCH offers acute care in its 151-bed facility as well as occupational medicine, wellness medicine, walk-in urgent care, and home health care. CMCH has been recognized as one of the top 100 hospitals in the United States.

Student Learning Objective

To understand the complexity of the external environment and how it affects all organizations, specifically the health care provider.

Critical Thinking Questions

1. Who are Central Michigan Community Hospital's customers, and how do they affect CMCH?

2. How do technology, competition, physicians (labor force), and the government af CMCH?

SKILLS

The difference between learning about management and learning to be a manager is the acquisition of skills. This text focuses on skill development so students can use what they learn on the job. The skill material is integrated throughout the text, but instructors can choose how to incorporate the material into their classroom experience—individually or as groups, inside the class or as outside group projects. Instructors can also determine the extent to which they want to use behavior modeling as the basis for skill development in their classroom, if at all.

I use the term "skill building" in this text only if students can actually develop a skill that can be used on the job. The features listed on the next page include true skill building, such as step-by-step models, skill-building exercises, and behavior model videos. Other features support skill building, such as self-assessments and group exercises. Students will know they are working on a skill when they see this icon in the margin.

skillbuilder

Skill Development Goals

Following a chapter's Learning Objectives, the chapter's Skill Development Goals are listed. Specific skills that can be learned through the use of the chapter and its exercises are detailed. The goals identify the management function, skill, role, and SCANS competencies taught in that chapter.

step 1.

Step-by-Step Models

The book contains 25 detailed sets of how-to steps for handling day-to-day management functions. They are integrated into the context of the chapter or skill-building exercise being taught. For example, models teach students how to set objectives and priorities, how to handle a complaint, how to discipline an employee, etc. This feature directly teaches students how to be managers.

Skill-Building Exercises

Each chapter contains at least one Skill-Building Exercise, all of which have been class-tested to be the best found in any text in the market. Full support of 37 activities can be found in the Instructor's Manual including detailed information, timing, answers, etc. All exercises and their use are optional in the classroom. There are three primary types of exercise. Each type of exercise is identified by its own icon.

I

A. Individual Focus: Eighteen exercises (48 percent) are those in which participants are required to make individual decisions prior to or during class. These answers can be shared in class for discussion, or the instructor may elect to go over recommended answers.

G

B. Group Focus: 8 exercises (22 percent) are those in which participants discuss the material presented and may select group answers.

R

C. Role Play Focus: 11 exercises (30 percent) are those in which participants are presented with a model and given the opportunity to use the model, usually in groups of three.

Behavior Model Videos

To reinforce the development of skills for students, the Lussier package includes 12 Behavior Model Videos, unique to the Management curriculum. The videos demonstrate managers successfully performing common management functions such as handling complaints, delegating tasks, conducting job interviews, etc. Students learn from watching the videos and/or using them in conjunction with Skill-Building Exercises. Material in the text integrates the videos into the chapters. Ideas for using all videos are detailed in the Instructor's Manual.

Self-Assessment Exercises

Scattered throughout the text are 18 Self-Assessment Exercises. Students complete these assessments to gain personal knowledge of self. All information for completing and scoring the assessments is contained within the text. Self-knowledge leads students to an understanding of how they can and will operate as managers in the real world. Many of the assessments are tied to exercises within the book, thus enhancing the impact of the activities.

Exercises

Many chapters contain exercises that enhance classroom learning but are not directly tied to developing skills. These exercises tend to center around group projects and classroom discussions for the creation of an active learning environment.

Test Bank (Assessing Skill Development) and Instructor's Manual Reinforcement of Skills

Every Skill-Building Exercise in the text has reinforcement and assessment questions for it in the corresponding test bank chapter, a unique feature of the Lussier text package. The Instructor's Manual contains detailed answers for all of the skills features in the text, including timing, information, answers, logistics for instructor use, and follow-up questions for student debriefing. The manual also explains how to test on skill building.

---

24 / Chapter 1 • Managing

BEHAVIOR MODEL VIDEO EXERCISE 1-1

Behavior Model Video 1–1 (11 minutes), Situational Management, shows Laura, a bank branch manager, who manages tellers who are not collecting fees. Laura's boss, Celeste, discusses the situation with her. The video illustrates the four management styles, explained in Skill-Building Exercise 1–1.

Objective
To better understand the four situational management styles.

Procedure 1 (10–20 minutes)
The instructor shows Behavior Model Video 1–1. As you view each of the four scenes, identify the four situational management styles and select the one being used by the manager.

Scene 1. __   a. autocratic (S1A)
Scene 2. __   b. consultative (S2C)
Scene 3. __   c. participative (S3P)
Scene 4. __   d. empowerment (S4E)

After viewing each of the four scenes, identify/match the style used by the manager by placing the letter of the style on the scene line.

Option A: View all four scenes and identify the style used by the manager. After viewing all four scenes, discuss them. The correct answers are given in the video.

Option B: After each scene, the class discusses the style used by the manager. The instructor states the correct answer after each of the four scenes.

Procedure 2 (2–5 minutes)
Select the one style that you would use in this situation. Are other styles also appropriate? Which style would you not use (not appropriate) for this situation? Next to each style listed above, write the letter A for appropriate or N for not appropriate.

Discussion
Option A: In groups of four to six, answer the following questions.
Option B: As a class answer the following questions.
1. Which style(s) are not appropriate to use in this situation?
2. Which styles(s) are appropriate to use in this situation?
3. Is there one style most appropriate in this situation? If yes, which one?

Conclusion
The instructor may make concluding remarks.

Application (2–4 minutes)
What did I learn from this exercise? How will I use this knowledge in the future?

_____

Sharing
Volunteers give their answers to the application section.

ANCILLARY SUPPORT

Just as businesses must be integrated across functions and departments for success, text and ancillary material must also integrate to create the optimum student learning experience. Many of our key supplements have been described to you as part of the support for our three-pronged approach to the management curriculum. The list below describes all elements of the text package to create a successful classroom environment. I personally wrote the Instructor's Manual, wrote and reviewed much of the test bank, and edited every Behavior Model Video script to ensure the development of the best integrated learning features for management.

Instructor's Manual

I wrote the Instructor's Manual to ensure that every faculty member would receive complete integrated support for teaching. The manual contains the following for each chapter of the book: a detailed outline for lecture enhancement, Work Application Student Sample Answers, Review and Discussion Question Answers, Applying the Concept Answers, Case and Video Case Question Answers, Instructions on Use of Videos, and Skill-Building Exercise and other Exercise Ideas (including set-up and timing). The Instructor's Manual also includes ideas on how to use the special features of the text in the classroom with emphasis on creating an interactive learning environment.

Test Bank

A unique feature of the text package is the test bank structured around the three-pronged approach of the book: concepts, applications, and skills. Questions assessing each aspect of student learning in these three areas are delineated and included for each chapter. No other book on the market attempts to assess student skill development.

Thomson Learning Testing Tools

All test questions are available in electronic Windows-based format for automatic test generation.

PowerPoint

Teaching transparencies are available in electronic format for a more flexible and professional presentation in the classroom.

Behavior Model Videos

To reinforce the development of skills for students, the Lussier package includes 12 Behavior Model Videos, unique to the Management curriculum.

The videos demonstrate managers successfully performing common management functions such as handling complaints, delegating tasks, conducting job interviews, etc. Students learn from watching the videos and/or using them in conjunction with Skill-Building Exercises. Material in the text integrates the videos into the chapters. Ideas for using all videos are detailed in the Instructor's Manual.

BusinessLink Video Cases

Accompanying and integrated within the text are 9 BusinessLink Video Cases. Each case centers around topics key to management understanding within a profile of a real business organization solving real-world problems. They create added variety in the classroom presentation and stimulate students to learn about organizations, teams, and management.

SUMMARY OF KEY INNOVATIONS

My goal is to make both students and instructors successful in the classroom by providing learning features that not only teach about management but also help students become managers. Here are the special ways in which we do it:

- The three-pronged approach to the curriculum: concepts, applications, skills.
- Assessment of this approach through a three-section test bank: concepts, applications, skills.
- Flexibility—use any or all of the features that work for you!
- Unique skill-building exercises that develop skills for use on the job.
- An Internet appendix that provides helpful information on using the Internet.
- An unsurpassed video package: 12 Behavior Model Videos; 9 BusinessLink Video Cases.

ACKNOWLEDGMENTS

The authorship of a publishing project of this magnitude is only one aspect of a complex process. Many hardworking individuals gave great effort to create this text and package. I wish to express my gratitude to many of these key contributors, especially the fine people at South-Western College Publishing/ITP. Having worked with a number of major publishers over the years, South-Western is the best. Specifically, I would like to thank my executive editor, John Szilagyi; my marketing manager, Rob Bloom; my developmental editor, Leslie Kauffman; my production editors, Mardell Toomey and Sharon Smith; my art director, Jennifer Mayhall; and my media technology editor, Kevin von Gillern. My secretary, Mechele Holbrook, also provided great support.

I wish to thank my mentor and coauthor of many publications, Joel Corman, for his advice and encouragement during and after my graduate education at Suffolk University. I also wish to thank Dr. Abbas Nadim, Dr. David Morris, and Dr. Judith Neal, doctoral faculty at the University of New Haven. Thanks, Dr. Nadim (Ph.D., Wharton School; protégé of Russell Ackoff), for educating me in the ways of systems theory, which is used throughout this book. Thanks, too, to Dr. Morris for influencing the development of more figures that integrate the material through the use of visuals.

In addition, the reviewers of the project provided me with great ideas and inspiration for writing. The reviewers overwhelmingly confirmed the basic philosophical premise behind the book—teaching students how to *BE* managers—and I am very grateful for their valuable input:

James O. Armstrong II	John Tyler Community College
Harold Babson	Columbus State Community College
Brenda Barfield	Surry Community College
C. Richard Bartlett	Muskingum Area Technical College
Verona K. Beguin	Eastern Oregon State College
Julia G. Derrick	Brevard Community College
Joe Dobson	Western Illinois University
Charles Peter Duffy	Iona College
Michael R. Evans	Appalachian State University
James Genseal	Joliet Junior College
Nancy B. Higgins	Montgomery College
Anna M. McCormick	West Virginia University Institute of Technology
Tom D. McFarland	South College
Nancy Ray-Mitchell	McLennan Community College
Duane Schecter	Muskegon Community College
James Thornton	Champlain College
Randall E. Wade	Rogue Community College
Dave Wilderman	Wabash Valley College

I hope everyone who uses this text enjoys teaching from these materials as I do.

Robert N. Lussier
Springfield College

PHOTO CREDITS

About the Author

Robert N. Lussier is a professor of management at Springfield College and has taught management for more than 25 years. He has developed some innovative and widely copied methods for applying concepts and developing skills that can be used in one's personal and professional life. He is also the director of Israel Programs and goes twice a year to visit the Branch and to teach courses. Other international experience includes Namibia and South Africa.

Dr. Lussier is a prolific writer, with over 150 publications to his credit. His articles have been published in the *Academy of Entrepreneurship Journal*, *Business Horizons*, *Business Journal*, *Entrepreneurial Executive*, *Journal of Business & Entrepreneurship*, *Journal of Business Strategies*, *Journal of Small Business Management*, *Journal of Small Business Strategy*, *SAM Advanced Management Journal*, and others.

When not writing, he consults to a wide array of commercial and nonprofit organizations. In fact, some of the material in the book was developed for such clients as Baystate Medical Center, Coca-Cola, Friendly Ice Cream, Institute of Financial Education, Mead, Monsanto, Smith & Wesson, the Social Security Administration, the Visiting Nurses Assoc., and YMCAs.

Dr. Lussier holds a bachelor of science in business administration from Salem State College, two master's degrees in business and education from Suffolk University, and a doctorate in management from the University of New Haven.

1 Managing

Learning Objectives

After studying this chapter, you should be able to:

1. Describe a manager's responsibility.
2. List and explain the three management skills.
3. List and explain the four management functions.
4. Explain the three management roles: interpersonal, informational, and decisional.
5. List the hierarchy of management levels.
6. Describe the three different types of managers: general, functional, and project.
7. Describe the differences among management levels in terms of skills needed and functions performed.
8. Define the following **key terms** (in order of appearance in the chapter):

manager	management functions
manager's resources	planning
performance	organizing
management skills	leading
technical skills	controlling
human and communication skills	management role categories
conceptual and decision-making skills	levels of management
	types of managers

*skillbuilder

1. You should develop your situational management skills (Skill-Building Exercise 1–1).

   To be more specific, you should develop your conceptual and decision-making management skills by analyzing situations and selecting the appropriate management style that best meets the needs of the situation. Using the most appropriate management style for a given situation will help you understand the appropriate human and communication skills to use for the situation. The primary management function skill developed is leadership. The primary management roles developed through this exercise are the interpersonal role and the decisional role. The SCANS skill competencies of information and systems, as well as basic and thinking foundation skills, are developed.

The Gap, Inc., started with a single Gap store on Ocean Avenue in San Francisco in 1969. Within 25 years it grew to become a leader in retailing with over 1,500 stores. The Gap is a specialty retailer that operates stores selling casual apparel for men, women, and children under five brand names: Gap, Gap Kids, babyGap, Old Navy, and Banana Republic. Some of the Gap stores combine these product lines, and others are single-line stores. Personal care products and shoes have been introduced at The Gap to provide customers with still more reasons to shop the stores.

Stores in the United States are located in 48 states, including all of the 50 largest metropolitan statistical areas. Gap international stores are in Puerto Rico, Canada, the United Kingdom, France, Japan, Wales, and Scotland. Virtually all stores are leased, and no stores are franchised or operated by others.

The Gap is customer-driven. In other words, all Gap employees focus on the customer as the most important part of the job. Evidence of this dedication to customers is The Gap's policy of greeting each customer at the door to make him or her feel welcome and to determine how the employees can help the customer. All store managers work with customers and are evaluated and promoted according to how well they deal with customers.

The Gap offers college graduates challenging management careers and internship positions to college students. It has a promotion policy that enables the talented, harder-working managers to continually advance. Those who are willing to relocate increase the speed at which they climb the corporate ladder. Important management practices at The Gap include goal setting and training.[1]

For current information on The Gap, use Internet address **http://www.gap.com**. For ideas on using the Internet, see Appendix B.

Organizations are looking for employees with good general management skills[2] because enlightened management is rare in conventional practice.[3] Managers have a direct impact on employee satisfaction. Research has shown that most people who are not happy on the job are actually dissatisfied with their managers rather than the job itself.[4] Think about the jobs you have had that you liked most and least. Was management a determining factor in your selection? This book was written so that you can learn how to be a good manager by developing management skills. Regardless of whether you become a manager, the skills you will develop through this course apply to both your personal life and professional life. In this chapter you will learn what a manager is, what it takes to be a successful manager, what managers do, and differences among managers.

WHAT IS MANAGEMENT?

An Interview with a Manager

This interview with Bonnie Castonguary, a store manager at The Gap, provides an overview of the manager's job and responsibility.

Author: When did you start with The Gap and what was your progression to your present job as store manager?

Bonnie: I started in November of 1990 as a store manager in training. In September of 1991 I replaced a woman on maternity leave as acting store manager. In January of 1992 I had my first store. In August of 1993 and October of 1994 I was promoted to larger stores with more sales volume. In 1997, I was promoted to manager of The Gap outlet store in Clinton. My next career advancement is to general manager whereby I would still be in one store, but I would assist the district manager by overseeing other stores in my district.

Author: Briefly describe your job.

Bonnie: The following general summary is taken from "The Gap, Inc. Position Overview Store Management" form, which is two pages long. It begins with the general summary and is followed by details of each part of the summary for each level of management.

The Store Management team manages the sales, operations, and personnel functions of the store to ensure maximum profitability and compliance with company procedures. The team includes Assistant Managers, Associate Managers, the Store Manager, and/or the General Manager.

In Figure 1–1, Bonnie describes a typical Monday.

Figure 1–1
A Day in the Life of a Manager

8:00 A.M.
- Enter the store and walk the sales floor to ensure a proper close took place the night before.
- Project the payroll cost for the week as a percentage of my forecasted sales, and call it in.
- Perform opening procedures on the controller (computer that records sales transactions and inventory count for all cash registers in the store).

8:30 A.M.
- Walk the sales floor with visual staff and assign projects for them to create new displays for merchandise during the day (create a "to do" list for employees and myself).

9:00 A.M.
- Before the store opens, call voice mail for messages left by other store managers or my boss, the district manager.
- Make business telephone calls for the day.

9:30 A.M.
- Assign sales associates to store zones.
- Put money in computer cash register drawers.

10:00 A.M.
- Open the store.
- Make sure sales associates are zoned out on the floor for proper floor coverage.
- Make sure everyone who enters the store is greeted and has his or her needs determined.
- Provide floor coverage. (Help out as needed—greet customers, assist customers with sales, stock shelves, assist at the changing room, etc.)

12:00 P.M.
- Do business analysis for previous month from operating statement and gross margin reports.

12:30 P.M.
- Provide floor coverage as needed for staggered employee breaks.

1:30–2:30 P.M. My break then:
- Prepare customer request transfers (merchandise our store has but other stores do not have) to be delivered. Enter transfers into computer and get merchandise.

3:00 P.M.
- Leave for district meeting.

3:15 P.M.
- Drop off transfers and pick up another store manager; continue on to district meeting.

4:00 P.M.
Meeting is conducted by district manager with the seven general and store managers. Meeting begins with discussion of the following topics and ends with a walk-through of the store at which the meeting is held.
- Previous week's sales, previous week's payroll, payroll projections for next month (cost as a percentage of sales), cleanliness, and standards of the stores.
- New information items, mail, general discussion, questions, etc.
- Store walk-through. During a walk-through, the host store manager discusses new display ideas that the other store managers may want to use. In addition, the other store managers give the host manager ideas for improving the store visualization. In other words, this is a time to share ideas that will help all team members in the Gap district.

6:00 P.M.
- Call my store to see how sales are going for the day, then leave for home.

Author: What do you like best about being a manager?

Bonnie: You don't have time to get bored on the job because you are always doing something different.

Author: What do you like least about being a manager?

Bonnie: Dealing with difficult performance problems of employees and customers, and always being on call. When I'm not at work, I'm still on call when there are problems at the store. This could mean going to the store at 2:00 A.M. to shut off the alarm.

Author: What advice would you give to college graduates without any full-time work experience who are interested in a management career after graduation?

Bonnie: You need to be dedicated and hard working. You must take great pride in your work. You have to be willing to take on a lot of responsibility. Remember, your employees are always looking to you to set the example; when you make a mistake (which you will do), it affects your staff. You have to be a self-starter. As a store manager you have to motivate employees, but your boss is not around much to motivate you.

The Manager's Responsibility

1. Describe a manager's responsibility.

manager
The individual responsible for achieving organizational objectives through efficient and effective utilization of resources.

manager's resources
Human, financial, physical, and informational resources.

A **manager** *is responsible for achieving organizational objectives through efficient and effective utilization of resources.* A few terms in this definition should be explained. *Efficient* refers to doing things right, to maximizing the utilization of resources. *Effective* refers to doing the right thing in order to attain the objective, or the degree to which a manager achieves objectives. *The* **manager's resources** *include human, financial, physical, and informational.*

Human Resources. Human resources are people. Managers are responsible for getting the job done through employees. People are the manager's most valuable resource.[5] Note that in the day in a life of a manager, Bonnie did not attempt to create all the visual displays herself. She accomplished this objective through her staff. As a manager you should hire the best people available. These employees must then be trained to use the organization's other resources to maximize productivity. Throughout this book we will focus on working with employees to accomplish organizational objectives.

Financial Resources. Most managers have a budget stating how much it should cost to operate their department/store for a set period of time. In other words, a budget defines the financial resources available. The manager is responsible for seeing that the department does not waste any of the available resources.[6] Bonnie placed cash in the drawers before opening the store. She also projected payroll cost as a percentage of sales to reach profit objectives. Bonnie is responsible for maximizing profitability at The Gap.

Physical Resources. Getting the job done requires effective and efficient use of physical resources. In a retail store like Bonnie's, this includes the store building, the merchandise to be sold, the fixtures that display the merchandise, and the computer used to record sales and inventory. It also involves the inventory in the back room and supplies such as price tags, hangers, charge slips, and so on. Managers are responsible for keeping equipment in working condition and for making sure that necessary materials and supplies are available. Deadlines might be missed and present sales and future business lost if physical resources are not available and used and maintained properly.

Informational Resources. Managers need information from a variety of sources.[7] The controller (computer) is used to store and retrieve information within and among Gap stores. When Bonnie was checking her voice mail, making calls, giving employees directions on setting up displays, and attending the district meeting with store walk-through, she was using informational resources. Sharing information with teammates will influence your success as a manager.[8] Information continues to increase in importance as a means of increasing the speed of doing business in a competitive global environment.

The level of organizational **performance** *is based on how effectively and efficiently managers utilize resources to achieve objectives.* Managers are responsible for and evaluated on how well they meet organizational objectives through effective and efficient utilization of resources. The current trend is to require managers to achieve objectives with fewer resources.[9] Today's managers are expected to work as team leaders with a diversity of team members.[10]

WHAT DOES IT TAKE TO BE A SUCCESSFUL MANAGER?

Now that you have an idea of what management is, you will learn some of the qualities and skills necessary to be a successful manager.

Management Qualities

Over the years, numerous researchers have attempted to answer the question, "What does it take to be a successful manager?" In a *Wall Street Journal* Gallup survey, 782 top executives in 282 large corporations were asked, "What are the most important traits for success as a supervisor?"[11] Before you read what these executives stated, complete Self-Assessment Exercise 1–1 to find out if you have what it takes to become a successful manager.

The executives in the Gallup survey identified integrity, industriousness, and the ability to get along with people as the three most important traits for successful managers. Other traits included business knowledge, intelligence, leadership ability, education, sound judgment, ability to communicate, flexibility, and ability to plan and set objectives. The executives also identified seven traits that lead to failure in a manager: having a limited viewpoint, not being able to understand others, not being able to work

WORK APPLICATION

1. Describe the specific resources used by your present/past boss. Give the manager's job title and department.

performance
Means of evaluating how effectively and efficiently managers use resources to achieve objectives.

WORK APPLICATION

2. Identify a specific manager, preferably one who is or was your boss, and explain what makes him or her successful or unsuccessful. Give examples.

Self-Assessment Exercise 1-1

Management Traits Questionnaire

The following 15 questions relate to some of the qualities needed to be a successful manager. Rate yourself on each item by placing the numbers 1–4 that best describes your behavior for each item.

4—The statement is not very descriptive of me.

3—The statement is somewhat descriptive of me.

2—The statement is descriptive of me.

1—The statement is very descriptive of me.

_____ 1. I enjoy working with people. I prefer to work with others rather than working alone.

_____ 2. I can motivate others. I can get people to do things they may not want to do.

_____ 3. I am well liked. People enjoy working with me.

_____ 4. I am cooperative. I strive to help the team do well, rather than to be the star.

_____ 5. I am a leader. I enjoy teaching, coaching, and instructing people.

_____ 6. I want to be successful. I do things to the best of my ability to be successful.

_____ 7. I am a self-starter. I get things done without having to be told to do them.

_____ 8. I am a problem-solver. If things aren't going the way I want them to, I take corrective action to meet my objectives.

_____ 9. I am self-reliant. I don't need the help of others.

_____ 10. I am hard working. I enjoy working and getting the job done.

_____ 11. I am trustworthy. If I say I will do something by a set time, I do it.

_____ 12. I am loyal. I do not do or say things to intentionally hurt my friends, relatives, or coworkers.

_____ 13. I can take criticism. If people tell me negative things about myself, I give them serious thought and change when appropriate.

_____ 14. I am honest. I do not lie, steal, or cheat.

_____ 15. I am fair. I treat people equally. I don't take advantage of others.

_____ Total score (add numbers on lines 1–15; the range of your score is 15–60)

In general, the lower your score, the better your chances of being a successful manager. If you are interested in being a manager someday, you can work on improving your integrity (items 11–15), industriousness (items 6–10), and ability to get along with people (items 1–5) both in this course and in your personal life. As a start, review the traits listed here. Which ones are strongest and weakest? Think about how you can improve in the weaker areas, or preferably, write out a plan.

with others, being indecisive, lacking initiative, not assuming responsibility, and lacking integrity. Other failure traits included lack of ability to change, reluctance to think independently, inability to solve problems, and desire for popularity.

Management Skills

Today, there is a need for good management skills.[12] Experience, training, and education in courses similar to this one will help you develop good management skills.[13] Because management skills are so important, the focus of this book is on skill building. The key to success is perseverance through hard work. If you work at it, you can develop your management skills through this course. The concepts in this book also can and should be used in your daily life.

Robert Katz conducted a study over 20 years ago that is still widely quoted today. Katz identified three skills needed to be an effective administrator: technical, human, and conceptual.[14] Over the years other researchers have added administrative, communication, political, and problem-solving and decision-making skills. For our purposes, **management skills** *include (1) technical, (2) human and communication, and (3) conceptual and decision-making skills.*

Technical Skills. **Technical skills** *are the ability to use methods and techniques to perform a task.* When managers are working on budgets, they may need computer skills in spreadsheet software such as Lotus 1-2-3 or Excel. Bonnie needs computer skills to open the store, record transfers, and record sales. Most employees are promoted to their first management position primarily because of their technical skills. Technical skills vary widely from job to job;[15] therefore, this course does not focus on developing technical skills. However, in Chapters 5 and 14 you will learn to use planning and decision-making tools and financial and budgetary tools.

Human and Communication Skills. **Human and communication skills** *are the ability to work with people in teams.* Without communication skills, you cannot be an effective team member or manager.[16] Today, employees want to participate in management.[17] Therefore, there is an increase in the use of teams with an emphasis on good human relations.[18] Another area of human skills includes political skills. How well you get along with employees will affect your management success. You do not have to like people—although it does help—to have a good working relationship. Most of Bonnie's day was spent working with employees and customers. The Gap position overview for store managers states that excellent communication skills are needed to be a manager. Throughout this book, you will learn how to work with a diversity of people, develop human resource skills, improve communication skills, motivate and lead others, manage teams, develop power and political skills, manage conflict, and improve employee performance.

Conceptual and Decision-Making Skills. **Conceptual and decision-making skills** *are the ability to understand abstract ideas and select alternatives to solve problems.* Another term for conceptual skills is *systems thinking,* or the ability to understand an organization/department as a whole and the interrelationship among its parts. As businesses compete in a continually

2. List and explain the three management skills.

management skills
(1) technical, (2) human and communication, and (3) conceptual and decision-making.

technical skills
The ability to use methods and techniques to perform a task.

human and communication skills
The ability to work with people in teams.

conceptual and decision-making skills
The ability to understand abstract ideas and select alternatives to solve problems.

Figure 1–2
Management Skills

WORK
APPLICATION

3. Select a manager,
preferably one who
is or was your boss,
and state the specific
technical, human,
communication, con-
ceptual, and decision-
making skills he or
she uses on the job.

diversifying global environment, creative analysis and judgment, currently referred to as *critical thinking*, are needed to resolve conflict and solve problems.[19]
An important part of Bonnie's job is to make decisions about what merchandise to carry, how to display the merchandise, and which people to hire.
Throughout this book, you will learn how to develop your conceptual and decision-making skills. For a review of the management skills, see Figure 1–2.

Skills and Tasks for Jobs: SCANS

The U.S. Secretary of Commerce's Commission on Achieving Necessary
Skills (SCANS) conducted a study to determine the necessary skills and
tasks for jobs. The commission members identified five competencies
(resources, interpersonal skills, information, systems, and technology) and a
three-part foundation (basic skills, thinking skills, and personal qualities) of
skills for personal qualities needed for solid job performance. A more detailed explanation of the skills identified by SCANS will be presented later
in this chapter.

The Ghiselli Study

Professor Edwin Ghiselli conducted a study to determine the traits necessary
for success as a manager.[20] Ghiselli identified six traits as important,
although not all are necessary for
success. These six traits, in reverse
order of importance, include (6)
initiative, (5) self-assurance, (4)
decisiveness, (3) intelligence, (2)
need for occupational achievement, and (1) supervisory ability.
The number-one trait, supervisory
ability, includes skills in planning,
organizing, leading, and controlling. Ghiselli's four areas of supervisory ability are more commonly
referred to as the *management
functions,* which you will learn
about in the next section.

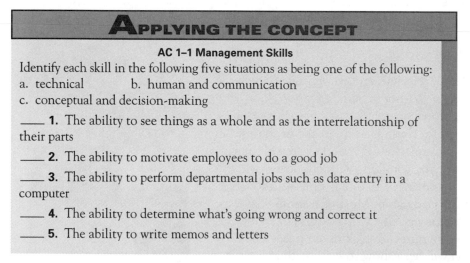

APPLYING THE CONCEPT

AC 1–1 Management Skills
Identify each skill in the following five situations as being one of the following:
a. technical   b. human and communication
c. conceptual and decision-making

_____ **1.** The ability to see things as a whole and as the interrelationship of
their parts

_____ **2.** The ability to motivate employees to do a good job

_____ **3.** The ability to perform departmental jobs such as data entry in a
computer

_____ **4.** The ability to determine what's going wrong and correct it

_____ **5.** The ability to write memos and letters

WHAT DO MANAGERS DO?

Having discussed what management is, and what it takes to be a successful
manager, our next question is, "What do managers do?" In this section, you
will learn about the four functions performed by managers and the three
roles that all managers play.

Management Functions

As stated earlier, managers get the job done through others. A manager plans, organizes, leads, and controls resources to achieve organizational objectives.[21] If managers run a machine, wait on customers, or put up a store display, they are performing nonmanagement or employee functions. *The four* **management functions** *include the following:*

- *Planning*
- *Organizing*
- *Leading*
- *Controlling*

3. List and explain the four management functions.

management functions
Planning, organizing, leading, and controlling

This book is organized around the four management functions. Each of the four management functions serves as a title for a part of the book, and three to five chapters are devoted to developing skills in each functional area. Here, and in later chapters, each function is explained separately. However, you should realize that the four functions are a systems process; they are interrelated and are often performed simultaneously.

Planning. Planning is typically the starting point in the management process. To be successful, organizations need a great deal of planning.[22] People in organizations need goals and plans to achieve them. **Planning** *is the process of setting objectives and determining in advance exactly how the objectives will be met.* Managers commonly have to schedule employees and the work to be performed and develop budgets. Bonnie has to schedule employees to work and select merchandise to be sold. At 8:30 A.M. Bonnie planned what displays the visual staff would create. The ability to perform the planning function is based on conceptual and decision-making management skills.

planning
The process of setting objectives and determining in advance exactly how the objectives will be met.

Organizing. To be successful requires organization. A manager must also design and develop an organizational system to implement the plans.[23] **Organizing** *is the process of delegating and coordinating tasks and resources to achieve objectives.* Managers allocate and arrange resources. An important part of coordinating human resources is to assign people to various jobs and tasks. At 8:30 A.M. Bonnie delegated the responsibility to develop the merchandise displays to the visual staff. At 9:30 A.M. Bonnie assigned sales associates to zones to fill the sales floor. An important part of organizing, sometimes listed as a separate function, is staffing. *Staffing is the process of selecting, training, and evaluating employees;* Bonnie has full responsibility for staffing her store. The ability to organize is based on a blend of conceptual and decision-making skills and human and communication skills.

organizing
The process of delegating and coordinating tasks and resources to achieve objectives.

Leading. In addition to planning and organizing, a manager must work with employees as they perform their tasks on a daily basis. **Leading** *is the process of influencing employees to work toward achieving objectives.* Managers must communicate the objectives to employees and motivate them to

leading
The process of influencing employees to work toward achieving objectives.

achieve the objectives.[24] An important part of Bonnie's job involves communicating with, motivating, and leading individuals and teams. Bonnie coaches her employees as they perform their jobs. The ability to lead is based on human and communication skills.

Controlling. Only three out of ten people do the things they say they will do.[25] Therefore, objectives will not be met without follow-through. **Controlling** *is the process of establishing and implementing mechanisms to ensure that objectives are achieved.* An important part of controlling is measuring progress toward the achievement of the objective and taking corrective action when necessary.[26] Throughout the day Bonnie was controlling. She started her day by checking the previous night's closing and turning on the computer. From 10:00 to 12:00 and 12:30 to 1:30 Bonnie was making sure there was full floor coverage at all locations, and filling in where needed to maintain coverage. The ability to control is based on conceptual and decision-making and human and communication skills.

controlling
The process of establishing and implementing mechanisms to ensure that objectives are achieved.

Nonmanagement Functions

All managers perform the four functions of management as they get the work done through employees. However, many managers also perform nonmanagement, or employee, functions as well. For example, Bonnie spent from 10:00 to 12:00 and 12:30 to 1:30 primarily waiting on customers, which is an employee or nonmanagement function. If Bonnie personally made a photocopy of the business analysis she was working on, this would be a nonmanagement function as well. Many managers, like Bonnie, are called working managers because they perform both management and employee functions. When Bonnie is promoted to general manager, she will spend less time performing nonmanagement functions and virtually no time when she becomes a district manager.

The Systems Relationship among the Management Functions

The management functions are not a linear process. Managers do not usually plan, then organize, then lead, and then control. The functions are distinct yet interrelated. Managers often perform these functions simultaneously. In

---

WORK APPLICATION

4. Identify a specific manager, preferably one who is or was your boss, and give examples of how that person performs each of the four management functions.

APPLYING THE CONCEPT

AC 1–2 Management Functions

Identify whether each of the five situations describes one of the four management functions listed or is a nonmanagement function.

a. planning b. organizing c. leading d. controlling e. nonmanagement

_____ **6.** The manager is showing an employee how to set up a machine for production.

_____ **7.** The manager is determining how many units were produced during the first half of the shift.

_____ **8.** An employee has been absent several times. The manager is discussing the situation and trying to get the employee to improve attendance.

_____ **9.** The manager is conducting a job interview to fill the position of a retiring employee.

_____ **10.** The manager is fixing a broken machine.

addition, each function depends on the others. For example, if you start with a poor plan, the objective will not be met even though things are well organized, led, and controlled. Also, if you start with a great plan, but are poorly organized, or poorly lead, the objective may not be met. Plans without controls are rarely implemented effectively. Figure 1–3 illustrates this process. Remember that the management functions are based on setting (planning) and achieving (organizing, leading, and controlling) objectives.

SCANS and the Management Functions

To better understand the relationship among SCANS and the management skills and functions, see Figure 1–4. Following each SCANS skill is a listing (in parentheses) of the management skills and functions that help to develop the SCANS skill.

Management Roles

Henry Mintzberg identified ten roles that managers undertake to accomplish the management functions of planning, organizing, leading, and controlling. A *role* is a set of expectations of how one will behave in a given situation. Studies have supported Mintzberg's management role theory.[27, 28, 29] Mintzberg grouped these roles into three categories.[30] *The* **management role categories** *include the following:*

- *Interpersonal*
- *Informational*
- *Decisional*

    Interpersonal Roles. Interpersonal roles include figurehead, leader, and liaison. When managers play interpersonal roles, they use their human and communication management skills as they perform the necessary management function. Managers play the *figurehead role* when they represent the organization or department in ceremonial and symbolic activities. Bonnie played the figurehead role when she greeted visitors and gave them a tour of the store. Managers play the *leader role* when they motivate, train, communicate with, and influence others. Throughout the day, Bonnie performed the leader role as she directed employees to maintain floor coverage. Managers play the *liaison role* when they interact with people outside of their unit to gain information and favors. Bonnie was a liaison at the district meeting, which included the store walk-through.

    Informational Roles. Informational roles include monitor, disseminator, and spokesperson. When managers play informational roles, they use

Figure 1–3
Management Skills and Functions

4. Explain the three management roles: interpersonal, informational, and decisional.

management role categories
Interpersonal, informational, and decisional.

WORK APPLICATION

5. Identify a specific manager, preferably one who is or was your boss, and give examples of how that person performs each of the three manager role categories. Be sure to identify at least one of the three or four roles listed under interpersonal, informational, and decisional roles.

Workplace Know-How

The know-how identified by SCANS is made up of five competencies and a three-part foundation of skills and personal qualities needed for solid performance. These include:

COMPETENCIES. Effective workers can productively use:

1. **Resources.** Allocating time, money, materials, space, staff. (Resources relates to the technical and conceptual and decision-making skills and to the planning, organizing, and controlling management functions.)

2. **Interpersonal Skills.** Working on teams, teaching others, serving customers, leading, negotiating, and working well with people from culturally diverse backgrounds. (Interpersonal skills relates to the human and communication skills and to the organizing and leading management functions.)

3. **Information.** Acquiring and evaluating data, organizing and maintaining files, interpreting and communicating, and using computers to process information. (Information relates to the technical, human, and communication management skills and to the organizing, leading, and controlling management functions.)

4. **Systems.** Understanding social, organizational, and technological systems, monitoring and correcting performance, and designing or improving systems. (Systems relates to the conceptual and decision-making management skills and to the planning, organizing, and controlling management functions.)

5. **Technology.** Selecting equipment and tools, applying technology to specific tasks, and maintaining and troubleshooting technologies. (Technology relates to the technical management skill and to the planning, organizing, and controlling management functions. Chapters 5, 6, 14, and 15 help to develop technology skills.)

THE FOUNDATION. Competence requires:

1. **Basic Skills.** Reading, writing, arithmetic and mathematics; speaking and listening. (All the management skills and functions need the basic skills. Reading skills can be developed through reading this book. Chapters 5 and 15 require some math. Speaking skills can be developed through class activities. Chapter 11 provides suggestions for improving writing, speaking, and listening skills.)

2. **Thinking Skills.** Thinking creatively, making decision, solving problems, seeing things in the mind's eye, knowing how to learn, and reasoning. (All the management skills and functions need the thinking skills, especially conceptual and decision-making management skills. Chapter 3 focuses exclusively on thinking skills.)

3. **Personal Qualities.** Individual responsibility, self-esteem, sociability, self-management, and integrity. (Personal qualities affect our management skills and how we perform the mangement functions. Personal qualities can be developed throughout this book; each chapter has one or more self-learning exercises which focus on personal qualities.)

Source: U.S. Secretary's Commission on Achieving Necessary Skills. *Skills and Tasks for Jobs: A SCANS Report for America 2000*. Washington, DC: U.S. Department of Commerce, National Technical Information Services, 1992, p. 6.

Information in parentheses added by the author.

Figure 1–4
The Relationship among SCANS and the Management Skills and Functions

their human and communication management skills. Managers play the *monitor role* when they read and talk to others to receive information. Bonnie was continually monitoring the situation to ensure full floor coverage. Managers play the *disseminator role* when they send information to others. Bonnie played the disseminator role when she was at the district meeting. Managers play the *spokesperson role* when they provide information to people outside the organization. Bonnie played the spokesperson role when she made business calls in the morning and gave the interview to the author of this book.

*Note that the starting place is with organizational objectives. Therefore, read the boxes from left to right.
**Managers play the necessary roles, while performing management functions, to achieve organizational objectives.

Figure 1–5
Ten Roles Managers Play

Decisional Roles. Decisional roles include entrepreneur, disturbance handler, resource allocator, and negotiator. When managers play decisional roles, they use their conceptual and decision-making management skills. Managers play the *entrepreneur role* when they innovate and initiate improvements. Bonnie had the visual staff set up new displays to help improve store sales. Managers play the *disturbance-handler role* when they take corrective action during disputes or crisis situations. Bonnie had to deal with a customer who was not satisfied that an employee would not give a cash refund for merchandise returned. Managers play the *resource-allocator role* when they schedule, request authorization, and perform budgeting and programming activities. Bonnie allocated sales associates to cover the floor. Managers perform the *negotiator role* when they represent their department or organization during nonroutine transactions to gain agreement and commitment. Bonnie played the negotiator role when she made business calls to outside contractors.

APPLYING THE CONCEPT

AC 1–3 Management Roles

Identify each of the five roles below as:
a. interpersonal   b. informational   c. decisional

_____ **11.** The manager discusses the new union contract with union representatives.

_____ **12.** The manager shows an employee how to fill out a form.

_____ **13.** The manager reads *The Wall Street Journal* with a cup of coffee first thing in the morning.

_____ **14.** The manager develops new total quality management (TQM) techniques.

_____ **15.** The sales manager discusses a complaint with a customer.

As businesses continue to compete in a diversified global economy, environment and technology affect interpersonal, informational, and decisional roles.[31] See Figure 1–5 for a review of these three categories of ten roles.

5. List the hierarchy of management levels.

DIFFERENCES AMONG MANAGERS

Differences occur in levels of management, types of managers, management skills needed, management functions performed,[32] roles played,[33] large versus small business managers, and profit versus not-for-profit managers.

The Three Levels of Management (and Operative Employees)

levels of management
Top, middle, and first-line.

The three **levels of management** *include top, middle, and first-line.* They are also called strategic, tactical, and operational. The three levels relate to each other as described here. See Figure 1–6 for an illustration of the three levels of management and operative employees.

Top Managers. These executive positions have titles such as chairman of the board, chief executive officer (CEO), president, or vice president. Most organizations have relatively few top management positions. Top managers are responsible for managing the entire organization or major parts of it. They develop and define the organization's purpose, objectives, strategies, and long-term plans. They report to other executives or boards of directors and supervise the activities of middle managers.

Middle Managers. People holding these positions have titles such as sales manager, branch manager, or department head. Middle managers are responsible for implementing top management's strategy by developing short-term operating plans. They generally report to executives and supervise the work of first-line managers.

First-Line Managers. Examples of the titles at this level include crew leader, supervisor, head nurse, and office manager. These managers are responsible for implementing middle managers' operational plans. They generally report to middle managers. Unlike those at the other two levels of management, first-line managers do not supervise other managers; they supervise operative employees.

Operative Employees. Operative employees are the workers in an organization who do not hold management positions. They report to first-line managers. They make the products, wait on customers, perform repairs, and so on.

Based on The Gap's organization structure, Bonnie is a first-line manager because she has operative employees reporting directly to her. Recall that Bonnie told the visual staff what to do for the day. How-

WORK APPLICATION

6. Identify the three levels of management in a specific organization by level and title. Be sure to list the organization's name.

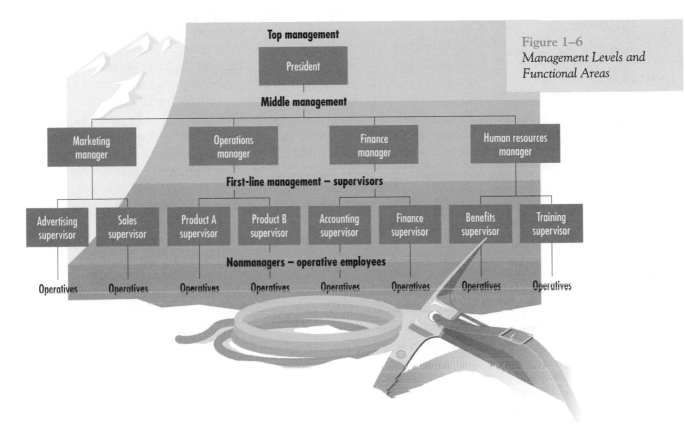

Figure 1–6
*Management Levels and
Functional Areas*

ever, within her store, she is in a sense the top manager. Bonnie is also a middle manager in the sense that she reports to a higher-level district manager and has three first-line managers—two associate managers and one assistant manager—reporting directly to her. Bonnie's store usually has a minimum of 30 operative employees. But during the busy seasons of Christmas and back-to-school, there are as many as 50 employees working at her store.

Types of Managers

The three **types of managers** *include general, functional, and project.* Top-level and some middle managers are *general managers* because they supervise the activities of several departments that perform several different activities. Middle and first-line managers are often *functional managers* that supervise the activities of related tasks. Bonnie is a functional manager because she is responsible for overseeing the functions performed at her store.

The four most common functional areas include marketing, operations/production, finance/accounting, and human resources/personnel management. A marketing manager is responsible for selling and advertising products and services. A production manager is responsible for making a product

6. Describe the three different types of managers: general, functional, and project.

types of managers
General, functional, and project.

such as a Ford Mustang, whereas an operations manager is responsible for providing a service such as a loan by Bank America. However, both product and service organizations now use the broader term *operations*. The accounting manager is responsible for keeping records of sales and expenses (accounts receivable and payable) and determining profitability, whereas the financial manager is responsible for obtaining the necessary funds and investments. The term *finance* is commonly used to mean both accounting and financial activities. The human resources (replaces the old term *personnel*) manager is responsible for forecasting future employee needs and recruiting, selecting, evaluating, and compensating employees. This manager also ensures that employees follow legal guidelines and regulations.

A *project manager* coordinates employees and other resources across several functional departments to accomplish a specific task, such as to develop and produce a new breakfast cereal for Kellogg's or General Mills, or a new model aircraft at Boeing.

The current business trend is to cut management levels,[34] particularly middle managers, and to bridge the gap between levels. Organizations are also developing less rigid management structures, such as self-managed teams, which increases the need for human relations and communication skills.

Management Skills

All managers need technical, human and communication, and conceptual and decision-making skills. However, the need for these skills varies with the level of management.[35] Although various studies have been conducted to determine the exact need for each skill by each level of management, discrepancies in the results exist. It is generally agreed that at all three levels of management, the need for human and communication skills remains fairly constant. However, top-level managers have a greater need for conceptual and decision-making skills, whereas first-line managers have a greater need for technical skills. This is logical because as you move up the management levels, you have to be able to conceptualize how more departments interrelate. At the first-line level you need to be concerned primarily with day-to-day production of the product or service.[36] Middle managers tend to need a balance of all three skills, but needs vary from organization to organization.

Management Functions

All managers perform the four management functions: planning, organizing, leading, and controlling. However, the time spent on each function varies with the level of management.[37] Studies of the amount of time managers spend on each function are inconclusive. However, it is generally agreed that first-line managers spend more time leading and controlling, middle-level managers spend equal time on all four functions, and top managers spend more time planning and organizing. Figure 1–7 summarizes the differences in management levels as well as the varying skills needed.

7. Describe the differences among management levels in terms of skills needed and functions performed.

Management Level	Primary Management Skills Needed	Primary Management Functions Performed
Top	Conceptual and human skills	Planning and organizing
Middle	Balance of all three	Balance of all four
First-Line	Technical and human skills	Leading and controlling

Figure 1–7
Differences among Management Levels in Skills Needed and Functions Performed

Large versus Small Business Managers

There are many different definitions of small business. For our purposes, based on one Small Business Administration (SBA) definition, a small business is independently owned and operated, is not dominant in its field, and has fewer than 500 employees. Bonnie works for a large organization—The Gap. Her independent store resembles a small business, but it has the support of a large organization. See Figure 1–8 for a list of differences between large and small businesses. However, realize that these are general statements. Many large and small businesses share certain characteristics.

Today, large businesses are seeking people with entrepreneurial skills. *Entrepreneurs* start new businesses. In large organizations, *intrapreneurs* start new lines of business within a larger business with the support of its resources. Companies such as 3M, General Electric, and Bristol Myers encourage intrapreneurship.

Figure 1–8
Differences between Large and Small Businesses

Functions and Roles	Large Business	Small Business
Planning	Commonly have formal written objectives and plans with a global business focus.[38]	Commonly have informal objectives and plans that are not written with a global focus.
Organizing	Tend to have formal organization structures with clear policies and procedures, with three levels of management. Jobs tend to be specialized.	Tend to have informal structures without clear policies and procedures, with fewer than three levels of management. Jobs tend to be more general.
Leading	Managers tend to be more participative, giving employees more say in how they do their work and allowing them to make more decisions.	Entrepreneurs tend to be more autocratic and want things done their way, often wanting to make the decisions.
Controlling	Tend to have more sophisticated computerized control systems.	Tend to use less sophisticated control systems and to rely more on direct observation.
Important management roles	Resource allocator.[39]	Entrepreneurial and spokesperson.[40]

APPLYING THE CONCEPT

AC 1–4 Differences among Management Levels

Five descriptions follow (16–20). Identify the level of management as:
a. top   b. middle   c. first-line

_____ **16.** Supervises the operative employees.

_____ **17.** Has greater need for conceptual than technical skills.

_____ **18.** Spends more time leading and controlling.

_____ **19.** Reports to an executive.

_____ **20.** Has a more balanced need for the management skills and functions.

Most large businesses started as small businesses. The importance of small business grew during the 1990s. Small businesses now produce more than one-third of the U.S. gross national product (GNP) and create more than 80 percent of all new jobs.[41] Thus, when you graduate, you may end up working for a small business. In addition, one-third of businesses are now owned by women.[42]

Profit versus Not-for-Profit Managers

Is the manager's job the same in profit and not-for-profit organizations? Although some noteworthy differences exist, the answer is yes. All managers need management skills, perform the same management functions, and play the same roles regardless of the organization type. Bonnie works for a profit business. Government employees work for the public (not-for-profit) sector.

Two primary areas of difference between profit and not-for-profit organizations include measuring performance and staffing. The primary measure of performance for profit organizations is bottom-line profit. Not-for-profit organizations have no universal measure of performance. The United Way, Boy Scouts and Girl Scouts, library, and registry of motor vehicles have different performance measurements. In addition, profit organizations pay workers. However, in many not-for-profit organizations some of the workers are unpaid volunteers.

Throughout this text you will develop management skills that are universally valuable to all organizations. But, more importantly, you will develop skills that will help you become the person that you want to be in your private and professional lives.

CHAPTER SUMMARY AND GLOSSARY

The chapter summary is organized to answer the eight learning objectives for Chapter 1.

1. Describe a manager's responsibility.

A manager is responsible for achieving organizational objectives through efficient and effective use of resources. _Efficient_ refers to doing things right, and _effective_ refers to doing the right thing. The manager's resources include human, financial, physical, and informational.

2. List and explain the three management skills.

The three management skills are technical, human and communication, and conceptual and decision making. Technical skills are the ability to use methods and techniques to perform a task. Human and communication skills are the ability to work with people in teams. Conceptual and decision-making skills are the ability to understand abstract ideas and select alternatives to solve problems.

3. List and explain the four management functions.

The four management functions are planning, organizing, leading, and controlling. Planning is the process of setting objectives and determining in advance exactly how the objectives will be met. Organizing is the process of delegating and coordinating tasks and resources to achieve objectives. Leading is the process of influencing employees to work toward achieving objectives. Controlling is the process of establishing and implementing mechanisms to ensure that the organization achieves its objectives.

4. Explain the three management roles: interpersonal, informational, and decisional.

Managers play the interpersonal role when they act as figurehead, leader, and liaison. Managers play the informational role when they act as monitor, disseminator, and spokesperson. Managers play the decisional role when they act as entrepreneur, disturbance handler, resource allocator, and negotiator.

5. List the hierarchy of management levels.

The three hierarchy levels are top (operations executive), middle (marketing manager), and first-line (accounting supervisor).

6. Describe the three different types of managers: general, functional, and project.

A general manager supervises the activities of several departments/units that perform different activities. Functional managers supervise related activities such as marketing, operations, finance, and human resources management. A project manager coordinates employees and other resources across several functional departments to accomplish a specific task.

7. Describe the differences among management levels in terms of skills needed and functions performed.

Top managers have a greater need for conceptual and decision-making skills than first-line managers. Middle managers have a need for a balance of all three skills. First-line managers have a greater need for technical skills than top managers.

8. Define the following key terms (in order of appearance in the chapter):

Select one or more methods: (1) fill in the missing key terms from memory, (2) match the key terms from the end of the summary with their definitions below, or (3) copy the key terms in order from the list at the beginning of the chapter.

A _____ is responsible for achieving organizational objectives through efficient and effective utilization of resources.

The _____ include human, financial, physical, and informational.

The level of organizational _____ is based on how effectively and efficiently managers use resources to achieve objectives.

_____ include technical, human and communication, and conceptual and decision-making.

_____ are the ability to use methods and techniques to perform a task.

_____ are the ability to work with people in teams.

_____ are the ability to understand abstract ideas and select alternatives to solve problems.

The four _____ include planning, organizing, leading, and controlling.

_____ is the process of setting objectives and determining in advance exactly how the objectives will be met.

_____ is the process of delegating and coordinating tasks and resources to achieve objectives.

_____ is the process of influencing employees to work toward achieving objectives.

_____ is the process of establishing and implementing mechanisms to ensure that objectives are achieved.

The _____ include interpersonal, informational, and decisional.

There are three _____: top, middle, and first-line.

There are three _____: general, functional, and project.

KEY TERMS

conceptual and decision-making skills   9
controlling   12
human and communication skills   9
leading   11
levels of management   16

management functions   11
management role categories   13
management skills   9
manager   6
manager's resources   6
organizing   11

performance   7
planning   11
technical skills   9
types of managers   17

REVIEW AND DISCUSSION QUESTIONS

1. What is management, and why is it important to learn about management?

2. What are the three management skills? Do all managers need these skills?

3. What are the four functions of management? Do all managers perform all four functions?

4. What are the three management roles? Do all managers perform all three roles?

5. What are the three types of managers? Is there really a difference among them?

OBJECTIVE CASE 1

Microsoft Corporation

In 1978, Bill Gates and Paul Allen launched Microsoft, which grew from a small business into a giant. Microsoft quickly surpassed the value of IBM. Bill Gates's 30 percent stock ownership has been valued at over $70 billion. The phenomenal growth of Microsoft is directly related to Gates's dedication to innovation and hard work.

Bill Gates, known as a demanding boss, encourages creativity and recognizes employee achievements. He demands that his colleagues be well informed, logical, vocal, and thick-skinned. Employees often spend long hours interacting in teams. Teams that develop and market programming languages must present their ideas at the so-called "Bill" meeting. During Bill meetings, Gates often interrupts presentations to question facts and assertions. He is known to shout criticism and challenges at team members, who are expected to stand up to him with good answers.

Bill Gates actively participates in and coordinates small units devoted to functional areas such as programming and marketing, but he delegates authority to managers to run their departments. Each part of the company is independent, yet Gates is the glue that holds it all together. Gates's overall business goals and plan for Microsoft, known as the Microsoft Vision, are clearly stated and effectively communicated throughout the company. His long-range vision, "Information at Your Fingertips," will take at least a decade to realize. He believes that any piece of information that the public wants should be available. Gates talks about how the company's current success sprang from the bets it made years ago and stuck with.

Bill Gates also wants to control the software market for the World Wide Web Internet. However, he has been accused of trying to monopolize the market and has run into some legal problems with the Department of Justice, to which he admitted that Microsoft restricts the ability of its Internet partners to deal with its rivals.[43]

Select the best alternative for the following questions. Be sure you are able to explain your answers.

____ 1. Which resource played the most important role in the success of Microsoft?

    a. human   c. financial

    b. physical   d. informational

____ 2. Which of the management skills is stressed most in the case study?

    a. technical

    b. human and communication

    c. conceptual and decision-making

____ 3. Which one of the management functions is stressed most in the case study?

    a. planning   c. leading

    b. organizing   d. controlling

____ 4. Bill Gates's participation in and coordination of small units, but delegating authority to managers to run them, is an example of the ____ management function.

    a. planning   c. leading

    b. organizing   d. controlling

____ 5. Which primary management role did Bill Gates use to achieve success?

    a. interpersonal–leader

    b. informational–monitor

    c. decisional–negotiator

____ 6. Bill Gates is at which level of management?

    a. top

    b. middle

    c. first-line

____ 7. Which type of manager is Bill Gates?

    a. general   b. functional   c. project

OBJECTIVE CASE 1

(continued)

___ **8.** As CEO, Bill Gates has greater need for which skills?

    a. technical over conceptual

    b. conceptual over technical

    c. a balance

___ **9.** As CEO, how does Bill Gates spend more of his time?

    a. planning and organizing

    b. leading and controlling

    c. a balance

___ **10.** Would Ghiselli agree that Bill Gates has supervisory ability?

    a. yes   b. no

11. Give examples of some of the tasks Bill Gates performs in each of the four management functions.

12. Give examples of some of the tasks Bill Gates performs in each of the three management roles.

13. Do you think you would like to work for Bill Gates? Explain your answer.

For current information on Microsoft, use Internet address http://www.microsoft.com. For ideas on using the Internet, see Appendix B.

BEHAVIOR MODEL VIDEO EXERCISE 1-1

Behavior Model Video 1–1 (11 minutes), Situational Management, shows Laura, a bank branch manager, who manages tellers who are not collecting fees. Laura's boss, Celeste, discusses the situation with her. The video illustrates the four management styles, explained in Skill-Building Exercise 1–1.

Objective
To better understand the four situational management styles.

Procedure 1 (10–20 minutes)
The instructor shows Behavior Model Video 1–1. As you view each of the four scenes, identify the four situational management styles and select the one being used by the manager.

Scene 1. ___   a. autocratic (S1A)

Scene 2. ___   b. consultative (S2C)

Scene 3. ___   c. participative (S3P)

Scene 4. ___   d. empowerment (S4E)

After viewing each of the four scenes, identify/match the style used by the manager by placing the letter of the style on the scene line.

Option A: View all four scenes and identify the style used by the manager. After viewing all four scenes, discuss them. The correct answers are given in the video.

Option B: After each scene, the class discusses the style used by the manager. The instructor states the correct answer after each of the four scenes.

Procedure 2 (2–5 minutes)
Select the one style that you would use in this situation. Are other styles also appropriate? Which style would you not use (not appropriate) for this situation? Next to each style listed above, write the letter A for appropriate or N for not appropriate.

Discussion
Option A: In groups of four to six, answer the following questions.

BEHAVIOR MODEL VIDEO EXERCISE 1-1

Option B: As a class answer the following questions.
1. Which style(s) are not appropriate to use in this situation?
2. Which styles(s) are appropriate to use in this situation?
3. Is there one style most appropriate in this situation? If yes, which one?

Conclusion
The instructor may make concluding remarks.

Application (2–4 minutes)
What did I learn from this exercise? How will I use this knowledge in the future?

_____

_____

Sharing
Volunteers give their answers to the application section.

Skill-Building Exercise 1–1

*skillbuilder

1 G

Situational Management

Preparing for Skill-Building Exercise 1-1
In this exercise you will learn your preferred management style and how to analyze a situation in order to select the appropriate management style.

Determining Your Preferred Management Style
Before reading about situational management, complete Self-Assessment Exercise 1–2 which follows to determine your preferred management style.

Self-Assessment Exercise 1–2

Determining Your Preferred Management Style

Following are 12 situations. Select the one alternative that most closely describes what you would do in each situation. Don't be concerned with trying to pick the right answer; select the alternative you would really use. Circle a, b, c, or d. Ignore the C ___ and S ___ ,

which will be explained later in this chapter and used in class in Skill-Building Exercise 1–1.

C ___ 1. Your rookie crew seems to be developing well. Their need for direction and close supervision is diminishing. What do you do?

a. Stop directing and overseeing performance unless there is a problem. S ____

b. Spend time getting to know them personally, but make sure they maintain performance levels. S ____

c. Make sure things keep going well; continue to direct and oversee closely. S ____

d. Begin to discuss new tasks of interest to them. S ____

C ____ 2. You assigned Jill a task, specifying exactly how you wanted it done. Jill deliberately ignored your directions and did it her way. The job will not meet the customer's standards. This is not the first problem you've had with Jill. What do you decide to do?

a. Listen to Jill's side, but be sure the job gets done right. S ____

b. Tell Jill to do it again the right way and closely supervise the job. S ____

c. Tell her the customer will not accept the job and let Jill handle it her way. S ____

d. Discuss the problem and solutions to it. S ____

C ____ 3. Your employees work well together; the department is a real team. It's the top performer in the organization. Because of traffic problems, the president okayed staggered hours for departments. As a result, you can change your department's hours. Several of your workers have suggested changing. What action do you take?

a. Allow the group to decide the hours. S ____

b. Decide on new hours, explain why you chose them, and invite questions. S ____

c. Conduct a meeting to get the group members' ideas. Select new hours together, with your approval. S ____

d. Send around a memo stating the hours you want. S ____

C ____ 4. You hired Bill, a new employee. He is not performing at the level expected after one month's training. Bill is trying, but he seems to be a slow learner. What do you decide to do?

a. Clearly explain what needs to be done and oversee his work. Discuss why the procedures are important; support and encourage him. S ____

b. Tell Bill that his training is over and it's time to pull his own weight. S ____

c. Review task procedures and supervise his work closely. S ____

d. Inform Bill that his training is over and that he should feel free to come to you if he has any problems. S ____

C ____ 5. Helen has had an excellent performance record for the last five years. Recently you have noticed a drop in the quality and quantity of her work. She has a family problem. What do you do?

a. Tell her to get back on track and closely supervise her. S ____

b. Discuss the problem with Helen. Help her realize that her personal problem is affecting her work. Discuss ways to improve the situation. Be supportive and encourage her. S ____

c. Tell Helen you're aware of her productivity slip and that you're sure she'll work it out soon. S ____

d. Discuss the problem and solution with Helen and supervise her closely. S ____

C ____ 6. Your organization does not allow smoking in certain areas. You just walked by a restricted area and saw Joan smoking. She has been with the organization for ten years and is a very productive worker. Joan has never been caught smoking before. What action do you take?

a. Ask her to put the cigarette out and then leave. S ____

b. Discuss why she is smoking and what she intends to do about it. S ____

c. Give her a lecture about not smoking and check up on her in the future. S ____

d. Tell her to put the cigarette out, watch her do it, tell her you will check on her in the future. S ___

C ___ 7. Your employees usually work well together with little direction. Recently a conflict between Sue and Tom has caused problems. What action do you take?

    a. Call Sue and Tom together and make them realize how this conflict is affecting the department. Discuss how to resolve it and how you will check to make sure the problem is solved. S ___

    b. Let the group resolve the conflict. S ___

    c. Have Sue and Tom sit down and discuss their conflict and how to resolve it. Support their efforts to implement a solution. S ___

    d. Tell Sue and Tom how to resolve their conflict and closely supervise them. S ___

C ___ 8. Jim usually does his share of the work with some encouragement and direction. However, he has migraine headaches occasionally and doesn't pull his weight when this happens. The others resent doing Jim's work. What do you decide to do?

    a. Discuss his problem and help him come up with ideas for maintaining his work; be supportive. S ___

    b. Tell Jim to do his share of the work and closely watch his output. S ___

    c. Inform Jim that he is creating a hardship for the others and should resolve the problem by himself. S ___

    d. Be supportive but set minimum performance levels and ensure compliance. S ___

C ___ 9. Barbara, your most experienced and productive worker, came to you with a detailed idea that could increase your department's productivity at a very low cost. She can do her present job and this new assignment. You think it's an excellent idea. What do you do?

    a. Set some goals together. Encourage and support her efforts. S ___

    b. Set up goals for Barbara. Be sure she agrees with them and sees you as being supportive of her efforts. S ___

    c. Tell Barbara to keep you informed and to come to you if she needs any help. S ___

    d. Have Barbara check in with you frequently so that you can direct and supervise her activities. S ___

C ___ 10. Your boss asked you for a special report. Frank, a very capable worker who usually needs no direction or support, has all the necessary skills to do the job. However, Frank is reluctant because he has never done a report. What do you do?

    a. Tell Frank he has to do it. Give him direction and supervise him closely. S ___

    b. Describe the project to Frank and let him do it his own way. S ___

    c. Describe the benefits to Frank. Get his ideas on how to do it and check his progress. S ___

    d. Discuss possible ways of doing the job. Be supportive; encourage Frank. S ___

C ___ 11. Jean is the top producer in your department. However, her monthly reports are constantly late and contain errors. You are puzzled because she does everything else with no direction or support. What do you decide to do?

    a. Go over past reports, explaining exactly what is expected of her. Schedule a meeting so that you can review the next report with her. S ___

    b. Discuss the problem with Jean and ask her what can be done about it; be supportive. S ___

c. Explain the importance of the report. Ask her what the problem is. Tell her that you expect the next report to be on time and error-free. S ＿＿

d. Remind Jean to get the next report in on time without errors. S ＿＿

C ＿＿12. Your workers are very effective and like to participate in decision making. A consultant was hired to develop a new method for your department using the latest technology in the field. What do you do?

a. Explain the consultant's method and let the group decide how to implement it. S ＿＿

b. Teach them the new method and supervise them closely. S ＿＿

c. Explain the new method and the reasons that it is important. Teach them the method and make sure the procedure is followed. Answer questions. S ＿＿

d. Explain the new method and get the group's input on ways to improve and implement it. S ＿＿

To determine your preferred management style, follow these steps:

1. Circle the letter you selected for each situation. The column headings (S-A through S-E) represent the management style you selected. S1A =

Autocratic, S2C = Consultative, S3P = Participative, S4E = Empowerment

	S1A	S2C	S3P	S4E
1.	c	b	d	a
2.	b	a	d	c
3.	d	b	c	a
4.	c	a	d	b
5.	a	d	b	c
6.	d	c	b	a
7.	d	a	c	b
8.	b	d	a	c
9.	d	b	a	c
10.	a	c	d	b
11.	a	c	b	d
12.	b	c	d	a
Totals	＿＿	＿＿	＿＿	＿＿

2. Add up the number of circled items per column. The highest is your preferred management style. Is this the style you tend to use most often?

Your management style flexibility is reflected in the distribution of your answers. The more evenly distributed the numbers are between S-A, S-C, S-P, and S-E, the more flexible your style is. A score of 1 or 0 in any column may indicate a reluctance to use the style.

Note: There is no "right" management style. This part of the exercise is designed to enable you to better understand the style you tend to use or prefer to use.

Analyzing the Situation

Now that you have determined your preferred management style, you will learn about the four management styles and when to use each. According to contingency theorists (see Appendix A), there is no best management style for all situations. Instead, effective managers adapt their style to individual capabilities or a group situation.[44] Studies have shown that manager–employee interactions can be classified into two distinct categories: directive and supportive.

- *Directive behavior.* The manager focuses on directing and controlling behavior to ensure that the task gets done. The manager tells employees what to do and when, where, and how to do the task and closely oversees performance.

- *Supportive behavior*. The manager focuses on encouraging and motivating behavior without telling the employee what to do. The manager explains things and listens to employee views, helping employees make their own decisions through building up confidence and self-esteem.

In other words, when you, as a manager, interact with your employees, you can focus on directing (getting the task done), supporting (developing relationships), or both.

These definitions lead us to the question, "What style should I use and why?" The answer depends on the situation, which is determined in part by the capability of the employees. In turn, there are two distinct aspects of capability:

- *Ability*. Do the employees have the knowledge, experience, education, skills, and so forth to do a particular task without direction from you as the manager?

- *Motivation*. Do the employees have the confidence to do the task? Do they want to do the task? Are they committed to performing the task? Will they perform the task without your encouragement and support?

Determining Employee Capability

Employee capability may be measured on a continuum from low to outstanding, which you, as a manager, determine. You select the capability level that best describes the employees' ability and motivation for the specific task.

- *Low (C1)*. The employees can't do the task without detailed directions and close supervision. Employees in this category are either unable or unwilling to do the task.

- *Moderate (C2)*. The employees have moderate ability and need specific direction and support to get the task done properly. The employees may be highly motivated but still need direction due to lack of ability.

- *High (C3)*. The employees have high ability but may lack the confidence to do the job. What they need most is support and encouragement to motivate them to get the task done.

- *Outstanding (C4)*. The employees are capable of doing the task without direction or support.

Most people perform a variety of tasks on the job. It is important to realize that employee capability may vary depending on the specific task. For example, a bank teller may be a C4 for routine transactions but a C1 for opening new or special accounts. Employees tend to start working with a C1 capability, needing close direction. As their ability to do the job increases, you can begin to be supportive and probably stop supervising closely. As a manager, you must gradually develop your employees from C1 to C2 to C3 or C4 levels over time.

The Four Management Styles

As mentioned, the correct management style depends on the situation, which in turn, is a function of employee capability. Each of the four management styles also involves various degrees of supportive and directive behavior. The four situational management styles are autocratic, consultative, participative, and empowerment.

- *Autocratic style (S1A)* involves high-directive/low-supportive behavior (HD/LS) and is appropriate when interacting with low-capability employees (C1). When interacting with employees, give very detailed instructions describing exactly what the task is and when, where, and how to perform it. Closely oversee performance and give some support. The majority of time with the employees is spent giving directions. Make decisions without input from the employees.

- *Consultative style (S2C)* involves high-directive/high-supportive behavior (HD/HS) and is appropriate when interacting with moderately capable employees (C2). Give specific instructions as well as overseeing performance at all major stages through completion. At the same time, support the employees by explaining why the task should be performed as requested and answering their questions. Work on relationships as you sell the benefits of completing the task your way. Give fairly equal amount of time to directing and supporting employees. When making decisions, you may consult employees, but still have the final say. Once you make the decision, which can incorporate employees' ideas, direct and oversee their performance.

- *Participative style (S3P)* is characterized by low-directive/high-supportive behavior (LD/HS) and is appropriate when interacting with employees with high capability (C3). When interacting with employees, spend a small amount of time giving general directions and a great deal of time giving encouragement. Spend limited time overseeing performance, letting employees do the task their way while focusing on the end result. Support the employees by encouraging them and building up their self-confidence. If a task needs to be done, don't tell them how to do it; ask them how they will accomplish it. Make decisions together or allow employees to make the decision subject to your limitations and approval.

- *Empowerment style (S4E)* entails low-directive/low-supportive behavior (LD/LS) and is appropriate when interacting with outstanding employees (C4). When interacting with these employees, merely let them know what needs to be done. Answer their questions, but provide little, if any, direction. It is not necessary to oversee performance. These employees are highly motivated and need little, if any, support. Allow these employees to make their own decisions subject to your limitations, although approval will not be necessary. Other terms for empowerment would be *laissez-faire* or *hands off*; let them alone to do their own thing.

Model 1–1 summarizes the four management styles.

Applying the Situational Management Model

You're already familiar with the following situation from Self-Assessment Exercise 1–2, which was part of the exercise for determining your management style. Now you're going to apply the information in Model 1–1 to this situation. (Later, in Skill-Building Exercise 1–1, you may deal with the remaining 11 situations in class.)

To begin, identify the employee capability level in each situation, listed in the top of Model 1–1. Indicate the capability level by placing the number 1 through 4 on the line marked "C" to the left of the situation. Next, determine the management style that each response (a, b, c, or d) represents and indicate that style by placing the letter A, C, P, or E on the line marked "S" at the end of each response. Finally, identify the response you think is most appropriate by placing a checkmark next to it. Now use Model 1–1 to select the management style that will result in the optimum performance of the task.

C ___ 1. Your rookie crew seems to be developing well. Their need for close supervision is diminishing. What do you do?
   a. Stop directing and overseeing performance, unless there is a problem. S ___
   b. Spend time getting to know them personally, but make sure they maintain performance levels. S ___
   c. Make sure things keep going well; continue to direct and oversee closely. S ___
   d. Begin to discuss new tasks of interest to them. S ___

Let's see how well you did.

1. As a rookie crew, their capability started at C-1, but they have now developed to the C-2 level. If you put the number 2 on the C line, you were correct.

2. Alternative a is the E—empowerment style. There is low direction and support. Alternative b is the C—consultative style. There is both high direction and support. Alternative c is the A—autocratic style. There is high direction but low support. Alternative d is the P—participative

Step 1. Determine capability level of employees on a continuum from C1 to C4; follow arrow left to right.

Step 2. Match the management style (S-A, S-C, S-P, S-E) with the employee capability level; follow the arrow down from the capability level box to the management style box.

Model 1–1
Situational Management Model

CAPABILITY LEVELS (C)
[Employee Ability and Motivation to Perform the Task]

(C1) Low Low Ability or Low Motivation	(C2) Moderate Low Ability/ High Motivation	(C3) High High Ability/ Low Motivation	(C4) Outstanding High Ability/ High Motivation
Employees are unable to perform the task, or totally lack motivation (unwilling to perform without coercion).	Employees have moderate ability and are motivated (confidence) to do the task with direction.	Employees have the ability to do the task but need motivation (reluctant or need confidence buildup).	Employees have the ability and motivation to perform the task without direction or support.

MANAGEMENT STYLES (S)
[Directive and Supportive Behavior Manager Needs to Give Employees to Perform the Task]

(S1A) Autocratic High Directive/ Low Supportive	(S2C) Consultative High Directive/ High Supportive	(S3P) Participative Low Directive/ High Supportive	(S4E) Empowerment Low Directive/ Low Supportive
Manager tells employees what to do and how to do it and closely oversees task performance. Manager makes decisions without employee input.	Manager sells employees on doing the task and oversees performance. Manager includes employee input in decisions while developing a supportive relationship.	Manager develops motivation by developing confidence through shared decision-making in a supportive relationship.	Manager gives employees authority to do the task their way; employees make decisions without the manager's input.

style. There is low direction and high support (in discussing employee interests).

3. If you selected b as the match, you were correct. However, in the business world there is seldom only one way to handle a situation successfully. Therefore, in this exercise, you are given points based on how successful your behavior would be in each situation. In situation 1, b is the most successful alternative because it involves developing the employees gradually; it's a three-point answer. Alternative c is the next best alternative, followed by d. It is better to keep things the way they are now rather than trying to rush employee development, which would probably cause problems. So c

is a two-point answer, and d gets one point. Alternative a is the least effective because you are going from one extreme of supervision to the other. This is a zero-point answer because the odds are great that this style will cause problems that will negatively affect your management success.

The better you match your management style to employees' capabilities, the greater your chances of being a successful manager. During the in-class part of Skill-Building Exercise 1–1, you will apply the model to the remaining situations and be given feedback on your success at applying the model as you develop your situational management skills.

Doing Skill-Building Exercise 1–1 In Class

Objectives

1. To learn to use the situational management model.
2. To develop your ability to supervise employees using the appropriate situational management style for their capability level.

Procedure
You will apply the Situational Management Model 1–1 to the situations in Self-Assessment Exercise 1–2. Your instructor will give you the recommended answers which will enable you to determine your success at selecting the appropriate style.

Video (11 minutes)
Behavior Model Video 1–1 may be shown to illustrate how to use the situational management model and the four management styles. Use the form on page 24 to record answers.

Step 1 (3–8 minutes)

The instructor reviews the situational management model and explains how to use the model for situation 2 in Self-Assessment Exercise 1–2.

1. Determine the capability level of employees. For each situation, use the top row in Model 1–1 to identify the employee capability level the situation describes. Write the level (1 through 4) on the line marked "C" to the left of each situation.

2. Match the management style with the employee capability level. The management match is below the capability level in the model. Identify the management style that each response (a through d) represents. Indicate the style (S1A, S2C, S3P, or S4E) on the line marked "S" at the end of each response. Finally, choose the management style best for each situation by making a checkmark next to the appropriate response (a, b, c, or d).

Step 2 (25–45 minutes)

1. Turn to situation 3 in Self-Assessment Exercise 1–2 and to Model 1–1. Apply the model to the situation and select the best course of action (3 to 4 minutes). The instructor will go over the answers and scoring (3 to 4 minutes).

2. Divide into teams of two or three. Apply the model as a team to situations 4 through 6. Team members may select different answers if they don't agree (6 to 10 minutes). Do not do situations 7 through 12 until you are told to do so. Your instructor will go over the answers and scoring for situations 4 through 6 (5 to 8 minutes).

3. As a team, select your answers to situations 7 through 12 (11 to 15 minutes). Your instructor will go over the answers and scoring for situations 7 through 12 (2 to 4 minutes).

Conclusion
The instructor may lead a class discussion and make concluding remarks.

Application (2–4 minutes)
What did I learn from this experience? How will I use this knowledge in the future?

_____

_____

Sharing
Volunteers give their answers to preceding applications.

Exercise 1–1

G

Getting to Know You

Objectives

1. To get acquainted with some of your classmates.

2. To gain a better understanding of what the course covers.

3. To get to know more about your instructor.

Procedure 1 (5–8 minutes)
Break into groups of five or six, preferably with people you do not know. Each member tells his or her name and two or three significant things about himself or herself. After all the members are finished, they may ask each other questions to get to know each other better.

Procedure 2 (4–8 minutes)
Can anyone in the group call the others by name? If so, he or she should do so. If not, have each member repeat his or her name. Follow with each member calling all members by name. Be sure each person knows everyone's first name.

Discussion Question
What can you do to improve your ability to remember people's names?

_____

_____

_____

Procedure 3 (5–10 minutes)
Elect a spokesperson or recorder for your group. Look over the following categories and decide what specific statements or questions you would like your spokesperson to ask the instructor based on these categories.

The spokesperson will not identify who asked the questions. You do not have to have questions for each area.

1. *Course expectations.* What do you hope to learn from this course? Your instructor will comment on your expectations and tell the class whether the topics are a planned part of the course.

2. *Doubts or concerns.* Is there anything about the course that you don't understand? Express any doubts or concerns that you may have or ask questions for clarification.

3. *Questions about the instructor.* List questions to ask the instructor in order to get to know him or her better.

Procedure 4 (10–20 minutes)
Each spokesperson asks the instructor one question at a time until all questions from Procedure 3 have been answered. Spokespeople should skip questions already asked by other groups.

Conclusion
The instructor may make concluding remarks.

Application (2–4 minutes)
What did I learn from this experience? How will I use this knowledge in the future?

_____

_____

Sharing
Volunteers may give their answers to the preceding questions.

Appendix A: A Brief History of Management

Learning Objectives

After studying this appendix, you should be able to:

1. State the major similarity and difference between the classical and behavioral theorists.

2. Describe how the systems theorist and the contingency theorist differ from the classical and behavioral theorists.

3. Define the following **key terms** (in order of appearance in the appendix):

classical theorists
behavioral theorists
management science theorists

systems theorists
sociotechnical theorists
contingency theorists

1. State the major similarity and difference between the classical and behavioral theorists.

There are two primary reasons why you should be concerned about the history of management: to better understand current developments and to avoid repeating mistakes. Early literature on management came from management practitioners who wrote about their experiences and attempted to extrapolate basic principles. More recent literature comes from researchers. There are different classifications of management approaches, or what are often called schools of management thought. In this section you will learn about five approaches to management: classical, behavioral, quantitative, systems, and contingency.

Classical Theory

classical theorists
Researchers who focus on the job and management functions to determine the best way to manage in all organizations.

The **classical theorists** *focus on the job and management functions to determine the best way to manage in all organizations.* In the early 1900s, managers began an organized approach to increasing performance by focusing on the efficiency of managing jobs. This focus later changed to a concern for managing departments and organizations. Scientific management stressed job efficiency through the development of technical skills, while administrative theory stressed rules and the structure of the organization.

Scientific Management. Frederick Winslow Taylor (1856–1915), an engineer known as the Father of Scientific Management, focused on analyzing and redesigning jobs more efficiently. He searched for the best way to maximize performance. As a result of his work, he developed several "scientific management" principles. Some of his major principles include the following:

1. Develop a procedure for each element of a worker's job.
2. Promote job specialization.
3. Scientifically select, train, and develop workers.
4. Plan and schedule work.
5. Establish standard methods and times for each task.
6. Use wage incentives such as piece rates and bonuses.[1]

Frank Gilbreth (1868–1924) and his wife Lillian Gilbreth (1878–1972) developed time and motion studies to develop more efficient work procedures. Their work was popularized in a book, movie, and television sitcom entitled *Cheaper by the Dozen*, a reference to their application of scientific management practices to their family of 12 children. When Frank died, their children ranged in age from 2 to 19 years old. Lillian continued her work as a consultant. However, she changed the focus of her work to pioneer industrial psychology. Lillian became a professor of management at Purdue University, and is commonly referred to as the First Lady of Management.

Another person who made important contributions to scientific management was Henry Gantt (1861–1919). He developed a method for scheduling work over a period of time that is still widely used today. You will learn how to develop a Gantt Chart in Chapter 5.

Administrative Theory. Henri Fayol (1841–1925) was a French engineer known as the Pioneer of the Principles and Functions of Management. He made a clear distinction between operating and managerial activities. Fayol identified five major functions of management: planning, coordinating, organizing, controlling, and commanding. In addition to his five management functions, Fayol also developed 14 principles that are still used today.[2] Most principles of management textbooks are organized and presented based on the functions of management.

Two other contributors to administrative management are Max Weber (1864–1920) and Chester Barnard (1886–1961). Max Weber was a German sociologist who developed the *bureaucracy concept.* His concept of bureaucracy did not include a lot of red tape and inefficiency: its aim was to develop a set of rules and procedures to ensure that all employees were treated fairly. Chester Barnard studied authority and power distributions in organizations. He raised awareness of the informal organization—cliques and naturally occurring social groupings within formal organizations.

Mary Parker Follett (1868–1933) stressed the importance of people rather than engineering techniques. Follett contributed to administrative theory by emphasizing the need for worker participation, conflict resolution, and shared goals. The trend today is toward increasingly higher levels of employee participation. Barnard and Follett's contributions led to the development of behavioral theory.

Companies still successfully use classical management techniques today. McDonald's system of fast food service is one good example of a company using these techniques. Managers at Monsanto also use classical techniques, such as time and motion studies, and organization principles that you will learn about in Chapter 6. Large organizations that are downsizing to cut costs by laying off employees and becoming more efficient are using a classical management approach.

Behavioral Theory

The **behavioral theorists** *focus on people to determine the best way to manage in all organizations.* In the 1920s, management writers began to question the classical approach to management and changed their focus from the job itself to the people who perform the job. Like the classicists, behaviorists were looking for the best way to manage in all organizations. However, the behavioral approach to management stressed the need for human skills rather than technical skills.

Elton Mayo (1880–1949) pioneered the *human relations* movement. Mayo headed a group of Harvard researchers in conducting the Hawthorne Studies, a landmark study of human behavior in Western Electric's Hawthorne plant (Cicero, Illinois) from 1927 to 1932. Like Taylor, Mayo wanted to increase

behavioral theorists
Researchers who focus on people to determine the best way to manage in all organizations.

performance; however, he wanted to determine the best work environment as his means to the end result. These researchers suggested that a manager's treatment of people had an important impact on their performance. In other words, treating people as special and meeting their needs frequently results in increased performance. The *Hawthorne effect* refers to the phenomenon that just studying people affects performance.[3]

Abraham Maslow (1908–1970) developed the *hierarchy of needs theory*.[4] Maslow is one of the earliest researchers to study motivation, and motivation is still a major area of research. You will learn more about Maslow's hierarchy of needs and other motivation theories in Chapter 12.

Douglas McGregor (1906–1964) developed *Theory X* and *Theory Y*. McGregor contrasted the two theories, based on the assumptions that managers make about workers. Theory X managers assume that people dislike work and need managers to plan, organize, and closely direct and control their work in order for them to perform at high levels. Theory Y managers assume that people like to work and do not need close supervision. McGregor did not give specific details on how to manage; he suggested a reorientation in managerial thinking.[5]

Behaviorists felt that a happy employee would be productive. However, later research suggested that a happy worker is not necessarily a productive worker. As you can see, the classical and behavioral theories are very different, yet both claimed to have the best method of managing in all organizations.

The behavioral approach to management is still evolving and is being used in organizations. The current term for studying people at work is the *behavioral science approach*, which draws from economics, psychology, sociology, and other disciplines. Most of the material in the organizing and leading chapters is based on behavioral science research. Bonnie and managers all over the globe use behavioral sciences in dealing with people.

Management Science

management science theorists
Researchers who focus on the use of mathematics to aid in problem-solving and decision-making.

The **management science theorists** *focus on the use of mathematics to aid in problem solving and decision making.* During World War II (1940s) a research program began to investigate the applicability of quantitative methods to military and logistics problems. After the war, business managers began to use management science (math). Some of the mathematical models are used in the areas of finance, management information systems (MIS), and operations management. The use of computers has led to an increase in the use of quantitative methods by managers all over the globe. Because management science stresses decision-making skills and technical skills, it is more closely aligned with classical management theory than behavioral theory. You will learn more about management science in the planning and controlling chapters. Management science is not commonly used in the organizing and leading management functions.

Integrative Perspective

The integrative perspective has three components: systems theory, sociotechnical theory, and contingency theory.

Systems Theory. The **systems theorists** *focus on viewing the organization as a whole and as the interrelationship of its parts.* In the 1950s, there was an attempt to integrate the classical, behavioral, and management science theories into a holistic view of the management process. An organizational system transforms inputs (resources) into outputs (products and/or services).

According to Russell Ackoff, the commonly used classical approach to problem solving is a reductionism process. Managers tend to break an organization into its basic parts (departments), understand the behavior and properties of the parts, and add the understanding of the parts together to understand the whole. They focus on making independent departments operate as efficiently as possible. The reductionism approach cannot yield an understanding of the organization, only knowledge of how it works. Because the parts of a system are interdependent, even if each part is independently made to perform as efficiently as possible, the organization as a whole will not perform as effectively as possible. For example, all-star athletic teams are not known to be the best teams and may not be able to beat an average team in the league.[6]

Systems theory stresses the need for conceptual skills in order to understand how the subsystems (departments) interrelate and contribute to the organization as a whole. For example, the marketing, operations, and financial departments' (subsystems) actions affect each other; if the quality of the product goes down, sales may decrease, causing a decrease in finances. Before managers in one department make a decision, they should consider the interrelated effects it will have on the other departments. The organization is a system (departments), just as the management process is a system (planning, organizing, leading, and controlling), with subsystems (parts of departments) that affect each other. So, in other words, when you have a problem to solve, do not break it into pieces; focus on the whole.

According to Harold Koontz,[7] Daniel Katz and Robert Kahn,[8] and others, the systems approach recognizes that the organization is an open system because it interacts with, and is affected by, the external environment. For example, government laws affect what the organization can and cannot do, the economy affects the organization's sales, and so on. You will learn more about open systems and the organizational environment in the next chapter.

Over the years, systems theory lost some of its popularity. However, today one of the major trends is toward total quality management (TQM), which takes a systems approach to management. You will learn more about TQM in Chapters 2, 7, and 15.

Sociotechnical Theory. The **sociotechnical theorists** *focus on integrating people and technology.* Also during the 1950s and 1960s, Trist, Bamforth,

---

2. Describe how the systems theorist and the contingency theorist differ from the classical and behavioral theorists.

systems theorists
Researchers who focus on viewing the organization as a whole and as the interrelationship of its parts.

sociotechnical theorists
Researchers who focus on integrating people and technology.

Emery,[9] and others developed sociotechnical systems. They realized, as today's managers do, that you must integrate both people and technology. To focus on one at the exclusion of the other leads to lower levels of performance. Much of current behavioral science work is in agreement with sociotechnical theory.

contingency theorists
Researchers who focus on determining the best management approach for a given situation.

Contingency Theory. The **contingency theorists** *focus on determining the best management approach for a given situation.* In the 1960s and 1970s, management researchers wanted to determine how the environment and technology affected the organization.

Tom Burns and George Stalker conducted a study to determine how the *environment* affects a firm's organization and management systems. They identified two different types of environments: stable (where there is little change) and innovative (great changes); and two types of management systems: mechanistic (similar to bureaucratic classical theory) and organic (nonbureaucratic, more similar to behavioral theory). They concluded that in a stable environment the mechanistic approach works well, whereas in an innovative environment the organic approach works well.[10]

Joan Woodward conducted a study to determine how technology (the means of producing products) affects organizational structure. She found that organizational structure did change with the type of technology. Woodward concluded that the mechanistic or classical approach worked well with mass-production technology (autos on an assembly line), whereas the organic or behavioral approach worked well with small-batch (custom-made products) and long-run process (oil refinery) technology.

Comparing Theories

See Figure A–1, Comparing Theories, for a review of this Appendix. Throughout this book, you will learn to take an intergrative perspective using systems and contingency theories, with some management science, to ensure that you maximize development of your management skills. For example, the skill-building exercise at the end of Chaper 1, Situational Management, uses a contingency approach.

Figure A-1
Comparing Theories

Classical	Behavioral	Management Science	Systems	Contingency
Attempt to develop best way to manage in all organizations by focusing on the jobs and structure of the firm.	Attempt to develop one best way to manage in all organizations by focusing on people and making them happy.	Recommend using math (computers) to aid in problem solving and decision making.	Manage by focusing on the organization as a whole and the interrelationship of its departments, rather than reductionism.	Recommend using other theories, one or a combination, that best meet the given situation.

APPENDIX SUMMARY AND GLOSSARY

The appendix summary is organized to answer the three learning objectives for Appendix A.

1. State the major similarity and difference between the classical and behavioral theorists.

Both the classical and behavioral theorists wanted to find the best way to manage in all organizations. However, the classicist focused on the job and management functions, whereas the behaviorist focused on people.

2. Describe how the systems theorist and the contingency theorist differ from the classical and behavioral theorists.

The classical and behavioral and the systems theorists differ in the way they conceptualize the organization and its problems. The classical and behavioral theorists use a reductionist approach by breaking the organization into its component parts to conceptually understand the whole (sum of parts = whole). Systems theorists look at the organization as a whole and the interrelationship of its parts to conceptually understand the whole (whole = interrelationship of parts).

The classical and behavioral theorists seek the best management approach in all organizations. The contingency theorists propose that there is no best approach for all organizations; they seek to determine which management approach will work best in a given situation.

3. Define the following key terms (in order of appearance in the appendix):

Select one or more methods: (1) fill in the missing key terms from memory, (2) match the key terms from the end of the summary with their definitions below, or (3) copy the key terms in order from the list at the beginning of the appendix.

The _____ focus on the job and management functions to determine the best way to manage in all organizations.

The _____ focus on people to determine the best way to manage in all organizations.

The _____ focus on the use of mathematics to aid in problem-solving and decision-making.

The _____ focus on veiwing the organization as a whole and as the interrelationship of its parts.

The _____ focus on integrating people and technology.

The _____ focus on determining the best management approach for a given situation.

KEY TERMS

behavioral theorists 37

classical theorists 36

contingency theorists 40

management science theorists 38

sociotechnical theorists 39

systems theorists 39

2 The Environment: Globalization, Ethics, and Social Responsibility

Learning Objectives

After studying this chapter, you should be able to:

1. Explain the five internal environmental factors: management, mission, resources, systems process, and structure.

2. List and explain the need for the two primary principles of total quality management (TQM).

3. Describe how the nine external environmental factors—customers, competitors, suppliers, labor force, shareholders, society, technology, economies, and governments—can affect the internal business environment.

4. State the difference between a domestic, an international, and a multinational business.

5. Of the six ways to take a business global, list the lowest and the highest in cost and risk.

6. Describe how global diversity affects the implementation of the management functions.

7. Explain the stakeholders' approach to ethics.

8. Discuss the differences in the four levels of social responsibility: obstruction, obligation, reaction, and involvement.

9. Explain the difference between downsizing and re-engineering.

10. Define the following **key terms** (in order of appearance in the chapter):

internal environment
mission
stakeholders
systems process
quality
customer value
total quality management (TQM)
external environment
international business
multinational corporation (MNC)

global sourcing
joint venture
direct investment
ethics
stakeholders' approach to ethics
social responsibility
downsizing
re-engineering

Skill Development

*skillbuilder

1. You should develop your skill to analyze a company's environment and management practices (Skill-Building Exercise 2–1).

   This analysis requires conceptual skills. Having the skill to analyze your company's environment and management practices and those of its competitors will make you a more valuable employee. This skill is especially important if you want to progress to higher levels of management. The primary management function skill developed is planning. The primary management roles developed are informational and decisional. The SCANS skill competencies of resources, information, and especially systems, as well as basic and thinking foundation skills, are developed.

Frederick W. Smith thought of the idea of an overnight delivery system by air freight to accommodate time-sensitive shipments such as medicines, computer parts, and electronics. Smith presented the idea in a term paper to a professor in college and received a grade of "C." On March 12, 1973, Smith tested his service by delivering six packages. FedEx began operations officially on April 17 with a total of 186 packages shipped. FedEx lost a million dollars a month for the first 27 months.

FedEx developed the hub-and-spokes system now widely imitated in the airline industry. Using this system, all shipments are flown to a centralized hub, sorted, loaded onto planes, and dispatched. By November 1988, Federal Express was able to deliver as many as a million packages in one night. FedEx was the first in its industry to offer innovative ideas and services, including overnight package delivery, the Overnight Letter (1981), 10:30 A.M. next-day delivery (Fall 1982), package tracking in vans, real-time package tracking over the phone (1981), time-definite service for freight, Saturday delivery, and pickup service. FedEx now delivers an average of two million pieces per night to 186 countries. As you will learn in this chapter, FedEx's success is based on its internal environment and its ability to adapt to its external environment.[1]

For current information on Federal Express, use Internet address **http://www.fedex.com**. For ideas on using the Internet, see Appendix B.

1. Explain the five internal environmental factors: management, mission, resources, systems process, and structure.

internal environment
Factors that affect an organization's performance from within its boundaries.

mission
An organization's purpose or reason for being.

WORK APPLICATION

For each application in this chapter use a different, or several different, organizations for your examples.

1. State the mission of an organization, preferably an organization you work or have worked for.

stakeholders
People whose interests are affected by organizational behavior.

THE INTERNAL ENVIRONMENT

Profit and nonprofit organizations are created to produce products and/or services for customers. *The organization's* **internal environment** *includes the factors that affect its performance from within its boundaries.* They are called internal factors because they are within the organization's control, as opposed to external factors, which are outside the organization's control.[2] The five internal environmental factors that you will learn about in this section are management, mission, resources, the systems process, and structure.

Management

Managers are responsible for the organization's performance. They perform the functions of planning, organizing, leading, and controlling. The leadership style used and the decisions made by managers from the top down affect the performance of the organization.[3] Top managers often receive credit for the success or failure of the organization because they have control over their behavior, even though it is affected by the external environment. Clearly, FedEx would not be the success it is today without its founder and CEO, Frederick W. Smith. Bonnie Castonguary (Chapter 1) directly affects the performance of her Gap store.

Mission

The organization's **mission** *is its purpose or reason for being.* Developing the mission is top management's responsibility. The mission should identify present and future products.[4] The term *product* is commonly used to include both goods and services. The major reason businesses fail is that management doesn't look ahead. The organization produces the wrong product—one with no market or too small a market.[5] Managers with vision change the organization's mission by offering products in demand by customers.[6] Managers must develop and convey missions with clear objectives.[7] Figure 2–1 shows that Federal Express has a clear mission statement. Notice the objective to satisfy each customer.

Professor and consultant Russell Ackoff stated that the mission should include objectives that allow for measurement and evaluation of performance. The mission should state how the organization differs from its competitors. What unique advantage does the organization have to offer customers?[8] The mission should be relevant to all stakeholders.[9] **Stakeholders** *are people whose*

Federal Express is committed to our PEOPLE–SERVICE–PROFIT philosophy. We will produce outstanding financial returns by providing totally reliable, competitively superior global air-ground transportation of high priority goods and documents that require rapid, time-certain delivery. Equally important, positive control of each package will be maintained utilizing real-time electronic tracking and tracing systems. A complete record of each shipment and delivery will be presented with our request for payment. We will be helpful, courteous, and professional to each other and the public. We will strive to have a completely satisfied customer at the end of each transaction.

Figure 2-1
Federal Express Mission Statement

systems process
The method used to transform inputs into outputs.

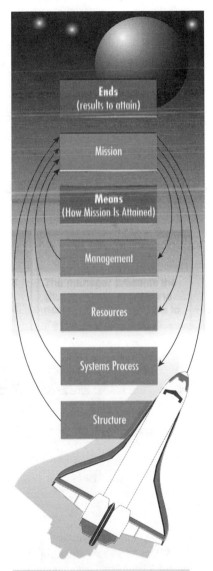

interests are affected by organizational behavior. Some of the stakeholders include employees, shareholders, customers, suppliers, the government, and so on. More about these stakeholders appears throughout this chapter.

The mission is also known as the ends the organization strives to attain. The other internal environmental factors are considered the means to achieve the ends. See Figure 2–2 for an illustration. Note that managers develop the mission and set objectives, but the managers are a means to the end. As a manager, you may not write the mission statement, but you will be responsible for helping to achieve it.

Resources

Organizations have resources to accomplish their mission.[10] As stated in Chapter 1, organizational resources include human, financial, physical, and informational. *Human resources* are responsible for achieving the organization's mission and objectives. FedEx's People–Service–Profit philosophy states that when the company puts its people first, they will provide outstanding service, which in turn will lead to profits. FedEx has thousands of employees delivering millions of packages daily worldwide. *Physical resources* at FedEx include aircraft and ground vehicles. COSMOS, the FedEx computer system, is critical to timed delivery with tracking. *Financial resources* are necessary to purchase and maintain the physical resources and to pay employees. *Informational resources* come primarily through COSMOS, but FedEx also has its own internal TV network called FXTV that reaches facilities worldwide via a closed-circuit satellite hookup. As a manager, you will be responsible for using these four resources to achieve the organization's mission.

The Systems Process

The **systems process** *is the method used to transform inputs into outputs.* The systems process has four components:

1. *Inputs.* Inputs are the startup forces that provide the organization with operating necessities. The inputs are the organization's resources (human, financial, physical, and informational). At FedEx, the primary input is the millions of packages to be delivered worldwide daily.

Figure 2-2
Internal Environment Means and Ends

WORK APPLICATION

2. Illustrate the systems process for an organization, preferably one you work or have worked for.

Internal Environment

Figure 2-3
The Systems Process

quality
Comparing actual use to requirements to determine value.

customer value
The purchasing benefits used by customers to determine whether or not to buy a product.

2. *Transformation.* Transformation is the conversion of the inputs into outputs.[11] At FedEx, the packages (input) go to the hub (transformation), where they are sorted for delivery.

3. *Outputs.* Outputs are the products offered to customers. At FedEx, the packages are delivered to customers.

4. *Feedback.* Feedback provides a means of control to ensure that the inputs and transformation process are producing the desired results. COSMOS is used as a means of feedback to help ensure that all packages are delivered on time.

Managers with a systems perspective view the organization as a process rather than as separate departments for finance, marketing, operations, and human resources.[12] The focus is on the interrelationship of all of these functions as the inputs are converted into outputs. See Figure 2–3 for an illustration of the systems process.

Quality. Quality is an internal factor because it is within the control of the organization. *Customers determine* **quality** *by comparing actual use to requirements to determine value.* **Customer value** *is the purchasing benefits used by customers to determine whether or not to buy a product.* Customers don't simply buy a product itself. They buy the benefit they expect to derive from that product. Value is what motivates us to buy products. When the author bought a computer and software, it was not for the equipment itself; it was for the benefits of being able to word process this book's manuscript.

Quality and value are important components of all organizations because they attract and retain customers.[13]

Total Quality Management (TQM). TQM is the commonly used term for stressing quality within an organization.[14] TQM uses a systems perspective because it is not a program for one department, but a responsibility of everyone (total) in the organization. **Total quality management (TQM)** *is the process that involves everyone in the organization focusing on the customer to continually improve product value.* The two primary principles of TQM are (1) to focus on delivering customer value[15] and (2) to continually improve the system

APPLYING THE CONCEPT

AC 2–1 The Internal Environment
Identify each statement by its internal environmental factor.
a. management   c. resources   e. structure
b. mission   d. systems process

_____ 1. "We take these chemicals and make them into a liquid, which then goes into these molds. When it's hard, we have outdoor chairs."

_____ 2. "We deliver pizza and buffalo wings."

_____ 3. "It's the people here that make this company what it is."

_____ 4. "As we grew we added a new department for human resources services."

_____ 5. "Management does not trust us. All the major decisions around here are made by top-level managers."

and its processes.[16] The Japanese term for continuous improvement is *Kaizen*. You will learn more about quality and TQM in Chapters 7 and 15.

Structure

Structure refers to the way in which the organization groups its resources to accomplish its mission. As discussed in Chapter 1, an organization is a system. Being a system, it is structured into departments such as finance, marketing, production, personnel, and so on. Each of these departments affects the organization as a whole, and each department is affected by the other departments. Organizations structure resources to transform inputs into outputs. All of the organization's resources must be structured effectively to achieve its objectives.[17] As a manager you will be responsible for part of the organization's structure—a department. You will learn more about organizational structure in Chapters 6 through 8. See Figure 2–4 for a review of the internal environment components.

THE EXTERNAL ENVIRONMENT

The organization's **external environment** *includes the factors that affect its performance from outside its boundaries.* Although managers can control the internal environment, they have very limited influence over what happens outside the organization. The nine major external factors are customers, competition, suppliers, labor force/unions, shareholders, society, technology, the economy, and governments.

Customers

Customers have a major effect on the organization's performance through purchasing products.[18] Without customers there is no need for an organization. Effective managers today realize the need to offer customers products of value to them. Continually improving customer value is often the difference between success and failure in business. Customer value changes over time, and if products don't change with them, companies lose customers to competitors. Changing tastes dented Campbell's canned-soup sales.[19]

Is Customer Service Important? A study revealed that the organizations with high service strategies have higher market share and return on sales than organizations with low service strategies. So there is no question that service has an economic impact.[20] Service is an important part of value. This, among other reasons, is why TQM focuses on creating customer value. The better you create customer value, the more successful your management career will be.

---

total quality management (TQM)
The process that involves everyone in the organization focusing on the customer to continually improve product value.

2. List and explain the need for the two primary principles of total quality management (TQM).

3. Describe how the nine external environmental factors—customers, competitors, suppliers, labor force, shareholders, society, technology, economies, and governments—can affect the internal business environment.

external environment
The factors that affect an organization's performance from outside its boundaries.

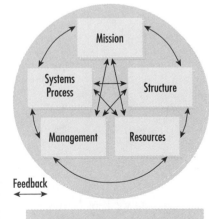

Figure 2-4
Internal Environment Components

Competition

Organizations must compete for customers. Competitors' strategic moves affect the performance of the organization.[21] FedEx was the first to offer overnight delivery by 10:30 A.M., but its primary competitor, United Parcel Service (UPS), was first to introduce overnight delivery by 8:30 A.M. followed by same-day delivery. FedEx is matching UPS's services to keep its customers. Other major competitors of FedEx include Roadway Package System (RPS), Airborne, and Express Mail–U.S. Postal Service, plus many other regional companies.

Another important area of customer value is pricing. When a competitor changes prices, firms tend to match prices to keep customers; for example, the increasing speed and dropping prices of PCs. Competition is increasing as the global economy expands.

Effective managers develop missions with strategies that offer a unique advantage over the competition.[22] Domino's Pizza developed free delivery guaranteed within 30 minutes (which was later changed), and took business away from Pizza Hut and others. Now, because of the competition, Pizza Hut and others also offer free delivery.

Time-based competition, which focuses on increasing the speed of going from product idea to delivery to customers, is a current trend. You will learn about time-based competition in Chapters 4 and 15.

WORK APPLICATION

4. Give an example of how one firm's competitors have affected that business.

Suppliers

Many organizations' resources come from outside the firm. Organizations often buy land, buildings, machines, equipment, natural resources, and component parts from suppliers.[23] Therefore, an organization's performance is affected by suppliers. General Motors (GM) built the Saturn plant and developed a separate Saturn dealership network to sell its cars. However, in its first year, because of production problems, Saturn dealers received only half of their allocation of cars. The dealer's performance was adversely affected. To be an effective manager you need to realize the importance of suppliers and develop close working relationships with them; this is an important part of TQM.[24]

Labor Force

The employees of the organization have a direct effect on its performance. Management recruits human resources from the available labor force outside its boundaries. The firm's mission, its structure, and its systems process are major determining factors of the capability levels employees need to meet objectives. The skills needed by FedEx employees differ from those needed by Gap employees.

Unions also provide employees for the organization. Unions are considered an external factor because they become a third party when dealing with the organization. Most UPS employees are members of the Teamsters

Union, whereas FedEx employees do not have a major union. The union has the power to strike. When a union strikes, revenues and wages are lost. The 1994 baseball strike, the 1997 UPS strike, which helped FedEx, and the GM strike of 1998[25] are examples.

Shareholders

The owners of a corporation, known as shareholders, have a significant influence on management. Most shareholders of large corporations are generally not involved in the day-to-day operation of the firm, but they do vote for the directors of the corporation. The board of directors is also generally not involved in the day-to-day operation of the firm. However, it hires and fires top management. The top manager reports to the board of directors. If the organization does not perform well, managers can be fired.

Society

Members of society may also exert pressure on the management of an organization to change.[26] Individuals and groups have formed to pressure business for changes. People who live in the area of a business do not want it to pollute the air or water or otherwise abuse the natural resources. Societal pressures have brought about tougher pollution requirements. Tuna companies used to kill dolphins when catching tuna. However, because of societal pressure, many companies now put claims on tunafish cans stating that they are "dolphin safe." Society is pressuring business to be socially responsible and ethical. You will learn more about ethics and social responsibility later in this chapter.

Technology

The rate of technological change will continue to increase.[27] Few organizations operate today as they did even a decade ago. Products not envisioned a few years ago are now being mass-produced. The computer has changed the way organizations conduct and transact business. Computers are often a major part of a firm's systems process. Telecommunications has been growing for a century and may be poised to explode into a wave of new products.

The Internet has been changing the way people do business. The Internet is blurring roles in the supply chain and giving small companies the chance to work with and compete against large businesses on an even footing.[28] The Internet is creating global opportunities for many organizations. Companies that do not use it or are slow to change face the threat of lost business to competitors. New technology creates opportunities for some companies and is a threat to others.

FedEx prides itself in using technology. FedEx was the first to develop the hub system that enabled overnight delivery and its real-time tracking system for all packages using COSMOS. On the other hand, the fax machine and

WORK APPLICATION

5. Give an example of how technology has affected one or more organizations, preferably one you work or have worked for.

e-mail created a threat to FedEx, offering instant delivery. Fortunately, the bulk of FedEx revenues comes from packages. If you want your management career to continue, you must keep up with the latest technology in your field. Be the first to volunteer to learn new things.

Economy

The organization has no control over economic growth, inflation, interest rates, foreign exchange rates, and so on, yet these things have a direct impact on its performance. In general, as measured by gross domestic product (GDP), businesses do better when the economy is growing than during times of decreased GDP, or recession. If business activity is slow, there are less packages to ship, so FedEx is affected as well.

During periods of inflation, businesses experience increased costs, which cannot always be passed along to consumers. This results in decreased profits. When interest rates are high, it costs more to borrow money, which may affect profits. Foreign exchange rates affect businesses both at home and abroad. When the dollar is weak, foreign goods are more expensive in the United States, and vice versa. A weak dollar helps to create opportunities for the United States. An understanding of economics, and more importantly global economics, can help you to advance to top-level management.

Governments

Foreign, federal, state, and local governments all set laws and regulations that businesses must obey. These laws remain pretty much intact through generations of political turnover, even though their interpretations, guidelines, and enforcement do depend heavily on the government officials of the time. The government environment is sometimes referred to as the political and legal environment.

The auto industry has been required to decrease the amount of pollution its cars emit into the air. Airlines have been told to decrease the noise level of their planes. Businesses can no longer dump their waste in our waterways. The Occupational Safety and Health Administration (OSHA) sets safety standards that must be met. Organizations cannot sell drugs without FDA approval. The Americans with Disabilities Act (ADA) compelled businesses to change many employment practices. In other words, to a large extent, business may not do whatever it wants to do; the government tells business what it can and cannot do. Sears-owned Allstate Insurance left the state of Massachusetts because of the unfavorable government environment.

Governments create both opportunities and threats for businesses. A number of years ago, the state of Maine changed the legal drinking age from 21 to 18. Dick Peltier opened a bar targeted for the 18- to 20-year-old group that became very successful. However, a few years later, the state increased the legal drinking age. Dick virtually lost his business overnight.

Global Government Trade Agreements. Organizations and governments are working together to develop free trade between countries. The General Agreement on Tariffs and Trade (GATT) is an international organization to which over 100 countries belong. GATT works to develop general agreements between all members and acts as a mediator between member countries who cannot resolve differences or when one country feels another is using unfair practices. A GATT panel can order unfair practices stopped or allow the country claiming unfair practices to retaliate.

There are European trade alliances, the largest being the European Union (EU), formerly called the European Community, which consists of 15 full-member states and countries: Austria, Belgium, Denmark, Finland, France, Greece, Ireland, Italy, Luxembourg, The Netherlands, Portugal, Spain, Switzerland, the United Kingdom, and Germany. Since late 1992, the EU has been a single market without national barriers to travel, employment, investment, and trade. EU members plan to have a single currency to create an Economic and Monetary Union (EMU). Some 13 billion new *euro* bank notes will be circulated, and some 280 million Europeans in 11 EU countries from Portugal to Finland will use the new currency.[29] The euro will make conducting business and traveling much easier in this trading block. Other countries plan to join the EU, and others have agreed to open their markets to EU products by the end of the decade.

The U.S.–Canada agreement was expanded to include Mexico in the North American Free Trade Agreement (NAFTA), which was created in 1993 and implemented in 1994. In the next 10 to 15 years, as many as 20,000 separate tariffs are expected to be eliminated to allow free trade among member countries. There is talk of expanding NAFTA to include alliances with Central and South America.

The Pacific Rim countries—Japan, China, Korea, Taiwan, Indonesia, Malaysia, the Philippines, Thailand, Hong Kong, and Singapore—do not have a formal alliance but do create an important growing market. For an illustration of these trading blocs, see Figure 2–5. These agreements between governments also affect the way firms conduct business in a global environment.

Chaos and Interactive Management

In many industries the environment is changing at an incredibly fast pace. It is commonly referred to as being in chaos. *Chaos theory* refers to the need for managers to make quick changes. Today's managers must be able to thrive on chaos.[30] But at the same time, change should be interactive.

According to Russell Ackoff, unlike reactive managers (who make changes only when forced to by external factors) and responsive managers (who try to adapt to the environment by predicting and preparing for change before they are required to do so), interactive managers design a desirable future and invent ways of bringing it about. They believe they are

NAFTA

EU

Pacific Asia

Figure 2-5
Trading Blocs

APPLYING THE CONCEPT

AC 2–2 The External Environment

Identify each statement by its external environmental factor.

a. customers	d. labor force	g. technology
b. competition	e. shareholders	h. governments
c. suppliers	f. society	i. economy

_____ **6.** "Procter & Gamble has developed a new biodegradable material to replace the plastic liner on its diapers so that they don't take up landfill space for so long."

_____ **7.** "At one time, AT&T was the only long-distance company, but then MCI, Sprint, and others came along and have taken away some of its customers."

_____ **8.** "I applied for a loan to start my own business, but I might not get it because money is tight these days, even though interest rates are high."

_____ **9.** "The owners of the company have threatened the CEO. They say they will fire the CEO if the business does not improve this year."

_____ **10.** "Management was going to sell our company to PepsiCo, but the government said we would be in violation of antitrust laws. What will happen to our company now?"

capable of creating a significant part of the future and controlling its effects on them. They try to prevent, not merely prepare for, threats and to create, not merely exploit, opportunities. Rather than react or respond, interactive managers make things happen for their benefit and for that of their stakeholders. In the early 1970s, people believed that overnight delivery was not possible, but this did not stop Smith from making overnight delivery become a reality through Federal Express. Do you have any great ideas for a new business or a way to help an existing business create customer value?

As a business grows, the complexity of its internal and external environments increases. The ma-

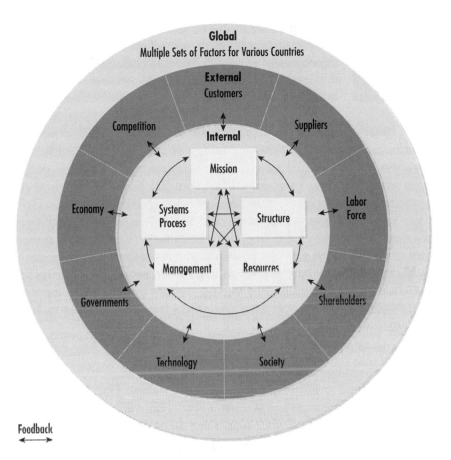

Figure 2-6
*The Organizational
Environment*

jor factor increasing the complexity of the environment is the globalization of markets.[31] For a review of the organizational environment, see Figure 2–6. Think about the complexity of FedEx's environment. FedEx does business worldwide. Therefore, it has to follow the rules and regulations of different governments in countries with different economies, labor forces, societies, and so on. In the next section you will learn about conducting business in a global environment.

CONDUCTING BUSINESS IN A GLOBAL ENVIRONMENT

In this section you will learn about global business, how to take a business global, practices of large global companies and small international businesses, and global diversity.

Competing in the global environment is necessary to any company's survival.[32] Even most small local businesses do, or will, compete with global companies at home. Managers, particularly in large companies, are embracing global management systems.[33] Of the largest 500 global companies,

4. State the difference between a domestic, an international, and a multinational business.

grouped according to country, the United States has more than any other country.[34] The global environment is characterized by rapidly transforming economies, instant communication, interconnected business alliances, close relationships with suppliers, and rapidly changing technology.[35] The question is no longer, "Should the business go global?" It's "How do we go global and how fast?"[36]

The primary reason for conducting business globally is to increase sales and profits.[37] If you start a *domestic business* (business conducted in only one country) in the United States, you have around 268 million people as potential customers. If you expand to transact business (buy and sell some inputs and outputs) in Canada and Mexico (NAFTA countries), you increase your population market to around 375 million. At this point, you would have an international business. An **international business** is *primarily based in one country but transacts business in other countries*. If you expand to the EU by setting up business operations in one of the 15 countries and transact business throughout the EU, you have 350 million more potential customers, for a total of around 725 million. Go to China and India and your market is up to around 3 billion people.[38] At the point when you have significant operations (an established place of conducting business at home and in at least one other country and have sales outside your home country of 25 percent or more), you would have a multinational or global business.[39]

international business
A business primarily based in one country that transacts business in other countries.

A **multinational corporation (MNC)** *has significant operations in more than one country*. Larger MNCs with established places of conducting business in many countries and with sales outside the home country exceeding 50 percent include Gillette, Colgate, Coca-Cola, IBM, Digital Equipment, NCR, Dow Chemical, Xerox, Alfac, Rhône-Poulene Rorer, Exxon, Mobil, Texaco, Motorola, Citicorp, BankBoston, Avon, and Hewlett-Packard. Nestlé is based in Vevy, Switzerland, and gets over 98 percent of its revenues and has over 95 percent of its assets outside of Switzerland. You may never start your own global business, but you may become an international manager. An *international manager* manages across a number of countries and cultures simultaneously.

multinational corporation (MNC)
A business with significant operations in more than one country.

5. Of the six ways to take a business global, list the lowest and the highest in cost and risk.

Taking a Business Global

A domestic business can go global in six major ways: global sourcing, importing and exporting, licensing, contracting, joint ventures, and direct investment. Figure 2–7 presents them in order by cost and risk and international versus MNC use.

Global Sourcing. **Global sourcing** *is the use of worldwide resources*. It is also called *outsourcing*.[40] The difference between a domestic manager and a global manager is where they look for the best deal on inputs and a location for transforming inputs into outputs. GM, Ford, and Chrysler use foreign material, supplies, and parts in their U.S.-made cars. For several years now,

global sourcing
The utilization of worldwide resources.

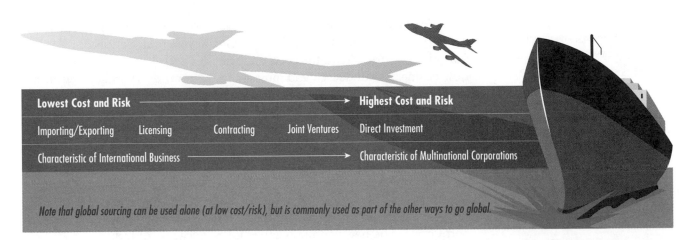

Lowest Cost and Risk			→	Highest Cost and Risk
Importing/Exporting	Licensing	Contracting	Joint Ventures	Direct Investment
Characteristic of International Business		→		Characteristic of Multinational Corporations

Note that global sourcing can be used alone (at low cost/risk), but is commonly used as part of the other ways to go global.

Figure 2-7
Taking a Business Global

Chrysler has been making cars in Canada that are sold in the United States. One of the major barriers to passing NAFTA was the threat of losing jobs to Mexico through maquiladoras. *Maquiladoras* are light-assembly plants built in Mexico, near the U.S. border, to take advantage of the low-cost labor. Both international corporations and MNCs use global sourcing.[41] As an international manager you will need to scan the globe, not just the United States, for the best deals.

Importing and Exporting. With *importing*, the domestic firm buys the products from the foreign firms and sells them at home. Pier 1 Imports and U.S. auto dealerships that sell Japanese and German cars are examples. With *exporting*, the domestic firm sells its products to a foreign buyer. Ford exports cars to Japanese dealerships.

Licensing. Under a *licensing* agreement, one company allows another to use its assets, such as brand name, trademark, technology, patent, and copyright. For a fee, Walt Disney allows companies around the world to make all kinds of products using Mickey Mouse and other characters. A common form of licensing is the *franchise* in which the franchiser provides a combination of trademark, equipment, materials, training, managerial guidelines, consulting advice, and cooperative advertising to the franchisee for a fee and a percentage of the revenues. McDonald's, Pizza Hut, Subway, and Holiday Inn, for example, have franchise operations all over the world.

Contracting. With *contract manufacturing*, a company has a foreign firm manufacture the goods while retaining the marketing process. Sears uses this approach in Latin America and Spain. Contract manufacturers make products with Sears' name on them, and Sears sells them in its stores. With *management contracting*, the seller provides management services for the foreign firm. Hilton operates hotels all over the world for local owners. All kinds of contract services can be provided.

joint venture
Created when firms share ownership (partnership) of a new enterprise.

direct investment
Occurs when a company builds or purchases operating facilities (subsidiaries) in a foreign country.

Joint Venture. A **joint venture** *is created when firms share ownership (partnership) of a new enterprise.* Toyota and GM have a joint venture in California. The two firms share the costs and risk, but both lose some control over how business is conducted and must share the rewards. A *strategic alliance* is an agreement but does not necessarily involve shared ownership. Kodak, Fuji, Canon, and Minolta have agreed to work together to develop new types of film. Kodak and Fuji will manufacture the film and Canon and Minolta will produce cameras to use it.

It is important to compete globally.[42] Thus over half of America's fastest-growing companies have teamed with others during the past three years to improve products or create new ones.[43] To be more competitive with FedEx, UPS entered a joint venture with local New Zealand company Fliway Transport Group. The new venture is called UPS-Fliway (NZ) Ltd.[44]

Direct Investment. **Direct investment** *occurs when a company builds or purchases operating facilities (subsidiaries) in a foreign country.* Ford and GM have production facilities in Europe. Becoming an MNC takes at least a joint venture, but the auto industry uses a combination of joint ventures and direct investments. The auto company trend is to make the cars closer to where they are sold.

In its pursuit of global expansion, FedEx made direct investments by purchasing 20 different companies. Clearly, FedEx is an MNC.

Practices of Large Global Companies

MNCs compete in a *global village*. This world has no boundaries, since MNCs will do business anywhere in the world using all six methods of going global.

MNCs have a global management team, strategy, operations and products, technology and R & D, financing, and marketing.[45]

Global Management Team. Leading global companies have top-level managers who are foreign nationals and subsidiaries managed by foreign nationals. Cross-culturally trained managers frequently travel to understand the cultures in which they do business. The fast management track now leads overseas; global companies want top managers who have been around the world.

Global Strategy. The entire global company has one strategy and structure, not one per subsidiary. Global dimensions are balanced for worldwide coordination to attain economies of scale and the local dimension that enables the country manager to respond to local consumer needs and counter local competition. There is no home-country preference. Global strategy utilizes direct investment, joint ventures, and strategic alliances.

Global Operations and Products. Global companies have standardized operations worldwide to attain economies of scale, and they make products to be sold worldwide, not just in local markets. In the mid-1990s Ford sold different cars in Europe and the United States with different operating equipment. However, Ford's stated goal is to have the same type of facilities producing the same cars that will be sold in NAFTA, EU, and other countries by the year 2000. Unit headquarters are placed in the country with the best resources to do the job, rather than in the home country. AT&T's corded telephone operation is headquartered in France, Du Pont's electronics in Japan, and IBM's networking systems in the United Kingdom.

Global Technology and R&D. Technology and research and development (R&D) are centralized in one country, rather than duplicated at each subsidiary, to develop world products. Global sourcing of technology and R&D is used. For example, Ford had Mazda develop its Probe, which Ford produces.

Global Financing. MNCs search world markets to get the best rates and terms when borrowing money for the long term; short-term financing is largely in individual countries using local financial institutions. Product prices are quoted in foreign currencies, rather than the home currency. MNCs sell stock in their subsidiary to the people in that country. They manage currency exchange—as well as global purchasing, currency hedging, currency risk exposure, and other important corporate functions—on an international basis.

Global Marketing. Global products and marketing are adapted for local markets. When McDonald's went to India, it had a problem. Can you guess what it was? If you said the cow is sacred in India and most people there will not eat an all-beef patty, you were correct. So McDonald's sells its Big Mac in India, but it's not beef. Advertisements are often developed by local agencies. Products used to be developed in the home market and then brought to other countries later, but the trend is toward global introduction of products (time-based competition). Gillette introduced its Sensor razor in the United States (during the 1990 Super Bowl) and 19 other countries at virtually the same time with the same advertisement.

FedEx follows these practices with strong emphasis on global delivery of packages using standardized operations. For a review of the list of practices of large global companies, see Figure 2–8.

Practices of Small International Companies

You do not have to be a big fish to swim in international waters. CEOs, even of small companies, need to think globally or they will be unemployed. It is actually easier for small companies to operate without much regard for national boundaries, and they can usually make changes much faster than large MNCs. The most successful global companies are small specialized niche players with one product or product line.[46] However,

Figure 2-8
Practices of Large Global Companies

Global Management Team

Global Strategy

Global Operations and Products

Global Company

Global Technology and R & D

Global Financing

Global Marketing

large MNCs have more resources than small businesses. Therefore, small firms tend to be international businesses rather than global companies, and they cannot follow all six practices of leading MNCs.[47] Let's examine the differences between large MNCs and small international businesses using the six practices.

Global Management Team. Small business owners often do not have, and cannot afford to hire, foreign managers.[48] However, consultants and agents can be hired to do the job.

Global Strategy. Whereas MNCs can afford to use direct investment and joint ventures as their strategy for going global, most small businesses don't have the money. They tend to use importing and exporting and global sourcing strategies to go global.

Global Operations and Products. While MNCs can afford to have their own operating facilities in many countries, most small businesses cannot. Therefore, they tend to provide fewer operating facilities, use contracting, or export to others who have the operating facilities. Small businesses can make standard products that can be sold globally.

Global Technology and R&D. Other than high-tech companies, most small businesses have a small or no budget for technology and R&D. However, many scan the globe and copy the latest developments quickly rather than developing them.

Global Financing. Generally, unlike MNCs, small businesses cannot borrow money from one country and invest it in another. To go global, many small business owners turn to the Export-Import Bank. Eximbank is a government agency responsible for aiding the export of U.S. goods and services through a variety of loan guarantees and insurance programs. Besides Eximbank, a small business may be able to get a loan in the country in which it plans to do business. This should be a consideration when selecting a country in which to do business.

Global Marketing. Small businesses can use export management companies, agents, and distributor services to conduct their marketing. In addition, small business managers can attend trade shows, network through trade centers, and advertise in industry publications.

WORK APPLICATION

6. Select a business and identify its level of globalization and as many of its global practices as you can.

Global Diversity

U.S. managers using traditional American management styles often fail in an overseas business culture.[49] Companies need to train employees in language, local culture, and local business practices so they can be successful globally.[50] When conducting business with foreign firms, and more importantly in foreign countries, be aware of cultural differences. To have successful human relations, you must be flexible and adapt to other peoples' ways of behaving; you are the foreigner and cannot expect others to change for you.

In this section you will learn about diversity in customs, attitude toward time, work ethic, pay, laws and politics, ethics, and participative management. Figure 2–9 lists global diversities. As you read, realize that you are presented with stereotypical generalities in which exceptions occur. The examples are not meant to judge "right" and "wrong" behavior. They are intended to illustrate cross-cultural differences that affect human relations and management.

Diversity in Customs. *Customs* are the accepted way of conducting business. The Japanese place a high priority on human relations, participative management, and teamwork.[51] If you try to be an individual star, you will not be successful in Japan. If you are very outspoken, you will be considered impolite in Japan. If you refuse to be involved in receiving and giving gifts, you will offend Japanese people. Many Japanese companies start the day with exercises and company cheers. If you do not actively participate, you will be an outsider.

In Europe, management has more cultural than technical aspects. It deals with value systems and religious backgrounds and is organized more as a language than as a set of techniques.[52] Power and politics (Chapter 9) are important in the United States, but they are even more important in France. It is important for a French manager to be seen as holding great power. Teamwork is less important in France. An essential part of the French morning routine for many men is to kiss most of the women of equivalent class to themselves. Unexpected kissing could create an embarrassing situation for you.

Americans prefer to speak face-to-face from a greater distance than people of most other countries. If you back away or turn to the side from others, they may follow you and create a dance, and you may be considered cold and stand-offish. During face-to-face communications, Latinos tend to touch each other more than Americans. Jumping when unexpectedly touched could create an embarrassing situation.

Gestures vary from country to country. For example, Americans prefer eye contact. However, if you talk to young Puerto Ricans they will look down as a mark of respect when speaking to adults because eye contact is considered rude. In Australia making the "V" sign with the hand is considered an obscenity rather than a sign of victory. Former President Bush found this out after flashing the "V" sign to the Australian crowds in 1992.

Diversity in Attitudes Toward Time. Americans typically view time as a valuable resource that is not to be wasted, and socializing is often considered a waste of time. However, it would be considered impolite to start a business meeting with Hispanics without engaging in a certain amount of relaxed small talk. If you try to rush business deals without slowly developing personal relationships with Japanese managers, you will not be successful in obtaining Japanese business accounts.

Figure 2-9
Global Diversities

American and Swiss businesspeople usually expect you to be precisely on time for an appointment. However, if you arrive on time for an appointment with a manager in other countries, you may be kept waiting for an hour. If you call a meeting in some countries, most members will be late and some may not show up at all. When they do show up they may express that punctuality was not one of their priorities. They may expect you to wait up to an hour for them. If you get angry and yell, you could harm human relations.

Diversity in Work Ethic. The work ethic—viewing work as a central interest and a desirable goal in life—varies all over the world. Generally, the Japanese have a higher work ethic than Americans and Europeans. With a high work ethic, and the acceptance of automation, many Japanese plants are the most productive in the world. Although there is not much difference in work ethic between Americans and Europeans, Americans are more productive even though Europeans are usually better trained than Americans.

Americans are relatively good at extracting value from poorly prepared workers, which is important when working with illiterate people all over the world. However, in some cultures, managers and employees have little interest in being productive. These relaxed attitudes do not do much for the bottom line of global businesses that are trying to change work ethic.

Diversity in Pay. Americans, in general, are no longer the world's highest-paid employees. The Japanese and Europeans have caught up and earn as much as Americans. Employees of Third World countries are paid much less than employees in developed countries.

Pay systems also must vary in some countries to meet employee values. One of the trends in American pay has been pay for performance. However, some countries value being paid for loyalty and following orders. Paying a salary works well in some countries, but not in others.

Diversity in Laws and Politics. The legal and political environment becomes increasingly complex as the multinational company does business all over the world. Employee health and safety laws are generally more protective of employees in developed countries than in Third World countries. Labor laws also vary widely from country to country. Western European nations offer good benefits, including a required four- to six-week vacation, paid holidays, and sick and family leave. It is also easier to terminate employees in some countries than in others.

In some countries, government structure and politics are much more stable than in others. A change in government can mean changes in business practices overnight. Some countries have literally taken away American business plants and equipment and sent the Americans home without any compensation.

Diversity in Ethics. When conducting global business you must rethink business ethics.[53] In the United States and other countries, it is illegal to take and give bribes for doing business. However, in many countries bribing is the standard practice of doing business. An American businessperson complained to a local telephone company manager that the service person showed up and asked for a bribe, which was refused, so the telephone worker left without installing the phone. The telephone company manager told the businessperson that the matter would be investigated, for a fee (bribe).

Diversity in Participative Management. In Third World nations, employees need basic skills training and are not capable of participating in management decisions without being trained to do so. Some cultures value participation in management whereas others are not interested. In some cultures employees simply want, and need, to be told what to do.

Management–labor relations vary globally. In France, management and labor are more polarized than in America, whereas in Japan they are more cooperative. Management and human relations become more complex as management styles change from country to country.

Global Diversity and the Functions of Management. What works well in the United States does not necessarily work in other countries. To successfully manage globally, the international manager must plan, organize, lead, and control differently according to the characteristics of the culture of the country. It is fine to come up with a general set of principles, but global companies cannot try to detail everything. With restaurants in more than 70 countries, McDonald's employment practices and philosophies, in essence, are similar around the world. However, this does not mean that McDonald's implements these practices the same way from one country to the next. To do so would be unfair and culturally inappropriate.[54]

6. Describe how global diversity affects the implementation of the management functions.

BUSINESS ETHICS

Business graduates have been called ethically naïve.[55] In recent years there has been an increased emphasis on business ethics.[56] You cannot go too many days without hearing or reading, in the mass media, some scandal related to unethical and/or unlawful behavior. **Ethics** *are the standards of right and wrong that influence behavior.* Right behavior is considered ethical, and wrong behavior is considered unethical. Government laws and regulations are designed to govern business behavior. However, ethics go beyond legal requirements. What is considered ethical in one country may be unethical in another. It is not always easy to distinguish between ethical and unethical behavior, such as a gift (ethical) versus a bribe (unethical). Secretaries' top pet peeves include bosses who lie and ask them to lie for them.[57, 58] Are little white lies ethical, and what is the difference between an unethical lie and a little white one? In this section you will learn that ethical behavior does pay; you will also learn about some simple guides to ethical behavior and about managing ethics.

ethics
Standards of right and wrong that influence behavior.

Does Ethical Behavior Pay?

Generally, the answer is yes. Recall from Chapter 1 that one of the qualities necessary to being a successful manager is integrity. Using ethical behavior is part of integrity. Ben and Jerry claim that the success of their ice cream business is based on their ethics and social responsibility.[59] At first, you may be richly rewarded for acting unethically, but retaliation follows, trust is lost, and productivity declines.[60] If you get caught in a lie, people will not trust you and it becomes difficult to get ahead in the organization. Organizations are interviewing job applicants carefully to avoid hiring unethical employees.[61] Good business and good ethics are synonymous. Ethics is at the heart and center of business, and profits and ethics are intrinsically related.[62]

Simple Guides to Ethical Behavior

Every day in your personal and professional life you face decisions in which you can make ethical or unethical choices. You make your choices based on your past learning experiences from parents, teachers, friends, managers, coworkers, and so forth. Your combined past makes up what many refer to as your conscience, which helps you choose right from wrong in a given situation. Following are some guides that can help you make the right decisions.

Golden Rule. Following the Golden Rule will help you be ethical. The golden rule is as follows:

"Do unto others as you want them to do unto you."

or

"Don't do anything to anyone that you would not want them to do to you."

Four-Way Test. Rotary International developed the four-way test of the things we think and do to guide business transactions. The four questions are (1) Is it the truth? (2) Is it fair to all concerned? (3) Will it build goodwill and better friendship? (4) Will it be beneficial to all concerned? When making your decision, if you can answer yes to these four questions it is probably ethical.

7. Explain the stakeholders' approach to ethics.

stakeholders' approach to ethics
Creating a win-win situation for all stakeholders so that everyone benefits from the decision.

Stakeholders' Approach to Ethics. Under the **stakeholders' approach to ethics,** *when making decisions, you try to create a win-win situation for all relevant stakeholders so that everyone benefits from the decision.* The higher up in management you go, the more stakeholders you have to deal with.[63] You can ask yourself one simple question to help you determine if your decision is ethical from a stakeholders' approach:

"Am I proud to tell relevant stakeholders my decision?"

If you are proud to tell relevant stakeholders your decision, it is probably ethical. If you are not proud to tell others your decision or you keep rationalizing it, the decision may not be ethical. If you are unsure if a decision is ethical, talk to your boss, higher-level managers, ethics committee members, and other people with high ethical standards. If you are reluctant to ask others for advice on an ethical decision because you may not like their answers, the decision may not be ethical.

Unfortunately, sometimes decisions must be made that do not benefit all stakeholders. For example, if business is slow, a layoff may be necessary. Usually, the employees who get laid off do not benefit from the decision. Many large companies that permanently lay off employees offer severance pay and outplacement services to help the employees get jobs with other organizations.

Managing Ethics

An organization's ethics are based on the collective behavior of its employees. If each individual is ethical, the organization will be ethical too. The starting place for ethics is you.[64] Are you an ethical person? Exercise 2–1 at the end of this chapter will help you answer this question. From the management perspective, managers should set guidelines for ethical behavior, set a good example, and enforce ethical behavior.

Codes of Ethics. Codes of ethics, also called codes of conduct, state the importance of conducting business in an ethical manner and provide guidelines for ethical behavior.[65] Most large businesses have written codes of ethics. See Figure 2–10 for the code of ethics at Exxon Company, U.S.A.

Top Management Support. It is the responsibility of management from the top down to develop codes of ethics, to ensure that employees are trained and instructed on what is and what is not considered ethical behavior, and to enforce ethical behavior.[66] However, the primary responsibility is

---

Business Ethics
- Our Company policy is one of strict observance of all laws applicable to its business.
- A reputation for scrupulous dealing is itself a priceless Company asset.
- We do care how we get results.
- We expect candor at all levels and compliance with accounting rules and controls.

Conflict of Interest
- Competing or conducting business with the Company is not permitted, except with the knowledge and consent of management.
- Accepting and providing gifts, entertainment, and services must comply with specific requirements.
- An employee may not use Company personnel, information, or other assets for personal benefit.
- Participating in certain outside activities requires the prior approval of management.

Figure 2-10
Summary Code of Ethics of Exxon Company, U.S.A.

to lead by example. Employees tend to look to managers, especially top managers, for examples of behavior. If managers are not ethical, employees will not be ethical. Jack S. Llewellyn, President and CEO of Ocean Spray, believes that the CEO has to be the model for ethical standards, and that managers will treat customers and workers fairly if the CEO does.

Enforcing Ethical Behavior. If employees are rewarded rather than punished for their unethical behavior, they will conduct unethical business practices. Many organizations have developed ethics committees that act as judge and jury to determine if unethical behavior has been conducted and what the punishment should be for violating company policy. More companies are establishing ethics offices, with a director or vice president who reports directly to the CEO, to establish ethics policies, listen to employees' complaints, conduct training, and investigate abuses such as sexual harassment.

As a means of enforcing ethical behavior, employees should be encouraged to engage in internal whistle-blowing.[67] *Whistle-blowing* occurs when employees expose what they believe to be unethical behavior by their fellow employees. Whistle-blowers can go internally to management and report unethical behavior or they can go to external sources like the government or newspapers. According to the law and ethics, whistle-blowers should not suffer any negative consequences. Would you report unethical behavior by fellow employees to your boss or upper-level managers? If upper-level managers engage in, or support, unethical behavior, would you go outside the organization to report it? It is not easy to say whether or not you would be a whistle-blower without being in a specific situation, but some day you may be faced with that decision.

By living its People–Service–Profits philosophy, FedEx is considered to be an ethical company. FedEx has a code of ethics that stresses the achievement of the highest possible standards of business and personal ethics.

WORK APPLICATION

7. Select a business and identify how it manages ethics.

SOCIAL RESPONSIBILITY

social responsibility
The conscious effort to operate in a manner that creates a win-win situation for all stakeholders.

Ethics and social responsibility are closely related. **Social responsibility** *is the conscious effort to operate in a manner that creates a win-win situation for all stakeholders.* Ethical behavior is often socially responsible and vice versa. In this section you will learn about social responsibility to stakeholders, that it pays to be socially responsible, and the four levels of social responsibility.

Social Responsibility to Stakeholders

Companies have a social responsibility to try to create a win-win situation with all nine external categories of stakeholders, as well as with the internal stakeholders—the employees you learned about earlier in this chapter. For *customers*, the company must provide safe products and services with customer value. For *society*, the company should improve the quality of life, or at least not destroy the environment. Senior executives of large global corporations acknowledge their responsibility to control pollution. Businesses that have developed environmental programs state that they are more efficient and competitive.[68] The company must compete fairly with *competitors*. Through *technology*, the company should develop new ways of increasing customer value and the

APPLYING THE CONCEPT
AC 2–3 Stakeholders

Identify each statement by its stakeholder:

a. employees c. society   e. suppliers
b. customers d. competitors f. government

____ **11.** "We are going to fight that utility company to stop it from putting a nuclear power plant in our town."

____ **12.** "I bought this cigarette. It exploded in my face when I lit it, causing me injury."

____ **13.** "The town board is very political, so you have to play games if you want to get a liquor license."

____ **14.** "I'm sorry to hear your retail sales are down; we will have to cut back our production."

15. "I bid on the job, but PIP's got the contract to print the material."

quality of life. The company must work with *suppliers* in a cooperative manner. It must abide by the laws and regulations of *government*. The company must strive to provide equal employment opportunities for the *labor force*. It must be financially responsible in relation to the *economy*. The company must provide *shareholders* with a reasonable profit. It must provide *employees* with safe working conditions with adequate pay and benefits.[69]

Does It Pay to Be Socially Responsible?

Various researchers have tried to determine the relationship between social responsibility and financial performance. However, results based on financial performance alone have been inconsistent. An alternative performance measure based on stakeholders' response was tested and a relationship was established between social responsibility and performance.[70] Overall stock prices do not fall based on the announcement of some corporate illegalities, but they do fall when bribery, tax evasion, or violations of government contracts are announced.[71] In a survey, 88 percent of respondents stated that they were more inclined to buy from companies that are socially responsible than from companies that are not.[72] Although there is no clear link between social responsibility and bottom-line profits, we can at least say that it does not hurt performance. Therefore, social responsibility does pay because company stakeholders benefit.[73] Ben & Jerry's ice cream is a leader in social responsibility because owners Ben Cohen and Jerry Greenfield are committed to the dual aims of bottom-line profits and social responsibility. Ben & Jerry's is the most generous company: it gives 7.5% of its profits for socially responsible activities. Ben & Jerry's started with $8,000 in savings from a converted gasoline station in Vermont in 1978 to become an international distributor of prepackaged ice cream yielding annual sales of more than $170 million.[74]

8. Discuss the differences in the four levels of social responsibility: obstruction, obligation, reaction, and involvement.

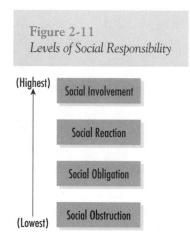

Figure 2-11
Levels of Social Responsibility

(Highest)

Social Involvement

Social Reaction

Social Obligation

(Lowest) Social Obstruction

WORK APPLICATION

8. Select a business and identify its level of social responsibility for a specific issue.

Levels of Social Responsibility

Historically, capitalism was based on economist Adam Smith's ideas and practices. Smith stated that in the long run public interests are served by individuals and businesses that pursue their own self-interest, and that government should play a limited role. Milton Friedman, economist and Nobel laureate, agrees with Smith; when a business makes a profit, it is being socially responsible. A corporation has no responsibility to society beyond that of obeying the law and maximizing profits for shareholders.[75] On the other extreme, CEOs have been accused of not placing a high value on social responsibility. Most managers' and employees' views fall between these two extremes. Four levels of social responsibility have been identified: social obstruction, social obligation, social reaction, and social involvement. For an illustration of the four levels of social responsibility, see Figure 2–11.

Social Obstruction. Under *social obstruction*, managers deliberately perform, or request employees to perform, unethical or illegal business practices. For example, Ashland Oil was found guilty of setting prices with other contractors in order to charge higher prices for highway work in Tennessee and North Carolina. Ashland managers also wrongfully fired two employees because they refused to cover up illegal company payments. In such cases, whistle-blowing and strong government penalties can help prevent social obstruction.

Social Obligation. Under *social obligation*, managers meet only the minimum legal requirements. Compliance is an approach in which firms rely on end-of-pipe types of pollution control and often resist the passage and enforcement of environmental regulations.[76]

Social Reaction. Under *social reaction*, managers respond to appropriate societal requests. The most common type of social reaction takes place when civic groups go to a company and ask for donations for the arts, college scholarships, antidrug programs; sponsorship of sports teams; or the use of company facilities for meetings or sports team use. Companies, including IBM and Exxon, also match employee contributions to worthwhile charitable causes.

Social Involvement. Under *social involvement*, managers voluntarily initiate socially responsible acts. McDonald's was socially involved when it established Ronald McDonald houses to help the families of sick children. FedEx is at the social involvement level of social responsibility. FedEx was the first to invest in a noise-reduction program to enable 727-100 aircraft to fly at Stage 3 noise levels (the quietest noise levels certified by the FAA). FedEx encourages employees to devote personal time to community service through volunteerism.

Many organizations can be classified as being at one of the four levels of social responsibility. However, an organization can be on different levels for different issues.

Social Audit. A *social audit* is a measure of a firm's social behavior. Many large businesses set social objectives and thus try to measure if they have met the objectives. Many large corporations include a social audit in their annual report.

Are Downsizing, Re-engineering, and Contingent Workers Socially Responsible?

To increase *productivity*, many firms are downsizing. **Downsizing** *is the process of cutting organizational resources to get more done with less as a means of increasing productivity.* The primary area of cutting is human resources. Many large organizations have cut jobs by the thousands as part of cost-cutting programs. To be competitive in a global market, companies must do more with less, but simply cutting jobs and requiring the remaining employees to do the same jobs of two or three people does not work in the long run. An alternative to downsizing is re-engineering, which involves downsizing in a systematic manner.

Re-engineering *involves the radical redesign of work to combine fragmented tasks into streamlined processes that save time and money* (time-based competition). With re-engineering you start with a fresh approach that assumes there are no current jobs. You design the process so that *teams* are involved in *participative management*, from acquiring inputs all the way through to transforming them into outputs. Re-engineered work usually requires fewer workers and far fewer managers. With re-engineering, teams work on a whole process and have a real sense of closure because they have the power to make decisions and can point to an outcome and say, "I made that happen." Re-engineered jobs tend to be much more rewarding than traditional jobs.[77] However, the employees who lose their jobs don't benefit.

To cut costs, many organizations use contingent workers. *Contingent workers* are part-time, temporary, and freelance laborers. Organizations primarily use contingent workers because they generally do not give these workers any benefits. It is less costly to have two part-time workers than one full-time employee. Wal-Mart keeps its costs down in part by keeping its compensation level low. Contingent workers make up 25 percent of the

---

APPLYING THE CONCEPT

AC 2–4 Levels of Social Responsibility
Identify each statement by its level of social responsibility.
a. social obstruction   c. social reaction
b. social obligation   d. social involvement

____ **16.** "I agree that a Boys and Girls Club downtown would be beneficial to our city. We will give you $1,000 for the project."

____ **17.** "I'm disappointed with the reading levels of employees coming from our local high school. Betty, I want you to contact the principal and see if you can work together to develop a program to improve reading skills."

____ **18.** "Bill, the auditor will be here next week, so we'd better make sure that the inventory we took does not show up as missing."

____ **19.** "We stopped killing seals with clubs because of the bad press we were receiving. Now we use guns, which is more expensive."

____ **20.** "As of June 1 the new regulations go into effect. We will have to cut the amount of waste we dump into the river by half. Get the lowest bidder to pick up the other half and dispose of it."

---

9. Explain the difference between downsizing and re-engineering.

downsizing
The process of cutting organizational resources to get more done with less as a means of increasing productivity.

re-engineering
The radical redesign of work to combine fragmented tasks into streamlined processes that save time and money.

work force and outnumber all employees of the Fortune 500 companies combined.[78]

Downsizing and re-engineering have not been successful at many organizations because management is focusing on cost cutting and has not made the necessary investment in human resources. According to Hammer, co-author of the book that coined the term *re-engineering*, "The biggest lie told by most corporations, and they tell it proudly, is that people are our most important assets. Total fabrication. They treat people like raw materials. If you're serious about treating people as an asset, we're looking at a dramatic increase in investment in them."[79] "I tell companies they need to quintuple their investment in education. Training is about skills; education is about understanding broad knowledge. Everybody who works in a company needs to understand the business." This includes complete understanding of the company mission, objectives, and strategy (Chapter 4).[80]

Downsizing and re-engineering have not been successful.[81] The price was paid by U.S. workers, who were needlessly laid off in record numbers through downsizing for the sake of higher stock values.[82] And the growth in the number of contingent workers is bad news for workers who want full-time jobs with benefits.[83]

CHAPTER SUMMARY AND GLOSSARY

The chapter summary is organized to answer the ten learning objectives for Chapter 2.

1. Explain the five internal environment factors: management, mission, resources, systems process, and structure.

Management refers to the people responsible for an organization's performance. Mission is the organization's purpose or reason for being. The organization has human, physical, financial, and informational resources to accomplish its mission. The systems process is the method of transforming inputs into outputs as the organization accomplishes its mission. Structure refers to the way in which the organization groups its resources to accomplish its mission.

2. List and explain the need for the two primary principles of total quality management (TQM).

The two primary principles of TQM are (1) focus on delivering customer value and (2) continually improve the system and its processes. To be successful, businesses must continually offer value to attract and retain customers. Without customers you don't have a business.

3. Describe how the nine external environmental factors—customers, competitors, suppliers, labor force, shareholders, society, technology, economies, and governments—can affect the internal business environment.

Customers should decide what products the business offers, for without customer value there are no customers or business. *Competitors'* business practices, such as features and prices, often have to be duplicated in order to maintain customer value. Poor-quality inputs from *suppliers* result in poor-quality outputs without customer value. Without a qualified *labor force* or employees, products and services will have little or no customer value. *Shareholders*, through an elected board of directors, hire top managers and provide directives for the organization. *Society* pressures business to perform or not perform certain activities, such as pollution control. The business must develop new *technologies*, or at least keep up with them, to provide customer value. *Economic* activity affects the organization's ability to provide customer value. For example, inflated prices lead to lower customer value. *Governments* set the rules and regulations that business must adhere to.

4. State the difference between a domestic, an international, and a multinational business.

A domestic firm does business in only one country. An international firm is primarily based in one country but transacts business with other countries. Multinational corporations (MNCs) have significant operations in more than one country.

5. Of the six ways to take a business global, list the lowest and the highest in cost and risk.

Importing and exporting is the lowest and direct investment is the highest in cost and risk; global sourcing can be part of either method.

6. Describe how global diversity affects the implementation of the management functions.

Because of global diversity, management practices that work well in one country may not work at all in another. Therefore, when performing the management functions of planning, organizing, leading, and controlling, the manager must understand the customs and culture of the country.

7. Explain the stakeholders' approach to ethics.

Under the stakeholders' approach to ethics, you create a win-win situation for the relevant parties affected by the decision. If you are proud to tell relevant stakeholders about your decision, it is probably ethical. If you are not proud to tell stakeholders, or if you keep rationalizing the decision, it may not be ethical.

8. Discuss the differences in the four levels of social responsibility: obstruction, obligation, reaction, and involvement.

Participation in social responsibility goes from a low to high level. Under social obstruction, managers conduct unethical, illegal behavior. Under social obligation, managers meet only the minimum legal requirements. Under social reaction, managers respond to societal requests. Under social involvement, managers voluntarily initiate socially responsible acts.

9. Explain the difference between downsizing and re-engineering.
Downsizing is the process of cutting organizational resources to get more done with less as a means of increasing productivity. Re-engineering involves the radical redesigning of work to combine fragmented tasks into streamlined processes that save time and money. Downsizing simply focuses on cutting resources, whereas re-engineering focuses on developing new jobs.

10. Define the following key terms (in order of appearance in the chapter):
Select one or more methods: (1) fill in the missing key terms from memory, (2) match the key terms from the end of the summary with their definitions below, or (3) copy the key terms in order from the list at the beginning of the chapter.

The organization's _____ includes the factors that affect the organization's performance from within its boundaries.

The organization's _____ is its purpose or reason for being.

_____ are people whose interests are affected by organizational behavior.

The _____ is the method for transforming inputs into outputs.

Customers determine _____ by comparing actual use to requirements to determine value.

_____ is the purchasing benefits expected by customers to determine whether or not to buy a product.

_____ is a process that involves everyone in the organization focusing on the customer to continually improve product value.

The organization's _____ includes the factors that affect its performance from outside its boundaries.

An _____ is primarily based in one country but transacts business in other countries.

A _____ has significant operations in more than one country.

_____ is the utilization of worldwide resources.

A _____ is created when firms share ownership (partnership) of a new enterprise.

_____ occurs when a company builds or purchases operating facilities (subsidiaries) in a foreign country.

_____ are the standards of right and wrong that influence behavior.

Under the _____, when making decisions you try to create a win-win situation for all relevant stakeholders so that everyone benefits from the decision.

_____ is the conscious effort to operate in a manner that creates a win-win situation for all stakeholders.

_____ is the process of cutting organizational resources to get more done with less as a means of increasing productivity.

_____ involves the radical redesign of work to combine fragmented tasks into streamlined processes that save time and money.

KEY TERMS

customer value   46

direct investment   56

downsizing   67

ethics   61

external environment   47

global sourcing   54

internal environment   44

international business   54

joint venture   56

mission   44

multinational corporation (MNC)   54

quality   46

re-engineering   67

social responsibility   64

stakeholders   44

stakeholders' approach to ethics   62

systems process   45

total quality management (TQM)   47

REVIEW AND DISCUSSION QUESTIONS

1. Do you believe that most organizations really focus on creating customer value? Explain.

2. Do you think that all organizations should use TQM? Explain your answer.

3. What is the relationship between management and mission, resources, the systems process, and structure? Which of these internal factors are ends and which are means?

4. What major technology change has had the greatest impact on the quality of your life?

5. Is NAFTA of more benefit or harm to the United States?

6. Should government regulation of business be increased, decreased, or remain the same as it is now?

7. Can you list any international and global companies in the area of your college?

8. For some of the companies you listed in question 7, can you identify their method(s) of going global?

9. Do you believe that if you use ethical behavior it will pay off in the long run?

10. Do you have your own guide to ethical behavior that you follow now? Will you use one of the guides from the text? If yes, which one and why?

11. Can ethics be taught and learned?

12. Do you believe that companies benefit from being socially responsible? If yes, how?

13. As a CEO, what level of social responsibility would you use?

14. With global sourcing, downsizing, and re-engineering, U.S. workers lose jobs. Are these practices ethical and socially responsible?

OBJECTIVE CASE

The Tobacco Industry

Over the years there has been pressure on the tobacco companies [major competitors include R.J. Reynolds (part of RJR Nabisco), Philip Morris, and Brown & Williamson] to limit or even stop the sale of tobacco products in the United States. With researchers reporting that cigarette smoking is hazardous to peoples' health, the Surgeon General mandated that warning labels be placed on all packs of cigarettes.

Tobacco companies have been accused of putting substances into their cigarettes to make them addictive. There is evidence that these companies knew of the health dangers of cigarettes many years ago and kept the information

OBJECTIVE CASE

(continued)

from the public and that they even destroyed such reports. The government is pushing for tobacco legislation as people and the government have been winning lawsuits against the tobacco companies for damages. According to the Treasury department, smoking costs the United States about $130 billion a year in shortened working lives and added health-care spending.[84] As the government unsuccessfully tries to prevent minors from smoking, many businesses continue to sell minors cigarettes illegally.

In spite of the pressure, tobacco companies are profitable and claim that they provide customers with a product they want. With cigarette profits, the sale of stock, and debt, tobacco companies have diversified to provide other means of income. Philip Morris bought Miller Beer, General Foods, and Kraft. R.J. Reynolds and Nabisco are now one company. Despite pressure and diversification, the tobacco companies are not about to stop selling cigarettes.

Tobacco companies do not force people to buy their cigarettes. As long as people continue to smoke, some business will provide the cigarettes, so why shouldn't it be RJR and Philip Morris? If either of these two companies stopped selling cigarettes, it would just mean more business for the other one. If they both stopped selling cigarettes, some new company would provide them, so long as it is profitable. Besides, the government collects a lot of taxes on the sale of cigarettes, and the tobacco companies pay taxes on their cigarette profits, which in turn help to pay for programs that help the poor. The tobacco industry provides many thousands of people with jobs, and thousands of businesses sell cigarettes at a profit.

Even before all the antismoking pressure in the United States, tobacco companies realized the potential for increased sales overseas. The Asian market alone sells more than $90 billion worth of cigarettes annually. In fact, over ten years ago, the U.S. government helped RJR and Philip Morris send cigarettes into the Asian market by threatening to boycott goods from Japan, Taiwan, and Korea.

Fewer than 10 percent of Asian women and adolescents smoke, and U.S. tobacco companies promised not to go after them. However, Philip Morris advertises a cigarette geared to women (Virginia Slims), and RJR sponsored three concerts featuring a popular Hong Kong rock star with the admissions price being five empty packs of Winston cigarettes. American and Taiwanese officials have complained that U.S. companies have hired people to hand out cigarettes to 12-year-olds at amusement parks.

Select the best alternative for the following questions. Be sure you are able to explain your answers.

____ 1. Tobacco companies provide a quality product with customer value.

    a. true   b. false

____ 2. RJR and Philip Morris have shareholders.

    a. true   b. false

____ 3. Technology has had a major effect on the tobacco industry.

    a. true   b. false

____ 4. The primary pressure on the tobacco industry is coming from the ___ external factors.

    a. customers and competition

    b. society and governments

    c. suppliers and labor

    d. economy and competition

    e. shareholders and technology

____ 5. GATT, NAFTA, EU, and Pacific Asia have the power to affect tobacco companies' performance.

    a. true   b. false

____ 6. RJR and Philip Morris are ___ companies.

    a. domestic   c. MNC

    b. international

OBJECTIVE CASE

(continued)

___ 7. Based on information in the case, the primary way RJR and Philip Morris took the business global to Asia was through ___ .

   a. exporting   d. joint venture

   b. licensing   e. direct investment

   c. contracting

___ 8. Tobacco companies have been accused of unethical practices.

   a. true   b. false

___ 9. Managers at RJR and Philip Morris appear to be strongly enforcing ethical behavior in Asia.

   a. true   b. false

___ 10. Overall, in the United States, tobacco companies are on the ___ level of social responsibility.

   a. social obstruction   c. social reaction

   b. social obligation   d. social involvement

11. Are the tobacco companies ethical? Explain your answer.

12. Are the tobacco companies socially responsible? In other words, do they make a conscious effort to operate in a manner that creates a win-win situation for all stakeholders?

13. If the U.S. government passed a law making the sale of cigarettes illegal, how would each of the nine external factors benefit and/or be hurt?

14. Should the U.S. government pass a law making the sale of cigarettes illegal?

For current information on RJR, use Internet address http://rjrnabisco.com, and for Philip Morris use http://pmdocs.com. For ideas on using the Internet, see Appendix B.

VIDEO CASE

Central Michigan Community Hospital I

(2-1 11½ min.)

Case Summary

Central Michigan Community Hospital (CMCH) is a full-service, not-for-profit hospital serving the rural center of Michigan. CMCH offers acute care in its 151-bed facility as well as occupational medicine, wellness medicine, walk-in urgent care, and home health care. CMCH has been recognized as one of the top 100 hospitals in the United States.

Student Learning Objective

To understand the complexity of the external environment and how it affects all organizations, specifically the health care provider.

Critical Thinking Questions

1. Who are Central Michigan Community Hospital's customers, and how do they affect CMCH?

2. How do technology, competition, physicians (labor force), and the government affect CMCH?

Skill-Building Exercise 2–1

The Organizational Environment and Management Practices Analysis

Preparing for Skill-Building Exercise 2–1

For this exercise you will select a specific organization. It is recommended that you select an organization you work or have worked for. Answer the questions as they relate to the business you selected. You may contact people in the organization to get your answers. Write your answers to all questions.

The Internal Environment

1. Identify the top managers and briefly discuss their leadership style.

2. State the organization's mission.

3. Identify some of the organization's major resources.

4. Explain the organization's systems process. Discuss how the organization ensures quality and customer value.

5. Identify the organization's structure by listing its major departments.

The External Environment

(Within your answer to this section's questions, be sure to state how each of these external factors affects the organization.)

6. Identify the organization's target customers.

7. Identify the organization's major competitors.

8. Identify the organization's major suppliers.

9. What is the major labor force the organization recruits from?

10. Does the organization have shareholders? Is its stock listed on one of the three major stock exchanges? If yes, which one?

11. How does the organization affect society and vice versa?

12. Describe some of the past, present, and future technologies of the organization's industry. Is the organization a technology leader?

13. Identify the governments that affect the organization. List some of the major laws and regulations affecting the business.

14. Explain how the economy affects the organization.

Globalization

15. Is the organization a domestic, an international, or a global company?

16. If the organization is international or global, list and briefly describe its global activities (exporting, etc.).

17. If the organization is international or global, list and briefly describe its practices (management team, strategy, etc.).

Ethics

18. Does the organization have any guides to ethical behavior? If yes, explain.

19. How does the organization manage ethics? Does it have a code of ethics (what's in it)? Does top management lead by good ethical example? Are ethical behaviors enforced (how)?

Social Responsibility

20. Overall, on which level of social responsibility does the organization operate? Identify some of the things the organization does to be socially responsible and the level of social responsibility.

Doing Skill-Building Exercise 2–1 in Class

Objective

To develop the conceptual skill to analyze an organization's environmental and management practices.

Preparation

You should have completed the organizational environment preparation before class.

Experience
The primary skill building comes from the preparation for this exercise. Class members will share their preparation to reinforce learning.

Options (10–30 minutes)

1. The class breaks into groups of three to five members. Each member tells the others his or her answers to the preparation. One student's example may be selected and presented to the entire class.

2. The instructor calls one member of the class to give his or her answers to the preparation. Several students may be called on to give their answers.

3. The instructor calls on different students to give answers to different parts of the preparation.

Conclusion
The instructor may make concluding remarks.

Application (2–4 minutes)
What did I learn from this experience? How will I use this knowledge in the future?

_____

_____

Sharing
Volunteers give their answers to the application section.

Exercise 2–1

Ethics and Whistle-Blowing

I G   Self-Assessment Exercise 2–1

Preparing for Exercise 2–1
Is Your Behavior Ethical?
For this exercise you will be using the same set of statements twice. The first time you respond to them, focus on your own behavior and the frequency with which you use it. On the line preceding the question, place the number 1–5 that represents how often you did, do, or would do the behavior if you had the chance. These numbers will alow you to determine your level of ethics. You can be honest without fear of having to tell others your score in class. Sharing ethics scores is not part of the exercise.

The second time you use the statements, focus on other people in an organization that you work or have worked for. Place an "O" on the line after the number if you observed someone doing this behavior. Also place a "W" on the line if you reported this behavior (whistle-blowing) within the organization or externally.

Column 1   Frequently   Never

             1   2   3   4   5

Column 2   O—observed   W—reported

College

____ 1. ____ Cheating on homework assignments.

____ 2. ____ Passing in papers that were completed by someone else, as your own work.

____ 3. ____ Cheating on exams.

Job

____ 4. ____ Coming to work late and getting paid for it.

____ 5. ____ Leaving work early and getting paid for it.

____ 6. ____ Taking long breaks/lunches and getting paid for it.

_____ 7. _____ Calling in sick to get a day off, when not sick.

_____ 8. _____ Socializing or goofing off rather than doing the work that should be done.

_____ 9. _____ Using the company phone to make personal calls.

_____ 10. _____ Doing personal work while on company time.

_____ 11. _____ Using the company copier for personal use.

_____ 12. _____ Mailing personal things through the company mail.

_____ 13. _____ Taking home company supplies or merchandise and keeping it.

_____ 14. _____ Taking home company tools/equipment without permission for personal use and returning it.

_____ 15. _____ Giving company supplies or merchandise to friends or allowing them to take them without saying anything.

_____ 16. _____ Putting in for reimbursement for meals and travel or other expenses that weren't actually eaten or taken.

_____ 17. _____ Using the company car for personal business.

_____ 18. _____ Taking spouse/friends out to eat and charging it to the company expense account.

_____ 19. _____ Taking a spouse/friend on business trips and charging the expense to the company.

_____ 20. _____ Accepting gifts from customers/suppliers in exchange for giving them business.

To determine your ethics score, add up the numbers 1–5. Your total will be between 20 and 100. Place the number here _____ and on the continuum below that represents your score.

Unethical   Ethical

20—30—40—50—60—70—80—90—100

Discussion Questions

1. For the college items 1–3, who is harmed and who benefits from these unethical behaviors?

2. For job items 4–20, select the three (circle their numbers) you consider the most severe unethical behavior. Who is harmed and who benefits by these unethical behaviors?

3. If you observed unethical behavior but didn't report it, why didn't you report the behavior? If you did blow the whistle, why did you report the unethical behavior? What was the result?

4. As a manager it is your responsibility to uphold ethical behavior. If you know employees are doing any of these unethical behaviors, will you take action to enforce compliance with ethical standards?

Doing Exercise 2–1 in Class

Objective

To better understand ethics and whistle-blowing and what you will do about unethical behavior.

Preparation

You should have completed the preparation for this exercise.

Experience

You will share your answers to the preparation questions, but are not requested to share your ethics score.

Procedure 1 (5–10 minutes)

The instructor writes the numbers 1–20 on the board. For each statement students raise their hands if they observed this behavior, and again if they reported the behavior. The instructor writes the numbers on the board. (Note: Procedures 1 and 2A may be combined.)

Procedure 2 (10–20 minutes)

Option A: As the instructor takes a count of the students who have observed and reported unethical behavior, he or she leads a discussion on the statements.

Option B: Break into groups of four to six and share your answers to the four discussion questions at the end of the preparation part of this exercise. The groups may be asked to report their general consensus to the entire class. If so, select a spokesperson before the discussion begins.

Option C: The instructor leads a class discussion on the four discussion questions at the end of the preparation part of this exercise.

Conclusion

The instructor may make concluding remarks.

Application (2–4 minutes)

What did I learn from this exercise? How will I use this knowledge in the future?

_____

_____

Sharing

Volunteers give their answers to the application section.

3 Creative Problem Solving and Decision Making

Learning Objectives

After studying this chapter, you should be able to:

1. Explain the relationship among objectives, problem solving, and decision making.

2. Explain the relationship among the management functions, decision making, and problem solving.

3. List the six steps in the decision-making model.

4. Describe the difference between programmed and nonprogrammed decisions and among the conditions of certainty, uncertainty, and risk.

5. Describe when to use the decision-making model versus the bounded rationality model and group versus individual decision making.

6. State the difference between an objective and "must" and "want" criteria.

7. State the difference between creativity and innovation.

8. List and explain the three stages in the creative process.

9. Describe the differences among quantitative, Kepner-Tregoe, and cost-benefit analysis techniques for analyzing and selecting an alternative.

10. Define the following **key terms** (in order of appearance in the chapter):

problem	innovation
problem solving	creativity
decision making	creative process
decision-making model	devil's advocate
programmed decisions	brainstorming
nonprogrammed decisions	synectics
decision-making conditions	nominal grouping
criteria	consensus mapping

Skill Development

skillbuilder

1. You can develop your problem-solving and decision-making skills by learning to use the decision-making model (Skill-Building Exercise 3–1).

   This skill is part of conceptual and decision-making management skill. Decision making is used when performing all four management functions and the five SCANS competencies. This skill is part of the decisional management role and SCANS thinking skills.

skillbuilder

2. You can develop your skill at knowing which level of participation to use in a given decision-making situation (Skill-Building Exercise 3–2).

Coca-Cola was created by John Pemberton. It began as a 5-cents-a-glass local pharmacy soda fountain drink on May 8, 1886, and has become the world's favorite soft drink. The Coca-Cola Company is the world's largest producer and distributor of soft drink syrups and concentrates. Company products are sold through bottlers, fountain wholesalers, and distributors in more than 195 countries around the globe. Coca-Cola sells 1 billion servings of its products daily and has annual sales of over $19 billion and a net income of more than $4 billion.

The Coca-Cola script has become the best known and most admired trademark in the history of commerce, recognized by nearly all of the world's population. The Coca-Cola Company is clearly in touch with the simple desire of people everywhere to pause, refresh, and enjoy. Satisfying this need is the core of Coca-Cola's global success.

Coca-Cola is also the world's largest marketer and distributor of juice and juice drink products (Minute Maid, Powerade, Hi-C, Georgia, Fruitopia, Bright & Early, and Bacardi tropical fruit mixers). However, juice drinks are only a small part of the business being sold in 24 countries, with daily servings of 28 million.

Management's primary objective is to increase shareowner value over time, which it has done, led by M. Douglas Ivester, chairman of the board and CEO. The primary goal is to expand Coca-Cola's global business system to reach increasing numbers of consumers. CEO Ivester said, "This is a business in its infancy, a true growth company with true, incomparable growth opportunities all over the world."

The decision to go global started in Canada back at the turn of the 20th century. In 1906, bottling plants had been established in Cuba and Panama. However, in 1923, making Coca-Cola available around the world became an organized part of the business. This creative decision led to Coca-Cola being the world leader it is today. Along the way many problems needed to be solved, and many decisions led to its present success, as well as a few mistakes, including New Coke.[1]

For current information on Coca-Cola, use Internet address **http://www.cocacola.com**. For ideas on using the Internet, see Appendix B.

PROBLEM SOLVING AND DECISION MAKING: AN OVERVIEW

The ability to solve problems in innovative ways is one of the top four qualities employers want.[2] One of the major reasons managers are hired is to solve problems and make decisions.[3] Making bad decisions can destroy careers and companies.[4] Some decisions affect the health, safety, and well-being of consumers, employees, and the community. Some writers state that a manager makes about 80 decisions daily, or one every 5 or 6 minutes, and others claim the total is in the hundreds.[5] No one can say for sure how many decisions you will make as a manager, but you should realize that your problem-solving and decision-making skills will affect your career success. As with all the management skills, problem solving and decision making can be developed.[6]

This section will cover what a problem is and the relationship among objectives, problem solving, and decision making; the relationship among the management functions, decision making, and problem solving; the problem-solving and decision-making model; and your preferred decision-making style.

1. Explain the relationship among objectives, problem solving, and decision making.

The Relationship among Objectives, Problem Solving, and Decision Making

As a manager, you and your boss may set objectives together or your boss may simply assign objectives for you to achieve. When you do not meet your objectives, you have a problem. When you have a problem, you must make decisions.[7] The better you can develop plans that prevent problems before they occur, the fewer problems you will have and the more time you will have to take advantage of opportunities.[8] Seeking opportunities to continuously increase customer value requires the same consideration as solving existing problems.

A **problem** *exists whenever objectives are not being met.* In other words, you have a problem whenever a difference exists between what is actually happening and what you and your boss want to happen. If the objective is to produce 1,500 units per day but the department produces only 1,490, a problem exists. The system causes 85 percent of the problems in organizations, not its people. **Problem solving** *is the process of taking corrective action to meet objectives.* **Decision making** *is the process of selecting an alternative course of action that will solve a problem.* Decisions must be made when you are faced with a problem.[9] The first decision concerns whether or not to take corrective action.

Some problems cannot be solved, and others do not deserve the time and effort it would take to solve them. However, your job requires you to achieve organizational objectives. Therefore, you will have to attempt to solve most problems.

The Relationship among the Management Functions, Decision Making, and Problem Solving

All managers perform the same four functions: planning, organizing, leading, and controlling. While performing these functions, managers must make decisions. Recall (Chapter 1) that conceptual and decision-making skills are one of the three skills needed for success in management. In fact, making decisions precedes taking action. For example, when planning, managers must make decisions about objectives and when, where, and how they will be met. When organizing, managers must make decisions about what to delegate and how to coordinate the department's resources. When staffing, managers must decide who to hire and how to train and evaluate employees. To lead, managers must decide how to influence employees. To control, managers must select methods to ensure that they meet objectives. When managers perform management functions with skilled decision making, they have fewer problems to solve.

Pepsi Cola wanted to create an opportunity by increasing customer value. Pepsi had an objective to increase its market share by getting Coca-Cola drinkers to switch to Pepsi. To do so, Pepsi successfully created the "Pepsi challenge." Pepsi advertised that people preferred Pepsi to Coke. Pepsi did not change its product to increase customer value. Instead, the company used advertising to give people the perception of a superior product, and the perception itself created customer value. Coca-Cola had a problem because it was losing sales to Pepsi Cola. To solve the problem, Coca-Cola made the decision to introduce New Coke. The New Coke decision caused additional problems with Coke's loyal customers, who felt the decision decreased, rather than increased, customer value. Three months later, Coca-Cola admitted the poor decision and made the decision

problem
Occurs when objectives are not being met.

problem solving
The process of taking corrective action to meet objectives.

decision making
The process of selecting an alternative course of action that will solve a problem.

WORK APPLICATION

1. Give an example of when a job objective was not met. Identify the problem created and the decision made in regard to the objective not being met.

2. Explain the relationship among the management functions, decision making, and problem solving.

WORK APPLICATION

2. Give a job example of when a manager was performing a management function and made a poor decision. Explain the management function and the problem created by the poor decision.

3. List the six steps in the decision-making model.

decision-making model
The steps are (1) classifying and defining the problem or opportunity, (2) setting objectives and criteria, (3) generating creative and innovative alternatives, (4) analyzing alternatives and selecting the most feasible, (5) planning and implementing the decision, and (6) controlling.

to reintroduce Coca-Cola Classic. We'll discuss the New Coke decision in more detail as we cover the steps in the decision-making model.

The Decision-Making Model

The **decision-making model** *steps are (1) classifying and defining the problem or opportunity, (2) setting objectives and criteria, (3) generating creative and innovative alternatives, (4) analyzing alternatives and selecting the most feasible, (5) planning and implementing the decision, and (6) controlling.* Model 3–1 lists these steps. Notice that the steps do not simply go from start to finish. At any step you may have to return to a prior step to make changes. For example, if you are in the sixth step, controlling, and the implementation is not going as planned (step 5), you may have to backtrack to prior steps to take corrective action by generating and selecting a new alternative or changing the objective. If you have not defined the problem accurately, you may have to go back to the beginning.

Following the steps in the model will not guarantee that you make good decisions. However, using the model will increase your chances of success in problem solving and decision making.[10] Consciously use the model in your daily life, and you will improve your ability to make decisions. The remainder of this chapter provides the details of the model so that you can develop your creative problem-solving and decision-making skills. But before you do so, learn your preferred decision-making style in Self-Assessment Exercise 3–1.

Self-Assessment Exercise 3–1

Decision-Making Styles

Individuals differ in the way they approach decisions. To determine if your decision-making style is reflexive, reflective, or consistent, answer the eight questions by selecting the choice that best describes how you make decisions. Place a number 1–5 on the line before each question.

This behavior is common for me.

This behavior is not common for me.

1 ——— 2 ——— 3 ——— 4 ——— 5

___ 1. Overall, I make decisions quickly.

___ 2. When making decisions, I go with my first thought or hunch.

___ 3. When making decisions, I don't bother to recheck my work.

___ 4. When making decisions, I gather little or no information.

___ 5. When making decisions, I consider very few alternative options.

___ 6. When making a decision, I usually make it well before the deadline.

___ 7. When making a decision, I don't ask others for advice.

___ 8. After making a decision, I don't look for other alternatives or wish I had waited longer.

___ Total score

To determine your style, add up the numbers 1 through 5 that represent your answers. The total will be between 8 and 40. Place an X on the continuum line that represents your score.

Reflexive   Consistent   Reflective

8 ———— 20 ———— 30 ———— 40

Following is an explanation of each style. A group also has a preferred decision-making style, based on how its members make decisions. You could answer the eight questions by changing the "I" to "we" and referring to a group rather than to yourself.

Reflexive Style. A reflexive decision maker likes to make quick decisions (shooting from the hip) without taking the time to get all the information that may be needed and without considering all alternatives. On the positive side, reflexive decision makers are decisive; they do not procrastinate. On the negative side, making quick decisions can lead to waste and duplication when the best possible alternative is overlooked. Employees view a reflexive decision maker as a poor manager if the manager consistently makes bad decisions. If you use a reflexive style for important decisions, you may want to slow down and spend more time gathering information and analyzing alternatives.

Reflective Style. A reflective decision maker likes to take plenty of time to make decisions, gathering considerable information and analyzing several alternatives. On the positive side, the reflective type does not make hasty decisions. On the negative side, the reflective type may procrastinate and waste valuable time and other resources. The reflective decision maker may be viewed as wishy-washy and indecisive. If you use a reflective style, you may want to speed up your decision making. As Andrew Jackson once said, "Take time to deliberate; but when the time for action arrives, stop thinking and go on."

Consistent Style. Consistent decision makers tend to make decisions without rushing or wasting time. They know when they have enough information and alternatives to make a sound decision. Consistent decision makers tend to have the best record for making good decisions. They tend to follow the decision-making steps in Model 3–1 when appropriate. The next section will teach you when to make quick decisions without the model and when to take your time and use the model.

CLASSIFY AND DEFINE THE PROBLEM OR OPPORTUNITY

The first step in the decision-making model requires defining the problem or opportunity. In this section you will learn how to classify the problem, select the appropriate level of participation, and determine the cause of problems.

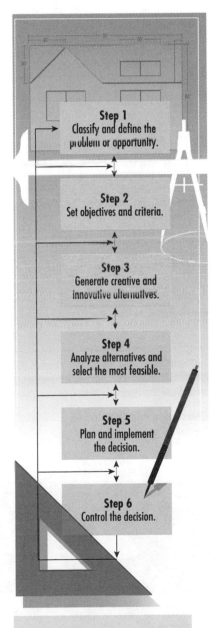

Step 1
Classify and define the problem or opportunity.

Step 2
Set objectives and criteria.

Step 3
Generate creative and innovative alternatives.

Step 4
Analyze alternatives and select the most feasible.

Step 5
Plan and implement the decision.

Step 6
Control the decision.

Model 3-1
The Decision-Making Model

APPLYING THE CONCEPT

AC 3–1 Steps in Decision Making

Identify the step in the decision-making model that each statement represents.

a. Step 1   b. Step 2   c. Step 3   d. Step 4   e. Step 5   f. Step 6

_____ 1. "We will use the brainstorming technique to solve the problem."

_____ 2. "Betty, is the machine still jumping out of sequence, or has it stopped?"

_____ 3. "I don't understand what we are trying to accomplish."

_____ 4. "What symptoms have you observed to indicate that a problem even exists?"

_____ 5. "Linear programming should be used to help us in this situation."

4. Describe the difference between programmed and nonprogrammed decisions and among the conditions of certainty, uncertainty, and risk.

programmed decisions
With recurring or routine situations, the decision maker should use decision rules or organizational policies and procedures to make the decision.

nonprogrammed decisions
With significant and nonrecurring and nonroutine situations, the decision maker should use the decision-making model.

decision-making conditions
Certainty, risk, and uncertainty.

Classify the Problem

Problems may be classified in terms of the decision structure involved, the conditions under which a decision will be made, and the decision-making model used.

Decision Structure. With **programmed decisions,** *recurring or routine situations, the decision maker should use decision rules or organizational policies and procedures to make the decision.* For example, a specified amount of inventory will be reordered every time stock reaches a specified level. *With* **nonprogrammed decisions,** *significant and nonrecurring and nonroutine situations, the decision maker should use the decision-making model.* To be significant, a decision must be expensive (purchasing major assets) and/or have major consequences (new product or reduction of employees) for the department or organization. Nonprogrammed decisions take longer to make than programmed decisions. The decision structure continuum is illustrated in Figure 3–1.

You must be able to differentiate between the two types of decision structures,[11] because they provide a guideline as to how much time and effort you should spend to make effective decisions. Coca-Cola made a nonprogrammed decision when it developed New Coke. Upper-level managers tend to make more of the nonprogrammed decisions than lower-level managers, who make more programmed decisions.

Decision-Making Conditions. *The three* **decision-making conditions** *are certainty, risk, and uncertainty.* When making a decision under the conditions of *certainty*, the manager knows the outcome of each alternative in advance. When making a decision under conditions of *risk*, the manager does not know the outcome of each alternative in advance but can assign probabilities to each outcome. Under conditions of *uncertainty*, lack of information or knowledge makes the outcome of each alternative unpredictable so the manager cannot determine probabilities.

When Coca-Cola introduced New Coke, it incurred a *risk*. If the company had been certain of the outcome of the decision, it would not have made it. It was a condition of risk because the company had conducted research with over 190,000 consumers through taste tests. The overwhelming majority preferred the taste of New Coke over Coca-Cola.

Nonprogrammed Decision
(Significant and nonrecurring and nonroutine)
(Longer period of time to make decisions)

Programmed Decision
(Nonsignificant, recurring, and routine)
(Shorter period of time to make decisions)

Figure 3-1
Decision Structure Continuum

Management makes most decisions under conditions of risk.[12] However, upper-level managers tend to make more uncertain decisions than lower-level managers. When making decisions under uncertainty, it is difficult to determine the needed resources to solve the problem or create an opportunity.[13] Although risk and uncertainty cannot be eliminated, they can be reduced. Figure 3–2 illustrates the decision-making conditions continuum.

Uncertainty	Risk	Certainty
(outcome of alternatives unpredictable)		(outcome of alternatives predictable)

Figure 3-2
Decision-Making Conditions Continuum

Decision-Making Model. There are two primary decision models: the rational model and the bounded rationality model. With the *rational model*, the decision maker attempts to use *optimizing*, selecting the best possible alternative. With the *bounded rationality model*, the decision maker uses *satisficing*, selecting the first alternative that meets the minimal criteria. The decision-making model presented as Model 3–1 is the rational model. With satisficing, only parts, or none, of the model would be used.

You need to remember which model to use and when. The more unstructured the decision and the higher the degree of risk and uncertainty, the greater the need to spend time conducting research with the aid of the decision-making model. Optimize (select the best possible alternative) when you are making nonprogrammed high-risk or uncertain decisions. Satisfice (select the first alternative that meets the minimum criteria) when you are making programmed low-risk or certain decisions. Figure 3–4 illustrates which model to use when, with other factors.

5. Describe when to use the decision-making model versus the bounded rationality model and group versus individual decision making.

WORK APPLICATION

3. Give an example of a programmed and a nonprogrammed decision and their decision conditions from an organization you work or have worked for.

Select the Appropriate Level of Participation

When a problem exists, the manager must decide who should participate in solving it. As a rule of thumb, only the key people involved with the problem should participate. However, the current trend in management favors increased employee participation.[14] Thus, the major question is not whether managers should allow employees to participate in problem solving and decision making, but when and how this should be done. When solving problems and making decisions, you should use the management style appropriate to the situation (autocratic, consultative, participative, or empowerment). You learned about situational management in Chapter 1 (Skill-Building Exercise 1–1). In Skill-Building Exercise 3–2 the situational management model is expanded to cover decision making. For now, you will learn about two levels of participation: individual and group decision making. However, realize that even though the trend is toward group decision making, some people want to be involved in group decision making and others do not.[15]

Figure 3–3 lists the potential advantages and disadvantages of using groups to make decisions. The key to success when using groups is to maximize the advantages while minimizing the potential disadvantages.

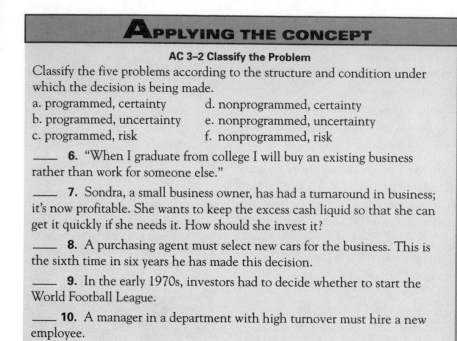

APPLYING THE CONCEPT

AC 3–2 Classify the Problem

Classify the five problems according to the structure and condition under which the decision is being made.

a. programmed, certainty
d. nonprogrammed, certainty

b. programmed, uncertainty
e. nonprogrammed, uncertainty

c. programmed, risk
f. nonprogrammed, risk

_____ **6.** "When I graduate from college I will buy an existing business rather than work for someone else."

_____ **7.** Sondra, a small business owner, has had a turnaround in business; it's now profitable. She wants to keep the excess cash liquid so that she can get it quickly if she needs it. How should she invest it?

_____ **8.** A purchasing agent must select new cars for the business. This is the sixth time in six years he has made this decision.

_____ **9.** In the early 1970s, investors had to decide whether to start the World Football League.

_____ **10.** A manager in a department with high turnover must hire a new employee.

Potential Advantages of Group Problem Solving and Decision Making. When group members have something to contribute, six potential advantages accrue:

1. *Better-quality decisions.* The old saying, "two heads are better than one," is generally true. Groups usually do a better job of solving complex problems than the best individual in the group. Using groups to solve problems and make decisions is appropriate for significant nonprogrammed decisions made under conditions of risk or uncertainty.

2. *More information, alternatives, creativity, and innovation.* A group of people usually has more information than an individual. A diverse group offers different points of view and a variety of alternative solutions. Creative or innovative ideas (or products) often do not come from the work of one person, but from the combined input of members building on each others' ideas.

3. *Better understanding of the decision.* When people participate in decision making, they usually understand the alternatives presented and why the one selected was the best alternative. This allows easier implementation of the decision.

4. *Greater commitment to the decision.* Researchers have shown that people involved in making a decision increase their commitment to make implementation of the decision a success.

Figure 3-3
Potential Advantages and Disadvantages of Using Group Decision Making

Potential Advantages
1. Better-quality decisions
2. More information, alternatives, creativity, and innovation
3. Better understanding of the decision
4. Greater commitment to the decision
5. Improved morale and motivation
6. Good training

Potential Disadvantages
1. Wasted time and slower decision making
2. Satisficing
3. Domination and goal displacement
4. Conformity and groupthink

5. *Improved morale and motivation.* Participation in problem solving and decision making is rewarding and personally satisfying to the people involved. People who can say "I was a part of making and implementing that decision" have higher levels of morale and motivation than people who cannot.

6. *Good training.* Group participation allows employees to better understand problems faced by the organization. With the trend toward using groups, allowing participation in decision making trains people to work in groups by developing group process skills.[16]

Potential Disadvantages of Group Problem Solving and Decision Making. Groups need to be careful to avoid the following disadvantages:

1. *Wasted time and slower decision making.* It takes longer for a group to make a decision. Employees involved in problem solving and decision making are not on the job producing. Thus group involvement costs the organization time and money. For programmed decisions of certainty or low risk, individual decision making would generally be more cost effective than group decision making.

2. *Satisficing.* Groups are more likely to satisfice than an individual, especially when group meetings are not run effectively. Members may take the attitude, "Let's get it over with and get out of here." Part of the reason groups satisfice more than individuals is responsibility. When one person is responsible, that person stands out if a good or poor decision is made. But with a group usually no one person gets the blame or credit for the decision, so attendance and commitment are often lower.

3. *Domination and goal displacement.* One group member, or subgroup, may dominate and nullify the group decision. Subgroups of individuals may develop and destructive conflict may result. *Goal displacement* occurs when an individual or subgroup tries to get its own decision accepted, or dominates for personal reasons, rather than meeting the original goal of finding the best solution.

4. *Conformity and groupthink.* Group members may feel pressured to go along with the group's decision without questioning it out of fear of not being accepted or not wanting to cause conflict. Groupthink occurs when members withhold different views to appear in agreement. This nullifies the advantage of diversity. Conformity is especially problematic in highly cohesive groups because members want to get along. Conformity is less problematic in groups that value diversity because group members seek differences.

In general, when you have a significant nonprogrammed decision with high risk or uncertainty, use group decision making. When you have a programmed decision with low risk or certainty, use individual decision making.

One individual did not simply make the New Coke decision. However, Coca-Cola may not have used the advantages and may have suffered from some of the disadvantages of group decision making.

WORK APPLICATION

4. Give an example of a group and individual decision made in an organization you work or have worked for. For the group decision, identify the potential advantages and disadvantages encountered by the group.

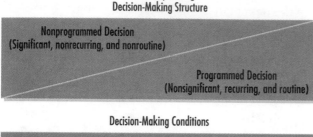

Relationship among:
Decision-Making Structure

Nonprogrammed Decision
(Significant, nonrecurring, and nonroutine)

Programmed Decision
(Nonsignificant, recurring, and routine)

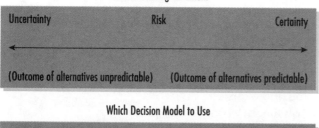

Decision-Making Conditions

Uncertainty	Risk	Certainty

(Outcome of alternatives unpredictable)   (Outcome of alternatives predictable)

Which Decision Model to Use

Decision-Making Model   Bounded Rationality Model

(Optimizing)   (Satisficing)

When to Use Group or Individual Decision Making

Group Decisions   Individual Decisions

Figure 3-4
Classifying the Problem or Opportunity Continuums

To be successful at decision making, you need to identify the type of problem to be solved, and the level of participation to use. However, this is a general guide; there may be exceptions to the rule. In Skill-Building Exercise 3–2, Situational Management: Decision Making, you will develop this skill. Figure 3–4 puts together the concepts from this section to help you better understand how to classify problems.

Define the Problem or Opportunity

After you have classified the problem or opportunity, you or the group must clearly define it accurately. Defining the problem accurately requires conceptual skills.

Because of job time pressures, especially in downsized organizations, managers must often hurry to solve problems and make decisions. In a hurry, they may neglect the first step in problem solving. Rushing to solve a problem that is not correctly defined often leads to a decision that does not solve the problem—haste makes waste. An important part of defining the problem is to distinguish symptoms from the cause of the problem.

Distinguish Symptoms from the Cause of the Problem. To do this, list the observable and describable occurrences (symptoms) that indicate a problem exists. Once you do this, you must determine the cause of the problem. If you eliminate the cause, the symptoms should disappear. For example, Sam, an employee with six years on the job, has been an excellent producer. However, in the last month, Sam has been out sick or late more times than he was in the past two years. What is the problem? If you say "absenteeism" or "lateness," you are confusing symptoms and causes. They are symptoms of the problem, but don't tell you why the problem has occurred. If you don't eliminate the original and subsequent causes, problem symptoms will reappear.

At Coca-Cola the symptom of the problem was lost market share to Pepsi. Coca-Cola defined the cause of the problem to be the taste of the product. Pepsi is sweeter than Coke. However, this was not the problem because New Coke was sweeter, but was not preferred.

On the opportunity side, Pepsi defined an opportunity in marketing its Crystal Pepsi product. However, under this nonprogrammed decision of risk, Crystal was not a success.

Remember that, as a decision maker, you must define the problem correctly in order to solve it. When making significant nonprogrammed decisions of high risk or uncertainty, you need to take your time and clearly distinguish symptoms from causes of the problem.

SET OBJECTIVES AND CRITERIA

Generally, with programmed decisions, the objective and criteria have been set. Therefore, you need not follow steps 2–4 of the decision-making model. However, with nonprogrammed decisions you should follow all the steps in the decision-making model. Therefore, the second step for the individual or group to follow in the model requires setting objectives and developing criteria.

Set Objectives. Setting objectives helps managers to make better decisions.[17] Groups take longer than individuals to set objectives and criteria, but groups that set their own objectives perform better than those that do not.[18] The objective must state what the decision should accomplish. It can be to solve a problem or to take advantage of an opportunity.

Set Criteria. You should also specify the criteria for achieving the objective. **Criteria** *are the standards that an alternative must meet to be selected as the decision that will accomplish the objective.*[19] Having multiple criteria helps to optimize the decision.[20] You should distinguish "must" and "want" criteria. "Must" criteria have to be met in order for the alternative to be acceptable, whereas "want" criteria are desirable but not necessary for the alternative to be acceptable. With satisficing, you stop with the first acceptable alternative; with optimizing, you seek to select the best possible option.

An example of an objective and criteria for hiring a manager might be as follows. The problem is that a store manager has quit and a new manager must be hired. The objective is to hire a store manager by June 30, 20XX. The required "must" criteria include a college degree and a minimum of five years' experience as a store manager. The preferred "want" criterion is that the person should be a minority group member. The hiring manager wants to hire a minority employee but will not hire one who does not meet the "must" criteria. In addition, if a significantly more qualified nonminority person applies for the job, he or she will be offered the job. In this situation you would optimize the decision rather than satisfice. We will discuss criteria again later in this chapter.

6. State the difference between an objective and "must" and "want" criteria.

criteria
The standards that an alternative must meet to be selected as the decision that will accomplish the objective.

WORK APPLICATION

6. Identify some of the qualification criteria (college degree, years of experience, etc.) for jobs at an organization you work or have worked for. Distinguish any "must" and "want" criteria.

GENERATE CREATIVE ALTERNATIVES

After the problem is defined and objectives and criteria are set, the decision maker may generate possible alternatives (step 3 of the decision-making model) for solving the problem or creating the opportunity. Usually many possible ways exist to solve a problem; in fact, if you don't have two or more alternatives, you don't have to make a decision.

With programmed decision making, the alternative is usually predetermined. However, with nonprogrammed decision making, more time and effort are needed to come up with new creative and innovative ideas. In this section you will find out about innovation and creativity, using information and technology to generate alternatives and group methods for generating creative alternatives.

7. State the difference between creativity and innovation.

innovation
The implementation of a new idea.

creativity
A way of thinking that generates new ideas.

8. List and explain the three stages in the creative process.

creative process
The three stages are (1) preparation, (2) incubation and illumination, and (3) evaluation.

Figure 3-5
Stages in the Creative Process

Innovation and Creativity

Innovation. An **innovation** *is the implementation of a new idea.* Two important types of innovations are product innovation (new things) and process innovation (new ways of doing things). *Product innovations* are changes in outputs (goods or service) to increase consumer value, or new outputs. *Process innovations* are changes in the transformation of inputs into outputs. Coca-Cola introduced New Coke, Diet Coke and other products, and has been working on its processes to cut cost. The success of innovation comes from creative problem solving.[21]

Creativity. **Creativity** *is a way of thinking that generates new ideas.* Adelphi University provides an example of a creative solution that became an innovation. The university wanted to expand its graduate business program. However, many potential students felt that they did not have the time to further their education. The alternative that Adelphi developed was the "classroom on wheels," which offers classes four days a week on commuter trains into and out of New York City. Some creative ideas are never converted successfully into products or processes. RJR Tobacco had a creative idea to sell smokeless cigarettes under the name Premier. RJR test marketed Premier in limited areas, but pulled the product from the market with an estimated loss of more than $300 million.[22]

The Creative Process. No definite relationship exists between intelligence and creativity; everyone has creative capability.[23] *The three stages in the* **creative process** *are (1) preparation, (2) incubation and illumination, and (3) evaluation.* Following these guidelines, summarized in Figure 3–5, can help you improve your creativity. As with the decision-making model, you may have to return to prior stages.

1. *Preparation.* The manager must become familiar with the problem by getting others' opinions, feelings, and ideas, as well as the facts.[24] When solving a problem or seeking opportunities, look for new angles, use imagination and invention, and don't limit yourself to the boundaries of past thinking.[25] Generate as many possible solutions as you can think of without making a judgment.

2. *Incubation and illumination.* After generating alternatives, take a break; sleep on the problem. Take some time before working on the problem again. During the incubation stage, you may gain an insight into the solution as your subconscious works on the problem—illumination. Have you ever worked hard on something and become discouraged but found that when you gave up or took a break, the illumination solution came to you? Illumination can also happen while working on the problem or during incubation. Illumination is sometimes referred to as the "Aha, now I get it" phenomenon.

3. *Evaluation.* Before implementing a solution, you should evaluate the alternative to make sure the idea is practical.[26] A good approach to use

when evaluating a decision, not before, is the devil's advocate. *With the* **devil's advocate** *approach, group members focus on defending the solution while others try to come up with reasons the solution will not work.* Devil's advocate evaluation usually leads to more creativity as the idea is improved upon.

Organizations encourage creativity; therefore, companies like Pitney Bowes, Fuji, Omron, Shimizu, and Shiseldo, for example, have developed training programs that emphasize creativity.

Using Information and Technology to Generate Alternatives

The ideal managers of the 21st century use facts, information, and knowledge to make decisions. Decisions should be based on solid information rather than simply intuition. However, when generating alternatives the question comes up, "How much information and alternatives do I need and where should I get it?" There is no simple answer. The more important the decision, generally, the more information and alternatives you need. To optimize, you select the best possible alternative. However, if you get too much information, the decision becomes too complex, and the optimal alternative may not be selected.[27]

Useful information has four characteristics: (1) timeliness, (2) quality, (3) completeness, and (4) relevance, which Figure 3–6 illustrates. *Timeliness* refers to whether or not you can get the information in time to make a decision. *Quality* refers to the accuracy of the information. People can be easily misled by false information, especially when it comes from group members.[28] Members may give false information to get the decision they want, or they may withhold information,[29] which is part of completeness. *Completeness* refers to the amount of data collected. *Relevance* refers to how closely and how importantly the information pertains or relates to the decision objectives. Good criteria will help you to select and eliminate information and alternatives.

Technology, especially telecommunications and computers, has shown considerable potential for problem solving and decision making. Computer idea-generating software does help individuals develop alternative solutions more creatively.[30]

Using Groups to Generate Creative Alternatives

A group usually has the potential difficulties of satisficing, dominance, and groupthink, especially with established work groups. To avoid these difficulties, you need to be careful that the group does not just list a limited number of alternatives and quickly move to accept one.[31]

When the problem has been classified as one a group should solve, a variety of methods are available using group participation to generate creative alternative solutions.[32] A discussion of five of the more popular techniques, which Figure 3–7 illustrates, follows.

devil's advocate
Group members focus on defending the solution while others try to come up with reasons the solution will not work.

WORK APPLICATION

7. Give an example of how you, or someone else, solved a problem using the stages in the creative process. Be sure to list the steps and whether illumination came during incubation or while working on the problem.

Figure 3-6
Characteristics of Useful Information

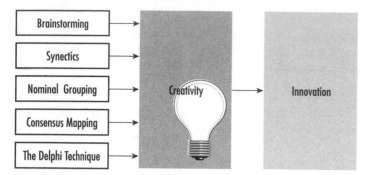

Figure 3-7
Group Decision-Making Techniques That Foster Creativity and Innovation

brainstorming
The process of suggesting possible alternatives without evaluation.

synectics
The process of generating novel alternatives through role playing and fantasizing.

nominal grouping
The process of generating and evaluating alternatives using a structured voting method.

Brainstorming. **Brainstorming** *is the process of suggesting many possible alternatives without evaluation.* The group is presented with a problem and asked to develop as many solutions as possible. Members should be encouraged to make wild, extreme suggestions. They should also build on suggestions made by others. However, members should not react in any way, favorably or unfavorably, to any of the members' contributions, including their own. When selecting members for a brainstorming group, try to include a diversity of people; 5 to 12 people make up a good-sized group. Status differences should be ignored. Everyone should have an equal voice. None of the alternatives should be evaluated until all possible alternatives have been presented. Brainstorming is commonly used[33] and companies are training employees to use it for problems requiring creative ideas such as solving problems[34] and naming a new product or service.

Electronic brainstorming (EBS) uses computers to generate alternatives. Participants synchronously send ideas without getting together. With EBS, people can be global without getting together, and numbers of participants do not have to be limited.[35]

Synectics. **Synectics** *is the process of generating novel alternatives through role playing and fantasizing.* Synectics focuses on generating novel ideas rather than a quantity of ideas. At first, the leader does not even state the exact nature of the problem so that group members avoid preconceptions. For example, when Nolan Bushnell wanted to develop a new concept in family dining, he began by discussing leisure activities generally. Bushnell then moved to leisure activities having to do with eating out. The idea that came out of this synectic process was a restaurant—electronic game complex where families could entertain themselves while eating pizza and hamburgers. The complex is called Chuck E. Cheese Showbiz/Pizza Time Inc.

Nominal Grouping. **Nominal grouping** *is the process of generating and evaluating alternatives using a structured voting method.* This process usually involves six steps:[36]

1. *Listing.* Each participant generates ideas in writing.
2. *Recording.* Each member presents one idea at a time and the leader records them where everyone can see them. This continues in a round-robin manner until all ideas are posted.
3. *Clarification.* Alternatives are clarified through a guided discussion, and any additional ideas are listed.
4. *Ranking.* Each employee rank-orders the top three ideas; low-ranked alternatives are eliminated.

5. *Discussion*. Rankings are discussed for clarification, not persuasion. During this time, participants should explain their choices and their reasons for making them.

6. *Vote*. A secret vote is taken to select the alternative.

Nominal grouping is appropriate to use in situations in which groups may be affected by domination, goal displacement, conformity, and groupthink, because it minimizes these effects.

Consensus Mapping. **Consensus mapping** *is the process of developing group agreement on a solution to a problem.* If a consensus cannot be reached, the group does not make a decision for change. It differs from nominal grouping because there can be no competitive battle in which a vote is taken and a solution is forced on some members of the group. The Japanese call this approach *Ringi*.[37] Consensus mapping can be used after brainstorming. The principal difference is that in consensus mapping the group categorizes or clusters ideas rather than choosing a single solution. A major benefit of consensus mapping is that because the solution is the group's, members generally are more committed to implementing it.

The Delphi Technique. The *Delphi technique* involves using a series of confidential questionnaires to refine a solution. Responses on the first questionnaire are analyzed and resubmitted to participants on a second questionnaire. This process may continue for five or more rounds before a consensus emerges. Managers commonly use the Delphi technique for technological forecasting, such as projecting the next computer breakthrough and its effect on a specific industry. By knowing what is to come, managers can make creative decisions to plan for the future.[38]

Upper-level managers commonly use synectics and the Delphi technique for a specific decision. Brainstorming, nominal grouping, and consensus mapping techniques are frequently used at the department level with work groups. Be on guard against responses that kill creativity. Figure 3–8 lists some of these statements. If your employees make such statements, make everyone realize that this demonstrates a negative attitude and is unproductive.

consensus mapping
The process of developing group agreement on a solution to a problem.

WORK APPLICATION

8. Give example decisions in which it would be appropriate for managers where you work or have worked to use brainstorming, nominal grouping, or consensus mapping.

APPLYING THE CONCEPT

AC 3–3 Using Groups to Generate Alternatives

In the five situations, identify the most appropriate group technique to use in generating alternatives.

a. brainstorming   b. synectics   c. nominal grouping
d. consensus mapping   e. Delphi technique

____ 11. Upper-level management wants to develop some new toys. They called in a consultant who is leading groups of employees and children together to come up with ideas.

____ 12. The department is suffering from morale problems and the manager doesn't know what to do about it.

____ 13. The manager must choose new matching desks for the ten employees in the office.

____ 14. The manager wants to reduce waste in the production department to cut cost and increase productivity.

____ 15. Top managers want to project future trends in the banking industry, as part of their long-range planning.

Figure 3-8
Responses That Kill
Creativity

- It can't be done.
- We've never done it.
- Has anyone else tried it?
- It will not work in our department/ company/industry.

- It costs too much.
- It isn't in the budget.
- Let's form a committee.

Decision Trees

After you come up with your alternatives, you may want to make a decision tree. A *decision tree* is a diagram of alternatives. The diagram gives a visual picture of the alternatives, which makes it easier for some people to analyze them. A decision tree appears in the case at the end of this chapter.

At Coca-Cola, to stop customers from switching to Pepsi, a few of the alternatives included: to do nothing, to come up with an advertising campaign to offset "the Pepsi challenge," to introduce New Coke while keeping Coca-Cola, and to replace Coca-Cola with New Coke.

9. Describe the differences among quantitative, Kepner-Tregoe, and cost-benefit analysis techniques for analyzing and selecting an alternative.

ANALYZE ALTERNATIVES AND SELECT THE MOST FEASIBLE

Notice that step 3 of the decision-making model, generate alternatives, and step 4, analyze alternatives and select the most feasible, are two different steps. This is because generating and evaluating alternatives at the same time tends to lead to satisficing and wasting time discussing poor alternatives rather than optimizing.

In evaluating alternatives, you should think forward and try to predict the possible outcome of each. Be sure to compare alternatives to the objectives and criteria; set in step 2 of the decision-making model. In addition, compare each alternative to the others.[39] This section presents three popular alternative analysis techniques: quantitative, Kepner-Tregoe, and cost-benefit.

Quantitative Techniques

One of the five approaches to management is management science (Appendix A), which uses math to aid in problem solving and decision making. Quantitative techniques objectively use math to aid in analyzing alternative solutions. Five quantitative techniques follow; Chapter 15 will present other quantitative techniques. This will make you aware of the techniques; it will not make you a mathematician. If you are interested in the actual calculations, you should take courses in quantitative analysis.

Managers may not be expected to compute the math for all types of quantitative techniques. However, if you know when to use these techniques, you can seek help from specialists within or outside the organization. Going to your boss and suggesting using any of these techniques appropriately will show initiative on your part.

Break-Even Analysis. Break-even analysis allows calculation of the volume of sales or revenue that will result in a profit. It involves forecasting the volume of sales and the cost of production. The break-even point occurs at the level where no profit or loss results. For example, Coca-Cola could have computed how many bottles of New Coke would have to be sold to break even.

Capital Budgeting. These techniques are used to analyze alternative investments. The payback approach allows calculation of the number of years it will take to recover the initial cash invested. The alternative having the quickest payback is preferred. Another technique computes the average rate of return. It is appropriate when the yearly returns differ. A more sophisticated technique, the *discounted cash flow* method, takes into account the time value of money. It assumes that a dollar today is worth more than a dollar in the future. Organizations including AMF, Kellogg, Procter & Gamble, and 3M use discounted cash flow. Coca-Cola used capital budgeting techniques when it made the decisions to buy Minute Maid and Hi-C brand juice and juice drinks. You will learn more about capital budgeting in Chapter 14.

Linear Programming. Optimum allocation of resources is determined using linear programming (LP). The resources that managers typically allocate include time, money, space, material, equipment, and employees. Companies primarily use LP for programmed decisions under conditions of certainty or low risk. LP is widely applied to product-mix decisions. Lear Siegler, Inc., uses LP when determining work flow, to optimize the use of its equipment and production. Bendix Corporation uses LP to minimize transportation (shipping) costs for its truck fleet.

Queuing Theory. This technique attacks waiting time. An organization can have any number of employees providing service to customers. If the organization has too many employees working at one time, they will not be waiting on customers and money paid to them is lost. If the organization has too few employees working at one time, it can lose customers who don't want to wait for service, which results in lost revenue. Queuing theory helps the organization balance these two costs. Retail stores use queuing theory to determine the optimum number of checkout clerks; airports to determine the optimum number of takeoffs and landings on runways; and production departments to schedule preventive maintenance on equipment.

Probability Theory. Probability theory enables the user to make decisions under the condition of risk. The user assigns a probability of success or failure to each alternative. The user then calculates the expected value, which is the payoff or profit from each combination of alternatives and

WORK APPLICATION

9. Give example decisions in which it would be appropriate for managers in an organization you work or have worked for to use the quantitative techniques of break-even analysis, capital budgeting, linear programming, queuing theory, and probability theory. Select any two.

outcomes. The calculations are usually done on a payoff matrix or decision tree by multiplying the probability of the outcome by the benefit or cost. Probability theory is used to determine whether to expand facilities and to what size; to select the most profitable investment portfolio; and to determine the amount of inventory to stock. You could use it to choose a job.

The Kepner-Tregoe Method

The Kepner-Tregoe method combines the objective quantitative approach with some subjectivity. The subjectivity comes from determining "must" and "want" criteria and assigning value weights to them. It is a technique for comparing alternatives using the criteria selected in step 2 of the problem-solving and decision-making model. It is helpful when comparing purchase options, such as machines, computers, and trucks, and when selecting people to be hired and promoted. Figure 3–9 shows an example of its use. You should refer to the exhibit to clarify the discussion.

Figure 3-9
The Kepner-Tregoe Method for Analyzing Alternatives

Must Criteria		Car 1	Car 2	Car 3	Car 4
Cost under $9,000		Yes	Yes	Yes	Yes
Available within one week		Yes	Yes	Yes	No
Want Criteria		**Meets Criteria**			
	Importance*	1 WS**	2 WS**	3 WS**	4 WS**
Gas mileage	7 ×	5 = 35	6 = 42	8 = 56	
Sporty	8 ×	5 = 40	7 = 56	4 = 32	
Blue	3 ×	10 = 30	0 = 0	0 = 0	
AM/FM stereo	5 ×	7 = 35	8 = 40	3 = 15	
Cruise control	2 ×	1 = 2	0 = 0	0 = 0	
Good condition	10 ×	5 = 50	6 = 60	8 = 80	
Low mileage	6 ×	6 = 36	4 = 24	5 = 30	
Few years old	7 ×	3 = 21	5 = 35	5 = 35	
Total weighted score		249	257	248	

*Indicates quantity of importance [on a scale of 10 (high) to 1 (low)] assigned to each as a weight.

**Weighted score.

step 1. **Compare each alternative to the "must" criteria.** Eliminate any alternative that does not meet the "must" criteria. To illustrate, let's state that our objective is to buy a car within two weeks. This is a nonprogrammed decision, which you will decide by yourself. Figure 3–9 lists the "must" and "want" criteria for each alternative. (These correspond to steps 2 and 3 in decision-making model 3–1.) As you can see, alternative car 4 does not meet all the "must" criteria and is eliminated.

step 2. **Rate each "want" criterion on a scale of 1 to 10 (10 being most important).** Figure 3–9 lists these in the "importance" column. They range from 2 to 10. Note that you do not rank from 1 to 8. The same number may be used more than once, 7 for example.

step 3. **Assign a value of 1 to 10 (10 being the highest)** to how well each alternative meets the "want" criteria. These values can be compared for each car; they are shown in the vertical columns labeled car 1 through 4. Again, many factors can have equal weight, 5 for example.

step 4. **Compute the weighted score (WS) for each alternative** by multiplying (horizontally) the importance value by the "meets criteria" value for each car. Next, add the total weight for each car, each "want" criterion (vertically).

step 5. **Select the alternative with the highest total weighted score** as the solution to the problem. Car 2 should be selected because it has the highest weighted score of 257 versus 248 and 249 for the other cars. Selecting car 2 assumes you rely entirely on your decision model and not partially on your own instinct, intuition, or judgment.

Cost-Benefit (Pros and Cons) Analysis

The management science approaches, quantitative methods, and Kepner-Tregoe method are objective mathematical approaches to comparing alternatives. However, times occur when the benefit received for the cost is uncertain, making management science approaches unusable. Cost-benefit analysis is a technique for comparing the cost and benefit of each alternative course of action using subjective intuition and judgment along with math. With the pros and cons analysis, you identify the advantages, which can be considered the benefits, and disadvantages, which can be considered the cost, of each alternative. Figure 3–10 compares the three approaches to analyzing and selecting alternatives.

Ben Franklin is said to have used the pros and cons, an offshoot of using cost-benefit. Ben would take a piece of paper and draw a line down the middle. On one side, he would list the pros and on the other the cons for using

Quantitative Techniques	Kepner-Tregoe Method	Cost-Benefit
(Objective)		(Subjective)
(Maximal use of math to make the decision)		(Minimal use of math to make the decision)

Figure 3-10
Alternative Analysis Techniques Continuum

each alternative. Ben would then select the best alternative. Many people think about the cost and benefits or pros and cons without writing them down. You should write them down to improve comparisons of alternatives for important nonprogrammed decisions.

Cost-benefit analysis is more subjective than management science techniques. Therefore, when using cost-benefit with groups, the group should do a critical evaluation of all alternatives.[40] Using a method such as the devil's advocate approach can help the group to avoid the potential problems of satisficing, dominance, and groupthink. The group should also be careful of the way alternatives are presented for evaluation,[41] as the order of presentation can affect the decision. Alternatives presented in a negative way tend not to be selected, and people tend to remember best what they hear first and last.

Research has been conducted to compare the quality of individual decisions when the person consults with others prior to making the final decisions. Results suggest that consulting others increases confidence but not the accuracy of the decision. This result may occur because people tend to consult others to seek information or approval for their decision, rather than to have the other person act as a devil's advocate and make them justify the solution.[42]

Regardless of the method used to analyze alternatives, the one selected should be the optimal alternative that meets the criteria established in step 2 of the decision-making model. If none of the alternatives meet the criteria, you have two basic options: (1) return to step 2 and change the criteria to select the best alternative or (2) return to step 3 and generate more alternatives.

Coca-Cola selected the alternative to replace Coca-Cola with New Coke rather than to offer it as an additional soft drink alternative for those who prefer a sweeter cola taste. After all, research taste tests indicated that people preferred New Coke to Coca-Cola.

WORK APPLICATION

10. Give an example decision in which it would be appropriate for managers where you work or have worked to use the Kepner-Tregoe method and cost-benefit analysis.

PLAN, IMPLEMENT THE DECISION, AND CONTROL

The final two steps in the decision-making model involve planning and implementing the decision, step 5, and controlling, step 6.

Plan. After making a decision, you develop a plan of action[43] with a schedule for implementation.[44] You will learn the details of planning in the next two chapters.

Implement the Plan. After a decision has been made and plans developed, the plans must be implemented.[45] Communicating the plan to all employees is critical to successful implementation. You will learn about communication in Chapter 11. It may be necessary to delegate assignments to others. You will learn about delegating in Chapter 6. Coca-Cola developed plans to make New Coke, to advertise it, and to deliver it.

Control. Control methods should be developed while planning. Checkpoints should be established to determine whether the chosen alternative is solving the problem.[46] If not, corrective action may be needed. Managers should not be locked into a decision and wind up throwing good money after bad. When managers will not admit that they made a bad decision and change, they are in the process known as *escalation of commitment.* When you make a poor decision, you should admit the mistake and try to rectify it by going back over the steps in the decision-making model. At Coca-Cola, three weeks after introducing New Coke, management admitted its mistake and brought back Coca-Cola, with the new name Coca-Cola "Classic" to distinguish it from New Coke.

CHAPTER SUMMARY AND GLOSSARY

The chapter summary is organized to answer the ten learning objectives for Chapter 3.

1. Explain the relationship among objectives, problem solving, and decision making.
The three terms are interrelated as follows. Managers are responsible for setting and achieving organizational objectives. When managers do not meet objectives, a problem results. When a problem exists, decisions must be made about what, if any, action must be taken.

2. Explain the relationship among the management functions, decision making, and problem solving.
The three terms are interrelated as follows. When managers perform the functions of planning, organizing, leading, and controlling, they make decisions. If managers lack proficiency at performing the management functions, they will have many problems.

3. List the six steps in the decision-making model.
The steps in the decision-making model are (1) defining the problem, (2) setting objectives and criteria, (3) generating alternatives, (4) analyzing alternatives and selecting the most feasible, (5) planning and implementing the decision, and (6) controlling.

4. Describe the difference between programmed and nonprogrammed decisions and among the conditions of certainty, uncertainty, and risk.
The difference between programmed and nonprogrammed decisions is in the recurrence, routine, and significance of the decision to be made. Nonprogrammed decisions include nonrecurring, nonroutine, significant decisions. Recurring, routine, and nonsignificant decisions are programmed decisions.

The difference in decision-making conditions is based on the degree of certainty of the outcome of the decision. With certainty you know the outcome of alternatives, with risk you can assign probabilities to the outcomes, and with uncertainty you do not know the outcomes of alternatives.

5. Describe when to use the decision-making model versus the bounded rationality model and group versus individual decision making.

Use the decision-making model with group decision making when a non-programmed decision with high risk or uncertainty exists. Use the bounded rationality model with an individual decision when a programmed decision with low risk or certainty exists. However, this is a general guide; there may be exceptions to the rule.

6. State the difference between an objective and "must" and "want" criteria.

An objective is the end result you want from making the decision. The "must" criteria are the requirements that an alternative must meet to be selected as the decision. The "want" criteria are desirable but are not necessary for the alternative to be selected as the decision.

7. State the difference between creativity and innovation.

Creativity is a way of thinking that generates new ideas. Innovation is the implementation of new ideas for products and processes.

8. List and explain the three stages in the creative process.

The three stages are: (1) preparation; familiarity with the problem; (2) incubation and illumination; incubation is taking a break from the problem and illumination is the point at which one gets the idea for the solution; (3) evaluation; making sure the idea will work before it becomes an innovation.

9. Describe the differences among quantitative, Kepner-Tregoe, and cost-benefit analysis techniques for analyzing and selecting an alternative.

Quantitative and Kepner-Tregoe are management science approaches; cost-benefit is not. Quantitative methods use math subjectively to select the alternative with the highest value. Kepner-Tregoe uses objective math, with some subjectivity in selecting and weighting criteria, to select the alternative with the highest value. Cost-benefit analysis is primarily based on subjective analysis, with some math, but alternatives do not have a final number value to compare.

10. Define the following key terms (in order of appearance in the chapter):

Select one or more methods: (1) fill in the missing key terms from memory, (2) match the key terms from the end of the summary with their definitions below, or (3) copy the key terms in order from the list at the beginning of the chapter.

A _____ exists whenever objectives are not being met.

_____ is the process of taking corrective action to meet objectives.

_____ is the process of selecting an alternative course of action that will solve a problem.

The _____ steps include (1) classifying and defining the problem or opportunity, (2) setting objectives and criteria, (3) generating alternatives,

(4) analyzing alternatives and selecting the most feasible, (5) planning and implementing the decision, and (6) controlling.

With _____, recurring or routine situations, the decision maker should use decision rules or organizational policies and procedures to make the decision.

With _____, significant and nonrecurring and nonroutine situations, the decision maker should use the decision-making model.

The three _____ include certainty, risk, and uncertainty.

_____ are the standards that an alternative must meet to be selected as the decision that will accomplish the objective.

_____ is the implementation of a new idea.

_____ is a way of thinking that generates new ideas.

The three stages in the _____ are (1) preparation, (2) incubation and illumination, and (3) evaluation.

With the _____ approach, group members focus on defending the solution while others try to come up with criticisms of why the solution will not work.

_____ is the process of suggesting many possible alternatives without evaluation.

_____ is the process of generating and evaluating alternatives using a structured voting method.

_____ is the process of developing group agreement on a solution to a problem.

KEY TERMS

brainstorming 92	**decision-making conditions** 84	**problem** 81
consensus mapping 93	**decision-making model** 82	**problem solving** 81
creative process 90	**devil's advocate** 91	**programmed decision** 84
creativity 90	**innovation** 90	**synectics** 92
criteria 89	**nominal grouping** 92	
decision making 81	**nonprogrammed decisions** 84	

REVIEW AND DISCUSSION QUESTIONS

1. Are problem solving and decision making really important? Explain.

2. Why is it necessary to determine the decision structure and decision-making conditions?

3. What is the current trend in using groups to solve problems and make decisions?

4. Which potential disadvantage of group problem solving and decision making do you think is most common?

5. Is a decrease in sales or profits a symptom or a cause of a problem?

6. Would a maximum price of $1,000 to spend on a stereo be an objective or a criterion?

7. Are creativity and innovation really important to all types of businesses? Is it important to evaluate creativity before it becomes an innovation?

8. Have you ever made a decision with information that was not timely, of quality, complete, and/or relevant? If yes, explain.

9. What is the major difference between nominal grouping and consensus mapping?

10. Why are generating and analyzing alternatives separate steps in the decision-making model?

11. Have you ever used any of the techniques for analyzing and selecting an alternative? If yes, which one?

12. Do you know anyone who has been the victim of escalation of commitment? If yes, explain.

OBJECTIVE CASE

Carolyn Blakeslee's Art Calendar®

In 1986, Carolyn Blakeslee founded *Art Calendar*, a monthly publication for visual artists. *Art Calendar* provides information (approximately 15 pages) about grants, shows, and other forums to which artists can submit their work, as well as some topical freelance columns.

Carolyn started *Art Calendar* as a part-time business in a room in her home. Eight out of the first ten years, circulation revenues doubled. *Art Calendar* grew to become artists' definitive source of information.

Carolyn did not expect the business to become so successful. Over the years the business became more complex and time-consuming. Without employees, it was no longer possible to read all the mail during her daily five miles on a stationary bike. The part-time hours became more than full-time. Carolyn, like many women, wants to have it all. She wants to meet financial goals and devote time to her family (she really enjoys motherhood, spending time with her husband), her own artwork, and leisure pursuits. Carolyn reached that point in the life of successful small businesses where she had to make a decision based on three major alternatives: (1) maintain, (2) expand, or (3) sell the business.

1. *Maintain the folksy nature of the publication.* In this area, she does have at least two subalternatives, shown below in the decision tree.

2. *Expand the business by making it more professional.* As shown below, this alternative has at least

Decision Tree

OBJECTIVE CASE
(continued)

three subalternatives. If this alternative is selected, decisions about expansion must be made.

3. *Sell the business.* If Carolyn does sell the business, she has to make a decision about future employment with at least four major alternatives (see decision tree).

With the decision tree you first write down all the alternatives that lead to one possible decision. Can you think of other alternatives not listed that should be? After listing the alternatives, you analyze them and select the alternative and the subalternative as the decision.

Select the best alternative to the following questions. Be sure you are able to explain your answers.

_____ 1. Carolyn Blakeslee does not perform the management function(s) of

    a. planning   c. leading
    b. organizing   d. controlling

_____ 2. The decision structure facing Carolyn is

    a. programmed   b. nonprogrammed

_____ 3. The decision-making condition facing Carolyn is

    a. certainty   b. risk   c. uncertainty

_____ 4. In making this decision, the ___ model would be appropriate.

    a. rational   b. bounded rationality

_____ 5. Should Carolyn set objectives and criteria for the decision?

    a. yes   b. no

_____ 6. In deciding to maintain, expand, or sell, creativity and innovation are not critical.

    a. true   b. false

_____ 7. The information in the case lacks the ___ that Carolyn needs to make her decision.

    a. timeliness   c. completeness
    b. quality   d. relevance

_____ 8. Which technique would be most appropriate for Carolyn's decision?

    a. brainstorming   d. consensus mapping
    b. synectics   e. Delphi
    c. nominal   f. none of these are
      grouping   appropriate

_____ 9. Which method for analyzing and selecting an alternative is most appropriate for Carolyn's decision?

    a. quantitative technique
    b. Kepner-Tregoe
    c. cost-benefit

_____ 10. Which alternative will be the most complex to plan, implement, and control?

    a. maintain
    b. expand
    c. sell

11. List the pros and cons for each alternative from Carolyn's perspective, which may be different from yours. Be sure to state the risk of not expanding and expanding.

12. If you were in Carolyn's situation, would you maintain, expand, or sell? Assume you could get a check in the amount equal to ten years' full-time salary upon the sale.

For current information on Folk Art Calendar, use Internet address http://folkart.org. For ideas on using the Internet, see Appendix B.

*skillbuilder

I G

Skill-Building Exercise 3–1

Making a Decision Using the Decision-Making Model

Preparing for Skill-Building Exercise 3–1

Select a significant problem or opportunity that you now face. Remember, a problem exists when objectives are not being met. In other words, there is a difference in what is happening and what you want to happen. The problem or opportunity may be from any facet of your life—work, college, sports, a relationship, a purchase to be made in the near future, where to go on a major date, and so on. Use the decision-making model outline below to write down and solve your problem or take advantage of the opportunity.

Step 1. Classify and Define the Problem or Opportunity

Decision structure. Do you need to make a programmed or nonprogrammed decision?

Decision condition. Is it uncertainty, risk, or certainty?

Decision-making model. Is the rational or bounded rationality model appropriate? (Continue to follow all steps in the decision-making model even if bounded rationality is appropriate.)

Select the appropriate level of participation. Should an individual or group be used? (If a group decision is appropriate, use a group for the following steps in the model. But remember to take advantage of, and minimize the disadvantages of, using groups as you make the decision.)

Define the problem or opportunity. List the symptoms and causes, then write a clear statement of the problem or opportunity you will make a decision about.

_____

_____

_____

Step 2. Set Objectives and Criteria

Write out what is to be accomplished by making the decision and the standards that the alternative must meet to be selected as the decision that will accomplish the objective. (Specify "must" and "want" criteria if appropriate for the decision.)

Objective: _____

_____

Criteria: (must) _____

    (want) _____

Step 3. Generate Creative Alternatives

What information do you need? (Remember that information must be timely, of quality, complete, and relevant to be useful.) Will you use any technology?

If you are using a group, will brainstorming, nominal grouping, or consensus mapping be used?

List your alternatives (at least three) below; number them. If a decision tree will be helpful, make one.

_____

_____

_____

_____

_____

_____

Step 4. Analyze Alternatives and Select the Most Feasible

Are quantitative, Kepner-Tregoe, or cost-benefit (pro and con) analysis appropriate? Use one below.

_____

_____

_____

_____

_____

Step 5. Plan and Implement the Decision

Write out your plan for implementing the decision. Be sure to state the controls you will use to make sure you know if the decision is working. How can you avoid escalation of commitment?

_____

_____

_____

_____

_____

_____

Step 6. Controlling

After implementing the decision, come back and make notes about progress on solving the problem or opportunity. Indicate any need for corrective action, and if you need to, return to prior steps in the decision-making model.

_____

_____

_____

_____

Doing Skill-Building Exercise 3–1 in Class

Objective
To develop your problem-solving and decision-making skills by learning to use the decision-making model.

Preparation
You should have made a personal decision using the model preparation pages for this exercise.

Experience
You will share your decision with a small group of students who will give you feedback.

Procedure (10–20 minutes)
1. Break into groups of three to five people. One at a time, go through the steps in making your decision. At each step, group members give feedback such as pointing out any errors, offering suggestions on how to improve the written statements, providing additional alternatives, listing more pros and cons not thought of, stating which alternatives others would select, and so on.

2. Same as 1, but the group selects the best decision to be presented to the entire class.

Conclusion
The instructor may lead a class discussion and/or make concluding remarks.

Application (2–4 minutes)
What did I learn from this experience? How will I use this knowledge in the future?

_____

_____

_____

Sharing
Volunteers give their answers to the application section.

BEHAVIOR MODEL VIDEO EXERCISE 3-1

Behavior Model Video 3–1 (13 minutes), Situational Management: Decision Making, shows the human resources director, Richard, meeting with a supervisor, Denise, to discuss training changes. The video illustrates the four situational management styles, explained in Skill-Building Exercise 3–2.

Objective
To better understand the four situational management decision-making styles.

Procedure 1 (10–20 minutes)
The instructor shows Video Module 3–1, Situational Management: Decision Making. As you

BEHAVIOR MODEL VIDEO EXERCISE 3-1 *(continued)*

view each of the four scenes, identify the management decision-making style being used by the manager. Write the letters and number of the style on the scene line after each scene.

Scene 1. _____ Autocratic (S1A)

Scene 2. _____ Consultative (S2C)

Scene 3. _____ Participative (S3P)

Scene 4. _____ Empowerment (S4E)

Option A. View all four scenes and identify the style used by the manager. Select the one style that you would use in this situation. Are other styles also appropriate? Which style would you not use (not appropriate) for this situation? Next to each style listed, write the letter A for appropriate or N for not appropriate. After everyone is done, the instructor leads a class discussion and/or gives the correct answers.

Option B. After each scene the class discusses the style used by the manager. The instructor states the correct answer after each of the four scenes.

Conclusion
The instructor may lead a class discussion and/or make concluding remarks.

Application (2–4 minutes)
What did I learn from this exercise? How will I use this knowledge in the future?

_____

_____

_____

Sharing
Volunteers give their answers to the application section.

*skillbuilder

I **G**

Skill-Building Exercise 3–2

Situational Management: Decision Making

Preparing for Skill-Building Exercise 3–2

Note: This exercise is an extension of the Situational Management Model from Skill-Building Exercise 1–1 (Chapter 1). If you have not read the preparation part of the exercise, read it before continuing.

Managers today recognize the trend toward participation in decision-making and are open to using participation.[47] It is frustrating for managers to decide when to use participation and when not to, and what level of participation to use. You are about to learn how to use a model that will develop your skill at selecting the appropriate management style to meet the needs of the situation. First, let's examine ways in which groups can be used to generate solutions.

Selecting the Appropriate Situational Management Decision Style

In addition to capability level, Situational Management Model, you must also consider time, information, and acceptance. As a manager you follow two steps in selecting the appropriate situational management decision style for problem solving and decision making: diagnosing the situation and selecting the appropriate style.

Step 1. Diagnose the Situation. The first step involves diagnosing the situational variables, including time, information, acceptance, and employee capability.

Time. You must determine whether you have enough time to include employees in decision making. View time as yes (you have time to use participation) or no (you do not have time to use participation). If you do not have time, you should use the autocratic style (S1A), regardless of preference. When you do not have time to include employees in problem solving and decision making, you ignore the other three variables; they are irrelevant if you do not have time. If you say yes you have time, any style may be appropriate. You use the other three variables to select the style. In other words, when there isn't enough time to include participation, time is the most important factor. However, when there is time, it becomes the least important factor.

Time is a relative term. In one situation, a few minutes may be considered a short time period, but in another a month may be a short period of time. Time is not wasted when the potential advantages of using participation are realized.

Information. You must decide if you have enough information to make a quality decision alone. The more information you have, the less need for participation; the less information you have, the greater the need for participation. If you have all the necessary information, you have no need for employee participation, and the autocratic style (S1A) is appropriate. When you have some information, but need more than can be obtained by asking questions, the consultative style (S2C) may be appropriate. If you have little information, the appropriate style may be participative (S3P—group discussion) or empowerment (S4E—group makes the decision).

Acceptance. You must decide whether employee acceptance of the decision is critical to implementing the decision. The more employees will like a decision, the less need for participation; the more employees will dislike a decision, the greater the need for participation. If you make the decision alone, will the employees or group willingly implement it? If the employees or group will be accepting, the appropriate style is probably autocratic (S1A). If the employees or group will be reluctant, the appropriate style may be consultative (S2C) or participative (S3P). If they will probably reject the decision, the participative (S3P) or empowerment style (S4E) may be appropriate. Recall that when groups make decisions, they are more understanding, accepting, and committed to implementing the decision.

Capability. You must decide whether the employees or group have the ability and motivation to be involved in problem solving and decision making.[48] Do the employees or group have the experience and information needed to be involved? Will employees put the organization's or department's goals ahead of personal goals? Do the employees want to be involved in problem solving and decision making? Employees are more willing to participate when the decisions personally affect them. If the employees' or group's capability level is low (C1), an autocratic style (S1A) may be appropriate. When capability is moderate (C2), a consultative style (S2C) may be appropriate. If capability level is high (C3), a participative style (S3P) might be adopted. If capability is outstanding (C4), choose the empowerment style (S4E). Note that you should only use the empowerment style with employees who have outstanding capability levels, regardless of the informational and acceptance factors. Remember that the employees' or group's capability level can change from situation to situation.

Step 2. Select the Appropriate Management Style. After considering the four variables, you select the appropriate style. In some situations, all variables will indicate that the same style is appropriate. In other cases, the appropriate style is not so clear. For example, you could be in a situation in which you have time to use any style, may have all the information necessary (autocratic), employees may be reluctant (consultative or participative), and their capability may be moderate (consultative). In situations where different styles are indicated for different variables, you must determine which variable should be given more weight. In the preceding example, assume that acceptance was critical for successful implementation of the decision. Acceptance takes precedence over information. Because the employees involved have moderate capability, the consultative style would be appropriate. Model 3–2 summarizes use of the four situational management styles in decision making.

Using the Situational Management: Decision-Making Model

We will apply the model to the following situation; more situations are presented later in this exercise.

_____ Manager Ben can give only one of his employees a merit pay raise. He has a week to make the decision. Ben knows how well each employee performed over the past year. The employees really have no option but to accept getting or not getting the pay raise, but they can complain to upper management about the selection. The employees' capability levels vary, but as a group they have a high capability level under normal circumstances.

_____ time   _____ information
_____ acceptance   _____ capability

Step 1. Diagnose the Situation. Ben has plenty of time to use any level of participation (place a Y for yes on the time line below the situation). He has all the information needed to make the decision (place S1A on the information line). Employees have no choice but to accept the decision (place S1A on the acceptance line). And the group's capability level is normally high (place S3P on the capability line).

Step 2. Select the Appropriate Style for the Situation. There are conflicting styles to choose from (autocratic and participative): yes time S1A information S1A acceptance S3P capability. The variable that should be given precedence is information. The employees are normally capable, but in a situation like this they may not put the department's goals ahead of their own. In other words, even if employees know who deserves the raise, they may fight for it anyway.

Such a conflict could cause future problems. Some possible ways to make the decision include the following:

Autocratic (S1A). The manager would select the person to be given the raise without discussing it with any employees. Ben would simply announce the decision after submitting it to the payroll department.

Consultative (S2C). The manager would get information from the employees concerning who should get the raise. Ben would then decide who would get the raise. He would announce the decision and explain the rationale for it. He might invite questions and discussion.

Participative (S3P). The manager could tentatively select the employee who gets the raise, but be open to change if a group member convinces him that someone else should. Or Ben could explain the situation to the group and lead a discussion concerning who should get the raise. After considering the group's input, Ben would make the decision and explain the rationale for it. Notice that the consultative style does not allow for discussion as the participative style does.

Empowerment (S4E). The manager would explain the situation and allow the group to decide who gets the raise. Ben may be a group member. Notice that this is the only style that allows the group to make the decision.

The autocratic style is appropriate for this situation. The consultative style is also a good approach. However, the participative and empowerment styles use too much participation for the situation. Your skill at selecting the appropriate decision-making management style should improve through using the model for the ten situations below.

Deciding Which Situational Management Decision-Making Style to Use

Following are ten situations calling for a decision. Select the appropriate problem-solving and decision-making style. Be sure to use Model 3–2 when determining the style to use. First determine the answers to the variables on the lines below the situation. Then place the style on the line before the number.

S1A—autocratic   S2C—consultative
S3P—participative   S4E—empowerment

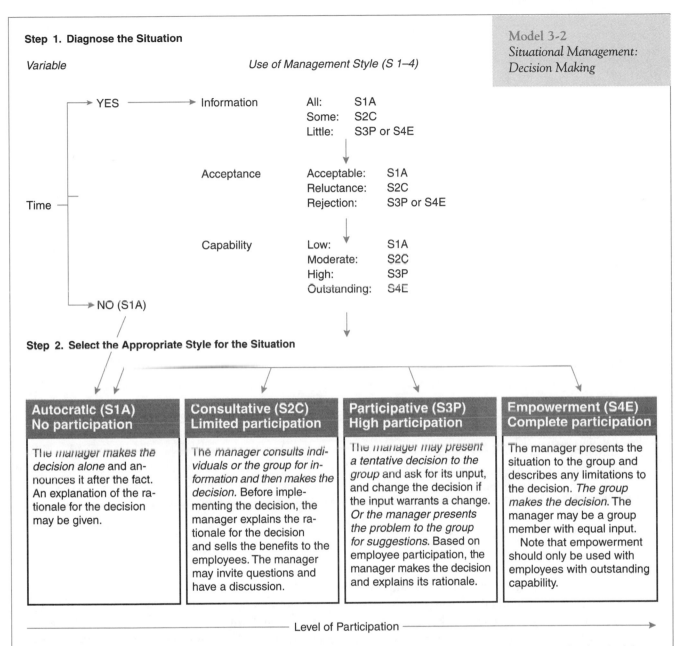

Step 1. Diagnose the Situation

Variable   *Use of Management Style (S 1–4)*

Model 3-2
Situational Management: Decision Making

Time — YES ——→ Information
- All: S1A
- Some: S2C
- Little: S3P or S4E

Acceptance
- Acceptable: S1A
- Reluctance: S2C
- Rejection: S3P or S4E

Capability
- Low: S1A
- Moderate: S2C
- High: S3P
- Outstanding: S4E

NO (S1A)

Step 2. Select the Appropriate Style for the Situation

Autocratic (S1A) No participation	Consultative (S2C) Limited participation	Participative (S3P) High participation	Empowerment (S4E) Complete participation
The *manager makes the decision alone* and announces it after the fact. An explanation of the rationale for the decision may be given.	The *manager consults individuals or the group for information and then makes the decision*. Before implementing the decision, the manager explains the rationale for the decision and sells the benefits to the employees. The manager may invite questions and have a discussion.	The *manager may present a tentative decision to the group* and ask for its input, and change the decision if the input warrants a change. *Or the manager presents the problem to the group for suggestions*. Based on employee participation, the manager makes the decision and explains its rationale.	The manager presents the situation to the group and describes any limitations to the decision. *The group makes the decision*. The manager may be a group member with equal input. Note that empowerment should only be used with employees with outstanding capability.

———— Level of Participation ————→

Note that with the autocratic, consultative, and participative styles the manager retains the power to make the decision; with empowerment the group makes the decision.

____ 1. You have developed a new work procedure that will increase productivity. Your boss likes the idea and wants you to try it in a few weeks. You view your employees as fairly capable and believe that they will be receptive to the change.

_____ time   _____ information

_____ acceptance   _____ capability

_____ 2. There is new competition in your industry. Your organization's revenues have been dropping. You have been told to lay off 3 of your 15 employees in two weeks. You have been supervisor for over three years. Normally, your employees are very capable.

_____ time _____ information

_____ acceptance _____ capability

_____ 3. Your department has been facing a problem for several months. Many solutions have been tried and failed. You've finally thought of a solution, but you're not sure of the possible consequences of the change required or of acceptance by your highly capable employees.

_____ time _____ information

_____ acceptance _____ capability

_____ 4. Flex-time has become popular in your organization. Some departments let each employee start and end work when he or she chooses. However, because of the cooperation required of your employees, they must all work the same eight hours. You're not sure of the level of interest in changing the hours. Your employees are a very capable group and like to make decisions.

_____ time _____ information

_____ acceptance _____ capability

_____ 5. The technology in your industry is changing too fast for the members of your organization to keep up. Top management hired a consultant who has made recommendations. You have two weeks to decide what to do about the recommendations. Your employees are usually capable; they enjoy participating in the decision-making process.

_____ time _____ information

_____ acceptance _____ capability

_____ 6. A change has been handed down by top management. How you implement it is your deci-sion. The change takes effect in one month and it will affect everyone in your department. Their acceptance is critical to the success of the change. Your employees are usually not interested in making routine decisions.

_____ time _____ information

_____ acceptance _____ capability

_____ 7. Your boss called to tell you that someone requested an order for your department's product; the delivery date is very short. She asked you to call her back with a decision about taking the order in 15 minutes. Looking over the work schedule, you realize that it will be very difficult to deliver the order on time. Your employees will have to push hard to make it. They are cooperative, capable, and enjoy being involved in decision-making.

_____ time _____ information

_____ acceptance _____ capability

_____ 8 Top management has decided to make a change that will affect all of your employees. You know that they will be upset because it will cause them hardship. One or two may even quit. The change goes into effect in 30 days. Your employees are very capable.

_____ time _____ information

_____ acceptance _____ capability

_____ 9. You believe that productivity in your department could be increased. You have thought of some ways to do it, but you're not sure of them. Your employees are very experienced; almost all of them have been in the department longer than you have.

_____ time _____ information

_____ acceptance _____ capability

_____ 10. A customer offered you a contract for your product with a quick delivery date. The offer is open for two days. To meet the contract deadline, employees would have to work nights and weekends for six weeks. You cannot require them to work overtime. Filling this profitable contract could help get you the raise you want and feel you deserve. However, if you take the contract and don't deliver on time, it will hurt your chances of getting a big raise. Your employees are very capable.

_____ time   _____ information

_____ acceptance   _____ capability

Doing Skill-Building Exercise 3–2 in Class

Objective
To develop your skill at knowing which level of participation to use in a given decision-making situation. You will learn to use the Situational Management: Decision-Making Model.

Preparation
You should have completed the preparation for this exercise unless told not to do so by your instructor.

Experience
You will try to select the appropriate problem-solving and decision-making style for each of the ten situations in the preparation for this exercise.

Procedure 1 (10–15 minutes)
Behavior Model Video 3–1 is shown to illustrate the four decision-making styles. Use the form on page 106 to record answers.

Procedure 2 (10–20 minutes)
Behavior Model Video 3–1, Situational Management: Decision Making, may be shown. The instructor reviews Model 3–2 and explains how to use it to select the appropriate management style for the first situation.

Procedure 3 (4–8 minutes)
Students working alone complete situation 2 using the model, followed by the instructor going over the recommended answers.

Procedure 4 (10–20 minutes)
Break into teams of two or three. Apply the model to situations 3 through 5 as a team. You may decide to change your original answers. The instructor goes over the recommended answers and scoring for situations 3 through 5. Do not continue with situation 6 until the instructor goes over the answers to situations 3 through 5.

Procedure 5 (10–20 minutes)
In the same teams, select decision-making styles for situations 6 through 10. The instructor will go over the recommended answers and scoring.

Conclusion
The instructor may lead a class discussion and/or make concluding remarks.

Application (2–4 minutes)
What did I learn from this experience? How will I use this knowledge in the future?

_____

_____

_____

Sharing
Volunteers give their answers to the application section.

4

The Strategic and Operational Planning Process

Learning Objectives

After studying this chapter, you should be able to:

1. Describe the differences between strategic and operational plans.
2. State the differences among the three levels of strategies: corporate, business, and functional.
3. Explain the reason for conducting an industry and competitive situation analysis.
4. Explain the reason for conducting a company situation analysis.
5. State how competitive advantage and benchmarking are related.
6. Discuss how goals and objectives are similar yet different.
7. List the steps in the writing objectives model.
8. Describe the four grand strategies: growth, stability, turnaround and retrenchment, and combination.
9. Describe the three growth strategies: concentration, integration, and diversification.
10. Discuss the three business-level adaptive strategies: prospecting, defending, and analyzing.
11. List the four major functional operational strategy areas.
12. Define the following **key terms** (in order of appearance in the chapter):

strategic planning	goals
operational planning	objectives
strategic process	writing objectives model
strategy	management by objectives (MBO)
three levels of strategies	
corporate-level strategy	grand strategy
business-level strategy	corporate growth strategies
functional-level strategy	merger
situation analysis	acquisition
SWOT analysis	business portfolio analysis
competitive advantage	adaptive strategies
benchmarking	functional strategies

Skill Development

✳**skillbuilder**
1. You can learn to write effective objectives (Skill-Building Exercise 4–1).

✳**skillbuilder**
2. You can learn to develop a strategic plan for a business (Skill-Building Exercise 4–2).

These skills are part of conceptual and decision-making management skills. These exercises develop your planning and decisional roles skills. The exercises also develop the SCANS skill competencies of using resources, information, and systems, as well as basic and thinking foundation skills.

Jiffy Lube of Utah began operations in Utah and Colorado. James Hindman bought the company and changed the name to Jiffy Lube International in 1979.

Hindman was the new football coach at Western Maryland College. After graduating with a physical education degree, Peter Clark worked as a graduate assistant coaching football and worked for Hindman for two years as he completed his master's degree and for another two years as a coach and teacher. Hindman asked Pete to work for him at Jiffy Lube. Hindman sent Pete to Utah for three months to learn how to operate Jiffy Lubes. Pete came back to Baltimore as director of training and began to teach people who bought Jiffy Lube franchises how to run them. Pete developed a procedures manual and later became operations manager. After setting up one hundred Jiffy Lubes, Pete decided to quit working for Jiffy Lube and become a franchisee.

Pete became a partner with Steve Spinelli in two Jiffy Lube service centers in western Massachusetts. Pete and Steve developed several more service centers. They then became partners with Rich Heritage and developed service centers in the Hartford, Connecticut area. Pete, Steve, and Rich joined with John Sasser to buy nine existing service centers in New York that were not being run well and to develop more service centers. This combined Jiffy Lube business was called American Oil Change, totaled 47 service centers in New England and New York, and employed around 700 people. Pennzoil bought Jiffy Lube International and began to aggressively buy back successful franchises. In 1991, Pete and his partners sold their 47 service centers to Pennzoil's Jiffy Lube.

At the same time, Pete became a partner with his two brothers, who started two centers in Pittsfield, Massachusetts. Pete and his brothers sold the Pittsfield Jiffy Lubes to Pennzoil's Jiffy Lube. Today, Pete and his wife are partners with Dave Macchia, who serves as the operations manager of six Jiffy Lubes in the Worcester area.

Since 1991, at age 37, Pete no longer works full time managing his Jiffy Lube operations. He presently helps Dave run the business, and spends more time in community service, coaching, and with his family. Pete spends many hours working for the Jimmy Fund. Pete has been a football coach at Trinity College, is the baseball coach at Agawam High School, and coaches his children's Agawam basketball, baseball, and softball teams.

Throughout this chapter you will learn more about the large businesses of Pennzoil and the small business franchise of Bowman-Clark, Inc. (Pete and his partners currently own six Jiffy Lubes that employ around 70 people).[1]

For current information on Jiffy Lube, use Internet address **http://www.jiffylube.com**. For ideas on using the Internet, see Appendix B.

---

1. Describe the differences between strategic and operational plans.

strategic planning
The process of developing a mission and long-range objectives and determining in advance how they will be accomplished.

operational planning
The process of setting short-range objectives and determining in advance how they will be accomplished.

WORK APPLICATION

1. Give an example strategic and operational objective from an organization you work or have worked for.

STRATEGIC AND OPERATIONAL PLANNING

In this section you will learn about the planning process and the levels of strategic planning. But first you should understand the importance of planning. Simply having a great idea does not automatically guarantee success. In fact, about eight of every ten (80 percent) product introductions fail. The primary reason for failure is poor planning.[2] A few examples include Weyerhaeuser's UltraSofts baby diapers, R.J. Reynolds' smokeless cigarette Premier, General Mills' Benefit cereal, Anheuser-Busch's LA Beer, and Grandmother Calendar Company, selling elaborate cut-rate personalized calendars.[3]

The Strategic Process

Strategic planning *is the process of developing a mission and long-range objectives and determining in advance how they will be accomplished.* **Operational planning** *is the process of setting short-range objectives and determining in advance how they will be accomplished.* The difference between planning, strategic planning, and operational planning is primarily the timeframe and management level involved. Planning does not specify a timeframe. Strategic planning includes developing a mission statement and long-term objectives. *Long-term* generally means that it will take longer than one year to achieve the objective. Strategic plans are commonly developed for five years, and reviewed and revised every year so that a five-year plan is always in place. Top-level managers develop strategic plans. Operational plans have *short-term* objectives that will be met in one year or less. Middle and first-line managers develop operational plans.

Through the strategic process, upper-level managers develop the long-range plans and middle and lower-level managers develop the operational plans to accomplish the long-range objectives. Following the means-end chain (Chapter 2), top managers determine the ends and middle- and lower-level managers determine the means to accomplish the ends. The key to a successful strategic process is the coordination of the strategic and operational plans—bridging the gap between levels.[4]

The steps in the **strategic process** *are (1) developing the mission, (2) analyzing the environment, (3) setting objectives, (4) developing strategies, and (5) implementing and controlling strategies.* Developing strategies takes place at three levels. This section presents developing strategies followed by developing the mission. Later sections of this chapter cover the other steps. See Figure 4–1 for an illustration of the strategic process. Notice that the process is not simply linear from steps 1–5 and then ends. As the arrows indicate, you need to return to prior steps and make changes as an ongoing process. You should also realize that the strategic process includes the four functions of management.

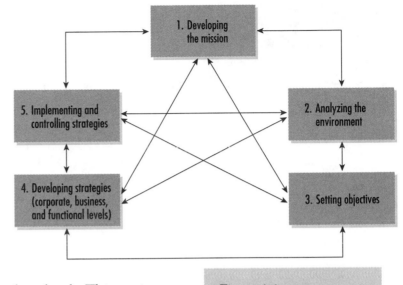

Figure 4-1
The Strategic Process

strategic process
The steps are (1) developing the mission, (2) analyzing the environment, (3) setting objectives, (4) developing strategies, and (5) implementing and controlling strategies.

Levels of Strategies

A **strategy** *is a plan for pursuing the mission and achieving objectives. The* **three levels of strategies** *are corporate, business, and functional.* You will learn more about these three levels of strategies in separate sections later in this chapter. For now, we will simply define each so that you will understand the differences among the three levels.

The **corporate-level strategy** *is the plan for managing multiple lines of businesses.* Many, especially large, companies actually consist of several businesses. Philip Morris has a Philip Morris tobacco line of business, Miller Beer, and Kraft General Foods. General Motors has GM Automobiles, Electronic Data Systems, and Hughes Electronics. Jiffy Lube is one of Pennzoil's lines of business. However, most, especially small, businesses are only in one line of business, Pete Clark's business being one example. Therefore, they do not require corporate strategy.

The **business-level strategy** *is the plan for managing one line of business.* Each of Philip Morris's and General Motors' lines of business has its own strategy for competing in its industry environment. Since 1906, Kellogg Company has continued to focus on cereal as a single line of business.

The **functional-level strategy** *is the plan for managing one area of the business.* The functional areas, discussed in prior chapters, are marketing, finance and accounting, operations/production, human resources, and others based

strategy
A plan for pursuing the mission and achieving objectives.

three levels of strategies
Corporate, business, and functional.

corporate-level strategy
The plan for managing multiple lines of businesses.

2. State the differences among the three levels of strategies: corporate, business, and functional.

business-level strategy
The plan for managing one line of business.

functional-level strategy
The plan for managing one area of the business.

WORK APPLICATION

2. Does a business you work or have worked for have multiple lines of business? If yes, list them.

on the line of business. Each of Pete's six Jiffy Lube managers is involved with these functional areas. See Figure 4–2 for an illustration of strategic and operational levels.

Developing the Mission

Developing the mission is the first step in the strategic process. However, after analyzing the environment you should reexamine the mission to see if it needs to be changed. The mission is important because it is the foundation of the other four steps in the strategic process. The organization's mission is its purpose or reason for being[5] (Chapter 2). The mission states what business(es) the company is in now and will be in the future.[6] A mission creates a vision of where the company is headed and why.[7] It contains the expectations the organization strives to achieve.[8] Pete stated his Jiffy Lube mission as: "Our business is the automobile oil-changing service business. We provide a timely, high-quality service to achieve customer satisfaction."

Pete and others realize the importance of focusing and developing a strategic process from the customer's perspective.[9] Employees strive to increase customer satisfaction by improving products and reducing delivery times (time-based competition). Pete has no clear definition of quality because the customer determines quality (Chapter 2). It is the customers' perception of how they were treated when they come in for service. If customers perceive they have been treated well, they will come back the next time they need their oil changed. Customer satisfaction is so important that many companies focus on it as a corporate strategy, and companies with a customer satisfaction strategy generally outperform those that are not customer satisfaction–oriented.

Figure 4-2
Strategic and Operational Levels

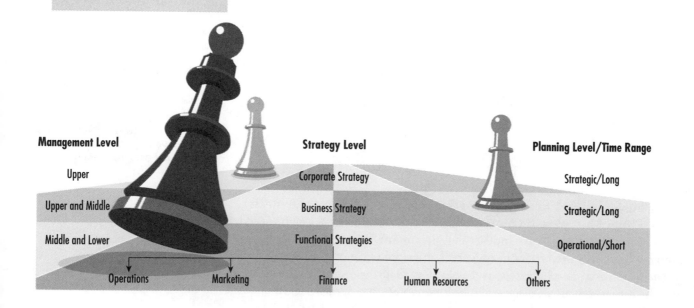

Management Level	Strategy Level	Planning Level/Time Range
Upper	Corporate Strategy	Strategic/Long
Upper and Middle	Business Strategy	Strategic/Long
Middle and Lower	Functional Strategies	Operational/Short

Operations   Marketing   Finance   Human Resources   Others

Over the past two decades, the strategic plan has become almost as common a management tool as the budget for large corporations.[10] To aid in the strategic planning process, a variety of software packages are available.[11]

ANALYZING THE ENVIRONMENT

A business strategy must be congruent with the capabilities of the firm and its external environment to create value.[12] The internal and external environmental factors (Chapter 2) are analyzed as step 2 in the strategic process, which determines congruence. Another term for analyzing the environment is situation analysis. A **situation analysis** *draws out those features in a company's environment that most directly frame its strategic window of options and opportunities.* The situation analysis has three parts: industry and competitive analysis, company situational analysis, and competitive advantage. Keep in mind that companies with multiple lines of business must conduct an environmental analysis for each line of business.

situation analysis
Draws out those features in a company's environment that most directly frame its strategic window of options and opportunities.

Industry and Competitive Situation Analysis

Industries vary widely in their business makeup, competitive situation, and growth potential.[13] Determining the attractiveness of an industry requires answering questions such as: How large is the market? What is the growth rate? How many competitors are there? Pete described his industry as the automotive service industry. The market size is around 250,000 people, and since the Worcester area is saturated with competitors, little growth potential exists. Pete's (six service centers) major direct competitors are Ready Lube (five service centers), Oil Doctor (two service centers), and the many independent gas stations, service centers (Firestone, Goodyear, etc.), and dealerships that also change oil. Michael Porter developed the five competitive forces as a tool for analyzing the competitive environment.[14]

3. Explain the reason for conducting an industry and competitive situation analysis.

Five Competitive Forces. Competition in an industry is a composite of five competitive forces:

1. *The rivalry among competing sellers in the industry.* Porter calls this the scrambling and jockeying for position. How do businesses compete for customers (price, quality, speed, and so on)? How competitive is the industry?[15] Coca-Cola and Pepsi and AT&T, MCI, and Sprint are competitive rivals. The company needs to anticipate competitive moves.

2. *Threat of substitute products and services.* Companies in other industries may try to take customers away. Very Fine Juice, Snapple, Gatorade, and others have targeted soda drinkers to substitute juice drinks.

3. *Potential new entrants.* How difficult and costly is it for new businesses to enter the industry as competitors? Does the company need to plan for new competition? Coke and Pepsi don't have to be too concerned

about new competition, but the local small business video store may have to compete with a new Blockbuster.

4. *Power of suppliers.* How much does the business depend on the supplier? If the business has only one major supplier, without alternatives available, the supplier has great bargaining power over the business. Coca-Cola has great power over independently owned Coca-Cola bottlers because it is the sole supplier. However, a small video store can buy its videos from any number of suppliers, who have little power over it.

5. *Power of buyers.* How much does the business depend on the buyer?[16] If the business has only one major buyer, or a few, without alternatives available, the buyer has great bargaining power over the business. GM told its suppliers that they would have to cut their prices or lose business. Many of the businesses that sell to GM had no bargaining power and lowered their prices.

Companies use industry and competitive situation analysis primarily at the corporate strategy level to make decisions regarding which lines of business to enter and exit and how to allocate resources among lines of business.[17] This process will be explained in more detail later in this chapter. Pennzoil bought Jiffy Lube because it was an attractive industry to enter. Pete also used industry and competitive analysis to make the decision to keep his Jiffy Lubes in the Worcester area rather than selling them to Pennzoil, which is still an option. See Figure 4–3 for a competitive analysis of Pete's Jiffy Lube. Overall, Pete does not think the industry is attractive to new entrants, but it is attractive for him to stay in this line of business in this area.

Company Situation Analysis (SWOT)

The company situation analysis is used at the business strategy level to determine the strategic issues and problems that need to be addressed through the next three steps of the strategic process. A complete company situation analysis has five key parts, listed in Figure 4–4:

1. *Assessment of the present strategy based on performance.* This assessment can be a simple statement or a more complex comparison of performance indicators[18] (market share, sales, net profit, return on assets, and so on) over the last five years.

2. *SWOT analysis. An organization's internal environmental strengths and weaknesses and external environmental opportunities and threats are determined through a* **SWOT analysis.** SWOT is a highly recommended strategic tool.[19] Wal-Mart asked its pet food suppliers to do a SWOT analysis; it sent them a 33-page vendor planning packet. Due to Wal-Mart's buying power of $49 billion, most suppliers completed the SWOT analysis.[20] The SWOT analysis is based on the environment covered in detail in Chapter 2. As a quick review, the internal environ-

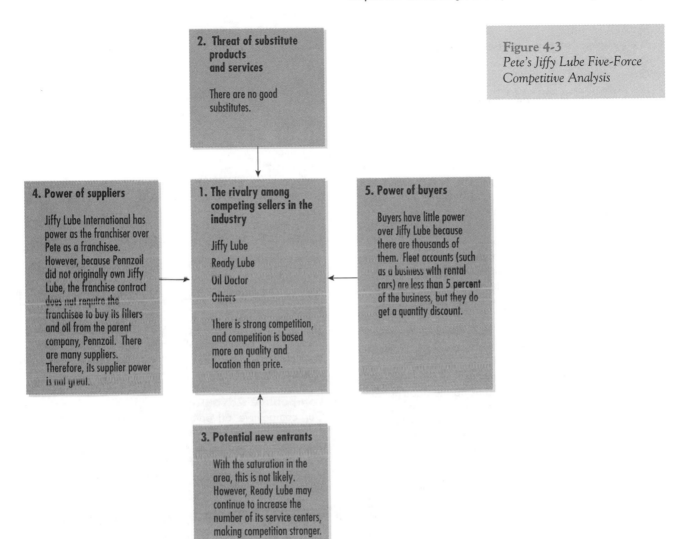

Figure 4-3
Pete's Jiffy Lube Five-Force Competitive Analysis

2. Threat of substitute products and services

There are no good substitutes.

4. Power of suppliers

Jiffy Lube International has power as the franchiser over Pete as a franchisee. However, because Pennzoil did not originally own Jiffy Lube, the franchise contract does not require the franchisee to buy its filters and oil from the parent company, Pennzoil. There are many suppliers. Therefore, its supplier power is not great.

1. The rivalry among competing sellers in the industry

Jiffy Lube
Ready Lube
Oil Doctor
Others

There is strong competition, and competition is based more on quality and location than price.

5. Power of buyers

Buyers have little power over Jiffy Lube because there are thousands of them. Fleet accounts (such as a business with rental cars) are less than 5 percent of the business, but they do get a quantity discount.

3. Potential new entrants

With the saturation in the area, this is not likely. However, Ready Lube may continue to increase the number of its service centers, making competition stronger.

mental factors analyzed for *strengths* and *weaknesses* are management, mission, resources, systems process, and structure. The external environmental factors analyzed for *opportunities* and *threats* are customers, competitors, suppliers, labor force, shareholders, society, technology, the economy, and governments. Figure 4–5 contains a SWOT analysis for Pete's Jiffy Lube. Pete's friend and former associate Hindman knew

Figure 4-4
Company Situation Analysis Steps

1. Assessment of the present strategy based on performance.

2. SWOT analysis.

3. Competitive strength assessment (competitive advantage?)

4. Conclusions concerning competitive position.

5. Determination of the strategic issues and problems that need to be addressed through the strategic process.

1. Assessment of the Present Strategy Based on Performance

Our present strategy is working well. Our performance has been profitable, even during economic downturn in the late 1980s into 1990–1991, but has been strong since 1992.

2. SWOT Analysis

Strengths. Our major strength is the reputation we have developed by being the first company to focus on quick oil change. Being first, we also have selected the prime locations for our service centers. We have a strong management team with a clear mission. A major strength is tight budgetary control over our resources. Our information resource computer enables us to have a complete history of all work done on each car. We continually focus on cost cutting. Our systems process and structure are strong and allow us to lube a car in 10 to 15 minutes.

Weaknesses. Our one weakness concerns employees who provide service and interact with customers. Changing oil is not a high-skill, high-paying job. Therefore, we have to be careful to hire employees capable of being responsible and using the good human relations skills we teach them. An irresponsible employee who makes a mistake, such as not putting the oil plug back in so the oil leaks as the person drives the car, can cost money and lose customers.

Opportunities. In the Worcester area, we could put in one more service center, and we could expand into other areas. I see our primary opportunity in offering new services, which we have done over the years. In addition to an oil change, we offer air conditioning, radiator, PVC, and lights services. Jiffy Lube International continues to test new services and advises franchises on which ones work. During better economic times we have the opportunity to service more cars.

Threats. Our major immediate threat comes from the government. Environmental protection requires us to meet standards. For example, new air conditioning systems that do not use freon require us to purchase new machines to service newer cars. This machine is expensive and takes up considerable space. The Occupational Safety and Health Administration (OSHA) also requires us to meet standards. Through government influence, a major long-term threat is the technology of the electric car. Electric cars do not need an oil change.

3. Competitive Strength Assessment

(rating: 1 (low) to 10 (high) for each firm) (rating × weight —)

Critical success factors	Weight	Jiffy Lube	Ready Lube	Oil Doctor
Training	.60	10—6.0	8—4.8	2—1.2
Quality perception	.20	9—1.8	7—1.4	2—0.4
Timely service	.20	8—1.6	8—1.6	3—0.6
Total	1.00	9.4	7.8	2.2

Note: There is a system effect among the critical success factors. Training is the most important factor, because through training employees learn to deliver quality perception by professional interaction with customers, and they learn to do the job right in a timely manner. Slow service will influence the quality perception.

3. Competitive Advantage

Our competitive advantage is our name recognition and quality image with key locations. Being an industry leader, Jiffy Lube does most of its benchmarking among its own service centers. Franchises are provided with numerous statistics that allow us to compare our business to others.

4. Conclusions Concerning Competitive Position

We are the leading, or strongest, competitor and will continue to be through continual improvement of quality service.

5. Determination of the Strategic Issues and Problems That Need to Be Addressed Through the Strategic Process

The three primary areas Jiffy Lube needs to focus on are: (1) keeping up with Jiffy Lube International research and using new ideas to improve business; (2) keeping up with the environmental issues; and (3) continuing to monitor Ready Lube, which is aggressively trying to take our customers. For example, they are moving across the street from us at their new location.

Figure 4-5
Pete's Jiffy Lube Company Situation Analysis

that oil should be changed every 3,000 miles, but that few people changed it that often because of the long wait at service centers. So Hindman took advantage of the opportunity to provide customer value by buying Jiffy Lube of Utah.

3. *Competitive strength assessment (competitive advantage?)*. For a strategy to be effective, it must be based on a clear understanding of competitors.[21] The critical success factors for the line of business are compared to each major competitor. *Critical success factors* are the few major things that the business must do well to be successful. Through the competitive strength assessment, the organization may elect to develop a competitive advantage; it is covered separately as the final part of this section. Organizations may apply two common approaches. The first approach assigns each factor a rating of 1 (weak) to 10 (strong) and adds up the ratings to determine the ranking of competitors. The second approach uses the same rating system, but weights the critical success factors by importance. The total of the weights equals 1.00. The weight is multiplied by the rating to get a score for each firm on each factor. Scores are totaled to determine the ranking of competitors. Figure 4–5 gives an example of the weighted method for Pete's Jiffy Lube.

4. *Conclusions concerning competitive position*. How is the business doing compared to its competition?[22] Are things improving, slipping, etc.?

5. *Determination of the strategic issues and problems that need to be addressed through the strategic process*. Based on steps 1 through 4, what needs to be done in the future to improve competitive position?

Competitive Advantage

Through strategic planning, a competitive advantage should be created.[23] Many organizations are focusing on developing competitive advantages based on high quality and time-based competition. A **competitive advantage** *specifies how the organization offers unique customer value*. It answers the questions: What makes us different from our competition? Why should a person buy our product or service rather than the competition's? A sustainable competitive advantage (1) distinguishes the organization from its competitors, (2) provides positive economic benefits, and (3) cannot be readily duplicated. The key to producing sustainable competitive advantage is effective management of people.[24]

Pizza Hut had a competitive advantage for restaurant dining before Domino's arrived. Domino's did not compete head-to-head with restaurants; it made free delivery its competitive advantage. Some competitive advantages are not sustainable because they are easily copied. Pizza Hut and many local pizza places started to deliver years ago. However, the creator, such as Domino's and Jiffy Lube, often gets the name recognition and

WORK APPLICATION

5. Does a company you work or have worked for have a competitive advantage? If yes, state it. If no, state how it is the same as competitors.

reputation that the followers don't have. If you ask people for the name of a company that delivers pizza and a place to get a quick oil change, most will say Domino's and Jiffy Lube.

Businesses also use low cost or price as a competitive advantage. If you walk into a supermarket to buy a cola, you will most likely find local brands priced lower than Coke and Pepsi in order to offer customer value. Many stations that compete with Mobil, Exxon, and other national gas stations sell gas at a lower price. The fast oil-change service centers in Pete's area charge about the same price.

If you ever consider starting a business, be sure to answer the questions: What will make my business different from the competition's? Why should a person buy my product or service rather than the competition's? If you don't have an answer, you will not have a competitive advantage, and you may not be able to get enough customers to have a successful business. Skill-Building Exercise 4–2 requires you to develop a strategic plan for a business that you may be interested in starting some day.

Two related concepts of competitive advantage are core competency and benchmarking. A *core competency* is what a firm does well. Core competencies are a strength. By identifying core competencies, new products and services can be created that take advantage of the company's strengths.[25] For example, Honda has a core competency in engines. Honda went from producing cars and motorcycles, which are based on engines, to garden tillers, lawn mowers, snowblowers, snowmobiles, power generators, and outboard motors.

benchmarking
The process of comparing an organization's products and processes with those of other companies.

Benchmarking *is the process of comparing an organization's products and processes with those of other companies.* The idea of benchmarking is to legally and ethically find out about other products and processes and to copy them or improve upon them. Most benchmarking takes place within a company or industry.[26] For example, Ready Lube and Oil Doctor basically resemble Jiffy Lube. Pizza Hut and Little Caesar copied Domino's delivery. However, looking at noncompetitors can provide good ideas that create a competitive advantage. McDonald's in mid-Manhattan copied free delivery as well.

After a company has evaluated itself and the competition by completing the situation analysis, it should then go back and review the mission to see if it needs to be changed. Remember that the situation analysis is an ongoing process, referred to as *scanning the environment*. It tells what is going on in the external environment that may require change to continually improve customer value. Refer back to Figure 4–5 for a company situation analysis.

SETTING OBJECTIVES

Successful strategic management requires a commitment to a defined set of objectives by management.[27] After developing a mission and completing a situation analysis, you are ready for the third step in the strategic process:

setting objectives that flow from the mission to address strategic issues and problems identified through the situation analysis. Managers should have multiple objectives[28] that are prioritized to allow focus on the more important ones. In Chapter 6 you will learn how to prioritize.

Objectives are end results; they do not state how the objective will be accomplished. In this section you will learn the difference between goals and objectives, how to write objectives, the criteria for effective objectives, and about management by objectives (MBO).

Goals and Objectives

Some people use the terms *goal* and *objectives* synonymously.[29] You should be able to distinguish between them. **Goals** *state general targets to be accomplished*. **Objectives** *state what is to be accomplished in singular, specific, and measurable terms with a target date*. Goals are commonly used and are very useful, but objectives are needed to develop plans and to know if the end result is achieved. Goals are often translated into objectives. For an example, see Figure 4-6.

Writing Objectives

To help ensure that they will be met, objectives should be written and kept in a visual place, such as on your desk or wall. Successful people have objectives. This positive relationship is why motivational gurus and career counselors swear by written objectives.[30] New Year's resolutions are common, and it has been said that if you do not have any objectives, your resolution should be to get some.[31] But don't wait for New Year's, do it as part of Skill-Building Exercise 4–1.

To help you to write effective objectives that meet the criteria you will learn next, use the writing objectives model. *The parts of the* **writing objectives model** *are (1) infinitive + (2) action verb + (3) singular, specific, and measurable result to be achieved + (4) target date*. Model 4–1 shows the

6. Discuss how goals and objectives are similar yet different.

goals
General targets to be accomplished.
objectives
What is to be accomplished in singular, specific, and measurable terms with a target date.

6. State one or more goals from an organization you work or have worked for.

7. List the steps in the writing objectives model.

writing objectives model
(1) infinitive + (2) action verb + (3) singular, specific, and measurable result to be achieved + (4) target date.

Goal
- To raise our performance to the top quartile of our peers.
- To reach the top quartile, we have set four specific objectives.

Objectives
- Annual reserve replacement of 180 percent.
- Replacement cost of $4.30 per barrel of oil equivalent (boe).
- Operating cost, including general and administrative, of $4.25/boe.
- Return on assets of 10 percent after taxes.

Figure 4-6
Pennzoil Goals and Objectives for its Oil and Gas Division

Model 4-1
Writing Objectives Model

Four parts of the model:
(1) infinitive +
(2) action verb +
(3) singular, specific, and measurable result to be achieved +
(4) target date

Example from Coca-Cola: [32]

To   increase sales to 50% of carbonated soft drinks in the U.S. by 2001.
(1) + (2) +   (3) +   (4)

model, which is adapted from Max E. Douglas's model. Other example objectives will be provided with each criterion.

Criteria for Objectives

An effective objective includes four "must" criteria. For each criterion, an example of an ineffective objective will be presented, followed by a correction of the objective to make it effective.

Singular Result. To avoid confusion, each objective should contain only one end result. With multiple objectives listed together, one may be met and the other(s) may not be. The example comes from Wal-Mart stores.

Ineffective Objective   To increase pet food sales by 25% and to achieve a 5.4% market share.

Effective Objectives   To increase pet food sales by 25% by December 2003.

                           To achieve a 5.4% market share of pet foods during 2003.

Specific. The objective should state the exact level of performance expected. Research has shown that people with specific goals have higher levels of task performance than those with general goals.[33] The first example is generic; the second is based on the American Paper Institute.

Ineffective Objectives   To maximize profits in 2001. (How much is "maximize"?)

                           To recycle 40% by year end 2001. ($40% of what—glass, paper? type of paper?)

Effective Objectives   To earn a net profit of $1 million in 2001.

                           To recycle 40% of all paper by year end 2001.

Measurable. If people are to achieve objectives, they must be able to observe and measure their progress regularly to determine if the objectives have been met.[34] The following example is a Jiffy Lube goal.

Ineffective Objective	Perfect service for every customer. (How do you measure service?)
Effective Objective	To attain a 90% customer "excellent" satisfaction rating for 2000.

Target Date. A specific date should be set for accomplishing the objective. When people have a deadline, they usually try harder to get the task done on time than when they are simply told to do it when they can.[35] The example is based on Logical Water (a software company that developed Quesheet, a program that helps businesses find better ways to achieve their objectives).

Ineffective Objective	To become a multimillionaire. (By when?)
Effective Objective	To become a multimillionaire by December 2004.

It is also more effective to set a specific date than to give a time span because you can forget when the period began and should end. The following example is based on GTE:

Somewhat Effective	To double international business to $5 billion annually within five years.
Effective Objective	To double international business to $5 billion annually by year end 2000.

Some objectives are ongoing and do not require a stated date. The target date is indefinite until it is changed. The following examples come from 3M and General Electric:

Effective Objectives	To have 25% of sales coming from products that did not exist five years ago.
	To be number one or two in world sales in all lines of business.

In addition to the four "must" criteria, there are three "want" criteria.

Difficult but Achievable (Realistic). A number of studies show that individuals perform better when assigned difficult but achievable objectives rather than objectives that are too difficult or too easy or when simply told to "do your best."[36] You will learn the details in Chapter 12. *Realistic* is a subjective concept; therefore, it is a "want" rather than a "must" criterion.

Participatively Set. Groups that participate in setting their objectives generally outperform groups with assigned objectives (Chapter 3). Managers should use the appropriate level of participation for the employees' capabilities.[37] Because it is not always appropriate to have the group set objectives, it is a "want" rather than a "must" criterion.

WORK APPLICATION

7. Using the writing objectives model, write one or more objectives for an organization you work or have worked for, which meet the criteria that objectives should meet.

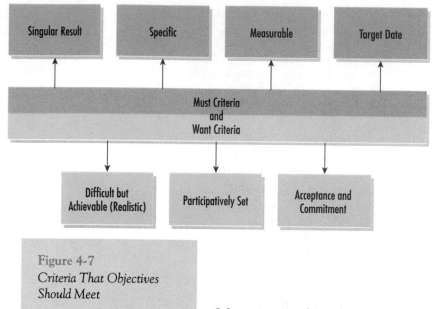

Figure 4-7
Criteria That Objectives Should Meet

management by objectives (MBO)
The process in which managers and their employees jointly set objectives for the employees, periodically evaluate the performance, and reward according to the results.

Acceptance and Commitment. For objectives to be met, employees must accept them. If employees do not commit to strive for the objective, even if you meet the preceding criteria, they may not meet the objective.[38] Participation helps get employees to accept objectives (Chapter 3). Because acceptance and commitment vary from individual to individual and times occur when managers must set objectives that employees will not like, acceptance and commitment are "want" criteria. For a review of the criteria that objectives should meet, see Figure 4–7.

Management by Objectives (MBO)

Management by objectives (MBO) *is the process in which managers and their employees jointly set objectives for the employees, periodically evaluate the performance, and reward according to the results.* Other names for MBO include work planning and review, goals management, goals and controls, and management by results.

MBO has met with both success and failure.[39] A major reason has been the lack of commitment and follow-through on management's part. MBO often fails because employees believe that management is insincere in its efforts to include employees in the decision-making process. Employees feel that management has already set the objectives and made the plans for implementation before talking to them. You can use the MBO process successfully with your subordinates if you commit and truly involve employees rather than trying to make them believe that your objectives are theirs.

The three steps of MBO include:

 Set individual objectives and plans. With each subordinate, the manager jointly sets objectives. The objectives are the heart of the MBO program and should meet the criteria discussed earlier.

step 2. **Give feedback and evaluate performance.** Communication is the key factor in determining MBO's success or failure. Thus, the manager and employee must meet frequently to review progress. The frequency of evaluations depends on the individual and the job performed. However, most managers probably do not conduct enough review sessions.

step 3. **Reward according to performance.** Employees' performance should be measured against their objectives. Employees who meet their objectives should be rewarded through recognition, praise, pay raises, promotions, and so on.

CORPORATE-LEVEL STRATEGY

After the mission has been developed, the situational analysis has been completed, and objectives have been set, the strategy, step 4 of the strategic process, should be developed at the corporate, business, and functional levels. In this section you will learn about corporate-level strategy: grand strategy, corporate growth strategies, portfolio analysis, and the product life cycle.

Grand Strategy

Grand strategy *is the overall corporate-level strategy of growth, stability, turnaround and retrenchment, or a combination thereof.* Each grand strategy reflects a different objective. Let's discuss each separately.

Growth. With a *growth strategy*, the company makes aggressive attempts to increase its size through increased sales. You will learn more about growth strategies under "Corporate Strategies."

Stability. With a *stability strategy*, the company attempts to hold and maintain its present size or to grow slowly. Many companies are satisfied with the status quo, for example, the WD-40 Company (petroleum-based lubricant) whose product is found in 75 percent of U.S. homes. Pete's Jiffy Lube has a stability strategy.

Turnaround and Retrenchment. *Turnaround strategy* is an attempt to reverse a declining business as quickly as possible. *Retrenchment strategy* is the divestiture or liquidation of assets. They are listed together because most turnarounds include retrenchment. Turnaround strategies generally attempt to improve cash flow by increasing revenues, decreasing costs, reducing assets, or combining these strategies. Texaco made one of the most successful U.S. turnarounds by selling $7 billion in assets.

Pennzoil sold substantially all of the domestic assets of its sulphur division. Pete and his partners sold 50 Jiffy Lubes to Pennzoil. A *spinoff* is a form of retrenchment in which the company sells one of its business units to form a separate company. ITT and AT&T both divided into three publicly traded companies in two of the largest-ever U.S. corporate breakups. James River had a spinoff of most of its nonconsumer paper and packaging operations.[40]

Combination. A corporation may pursue growth, stability, and turnaround and retrenchment across different lines of business. Pennzoil, like many other companies, has had the grand strategy to buy and sell business lines. You will learn more about this combination under "Portfolio Analysis."

Corporate Growth Strategies

The company that wants to grow has three major options. **Corporate growth strategies** *include concentration, backward and forward integration, and related and unrelated diversification.*

8. Describe the four grand strategies: growth, stability, turnaround and retrenchment, and combination.

grand strategy
The overall corporate-level strategy of growth, stability, turnaround and retrenchment, or a combination thereof.

9. Describe the three growth strategies: concentration, integration, and diversification.

corporate growth strategies
Concentration, backward and forward integration, and related and unrelated diversification.

Concentration. With a *concentration strategy*, the organization grows aggressively in its existing line(s) of business. Wal-Mart continues to open new stores. Pennzoil plans to aggressively increase the number of customers served by opening more Jiffy Lube service centers. Jiffy Lube opened service centers in Sears Auto-Service Centers around the United States.

Integration. With an *integration strategy*, the organization enters a forward or backward line(s) of business. *Forward integration* occurs when the organization enters a line of business closer to the final customer. *Backward integration* occurs when the organization enters a line of business far away from the final customer.[41] Pennzoil began refining oil in 1886 and it backward-integrated into extracting oil in 1989. When Pennzoil acquired Jiffy Lube, its forward integration objectives included gaining control over service centers that would be used to sell more of its motor oil. This acquisition gave Pennzoil three lines of business: (1) the extraction of oil (raw material), (2) the refinery to produce motor oil, to (3) the final consumer's auto engine at Jiffy Lube. Some manufacturers, like Bass shoes, have opened factory outlet stores to forward-integrate, thus bypassing traditional retail stores and selling their products directly to the customer.

Diversification. With a *diversification strategy*, the organization goes into a related or unrelated line of products. Pennzoil uses *related (concentric) diversification* by offering new products related to its motor oil through its Gumout line of automotive products. Nike used related diversification when it diversified from sports shoes to selling sports clothing. Sears used *unrelated (conglomerate) diversification* when it went from selling retail goods to selling insurance through its Allstate Insurance line of business. See Figure 4–8 for a review of strategies at the corporate level.

APPLYING THE CONCEPT

AC 4–1 Corporate Growth Strategies

Identify each statement by the type of growth strategy it would be making.

a. concentration
b. forward integration
c. backward integration
d. related diversification
e. unrelated diversification

_____ 1. Sears buys a tool company to make its Craftsman tools.

_____ 2. General Motors buys the Sea World theme park.

_____ 3. The Gap opens a new retail store in a mall.

_____ 4. Lee opens stores to sell its clothes.

_____ 5. Gateway 2000, a computer manufacturer, manufactures printers.

Common Growth Strategy Approaches. Common corporate approaches to growth include mergers, acquisitions, takeovers, joint ventures, and strategic alliances. A **merger** *occurs when two companies form one corporation.* Two companies become one new company. An **acquisition** *occurs when one business buys all or part of another business.* One business becomes a part of an existing business. Mergers and acquisitions often occur between competing companies to decrease competition; to compete more effectively with larger companies; to realize economies of size; to consolidate expenses; and to achieve access to markets, products, technology, resources,

merger
Occurs when two companies form one corporation.

acquisition
Occurs when one business buys all or part of another business.

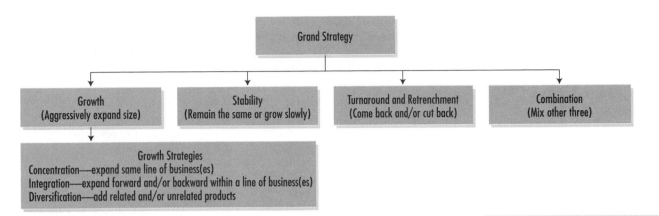

Figure 4-8
*Corporate Grand and
Growth Strategies*

and management talent. Companies often use acquisitions to enter new lines of businesses by buying an existing business rather than starting a new one.

When management of the target company rejects the purchasing company's offer, the purchasing company can make a bid to the target company shareholders to acquire the company through a *takeover.* Union Pacific Resources tried to acquire Pennzoil. Its board rejected the takeover and urged shareholders to reject a hostile takeover bid,[42] which they did.

Mergers and acquisitions have continued to grow year after year.[43] BankAmerica merged with NationsBank and Banc One merged with First Chicago.[44] Price and Costco warehouse membership clubs merged to become PriceCostco. Pennzoil acquired Jiffy Lube and recently acquired Quaker State and will merge the two best-known names in motor oil and quick oil change service centers.[45] Pennzoil also acquired Canadian oil and gas company Coenerco.

You learned about *joint ventures* (partners) and *strategic alliances* (work together without joint ownership), which are of increasing importance to growth (Chapter 2).[46]

Portfolio Analysis

Business portfolio analysis *is the corporate process of determining which lines of business it will be in and how it will allocate resources among them.* A *business line,* also called a *strategic business unit (SBU),* is a distinct business having its own customers that is managed reasonably independently of other businesses within the corporation. What constitutes an SBU varies from company to company, but it can be a division, subsidiary, or single product line.[47] Pennzoil has the following primary businesses: oil and gas (natural), motor oil and refined products, and franchise operations (Jiffy Lube). The industry and competitive situation analysis (five competitive forces) for each line of business, step 2 of the strategic process, is used to analyze a portfolio. Another method, the BCG Matrix, puts each line of business into one matrix.

business portfolio analysis
The corporate process of determining which lines of business it will be in and how it will allocate resources among them.

BCG Growth-Share Matrix. A popular approach to analyzing a portfolio is the Boston Consulting Group (BCG) Growth-Share Matrix. A BCG matrix for Pennzoil is shown in Figure 4–9. The four cells of the matrix are as follows:

- **Cash cows** generate more resources than they need, often with low growth, but with high market share. Examples of cash cows include Cola-Cola Classic and Crest toothpaste. Cash cows tend to have stability strategies.

- **Stars** are emerging businesses with high growth and market share. Stars require continuing investment of profits into the product, rather than using the funds with a "question mark," to continue growth until they become cash cows. The minivan became a star for Chrysler and Diet Coke became one for Coca-Cola. Stars tend to have growth strategies.

- **Question marks** are entries into any new businesses with negative returns in a high-growth market, beginning with low market share. Question marks need investments from other lines of business to develop into stars. But, they can become dogs. Maytag acquired Hoover's European unit in hopes of making it a star. However, about five years later it sold Hoover for a $170 million loss.[48] Question marks tend to have growth strategies.

- **Dogs** have low returns in a low-growth market and have low relative market share. Dogs are often divested or liquidated when they

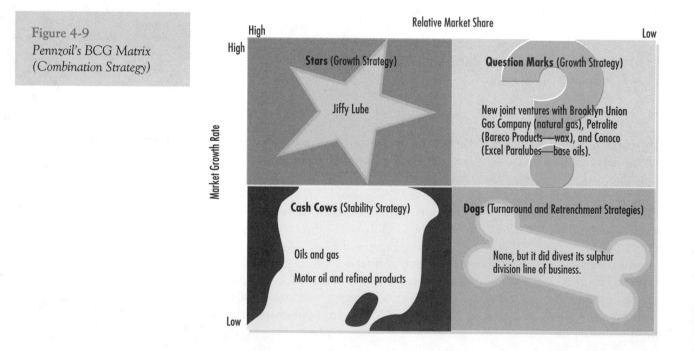

Figure 4-9
Pennzoil's BCG Matrix (Combination Strategy)

Relative Market Share

High — Low

Market Growth Rate — High / Low

Stars (Growth Strategy)

Jiffy Lube

Question Marks (Growth Strategy)

New joint ventures with Brooklyn Union Gas Company (natural gas), Petrolite (Bareco Products—wax), and Conoco (Excel Paralubes—base oils).

Cash Cows (Stability Strategy)

Oils and gas

Motor oil and refined products

Dogs (Turnaround and Retrenchment Strategies)

None, but it did divest its sulphur division line of business.

no longer provide acceptable profits. Black-and-white televisions, record turntables, and audio tape-players have become dogs. Dogs tend to have turnaround and retrenchment strategies.

The portfolio analysis (using combination strategy) provides managers with ideas about how to allocate cash and other resources among business lines (as well as which corporate strategies to use). Generally, managers take resources from the cash cows (stability strategy) and allocate them to the question marks and possibly the stars (growth strategies). Any cash from dogs is also given to question marks and stars, as well as any resources from their sale (retrenchment strategy). Seagram sold its Tropicana juice unit to help pay for the acquisition of music powerhouse PolyGram. Entertainment, not liquor, is now Seagram's main focus with over 70% of its revenues coming from music, movie, and theme-park divisions.[49]

A company in a single line of business cannot conduct a business portfolio analysis. However, it should perform a *product portfolio analysis*. The BCG business portfolio matrix can also be used to analyze a product line. For example, McDonald's started with a simple hamburger and fries. Over the years McDonald's introduced new products such as the Big Mac. The Big Mac started as a question mark, became a star, and then joined the cash cow hamburger and fries. McDonald's introduced pizza as a question mark, but rather than become a star it became a dog and was dropped from most restaurants.

The Entrepreneurial Strategy Matrix. The BCG Matrix was designed for large companies with multiple lines of business. Sonfield and Lussier[50] developed the Entrepreneurial Strategy Matrix (ESM) for small businesses. The ESM was developed to suggest strategies for new and ongoing entrepreneurial ventures that will lead to optimal performance in response to the identification of different combinations of innovation and risk. The matrix answers the questions: What venture situation are you in? What are the best strategic alternatives for a given venture?

Innovation is defined as the creation of something new and different. The newer and more different the product or service is, the higher the innovation. *Risk* is defined as the probability of a major financial loss. The entrepreneur determines the chances of the entrepreneurial venture failing and how serious the financial loss would be. The same dollar amount of possible loss might be more serious to one entrepreneur than to another. Combining innovation and risk, a four-cell matrix was created as shown in Figure 4–10.

The ESM also suggests appropriate strategies for each cell, which are presented in Figure 4–10 as well. Thus, entrepreneurs use the first part of the matrix to identify which cell their firms are in. Then, based on their cell, they utilize the appropriate suggested strategies for their matching cell in the second part of Figure 4–10.

Figure 4-10
*The Entrepreneurial
Strategy Matrix*

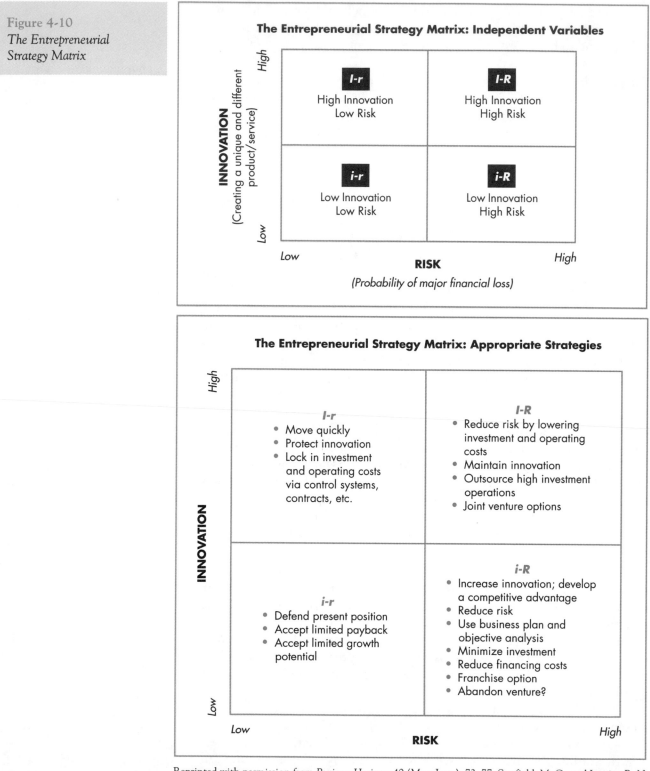

BUSINESS-LEVEL STRATEGY

Each line of business must develop its own mission, analyze its own environment, set its own objectives, and develop its own strategy. For the organization with a single line of products, such as Pete's Jiffy Lube, its corporate and business level strategies are the same. For the organization with multiple lines of business, linking corporate strategy with operations at the business unit level determines its success. In this section you will learn about adaptive strategies, competitive strategies, and how to change strategies during the product life cycle.

Adaptive Strategies

Each line of business needs its own strategy. However, it can be confusing to have the same strategy names at the corporate and business levels. The business level commonly uses the *adaptive strategies,* which correspond with the grand strategies. However, they emphasize adapting to changes in the external environment and entering new markets as a means of increasing sales. Figure 4–11 illustrates selecting the adaptive strategy based on the changing environment and growth rate, with corresponding grand strategies. Each adaptive strategy reflects a different objective. *The business-level* **adaptive strategies** *include prospecting, defending, and analyzing.*

Prospecting Strategy. The *prospecting strategy* calls for aggressively offering new products and/or entering new markets. Wal-Mart continues to open new stores to enter new markets. Pete's Jiffy Lube grew to operate over 50 service centers with the addition of partners. However, recall that growth has to be concentrated or related diversification. If it's integration or unrelated diversification, you need new lines of business and you no longer have a single line of business. The prospector strategy resembles the growth grand strategy and works appropriately in fast-changing environments with high growth potential.

Defending Strategy. The *defending strategy* calls for staying with the present product line and markets, and maintaining or increasing customers. Pete uses the defending strategy with his six Jiffy Lubes. Defending resembles the stability grand strategy, and works appropriately in a slow-changing environment with low growth potential.

10. Discuss the three business-level adaptive strategies: prospecting, defending, and analyzing.

adaptive strategies
Prospecting, defending, and analyzing.

WORK APPLICATION

10. Identify the adaptive strategy used by an organization you work or have worked for. Be sure to describe how it used the strategy.

Figure 4-11
Selecting Adaptive Strategies

Rate of Environmental Change	Potential Growth Rate	Adaptive Strategy	Similar to Grand Strategy
Fast	High	Prospector	Growth
Moderate	Moderate	Analyzer	Combination
Slow	Low	Defender	Stability

Analyzing Strategy. The *analyzing strategy* calls for a midrange approach between the prospector and defender. Analyzers move into new market areas at a cautious, deliberate pace and/or offer a core product group and seek new opportunities. Procter & Gamble has several established consumer products, including Pampers and Crest toothpaste, and occasionally offers innovations such as Aleve to compete with other pain relievers such as Bayer, Tylenol, and Advil. Analyzing resembles the combination grand strategy, and works appropriately in moderately changing environments with moderate growth potential.

Although the adaptive strategies have no strategy similar to turnaround and retrenchment, strategic business units may need to use this strategy to cut back or stop selling dog products. If the firm does not replace dogs with new products, it may eventually go out of business.

APPLYING THE CONCEPT

AC 4–2 Adaptive Strategies

Identify each statement by the type of adaptive strategy it represents.

a. prospecting   b. defending   c. analyzing

_____ **6.** Industry leader Coca-Cola's primary strategy in the saturated U.S. cola market.

_____ **7.** Nabisco comes out with new "umum" cookie to compete with Keebler's "umum" cookies.

_____ **8.** Friendly Ice Cream opens restaurants in the State of Washington.

_____ **9.** IBM pioneers a computer that can be folded up and put in your pocket.

_____ **10.** Domino's strategy when Pizza Hut started to copy delivering pizza.

Competitive Strategies

Michael Porter identified three effective business-level *competitive strategies:* differentiation, cost leadership, and focus.[51]

Differentiation Strategy. With a differentiation strategy, the company stresses its advantage over its competitors. Nike, Ralph Lauren Polo clothing, Calvin Klein, and others place their names on the outside of their products to create a prestigious differentiation from the competition. Differentiation strategy somewhat resembles the prospector strategy. According to Coca-Cola, the three keys to selling consumer products are differentiation, differentiation, differentiation,[52] which it does with its scripted name logo and contour bottle.

Cost Leadership. With a low-cost leadership strategy, the company stresses lower prices to attract customers. To keep its prices down, it must have tight cost control and an efficient systems process.[53] Wal-Mart also had success with this strategy. Cost leadership somewhat resembles the defender strategy. Bill Long, head of the successful low-cost leading Waremart Foods, says, "Growth demands high volume and high volume demands low prices."[54]

Focus. With a focus strategy, the company focuses on a specific regional market, product line, or buyer group. Within a particular target segment, or market niche, the firm may use a differentiation or cost leadership strategy.

Ed Boyd was hired by PepsiCo to direct what is believed to have been the first target marketing campaign for a major product. More than 50 years ago, Ed developed an African-American sales team to market Pepsi soft drinks to blacks.[55] *Ebony* and *Jet* magazines target African-Americans, MTV focuses on young people, and Rolex watches have a niche of upper-income people. Right Guard deodorant aims at men and Secret aims at women. The focus strategy somewhat resembles the analyzer strategy.

Product Life Cycle

The product life cycle refers to a series of stages that a product goes through over time.[56] The four stages of the *product life cycle* are introduction, growth, maturity, and decline. The speed at which products go through the life cycle varies. Many products, like Tide detergent, stay around for many years, while fad products, like pet rocks and pogs may only last months. Figure 4–12 illustrates the appropriate portfolio analysis, corporate grand strategy, and business-level adaptive strategy for each stage of the product life cycle for Pennzoil.

Pricing strategies are important to business.[57] Price strategies tend to change over the product life cycle. Prices tend to be higher in the introduction stage due to little if any competition. Prices decline with product age, but the number of products to market sustains a steady growth.[58]

Figure 4-12
Pennzoil Strategies Through the Product Life Cycle Stages

Product Life Cycle Stages Over Time			
Introduction Stage	**Growth Stage**	**Maturity Stage**	**Decline Stage**
Changing Strategies Over Time			
Growth Strategy / Prospector Strategy	Growth Strategy / Analyzer Strategy (New firms enter the market.)	Stability Strategy / Defender Strategy	Turnaround and Retrenchment Strategy / Prospector or Analyzer Strategy (To develop new products)
Portfolio Analysis Changes Over Time			
Question Marks (Pennzoil's three new joint ventures. A question mark can skip the star and cash cow stages and become a dog.)	Stars (Jiffy Lube)	Cash Cows (Oil and gas and motor oil and refined products)	Dogs (None—divested sulphur and is seeking new opportunities.)

Introduction Stage. As a growth strategy, the prospector introduces a new product that has a differentiation strategy because it is new; it can also use a focus strategy. It emphasizes getting the product accepted. Resources are used to promote (advertise) the product and to get production going. It is common to charge a high price to try to get back the investment. Jiffy Lube introduced the quick oil change. Introduction products are usually question marks in the business portfolio.

Growth Stage. As a continuing growth strategy, rapid sales growth takes place. When analyzers see that the prospector is doing well, they copy the product through benchmarking. Analyzers may use a differentiation, focus, or low-cost strategy to gain sales through the growth stage. Resource focus emphasizes quality and systems process improvements to gain economies of scale. Prices are often lowered, which reduces profits per unit, to gain market share. U.S. HealthCare cut prices to build market share. Analyzers (Ready Lube, Oil Doctor, and others) have copied Jiffy Lube and tend to use a focus strategy in regional markets. The portfolio stars, like Jiffy Lube, are usually in the growth stage.

Maturity Stage. At the maturity stage, sales growth continues slowly, levels off, and begins to decline. In a saturated market, the growth strategy changes to one of stability (defender). The low cost becomes more important, and cost-cutting efforts are emphasized. Quick oil change (Jiffy Lube) is still in the growth stage but growth is limited due to its nearing maturity. Mature products (Pennzoil oil and gas and motor oil and refined products) are usually cash cows in the portfolio.

Decline Stage. In the decline stage, sales drop. The strategy changes from stability–defend to turnaround and retrenchment and prospector or analyzer. Procter & Gamble uses a turnaround strategy with its personal care products, such as Tide, calling them new and improved to revitalize sales in order to prevent decline to the point of retrenchment. A product can be in the decline stage and remain profitable, such as black-and-white TVs, for many years. In the portfolio, products in the decline stage are dogs and may be divested. The prospector or analyzer strategy comes into play to develop new products.

Remember that the various grand and adaptive strategies complement one another. Select the appropriate strategy based on the mission, situation analysis, and objectives.

WORK APPLICATION

11. Identify the stage in the product life cycle for an organization you work or have worked for. Is the strategy you identified in Work Application 10 the appropriate strategy for this stage of the product life cycle? Explain your answers.

APPLYING THE CONCEPT

AC 4–3 Product Life Cycle

Select the stage of the product life cycle of each of the following products.

a. introduction b. growth c. maturity d. decline

_____ **11.** Mobil gasoline.

_____ **12.** Cassette tapes.

_____ **13.** Home carpeting (rugs).

_____ **14.** Cellular telephones.

_____ **15.** The fold-up computer that fits in your pocket.

FUNCTIONAL-LEVEL OPERATIONAL STRATEGIES

In prior sections you learned about long-range strategic planning. You will now learn about operational-level planning. The functional departments must develop strategies for achieving the business-level mission and objectives. **Functional strategies** *include marketing, operations, human resources, finance, and others*. The situation analysis also takes place at the functional levels to determine strengths and weaknesses. The functional departments also develop objectives and strategies for achieving them.

The implementation stage of the strategic process has remained a stumbling block as organizations have difficulty translating business strategies into cohesive competitive strategies. The need for greater intergration of corporate, business, and functional strategies within the organization has long been recognized. One of the foremost difficulties is achieving greater cooperation across functional departments. It has been suggested that functional strategies should be developed for each stage of the product life cycle, which can be used to integrate the functional areas.[59] We will briefly discuss each function. You may have taken, or will take, one or more entire courses on each function.

Marketing Strategy

The marketing department has the primary responsibility for knowing what the customer wants, or how to add customer value, and for defining the target market. Marketing has responsibility for the four Ps: product, promotion, place, and price. In other words, the marketing department makes decisions about which products to provide, how they will be packaged, how they will be advertised, where they will be sold and how they get there, and how much they will be sold for.

If the growth prospector business-level strategy is used, marketing will be involved in planning and implementing new products and/or markets to enter. If the stability defender strategy is selected, marketing will not be concerned about new products or markets or new product advertising. If the analyzer strategy is used, marketing will take a midrange approach between prospecting and defending. If the turnaround and retrenchment strategy is used, marketing will be involved in selecting products to drop and/or markets to exit.

Operations Strategy

The operations (or production) department is responsible for systems processes that convert inputs into outputs. Operations focuses on quality and efficiency in producing the products that marketing determines will provide customer value. You will learn more about operations in Chapter 15.

If the growth prospector business-level strategy is used, operations will be involved in planning for and producing the new products. Aggressive

---

11. List the four major functional operational strategy areas.

functional strategies
Marketing, operations, human resources, finance, and others.

growth may require new operations facilities. If the stability defender strategy is selected, operations will devote its full energy to improving quality and efficiency and cutting costs. If the analyzer strategy is used, operations will take a midrange approach between prospecting and defending. If the turnaround and retrenchment strategy is used, operations will be involved in cutting back systems processes.

Human Resources Strategy

The human resources department is responsible for working with all functional departments in the areas of recruiting, selecting, training, evaluating, and compensating employees. You will learn more about human resources in Chapter 8.

If the growth prospector business-level strategy is used, human resources will be involved in planning for and expanding the number of employees. If the stability defender strategy is selected, human resources will devote its full energy to improving quality and efficiency. If the analyzer strategy is used, human resources will take a midrange approach. If the turnaround and retrenchment strategy is used, human resources will be involved in laying off employees.

Finance Strategy

The finance strategy has at least two parts: (1) financing the business activities by raising money through the sale of stock (equity) or bonds/loans (debt), deciding on the debt-to-equity ratio, and paying off the debt and dividends (if any) to shareholders; and (2) keeping records of transactions, developing budgets, and reporting financial results (income statement and balance sheet). A third area of finance in many organizations includes optimum use of cash reserves, or the area of investing as a means of making money. Some organizations, including Texas Instruments and 3M, are developing separate strategic and operational budgets. You will learn more about finance in Chapter 14.

If the growth prospector business-level strategy is used, finance will be involved in planning for and raising money to pay for the functional area budgets, and dividends will be low, if any are given. If the stability defender strategy is used, finance will focus on paying off debt and will generally pay a dividend. If the analyzer strategy is used, finance will take a midrange approach. If the turnaround strategy is used, finance may both raise money and sell assets to pay for the comeback. With a retrenchment strategy, finance will be involved in the sale of assets, and dividends are generally not paid, or are low.

Other Functional Strategies

Based on the type of business, any number of other departments will also need to develop a strategy. One area that varies in importance is research and

WORK APPLICATION

12. Identify the functional area of an organization you work or have worked for. What was its operational strategy?

development (R&D). Businesses that sell a product usually allocate greater resources (budgets) for R&D than service businesses.

Pete has a small business; therefore, he does not have separate functional departments like Jiffy Lube International. Pete uses a stability defender strategy and gets advertising assistance from Jiffy Lube, but he also has an ongoing ad campaign run by a local ad agency.

APPLYING THE CONCEPT

AC 4–4 Functional Strategies

Identify each statement's type of functional strategy.

a. marketing   c. finance   e. other
b. operations   d. human resources

____ **16.** The department responsible for cleaning up and fixing things.

____ **17.** The department that sends out the bills.

____ **18.** The primary department that transforms inputs into outputs.

____ **19.** The department that decides where the product will be sold.

____ **20.** The department responsible for labor relations.

IMPLEMENTING AND CONTROLLING STRATEGIES

The first four steps in the strategic process involve planning. The fifth and final step involves implementing and controlling strategies to ensure that the mission and objectives, at all three levels, are achieved. Top and middle managers are more involved with the planning, whereas the lower-level functional managers and employees *implement* the strategies on a day-to-day basis. Successful implementation of strategies requires effective and efficient support systems throughout the organization. Although strategic planning usually goes well, implementation is often the problem. One reason is that strategic plans often end up buried in bottom drawers and no action is taken to implement the strategy.[60] Throughout Chapters 5 through 13, you will learn how to implement strategy.

As the strategies are being implemented, they must also be controlled. *Controlling* is the process of establishing and implementing mechanisms to ensure that objectives are achieved. An important part of controlling is measuring progress toward the achievement of the objective and taking corrective action when needed.[61] Another important part of controlling is staying within the budget when appropriate and being flexible and changing it when necessary to meet changes in the environment. You will develop your controlling skills in Chapters 14 and 15.

WORK APPLICATION

13. Give examples of controls used for an organization you work or have worked for.

CHAPTER SUMMARY AND GLOSSARY

The chapter summary is organized to answer the 12 learning objectives for Chapter 4.

1. Describe the differences between strategic and operational plans.
The primary differences are timeframe and management level involved.

Strategic planning involves developing a mission and long-range objectives and plans. Operational plans involve short-range objectives and plans. Upper-level managers develop strategic plans and lower-level managers develop operational plans.

2. State the differences among the three levels of strategies: corporate, business, and functional.

The primary differences are the focus, which narrows as strategy moves down the organization, and the management level involved in developing the strategy. Corporate-level strategy focuses on managing multiple lines of business. Business-level strategy focuses on managing one line of business. Functional-level strategy focuses on managing an area of a business line. Upper-level managers develop corporate- and business-level strategy, and lower-level managers develop functional strategy.

3. Explain the reason for conducting an industry and competitive situation analysis.

The industry and competitive situation analysis is used to determine the attractiveness of an industry. It is primarily used at the corporate strategy level to make decisions regarding which lines of business to enter and exit, and how to allocate resources among lines of business.

4. Explain the reason for conducting a company situation analysis.

The company situation analysis is used at the business strategy level to determine the strategic issues and problems that need to be addressed through the strategic process.

5. State how competitive advantage and benchmarking are related.

Competitive advantage and benchmarking are related because a company that decides to have a competitive advantage will use benchmarking against noncompetitors to be different from the competition. If the company decides not to have a competitive advantage, it will benchmark against the leading competitor and copy it. In addition, many firms will copy competitors' good ideas while trying to differentiate themselves in some other way.

6. Discuss how goals and objectives are similar yet different.

Goals and objectives are similar because they both state what is to be accomplished. Goals are often translated into objectives. They also differ in detail. Goals state general targets, whereas objectives state what is to be accomplished in singular, specific, and measurable terms with a target date.

7. List the steps in the writing objectives model.

The parts of the writing objectives model are: (1) infinitive + (2) action verb + (3) singular, specific, and measurable result to be achieved + (4) target date.

8. Describe the four grand strategies: growth, stability, turnaround and retrenchment, and combination.

With a growth strategy, the firm aggressively pursues increasing its size. With a stability strategy, the firm maintains the same size or grows slowly. With a turnaround strategy, the firm attempts a comeback; with retrenchment, it decreases in size. With a combination strategy, the other three strategies are used across different lines of business.

9. **Describe the three growth strategies: concentration, integration, and diversification.**

With a concentration strategy, the firm grows aggressively in its existing line(s) of business. With integration, the firm grows by entering a forward or backward line(s) of business. With diversification, the firm grows by adding related or unrelated products.

10. **Discuss the three business-level adaptive strategies: prospecting, defending, and analyzing.**

With the prospecting strategy, the firm aggressively offers new products/services and/or enters new markets. Prospecting is a growth strategy used in fast-changing environments with high growth potential. With the defending strategy, the firm stays with its product/line and markets. Defending is a stability strategy used in slow-changing environments with low growth potential. With the analyzing strategy, the firm moves into new markets cautiously and/or offers a core product group and seeks new opportunities. Analyzing is a combination strategy used in moderately changing environments with moderate growth potential.

11. **List the four major functional operational strategy areas.**

The four major functional operational strategy areas are marketing, operations, human resources, and finance. There are other functional department strategies based on the organization's needs.

12. **Define the following key terms (in order of appearance in the chapter):**

Select one or more methods: (1) fill in the missing key terms from memory, (2) match the key terms from the end of the summary with their definitions below, or (3) copy the key terms in order from the list at the beginning of the chapter.

_____ is the process of developing a mission and long-range objectives and determining in advance how they will be accomplished.

_____ is the process of setting short-range objectives and determining in advance how they will be accomplished.

The steps in the _____ are (1) developing the mission, (2) analyzing the environment, (3) setting objectives, (4) developing strategies, and (5) implementing and controlling strategies.

A _____ is a plan for pursuing the mission and achieving objectives.

The _____ include corporate, business, and functional.

The _____ is the plan for managing multiple lines of business.

The _____ is the plan for managing one line of business.

The _____ is the plan for managing one area of the business.

A _____ draws out those features in a company's environment that most directly frame its strategic window of options and opportunities.

Through a _____, the organization's internal environmental strengths and weaknesses and external environmental opportunities and threats are determined.

_____ specifies how the organization offers unique customer value.

_____ is the process of comparing the organization's products/services and processes with those of other companies.

_____ state general targets to be accomplished.

_____ state what is to be accomplished in singular, specific, and measurable terms with a target date.

The parts of the _____ are: (1) infinitive + (2) action verb + (3) singular, specific, and measurable result to be achieved + (4) target date.

_____ is the process in which managers and their employees jointly set objectives for the employee, periodically evaluate the progress, and reward according to the results.

_____ is the overall corporate-level strategy of growth, stability, turnaround and retrenchment, or a combination thereof.

_____ include concentration, backward and forward integration, and related and unrelated diversification.

A _____ occurs when two companies form one corporation.

An _____ occurs when one business buys all or part of another business.

The _____ is the corporate process of determining which lines of businesses it will be in and how it will allocate resources among them.

The business-level _____ include prospecting, defending, and analyzing.

_____ include marketing, operations, human resources, finance, and others.

KEY TERMS

REVIEW AND DISCUSSION QUESTIONS

1. In your own words, why are strategic and operational planning important?

2. Is there a difference between a plan and a strategy?

3. Should all businesses have corporate-, business-, and functional-level strategies?

4. Should a mission statement be customer-focused?

5. Why is a situational analysis part of the strategic process?

6. Should all businesses have a competitive advantage?

7. Is it ethical to copy other companies' ideas through benchmarking?

8. Are both goals and objectives necessary for a business?

9. Is it important to write objectives?

10. As a manager, would you use MBO?

11. Which growth strategy would you say is the most successful?

12. What is the difference between a merger and an acquisition?

13. Is there a difference between grand strategies and adaptive strategies?

14. Why would a business use a focus strategy rather than appeal to all customers?

15. Give examples of "other" functional departments.

OBJECTIVE CASE

Mattel Toy Company

Mattel, Inc., is the largest toy company in the world. Its competitors include Hasbro, Tyco Toys, and others. To offer a broader range of products, which helps it to compete on a global basis, the toy industry went through a great deal of consolidation. For example, Mattel bought Fisher-Price, but it keeps the Fisher-Price name on its product line of preschool and infant toys.

In addition, increased consolidation of retail distribution channels has affected the toy industry. The large specialty toy stores and discount retailers, including Toys 'R' Us, Wal-Mart, Kmart, and Target, have increased their share of the market. As a result, these retailers have increased their business with large toy companies that have financial stability and the ability to advertise and distribute toys on a global scale.

Large retailers are making it difficult to standardize toys because they each seem to want the product they sell to be a little bit different. They require changes in palletization, product packaging, and labeling. Retailers demand the product when they want it and in the quantity they want.

It is difficult to coordinate manufacturing and retail needs. Mattel acquired Pleasant Company, a direct marketer that makes the American Girl line, signaling a strategy to reduce its reliance on large retail stores.[62]

Mattel is changing the way it does business to meet the changing ways of retailers. Mattel has reengineered key business processes. It established a team of company and outside people to work on a project called Reengineering the Order Management Process (ROMP). ROMP determined the specific amount of each product available to every customer. Exchange of information between large retailers and Mattel is needed to allow them to keep up with "what's hot and what's not." Mattel now closely monitors consumer acceptance of particular products through electronic data interchange with large retailers. This system allows Mattel to quickly respond to the needs of the faster sales times in the retail store.

Mattel's approach to conducting business is to focus on a few core product lines that account for most of its revenues. The core product lines

OBJECTIVE CASE

(continued)

for Mattel include Barbie fashion dolls, clothing, and accessories; Hot Wheels vehicles and accessories; Disney products; and Fisher-Price products. With a strong core product line bringing most of the revenues, Mattel reduces its reliance on new products (question marks), which can be expensive and risky.

Mattel's core products spend a long time in the growth and maturity stages, but most of its new products tend to go through the product life cycle quickly. Mattel uses licensing agreements from companies with established images to help ensure success with new products. Mattel negotiates licensing agreements to create lines of dolls and other toys based on Disney's animated films. Mattel also has licensing agreements with companies such as Twentieth Century Fox, Turner Entertainment Co., and Viacom.

Mattel realized that buying Fisher-Price and aggressively expanding global distribution was the best way to compete. Globalization provides increased sales volume of core products and extends the product life cycles of new products. Mattel continues to use outsourcing of some of its basic business functions. Mattel purchases some designs from independent toy inventors, and it contracts with independent manufacturers to produce some of its products.

Select the best alternative for the following questions. Be sure you are able to explain your answers.

___ 1. The information in this case refers primarily to

    a. strategic planning
    b. operational planning

___ 2. Which of the five competitive forces is of major focus for Mattel?

    a. competitive rivalry
    b. threat of substitute products
    c. potential new entrants

    d. power of suppliers
    e. power of buyers

___ 3. Mattel does not have a competitive advantage over its competitors.

    a. true   b. false

___ 4. Mattel's global grand strategy is

    a. growth
    b. stability
    c. turnaround and retrenchment
    d. combination

___ 5. Mattel's corporate growth strategy is

    a. concentration
    b. forward integration
    c. backward integration
    d. related diversification
    e. unrelated diversification

___ 6. The Mattel and Fisher-Price strategic approach was a(n)

    a. merger   c. joint venture
    b. acquisition   d. strategic alliance

___ 7. The appropriate portfolio analysis for Mattel is

    a. business
    b. product

___ 8. Mattel's business-level adaptive strategy for products only, not markets, is

    a. prospecting
    b. defending
    c. analyzing

___ 9. Mattel's primary competitive strategy is

    a. differentiation
    b. cost leadership
    c. focus

OBJECTIVE CASE

(continued)

___ **10.** In the United States, toys are in which stage of the product life cycle?

    a. introduction c. maturity

    b. growth   d. decline

11. Should Mattel have the same adaptive strategy for markets as it does for products? Explain.

12. Should Mattel have the same adaptive strategy for global and domestic operations? Explain.

13. Conduct an industry and competitive situation analysis using the five-force competitive analysis. Use Figure 4–3 as an example.

14. Conduct a SWOT analysis for Mattel.

15. Write some possible goals and objectives for Mattel.

For current information on Mattel, use Internet address http://etoys.com to visit the toy site and/or http://mattelmedia.com. For ideas on using the Internet, see Appendix B.

VIDEO CASE

Kropf Fruit Company
(4–1 13½ minutes)

Case Summary

The Kropf Fruit Company is a four-generation family business in the rich apple-growing country of western Michigan. The business consists of orchards, a packing facility, and a storage facility. Kropf's enviroment changed as large grocery stores consolidated. The number of buyers for its products decreased, but the volume that each buyer purchased increased substantially. Small regional growers could not provide the volume of fruit these stores required nor did they have the storage facilities necessary to make the fruit available year-round. Thus, Kropf needed strategic planning.

Students' Learning Objective

To understand strategic planning and how a fruit company went through the strategic process.

Critical Thinking Questions

1. Should Kropf select a stability strategy and stay the same size or employ a growth strategy?

2. What types of tactical plans (functional-level operational strategies) must Kropf develop to accomplish its ten-year strategic plan?

Marketing

Operations

Human Resources

Finance

Skill-Building Exercise 4–1

Writing Objectives

Preparing for Skill-Building Exercise 4–1

For this exercise, you will first work at improving objectives that do not meet the criteria for objectives, then you will write nine objectives for yourself.

Part 1

For each of the following objectives, write the missing criteria and rewrite the objective so that it meets all "must" criteria. When writing objectives use the model:

infinitive + action verb + singular, specific, and

measurable result + target date

1. To improve our company image by year-end 2003.

Criteria missing: _____

Improved objective: _____

_____

2. To increase the number of customers by 10 percent.

Criteria missing: _____

Improved objective: _____

_____

3. To increase profits during 2001.

Criteria missing: _____

Improved objective:_____

_____

4. To sell 5 percent more hot dogs and soda at the baseball game on Sunday, June 13, 2002.

Criteria missing: _____

Improved objective: _____

_____

Part 2

Write three educational, personal, and career objectives you want to accomplish. Your objectives can be as short-term as something you want to accomplish today or as long-term as 20 years from now. Be sure your objectives meet the criteria for effective objectives.

Educational Objectives

1._____

_____

_____

2._____

_____

_____

3._____

_____

_____

Personal Objectives

1._____

_____

_____

2._____

_____

_____

3._____

_____

_____

Career Objectives

1._____

_____

_____

2._____

_____

_____

3._____

_____

_____

Doing Skill-Building Exercise 4–1 in Class

Objective
To develop your skill at writing objectives.

Preparation
You should have corrected and written objectives in the preparation before class.

Experience
You will get feedback on how well you corrected the four objectives and share your written objectives with others.

Options (8–20 minutes)

1. The instructor goes over suggested corrections for the four objectives in part 1 of the preparation, then calls on class members to share their written objectives (part 2) with the class.

2. The instructor goes over suggested corrections for the four objectives in part 1 of the preparation, then the class breaks into groups of four to six to share their written objectives.

3. Break into groups of four to six and go over the corrections for the four objectives in part 1. Tell the instructor when your group is done, but go on to part 2. Share your written objectives until all groups are finished with the four corrections. The instructor goes over the corrections and may allow more time for sharing objectives. Give each other feedback for improving your written objectives during part 2.

Conclusion
The instructor may lead a class discussion and/or make concluding remarks.

Application (2–4 minutes)
What did I learn from this experience? How will I use this knowledge in the future?

_____

_____

_____

Sharing
Volunteers give their answers to the application section.

---

*skillbuilder

Skill-Building Exercise 4–2

Entrepreneurial Strategic Planning

I **G**   Self-Assessment Exercise 4–1

Preparing for Skill-Building Exercise 4–2
Would you like to be your own boss? Have you ever given any thought to owning your own business? For this exercise you are asked to select a business you would like to start some day. To assess your entrepreneurial qualities on ten dimensions, complete Self-Assessment Exercise 4–1 before continuing with this exercise. Answer the questions honestly without fear of sharing your answers during class.

Entrepreneurial Qualities
Place a checkmark on the scale that best describes you.

1. I have a strong desire   I have a weak desire
   to be independent.   to be independent.

   ___ ___ ___ ___ ___ ___
    6   5   4   3   2   1

2. I enjoy taking reasonable risks.   I avoid taking risks.

| 6 | 5 | 4 | 3 | 2 | 1 |

3. I avoid making the same mistakes.   I repeat the same mistakes.

| 6 | 5 | 4 | 3 | 2 | 1 |

4. I can work without any supervision.   I need supervision to motivate me to work.

| 6 | 5 | 4 | 3 | 2 | 1 |

5. I seek out competition.   I avoid competition.

| 6 | 5 | 4 | 3 | 2 | 1 |

6. I enjoy working long, hard hours.   I enjoy taking it easy and having plenty of personal time.

| 6 | 5 | 4 | 3 | 2 | 1 |

7. I am confident of my abilities.   I lack self-confidence.

| 6 | 5 | 4 | 3 | 2 | 1 |

8. I need to be the best/successful.   I'm satisfied with being average.

| 6 | 5 | 4 | 3 | 2 | 1 |

9. I have a high energy level.   I have a low energy level.

| 6 | 5 | 4 | 3 | 2 | 1 |

10. I stand up for my rights.   I let others take advantage of me.

| 6 | 5 | 4 | 3 | 2 | 1 |

Scoring. Add up the 10 numbers below your checkmarks. The total number will be between 10 and 60. Place your score on the continuum below.

Entrepreneurial Qualities

Strong 60——50——40——30——20——10 Weak

Generally, the higher/stronger your entrepreneurial score, the better your chance of being a successful entrepreneur. However, simple paper-and-pencil surveys are not always good predictors. If you had a low score and really want to start a business, you may be successful. But, realize that you don't have all the typical entrepreneurial qualities.

An important part of any business plan is determining how much it will cost to start the business and to project the financial cash flow for the first five years. The financials are beyond the scope of this course, so just prepare a strategic plan without financials. Assume that money is not an issue because you hit the lottery for $50 million. Select a type of single-line business you want to start and give it a name and a general location with which you are familiar. To develop your strategy, use the following working strategic process papers. If you have absolutely no interest in owning your own business, you may select an existing business.

Before you begin the strategic process, list the name of the business and its major goods and/or services.

Company name: _____

Products: _____

_____

Step 1. Developing a Mission

Write a mission for your business. You may want to have a general mission in mind, but wait to write it after completing step 2.

_____

_____

_____

Step 2. Analyzing the Environment

Develop a five-force competitive analysis using Figure 4–3 as an example; then do a company situation analysis.

Five-Force Competitive Analysis

2. Threat of substitute products and services

4. Power of suppliers   1. The rivalry among competing sellers in the industry   5. Power of buyers

3. Potential of new entrants

Company Situation Analysis

1. SWOT analysis.

Strengths

_____

_____

_____

Weaknesses

_____

_____

Opportunities

_____

_____

_____

Threats

_____

_____

2. Competitive advantage (if any). You may do a competitive strength assessment, but it is not required

_____

_____

_____

3. Conclusions concerning competitive position.

_____

_____

_____

4. Determine the strategic issues and problems that need to be addressed through the strategic process.

_____

_____

_____

Step 3. Setting Objectives

List three goals or objectives.

_____

_____

_____

Step 4. Developing Strategies

Being in a single line of business, you do not need a grand strategy or to conduct a portfolio analysis. How-

ever, you should have an adaptive and competitive strategy based on the product life cycle.

Stage of the product life cycle: _____

Adaptive and competitive strategy (explain each briefly):

_____

_____

Step 5. Implementing and Controlling Strategies

List a few major controls you will use to implement the strategy. _____

_____

Doing Skill-Building Exercise 4–2 in Class

Objective

To develop your strategic planning skills.

Preparation

You should have completed the entrepreneurial strategic plan preparation.

Experience

You will share your entrepreneurial strategic plan in class.

Options (8–20 minutes)

1. Students present their strategic plan to the entire class.
2. Break into groups of three to five and share your strategic plans. Sharing answers to Self-Assessment Exercise 4–1 is not part of this exercise.
3. Same as option 1 but the group selects its best strategic plan to be presented to the entire class.

Conclusion

The instructor may lead a class discussion and/or make concluding remarks.

Application (2–4 minutes)

What did I learn from this experience? How will I use this knowledge in the future?

_____

_____

_____

Sharing

Volunteers give their answers to the application section.

5 Planning Tools

Learning Objectives

After studying this chapter, you should be able to:

1. State the difference between standing and single-use plans.
2. Explain why contingency plans are often needed.
3. Discuss the relationship between the strategic process and sales forecasting.
4. Describe the difference between qualitative and quantitative sales forecasting techniques.
5. Discuss the difference between the jury of executive opinion and the three composite sales forecasting techniques.
6. Explain the difference between the past sales and time series sales forecasting techniques.
7. Describe the similarities and differences between the planning sheet, Gantt chart, and PERT network.
8. Explain the use of a time log.
9. List and briefly describe the three steps in the time management system.
10. Define the following **key terms** (in order of appearance in the chapter):

standing plans
policies
procedures
rules
single-use plans
contingency plans
sales forecast
market share
qualitative sales forecasting
  techniques

quantitative sales forecasting
  techniques
time series
scheduling
planning sheets
Gantt charts
PERT
critical path
time management
time management system

Skill Development

*skillbuilder   1. You can develop your skill in using the Gantt chart and PERT network (Skill-Building Exercise 5–1).

*skillbuilder   2. You can develop your time management skills, which will enable you to get more done in less time with better results (Skill-Building Exercise 5–2).

These skills are part of conceptual and decision-making skills. These exercises develop your planning and resource-allocator decisional role skills. The SCANS skill competencies of using resources, information, and systems, basic and thinking foundation skills; and the personal quality of self-management are also developed.

atoya Washington graduated with a doctorate in business and began to teach at a western university. Latoya was a bit disappointed with her education because she felt it was too theoretical and without enough application and practical value—or skill building. She began to develop her own material and used it in her class, which students really liked. In her second year as a college professor, Latoya began a consulting firm, Washington Training and Development Services (WT&DS). Latoya developed a modular approach to offer skill development for business managers. Some of the modules she offers include setting objectives and developing plans, problem solving and decision making, participation in decision making, and time management.

Latoya developed a brochure as a means of promoting her services. The WT&DS mission statement, taken from the inside cover of her brochure, is: "We are dedicated to training people and developing their skills in order to maximize performance and productivity on the job, while enhancing individual careers."

Latoya began to market her business by cold-calling possible clients. Over the telephone she would briefly describe her business and try to get an appointment to go and meet with the person in charge of training and development to discuss her services in more detail, and to leave a brochure. After each meeting she would follow up the discussion with a thank-you letter, restating how the organization could benefit from her services. The letter was based on specific things the person told her during the meeting. The letter was an attempt to get the person to commit to a training program. The letter also stated that Latoya would follow up the letter with a phone call to answer questions, to close a sale.

After gaining some clients, Latoya started to market her business with a monthly letter to all prospective organizations (300) in the area. The letters gave updated information on training from publications, and always stated that a brochure was available upon request and that she would be pleased to make a personal visit if the person wanted more information. Latoya got to the point of not having to make any more cold calls because she developed a client base that kept her busy.[1]

Although the title of Chapter 4 is "The Strategic and Operational Planning Process," it placed more emphasis on strategic planning. This chapter places more emphasis on operational planning, which is also referred to as short-term action planning.[2] Sound business planning skills are important to your career success.[3] You need to know what you want to do (objectives) and then decide how to do it (planning).[4] As with decisions, different types of plans can be used.[5] Although the title of this chapter is "Planning Tools," it starts off by continuing to discuss the different types of planning, with a focus on short-term operational plans. Then, it explains the specific planning tools of sales forecasting, scheduling, and time management that you can use to improve your operational planning skills.

PLANS

In this section you will learn about the planning dimensions, standing plans versus single-use plans, contingency plans, why managers don't plan, and indicators of poor planning.

Planning Dimensions

Plans can be characterized by at least five dimensions: (1) The management *level* that develops the plan. (2) The *type of plan*—strategic or operational. (3) The *scope* of the plan covered. The plan can be broad in scope, such as for the entire organization, or for a business unit, or it can be narrow, such as for a functional department or for just a part of a department or even for one employee. (4) *Time*—long- or short-range. (5) *Repetitiveness*—single use or standing plan. The last chapter covered the first four dimensions. Next, you will cover the repetitiveness of plans. But, first see Figure 5–1 for an illustra-

Management Level	Type of Plan	Scope	Time	Repetitiveness
Upper and Middle	Strategic	Broad	Long-Range	Single-Use
Middle and Lower	Operational	Narrow	Short-Range	Standing Plan

Figure 5-1
Planning Dimensions

tion of the planning dimensions. Note that upper managers do more single-use planning and that lower levels deal more with standing plans. However, this does not mean that lower-level managers don't make single-use plans.

Standing versus Single-Use Plans

According to the repetitive dimension of plans, plans may be either *standing plans*, which are made to be used over and over again (repeated), or *single-use*, which are made to be used only once (nonrepetitive). Figure 5–2 illustrates the different types of standing and single-use plans.

Standing Plans. Operational strategies determine how objectives will be accomplished. This may be done by developing standing plans, which save future planning and decision-making time. **Standing plans** *include policies, procedures, and rules developed for handling repetitive situations.* Their purpose is to guide employees' actions in decision making. Union contract agreements become standing plans.

Policies *provide general guidelines to be followed when making decisions.* Policies exist at all levels within organizations. The board of directors develops policies, with the input of top management, for the entire organization. The manager implements these company policies.[6] In doing so, managers often establish policies for their own employees. External groups such as the government, labor unions, accrediting associations, and so forth dictate some policies. For example, the government requires organizations to offer equal opportunity to all, and labor unions require collective bargaining.

Examples of policy statements include: "The customer is always right." "We produce high-quality goods and services." "We promote qualified employees from within." "Employees will receive due process in grievances." Notice that policy statements are intentionally general guides that leave it to employees' discretion on how to implement them. As a manager, your daily decisions will be guided by policies. It will be your job to interpret, apply, and explain company policies to your employees. In situations where no policy exists, ask your boss to establish one or issue one yourself to be used when the situation recurs. Latoya's policy is: "To develop skills that will be used on the job to increase performance and productivity." How this policy is carried out varies from training program to training program. The policy helps Latoya to focus on this important issue.

1. State the difference between standing and single-use plans.

standing plans
Policies, procedures, and rules developed for handling repetitive situations.

policies
General guidelines to be followed when making decisions.

Figure 5-2
Standing versus Single-Use Plans

procedures
A sequence of actions to be followed in order to achieve an objective.

Procedures *are a sequence of actions to be followed in order to achieve an objective.* They are also called *standard operating procedures (SOPs)* and *methods.* Procedures are more specific than policies; they entail a series of decisions rather than a single decision and may involve more than one functional area. For example, sales, accounting, production, and shipping personnel may all have to follow a set procedure in order to meet a client's needs. Procedures ensure that all recurring, routine situations are handled in a consistent, predetermined manner.[7] Many organizations have procedures for purchasing, taking inventory, settling grievances, and so forth. Small firms often do not. Latoya teaches employees procedures, such as the steps in decision making (Chapter 3), as part of her training programs.

rules
State exactly what should or should not be done.

Rules *state exactly what should or should not be done.* Employees have no discretion on how to implement rules and regulations. Examples of rules include: "No smoking or eating in the work area." "Everyone must wear a hard hat on the construction site." "Stop at a red light." Violating rules usually involves penalties that vary in severity according to the seriousness of the violation and the number of offenses. As a manager, you will be responsible for establishing and enforcing rules in a uniform manner.[8] Latoya does have a no smoking rule during training.

Policies, procedures, and rules are all standing plans. However, they differ in terms of their definition and purpose. Policies provide general guides, procedures set a sequence of activities, and rules govern specific actions. The amount of detail varies for each type of standing plan, yet standing plans guide behavior in recurring situations. It is not always easy to distinguish between a policy, a procedure, and a rule. However, you should do so in order to know when you have the flexibility to do it your way and when you do not. The proper use of standing plans can help an organization meet objectives.[9]

Single-Use Plans. **Single-use plans** *include programs and budgets developed for handling nonrepetitive situations.* Single-use plans, unlike standing plans, are developed for a specific purpose and probably will not be used again in the same form. However, a single-use plan may be used as a model for future programs or budgets. A strategy is a single-use plan.

A *program* describes a set of activities and is designed to accomplish an objective over a specified time period. Programs are not meant to exist over the life of the organization. A program may have its own policies, procedures, budget, and so forth. It might take several years or less than a day to complete a given program. Examples include the development of a new product, expansion of facilities, or research and development to find a cure for a disease. Latoya develops programs for her clients.

When developing a program, you may find these procedure guidelines helpful: (1) Set project objectives. (2) Break the project down into a sequence of steps. (3) Assign responsibility for each step. (4) Establish starting and ending times for each step. (5) Determine the resources needed for each step. If you use the operational planning, shown later in Figure 5–4, page 162, you will be following these guidelines.

WORK APPLICATION

1. Give an example of a policy, a procedure, and a rule from an organization you work or have worked for.

single-use plans
Programs and budgets developed for handling nonrepetitive situations.

WORK APPLICATION

2. Give an example of a program you were involved in at work.

A *budget* is the funds allocated to operate a department for a fixed period of time. Many people fear budgets because they have low math or accounting skills. In reality, most budgets require planning skills rather than mathematical skills. When developed, a budget is a planning tool, and when implemented, it is a control tool. You will learn budgeting details in Chapter 14. Latoya uses a budget.

Contingency Plans

No matter how effectively you plan, there will be times when things go wrong that prevent you from achieving your objectives.[10] Things that go wrong are often beyond your control.[11] For example, a machine may break down or an employee may call in sick. When the uncontrollable occurs, you should be prepared with a backup, or contingency plan.[12] **Contingency plans** *are alternative plans to be implemented if uncontrollable events occur.* If a key employee calls in sick, another employee fills in to do the job. Construction work is usually contingent upon the weather. If it's nice, they work outside; if it is not, they work indoors. Shippers have contingency plans to use in case of a strike by the Teamsters truck driver union.

To develop a contingency plan for your department, you should answer three questions:

1. What might go wrong in my department?
2. How can I prevent it from happening?
3. If it does occur, what can I do to minimize its effect?

The answer to question 3 is your contingency plan. When developing single-use plans, ask everyone involved what can go wrong and what should be done if it does go wrong. Also ask others within and outside the organization who have implemented similar plans. They may have encountered problems you haven't thought of, and they may have good contingency plans to suggest.

Why Managers Don't Plan

In the course of conducting training programs for managers, Latoya has found that by far the most common reason for not planning is lack of time. "I'm too

---

APPLYING THE CONCEPT

AC 5–1 Identifying Plans

Identify each type of plan by categories:

Objective	*Standing Plan*	*Single-Use Plan*
a. objective	b. policy	e. program
	c. procedure	f. budget
	d. rule	

____ **1.** "Quality is job one." (Ford Motor Company)

____ **2.** President John F. Kennedy's plan to land someone on the moon.

____ **3.** To increase our market share by 10 percent next year.

____ **4.** Employees having babies will be given a two-month maternity leave.

____ **5.** How much will it cost to operate your department next month?

____ **6.** Wear safety glasses while touring the factory.

____ **7.** Forms for leaves of absence must be approved by the manager and submitted to the personnel office one month in advance of their effective dates.

____ **8.** Maintain the reject rate on staples under 5 percent.

____ **9.** "Never take unfair advantage of anyone the firm deals with." (J C Penney)

____ **10.** You may spend $1,000 to conduct that seminar.

---

2. Explain why contingency plans are often needed.

contingency plans
Alternative plans to be implemented if uncontrollable events occur.

WORK APPLICATION

3. Describe a situation in which a contingency plan is appropriate. Explain the plan.

busy putting out fires to plan" is a typical statement. This is one reason why you will learn about time management in this chapter. Latoya responds by asking the manager to think of the last few "fires," or crises, in the department. Were they caused by something the manager did or did not do? Many crises could have been avoided if the manager had planned.[13] Why can managers always find time to do a job over, but can't find the time to plan the job right the first time? Successful planners have fewer crises; they are in control of their departments. Nonplanners run out of control from one crisis to the next. Planning is a continuous activity. Plans do not have to be complicated or take a lot of time. Later in this chapter, you will learn about planning tools.

A second reason managers don't plan is their tendency toward action.[14] When a crisis occurs, many managers don't feel comfortable stopping to think and plan how to deal with it. They are more comfortable taking immediate action, but this often leads to further crises. There is an old saying, "When you fail to plan, you plan to fail."

Indicators of Poor Planning

Signs of poor planning include:

- *Objectives not met.* Missed deadlines, delivery dates, and schedules, or work not done on time.
- *Crises.* Pushing through rush jobs and using overtime to complete jobs.
- *Idle resources.* Physical, financial, or human resources kept waiting for the manager to assign tasks.
- *Lack of resources.* Necessary resources not available when needed.
- *Duplication.* The same task being done more than once.

3. Discuss the relationship between the strategic process and sales forecasting.

sales forecast
Predicts the units and/or dollar volume of products to be sold during a specified period of time.

SALES FORECASTING TOOLS

Forecasting is the process of predicting what will happen in the future. Organizations conduct a variety of forecasts during the environmental analysis, including economic forecasts, technological forecasts, and government regulation forecasts (Chapter 2).[15] However, the sales forecast is generally considered the most important organizational forecast.

A **sales forecast** *predicts the units and/or dollar volume of products to be sold during a specified period of time.* The sales forecast is important because of the systems effect. The short-term sales forecast is commonly conducted by the marketing department for one year and is set by the sales manager, with approval and possible adjustment by upper management.[16] However, the sales forecast affects the marketing department because it serves as the basis for the sales quotas for the sales representatives. The operations department uses the sales forecast to schedule how much of the product or service to produce. Marketing must monitor operations inventory levels and customer inventory levels to adjust sales forecasts as needed. The sales forecast affects the finance department because it has to determine how much money it will take in before it can determine how much money it can budget to spend; the sales forecast is the basis of the cash flow projection used to determine specific borrowing needs. The human resources department is affected by the need to increase or decrease the number of employees to meet the sales forecast. By improving its sales forcasting, Broadway Department Stores increased sales by 35 percent and turnover of merchandise by 18 percent in one year.

Company sales forecasts are commonly based on industry sales forecasts that consider the product life cycle.[17] For example, jet manufacturers U.S. Boeing and European Airbus conducted separate 20-year sales forecasts and predicted that total airplane sales will reach $1 trillion by 2014. Boeing puts global demand at about 15,400 airplanes and Airbus estimates about 15,000. In new industries it is more difficult to predict sales. For example, forecasted sales of volume for Web commerce range from a few billion dollars to as much as $100 billion.[18] Despite uncertainty, businesses have to be proactive so that they can build and retain customers.[19] Global sales of PCs priced at less than $1,000 were predicted to more than double by the year 2001.[20] Are sales increasing today? America Online (AOL) ran into operations problems when it dropped its rates and miscalculated the forecast for its online service and was accused of deceptive trade practices.[21] Was AOL's business practice an ethical error?

Based on the total number of products to be sold in an industry, many large companies predict what amount or percentage of industry sales they will make—their *market share*. A **market share** *is the percentage of industry sales made by one organization*. For example, Coca-Cola has 43 percent, Pepsi 31 percent, and all others a 26 percent market share of the U.S. carbonated soft drink industry. Coke's goal is to attain 50 percent of market share.[22]

Professional and trade publications are available that predict industry sales that you can use to help you when analyzing the environment and sales forecasting. You should take local conditions, especially competition, into account when predicting your company sales.

You should also realize that the sales forecast should be a part of the business-level strategy. When the prospector growth strategy is used, sales projections will go up at aggressive rates in future years. But with the analyzer, defender, or retrenchment strategies, sales will go up slightly, stay about the same, or go down, respectively.

Sales forecasting techniques can be classified as qualitative or quantitative. **Qualitative sales forecasting techniques** *use primarily subjective judgment, intuition, experience, and opinion to predict sales*. Some math may be used. **Quantitative sales forecasting techniques** *use objective, mathematical, past sales data to predict sales*. However, organizations commonly use a combination of quantitative and qualitative techniques to increase accuracy.[23] In this section you will learn about each sales forecasting technique, which Figure 5–3 illustrates.

market share
The percentage of industry sales made by one organization.

4. Describe the difference between qualitative and quantitative sales forecasting techniques.

qualitative sales forecasting techniques
Use primarily subjective judgment, intuition, experience, and opinion to predict sales.

quantitative sales forecasting techniques
Use objective, mathematical, past sales data to predict sales.

Qualitative (subjective)	Quantitative (objective)
Individual Opinion	Past Sales
Jury of Executive Opinion	Time Series
Sales Force Composite	Regression
Customer Composite	
Operating Unit Composite	
Survey	

Figure 5-3
Sales Forecasting Techniques

5. Discuss the difference between the jury of executive opinion and the three composite sales forecasting techniques.

Qualitative Sales Forecasting Techniques

Qualitative techniques include individual opinion, jury of executive opinion, sales force composite, customer composite, operating unit composite, and survey. You should realize that only qualitative techniques can be used with a new product or by a new company because they have no past sales on which to quantitatively base the forecast.

Individual Opinion. You probably predict what will happen in the future based on your personal experience and past events. People often use their intuition to make judgments about the future and to form an *individual opinion*. A person starting a new business all alone has no other option but to make an educated (based on industry analysis) individual opinion. Latoya used this sales forecasting technique when she started her business.

Jury of Executive Opinion. With the *jury of executive opinion*, a group of managers and/or experts use their pooled opinions to forecast sales. The common format is a group meeting to share ideas and to attempt to reach a consensus agreement of sales. However, the Delphi technique is also used. You have to decide if the group or individual decision-making style is appropriate (Chapter 3). Jury of executive opinion is commonly used with partners. Pete and Dave agree on the sales forecasts for their six Jiffy Lube service centers.

Sales Force Composite. The *sales force composite* combines the forecasts of each salesperson. Each salesperson predicts his or her sales for the future period; these are totaled to give a composite sales forecast for the company. Sales reps tend to know their customers and can be a good source. However, many company managers believe that their salespeople are too optimistic, and they balance the composite with other sales forecast techniques.[24] A sales force composite works well when professional sales reps sell relatively expensive products (or total orders) with a clear base of customers or territory, such as IBM mainframe computers.

Customer Composite. The *customer composite* is the total forecast of each major customer. You ask each major customer to predict how much they will buy during the future period. The total for each customer is added to give a composite sales forecast for the company. Customers tend to know their buying needs. Customer composite works well when an organization has relatively few customers with large volume sales, such as Mattel Toys with the large retailers Toys 'R' Us, Wal-Mart, Kmart, and Target.

Operating Unit Composite. An *operating unit composite* is the total sales forecast for multiple units. Businesses with multiple operating units, such as chain stores The Gap and Edwards Supermarkets, commonly predict the sales for each operating unit then add them together to get the total company sales forecast. Pete and Dave do this with their six Jiffy Lubes.

A variation of the operating unit composite is the *department composite*. A business with multiple revenue departments (such as a supermarket with meat, dairy, produce, etc.) can treat each department as an operating unit. Each department forecasts its sales and the composite is used to predict total sales for the operating unit. Edwards Supermarkets could use the department composite for each store and the operating unit composite for all stores.

An offshoot of the operating unit composite is the *product composite* in which a business with multiple products determines the sales for each product/service and combines them as a total operating unit sales forecast.

Survey. A *survey* utilizes mail questionnaires or telephone or personal interviews to predict future purchases. A sample of people is surveyed and a forecast for the entire population is made based on the responses. Businesses commonly use a survey to forecast the sales of a new product or service. For example, new Downy laundry softener samples were mass-mailed to all people in a given area. A week later, a sample of people were called to see if they used the product, if they liked the product, and if they would buy it the next time they need a softener. Surveys are also commonly used in the development of a new product to improve it before the final product is sold.

Quantitative Sales Forecasting Techniques

Quantitative techniques include past sales, time series, and regression. Any of the preceding qualitative techniques can be combined with quantitative techniques as long as the products and companies have existed long enough to have a history of sales. There is no definite time period for a history of sales. But time series and regression techniques need at least a year, and more years will give better results. Coca-Cola charts annual sales in each of the ten successive previous years.

Past Sales. The *past sales* technique assumes that past sales will be repeated, or may be subjectively adjusted for environmental factors. For example, a local pizza shop owner can say that on a typical Friday night it will sell 100 pizzas. Therefore, today it will prepare to sell 100 pizzas. However, if the weather was very poor, the forecast could increase to 125 pizzas. If it was a holiday when people tend to cook as a family, the sales forecast could be subjectively cut to 75.

Time Series. **Time series** *is used to predict future sales by extending the trend line of past sales volume over time.* With time series you plot the sales for a week, month, quarter, year, etc., to find a trend, which is then projected into the future to predict sales. The trend line can be extended by hand and the sales estimated (if the trend line is going up, you increase the sales forecast; if it is level, you keep it the same; and if it is going down, you decrease the sales forecast), but using a computer time series program is much more accurate. For example, the local pizza shop could plot sales by year to determine the trend and to predict sales by extending the trend line and possibly changing the 100-pizza standard.

Time series can also be used to plot days and months to determine day and month seasonal trends.[25] With time series, adjustments for environmental

5. Explain how any of the qualitative sales forecasting techniques can be, or preferably actually are, used by a company you work or have worked for.

6. Explain the difference between the past sales and time series sales forecasting techniques.

time series
Used to predict future sales by extending the trend line of past sales volume over time.

WORK APPLICATION

6. Explain how any of the quantitative sales forecasting techniques can be, or preferably actually are, used by a company you work or have worked for.

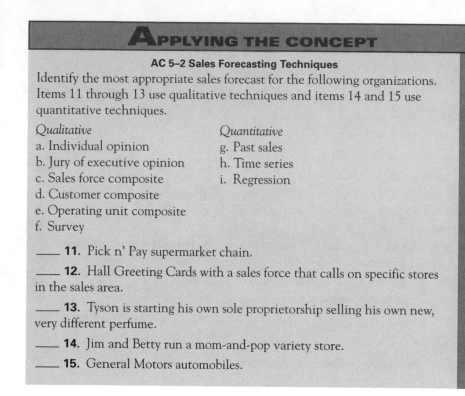

APPLYING THE CONCEPT

AC 5–2 Sales Forecasting Techniques

Identify the most appropriate sales forecast for the following organizations. Items 11 through 13 use qualitative techniques and items 14 and 15 use quantitative techniques.

Qualitative
a. Individual opinion
b. Jury of executive opinion
c. Sales force composite
d. Customer composite
e. Operating unit composite
f. Survey

Quantitative
g. Past sales
h. Time series
i. Regression

_____ **11.** Pick n' Pay supermarket chain.

_____ **12.** Hall Greeting Cards with a sales force that calls on specific stores in the sales area.

_____ **13.** Tyson is starting his own sole proprietorship selling his own new, very different perfume.

_____ **14.** Jim and Betty run a mom-and-pop variety store.

_____ **15.** General Motors automobiles.

factors are still used, but are more objective. Chatham Apothecary on Cape Cod used time series to predict monthly sales. Owners Bernie and Carolyn Young keep inventory levels that meet demand, but adjust them for environmental, seasonal, and weather factors to maximize sales. Latoya used time series to predict her second-year sales in business. She learned that July and August were slow months, but September and January were busy.

Regression. *Regression* is a mathematical modeling technique used to predict sales based on other variables.[26] Regression, beyond the scope of this book, is taught in statistics classes.

---

7. Describe the similarities and differences between the planning sheet, Gantt chart, and PERT network.

scheduling
The process of listing activities that must be performed to accomplish an objective; activities are listed in sequence with the time needed to complete each activity.

SCHEDULING TOOLS

After the marketing department has completed its sales forecast and received customer orders for the product, the operations department transforms inputs into outputs to create customer value. You will learn more about operations management in Chapter 15. To ensure customer value, many organizations include customer input in scheduling.[27] This is particularly important with just-in-time (JIT) operations. Schedules are the part of the operational plan that specify the details for transforming inputs into outputs. Recall that all employees are involved with transforming inputs into outputs, not just the operations department.

Scheduling *is the process of listing activities that must be performed to accomplish an objective; activities are listed in sequence with the time needed to complete each activity.* The details of the schedule answer the what, when, where, how, and who questions. When scheduling, you should define the job and ensure the availability of resources when needed.[28] All managers are involved in scheduling resources, including scheduling their time, which you will learn about in the next section on time management.

More organizations are using computers to schedule resources.[29] A variety of computer scheduling software programs are available. However, teaching you to schedule using a computer is beyond the scope of this course. You will, however, learn to use a simple planning sheet, a Gantt chart, and a PERT network by paper and pencil in this section. If you must do complex scheduling like that done at Westhoff Tool and Die, you will need to learn to use a computer. Westhoff uses a computer to track 80 projects. The computer schedules each machine in the plant on a chart, with copies given to six managers who supervise 60 operators.

Before learning about these three scheduling techniques, let's discuss two simple techniques you may have already used: the calendar and the to-do list. The *calendar* is used to write down important things that must be done on specific days, or times during the day. You can buy special planning calendars. The *to-do list* is commonly just a piece of paper (or you can buy special pads) used to write down the important things that must be done today, or soon. Scheduling calendars and to-do lists are also available in many inexpensive computer software packages. You will learn to use a more complex to-do list that includes setting priorities in the next chapter.

The Planning Sheet

Planning sheets *state an objective and list the sequence of activities, when each activity will begin and end, and who will complete each activity to meet the objective.* The planning sheet in Figure 5–4 shows a transformation process for a monthly marketing letter, developed by Latoya for WT&DS, which she mails to 300 potential customers. Stop reading to review Figure 5–4 and identify the plan used based on the five planning dimensions (Figure 5–1). The answer is at the bottom of the figure. The planning sheet works for plans with independent sequential steps of activities needed to accomplish the objective.

Set Objectives. Before you can determine how you will do something, you should decide what you want to accomplish.[30] So the first step in planning is to clearly state the end result you desire, using the writing objectives model in Chapter 4. After setting the objective, fill in who is responsible for achieving the objective, the starting and ending date, the priority (high, medium, low), and control checkpoints to monitor progress.

Plan and Schedule. List the sequence of steps stating what, where, how, resources needed, and so on in the first column. In the "when" column place the start and end time for each step. The third column contains the party responsible for each step.

Steps 2 through 4 and 7 could be eliminated if Latoya had all letters printed in their entirety on the word processor, rather than using a printer to duplicate them, and if she sent the letters first class instead of bulk rate. The reasons she included these steps were cost (first-class mail costs more than twice as much as bulk mail) and personalization.

You can easily make copies of the operational plan sheet for your own use by writing/typing in the bold information as a template.

Gantt Chart

Gantt charts *use bars to graphically illustrate a schedule and progress toward the objective over a period of time.* The different activities to be performed are

planning sheets
State an objective and list the sequence of activities, when each activity will begin and end, and who will complete each activity to meet the objective.

WORK APPLICATION

7. Give an example of a plan that would be appropriate to schedule using the planning sheet in an organization you work or have worked for.

Gantt charts
Use bars to graphically illustrate a schedule and progress toward the objective over a period of time.

Figure 5-4
WT&DS Operational Plan

OBJECTIVE: To mail a personalized form letter to all target clients by the 15th of each month.
Responsible: Joel   **Starting date:** 1st of each month
Due date: 15th of each month   **Priority:** High
Control checkpoints: 7th and 12th of each month

Activities (steps of what, where, how, resources needed, and so on)	When Start		End	Who
1. Type the letter on the word processor.	1st		2nd	Latoya
2. Deliver letter to printer.	3rd	or	4th	Joel
3. Letters are printed on WT&DS stationery.	5th		6th	printer
4. Pick up letters at printer.	6th	or	7th	Joel
5. Use mail merge to type names and addresses on letters and envelopes.	7th		9th	Joel
6. Each letter is signed by Latoya, folded, and put in an envelope.	10th		11th	Joel
7. Bundle to meet bulk mailing specifications.	12th		13th	Joel
8. Deliver to U.S. Postal Bulk Mail Center.	13th			Joel
9. Mail letters.	14th	or	15th	U.S. Mail

Based on the five planning dimensions: (1) This plan is developed by Latoya, who is the only manager; no real level. (2) The type of plan is operational. (3) The scope is narrow. (4) The time is short range. (5) Its repetitiveness is standing plan procedure.

usually shown vertically, with time shown horizontally. The resources to be allocated, such as people or machines, are commonly shown on the vertical axis. Or a variety of projects to be accomplished within a department can be shown on the same chart. Gantt charts, like the planning sheet, are appropriate for plans with independent sequential steps needed to accomplish the objective. The Gantt chart has the advantage over the planning sheet in that it places progress toward the objective on the chart as a control technique. In other words, a Gantt chart is both a planning and a control tool. Another important advantage of the Gantt chart over the planning sheet and PERT is that it can show multiple projects on one chart. This helps when prioritizing and scheduling project activities that use the same resources.[31]

Graphic illustrations of production were used when the Great Pyramids of Egypt were built. Henry Gantt popularized their use. Today, these bar diagrams are used extensively for allocating resources. WT&DS's planning sheet could be turned into a Gantt chart by changing the "when" column to show the days 1 through 15 instead of "start" and "end"; the rows would contain the bars to represent the number of days needed for each step. Though not shown in Figure 5–5, a Gantt chart can have a column for stat-

WORK APPLICATION

8. Give an example of a plan that would be appropriate to schedule using a Gantt chart in an organization you work or have worked for.

ing who, or what department or machine, and so on has responsibility for completing the activity or project, similar to the "who" column in the planning sheet. The "who" column especially helps when multiple people, departments, machines, and so on will be used to complete the project.

Figure 5–5 illustrates a Gantt chart for multiple orders in an operations department. Each order bar represents the starting to ending time, and the darker color part completion to date. Using the chart, you can see at a glance how orders are progressing. If you become aware that a project is behind schedule, you can take corrective action to get it back on schedule. Assume that today is day 1 of week 3 in May (end of dark color of bar should be directly under 3 to be on schedule). What is the status of each of the four projects on the chart in Figure 5–5? The answer is at the bottom of the figure.

Performance Evaluation and Review Technique (PERT)

Multiple activities are independent when they can be performed simultaneously; they are dependent when one activity must be completed before the next activity can begin. The planning sheet and Gantt chart are useful tools when the activities follow each other in a dependent series. However, when activities follow both dependent and independent series of each other, PERT (critical path) is more appropriate. PERT *is a network schedule that illustrates the dependence of activities.* Figure 5–6 shows a PERT network.

The key components to PERT are activities, events, times, the critical path, and possibly cost. With complex programs, it is common to have multiple activities represent one event. For example, in producing a car, building the engine would be an event because it requires multiple activities to complete. Time can be measured in a variety of ways (seconds, minutes, hours, days, weeks, months, years, etc.) to determine the critical path. The

PERT
A network schedule that illustrates the dependence of activities.

*Indicates today's date, the first day of the third week of May.

Bars indicate scheduled starting and ending of project.

▬ indicates part of project completed to date, while the blank space to the end of the bar indicates work still to be completed.

The GE project is done; IBM is right on schedule and should be completed this week; GM is behind schedule and should be complete during the fourth week in May; AT&T is ahead of schedule and should be completed during the first week of June.

Figure 5-5
Multiple-Project Gantt Chart (Order by Week)

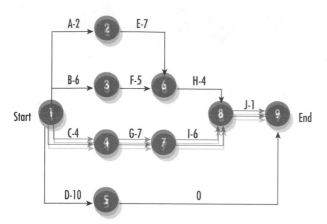

Circles = Events

Arrows and Letters = Activities

Numbers = Time in days

Double Arrows = The critical path, or how long it should take to complete the project

Figure 5-6
PERT Network

critical path
The most time-consuming series of activities in a PERT network.

WORK APPLICATION

9. Give an example of a plan that would be appropriate to schedule using a PERT network in an organization you work or have worked

skillbuilder

critical path is important to know because it determines the length of time it will take to complete a project by determining how long each activity will take. *The critical path is the most time-consuming series of activities in a PERT network.* It is shown by the double lines in Figure 5–6. Any delay of steps in the critical path will delay the entire project. Many organizations are focusing on shortening the time it takes to complete each activity to save time (time-based competition).[32] Cost for each activity can also be placed with the time.

Developing a PERT Network. The following steps explain how the PERT network in Figure 5–6 was completed:

  step 1. List all the activities/events that must be completed to reach the specific objective. Assign each a letter. In the example, we have ten activities labeled A through J.

step 2. Determine the time it will take to complete each activity/event. In Figure 5–6, time is measured in number of days as follows: A-2, B-6, C-4, D-10, E-7, F-5, G-7, H-4, I-6, and J-1.

step 3. Arrange the tasks on the diagram in the sequence in which they must be completed. In Figure 5–6, A must be completed before E can begin; E must be completed before H can begin; and H must be completed before J can begin. For example, before you can place a box of cereal on a shelf for sale (J), it must be ordered (A), received (E), and priced (H). Notice that activity D is independent. An arrow as well as a letter represents each activity. The numbered circles signify the completion of an event leading to the desired outcome. All activities originate and terminate at a circle. In Figure 5–6, 1 represents the start of the project and 9 its end or completion.

step 4. Determine the critical path. To do this, you must total the time it takes for each path from start (1) to end (9). Path 1–2–6–8–9 takes 2 + 7 + 4 + 1 days for a total of 14 days. Path 1–3–6–8–9 takes 6 + 5 + 4 + 1 days for a total of 16 days. Path 1–4–7–8–9 takes 4 + 7 + 6 + 1 days for a total of 18 days. Path 1–5–9 takes 10 + 0 days for a total of 10 days.

The critical path, indicated by the double arrow, is 1–4–7–8–9. The program or project should take 18 days to complete. If the job is supposed to be done in two weeks, you know before you even start that it cannot be done on time. You would have to change the completion date, or maybe even abandon the project.

To summarize this section, the operational planning sheet and Gantt chart are commonly used to develop procedures for routine standing plans, whereas PERT is commonly used for single-use program plans for a complex project with dependent activities. However, all three types of schedules can be used as either standing or single-use plans. There are computerized versions of Gantt charts and PERT networks. You will develop your scheduling skills through Skill-Building Exercise 5–1.

TIME MANAGEMENT TOOLS

Time has become an important aspect of a company's competitive advantage.[33] Fast delivery of products and services creates customer value. Companies such as Motorola, Cadillac, and Texas Instruments now focus on time, whereas Federal Express and Jiffy Lube based their business on time-based competition from the start. Motorola and other companies have discovered that poor productivity and inadequate customer service are related to poor time management.[34] Time management skills will have a direct effect on your productivity and career success.[35]

APPLYING THE CONCEPT

AC 5–3 Scheduling Tools

Select the most appropriate scheduling tool for each situation.

a. Planning Sheet   b. Gantt   c. PERT

____ **16.** A production department has six different types of machines and eight products.

____ **17.** Ted will develop a plan for building a new house.

____ **18.** Karen will develop procedures for a new method of providing a service.

____ **19.** A plan will be created for building a new submarine.

____ **20.** The training department wants to schedule the use of its rooms and courses.

Time management *refers to techniques that enable people to get more done in less time with better results.* Time is one of a manager's most valuable resources and time wasted can never be replaced. However, many managers do not use their time effectively, because they have never been taught the importance of prioritizing activities and using a time management system. Of the companies that do offer training, time management is a widely taught skill. Franklin Quest Company earns over $35 million a year from time management seminars and materials.[36] Latoya teaches time management skills to clients. Erskine Bowles, White House chief of staff, worked with President Clinton to develop his time management skills.[37] Unfortunately, many managers don't actually put the time management skills they learn into practice on the job on a regular basis.

In this section, you will learn ways to analyze your present use of time, how to use the time management system, and time management techniques. Developing time management skills is also an effective way to reduce stress (Chapter 9), increase personal productivity, and experience inner peace. You can possibly gain control of your life by controlling your time.

time management
Techniques that enable people to get more done in less time with better results.

Analyzing Time Use

The first step to successful time management requires determining how time is spent and wasted.[38] Working long hours is often a sign of poor time management; it's not how long or hard you work that counts—it's results that count. People often do not realize how they waste their time until they analyze time use. For example, managers waste an average of 15 minutes a day on hold on the telephone, which adds up to two weeks per year per person.[39] Managers who are aware of this time waster can plan to do something, such as read mail, while they wait, rather than do nothing. An analysis of how you use your time will indicate areas for improvement. You need to break habits that waste time.[40]

8. Explain the use of a time log.

The Time Log. The *time log* is a daily diary that tracks your activities and enables you to determine how you spend your time. You use one time log for each day. Figure 5–7 gives an example. You should keep track of your time every day over a period of one or two typical weeks. Try to keep the time log with you throughout the day. Fill in each 15-minute time slot, if possible, describing what you did. In Chapter 1, Figure 1–1, you saw the time log used by Bonnie, The Gap manager. Use Figure 5–7 as a template to develop your own time logs.

Analyzing Time Logs. After keeping time logs for five to ten working days, you can analyze the information recorded as follows. Write notes in the evaluation column, using the following abbreviations:

- Review the time logs to determine how much time you are spending on your primary responsibilities with high priorities (HP) and low priorities (LP). How do you spend most of your time?

- Identify areas where you spend too much time (TT).

- Identify areas where you do not spend enough time (NT).

- Identify major interruptions (I) that keep you from doing what you want to get done. How can you eliminate them?

- Identify tasks you are performing that you could delegate to someone else (D). Look for nonmanagement tasks. To whom can you delegate these tasks? (You will develop delegation skills in Chapter 6.)

Figure 5-7
Daily Time Log

Daily Time Log for: Day _____ Date _____	
Starting Time	Evaluation of Time Use
8:00	
8:15	
8:30	
8:45	
9:00	
9:15	
9:30	
9:45	
10:00	
etc., to Ending Time	

- How much time does your boss control (B)? How much time do your employees control (E)? How much time do others outside your department control (O)? How much time do you actually control (M)? How can you gain more control of your own time?

- Look for crisis situations (C). Were they caused by something you did or did not do? Do you have recurring crises? How can you plan to help eliminate recurring crises? Do you have effective contingency plans?

- Look for habits, patterns, and tendencies. Do they help or prevent you from getting the job done? How can you change them to your advantage?

- List three to five of your biggest time wasters (W). What can you do to help eliminate them?

- Ask yourself, "How can I manage my time more efficiently?"

After analyzing how President Clinton used his time, Bowles eliminated extraneous activities from his calendar.[41] Throughout the remainder of this section, you will learn ideas to help you answer these ten questions.

A Time Management System

Time management remains one of the most daunting challenges confronting people in unconventional work contexts.[42] The time management system you will learn has a proven record of success with thousands of managers. Managers should try it for three weeks. After that time, they can adjust it to meet their own needs.

The problem managers face is not a shortage of time, but effective use of their time. Could you use an extra two hours every day? Experts say that people waste at least this much time every day. The average manager could improve time use by 20 percent.

The four key components of the time management system are:

- *Priorities.* Seldom, if ever, do we have enough time to do everything we want to do. However, there is always time to do what is really important. Priorities determine what is more important and should be determined in terms of your major responsibilities. Spending time on high-priority tasks saves time on trivial concerns.[43]

- *Objectives.* Managers should develop goals. You should set weekly objectives following the guidelines stated in Chapter 4.

- *Plans.* You should develop operational plans to meet your objectives.

- *Schedules.* You can use the planning sheet, Gantt chart, and PERT for scheduling. You should schedule each week and work day.[44]

Time management systems all boil down to developing a plan and sticking to it as much as possible. *The **time management system** involves planning each week, scheduling each week, and scheduling each day.*

WORK APPLICATION

10. Identify your three biggest time wasters, preferably with the use of the time log. How can you cut down or eliminate these time wasters?

9. List and briefly describe the three steps in the time management system.

time management system
Planning each week, scheduling each week, and scheduling each day.

step 1. **Plan each week.** On the last day of each week, plan the coming week. You can also begin the week with planning it. Do this each and every week. Using your previous week's plan and departmental objectives, fill in a plan for the week on the weekly planner sheet, using Figure 5–8 as a template. Start by listing the objectives you want to accomplish during the week. These should be nonroutine things, not routine tasks you perform weekly or daily. For example, if an employee's annual review is coming up, set an objective to do it.

After setting a few major objectives, list major activities necessary to accomplish each objective[45] in column 1. If the objective calls for multiple activities, use one of the three scheduling tools. Priorities should be high, medium, or low. All high priorities must be done that week; others can be pushed into the next week if necessary. To continue our example, you will need to plan for completing the appraisal form, making an appointment with the employee, and planning for completing the performance review. The performance appraisal is a high (H) priority. You will develop performance appraisal skills in Chapter 8.

The last two columns to fill in are the "Time Needed" and "Day to Schedule." To continue our example, assume it will take you 20 minutes to prepare for the performance appraisal and about 30 minutes to complete it. The day to schedule could be your relatively quiet day. Total the time it will take to achieve your objectives for the week. Is the total time realistic considering you still need time for routine tasks and unexpected events? With experience, you will learn if you are too optimistic about how much you can plan for and accomplish in one week. Planning too much is frustrating and causes stress when you cannot get everything done. On the other hand, if you do not plan enough activities, you will end up wasting time.

step 2. **Schedule each week.** Scheduling your work gets you organized[46] to achieve your objectives for the week. You may make a schedule for the week while you plan it or afterwards, whichever you prefer. Planning and sched-

Figure 5-8
Weekly Planner

Plan for the week of: _____

Objectives:

Activities	Priority	Time Needed	Day to Schedule
Total time for the week			

Schedule for week of: _____					
	Mon.	Tues.	Wed.	Th.	Fri.
Starting Time					
8:00					
8:15					
8:30					
8:45					
9:00					
etc., to Ending Time					

Figure 5-9
Weekly Schedule

uling the week should take about 30 minutes. Figure 5–9 gives you a template for a weekly schedule. Start scheduling by filling in uncontrollable time slots, such as standing weekly meetings, for example. Then, schedule controllable events like performance appraisals. Most managers should leave about 50 percent of the week unscheduled to accommodate unexpected events. Your job may require more or less unscheduled time. With practice, you will perfect weekly planning and scheduling.

The key to time management is not to prioritize your schedule, but to schedule your priorities weekly and daily.[47]

| step 3. | **Schedule each day.** At the end of each day you should schedule the following day. Or you can schedule your day first thing in the morning. |

This should take 15 minutes or less. Base the day's schedule on your plan and schedule for the week, using the template in Figure 5–10. Going from the weekly to a daily schedule allows time to adjust for unplanned events. Begin by scheduling the activities over which you have no control, such as meetings you must attend. Leave your daily schedule flexible. As previously stated, most managers need about 50 percent of their time unscheduled to handle unexpected events. Some scheduling tips to follow include:

- Don't be too optimistic; schedule enough time to do each task. Many managers find that estimating the time something will take, and then doubling it, works well. With practice, you should improve.

- Once you have prioritized and scheduled tasks, focus on only one at a time.[48] A few people seem to do an incredible number of things. However, their impressive versatility is based mainly on doing one thing at a time.

- Schedule high-priority items during your "prime time," when you perform at your best. For most people it is early in the morning. However, some people are slow starters and perform better later in the day. Determine your

Figure 5-10
Daily Schedule

Schedule for day of: _____

Starting Time

8:00

8:15

8:30

8:45

9:00

etc., to Ending Time

prime time and schedule the tasks that need your full attention. Do routine things, such as checking your mail, at other times.[49]

- Try to schedule a time for unexpected events. Tell employees to see you with routine matters during a set time, such as 3 P.M. Have people call you, and call them, during this set time.

- Do not perform an unscheduled task before determining its priority. If you are working on a high-priority item and you receive a medium-priority matter, let it wait. Even the so-called urgent matters can often wait.

The time management system works well for managers who have to plan for a variety of nonrecurring tasks. For managers and employees who deal primarily with routine tasks, the time management system may not be necessary. For people in routine situations, the use of a good to-do list that prioritizes items may be all they need. In the next chapter you will learn about the to-do list. Skill-Building Exercise 5–2 gives you the opportunity to develop your time management skills by using the time management system. Forms similar to Figures 5–8 through 5–10 can be purchased in pad, book, and even computer versions. However, you can make your own full-page copies using the templates from the figures.

*skillbuilder

Time Management Techniques

Self-Assessment Exercise 5–1 contains 50 time management techniques arranged by management function. Planning and controlling are placed together because they are so closely related. Organizing and leading are separated.

After you have completed the Self-Assessment Exercise, implement the items you check as "should do." Once you are using all the "should do" items, work on your "could do" items to continually improve your time management skills. After implementing all the "should do" and "could do" items, reread the "does not apply" column to see if any of the items apply at that time.

WORK APPLICATION

11. From the 50 time management techniques listed in Self-Assessment Exercise 5–1, choose the three most important techniques you "should" be using. Explain how you will implement each technique.

Self-Assessment Exercise 5–1

Time Management Techniques

A list of 50 ideas that can be used to improve your time management skills follows. Place a checkmark in the appropriate box for each item.

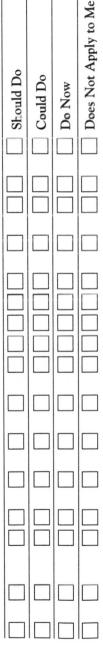

Planning and Controlling Management Functions

1. Use the time management system.

2. Use a to-do list and prioritize the items on it. Do the important things rather than the urgent things.

3. Get an early productive start on your top-priority items.

4. During your best working hours (prime time) do only high-priority items; schedule unpleasant or difficult tasks during prime time.

5. Don't spend time performing unproductive activities to avoid or escape job-related anxiety. It doesn't really work. Get the job done.

6. Throughout the day ask yourself, "Should I be doing this—now?"

7. Plan before you act.

8. Plan for recurring crises to eliminate crises (contingency planning).

9. Make decisions. It is better to make a wrong decision than none at all.

10. Schedule enough time to do the job right the first time. Don't be too optimistic about the amount of time it takes to do a job.

11. Schedule a quiet hour to be interrupted only by true emergencies. Have someone take messages or ask people to call you back.

12. Establish a quiet time for the entire organization or department. The first hour of the day is usually the best time.

13. Schedule large blocks of uninterrupted (emergencies-only) time for projects and so forth. If this doesn't work, hide somewhere.

14. Break large (long) projects into parts (time periods).

15. Before abandoning a scheduled item to do something unscheduled, ask the priority question: "Is the unscheduled event more important than the scheduled event?" If not, stay on schedule.

16. Schedule a time for doing similar activities (for example, make and return calls, write letters and memos).

	Should Do	Could Do	Do Now	Does Not Apply to Me

Organizing Management Function

17. Schedule unexpected event time and let people know the time. Ask people to see or call you during your scheduled unexpected time (professors have office hours), unless it's an emergency. Answer mail and do routine things while waiting for people to contact you. If people ask to see you—"Got a minute?"—ask whether it can wait until your scheduled unexpected event time.   ☐ ☐ ☐ ☐

18. Set a scheduled time, agenda, and time limit for all visitors, and keep on topic.   ☐ ☐ ☐ ☐

19. Keep a clean, well-organized work area/desk.   ☐ ☐ ☐ ☐

20. Remove all non-work-related or distracting objects from your work area/desk.   ☐ ☐ ☐ ☐

21. Do one task at a time.   ☐ ☐ ☐ ☐

22. With paperwork, make a decision at once. Don't read it again later and decide.   ☐ ☐ ☐ ☐

23. Keep files well arranged and labeled with an active and inactive file section. When you file an item, put a throwaway date on it.   ☐ ☐ ☐ ☐

24. Call rather than write and visit, when appropriate.   ☐ ☐ ☐ ☐

25. Delegate someone else to write letters, memos, and so forth.   ☐ ☐ ☐ ☐

26. Use form letters and form paragraphs in a word processor.   ☐ ☐ ☐ ☐

27. Answer letters (memos) on the letter itself.   ☐ ☐ ☐ ☐

28. Have someone read and summarize things for you.   ☐ ☐ ☐ ☐

29. Divide reading requirements with others and share summaries.   ☐ ☐ ☐ ☐

30. Have calls screened to be sure the right person handles it.   ☐ ☐ ☐ ☐

31. Plan before calling. Have an agenda and all necessary information ready; take notes on the agenda.   ☐ ☐ ☐ ☐

32. Ask people to call you back during your scheduled unexpected time. Ask about the best time to call them.   ☐ ☐ ☐ ☐

33. Have a specific objective or purpose for every meeting you conduct. If you cannot think of an objective, don't have the meeting.   ☐ ☐ ☐ ☐

34. For meetings, invite only the necessary participants and keep them only as long as needed.   ☐ ☐ ☐ ☐

35. Always have an agenda for a meeting and stick to it. Start and end as scheduled.   ☐ ☐ ☐ ☐

36. Set objectives for travel. List everyone you will meet with. Send (call) them agendas and have a file folder for each with all necessary data for your meeting.   ☐ ☐ ☐ ☐

37. Combine and modify activities to save time.   ☐ ☐ ☐ ☐

	Should Do	Could Do	Do Now	Does Not Apply to Me

Leading Management Function

38. Set clear objectives for subordinates with accountability; give them feedback and evaluate results often. ☐ ☐ ☐ ☐

39. Don't waste others' time. Don't make subordinates wait idly for decisions, instructions, or materials, in meetings, and so on. Wait for a convenient time, rather than interrupting your subordinates/others and wasting their time. ☐ ☐ ☐ ☐

40. Train your subordinates. Don't do their work for them. ☐ ☐ ☐ ☐

41. Delegate activities in which you do not need to be personally involved, especially non-management functions. ☐ ☐ ☐ ☐

42. Set deadlines earlier than the actual deadline. ☐ ☐ ☐ ☐

43. Use the input of your staff. Don't reinvent the wheel. ☐ ☐ ☐ ☐

44. Teach time management skills to your subordinates. ☐ ☐ ☐ ☐

45. Don't procrastinate; do it. ☐ ☐ ☐ ☐

46. Don't be a perfectionist—define "acceptable" and stop there. ☐ ☐ ☐ ☐

47. Learn to stay calm. Getting emotional only causes more problems. ☐ ☐ ☐ ☐

48. Reduce socializing without causing antisocialism. ☐ ☐ ☐ ☐

49. Communicate well. Don't confuse employees. ☐ ☐ ☐ ☐

50. If you have other ideas not listed above, add them here. ☐ ☐ ☐ ☐

CHAPTER SUMMARY AND GLOSSARY

This chapter summary is organized to answer the ten learning objectives for Chapter 5.

1. State the difference between standing and single-use plans.

The major difference is repetitiveness. Standing plans include policies, procedures, and rules developed for handling repetitive situations. Single-use plans include programs and budgets developed for handling nonrepetitive situations.

2. Explain why contingency plans are often needed.

Contingency plans are alternative plans to be implemented if uncontrollable events occur. There are many events that the manager cannot control, which could prevent objectives from being achieved. By predicting what could go wrong and planning how to handle it if it does, managers increase the chances of successfully achieving objectives.

3. Discuss the relationship between the strategic process and sales forecasting.

Sales forecasting is a part of the strategic process. A short-term (one-year) sales forecast is prepared at the functional operational level, usually by the marketing department. It is based on the environmental analysis and the business-level strategy.

4. Describe the difference between qualitative and quantitative sales forecasting techniques.

The difference between qualitative and quantitative sales forecasting is based on the objective use of math. Qualitative sales forecast techniques are based on subjective judgment, intuition, experience, and opinion, with some math. Quantitative techniques are based on objective mathematical past sales data to predict sales. However, a combination of the two methods can be used with existing products and organizations to improve forecasting.

5. Discuss the difference between the jury of executive opinion and the three composite sales forecasting techniques.

The jury of executive opinion seeks a consensus of agreement from managers and/or experts. The composite methods combine the forecasts of salespeople, customers, or operating units to get a total company sales forecast without an agreed-upon consensus. The composite techniques are more objective, based more on math, than the jury of executive opinion.

6. Explain the difference between the past sales and time series sales forecasting techniques.

With past sales, future sales are predicted to be the same or are subjectively adjusted for environmental factors. With time series, future sales are predicted based on extending the trend line according to sales volume over time. Adjustments for environmental factors are more objective.

7. Describe the similarities and differences between the planning sheet, Gantt chart, and PERT network.

Similarities include the fact that all three are scheduling techniques and list activities that must be performed to accomplish an objective. Activities are listed in sequence with the time needed to complete each. The primary difference concerns their format and use.

Planning sheets state an objective and list the sequence of activities, when each activity will begin and end, and who will complete each activity to meet the objective. *Gantt charts* use bars to graphically illustrate a schedule and progress toward the objective over a period of time. Gantt charts, like planning sheets, are appropriate for plans with independent sequential steps of activities needed to accomplish the objective. The Gantt chart has the advantage over the planning sheet in that it places progress toward the objective on the chart as a control technique. *PERT* is a network schedule that illustrates the dependence of activities. When activities are both dependent and independent of each other, PERT is more appropriate.

8. Explain the use of a time log.

A time log is a daily diary used to analyze how time is spent and wasted. Through a time log analysis, one knows areas to work on to improve time use.

9. List and briefly describe the three steps in the time management system.

The steps in the time management system are (1) Plan each week. The week is planned by determining the objectives and activities necessary to achieve the objective. (2) Schedule each week. The week is scheduled by selecting days and times to perform the activities necessary to achieve the week's objectives. (3) Schedule each day. The day is scheduled by selecting the times to perform the activities necessary to achieve the week's objectives. Going from a weekly to a daily schedule allows time to adjust for unplanned events.

10. Define the following key terms (in order of appearance in the chapter):

Select one or more methods: (1) fill in the missing key terms from memory, (2) match the key terms from the end of the summary with their definitions below, or (3) copy the key terms in order from the list at the beginning of the chapter.

_____ include policies, procedures, and rules developed for handling repetitive situations.

_____ provide general guidelines to be followed when making decisions.

_____ are a sequence of actions to be followed in order to achieve an objective.

_____ state exactly what should or should not be done.

_____ include programs and budgets developed for handling non-repetitive situations.

_____ are alternative plans to be implemented if uncontrollable events occur.

_____ is the prediction of the units and/or dollar volume of products to be sold during a specified period of time.

_____ is the percentage of industry sales made by one organization.

_____ use primarily subjective judgment, intuition, experience, and opinion to predict sales. Some math may be used.

_____ use objective, mathematical, past sales data to predict sales.

_____ is used to predict future sales by extending the trend line of past sales volume over time.

_____ is the process of listing activities that must be performed to accomplish an objective; activities are listed in sequence with the time needed to complete each.

_____ state an objective and list the sequence of activities, when each activity will begin and end, and who will complete each activity to meet the objective.

_____ use bars to graphically illustrate a schedule and progress toward the objective over a period of time.

_____ is a network schedule that illustrates the dependence of activities.

_____ is the most time-consuming series of activities in a PERT network.

_____ refers to techniques that enable people to get more done in less time with better results.

The _____ involves planning each week, scheduling each week, and scheduling each day.

KEY TERMS

contingency plans   155

critical path   164

Gantt charts   161

market share   157

PERT   163

planning sheets   161

policies   153

procedures   154

qualitative sales forecasting techniques   157

quantitative sales forecasting techniques   157

rules   154

sales forecast   156

scheduling   160

single-use plans   154

standing plans   153

time management   165

time management system   167

time series   159

REVIEW AND DISCUSSION QUESTIONS

1. What are the five planning dimensions?
2. What is the difference between a policy, a procedure, and a rule?
3. Why do some managers fail to plan?
4. Why is sales forecasting important?
5. When can't you use quantitative sales forecasting techniques?
6. Why is scheduling important?
7. What does a Gantt chart show that the planning sheet and PERT don't show?
8. When would you use a PERT network rather than a Gantt chart?
9. Why are time management skills important?
10. What does a time log show?
11. What are the four key components of the time management system?
12. If you schedule each week, why do you have to schedule each day too?
13. Can you think of any other important current management issues not listed?

OBJECTIVE CASE

Southwest Airlines

Southwest Airlines started as a small business with four planes in 1971. But its chairman, president, and CEO, Herb Kelleher, has turned Southwest into the fifth largest U.S. carrier. It has been profitable in all but its first two years. What makes this success story even more remarkable is the fact that other airlines, including TWA, Delta, American, and United, were reporting huge losses and retrenching while Southwest had a growth prospector strategy.

Southwest used a focus and low cost strategy to get where it is today. Rather than compete head-on with major airlines, Southwest selected a niche focus in short-haul, point-to-point flights. Its average flight is only 55 minutes. Therefore, it essentially has no hubs, and does not make connections with, or transfer baggage to, other carriers. Southwest flies to fewer cities, but it offers more frequent flights to those cities than its competitors.

In 1996, Southwest's cost per available seat mile was 6.5 cents versus 9 cents at American and 15 cents at USAir. Southwest's average yearly salary and benefits for each unionized worker was $43,707 versus $58,816 at Delta; the industry average is $45,692. Southwest has one of the lowest debt-to-equity ratios and the highest Standard & Poor's credit rating among U.S. airlines. Southwest planes spend an average of 20 minutes at the gate between flights, whereas the industry average is around 60 minutes. Therefore, Southwest planes spend about 11 hours per day in the air compared to the industry average of 8 hours, despite the fact that it has more frequent, shorter flights than the competition.

The mission at Southwest concerns inexpensive, simple, and focused airline service. Based on its low cost, it offers low fares. Needless to say, competitors had to drop their prices to compete with Southwest, and some decided to get out of Southwest's markets because they cannot compete. Southwest costs less than comparable intercity bus prices in most of its markets. CEO Kelleher has said, "Southwest has created a solid niche making the automobile our main competition."

To achieve its mission of inexpensive, simple service, Southwest has one type of plane: the fuel-efficient Boeing 737. This standardization allows lower inventory cost for spare parts, and allows specialization and minimizes training of flight and maintenance crews. Southwest has the lowest employee turnover in the industry.

To keep cost and fares down, Southwest uses a "no frills" approach to operations. It has no first-class or business section. It has no computerized reservation system because it does not offer reserved seats. Agents issue reusable numbered plastic cards on a first-come first-aboard to pick seats basis. Southwest does not offer meals or movies. However, low-cost and no frills do not mean low quality. In fact, Southwest is the only airline to win the U.S. Department of Transportation's "triple crown" monthly citation for the best on-time performance, fewest lost bags, and fewest overall complaints—not once, but four years in a row.

Select the best alternative for the following questions. Be sure you are able to explain your answers.

_____ 1. Southwest gains efficiency primarily from its

    a. standing plans   b. single-use plans

_____ 2. To be the low-cost operator in the airline business is a(n)

    a. objective c. procedure e. program
    b. policy   d. rule   f. budget

_____ 3. Being a "no-frills" airline is a company

    a. objective c. procedure e. program
    b. policy   d. rule   f. budget

_____ 4. To get its planes back in the air in about 15 minutes for an average of 11 trips a day, Southwest relies heavily on

    a. objective   d. rule
    b. policy   e. program
    c. procedure   f. budget

OBJECTIVE CASE

(continued)

___ **5.** Southwest most likely uses the ___ qualitative sales forecasting technique.

    a. sales force composite

    b. customer composite

    c. operating unit composite

    d. survey

___ **6.** Southwest most likely uses the ___ quantitative sales forecasting technique.

    a. past sales   b. time series

___ **7.** For scheduling flights, the ___ scheduling tool would be most appropriate for use at Southwest.

    a. planning sheet

    b. Gantt chart

    c. PERT

___ **8.** Following Southwest's growth strategy, the ___ scheduling tool would be most appropriate for entering new markets.

    a. planning sheet

    b. Gantt chart

    c. PERT

___ **9.** Time is a competitive advantage at Southwest.

    a. true   b. false

___ **10.** Time management skills are an important part of Southwest's success.

    a. true   b. false

11. Is Southwest customer-focused?

12. Could Southwest be as fast at getting its planes back into the air (15 minutes) if it offered long-distance flights?

13. Should Southwest grow by offering long-distance flights?

For current information on Southwest Airlines, use Internet address http://www.iflyswa.com. For ideas on using the Internet, see Appendix B.

VIDEO CASE

Next Door Food Stores I
(5–1 11½ Minutes)

Case Summary

Next Door Food Stores is a retail chain with unique opportunities to create a competitive advantage in the convenience store industry. This case illustrates how quality management decision making with single-use planning created a competitive edge. Day-to-day operational planning and implementation, such as just-in-time (JIT), are reillustrated.

Students' Learning Objective

To better understand decision making and operational planning.

Critical Thinking Questions

1. Should Next Door build and operate a warehouse or should it use wholesale distributors and vendors?

2. What are the risks and rewards for Next Door in accepting Coca-Cola's offer? Should it take the offer?

3. How does Next Door identify and respond to a merchandising trend?

Skill-Building Exercise 5–1

*skillbuilder

I G

Developing a Plan to Open a Record Shop

Preparing for Skill-Building Exercise 5–1

You have decided to open and manage (your name) Music Shop on April 1. It is now late December. You plan to move in one month before the store is scheduled to open in order to set up. During March, your assistant will help you set up and you will train him or her. You will start to implement the plan on January 2.

Assume that you have decided to use a (1) Gantt chart and (2) PERT network. Develop both, in order of your preference, following the text guides for their development, assuming that you have identified the activities and completion times listed below. (The activities may not be given in sequence.)

a. Lease the store fixtures to display your records/tapes/CDs; it will take two weeks to receive and arrange them.

b. Order and receive records/tapes/CDs. This takes one week.

c. Recruit and select an assistant (three weeks or less).

d. Install the fixtures, paint, decorate, and so on (two weeks).

e. Form a corporation (four weeks).

f. Make arrangements to buy records/tapes/CDs on credit (two weeks).

g. Find a store location (six weeks or less).

h. Unpack and display records/tapes/CDs (one week).

i. Train the assistant (one week).

j. Select the records/tapes/CDs you plan to stock (one week).

k. Determine start-up cost and cash outflow per month through April 30. Your rich uncle will lend you this amount (one week).

1. Gantt Chart. When developing the Gantt chart, use the following format, based on weeks. You may want to change the letter sequence to match starting dates.

Gantt Chart

Activity (letter)	January 1	2	3	4	February 1	2	3	4	March 1	2	3	4	April 1
___													
___													
___													
___													
___													
___													
___													
___													
___													
___													

2. PERT. When developing the PERT chart, from start draw arrows to your circle for the independent activities. Inside the circle place the letter of the activity. On the arrow to the activity, place the number of weeks it will take to complete it. Then draw an arrow to the end. Also from start, draw the first dependent activity followed by the next dependent activity and so on until the last one; then draw an arrow to end. Be sure to put the number of weeks and activity/event letters on your network. After all activities are listed, determine the critical path and draw the second arrow to indicate it. *Hint:* You should have five arrows to activities coming from start; you can start the process with selecting music independently or finding a store location.

PERT
(with critical path)

Start

End

Doing Skill-Building Exercise 5–1 in Class

Objective
To develop your planning skills using a Gantt chart and PERT network.

Preparation
You should have completed the Gantt and PERT to open your record shop.

Experience
You will be given feedback on your plans.

Procedure (10–20 minutes)
The instructor goes over the recommended Gantt and PERT.

Discussion and Conclusion
Is Gantt or PERT more appropriate for this type of plan?

Application (2–4 minutes)
What did I learn from this experience? How can I use this knowledge in the future?

_____

_____

Sharing
Volunteers give their answers to the application section.

Skill-Building Exercise 5–2

Time Management System

Preparing for Skill-Building Exercise 5–2

For this exercise you will need to make full-page copies of Figures 5–8 through 5–10 to serve as templates. Before using the time management system, it is helpful, but not necessary, to keep a time log (Figure 5–7) for one or two typical weeks to determine areas for improvement of time management.

Step 1. Plan Your Week. Using Figure 5–8, develop a plan for the rest of this week. Begin with today.

Step 2. Schedule Your Week. Using Figure 5–9, schedule the rest of this week. Be sure to schedule a 30-minute period to plan and schedule next week, preferably on the last day of this week.

Step 3. Schedule Your Day. Using Figure 5–10, schedule each day. Do this for every day at least until the class period for which this exercise is assigned.

Be sure to bring your plans and schedules to class.

Doing Skill-Building Exercise 5–2 in Class

Objective

To develop your time management skills to enable you to get more done in less time with better results.

Preparation

You need your completed time management plans and schedules.

Experience

You will share and discuss your plans and schedules for the week and your daily schedules.

Procedure 1 (5–10 minutes)

Break into groups of four to six and share and discuss your plans and schedules. Pass them around so that you can make comparisons. The comparisons serve as a guide to improving future plans and schedules.

Conclusion

The instructor leads a class discussion and makes concluding remarks.

Application (2–4 minutes)

What did I learn from this experience? How will I use this knowledge in the future?

_____

_____

Sharing

Volunteers give their answers to the application section.

6 Organizing and Delegating Work

Learning Objectives

After studying this chapter, you should be able to:

1. Explain the difference between a flat and a tall organization.
2. Describe the similarity and difference among liaisons, integrators, and boundary roles.
3. Discuss the difference between formal and informal and centralized and decentralized authority.
4. List and briefly explain the four levels of authority.
5. Describe the relationship between line and staff authority.
6. Explain what an organization chart is and list the four things it shows.
7. Discuss the difference between internal and external departmentalization.
8. State the similarities and differences between matrix and divisional departmentalization.
9. Explain the difference between job simplification and job expansion.
10. Describe the job characteristics model and what it is used for.
11. Explain how to set priorities by listing the three priority questions and how you assign and delegate high, medium, and low priority.
12. List the four steps in the delegation model.
13. Define the following **key terms** (in order of appearance in the chapter):

span of management	organization chart
responsibility	departmentalization
authority	divisional structure
delegation	job design
levels of authority	job enrichment
line authority	job characteristics model
staff authority	priority determination
centralized authority	questions
decentralized authority	delegation model

Skill Development

skillbuilder

1. You should develop your skill at setting priorities (Skill-Building Exercise 6–1).

   Setting priorities is an organizing skill that utilizes conceptual and decision-making skills. The exercise develops your decisional role skill of resource allocator. The SCANS skill competencies of using resources, information, and systems, as well as basic, thinking, and personal qualities foundation skills are also developed.

skillbuilder

2. You should develop your delegating skills (Skill-Building Exercise 6–2).

   Delegating is an organizing skill that utilizes human and communication skills. This exercise develops your interpersonal leader skills, informational skill of monitor, and decisional skill of resource allocator. The SCANS skills competencies of using resources, information, and systems, as well as basic, thinking, and personal qualities foundation skills are developed.

For a strategy to be implemented successfully, the organization must have a compatible structure. When the strategy changes, the structure follows (form follows function). As firms change, the organization structure must also change. The need for change will be illustrated throughout the chapter with the CMP Publications integrated case.

The husband and wife team of Gerry and Lilo Leeds founded CMP Publications in 1971. They have grown, at their goal of 20 percent a year, from 1 to 14 business newspapers and magazines. They compete in the high growth high-tech markets.

The Leeds's original structure called for centralized authority with Gerry and Lilo making all important decisions. As CMP grew, it became increasingly difficult for employees to personally meet with the Leeds. Employees began to line up outside the office at 8:00 in the morning and there was a constant waiting line. Important decisions that required a quick response, due to rapidly changing environments, were often delayed. The Leeds decided to reorganize CMP.

The Leeds broke the company into divisions, which essentially created semiautonomous companies within CMP. Each division had a manager who was given the authority to run the division and to make it grow. Division managers report to the publications committee, which oversees the divisions to ensure that they operate within CMP's mission and growth strategy. The publications committee consists of the Leeds and the division managers who meet regularly to discuss current business issues.

For current information on CMP Publications, use Internet address **http://www.techweb.com**. For ideas on using the Internet, see Appendix B.

PRINCIPLES OF ORGANIZATION

Organizing is the second function of management and was defined as the process of delegating and coordinating tasks and resources to achieve objectives. The four resources you organize are human, physical, financial, and information (Chapter 1). On an organizationwide basis, organizing refers to grouping activities and resources. As a manager, you must organize your departmental resources to achieve the functional operating objectives. Figure 6–1 lists the organization principles.

Unity of Command and Direction

Unity of command means that each employee should report to only one boss.[1] *Unity of direction* means that all activities should be directed toward the same objectives. Gerry and Lilo Leeds reorganized CMP into divisions with managers to provide unity of command. However, the divisions report to the publications committee, which provides unity of direction for the divisions.

Chain of Command

Chain of command, also known as the Scalar Principle, is the clear line of authority from the top to the bottom of the organization.[2] All members of the firm should know to whom they report and who, if anyone, reports to

WORK APPLICATION

1. Follow the chain of command from your present/ past position to the top of the organization. Start by identifying anyone who reported to you, then list your boss's title, your boss's boss's title, to the top manager's title.

Figure 6-1
Principles of Organization

- Unity of command and direction
- Chain of command
- Span of management (flat and tall organizations)
- Division of labor (specialization)
- Coordination
- Balanced responsibility and authority
- Delegation
- Flexibility
- Departmentalization
- Integration

them. The chain of command also identifies the formal path for communications. The chain of command forms a hierarchy[3] and is illustrated in the organization chart, which you will learn about in this chapter. CMP divisions set up a clear chain of command within each division. The Leeds now work closely with the division managers.

Span of Management

The **span of management** *refers to the number of employees reporting to a manager.* The fewer employees supervised, the smaller or narrower the span of management, also called *span of control*.[4] The more employees supervised, the greater or wider the span. There is no best number of employees to manage. The number of employees reporting to a manager should be limited to a number that can be effectively supervised. However, it is generally believed that lower-level managers can have a wider span of control than higher-level managers. The Leeds narrowed their span of control by organizing into divisions. Now they work with division managers rather than with all levels of employees as they did with the past structure.

With the span of management comes the height of the organizational levels. A *flat organization* exists when there are few levels with wide spans of management. A *tall organization* exists when there are many levels with narrow spans of management. Figure 6–2 illustrates flat versus tall organizations. Notice that the flat structure has only two levels of management and the tall structure has four. In recent years, organizations have cut management levels[5] and restructured with flattened management hierarchies.[6]

Division of Labor

With the *division of labor*, employees have specialized jobs. Related functions are grouped together under a single boss.[7] Employees generally have specialized jobs in a functional area such as accounting, production, or sales. Managers usually perform less specialized functions as they move up the management ladder. The Leeds developed a clear division of labor when they organized into divisions.

Lawrence and Lorsch coined the terms *differentiation* and *integration*.[8] Differentiation refers to the need to break the organization into departments, and integration refers to the need to coordinate the departmental activities.[9]

Coordination

Coordination means that all departments and individuals within the organization should work together to accomplish the strategic and operational objectives and plans.[10] Coordination is the process of integrating organizational/departmental tasks and resources to meet objectives.[11] Coordination requires conceptual skills. It is important that you coordinate all your resources.[12]

---

1. Explain the difference between a flat and a tall organization.

span of management
The number of employees reporting to a manager.

WORK APPLICATION

2. Identify your boss's span of management, or your own if you are or were a manager. How many levels of management are there in this organization? Is it a flat or a tall organization?

Flat Structure—Wide Span of Management

Tall Structure—Narrow Span of Management

Key:
Vice President **(VP)**
Manager **(M)**
Supervisor **(S)**

Figure 6-2
Flat versus Tall Organizations

All of the organization principles are used as coordination techniques. Other means of coordination include:

- *Direct contact* among people within and among departments.
- *Liaisons* who work in one department and coordinate information and activities with one or more other departments.
- *Committees* made up of people from the different departments being coordinated, such as the publications committee at CMP.
- *Integrators*, such as product or project managers, who do not work for any department but coordinate departmental activities to reach an objective.
- *Boundary roles* in which employees coordinate efforts with people in the external environment. Employees in sales, customer service, purchasing, public relations, and others play boundary roles.

2. Describe the similarity and difference among liaisons, integrators, and boundary roles.

Balanced Responsibility and Authority

Balanced responsibility and authority mean that the responsibilities of each individual in the organization are clearly defined. Each individual is also given the authority needed to meet these responsibilities and is held accountable for meeting them.[13] When you delegate, you do not give responsibility and authority away; you share them.

Responsibility *is the obligation to achieve objectives by performing required activities*. When strategic and operational objectives are set, the people responsible for achieving them should be clearly identified. Managers are responsible for the results of their organizations/divisions/ departments even though they do not actually make the goods or provide the services.

Authority *is the right to make decisions, issue orders, and use resources*. As a manager you will be given responsibility for achieving departmental objectives. You must also have the authority to get the job done. Authority is delegated. The chief executive officer (CEO) is responsible for the results of the entire organization and delegates authority down the chain of command to the lower-level managers who are responsible for meeting operational objectives.[14]

Accountability is the evaluation of how well individuals meet their responsibility. All members of the organization should be evaluated periodically and held accountable for achieving their objectives.[15] To this end, some companies keep track of the numbers and even names of employees who make the products. If the product is defective, they know who is responsible.

Managers are accountable for everything that happens in their departments. As a manager, you delegate responsibility and authority to perform tasks, but you should realize that you can never delegate your accountability.[16]

responsibility
The obligation to achieve objectives by performing required activities.

authority
The right to make decisions, issue orders, and use resources.

Delegation

Delegation *is the process of assigning responsibility and authority for accomplishing objectives*. Responsibility and authority are delegated down the chain of command. Delegation is an important skill for managers;[17] therefore, it will be covered in detail later in this chapter.

delegation
The process of assigning responsibility and authority for accomplishing objectives.

Flexibility

Flexibility means that there will always be exceptions to the rule.[18] Many employees focus on company rules rather than creating customer satisfaction.[19] For example, the rule is no sales slip with returned merchandise, no cash refund. This rule helps to protect the store from people who steal merchandise and then return it for cash. A well-known, excellent customer comes into the store and demands a cash refund without a sales slip. In analyzing the situation, the employee realizes that the store could lose a good customer. Should the employee follow the rules and lose a good customer, or be flexible and keep the good customer?

WORK APPLICATION

3. Does an organization you work or have worked for encourage following the standing plans or flexibility? Explain your answer.

APPLYING THE CONCEPT

AC 6–1 Principles of Organization

Identify each statement in terms of the following organizational principles:

a. unity of command and direction   e. coordination
b. chain of command   f. balanced responsibility and authority
c. span of management   g. delegation
d. division of labor   h. flexibility

_____ **1.** "Karl told me to pick up the mail. When I got to the post office, I did not have a key, so the postal worker wouldn't give me the mail."

_____ **2.** The players on the football team are on the offensive or defensive squad.

_____ **3.** "My job is frustrating at times because I work in a matrix structure. Sometimes my department manager tells me to do one thing but my project manager tells me to do something else at the same time."

_____ **4.** Middle manager: "I want an employee to deliver this package but I can't order one to do it directly. I have to have one of my supervisors give the order."

_____ **5.** "There has been an accident, and the ambulance is on the way. Juan, call Doctor Rodriguez and have her get to emergency room C in 10 minutes. Pat, get the paperwork ready. Karen, prepare emergency room C."

3. Discuss the difference between formal and informal and centralized and decentralized authority.

4. List and briefly explain the four levels of authority.

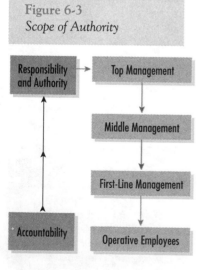

Figure 6-3
Scope of Authority

AUTHORITY

In this section, you will learn about formal and informal authority, levels of authority, line and staff authority, and centralized and decentralized organizational authority.

Formal and Informal Authority

Formal Authority. *Formal authority* (or structure) includes the specified relationships among employees. It is the sanctioned way of getting the job done. The organization chart illustrates formal authority and shows the lines of authority.[20]

Informal Authority. *Informal authority* (or structure) includes the patterns of relationships and communication that evolve as employees interact and communicate. It is the unsanctioned way of getting the job done. Informal authority can be used to overcome the burdens and limitations that formal authority imposes on employees.[21] Informally, employees can often get things done quicker.

Scope of Authority. The *scope of authority* narrows as it flows down the organization. The president has more authority than a vice president, who has more authority than a manager, who has more authority than a supervisor. Responsibility and authority are delegated and flow down the organization, whereas accountability flows up the organization, as Figure 6–3 illustrates.

Levels of Authority

You should know your formal authority.[22] For example, what level of authority does a nurse have to alter a medical record that is believed to be in error? Levels of authority can vary from task to task.

The **levels of authority** *are inform, recommend, report, and full.*

1. *Inform authority.* The person informs the boss of possible alternative actions. The boss has the authority to make the decision. People in secretarial and clerical positions often have only inform authority because the job calls for gathering data for others.

2. *Recommend authority.* The person lists alternative actions, analyzes them, and recommends one action. However, the person may not implement the recommendation without the boss's okay. The boss may require a different alternative if he or she does not agree with the recommendation. Committees are often given recommend authority.

3. *Report authority.* The person may freely select a course of action and carry it out. However, afterward the person must report the action taken to the boss. Nurses have the authority to alter medical records, when the situation calls for it. The doctor who wrote the original entry should be informed of the alteration.

4. *Full authority.* The person may freely make decisions and act without the boss's knowledge. For the most part, the Leeds gave the division managers full authority to run their semiautonomous divisions. However, even with full authority, many people consult their bosses for advice.

To illustrate, Tania, a manager, needs a new machine. If Tania had no authority, it would be up to her boss to get one. With inform authority, Tania would give her boss a list of possible machines to try and a description of their features, prices, and so forth. With recommend authority, Tania would analyze the machines' features and suggest which one to purchase. With report authority, Tania would actually purchase a machine, but would have to tell her boss about it, possibly by sending him or her a copy of the purchase order. With full authority, Tania would purchase the machine without having to tell her boss about it.

Line and Staff Authority

Line authority *is the responsibility to make decisions and issue orders down the chain of command.* Line managers are primarily responsible for achieving the organization's objectives, and staff people provide them with a service to help them.

Staff authority *is the responsibility to advise and assist other personnel.* Operations and marketing are usually line departments, but some organizations include financial activities, too. Human resources management, public relations, and data processing are almost always staff departments. The line departments are internal customers of the staff department. Therefore, line and staff department members should strive to form a collaborative partnership.[23]

Functional Authority. The staff's primary role is to advise and assist, but situations occur in which they can give orders to line personnel. *Functional authority* is the right of staff personnel to issue orders to line personnel in established areas of responsibility. For example, the maintenance department assists production by keeping the machines operating. If maintenance determines that a machine is unsafe, the department may issue an order to a line manager not to use the machine.

levels of authority
Inform, recommend, report, and full.

WORK APPLICATION

4. List and explain your level of authority for a specific task in an organization.

5. Describe the relationship between line and staff authority.

line authority
The responsibility to make decisions and issue orders down the chain of command.

staff authority
The responsibility to advise and assist other personnel.

Dual Line and Staff Authority. Staff managers may have both staff and line authority. For example, Ted, a public relations (staff) manager, advises and assists all departments in the organization. However, Ted also has line authority within his own department and issues orders (a line function) to his employees.

General and Specialist Staff. *General staff* work for only one manager. Often called "assistant to," they help the manager in any way needed. *Specialist staff* help anyone in the organization who needs it. Human resources, finance, accounting, public relations, and maintenance offer specialized advice and assistance.

The Leeds and division managers are all line managers. Division managers use the services of the printing, finance, and human resources staff departments.

Centralized and Decentralized Authority

The major difference between centralized and decentralized authority is who makes the important decisions. *With* **centralized authority,** *important decisions are made by top managers.* *With* **decentralized authority,** *important decisions are made by middle- and first-level managers.*

The major advantages of centralization include control (uniform procedures are easier to control, and fewer risks are taken) and reduced duplication of work (few employees perform the same tasks). The major advantages of decentralization include efficiency and flexibility (decisions are made quickly by people familiar with the situation) and development (managers are challenged and motivated to make decisions and solve their own problems). Which type of authority works best? There is no simple answer. Sears, General Electric, and General Motors have successfully used decentralized authority, and General Dynamics, McDonald's, and Kmart have successfully used centralized authority.

Authority is a continuum, with centralized and decentralized at each end.

Centralized authority —————————————————— Decentralized authority

With the exception of very small companies, which tend to be centralized, most organizations lie somewhere between the two extremes, but can be classified overall. The key to success seems to be having the right balance between the two extremes.[24] For example, production and sales are often decentralized, whereas finance and labor relations are centralized to provide uniformity and control throughout an organization. Top managers are decentralizing authority.[25]

The Leeds started CMP with centralized authority. However, as the company grew, it became too time-consuming to make all the decisions. Therefore, the Leeds decentralized authority to the division managers. See Figure 6–4 for a review of authority.

WORK APPLICATION

5. Identify one or more line and staff positions in an organization you work or have worked for. Also identify staff as general or specialist.

---

centralized authority
Important decisions are made by top managers.

decentralized authority
Important decisions are made by middle- and first-level managers.

WORK APPLICATION

6. Describe the type of authority (centralized or decentralized) used in an organization you work or have worked for.

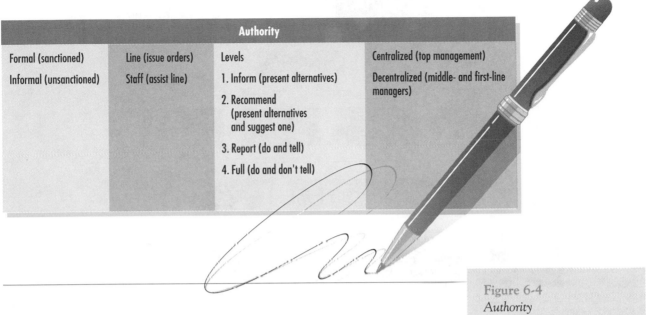

Authority			
Formal (sanctioned)	Line (issue orders)	Levels	Centralized (top management)
Informal (unsanctioned)	Staff (assist line)	1. Inform (present alternatives)	Decentralized (middle- and first-line managers)
		2. Recommend (present alternatives and suggest one)	
		3. Report (do and tell)	
		4. Full (do and don't tell)	

Figure 6-4
Authority

ORGANIZATIONAL DESIGN

Now you will learn about organizing an entire firm. *Organizational design* refers to the arrangements of positions into work units/departments and the interrelationship among them within the organization. The organizational design is illustrated through the organization chart and type of departmentalization.

Organization Chart

The formal organizational authority/structure defines the working relationships between the organization's members and their jobs and is illustrated through an organization chart. An **organization chart** *is a graphic illustration of the organization's management hierarchy and departments and their working relationships.* Each box represents a position within the organization, and each line indicates the reporting relationships and lines of communication.

Figure 6–5, an adaptation of General Motors' organization chart, illustrates four major aspects of a firm.

6. Explain what an organization chart is and list the four things it shows.

organization chart
A graphic illustration of the organization's management hierarchy and departments and their working relationships.

APPLYING THE CONCEPT

AC 6–2 Authority

Identify each statement by the type of authority.

a. formal   e. staff
b. informal   f. centralized
c. level   g. decentralized
d. line

_____ **6.** "My job is interesting, but it is frustrating when I recommend employees to the production and marketing managers and they do not hire them."

_____ **7.** "It is great working for an organization that encourages everyone to share information with everyone else."

_____ **8.** "Managers here have the autonomy to run their departments the way they want to."

_____ **9.** "I'm not sure if I'm supposed to get a list of company cars for Wendy or recommend one of them to her."

_____ **10.** "That is a great idea. I'll talk to our boss Pete, and if he likes it, he'll let us present the idea to his boss Jean."

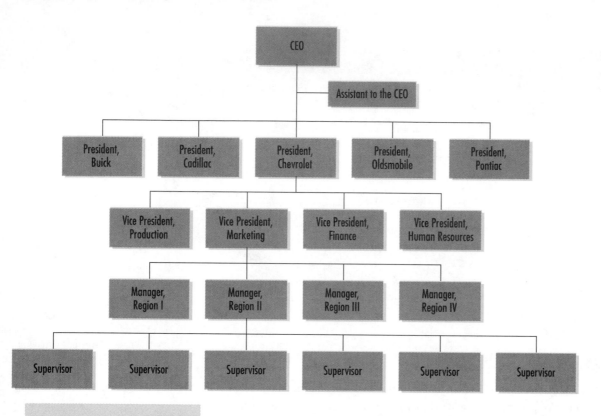

Figure 6-5
Organization Chart

- *The level of management hierarchy.* The CEO and presidents are top-level management, the vice presidents and managers are middle-level management, and the supervisors are first-level management.

- *Chain of command.* As you follow the vertical lines you can see that the division presidents report to the CEO. The managers report to vice presidents, and supervisors report to the managers.

- *The division and type of work.* GM divides work by type of automobile: Buick, Cadillac, Chevrolet, Oldsmobile, and Pontiac. Each vice president within a division is responsible for a function, or type of work, such as production, marketing, finance, or human resources. The production middle managers are responsible for specific automobile models such as Corvette or Camaro. The supervisors are responsible for specific phases of production: engine, frame, body, paint, and so forth.

- *Departmentalization.* An organization chart shows how the firm is divided into permanent work units. GM is organized primarily by product. Throughout this section organization charts will be used to illustrate the various types of departmentalization.

Note that each vice president of the Chevrolet division has middle managers reporting to him or her, and that each middle manager has supervisors reporting to him or her. The other four divisions—Buick, Cadillac, Oldsmobile, and Pontiac—all have their own vice presidents, middle managers, and supervisors. The assistant to the CEO is a *general* staff, and the finance and human resources departments are *specialist* staff.

An organization chart does not show the day-to-day activities performed or the structure of the informal organization.

To better focus on the customer, some organizations, including Dana Corporation, FedEx, Nordstrom, and Wal-Mart, have developed an upside-down organization chart with the customer at the top of the chart and management at the bottom. The upside-down chart reminds everyone in the organization that their job is to provide customer value, and informs managers that their role is to support employees in providing customer value.

Departmentalization

Departmentalization *is the grouping of related activities into units.* Departments may be created with an internal or external focus. Departmentalization around the internal operations or functions that the employees perform and the resources needed to accomplish the unit's work is called *functional departmentalization.* External or output departmentalization is based on activities that focus on factors outside the organization; this is called *product, customer, and territory departmentalization.*

Functional Departmentalization. Functional departmentalization involves organizing departments around essential input activities, such as production, sales, and finance, that are managerial or technological functions. The top of Figure 6–6 illustrates functional departmentalization.

The functional approach is the form most widely used by small organizations.[26] Large organizations that have a wide diversity of products or types of customers, or that cover a wide territory, cannot departmentalize effectively around functions.[27] Instead, they focus on factors external to the company.

Product (Service) Departmentalization. Product (service) departmentalization involves organizing departments around goods or services. Companies with multiple products commonly use product departmentalization. Each department may become a self-contained company, making and selling its own goods or service. Retail stores like Sears have product departments. The second organization chart in Figure 6–6 shows an example of product departmentalization.

Customer Departmentalization. Customer departmentalization involves organizing departments around the needs of different types of customers. The product or service may be the same or slightly different, but the needs of the customer warrant different marketing (packaging, sales staff, etc.) approaches. Motorola restructured to merge about six business units into two huge divisions—one geared to consumers and the other to industrial customers.[28] Organizations that offer a wide diversity of products often

7. Discuss the difference between internal and external departmentalization.

departmentalization
The grouping of related activities into units.

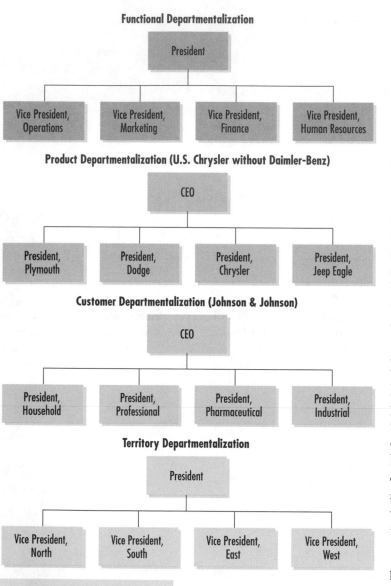

Functional Departmentalization

President

- Vice President, Operations
- Vice President, Marketing
- Vice President, Finance
- Vice President, Human Resources

Product Departmentalization (U.S. Chrysler without Daimler-Benz)

CEO

- President, Plymouth
- President, Dodge
- President, Chrysler
- President, Jeep Eagle

Customer Departmentalization (Johnson & Johnson)

CEO

- President, Household
- President, Professional
- President, Pharmaceutical
- President, Industrial

Territory Departmentalization

President

- Vice President, North
- Vice President, South
- Vice President, East
- Vice President, West

Figure 6-6
Departmentalization

8. State the similarities and differences between matrix and divisional departmentalization.

divisional structure
Departmentalization based on semiautonomous strategic business units.

use customer departments, as do some nonprofit organizations. For example, a counseling center may offer drug counseling, family counseling, and so on. However, these units usually are not self-contained. The third organization chart in Figure 6–6 illustrates customer departmentalization.

Territory (Geographic) Departmentalization. Territory (geographic) departmentalization involves organizing departments in each area in which the enterprise does business. The federal government uses this structure. For example, the Federal Reserve System is divided into 12 geographic areas centered in cities such as Boston, New York, and San Francisco. The last organization chart in Figure 6–6 illustrates territory departmentalization.

Multiple Departmentalization

Many organizations, particularly large, complex organizations, use several of the departmental structures described to create a *hybrid* organization. Any mixture of structures can be used. Some organizations have functional departments with one manufacturing facility, and sales are departmentalized by territory with separate sales managers and salespeople in different areas.

Matrix Departmentalization. Matrix departmentalization combines the functional and product departmental structures. With matrix departmentalization, the employee works for a functional department and is also assigned to one or more products or projects.[29] The major advantage of matrix departmentalization is flexibility. It allows the enterprise to temporarily organize for a project. The major disadvantage is that each employee has two bosses—a functional boss and a project boss—which violates the unity of command principle. Coordination can also be difficult. Rank Xerox and Boeing use a formal matrix structure. Figure 6–7 illustrates a matrix structure.

Divisional Departmentalization. **Divisional structure** *departmentalizes based on semiautonomous strategic business units* (Chapter 4). In essence, you have coordinated companies within a company. Within the divisional (or M-Form) structure, any mixture of the other forms of departmentalization

Figure 6-7
Matrix Departmentalization

● represents teams of functional employees working on a project.

may also be used by the company and within divisions. Divisional structure is common for large, complex global businesses with related goods and services to aid in portfolio management. Westinghouse uses divisional departmentalization to organize its dozens of divisions. The Leeds reorganized CMP into divisions.

The *conglomerate* (holding company or H-Form) structure departmentalizes based on autonomous profit centers. Companies with unrelated diversified business units use the conglomerate structure. Top management focuses on portfolio management to buy and sell businesses without great concern for coordinating divisions. ITT and Newell use the conglomerate structure. Johnson & Johnson has 166 separate companies that are encouraged to act independently.

Other Designs. Other designs include networks, new venture, and high involvement.

Network structures describe the interrelationship among different organizations. Networks are often flexible temporary arrangements among suppliers, customers, and/or competitors. Companies using strategic alliances and outsourcing form networks held together by contract and performance agreements.[30] For example, Apple Computer lacked the capacity to produce its entire line of PowerBook computers, so it contracted with Sony to manufacture the least expensive version.

New venture units, or skunkworks, consist of a group of employees who volunteer to develop new products or ventures for companies. They use a form of matrix structure. New products become a part of traditional departmentalization, are developed into new departments, or grow into divisions. Boeing, Genentech, Hewlett-Packard, IBM, Monsanto, NCR,

WORK APPLICATION

7. Draw a simple organization chart for an organization you work or have worked for. Identify the type of departmentalization and staff positions, if any, used.

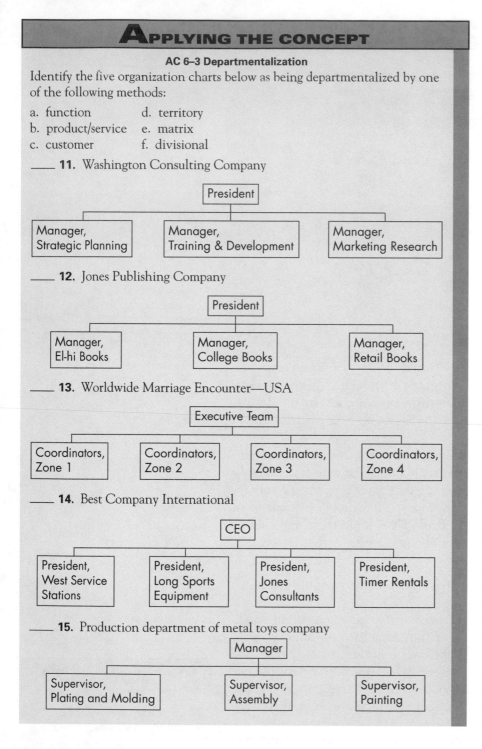

APPLYING THE CONCEPT

AC 6–3 Departmentalization

Identify the five organization charts below as being departmentalized by one of the following methods:

a. function   d. territory
b. product/service   e. matrix
c. customer   f. divisional

____ **11.** Washington Consulting Company

President
- Manager, Strategic Planning
- Manager, Training & Development
- Manager, Marketing Research

____ **12.** Jones Publishing Company

President
- Manager, El-hi Books
- Manager, College Books
- Manager, Retail Books

____ **13.** Worldwide Marriage Encounter—USA

Executive Team
- Coordinators, Zone 1
- Coordinators, Zone 2
- Coordinators, Zone 3
- Coordinators, Zone 4

____ **14.** Best Company International

CEO
- President, West Service Stations
- President, Long Sports Equipment
- President, Jones Consultants
- President, Timer Rentals

____ **15.** Production department of metal toys company

Manager
- Supervisor, Plating and Molding
- Supervisor, Assembly
- Supervisor, Painting

Westinghouse, and 3M have used skunkworks.

High involvement, or greenfields, uses a team approach to organize a new facility. Rather than change a traditional facility, many organizations are creating new smaller facilities, between 100 and 200 employees, based on the input of employees. High involvement organizations are flat; employee work teams make the decisions. You will learn about these work teams in the next section. Cummins Engine, General Foods, Mead, Procter & Gamble, Sherwin-Williams, and TRW have all developed greenfields.

JOB DESIGN

Tasks to be performed by organizations are grouped into functional departments, and the tasks are further grouped into jobs for each employee. **Job design** *is the process of combining tasks that each employee is responsible for completing.* Job design is crucial because it affects job satisfaction and productivity.[31] Empowering employees to be involved in designing their own jobs motivates them to increase productivity.[32] Many organizations, including GE and Pizza Hut, are asking employees to suggest ways to redesign their work.

As you will learn in this section, jobs can contain few tasks, called simplified, or they can contain many tasks, called expanded. You can use a job characteristics model to design jobs. Jobs are also being designed for work teams.

job design
The process of combining tasks that each employee is responsible for completing.

Job Simplification

Job simplification is used to make jobs more specialized.[33] It is based on the organizing principle of division of labor and Taylor's scientific management (Appendix A). The idea behind job simplification is to work smarter not harder. *Job simplification* is the process of eliminating, combining, and/or changing the work sequence to increase performance. Have employees break the job down into steps (flowchart) and see if they can:

- *Eliminate*. Does the task have to be done at all? If not, don't waste time doing it.
- *Combine*. Doing more than one thing at a time often saves time. Make one trip to the mail room at the end of the day instead of several throughout the day.
- *Change sequence*. Often a change in the order of doing things results in a lower total time.

Jobs that are too simple and boring can lead to lower levels of productivity. However, when used appropriately, work simplification can motivate employees. Often, people don't hate the job, just some aspect of it. Rather than ignoring or simply putting up with these hated aspects, they can change them. Intel decided that it was not necessary to fill out a voucher for expenses amounting to less than $100. Work volume went down by 14 percent in 30 days. GE developed its Work Out Program to improve and eliminate work, and Pizza Hut credits up to a 40 percent increase in store sales due to job simplification. The Leeds simplified jobs at CMP when they created specialized divisions.

Job Expansion

Job expansion is the process of making jobs less specialized. Jobs can be expanded through job rotation, job enlargement, and job enrichment.

Job Rotation. Job rotation involves performing different jobs for a set period of time. For example, employees making a car on a Ford assembly line could rotate so that they get to work on different parts. Many organizations develop conceptual skills in management trainees by rotating them through various departments. A few of the companies that have used job rotation include Bethlehem Steel, Dayton Hudson, Ford, Motorola, National Steel, and Prudential Insurance. Unfortunately, once employees master the various jobs, those jobs can be considered specialized and boring.

Related to job rotation is *cross-training*. With cross-training, employees learn to perform different jobs so they can fill in for one another when others are not on the job. As skills increase, employees become more valuable to the organization.

9. Explain the difference between job simplification and job expansion.

WORK APPLICATION

8. Describe how a job at an organization you work or have worked for could be simplified. Be sure to specify if you are eliminating, combining, or changing the sequence of the job.

job enrichment
The process of building motivators into the job by making it more interesting and challenging.

WORK APPLICATION

9. Describe how a job at an organization you work or have worked for could be expanded. Be sure to specify if you are using job rotation, job enlargement, or job enrichment and how the job is changed.

Job Enlargement. Job enlargement involves adding tasks to broaden job variety. For example, rather than rotate jobs, the car workers could combine tasks into one job. There could be two jobs instead of four. AT&T, Chrysler, GM, IBM, and Maytag are a few of the companies that have used job enlargement. Unfortunately, adding more simple tasks to a simple job is often not a great motivator.

Job Enrichment. **Job enrichment** *is the process of building motivators into the job itself by making it more interesting and challenging.* Job enrichment works for jobs of low motivation potential with employees who want their jobs enriched. Some employees are happy with the jobs the way they are. Organizations including AT&T, General Motors, IBM, Maytag, Monsanto, Motorola, Polaroid, and Traveler's Insurance Company have successfully used job enrichment. The Leeds created enriched jobs for the division managers by giving them the power to run their divisions as semiautonomous companies.

A simple way to enrich jobs is for the manager to delegate more variety and responsibility to employees.

Work Teams

The traditional approach to job design has been to focus on individual jobs. Today, the trend is shifting to designing jobs for work teams, or rather, teams are redesigning members' jobs.[34] The development of work teams is a form of job enrichment. Two common types of work teams are integrated and self-managed.

Integrated Work Teams. Integrated work teams are assigned a number of tasks by the manager, and the team gives specific assignments to members and is responsible for rotating jobs. For example, the foreman of a cleaning company could drop off groups of employees at job sites and go over tasks to be completed. The teams would decide who does what and how. The foreman would go to the various job sites to see how the work was progressing, and to transport employees to new job sites when they have finished.

WORK APPLICATION

10. Describe how an organization you work or have worked for uses, or could use, teams. Be sure to specify if the teams are integrated or self-managed.

Self-Managed Work Teams. Self-managed work teams are assigned a goal, and the team plans, organizes, leads, and controls to achieve the goal. Usually, self-managed teams operate without a designated manager; the team is both manager and worker. Teams commonly select their own members and evaluate each other's performance.[35] The cleaning company integrated work team could become a self-managed team by assigning the goal (number of sites to be cleaned for the day/week) and allowing the team, not the foreman, to determine the sequence of job sites. The team, not the foreman, would check its own progress. High-involvement greenfields are characterized by self-managed teams. Chrysler used teams to develop the Viper sports car.

Work teams have been successful.[36] Team-based work systems are emerging as a key source of sustained competitive advantage. However, members need to be trained to work together as a team.[37] In Chapter 10 you will learn about, and be trained in, teamwork. See Figure 6–8 for a review of the types of job designs and the job characteristics model, to be discussed next.

The Job Characteristics Model

The job characteristics model provides a conceptual framework for designing enriched jobs.[38] Individuals or a team can use the model to enrich jobs. *The* **job characteristics model** *comprises core job dimensions, critical psychological states, and employee growth-need strength to improve quality of working life for employees and productivity for the organization.* Hackman and Oldham[39] developed the job characteristics model.

Core Job Dimensions. Five core dimensions determine a job's personal (quality of working life for employees) and work (productivity for the organization) outcomes. By increasing each dimension, you can increase both personal and work outcomes.

1. *Skill variety* is the number of diverse tasks that make up a job and the number of skills used to perform the job.
2. *Task identity* is the degree to which an employee performs a whole identifiable task. Have an employee put together an entire television, rather than just place the screen in the set.
3. *Task significance* is the perception of the importance of the task to others—the organization, the department, coworkers, and/or customers.
4. *Autonomy* is the degree to which the employee has discretion to make decisions in planning, organizing, and controlling the task performed.
5. *Feedback* is the extent to which employees find out how well they perform their tasks.

Critical Psychological States. As the three critical psychological states—developed through core job dimensions—increase, so do the job's personal and work outcomes.

A. *Experienced meaningfulness of the work* is based on (1) skill variety, (2) task identity, and (3) task significance. The greater these core dimensions are, the greater the experienced meaningfulness of work.

10. Describe the job characteristics model and what it is used for.

job characteristics model
Comprises core job dimensions, critical psychological states, and employee growth-need strength to improve quality of working life for employees and productivity for the organization.

Figure 6-8
Job Designs

Job Design Options

Job Simplification	Job Expansion	Work Teams	Job Characteristics Model
Eliminate	Job rotation, switch jobs	Integrated	Core dimensions
Combine	Job enlargement, more tasks	Self-managed	Critical psychological states
Change sequence	Job enrichment, delegate		Performance and work outcomes
			Employee growth-need strength

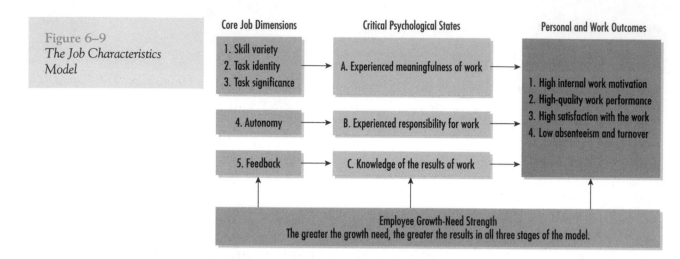

Figure 6–9
The Job Characteristics Model

Core Job Dimensions
1. Skill variety
2. Task identity
3. Task significance
4. Autonomy
5. Feedback

Critical Psychological States
A. Experienced meaningfulness of work
B. Experienced responsibility for work
C. Knowledge of the results of work

Personal and Work Outcomes
1. High internal work motivation
2. High-quality work performance
3. High satisfaction with the work
4. Low absenteeism and turnover

Employee Growth-Need Strength
The greater the growth need, the greater the results in all three stages of the model.

APPLYING THE CONCEPT

AC 6–4 Job Designs

Identify the way each of the jobs is being designed as:

a. job simplification   c. job enlargement   e. work teams
b. job rotation   d. job enrichment   f. job characteristics model

_____ **16.** "Jill, I'm delegating a new task to you to provide you with more challenge."

_____ **17.** "Sales reps who have business lunches with clients that are under $20 no longer need to provide a sales receipt."

_____ **18.** "We'd like to change your job so that you can develop new skills, complete entire jobs by yourself so that the job is more meaningful, let you do the job the way you want to, and let you know how you are doing."

_____ **19.** "To make your job less repetitive, we are going to add three new tasks to your job responsibility."

_____ **20.** "I'd like you to learn how to run the switchboard so that you can fill in for Ted while he is at lunch."

B. *Experienced responsibility for outcomes of the work* is based on dimension 4, autonomy. The greater the autonomy, the greater the experienced responsibility for outcomes of the work.

C. *Knowledge of the actual results of the work activities* is based on dimension 5, feedback. The greater the feedback, the greater the knowledge of results of the work.

Performance and Work Outcomes. Performance and work outcomes are the four benefits of the critical psychological states that are created by the five core job dimensions:

1. High internal work motivation.
2. High-quality work performance.
3. High satisfaction with the work.
4. Low absenteeism and turnover.

Employee Growth-Need Strength. Employee growth-need strength determines the employees' interest in having the five core dimensions improved, which determines the critical psychological states and personal and work outcomes. Figure 6–9 illustrates this process. Note that if employees are not interested in enriching their jobs, the job characteristics model will fail. You will learn more about needs and motivation in Chapter 12.

ORGANIZING YOURSELF AND DELEGATING

Successful managers are effective at setting priorities[40] and delegating work.[41] Recall that planning entails setting objectives and that organizing is the process of delegating and coordinating resources to achieve objectives. Thus, prioritizing these objectives is important,[42] because some objectives are more important than others,[43] and as a manager you get the work done by delegating it to employees.[44]

Now that you understand how organizations and jobs are designed, it's time to learn how to organize yourself by setting priorities and delegating work. Let's start by completing Self-Assessment Exercise 6–1, Personal Priorities, to determine what is important to you personally (your values) by prioritizing.

Self-Assessment Exercise 6–1

Personal Priorities

Below are 16 items. Rate how important each one is to you on a scale of 0 (not important) to 100 (very important). Write the number 0–100 on the line to the left of each item.

Not important					Somewhat important					Very important
0	10	20	30	40	50	60	70	80	90	100

____ 1. An enjoyable, satisfying job.

____ 2. A high-paying job.

____ 3. A good marriage.

____ 4. Meeting new people, attending social events.

____ 5. Involvement in community activities.

____ 6. My relationship with God/my religion.

____ 7. Exercising, playing sports.

____ 8. Intellectual development.

____ 9. A career with challenging opportunities.

____ 10. Nice cars, clothes, home, etc.

____ 11. Spending time with family.

____ 12. Having several close friends.

____ 13. Volunteer work for not-for-profit organizations like the cancer society.

____ 14. Meditation, quiet time to think, pray, etc.

____ 15. A healthy, balanced diet.

____ 16. Educational reading, TV, self-improvement programs, etc.

Below, transfer the numbers for each of the 16 items to the appropriate column, then add the two numbers in each column.

	Professional	Financial	Family	Social
	1. ____	2. ____	3. ____	4. ____
	9. ____	10. ____	11. ____	12. ____
Totals	____	____	____	____

	Community	Spiritual	Physical	Intellectual
	5. ___	6. ___	7. ___	8. ___
	13. ___	14. ___	15. ___	16. ___
Totals	___	___	___	___

The higher the total in any area, the higher the value you place on that particular area. The closer the numbers are in all eight areas, the more well-rounded you are.

Think about the time and effort you put forth in your top three values. Is it sufficient to allow you to achieve the level of success you want in each area? If not, what can you do to change? Is there any area in which you feel you should have a higher value total? If yes, which area, and what can you do to change?

Setting Priorities[45]

11. Explain how to set priorities by listing the three priority questions and how you assign and delegate high, medium, and low priority.

One important aspect of organizing a department, a job, and yourself is setting priorities.[46] At any given time, several tasks must be performed. How you, as a manager, select the *priority* order in which these tasks will be completed will affect your career success.[47] To prioritize successfully, list tasks that you must perform on a to-do list[48] and then assign each task a priority[49] to rank the order of performance. After prioritizing tasks, focus on accomplishing only one task at a time.

Priority Determination Questions. In order to determine the importance of tasks, you should ask yourself three questions about the task that needs to be completed. **Priority determination questions** *ask: Do I need to be personally involved? Is the task my responsibility or will it affect the performance or finances of my department? When is the deadline? Is quick action needed?* Figure 6–10 also lists the priority determination questions.

priority determination questions
Do I need to be personally involved? Is the task my responsibility or will it affect the performance or finances of my department? When is the deadline? Is quick action needed?

1. *Do I need to be personally involved* because of my unique knowledge or skills? (yes or no) Often, you are the only one who can do the task, and you must be involved.

2. *Is the task within my major area of responsibility or will it affect the performance or finances of my department?* (yes or no) You must oversee the performance of your department and keep the finances in line with the budget.

3. *When is the deadline? Is quick action needed?* (yes or no) Should you work on this activity right now, or can it wait? Time is a relative term. The key is to start the task soon enough so that you will meet the deadline. People often miss deadlines because they don't start the task soon enough.

Assigning Priorities. After the three questions are answered, a high, medium, or low priority can be assigned to each activity:

- *Delegate (D) Priority:* The task is delegated if the answer to question 1 is no. If the answer to question 1 is no, it is not necessary to answer questions 2 and 3 because a priority is not assigned to the task. However, planning the delegation and delegating the task are prioritized.

- *High (H) Priority:* A high priority is assigned if you answer yes to all three questions.

- *Medium (M) Priority:* A medium priority is assigned if you answer yes to question 1 but no to question 2 or no to question 3.

- *Low (L) Priority:* A low priority is assigned if you answer yes to question 1 but no to both questions 2 and 3.

The Prioritized To-Do List. Refer to Model 6–1 for a copy of the prioritized to-do list; make copies of it and use it on the job. The steps for using the prioritized to-do list are:

1. *Write the task* that you must perform on the task line.

2. *Answer the three priority questions* by placing a Y (yes) or N (no) in the column. Also place the deadline and time needed to complete the task in the respective column. The deadline and time needed are used with lower-level priorities that change into high priorities as the deadline approaches. You may want to write in the deadline to start the task rather than the completion deadline.

3. *Assign a priority* to the task by placing the letter D (delegate), H (high), M (medium), or L (low) in the priority column. Use the box at the top left of the prioritized to-do list to determine priority based on the Y or N answers to the priority determination questions. If you write D, set a priority on when to delegate the task.

4. *Determine which task to complete now.* You may have more than one high priority, so select the most important one. When all high priorities are completed, go to medium followed by low.

Update the tasks on the prioritized to-do list and *add new ones*. As time passes, the items prioritized medium and low become high. There is no set rule for how often to update, but do it at least daily. As new tasks come up, be sure to add them to your to-do list and prioritize them. In doing so, you will avoid suspending a high-priority task to work on a lower-level task.

As stated in Chapter 5, if you have a management job with a large variety of changing tasks with the need for more long-range planning, you may want to use the time management system. You can use the prioritized to-do list with the time management system for daily scheduling. If you have a job with a small variety of changing tasks and short-range time planning, you

---

1. Do I need to be personally involved because of my unique knowledge or skills? (yes or no)

2. Is the task within my major area of responsibility or will it affect the performance or finances of my department? (yes or no)

3. When is the deadline? Is quick action needed? (yes or no)

Figure 6-10
Priority Determination Questions

WORK APPLICATION

11. Using Model 6–1, list three to five tasks you must complete in the near future and prioritize them.

Assigning a Priority	Priority Determination Questions				Priority
	#1	#2	#3		
D Delegate priority (N) No to question 1 H High priority (YYY) Yes to all three questions M Medium priority (YNY or YYN) Yes to questions 1 and 2 or 3 L Low priority (YNN) Yes to question 1 and No to questions 2 and 3 **Task**	1. Do I need to be personally involved?	2. Is it my responsibility or will it affect performance or finances of my department?	3. Is quick action needed?	Deadline/Time needed	P r i o r i t y

Model 6-1
Prioritized To-Do List

skillbuilder

may simply use the prioritized to-do list to keep yourself organized and focused on high-priority tasks. Complete Skill-Building Exercise 6–1 to develop your skill at setting priorities using the prioritized to-do list.

Delegation

Delegation is the process of assigning responsibility and authority for accomplishing objectives. Telling employees to perform tasks that are part of their job design is issuing orders not delegating. Delegating refers to giving employees new tasks. The new task may become a part of a redesigned job, or it may simply be a one-time task.

Benefits of Delegation. When managers delegate, they have more time to perform high-priority tasks.[50] Delegation gets tasks accomplished and increases productivity.[51,52] Delegation trains employees and improves their self-esteem; it also eases the stress and burden on managers.[53] Delegating is a means of enriching jobs and can result in improved personal and work outcomes.

Obstacles to Delegation. Managers become used to doing things themselves.[54] Managers fear that the employee will fail to accomplish the task, or will show them up. Recall that you can delegate responsibility and authority, but not accountability.[55] Managers believe they can perform the task more efficiently than others.[56] Some managers don't realize that delegation is an important part of their job, others don't know what to delegate, and some don't know how to delegate. You should realize that delegating is an important management skill,[57] so don't let these or other obstacles stop you from delegating by using Model 6–1. The Leeds set up a division structure and delegated the responsibility for running the divisions to the division managers.

Signs of Delegating Too Little. The signs of delegating too little include: (1) taking work home, (2) performing employee tasks, (3) being behind in work, (4) continual feeling of pressure and stress, (5) rushing to meet deadlines, (6) not meeting deadlines, and (7) employees' seeking approval before acting.

WORK APPLICATION

12. Describe an obstacle to delegation or sign of delegating too little that you have observed.

Delegation Decisions

An important part of delegation is knowing which tasks to delegate. Successful delegation is often based on selecting what task to delegate and to whom to delegate it.[58]

What to Delegate. As a general guide, use your prioritized to-do list and delegate anything that you do not have to be personally involved with because of your unique knowledge or skill. Some possibilities include the following: (1) *Paperwork.* Have employees write reports, memos, letters, and so on. (2) *Routine tasks.* Have employees check inventory, schedule, order, and so on. (3) *Technical matters.* Have top employees deal with technical questions and problems. (4) *Tasks with developmental potential.* Give employees the opportunity to learn new things. Prepare them for advancement by enriching their jobs. (5) *Solving employees' problems.* Train them to solve their own problems; don't solve problems for them unless they lack capability.

What Not to Delegate. As a general guide, do not delegate anything that you need to be personally involved with because of your unique knowledge or skill. Typical examples include: (1) *Personnel matters.* Performance appraisals, counseling, disciplining, firing, resolving conflicts, and so on. (2) *Confidential activities.* Unless you have permission to do so. (3) *Crises.* There is no time to delegate. (4) *Activities delegated to you personally.* For example, if you are assigned to a committee, do not assign someone else without permission.

Determining to Whom to Delegate. Once you have decided what to delegate, you must select an employee to do the task. When selecting an employee, be sure that he or she has the capability to get the job done right by the deadline. Consider your employees' talents, interests, and motivation when making a selection. You may consult with several employees to determine their interest before making the final choice.

12. List the four steps in the delegation model.

delegation model
(1) explain the need for delegating and the reasons for selecting the employee; (2) set objectives that define responsibility, the level of authority, and the deadline; (3) develop a plan; (4) establish control checkpoints and hold employees accountable.

Delegating with the Use of a Model

After determining what to delegate and to whom, you must plan for and delegate the tasks. *The* **delegation model** *steps are: (1) explain the need for delegating and the reasons for selecting the employee; (2) set objectives that define responsibility, the level of authority, and the deadline; (3) develop a plan; (4) establish control checkpoints and hold employees accountable.* Following these four steps can increase your chances of successfully delegating. As you read, you will see how the delegation model is used with the job characteristics model, core job dimensions, and critical psychological states to influence performance and work outcomes.

 Explain the need for delegating and the reasons for selecting the employee. It is helpful for the employee to understand why the assignment must be completed. In other words, how will the department or organization benefit? Informing employees helps them realize the importance of the task (experienced meaningfulness of work). Telling the employee why he or she was selected should make him or her feel valued. Don't use the "it's a lousy job but someone has to do it" approach. Be positive; make employees aware of how they will benefit from the assignment. If step 1 is completed successfully, the employee should be motivated, or at least willing, to do the assignment.

 Set objectives that define responsibility, the level of authority, and the deadline. The objectives should clearly state the end result the employee is responsible for achieving by a specific deadline.[59] Define the level of authority the employee has (pp. 188–189).

 Develop a plan. Once the objectives are set, a plan is needed to achieve them. It is helpful to use an operational plan sheet (Chapter 5 Figure 5–4).

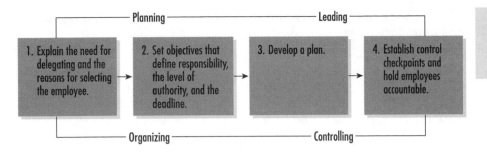

Model 6-2
Steps in the Delegation Model

The level of autonomy for developing the plan to accomplish the task should be based on the employee's capability level. Refer to Skill-Building Exercise 1–1 for details on selecting the management style appropriate for the employee's capability level.

step 4. **Establish control checkpoints and hold employees accountable.** For simple, short tasks, a deadline without control checkpoints is appropriate. However, it is often advisable to check progress at predetermined times (control checkpoints) for tasks that have multiple steps and/or that will take some time to complete. This approach builds information flow into the delegation system from the start. You and the employee should agree on the form (phone call, visit, memo, or detailed report) and timeframe (daily, weekly, or after specific steps are completed but before going on to the next step) for information regarding the assignment. When establishing control, consider the employee's capability level. The lower the capability, the more frequent the checks; the higher the capability, the less frequent the checks.

It is helpful to list the control checkpoints in writing on an operational planning sheet, making copies of the finished plan so that the parties involved and you as the delegating manager have a record. In addition, all parties involved should record the control checkpoints on their calendars. If the employee to whom the task was delegated does not report as scheduled, follow up to find out why the person did not report.[60] You should evaluate performance at each control checkpoint to date and upon completion to provide feedback that develops knowledge of the results of work. Providing praise for progress and completion of the task motivates employees to do a good job.[61] You will learn how to give praise in Chapter 12.

Model 6–2 summarizes the four steps of the delegation process. In Skill-Building Exercise 6–2, you will be given the opportunity to use the model to delegate a task to develop your delegation skills.

> **WORK APPLICATION**
>
> 13. Select a manager you work or have worked for and analyze how well he or she implements the four steps of delegation. Which steps does the manager typically follow and not follow?

*skillbuilder

CHAPTER SUMMARY AND GLOSSARY

The chapter summary is organized to answer the 13 learning objectives for Chapter 6.

1. Explain the difference between a flat and a tall organization.
A flat organization has few levels of management with wide spans of management. A tall organization has many levels of management with narrow spans of management.

2. Describe the similarity and difference among liaisons, integrators, and boundary roles.

They are similar because they are all coordination techniques. Liaisons and integrators are similar because they coordinate internally, whereas boundary roles coordinate efforts with customers, suppliers, and other people in the external environment. Liaisons and integrators are different because liaisons work in one department and coordinate with other departments, whereas integrators coordinate department activities without working for any department.

3. Discuss the difference between formal and informal and centralized and decentralized authority.

Formal authority is the sanctioned relationships and ways of getting the job done, whereas informal authority is the unsanctioned relationships and ways of getting the job done. With centralized authority top managers make important decisions; with decentralized authority middle- and first-line managers make important decisions.

4. List and briefly explain the four levels of authority.

(1) *Inform*—the person simply presents an alternative. (2) *Recommend*—the person presents alternatives and suggests one. (3) *Report*—the person takes action and then tells the boss. (4) *Full*—the person takes action and does not have to tell the boss about it.

5. Describe the relationship between line and staff authority.

The staff personnel advise and assist line personnel, who are responsible for making decisions, and issue orders down the chain of command.

6. Explain what an organization chart is and list the four things it shows.

An organization chart is a graphic illustration of the organization's management hierarchy and departments and their working relationships. It shows the level of management hierarchy, chain of command, division and type of work, and departmentalization.

7. Discuss the difference between internal and external departmentalization.

Internal, or input, departmentalization focuses on functions performed within the organization. External, or output, departmentalization focuses on the product, customer, or territory in which the organization does business.

8. State the similarities and differences between matrix and divisional departmentalization.

They are similar because they are both multiple departmentalization methods. Matrix combines the functional and product departmental structures to focus on projects. Divisional structure departmentalizes based on semiautonomous strategic business units to focus on portfolio management.

9. Explain the difference between job simplification and job expansion.

Job simplification is used to make jobs more specialized by eliminating, combining, and/or changing the sequence of work. Job expansion is used to make jobs less specialized by rotating employees, enlarging the job, and/or enriching the job to make it more interesting and challenging.

10. Describe the job characteristics model and what it is used for.
The job characteristics model is a conceptual framework for designing enriched jobs. It comprises core job dimensions, critical psychological states, and employee growth-need strength. It is used to improve the quality of working life for employees and productivity for the organization.

11. Explain how to set priorities by listing the three priority questions and how you assign and delegate high, medium, and low priority.
(1) Do I need to be personally involved because of my unique knowledge or skills? (2) Is the task within my major area of responsibility or will it affect the performance or finances of my department? (3) When is the deadline? Is quick action needed? A delegate priority is assigned when the answer to question 1 is no (N). A high priority is assigned when the answers to questions 1–3 are yes (YYY). A medium priority is assigned when the answer to question 1 is yes and the answer to questions 2 or 3 is no (YNY or YYN). A low priority is assigned when the answer to question 1 is yes and the answers to questions 2 and 3 are no (YNN).

12. List the four steps in the delegation model.
The delegation model steps are: (1) explain the need for delegating and the reasons the employee was selected; (2) set objectives that define responsibility, the level of authority, and the deadline; (3) develop a plan; (4) establish control checkpoints and hold employees accountable.

13. Define the following key terms (in order of appearance in the chapter):
Select one or more methods: (1) fill in the missing key terms from memory, (2) match the key terms from the end of the summary with their definitions below, or (3) copy the key terms in order from the list at the beginning of the chapter.

The _____ refers to the number of employees reporting to a manager.

_____ is the obligation to achieve objectives by performing required activities.

_____ is the right to make decisions, issue orders, and use resources.

_____ is the process of assigning responsibility and authority to achieve objectives.

The _____ are inform, recommend, report, and full.

_____ is the responsibility to make decisions and issue orders down the chain of command.

_____ is the responsibility to advise and assist other personnel.

With _____, important decisions are made by top managers.

With _____, important decisions are made by middle- and first-line managers.

An _____ is a graphic illustration of the organization's management hierarchy and departments and their working relationships.

_____ is the grouping of related activities into units.

_____ departmentalizes based on semiautonomous strategic business units.

_____ is the process of combining tasks that each employee is responsible for completing.

_____ is the process of building motivators into the job by making it more interesting and challenging.

The _____ comprises core job dimensions, critical psychological states, and employee growth-need strength to improve quality of working life for employees and productivity for the organization.

_____ ask: Do I need to be personally involved? Is the task my responsibility or will it affect the performance or finances of my department? When is the deadline? Is quick action needed?

The _____ steps are: (1) explain the need for delegating and the reasons for selecting the employee; (2) set objectives that define responsibility, the level of authority, and the deadline; (3) develop a plan; (4) establish control checkpoints and hold employees accountable.

KEY TERMS

authority   187
centralized authority   190
decentralized authority   190
delegation   187
delegation model   206
departmentalization   193

divisional structure   194
job characteristics model   199
job design   196
job enrichment   198
levels of authority   189
line authority   189

organization chart   191
priority determination questions   202
responsibility   187
span of management   185
staff authority   189

REVIEW AND DISCUSSION QUESTIONS

1. What is the difference between unity of command and unity of direction?

2. What is the relationship between the chain of command and the span of management?

3. What do the terms *differentiation* and *integration* mean?

4. What is the difference between responsibility and authority?

5. Can accountability be delegated?

6. How does the scope of authority change throughout the organization and what is the flow of responsibility, authority, and accountability?

7. What is the difference between a general staff and a specialist staff?

8. What does an organization chart show? What doesn't it show?

9. What is the difference between product and customer departmentalization?

10. What is the difference between a network structure, skunkwork, and greenfield?

11. What is job design and why is it necessary?

12. What is the difference between an integrated and a self-managed work team?

13. What is the importance of employee growth-need strength to the job characteristics model?

14. Why is it important to update priorities on a to-do list?

15. As a simple guide, what one question do you ask to determine what and what not to delegate?

16. Why is each of the four steps in the delegation model necessary?

OBJECTIVE CASE

General Motors and Saturn

In the 1980s, and even earlier, GM was having problems. GM was slow to respond to changing consumer taste. More Americans were buying Japanese cars because they liked the designs and high quality. GM also lost market share while its major domestic competitor Ford increased market share. By the early 1990s, GM was losing tens of billions of dollars a year, which forced its board of directors to install new management. GM returned to profitability under president John Smith, Jr.

Back in the early 1980s, GM set the goal to make cars that were every bit as good as those made by the Japanese with a lower price. However, GM did not want its image and present business systems and processes at that time to influence the achievement of its goal. So, it made the decision to set up an entirely new division called Saturn. GM invested over $3.5 billion in the Saturn project before it sold a single car in the fall of 1990.

The new Saturn plant was built in Spring Hill, Tennessee. A team of 99 people from the United Auto Workers and GM literally designed the company from scratch. Team members used benchmarking to come up with a superior-built car. They scoured the globe examining successful manufacturing operations to learn what they could do to improve quality and cut costs. The plant was designed with flexible equipment so that one assembly line could make different car models in response to changing market demands. Unlike the traditional assembly line in which workers stay put and the line moves, Saturn teams of assembly workers ride along with the car bodies on a slowly moving platform so they remain engaged with the evolving car shell. The platform can be raised and lowered.

Saturn's 4,500 workers participate in decision-making at all levels because union members sit on major committees. Saturn has fewer managers than the typical GM plant, and their role is different. At Saturn, they are advisors to the teams of 15 or so workers who have full responsibility and authority to do the job the way they want to. Team members can work with anyone in the organization to get the job done. Team members are trained technically and learn how to perform as an effective team. For example, they learn cooperative work methods, conflict management, and group dynamic skills. Original workers received 700 hours of training; new workers receive around 175 hours of training.

Saturn has been a design and sales success. Customers like the reliability, low price, and courteous dealer service. However, Saturn has not been the profit success it planned for.

Saturn has had problems producing the quantity of high-quality cars it needs to be profitable. The company has had trouble meeting production objectives. In its first year, the objective was to build 150,000 cars; it actually built

OBJECTIVE CASE

(continued)

50,000. To meet consumer demand and become profitable, management added a second and third shift to boost production to 310,000 cars. However, as production has gone up, quality has suffered.

Employees have stated that management is willing to trade off quality for quantity, and that the cooperative spirit between management and labor is threatened. Saturn employees are paid less than other GM workers, but they have a bonus system that allows them to make more than GM workers. However, in 1998, Saturn workers were being paid less than GM workers.

Select the best alternative for the following questions. Be sure you are able to explain your answers.

___ 1. The Saturn plant is a move toward greater unity of direction than other GM plants.
    a. True   b. False

___ 2. Saturn developed ___ as the primary means of coordination.
    a. direct contact   d. integrators
    b. liaisons   e. boundary roles
    c. a committee

___ 3. The Saturn plant was designed to be a ___ structure than other GM plants.
    a. flatter   b. taller

___ 4. Within the Saturn plant, authority is
    a. centralized   b. decentralized

___ 5. Today, GM uses ___ departmentalization.
    a. functional   d. territory
    b. product   e. matrix
    c. customer   f. divisional

___ 6. Saturn is based primarily on ___ design.
    a. network   c. greenfield
    b. skunkworks

___ 7. The Saturn plant primarily uses job
    a. simplification   c. enlargement
    b. rotation   d. enrichment

___ 8. Saturn uses ___ work teams.
    a. integrated   b. self-managed

___ 9. Based on the job characteristics model, jobs at Saturn have ___ levels of core job dimensions and critical psychological states.
    a. high   b. low

___ 10. Managers at Saturn are reluctant to delegate.
    a. True   b. False

11. Which TQM concepts does Saturn use?

12. Are production volume and high quality incompatible objectives?

13. Do you think Saturn will become a major profitable success story for GM? Go to the library and/or on the Internet and find out how it is doing by using Saturn in a computer search.

For current information on Saturn, use Internet address http://www.Saturncars.com. For ideas on using the Internet, see Appendix B.

Skill-Building Exercise 6–1

Setting Priorities

Preparing for Skill-Building Exercise 6–1

For this exercise assume that you are the first-line manager of a production department in a large company. A prioritized to-do list with ten tasks is on the next page. Assign priorities to each task by following the prioritized to-do list steps:

1. Write the task that you must perform on the task line. The ten tasks have been written in for you. When you use the to-do list for your own tasks, it is not recommended that you number them. They are numbered for class use so it is easier to know which task is being discussed.

2. Answer the three priority determination questions by placing a Y for yes or N for no in the columns labeled 1, 2, and 3. Because you are not the actual manager of this department, do not fill in the deadline/time needed column.

3. Assign a priority to the task by placing the letter D (delegate), H (high), M (medium), or L (low) in the priority column. Use the box at the top left of the prioritized to-do list to determine the priority based on the Y or N answers to the priority questions.

4. Determine which task to complete now. You may have more than one high priority, so select the most important one to do now—or first.

Doing Skill-Building Exercise 6–1 in Class

Objective

To develop your skill at setting priorities.

Preparation

You should have assigned a priority to the ten tasks on the to-do list preparation.

Experience

You will get feedback on how well you prioritized.

Procedure (10–30 minutes)

Option 1. Break into groups of four to six and share your priorities. Try to reach a group consensus on each of the ten priorities. After a group has finished, one member records priorities for the entire class to see. After all groups have finished, the instructor goes over the recommended answers.

Option 2. The instructor calls on students to get their priorities to each task. The instructor goes over the recommended answer for each item after a student(s) gives a priority.

Option 3. The instructor goes over the recommended answers without student involvement.

Conclusion

The instructor leads a class discussion and/or makes concluding remarks.

Application (2–4 minutes)

What did I learn from this experience? How will I use this knowledge in the future?

Sharing

Volunteers share their priorities lists with the class.

Prioritized To-Do List				Priority Determination Questions				
Assigning a Priority				#1	#2	#3		
D Delegate priority	(N) No to question 1			1. Do I need to be personally involved?	2. Is it my responsibility or will it affect performance or finances of my department?	3. Is quick action needed?	Deadline/Time needed	P r i o r i t y
H High priority	(YYY) Yes to all three questions							
M Medium priority	(YNY or YYN) Yes to questions 1 and 2 or 3							
L Low priority	(YNN) Yes to question 1 and No to questions 2 and 3							
Task								
1. Tom, the sales manager, told you that three customers stopped doing business with the company because your products have decreased in quality.								
2. Your secretary, Michele, told you that there is a salesperson waiting to see you. He does not have an appointment. You don't do any purchasing.								
3. Molly, a vice president, wants to see you to discuss a new product to be introduced in one month.								
4. Tom, the sales manager, sent you a memo stating that the sales forecast was incorrect. Sales are expected to increase by 20 percent starting next month. There is no inventory to meet the unexpected sales forecast.								
5. Dan, the personnel director, sent you a memo informing you that one of your employees has resigned. Your turnover rate is one of the highest in the company.								
6. Michele told you that a Bob Furry called while you were out. He asked you to return his call, but wouldn't state why he was calling. You don't know who he is or what he wants.								
7. Phil, one of your best workers, wants an appointment to tell you about a situation that happened in the shop.								
8. Tom called and asked you to meet with him and a prospective customer for your product. The customer wants to meet you.								
9. John, your boss, called and said that he wants to see you about the decrease in the quality of your product.								
10. In the mail you got a note from Randolf, the president of your company, and an article from *The Wall Street Journal*. The note says FYI (for your information).								

BEHAVIOR MODEL VIDEO

Behavior Model Video 6–1 (4½ minutes), Delegation, shows Steve, production manager, delegating the completion of production output forms to Dale, following the steps in Model 6–2.

This video serves as a behavior model that can be used prior to conducting Skill-Building Exercise 6–2, Delegating Authority.

*skillbuilder

R

Skill-Building Exercise 6–2

Delegating Authority

Preparing for Skill-Building Exercise 6–2
Read and understand the material on delegating.

Doing Skill-Building Exercise 6–2 in Class

Objective
To experience and develop skills in delegating authority.

Preparation
You should have read, and understood, the text material on delegating with the use of a model.

Experience
You will delegate, be delegated to, and observe the delegation of a task, and then evaluate the effectiveness of the delegated task. You may also see a video example of how to delegate using the delegation model.

Procedure 1 (4–8 minutes)
Break into as many groups of three as possible with the remainder in groups of two. Each person in the group picks a number 1, 2, or 3. Number 1 will be the first to delegate a task, then 2, and then 3. The level of difficulty of the delegation will increase with the number.

Each person then reads his or her delegation situation (1, 2, or 3) and plans how he or she will delegate the task. If you prefer, you can use an actual delegation from a past or present job. Just be sure to fully explain the situation to the delegatee. Be sure to follow the four delegation steps in this chapter. You may

use the operational planning sheet in Figure 5–4 to help you when you delegate. An observer sheet is included at the end of this exercise for giving feedback on each delegation.

Delegation Situation 1
Delegator (No. 1). You are a college student with a paper due in three days for your 10 A.M. class. It must be typed. You don't type well, so you have decided to hire someone to do it for you. The going rate is $1.50 per page. Think of an actual paper you have done in the past or will do in the future. Plan to delegate (you may use the operational planning sheet). Be sure to include the course name, paper title, special typing instructions, and so on. Assume that you are meeting the typist for the first time. He or she doesn't know you.
Delegatee (No. 2). Assume that you do typing and are willing to do the job.

Delegation Situation 2
Delegator (No. 2). You are the manager of a fast-food restaurant. In the past, you have scheduled the workers. Your policy is to keep changing the workers' schedules. You have decided to delegate the scheduling to your assistant manager. This person has never done any scheduling but appears to be very willing and confident about taking on new responsibility. Plan your delegation (you may use the operational planning sheet).

Delegatee (No. 3). Assume that you are interested in doing the scheduling if the manager delegates the task effectively.

Delegation Situation 3

Delegator (No. 3). You own and manage your own business. You have eight employees, one of whom is the organization's secretary. The secretary presently uses an old memory typewriter, which needs to be replaced. You are not sure whether it should be replaced with a word processor or a computer (with word-processing software). You can afford to spend up to $2,500. You try to keep costs down and get the most for your money. Because the secretary will use the new machine, you believe that this employee should be involved in, or maybe even make, the decision. The secretary has never purchased equipment and you believe will be somewhat insecure about the assignment. Plan your delegation (you may use the operational planning sheet).

Delegatee (No. 1). Assume that you are able to do the job but are somewhat insecure. Accept the task if the delegator "participates" effectively.

Procedure 2 (7–10 minutes)

A. *Delegation Situation 1.* Delegator 1 delegates the task (role-play) to number 2. Number 3 is the observer. As the delegation takes place, the observer uses the form at the end of this exercise to provide feedback on the effectiveness of the delegator. Answer the questions on the form.

B. *Integration.* The observer (or number 3) leads a discussion of the effectiveness of the delegation, although all team members should participate. Do not continue until you are told to do so.

Procedure 3 (7–10 minutes)

A. *Delegation Situation 2.* Follow procedure 2A, except number 2 is now the delegator, number 3 is the delegatee, and number 1 is the observer.

B. *Integration.* Follow procedure 2B with number 3 as the observer. Do not continue until you are told to do so.

Procedure 4 (7–10 minutes)

A. *Delegation Situation 3.* Follow procedure 2A, except number 3 is now the delegator, number 1 is the delegatee, and number 2 is the observer. If you are in a group of two, be an additional observer for another group.

B. *Integration.* Follow procedure 2B with number 1 as observer.

Conclusion

The instructor may lead a class discussion and make concluding remarks.

Application (2–4 minutes)

What did I learn from this experience? How will I use this knowledge in the future?

Sharing

Volunteers give their answers to the application section.

Note: Remember that the process does not end with delegating the task; you must control (check progress at control points and help when needed) to ensure that the task is completed as scheduled.

Observer Form

During the delegation process, the observer checks off the items performed by the delegators. Items not checked were not performed. After the delegation, the delegator and delegatee also check off the items. This sheet is used for all three situations. Use the appropriate vertical column for each situation.

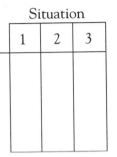

Delegation items for all situations	Situation		
	1	2	3

Did the delegator follow these steps:

Step 1. Explain the need for delegating and the reason for selecting the employee?

Step 2. Set an objective that defines responsibility and level of authority, and set a deadline?

Step 3. Develop a plan? Was it effective?

Step 4. Establish control checkpoints and hold the employee accountable?

Did the delegatee clearly understand what was expected of him or her and how to follow the plan?

_____

_____

How could the delegation be improved if done again?

_____

_____

_____

_____

7 Managing Change: Culture, Innovation, and Diversity

Learning Objectives

After studying this chapter, you should be able to:

1. Identify where the forces for change initiate.
2. List the four types of changes.
3. State the difference between a fact, a belief, and a value.
4. Describe the three levels of organizational culture and their relationship.
5. Explain intrapreneurship and its three roles.
6. State the core values of TQM.
7. Describe a learning organization's culture.
8. Discuss the relationship among diversity, innovation, and quality.
9. State the difference in the use of forcefield analysis and survey feedback.
10. Explain the difference between team building and process consultation.
11. Define the following **key terms** (in order of appearance in the chapter):

   types of change
   management information systems (MIS)
   stages of the change process
   organizational culture
   levels of culture
   core values of TQM
   learning organization

   organizational development (OD)
   OD interventions
   forcefield analysis
   survey feedback
   team building
   process consultation

Skill Development

skillbuilder **1.** You can develop your skill at identifying resistance to change so that you can implement change (Skill-Building Exercise 7–1).

Overcoming resistance to change is an organizing skill that utilizes conceptual and decision-making skills and human and communication skills. The exercise develops your interpersonal leader role and the decisional role of entrepreneur. The SCANS skill competencies of using resources, interpersonal skills, information, and systems, as well as the basic, thinking, and personal qualities foundation skills are also developed.

IBM has two fundamental missions. First, the company strives to lead in the creation, development, and manufacture of the industry's most advanced information technologies, including computer systems, software, networking systems, storage devices, and microelectronics. Second, IBM translates these advanced technologies into value for its customers worldwide—through its sales and professional services units in North America, Europe/Middle East/Africa, Asia Pacific, and Latin America. The company strives to provide products and services that improve customers' competitive position, enhance their own customer service, increase their productivity, and enrich their personal lives. IBM is making technology easier to use and manage. IBM's companywide crusade is translating technology into value for customers.

IBM has six strategic imperatives: (1) Exploiting its technology. (2) Increasing its share of the client/server computing market. (3) Establishing leadership in the emerging network-centric computing world. (4) Realigning the way it delivers value to customers. (5) Rapidly expanding its position in key emerging geographic markets. (6) Leveraging its size and scale to achieve cost and market advantages.

IBM invented the personal computer (PC) and held the strong leading market share for several years. However, with its higher prices and the increasing quality of its clones, IBM's market share dropped below 5 percent. Compaq is now the strong market leader, and Packard Bell also outsells IBM. Dell and Gateway are coming on strong. Who would have bet that the small upstart Compaq would overtake the giant IBM? Watching the great success of Microsoft, IBM decided that it should become a major player in the software and networking operation industry. Who

would have bet that the small upstart Microsoft would become larger than the giant IBM?

In June 1995, IBM acquired Lotus Development Corporation for $3.5 billion. Lotus's main products include 1-2-3, Ami Pro, Freelance, Notes, and cc: Mail. IBM wanted Notes to compete against Microsoft in the battle to control the market for "groupware" that runs on computers linked into networks. Throughout this chapter, we focus on the changes brought about through IBM's acquisition of Lotus.[1]

For current information on IBM, use Internet address **http://www.ibm.com**. For ideas on using the Internet, see Appendix B.

MANAGING CHANGE

Plato said, "Change takes place no matter what deters it." Managers are undergoing revolutionary changes in response to the global marketplace.[2] An organization's long-term success is determined by its ability to mange change.[3] Unfortunately for IBM, it was slow to change its PCs and lost market share, and it was slow to take advantage of the software opportunities when Compaq and Microsoft were quick to change.

Your ability to flexibly change with the diversifying global environment will affect your career success. Your college education should help prepare you to continue your lifelong journey of learning and changing. In this section, you will learn about the forces for change, types of change, stages in the change process, resistance to change, overcoming resistance to change, and change models.

1. Identify where the forces for change initiate.

Forces for Change

The Environment. The changing business environment presents many challenges.[4] An organization interacts with its external and internal environment. Review Chapter 2 for more details on how these factors require change in organizations and how the organization should proact and interact, rather than merely react, with the environment.

The Management Functions and Change. Most plans that managers develop require changes. When managers organize and delegate tasks, they often require employees to make some changes in their regular routine. When managers hire, orient, train, and evaluate performance, change is re-

WORK APPLICATION

1. Give an example of a force that resulted in a change in an organization you work or have worked for.

quired. Leadership calls for influencing employees, often to change in some way, and control may require new methods or techniques. Acquiring Lotus was part of IBM's plan to achieve its goal in software leadership. Adding Lotus to the company required some reorganization of IBM. IBM required changes at Lotus.

Types of Change

The types of change refer to what the organization will actually be changing. The four **types of change** *are strategy, structure, technology, and people*. Figure 7–1 presents the four types of change. Because of the systems effect, you need to consider the repercussions a change in one variable (type of change) will have on the other variables and plan accordingly.

Strategy. An organization may change its strategy at the corporate, business, and/or functional level. At the corporate level, IBM lost money from 1991 to 1993. During this time, IBM had a turnaround and retrenchment strategy. In 1995, IBM stabilized, changed its strategy to growth, and acquired Lotus as a related diversification growth strategy.

Structure. Structure commonly follows strategy. In other words, a change in strategy results in a change in structure. When IBM acquired Lotus, its organizational design changed. Over time, organizations often make changes in their structure. In the last chapter you learned about organizational structure; Figure 7–1 summarizes the areas. With the trend toward the global environment, organizations are restructuring, and the use of self-managed work teams continues.

2. List the four types of changes.

types of change
Strategy, structure, technology, and people.

Figure 7-1
Types of Organizational Change

STRATEGY	STRUCTURE	TECHNOLOGY	PEOPLE
Corporate (growth, stability, and turnaround and retrenchment)	**Principles** (unity of command and direction, chain of command, span of management, division of labor, coordination, balanced responsibility and authority, delegation, and flexibility)	**Machines** **Systems Process** **Information Process** **Automation**	**Skills** **Performance** **Attitudes** **Behavior**
Business Level (prospecting, defending, and analyzing)	**Authority** (formal and informal, levels of, line and staff, and centralized and decentralized)		
Functional (marketing, operations, finance, and human resources)	**Organizational Design** (departmentalization)		
	Job Design (job simplification, rotation, enlargement, enrichment, and work teams)		

management information systems (MIS)
Formal systems for collecting, processing, and disseminating the necessary information that aids managers in decision making.

Technology. Technological changes, such as the computer, fax, e-mail, and the Internet, have increased the rate of speed at which change takes place. Technology is a commonly used method of increasing productivity to gain competitive leverage.[5] Wal-Mart is committed to technology; operating costs are less than its competitors as a result.

Technology often leads to a change in strategy or structure. Lotus's new groupware was a major factor in IBM's changing its strategy and structure through the acquisition. Some of the major areas of technology change include:

- *Machines.* New machinery or equipment is introduced on an ongoing basis. The computer is a sophisticated machine that is also a part of many other machines.

- *Systems Process.* Systems process refers to how the organization transforms inputs into outputs. Changes in the systems process, such as the sequence of the work, is a technology change.

- *Information Process.* With the aid of the computer, organizations have changed the way they process information. **Management information systems (MIS)** *are formal systems for collecting, processing, and disseminating the necessary information that aids managers in decision making.* MIS attempt to centralize and integrate all or most of the organization's information, such as finance, production, inventory, and sales. In this way the departments can coordinate their efforts in working with the systems effect. IBM is in the information technology business to help other organizations use information technology.

- *Automation. Automation* is the simplification or reduction of human effort to do a job. Computers and other machines have allowed robots to replace people.[6] Automation does not take away jobs; it changes the types of jobs.[7] The need for training and higher levels of skill will continue into the future.[8] Your college education should help you to become flexible and to continue to upgrade your skills with technology changes. If you want raises and promotions, be the first to voluntarily learn new technologies.[9]

People. Tasks refer to the day-to-day things that employees do to perform their jobs, and tasks change with technology and structural changes. As tasks change, people's *skills* and *performance* must change. Organizations often attempt to change employees' *attitudes* and *behavior*. A change in organizational culture is also considered a people change. You will learn about culture in the next section.

People develop and implement strategy and structure. People also create, manage, and use technology; therefore, people are the most important resource. Change in other variables will not be effective without people. So it is important to get the input and participation of those who will be most affected by changes.[10] IBM was not doing well, so it replaced its chairman and CEO John Akers with Louis Gerstner, who had no computer experience, to turn IBM around.

Stages in the Change Process

People go through four distinct stages in the change process. *The four* **stages of the change process** *are denial, resistance, exploration, and commitment.*[11]

1. *Denial.* When people first hear the rumors though the grapevine that change is coming, they deny that it will happen at all, or to them. Originally, managers at Lotus were against the sale to IBM. Lotus's chairman and CEO, Jim Manzi, told IBM that Lotus was not for sale.

2. *Resistance.* Once people get over the initial shock and realize that change is going to be a reality, they resist the change. You need to accept the fact that resistance to change is part of human nature.[12] Lotus began to take steps to stop the sale to IBM. There were rumors that Manzi would quit or be let go if IBM bought Lotus.

3. *Exploration.* When the change begins to be implemented, employees explore the change, often through training, and better understand how it will affect them. After discussions with CEO Gerstner, and thinking about IBM's offer for him to stay as chairman and CEO of Lotus, Manzi accepted the offer.

4. *Commitment.* Through exploration, employees determine their level of commitment to making the change a success. The level of commitment can change. Manzi's eventual resignation showed lack of commitment to Lotus being part of IBM.

Figure 7–2 illustrates the change process. Notice that the stages are in a circular formation because change is an ongoing process not a linear one, and people can regress as the arrows show.

Resistance to Change and How to Overcome It

Most change programs fail because of employee resistance.[13] You will now learn why people resist change, and how to overcome resistance to change. See Figure 7–3 for an overview.

---

stages of the change process
Denial, resistance, exploration, and commitment.

Figure 7-2
Stages in the Change Process

Resistance to Change	Overcoming Resistance
Uncertainty	Trust climate for change
Inconvenience	Plan
Self-interest	State why change is needed and how it will affect employees
Loss	Create a win-win situation
Control	Involve employees
	Provide support

Figure 7-3
Resistance to Change and Ways to Overcome Resistance

Resistance to Change. Five of the major reasons employees resist change are:

- *Uncertainty.* Fear of the unknown outcome of change is common. People often get anxious and nervous and resist change in order to cope with their feelings.[14] Employees at Lotus were uncertain about how the company would change with IBM ownership. Would their jobs change, or worse, would they be eliminated?

- *Inconvenience.* People usually do not want to disrupt the way things are because they are comfortable. At a minimum, employees have to learn new ways, and they may need training to learn new skills. Employees of Lotus were inconvenienced by IBM.

- *Self-Interest.* People resist change that threatens their own self-interest. Employees are commonly more concerned about their best interest than the organization's. If Lotus CEO Manzi knew he would be fired if IBM bought Lotus, he may have resisted the acquisition.

- *Loss.* With change, jobs may possibly be lost. Change may require an economic loss due to a pay cut, which has happened in the airline industry. A change in work assignments or schedules may create a loss of social relationships.

- *Control.* Change can also result in an actual or perceived loss of power, status, security, and especially control. People may resent the feeling that their destiny is being controlled by someone else. Lotus employees were concerned about IBM taking control. How much control, and what types of control, would IBM use?

Overcoming Resistance to Change. Six of the major things you can do to overcome resistance to change follow. IBM could have used all of these methods to overcome resistance to change at Lotus.

1. *Develop a Positive Trust Climate for Change.* Develop and maintain good human relations. Make employees realize you have their best interest in mind and develop mutual trust. Constantly look for better ways to do things. Encouraging employees to suggest changes and implementing their ideas are important parts of continuous improvement.[15]

2. *Plan.* To implement changes successfully takes good planning. You need to identify the possible resistance to change and plan how to overcome it. View change from the employee's position. Set clear objectives so employees know exactly what the change is and how it affects them. The next four methods should be part of your plan.

3. *Clearly State Why the Change Is Needed and How It Will Affect Employees.* Communication is the key to change. Employees want and need to know why the change is necessary and how it will affect them both positively and negatively. Be open and honest with employees. Giving employees the facts as far in advance as possible helps them to overcome the fear of the unknown. If the grapevine starts to send incorrect facts, correct the information as quickly as possible.

4. *Create a Win-Win Situation.* The goal of human relations is to meet employee needs while achieving departmental/organizational objectives. To overcome resistance to change, be sure to answer the other parties' unasked question, "What's in it for me?" When people can see how they benefit, they are more willing to change. If the organization is going to benefit by the change, so should the employees.

5. *Involve Employees.* To create a win-win situation, involve employees. A commitment to change is usually critical to its successful implementation. Employees who participate in developing changes are more committed to them than employees who have changes assigned to them.[16]

6. *Provide Support.* Since training is very important to successful change, give as much advance notice and training as possible before the change takes place. Giving thorough training helps reduce frustration and helps employees realize they can be successful with the change. Mistakes should be used as learning experiences toward the change.[17]

A Model for Identifying and Overcoming Resistance to Change

Before making changes, you should anticipate how employees will react. Resistance to change involves the variables of intensity, source, and focus, and explains why people are reluctant to change.[18]

Intensity. People have different attitudes toward change. Some thrive on it and some are upset by it; many resist it at first but gradually accept it. As a manager of change, you must anticipate if resistance will be strong, weak, or somewhere in between. Intensity will be lower if you use the six methods for overcoming resistance to change.

3. State the difference between a fact, a belief, and a value.

Source. There are three major sources of resistance:

1. *Facts.* The facts (provable statements that identify reality) of the change are often circulated inaccurately through the grapevine. People tend to use facts selectively to prove their point. Facts used correctly help to overcome fear of the unknown.

2. *Beliefs.* Facts can be proven; beliefs cannot. Beliefs are subjective opinions that can be shaped by others. Our beliefs lead us to think and feel that a change is correct or incorrect or good or bad. Differences in perception can cause resistance to change.

3. *Values.* Values are what people believe are worth pursuing or doing. What we value is important to us. Values pertain to right and wrong and prioritization.

Focus. There are three major focuses of resistance:

1. *Self.* People naturally want to know "What's in it for me? What will I gain or lose?" When the facts of change have a negative effect on employees, creating a perceived loss, employees resist the change.

2. *Others.* After considering what's in it for them, or when the change does not affect them, people tend to consider how the change will affect their friends, peers, and colleagues. If employees analyze the facts and believe the change will affect others negatively, they may be resistant to the change.

3. *Work Environment.* The work environment includes the physical setting, the work itself, and the climate. People like to be in control of their environment, and they resist changes that take away their control.

Model 7–1 shows a resistance matrix with examples of each area of resistance. Use the matrix to identify the intensity, source, and focus of resistance. Once you have identified the probable resistance to change, you can work at overcoming it. Note that intensity is outside the matrix because it can be strong, moderate, or weak for each of the nine matrix boxes. In Skill-Building Exercise 7–1, you will use the resistance matrix to identify the source and focus of change.

WORK APPLICATION

4. Identify your resistance to change in Work Application 3. Use the resistance matrix and identify the box number, source, and focus name.

ORGANIZATIONAL CULTURE

organizational culture
The shared values, beliefs, and assumptions of how its members should behave.

An **organizational culture** *consists of the shared values, beliefs, and assumptions of how its members should behave.* Organizational culture is an approach to understanding how organizations function, or it gives meaning to the organization's way of doing things. Think of culture as the organization's personality. Members of an organization need to understand its culture.[19, 20, 21] In this section, you will learn about the three levels of culture, strong and weak cultures, and changing cultures.

Sources of Resistance (fact → belief → value)

Model 7-1
Resistance Matrix

Focus of Resistance (work → other → self)

1. Facts about self	4. Beliefs about self	7. Values pertaining to self
• I never did the task before. • I failed the last time I tried.	• I'm too busy to learn it. • I'll do it, but don't blame me if it's wrong.	• I like the way I do my job now. Why change? • I like working in a group.
2. Facts about others	5. Beliefs about others	8. Values pertaining to others
• She has the best performance record in the department. • Other employees told me it's hard to do.	• He just pretends to be busy to avoid extra work. • She's better at it than I am; let her do it.	• Let someone else do it; I do not want to work with her. • I like working with him. Don't cut him from our department.
3. Facts about the work environment	6. Beliefs about the work environment	9. Values pertaining to the work environment
• Why don't you pay me more to do it? • It's over 100 degrees. Can't we wait?	• This is a lousy job. • The pay here is too low.	• I don't care if we meet the goal or not. • The new task will make me work inside. I'd rather be outside.

Intensity (high, medium, or low for each box)

Source: Adapted from Ken Hultman, *Resistance Matrix: The Path of Least Resistance* (Austin, Texas: Learning Concepts, 1979).

Three Levels of Culture

The three **levels of culture** *are behavior, values and beliefs, and assumptions.*[22] Figure 7–4 illustrates the three levels of culture.

Level 1. Behavior. Behavior is the observable things that people do and say, or the actions employees take. *Artifacts* result from behavior and include written and spoken language, dress, material objects, and so on. Other terms used to describe level 1 behavior include rites, celebrations, ceremonies, heroes, jargon, myths, and stories.

Managers, particularly top managers who founded the organization, have a strong influence on culture. The late Sam Walton, founder of Wal-Mart; Tom Watson, founder of IBM; Ray Kroc, founder of McDonald's; and Mary Kay, founder of Mary Kay Cosmetics, are heroes to employees who tell stories about them.

4. Describe the three levels of organizational culture and their relationship.

levels of culture
Behavior, values and beliefs, and assumptions.

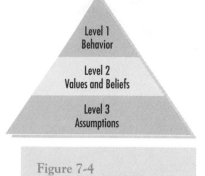

Figure 7-4
Three Levels of Culture

Level 2. Values and Beliefs. Values represent the way we ought to behave and beliefs represent if-then statements. If I do X, then Y will happen. Values and beliefs provide the operating principles that guide decision making and behavior that result in level 1 culture. We can observe behavior, but not values and beliefs. We can only infer from peoples' behavior what they value and believe. Values and beliefs often come from the mission statement; some organizations have formal statements of their values and beliefs, often called philosophy or ideology. Values identify what it takes to be successful; for example, McDonald's has "Q, S, C, V—Quality, Service, Cleanliness, and Value." Larry Robinson, head of a Cleveland-based chain of jewelry stores, says that the golden rule, "Do unto others as you would have them do unto you," has been the base of the company's corporate culture that took the chain from 2 to 72 stores. Organizations also use slogans to convey values, such as Ford's "Quality Is Job 1."

Level 3. Assumptions. *Assumptions* are values and beliefs that are deeply ingrained as unquestionably true. Employees tend to unquestionably understand how things are. Because assumptions are shared, they are rarely discussed. They serve as an automatic pilot to guide behavior. In fact, people often feel threatened when assumptions are challenged. If you question employees on why they do something, or suggest a change, they often respond with statements like, "That's the way it's always been done." Assumptions are often the most stable and enduring part of culture and are difficult to change.

Notice that behavior is at the top of the diagram in Figure 7–4. However, the assumptions and values and beliefs affect the behavior, not the other way around, or cause and effect work from the bottom up.

Strong and Weak Cultures

Organizational cultural strength is on a continuum from strong to weak. Organizations with *strong cultures* have employees who unconsciously know the shared assumptions; consciously know the values and beliefs; agree with the shared assumptions, values, and beliefs; and behave as expected. Organizations with many employees who do not behave as expected have weak cultures. When employees do not agree with the generally accepted shared values, they may become rebels and fight the culture.

Fortune magazine has an annual edition of "Most Admired Companies" that have the characteristics of strong organizational culture. Companies with strong cultures include Amdahl, Boeing, Dana Corporation, Digital, Emerson Electric, Fluor, IBM, Johnson & Johnson, Marriott, Procter & Gamble, and 3M.

The primary benefits of a strong culture include easier communication and cooperation. Unity of direction is common, and consensus is easier to reach. The primary disadvantage is the threat of becoming stagnant. To

WORK APPLICATION

5. Describe the organizational culture at all three levels for a firm you work or have worked for. Does the organization have a strong or weak culture?

change with the environment requires questioning the assumptions, values, and beliefs and changing them when necessary. One of the major reasons Gerstner was hired as CEO of IBM was because he was an outsider not prejudiced by the culture.

Managing and Changing Cultures

Organizational culture can be managed and changed.[23] Organizations that have changed and managed culture include the City of San Diego, Fiat, Ford, GM, Pacific Mutual, Pacific Telsis, Polaroid, Procter & Gamble, Tektronix, and TRW. Part of Gerstner's job when he was hired as CEO was to change IBM's culture. Successful organizations realize that managing culture is not a program with a starting and ending date. It is an ongoing organizationwide process called *organizational development* (OD).[24] You will learn about OD later in this chapter.

A change in culture is considered a *people-type* change. When changing culture, it must be changed at all three levels. A culture of success changes over time, and businesses that fail to change their culture lose their competitive advantage.[25]

Culture is an important consideration when merging with or acquiring a business. A mismatch in cultures can lead to failure. It is common for larger businesses to acquire small companies and to try to change their culture to match their own without success.[26] IBM has had a history of problems with acquisitions. IBM and Lotus had different cultures. IBM was larger and more bureaucratic than freewheeling Lotus. IBM planned to maintain Lotus as a freestanding company. But, at the same time, IBM had to integrate Lotus products into its own to make the entire IBM company a success.

When developing or changing culture, remember that it's not what you, as a manager, say is a value; it's what you measure, reward, and control that will influence behavior. For example, if management says ethics are important, but does not punish people for unethical behavior or reward ethical behavior, employees will not be ethical.

You will learn in the next two sections how organizations are creating organizational cultures to manage innovation, quality, and diversity.

APPLYING THE CONCEPT

AC 7–2 Strong and Weak Cultures

Identify each statement as being characteristic of an organization with a
a. strong culture   b. weak culture

_____ **6.** "Walking around this department during my job interview, I realized I'd have to wear a jacket and tie every day."

_____ **7.** "I'm a little tired of hearing about how our company founders conducted business. We all know the stories, so why do people keep telling them?"

_____ **8.** "I've never attended a meeting with people who all seem to act differently. I guess I can just be me rather than trying to act in an acceptable manner to others."

_____ **9.** "It's hard to say what is really important because management says quality is important. They force us to work at too fast a pace and they know we send out defective products just to meet orders."

_____ **10.** "I started to tell this ethnic joke and the other employees all gave me a dirty look."

INNOVATION

Recall from Chapter 3 that *creativity* is a way of thinking that generates new ideas and an *innovation* is the implementation of a new idea. Two important types of innovations are product innovation (new things) and process innovation (new ways of doing things).

Organizations need to develop technological innovations to keep ahead of competition, or at least to keep up with competitors.[27] Successful companies use innovation as a competitive advantage.[28] In this section, you will learn about organizational structures and cultures that stimulate creativity and innovation and about quality.

WORK APPLICATION

6. Give an example of an innovation from an organization you work or have worked for. Be sure to specify if it was a product or process innovation.

Innovative Organizational Structures

Organizational structures (Chapter 6) that stimulate innovation are commonly flat organizations with limited bureaucracy, have a generalist division of labor, coordinate with cross-functional teams, and are flexible. Use of the informal system is common and authority is decentralized. Job design includes job enrichment and work teams based on sociotechnical systems.

Large companies commonly use divisional structure to create small units that can be innovative. Innovative organizations commonly create separate systems for innovative groups,[29] such as new venture units (skunkworks). To develop the Macintosh computer, Steve Jobs took a small group of engineers and programmers and set up operations apart from the remainder of the plant. Colgate-Palmolive created Colgate Venture Company as a separate unit, and General Foods developed Culinova Group as a unit to which employees can take their ideas for possible development.

Within the human resources function, creative employees are *recruited* and *trained*, and a *reward* system that encourages creativity and innovation is developed.[30] Rewarding innovation leads to increased creativity. Many organizations provide financial and nonfinancial rewards to employees, as individuals and groups, that develop innovations. Organizations commonly use cash, prizes (such as trips), praise, and recognition to encourage people to be creative. Many companies give a percentage of the savings/earnings for the first year. Monsanto gives $50,000 each year to the individual or group that develops the biggest commercial breakthrough.

Innovative Organizational Cultures

The best corporate cultures encourage creativity and innovation.[31] In other words, cultures that value innovation, develop the proper environment of believing it is possible, and assume that it is part of the job have innovative employee behavior.[32] Organizations known to have strong innovative cultures include Corning, Hewlett-Packard, Intel, Johnson & Johnson, Merck, Monsanto, Procter & Gamble, Rubbermaid, Texas Instruments, and 3M.

Such organizations develop structures to match, and become a part of, their innovative culture.

Innovative organizations tend to have similar cultures that encourage experimentation.[33] They usually have strong cultures and innovative organizational structures as discussed. Innovative cultures commonly have the following six characteristics:

- *Encouragement of Risk-Taking.* They encourage employees to be creative without fear of punishment due to failure. Mistakes and failure are expected, but they are not punished unless due to negligence. They are viewed as a learning experience. At 3M, around 60 percent of the innovations do not succeed in the marketplace.

- *Intrapreneurship.* Intrapreneurship encourages the development of new products and services that might become separate business units. Intrapreneurship commonly has three roles in large organizations. The *inventor* is the one who comes up with the creative idea. However, inventors often lack the skill to transform the idea into an innovation. The *champion* is the one responsible for transforming the idea into an innovation. The champion, usually a middle manager, believes in the idea and promotes it by finding a sponsor to provide the resources needed for the innovation. The *sponsor*, a top-level manager, supports the innovation by providing the resources and structure for the innovation. Sponsors deal with the politics necessary to get the resources. At Texas Instruments, only creative ideas with an acknowledged inventor, champion, and sponsor are formally transformed into innovations.

- *Open Systems.* Organizational members constantly scan the environment for creative ideas. Benchmarking (Chapter 4) is commonly used.

- *Focus on Ends Rather Than Means.* They tell employees the objectives (ends) but the employees decide on the means to achieve them.

- *Acceptance of Ambiguity and Impractical Ideas.* Requiring clear, practical ideas stifles creativity. They encourage employees to work on creative ideas even when it is not clear to managers what the employees are doing, and they do not have to have an immediate practical value for the ideas. What seems ambiguous and impractical sometimes ends up as a great innovation.

- *Tolerance of Conflict.* They encourage diversity of opinions as a means of coming up with creative ideas and improving on them.

3M is generally recognized as the leader in innovation. 3M uses six rules, listed in Figure 7–5, to stimulate innovation. These six rules, which have been copied by other companies, are deeply engraved into 3M's culture.

5. Explain intrapreneurship and its three roles.

WORK APPLICATION

7. Identify and explain how an organization you work or have worked for does or does not have each of the six characteristics of innovative cultures. Overall, does the organization have a creative culture?

Figure 7-5
3M's Rules for an Innovative Culture

- **Set goals for innovation.** 3M's goal is to have 25 to 30 percent of annual sales come from products that are five years old or less. About one-third of 3M's revenues come from new products.

- **Commit to research and development.** 3M invests close to twice as much in R&D as the average U.S. company. 3M has a goal to cut the time it takes to introduce new products in half.

- **Inspire intrapreneurship.** Champions are allowed to manage their products as if they were running their own businesses. 3M employees can spend 15 percent of their time on personal research interests unrelated to their current job.

- **Facilitate, don't obstruct.** Divisions are small and autonomous and have access to information and technical resources throughout the entire company. Researchers with good ideas receive $50,000 Genesis grants to develop their creative ideas into innovative products.

- **Focus on the customer.** Quality is defined by the customer.

- **Tolerate failure.** Managers know that mistakes will be made and that destructive criticism kills creativity. Employees know that if an idea fails, they will be encouraged to pursue other ideas.

APPLYING THE CONCEPT

AC 7–3 Innovative and Noninnovative Cultures

Identify each statement as being characteristic of an organization with an

a. innovative culture   b. noninnovative culture

_____ **11.** "We have a very tall organization."

_____ **12.** "I worked on trying to develop a faster rotating blade, but it didn't work. However, my boss gave me a very sincere thank you for trying."

_____ **13.** "It drives me crazy when I'm delegated a task and the boss tells me the details of how to do the job. Why can't I meet the objective my way for a change?"

_____ **14.** "This company makes heavy use of policies, procedures, and rules."

_____ **15.** "We have jobs that are broad in scope and a lot of autonomy to do the job the way the team wants to do it."

After all, it invented the PC. However, IBM will need some innovations to regain its leading PC position. Lotus had a more creative structure and culture than IBM, and it was important for IBM to stimulate creativity at its traditional divisions and especially at its new Lotus division.

QUALITY

An organizational culture can value both innovation and quality. In fact, the innovation structure is essentially the same for a total quality management (TQM) culture. Because all organizations have different cultures, they generally don't say they have a culture of innovation, not quality, or vice versa. Both innovation and quality cultures focus on creating customer value. One slight difference is the emphasis on innovation. Organizations that focus primarily on innovation, like 3M, tend to place more emphasis on developing new products. However, organizations that focus primarily on TQM place more emphasis on continuous improvement of their products and services through their systems and processes.[34] TQM is based on continuous innovation.[35]

Core Values of TQM. *The* **core values of TQM** *are (1) to focus every-one in the organization on delivering customer value and (2) to continuously im-prove the system and its processes.* The values of a TQM culture emphasize the importance of trust, open communication, willingness to confront and solve problems, openness to change, internal cooperation against external com-petition, and adaptability to the environment. TQM values people as the most important resource. Employees are well trained, and they work in teams.[36] Employees collect data and use science to improve customer value. A TQM culture is a strong culture in which values are directed toward the strategic purpose of aligning people, processes, and resources to create value for customers through continuous improvement for strategic purposes.

The late W. Edwards Deming developed 14 points for creating the TQM culture. Deming's points improve employees' perceptions of their own job satisfaction, organization quality, productivity, overall organizational ef-fectiveness, and organizational competitiveness.[37] Figure 7–6 presents the 14 points.

6. State the core values of TQM.

core values of TQM

(1) To focus everyone in the organization on delivering customer value and (2) to continuously improve the system and its processes.

WORK APPLICATION

8. Identify and explain TQM values that are part of the culture in an organization that you work or have worked for.

Figure 7-6
Deming's 14 Points for Creating the Total Quality Culture

1. Create constancy of purpose toward improvement of product and service, with the aim to become competitive, to stay in business, and to provide jobs.
2. Adopt a new philosophy. We are in a new economic age created by Japan. We can no longer live with commonly ac-cepted styles of American management, nor with commonly accepted levels of delays, mistakes, or defective products.
3. Cease dependence on inspection to achieve quality. Eliminate the need for inspection on a mass basis by building quality into the product in the first place.
4. End the practice of awarding business on the basis of price tag. Instead, minimize total cost.
5. Improve constantly and forever the system of production and service to improve quality and productivity, and thus constantly decrease costs.
6. Institute training on the job.
7. Institute supervision. The aim of supervision should be to help people, machines, and gadgets to do a better job. Supervision of management is in need of overhaul, as well as supervision of production workers.
8. Drive out fear so that everyone may work effectively for the company.
9. Break down the barriers between departments. People in research, design, sales, and production must work as a team to foresee problems of production and use that may be encountered with the product or service.
10. Eliminate slogans, exhortations, and targets for the work force that ask for zero defects and new levels of productiv-ity. Such exhortations only create adversarial relationships. The bulk of the causes of low productivity belong to the system, and thus lie beyond the power of the work force.
11. Eliminate work standards that prescribe numerical quotas for the day. Substitute aids and helpful supervision.
12. Remove the barriers that rob the hourly worker of his or her right to pride of workmanship. The responsibility of su-pervisors must be changed from sheer numbers to quality. Remove the barriers that rob people in management and engineering of their right to pride of workmanship. This means abolishment of the annual rating, or merit rating, and management by objectives.
13. Institute a vigorous program of education and retraining.
14. Put everybody in the company to work to accomplish the transformation.

The Continuous Improvement (TQM) Culture. Research indicates a relationship between culture and quality, and between culture and employee performance.[38] TQM has been successful. The TQM focus on service increases customer perception of service quality,[39] which can lead to higher sales. Techneglas developed TQM that resulted in significant productivity and quality gains.[40] Emerson Electric Rosemount reduced manufacturing costs by 50 percent and cut cycle time by 62 percent in three years due to TQM.[41] Hoewever, TQM has also had its problems; it has been said that it has had more failure than success.[42] One of the reasons for its lack of success is the fact that TQM is not a program. Many organizations that have failed implemented TQM as a program, rather than as a culture with TQM values of continuous improvement and change. A culture of resistance to change is the biggest hurdle in implementing quality initiatives. Even organizations that have successfully implemented TQM systems nevertheless exhibit a reluctance to change much of their organizational culture. A true quality culture is one in which the organization is willing to change its culture through continuous quality improvements.[43] A learning organization changes its culture as needed.[44]

7. Describe a learning organization's culture.

The Learning Organization

The concept of the learning organization has developed out of the systems view of organizations. In a learning organization, everyone in the organization understands that the world is changing rapidly, that they must be aware of these changes, adapt to changes and, more important, be forces for change. *The **learning organization** has a culture with a capacity to learn, adapt, and change with its environment to continuously increase customer value.*

learning organization
The organization has a culture with a capacity to learn, adapt, and change with its environment to continuously increase customer value.

Organizations need to focus on building corporate learning instead of only developing individual skills and knowledge.[45] Many organizations are building learning organizations.[46] The learning organization appears to be the model for a fast-changing work enviroment.[47] A learning organization culture needs to include good human resources policies for recruiting, retaining, and developing highly skilled people; facilitate horizontal knowledge flows to allow the transfer, sharing, and leveraging of individual knowledge and expertise; and create a culture that is based on trust to fully exploit knowledge and expertise.[48] CEO Gerstner seems to be moving IBM toward becoming a learning organization.

8. Discuss the relationship among diversity, innovation, and quality.

DIVERSITY

Diversity programs have replaced most equal employment opportunity (EEO) and affirmative action (AA) programs. EEO stressed treating all employees equally, whereas AA was created to correct the past exclusion of women and minorities from organizations. AA established percentages and quotas. Then came reverse discrimination and essentially the end of AA. Some argue that AA has proven detrimental to the very people it was designed to help.[49] Although quotas are no longer used, many organizations are actively recruiting a diverse work force,[50] because they realize that a diverse workplace responds better to problems. A greater variety of backgrounds ceates a greater variety of solutions.[51] Diversity programs help the individual, group, and organization.[52] Knowing the value of a diverse work force, major hotels, as one example, are implementing strong initiatives to promote diversity.[53] In this section you wil learn about diversity and culture, valuing versus managing diversity, gender diversity, and mentors.

Diversity and Culture

An organizational culture can value innovation, quality, and diversity. In fact, the same organization structure supports all three values. According to the National Performance Review report, a relationship exists between quality and diversity. The report stated that before organizations can improve the quality of their services, they must first understand and address the requirements of all their employees.

While all organizations have different cultures, they can develop cultures that value diversity.[54] The approach to developing a culture that values diversity is to recognize the realities of the new work force and how this affects the efficiency and effectiveness of the organization as a system.

When we talk about diversity, we are referring to characteristics of individuals that shape their identities and their experiences in the workplace. *Diversity* refers to the degree of differences among members of a group or an organization. If you are wondering if diversity is really all that important, the answer is yes. There is a total lack of homogeneity in this world. Over the next decade, 85 percent of the labor force increase will be minorities and women.[55] It has been estimated that by the year 2030 less than 50 percent of the U.S. population will be white. Diversity in the workplace is a major concern of managers. Therefore, managing diversity will constitute a large portion of management's agenda throughout the next century.[56]

People are diverse in many ways. Within the work force, the major groups include race/ethnicity, religion, gender, age, ability, and other. A few of the commonly listed "other" differences include military status, sexual preference, expectations and values, lifestyles, socioeconomic class, work styles, and function and/or position within the organization. As an employee and manager, you should deal with all people in an ethical and legal manner.

Valuing Diversity versus Managing Diversity

Valuing diversity emphasizes training employees of different races and ethnicity, religions, genders, ages, and abilities and with other differences to function together effectively. To be creative and innovative and to continuously improve customer value, employees must work in an atmosphere of dignity and trust to work together as a team. A poor atmosphere compromises employees' ability to cooperatively execute the processes through which work gets done. Diversity affects bottom-line profits. In other words, if people don't work well together, the organization does not work well.

Managing diversity emphasizes fully utilizing human resources through organizational actions that meet all employees' needs. Managing diversity can only be successful with a change in culture.[57] Managing diversity requires an organizational culture that values diversity and meets the needs of all groups of workers.

As illustrated in Figure 7–7, managing diversity requires four components. The first is top management support and commitment. Employees throughout the organization look to top management for examples. If top management is committed and supports diversity, so will others at all levels. Diversity leadership refers to having top-level managers responsible for managing diversity. The diversity leaders must develop diversity policies and practices so that diversity funnels throughout the organization. The last and very important part of managing diversity is to provide employees with diversity training so that the diverse workers can work as a team. Exercise 7–1, Diversity Training, is an example diversity training session to better understand differences.

Gender Diversity

Before you learn about gender, complete Self-Assessment Exercise 7–1 to determine your attitude toward women at work.

The traditional family in which the husband worked and the wife was not employed is no longer the majority; two-income marriages are now the

Figure 7-7
Managing Diversity

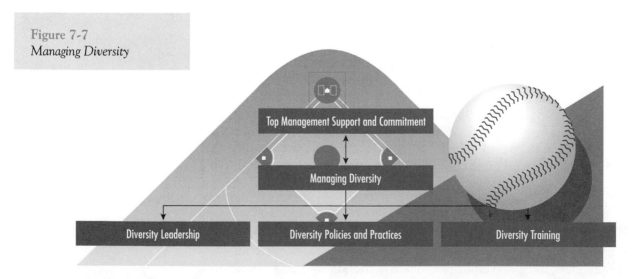

Self-Assessment Exercise 7–1

Women at Work

For each of the following ten statements, select the response that best describes your honest belief about women at work. Place the number 1, 2, 3, 4, or 5 on the line before each statement.

5—Strongly agree   4—Agree   3—Not sure
2—Disagree   1—Strongly disagree

____ 1. Women lack the education necessary to get ahead.

____ 2. Women working has caused rising unemployment among men.

____ 3. Women are not strong enough or emotionally stable enough to succeed in high-pressure jobs.

____ 4. Women are too emotional to be effective managers.

____ 5. Women managers have difficulty in situations calling for quick and precise decisions.

____ 6. Women work to earn extra money rather than to support a family.

____ 7. Women are out of work more often than men.

____ 8. Women quit work or take long maternity leaves when they have children.

____ 9. Women have a lower commitment to work than men.

____ 10. Women lack motivation to get ahead.

____ Total

To determine your attitude score, add up the total of your ten answers and place it on the total line and on the following continuum.

10 ———— 20 ———— 30 — ——— 40 ———— 50
Positive attitude   Negative attitude

Each statement is a commonly held attitude about women at work. However, through research, all of these statements have been shown to be false, or are considered myths about women at work. Such statements stereotype women unfairly and prevent women from gaining salary increases and promotions.

norm. However, on average, men put in less than half as much time as women on housework and child care.[58] According to the U.S. Bureau of Labor Statistics, by the year 2000 nearly 80 percent of women of working age are expected to be employed, and women will comprise almost half of the total work force.

Do women get equal treatment at work today? According to the Census Bureau, in spite of the Equal Pay Act, which requires equal pay for the same job, women's average hourly earnings are 70 percent of men's.[59] Although there has been progress in the promotion of minority group members and women, the glass ceiling still exists. The *glass ceiling* refers to the invisible barrier that prevents minorities and women from advancing beyond a certain level in organizations. Women hold about 37 percent of all domestic U.S. management positions.[60] However, women hold less than 5 percent of top management positions at large companies.[61] Women are also more commonly sexually harassed than men at work. *Sexual harassment* is any unwelcome behavior of a sexual nature.

APPLYING THE CONCEPT

AC 7–4 Sexual Harassment

Identify whether the following behavior is

a. sexual harassment   b. not sexual harassment

____ **16.** Ted tells Claire she is sexy and he'd like to take her out on a date.

____ **17.** Sue tells Josh he will have to go to a motel with her if he wants to be recommended for a promotion.

____ **18.** On the walls near Joel and Kathy's desks, they each hung pictures of nude men and women in view of other employees who walk by.

____ **19.** For the third time, after being politely told not to, Pat tells Chris an explicitly sexual joke.

____ **20.** Ray puts his hand on his secretary Lisa's shoulder as he talks to her.

- *Women want* recognition as equal partners and the active support of male colleagues. They want organizations to proactively address work and family issues.

- *Men want* the same freedom to express their emotions as women have. They want to be perceived as allies, not as the enemy. They also want to bridge the gap between dealing with women at home and work.[62]

As a manager you should realize that both males and females want a balance between work and family.

Mentoring. *Mentors* are higher-level managers who prepare high-potential employees for advancement. Mentoring is a program that enhances management skills, encourages diversity, and improves productivity.[63] Top-level managers should be mentors, and the program should not be limited to managers.[64] Mentoring programs have helped women and minorities to advance in organizations, thus helping to break the glass ceiling. However, if women and minorities who are less qualified are given special treatment it can result in reverse discrimination and may cause problems.[65] Having mentors who are willing and capable of working with you to develop your knowledge, abilities, and skills can help you in both your professional and personal life. So, regardless of gender and race, ask about mentoring opportunities at work. If the organization you work for does not have a mentoring program, select a possible mentor and ask the person to mentor you.

ORGANIZATIONAL DEVELOPMENT

organizational development (OD)
The ongoing planned process of change used as a means of improving performance through interventions.

In the first section of this chapter, you learned about change. Organizational development (OD) is the commonly used method of managing change.[66, 67] **Organizational development** *is the ongoing planned process of change used as a means of improving performance through interventions.* The human resources management department, discussed in the next chapter, is usually responsible for OD throughout the organization.[68] The *change agent* is the person selected by human resources management to be responsible for the OD program. The change agent may be a member of the organization or a hired consultant. In this section, you will learn about change models and interventions.

Change Models

Lewin's Change Model. In the early 1950s, Kurt Lewin developed a technique that is still used today for changing people's behavior, skills, and attitudes. Lewin's change model consists of three steps, listed in Figure 7–8.

1. *Unfreezing.* This step usually involves reducing the forces that are maintaining the status quo. Organizations sometimes accomplish unfreezing by introducing information that shows discrepancies between desired performance and actual performance.
2. *Moving.* This step shifts the behavior to a new level. This is the change process in which employees learn the new desirable behavior, values, and attitudes. Strategy, structure, technology, and people/culture changes may take place to reach desirable performance levels.
3. *Refreezing.* The desirable performance becomes the permanent way of doing things or the new status quo. Refreezing often takes place through reinforcement and support for the new behavior.

A Comprehensive Change Model. Lewin's change model requires a new formula for today's rapidly evolving business environment.[69] The model consists of five steps, listed in Figure 7–8:

1. *Recognize the Need for Change.* Clearly state the change needed—set objectives. Don't forget the systems effects. How will the change affect other areas of the organization?
2. *Identify Possible Resistance to the Change and Plan How to Overcome It.* Follow the guidelines in step 1.
3. *Plan the Change Interventions.* Based on the diagnosis of the problem, the appropriate intervention must be selected. You will learn some of the interventions used to facilitate change in this section. The change agent may select one or more interventions.

Lewin's Change Model	A Comprehensive Change Model	Figure 7-8 *Change Models*
Step 1. Unfreezing.	*Step 1.* Recognize the need for change.	
Step 2. Moving.	*Step 2.* Identify possible resistance to the change and plan how to overcome it.	
Step 3. Refreezing.	*Step 3.* Plan the change interventions.	
	Step 4. Implement the change interventions.	
	Step 5. Control the change.	

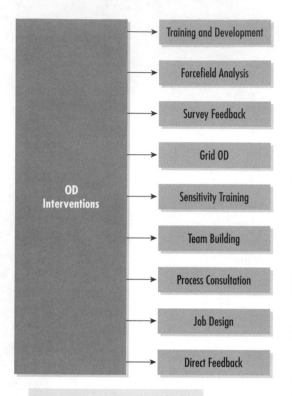

OD Interventions

- Training and Development
- Forcefield Analysis
- Survey Feedback
- Grid OD
- Sensitivity Training
- Team Building
- Process Consultation
- Job Design
- Direct Feedback

Figure 7-9
OD Interventions

OD interventions
Specific actions taken to implement specific changes.

9. State the difference in the use of forcefield analysis and survey feedback.

forcefield analysis
An OD intervention that diagrams the current level of performance, the hindering forces toward change, and the driving forces toward change.

survey feedback
An OD intervention that uses a questionnaire to gather data to use as the basis for change.

4. *Implement the Change Interventions.* The change agent, or someone selected, conducts the intervention to bring about the desired change.

5. *Control the Change.* Follow up to ensure that the change is implemented and maintained. Make sure the objective is met. If not, take corrective action.

Organizational Development Interventions

OD interventions *are specific actions taken to implement specific changes.* You will now learn about nine of the many OD interventions, listed in Figure 7–9.

Training and Development. Training and development are presented first because the other interventions often include some form of training. Training is the process of developing skills, behaviors, and attitudes to be used on the job.[70] You will learn about training in the next chapter. Recall that training is an important part of valuing diversity. Levi Strauss & Company has a $5-million-a-year valuing diversity educational program designed to get employees to become more tolerant of personal differences. IBM is highly regarded as one of the top companies in commitment to and quality of its training and development programs.

Forcefield Analysis. Forcefield analysis is particularly useful for small group (4 to 18 members) problem solving. **Forcefield analysis** *is an OD intervention that diagrams the current level of performance, the hindering forces toward change, and the driving forces toward change.* The process begins with an appraisal of the current level of performance. The present level of performance appears in the middle of the diagram. The hindering forces holding back performance are listed on the top or left part of the diagram. The driving forces keeping performance at this level are listed on the bottom or right of the diagram. After viewing the diagram, you develop strategies for maintaining or increasing the driving forces with simultaneous steps for decreasing hindering forces. For example, Figure 7-10 was developed for IBM's PC unit, which has dropped in market share. The solution selected should focus on the production problems and sales forecasting by marketing. After group members agree on the diagram, the solution often becomes clear to them as they develop a plan to change the present situation.

Survey Feedback. Survey feedback is one of the oldest and most popular OD techniques. **Survey feedback** *is an OD intervention that uses a questionnaire to gather data to use as the basis for change.* Survey feedback is commonly used in step 1 of the change model.[71] Different change agents will use slightly different approaches; however, a commonly used survey feedback program includes six steps:

1. Management and the change agent do some preliminary planning to develop an appropriate survey questionnaire.

2. The questionnaire is administered to all members of the organization/unit.

3. The survey data is analyzed to uncover problem areas for improvement.

4. The change agent feeds back the results to management.

5. Managers evaluate the feedback and discuss the results with their subordinates.

6. Corrective intervention action plans are developed and implemented.

Figure 7-10
Forcefield Analysis

Grid OD. Robert Blake and Jane Mouton developed a "packaged" approach to OD.[72] They developed a standardized format, procedures, and fixed goals. Grid OD is a six-phase program designed to improve management and organizational effectiveness. The six phases are:

1. *Training.* Teams of five to nine managers, ideally from different functional areas, are formed. During a week-long seminar, each team member assesses his or her leadership style by determining his or her position on the grid. (You will learn about the grid in Chapter 13.) They work at becoming 9,9 managers by developing skills in the areas of team building, communication, and problem solving.

2. *Team Development.* Managers return to the job and try to use their new skills as 9,9 managers, who show high concern for production and people.

3. *Intergroup Development.* Work groups improve their ability to cooperate and coordinate their efforts. This fosters joint problem-solving activities.

4. *Organizational Goal Setting.* Management develops an organization model it should strive to achieve.

5. *Goal Attainment.* The changes needed to become the model organization are determined and implemented.

6. *Stabilization.* The first five phases are evaluated to determine and stabilize positive changes and to identify areas for improvement or alteration.

Sensitivity Training. Sensitivity training includes a training group (or T-group) of 10 to 15 people. The training sessions have no agenda. People learn about how their behavior affects others and how others' behavior affects theirs. The popularity of T-groups peaked in the 1970s as organizations questioned the on-the-job value gained through the training. Although T-groups are still used,[73] they have largely been replaced by team building and process consultation.

10. Explain the difference between team building and process consultation.

team building
An OD intervention designed to help work groups increase structural and team dynamics performance.

Team Building. Team building is probably the most widely used OD technique today, and its popularity will continue as more companies use work teams.[74] The effectiveness of each team and all the teams working together directly affects the results of the entire organization. **Team building is an OD intervention designed to help work groups increase structural and team dynamics performance.** Team building can be used as a comprehensive OD technique in which the top executives go through the program by themselves, and then go through it with their middle managers, who then go through it with their supervisors, who then go through it with their employees. However, team building is more widely used as a means of helping new or existing groups in need of improving effectiveness.

Team-Building Goals. The goals of team-building programs will vary considerably, depending on the group's needs and the change agent's skills. Some of the typical goals include:

- To clarify the objectives of the team and the responsibilities of each team member.
- To identify problems preventing the team from accomplishing its objectives.
- To develop team problem-solving, decision-making, objective-setting, and planning skills.
- To develop open, honest working relationships based on trust and an understanding of group members.

The Team-Building Program. The team-building agendas and length of time vary with team needs and the change agent's skills. Typical programs go through six stages:

1. *Climate building and goals.* The program begins with the change agent trying to develop a climate of trust, support, and openness. The change agent discusses the program's purpose and goals based on data gathered prior to the program. Team members learn more about each other and share what they would like to accomplish—goals—through team building.

2. *Structure and team dynamics evaluation.* Team building is an intervention designed to improve both how the work is done (structure) and how team members work together as they do the work (team dynamics). The team evaluates its strengths and weaknesses in both areas. Team dynamics will be explained with process consultation, the next OD intervention.

3. *Problem identification.* The team identifies its strengths then its weaknesses or areas where it can improve. The problems come from the change

agent's interviews and/or the feedback survey. The team first lists several areas where it can improve. Then it prioritizes them in terms of how they will help the team improve performance.

4. *Problem solving.* The team takes the top priority and develops a solution. It then moves to the second priority, followed by the third, then fourth, and so on. Forcefield analysis can be used for problem solving.

5. *Training.* Team building often includes some form of training that addresses the problem(s) facing the group.

6. *Closure.* The program ends with a summarization of what has been accomplished. Team members commit to specific improvements in performance. Follow-up responsibility is assigned and a future meeting is set to evaluate results.[75]

APPLYING THE CONCEPT

AC 7–5 OD Interventions

Identify the appropriate OD intervention for the change in each statement as:

a. training and development   f. team building
b. forcefield analysis   g. process consultation
c. survey feedback   h. job design
d. grid OD   i. direct feedback
e. sensitivity training

____ 21. "Things are going well, but I think we could benefit from an organizationwide intervention to improve management and organizational effectiveness."

____ 22. "Morale and motivation have fallen throughout the division in recent months. We need an intervention that can identify the problems so we can change the situation."

____ 23. "We have outgrown our present inventory system, which is also dated. What intervention should we use to develop a new one?"

____ 24. "The new offset printing machine is installed. Who are we going to teach to run it and what intervention should we use?"

____ 25. "What intervention should we use to prepare our employees to put the product together as a group rather than each person continuing to produce one part of it?"

Process Consultation. Process consultation is often part of the second stage of team building, but it is commonly used as a separate, more narrowly focused intervention. **Process consultation** *is an OD intervention designed to improve team dynamics.* Team building may focus on the process of getting the job itself done, but process consultation focuses on how people interact as they get the job done. Team dynamics (or process) include how the team communicates, allocates work, resolves conflict, and handles leadership, and how the group solves problems and makes decisions. The change agent observes the group members as they work in order to give them feedback on team process. During team process consultation, the team discusses its process and how to improve it. Training may also be conducted to improve group process skills. The ultimate objective is to train the group so that process consultation becomes an ongoing team activity. You will learn more about team dynamics in Chapter 10.

process consultation
An OD intervention designed to improve team dynamics.

Job Design. Job design, which you already learned about in Chapter 6, is an OD intervention. Job enrichment is the commonly used intervention.

Direct Feedback. Situations occur, particularly with technology changes, in which the change agent is an outside consultant who comes in and recommends a direct solution. For example, IBM consultants work with

WORK APPLICATION

9. Give an example of one or more OD interventions used in an organization that you work or have worked for.

organizations to recommend information systems. Once installed, IBM often trains the employees to operate the new system.

CHAPTER SUMMARY AND GLOSSARY

The chapter summary is organized to answer the 11 learning objectives for Chapter 7.

1. Identify where the forces for change initiate.

The forces for change come from the external and internal environment.

2. List the four types of change.

The four types of change are strategy, structure, technology, and people.

3. State the difference between a fact, a belief, and a value.

A fact is a provable statement that identifies reality. A belief cannot be proven because it is an opinion. A value is what is important to people; values are used to prioritize.

4. Describe the three levels of organizational culture and their relationship.

Level 1 is behavior—the actions employees take. Level 2 is values and beliefs. Values represent the way we ought to behave and beliefs represent if-then statements. Level 3 is assumptions—values and beliefs that are deeply ingrained as unquestionably true. Values, beliefs, and assumptions provide the operating principles that guide decision making and behavior.

5. Explain intrapreneurship and its three roles.

Intrapreneurship is the development of new products that might become separate business units. The *inventor* comes up with the creative idea. The *champion* is responsible for the transformation of the idea into an innovation. The champion finds a *sponsor* who provides the resources needed for the innovation.

6. State the core values of TQM.

The core values of TQM are (1) to focus everyone in the organization on delivering customer value and (2) to continuously improve the system and its processes.

7. Describe a learning organization's culture.

Learning organizations have a culture with a capacity to learn, adapt, and change with their environments to continuously increase customer value.

8. Discuss the relationship among diversity, innovation, and quality.

Diversity has a direct effect on innovation and quality. A diverse organization is generally more innovative and produces higher-quality products than nondiverse organizations.

9. State the difference in the use of forcefield analysis and survey feedback.

Forcefield analysis is used by a small group to diagnose and solve a specific problem. Survey feedback uses a questionnaire filled out by a large group to identify problems; the group does not work together to solve a problem. Forcefield analysis could be used to solve a problem identified through survey feedback.

10. Explain the difference between team building and process consultation.

Team building is broader in scope than process consultation. Team building is an intervention designed to improve both how the work is done and how team members work together as they do the work (team dynamics). Process consultation is designed to improve team dynamics.

11. Define the following key terms (in order of appearance in the chapter):

Select one or more methods: (1) fill in the missing key terms from memory, (2) match the key terms from the end of the summary with their definitions below, or (3) copy the key terms in order from the list at the beginning of the chapter.

The _____ are strategy, structure, technology, and people.

_____ are formal systems for collecting, processing, and disseminating the necessary information that aids managers in decision making.

The _____ are denial, resistance, exploration, and commitment.

_____ consists of the shared values, beliefs, and assumptions of how its members should behave.

The three _____ are behavior, values and beliefs, and assumptions.

The _____ are (1) to focus everyone in the organization on delivering customer value and (2) to continuously improve the system and its processes.

A _____ has a culture with a capacity to learn, adapt, and change with its environment to continuously increase customer value.

_____ is the ongoing planned process of change used as a means of improving performance through interventions.

_____ are specific actions taken to implement specific changes.

_____ is an OD technique that diagrams the current level of performance, the hindering forces toward change, and the driving forces toward change.

_____ is an OD technique that uses a questionnaire to gather data that are used as the basis for change.

_____ is an OD technique designed to help work groups increase structural and team dynamics performance.

_____ is an OD technique that is designed to improve team dynamics.

KEY TERMS

REVIEW AND DISCUSSION QUESTIONS

1. How do the management functions relate to change?

2. How does the systems effect relate to the four types of change?

3. List the four stages in the change process.

4. Which of the five reasons for resisting change do you believe is most common?

5. Which of the six ways to overcome resistance to change do you believe is the most important?

6. What is the difference between a strong and weak organizational culture?

7. What are the two types of innovations?

8. List the six characteristics of an innovative culture.

9. Do you agree with the core values of TQM or would you recommend changing them? If yes, state your core values for TQM.

10. Which change model do you prefer? Why?

OBJECTIVE CASE

Eastman Kodak

Eastman Kodak Company was a very strong leader in the U.S. market in the 1970s, but was losing its strong leadership position as competition increased. One of its problem areas of business, best known to the public, was its photographic products. The Japanese came out with the 35-millimeter camera, and Kodak ignored the market for too long, giving the first mover advantage to the Japanese companies. Kodak also unsuccessfully spent years and millions of dollars on developing an instant camera to compete with Polaroid, and got sued in the process for patent infringement. In the film area it lost market share to Fuji and other companies. On top of the heavy competition, the price of silver rose dramatically. Kodak was in a crisis because silver was a critical raw material in its photographic products.

Planning for Change

Top managers identified three major factors contributing to problems at Kodak. First, costs were too high. Second, information at the bottom of the operation was not being shared throughout the company, and managers were not being held accountable for performance. Third, staff specialists developed strategic planning but it was not implemented by the line managers. Based on these factors, departmentalization was considered to be the cause of many of Kodak's problems.

Kodak's functional departments focused on manufacturing, marketing, R&D, and finance. However, the top managers believed that the company had to respond to the global environ-

OBJECTIVE CASE

(continued)

ment based on businesses rather than functions. With functional departments, no one was responsible for performance. The decision was made to change from functional to divisional departmentalization. The next decision was how to plan and implement the departmental change. A common approach was to have a group of four or five managers make the new organization chart behind closed doors and then dictate the change.

Managers were concerned about making the reorganization a success, so they decided to use participative OD management to implement the change following these steps: The top three managers developed a new organization. Then they met with the nine line managers, who would be affected by the change, and explained the new organization and the rationale as to why it was required. Part of the rationale was to become more competitive by developing new products at a faster rate. Top managers simply told the nine line managers to go off and think about the reorganization and then come back and discuss it. Line managers were to challenge, question, understand, improve, and most importantly to feel as though it is "our" reorganization. After four months, the team of 12 had a reorganization plan.

The team of 12 was expanded to the top 50 managers who went through roughly the same process. At the end of five months, 62 managers had a reorganization plan. The 62 widened to the top 150 managers. However, their job was not to rework the departmentalization; they were to develop a specific plan for the divisional implementation.

The next step was to appoint people to the top jobs in the new organization. Appointments were made based on assessment of talent, with seniority second in importance. Most of the top 150 managers involved in the process had new jobs. But more important, the large majority of managers supported the reorganization regardless of their new jobs. The preparation for change took 14 months.

Implementing Change

Kodak's reorganization began with a 12 percent reduction of employees over a two-year period. Most left voluntarily for other jobs, retirement, and so on. Over time, the number of managers was reduced by about 25 percent, and Kodak stopped its habit of promoting managers from within.

Next, nearly 30 independent business units were created and given the responsibility for developing and implementing their own strategy and worldwide profit performance. The business units were grouped into traditional imaging businesses, image-intensive information technology, and plastic polymers. Kodak acquired Sterling Drug and expanded into pharmaceuticals as an additional business group.

To achieve better focus on the customer, markets, and technology, manufacturing and R&D were split up and distributed into the business units. The relationship between the business units and the different geographic areas where Kodak conducted its business were more clearly articulated.

Each business unit was subject to periodic evaluation of its earnings and value. Each was required to generate a return that exceeded an internally established cost of equity, reflecting its own level of risk and market conditions. Businesses unable to attain the required rate of return were put on probation, and if they did not reach the goal, they were dismantled or divested.

Kodak's reorganization was successful by most measures. It improved its financial, productivity, and market share performance. Kodak's performance improved at a rate four times the U.S. average for several years in a row.

OBJECTIVE CASE

(continued)

Select the best alternative for the following questions. Be sure you are able to explain your answers.

___ **1.** The forces for change at Kodak came from the ___ environment.

    a. external   b. internal   c. both

___ **2.** The type of change Kodak made was primarily a ___ change.

    a. strategy   c. technology

    b. structure   d. people

___ **3.** Top management at Kodak took so long, 14 months, coming up with a plan for change because it was concerned about the ___ stage in the change process.

    a. denial   c. exploration

    b. resistance   d. commitment

___ **4.** Managers at Kodak may have resisted the change for ___ reasons.

    a. uncertainty   d. loss

    b. inconvenience   e. control

    c. self-interest   f. all of these

___ **5.** The primary way to overcome resistance to change used at Kodak was

    a. develop a trust climate

    b. plan

    c. state why change is needed and how it will affect employees

    d. create a win-win situation

    e. involve employees

    f. provide support

___ **6.** Part of the reason for Kodak's change in departmentalization was to develop a more innovative culture.

    a. true   b. false

___ **7.** Kodak changed to a TQM culture.

    a. true   b. false

___ **8.** Kodak used OD in its change process.

    a. true   b. false

___ **9.** Kodak followed the steps in the comprehensive change model.

    a. true   b. false

___ **10.** Kodak's change can be considered an organizational revitalization.

    a. true   b. false

11. Discuss the systems effect of Kodak's reorganization.

12. It took 14 months to plan the change, and the organizational design was not changed dramatically from the original top three managers' plan. Would it have been faster just to have dictated the change? Using hindsight, would you have dictated the change or used participation as Kodak did?

For current information on Kodak, use Internet address http://www.kodak.com. For ideas on using the Internet, see Appendix B.

VIDEO CASE

Central Michigan Community Hospital II

(7-1 12 min.)
Case Summary

This is a continuation of the Chapter 2 video case. Central Michigan Community Hospital (CMCH) is a full-service, not-for-profit hospital serving the rural center of Michigan. CMCH

VIDEO CASE (continued)

offers acute care in its 151-bed facility as well as occupational medicine, wellness medicine, walk-in urgent care, and home health care. CMCH has been recognized as one of the top 100 hospitals in the United States.

Students' Learning Objective

To better understand the complexity of change and methods for managing change in an organization.

Critical Thinking Questions

1. What types of changes should Central Community Hospital make to compete in the next century?

2. What can CMCH do to make these changes successful?

---

*skillbuilder

🔲🔲

Skill-Building Exercise 7–1

Identifying Resistance to Change

Preparing for Skill-Building Exercise 7–1

Below are ten statements made by employees asked to make a change on the job. Identify the source and focus of their resistance using Model 7–1. Because it is difficult to identify intensity of resistance on paper, skip the intensity factor. However, when you deal with people on the job, you need to identify their intensity. Place the number of the box (1–9) that represents and best describes the major resistance.

____ 1. "But we never did the job that way before. Can't we just do it the same way as always?"

____ 2. The tennis coach asked Jill, the star player, to have Louise as her doubles partner. Jill said, "Come on, Louise is a lousy player. Betty is better; don't break us up." The coach disagreed and forced Jill to accept Louise.

____ 3. The manager, Winny, told Mike to stop letting everyone in the department take advantage of him by sticking him with extra work. Mike said, "But I like my coworkers and I want them to like me, too. If I don't help people they may not like me."

____ 4. "I can't learn how to use the new computer. I'm not smart enough to use it."

____ 5. The police sergeant asked Chris, the patrol officer, to take a rookie cop as her partner. Chris said, "Do I have to? I broke in the last rookie, Wayne. He and I are getting along well."

____ 6. The employee went to Chuck, the manager, and asked him if she could change the work-order form. Chuck said, "That would be a waste of time; the current form is fine."

____ 7. Diane, an employee, is busy at work. The manager tells her to stop what she is doing and begin a new project. Diane says, "The job I'm working on now is more important."

____ 8. "I don't want to work with that work team. It has the lowest performance record in the department."

____ 9. "Keep me in the kitchen part of the restaurant. I can't work in the bar because drinking is against my religion."

_____ 10. "But I don't see why I have to stop showing pictures of people burning in a fire to help get customers to buy our smoke detector system. I don't think it's unethical. Our competitors do it."

Doing Skill-Building Exercise 7–1 in Class

Objective
To develop your ability to identify resistance to change so that you can improve your skill at overcoming resistance and implement changes effectively.

Preparation
You should have determined the resistance to change for the ten preparation statements.

Experience
You will get feedback on how well you identified resistance to change.

Procedure (10–30 minutes)
Option 1. Break into groups of four to six and share your priorities. Try to reach a group consensus on each of the ten priorities. When the groups are finished, one member records priorities for the entire class to see. After all groups are finished, the instructor goes over the recommended answers.

Option 2. The instructor calls on students to get their priorities to each task. The instructor goes over the recommended answer for each item after a student(s) gives a priority.

Option 3. The instructor goes over the recommended answers without student involvement.

Conclusion
The instructor leads a class discussion and/or makes concluding remarks.

Application (2–4 minutes)
What did I learn from this experience? How will I use this knowledge in the future?

_____

_____

Sharing
Volunteers give their answers to the sharing questions.

Exercise 7–1

G

Diversity Training

Preparing for Exercise 7–1
In preparation for this exercise, write out the answers to the following questions.

Race and Ethnicity
1. I am of _____ race and ethnicity(s).
2. My name is _____. It is significant because it means _____ and/or I was named after _____.
3. One positive thing about being a _____ is _____.
4. One difficult or embarrassing thing about being a _____ is _____.

Religion
1. I am of _____ religion.

2. One positive thing about being a _____ is _____.
3. One difficult or embarrassing thing about being a _____ is _____.

Gender
1. I am of _____ gender.
2. One positive thing about being a _____ is _____.
3. One difficult or embarrassing thing about being a _____ is _____.
4. Men and women are primarily different in _____ because _____.

Age

1. I am _____ years old.

2. One positive thing about this age is _____.

3. One difficult or embarrassing thing about being this age is _____.

Ability

1. I am of _____ (high, medium, low) ability in college and on the job. I do/don't have a disability.

2. One positive thing about being of _____ ability is _____.

3. One difficult or embarrassing thing about being of _____ ability is _____.

Other

1. The major other way(s) in which I'm different from other people is _____.

2. One positive thing about being different in this way is _____.

3. One difficult or embarrassing thing about being different in this way is _____.

Prejudice, Stereotypes, Discrimination

1. Identify how you have been prejudged, stereotyped, and discriminated against.

_____

_____

_____

_____

_____

Doing Exercise 7–1 in Class

Objective

To increase your understanding of the value of diversity and being different. The more you value diversity, the more effort you will place on developing good human relations with a diversity of people.

Preparation

You should have answered the preparation questions for this exercise.

Experience

You will share your answers to the preparation questions for this exercise.

Procedure 1 (2–3 minutes)

Break into groups of four to six with as much diversity as possible. The instructor will check the diversity levels and reassign people to groups to improve diversity, if necessary. Select a spokesperson to give the group's best one or two example answers to the prejudice, stereotype, discrimination question; it is not necessary to report on any other areas.

Procedure 2 (10–30 minutes)

The instructor sets a time limit and selects the topics in the preparation to be discussed. Start with areas of differences first, but be sure to allow time, about 5 minutes, to complete the prejudice, stereotype, discrimination question. If you finish the question to be reported before the time is up, go over other areas of differences that were not assigned by the instructor.

Procedure 3 (5–20 minutes)

The spokesperson from each group gives the one or two best examples of prejudice, stereotype, discrimination.

Conclusion

The instructor may lead a class discussion and/or make concluding remarks.

Application (2–4 minutes)

What did I learn from this experience? How will I use this knowledge in the future?

_____

_____

Sharing

Volunteers give their answers to the application section.

8 Human Resources Management: Staffing

Learning Objectives

After studying this chapter, you should be able to:

1. List the four parts of the human resources management process.

2. Explain the difference between a job description and a job specification and why they are needed.

3. State the two parts of attracting employees and the difference between them.

4. Describe the difference between hypothetical and probing questions.

5. Discuss the difference between orientation and training and development of employees.

6. List the steps in job instructional training.

7. Explain the two types of performance appraisal.

8. Explain the concept, "You get what you reward."

9. State the major components of compensation.

10. Describe the difference between the use of job analysis and job evaluation.

11. Explain why most organizations do not have labor relations.

12. Define the following **key terms** (in order of appearance in the chapter):

human resources management process	assessment centers
	orientation
bona fide occupational qualification	training
	development
strategic human resources planning	vestibule training
	performance appraisal
job description	compensation
job specifications	job evaluation
recruiting	labor relations
selection	collective bargaining

1. You can develop your skill in selection interviewing (Skill-Building Exercise 8–1).

2. You can develop your skill at training employees (Skill-Building Exercise 8–2).

Selecting and training are organizing/staffing skills that utilize human, communication, conceptual, and decision-making skills. The exercises develop your interpersonal, informational, and decisional management roles. The SCANS skill competencies of using resources-staff, interpersonal skills, informational-teaching others, and systems, as well as basic, thinking, and personal qualities foundation are developed.

Scitor, of Sunnyvale, California, produces goods and services in program management, systems engineering, and customized computer information systems. Founder and CEO Roger Meade has developed a unique organizational culture at Scitor based on his approach to human resources management. Meade views employees as valuable assets: "Scitor is our people; our success depends on them." He believes that the key to productivity is taking care of employees' needs, and he takes good care of them. Meade sees Scitor's human resources programs as investments, not a cost of doing business.

Human resources investments have been paying off through 18 years of profitable growth. Meade's theory is that profits and growth are a byproduct of doing the job right and focusing on customer satisfaction. By satisfying the customers and making them successful, the company is successful.

The human resources management process focuses on making life on the job as agreeable and as easy to handle as possible. Some of Scitor practices include benefits to all employees who work at least 17.5 hours per week. Scitor provides unlimited sick leave with no lost wages and no tracing of sick days taken. Scitor provides a company-paid health care plan with a $1,400 fund for each employee for dental and vision care and unreimbursed medical expenses. New mothers get 12 weeks of paid maternity leave and the option of full- or part-time work when they return. Scitor offers job sharing (two employees completing one full-time job) and flextime (employees select starting and ending times).

Scitor gives every employee tickets to one 49ers football home game. The company organizes picnics, chili cook-offs, ski trips, fishing trips, wine-tasting trips, and road rallies.

Also, Scitor has an annual fiscal year kick-off meeting in a first-class resort that all employees attend. Scitor pays for transportation, food, and lodging for each employee and a guest for the three-day meeting.

Meade does not view his human resources policies as generous or liberal; it's simple economics. Everything Scitor does is driven toward increasing competitiveness and productivity. The benefits exist because they support the attract-and-retain employee objective. The money saved on attracting and training new employees pays for the benefits.

For current information on Scitor, use Internet address **http://www.scitor.com**. For ideas on using the Internet, see Appendix B.

---

1. List the four parts of the human resources management process.

human resources management process
Planning, attracting, developing, and retaining employees.

THE HUMAN RESOURCES MANAGEMENT PROCESS

The **human resources management process** *consists of planning, attracting, developing, and retaining employees.* It is also known as the *staffing* process. Figure 8–1 illustrates the process, and each of the four parts of the process is discussed as a major section of this chapter. Notice the arrows used to illustrate the systems effect. For example, planning and compensation affect attracting employees, labor relations affects planning, job analysis affects training, and so on. In this section, you will learn about the legal environment and the human resources department.

The Legal Environment

The external environment, especially the competitive and legal environment, has a major impact on human resources practices. When the organization does not offer the competitive pay and benefits that competitors offer, employees may change companies. Organizations are not completely free to hire whomever they want. The human resources department usually has the responsibility of seeing that the organization complies with the law. Some of the legal considerations follow.

Major laws affecting employment are Equal Employment Opportunity (EEO) and executive orders on Affirmative Action (AA). EEO, a 1972 amendment to the Civil Rights Act of 1964, prohibits employment discrimination on the basis of sex, religion, race or color, or national origin and applies to virtually all private and public organizations that employ 15 or more employees. Who is legally considered a minority? A minority is just about anyone who is not a white male, of European heritage, or adequately edu-

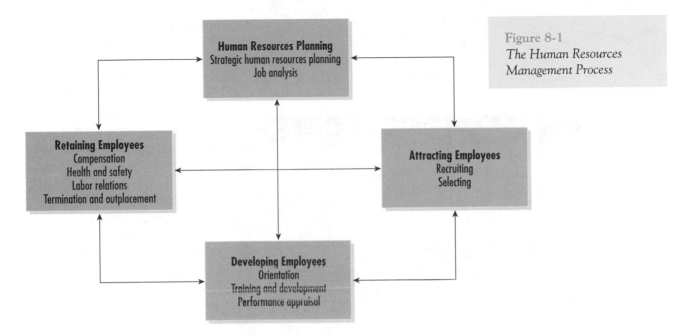

Figure 8-1
*The Human Resources
Management Process*

cated. The EEO minority guidelines list includes Hispanics, Asians, African-Americans, Native Americans, and Alaskan natives. The EEO also protects disadvantaged young people, disabled workers, and persons over 40 years of age. Although the law protects women from discrimination in employment, they are not considered to be a legal minority because they make up half of the population, and in some situations, are a majority.

The Equal Employment Opportunity Commission (EEOC) is responsible for legally enforcing equal opportunity for all. It has 47 field offices across the nation, and it operates a WATTS line (1-800-USA-EEOC) around the clock to provide information on employee rights. If you are not sure if what you are about to do, or are doing, is legal, call.[1]

Violation of the law can lead to investigation by the EEOC or to becoming a defendant in class-action or specific lawsuits. Courts find discrimination when selection criteria are vague, elusive, unstructured, undefined, or poorly conceived. As a manager, you should be familiar with your organization's EEO and AA program guidelines. Besides, offering equal opportunity to a diverse work force pays. The companies rated highest for hiring women and minorities outperformed the worst-rated companies.[2]

Preemployment Inquiries. On the application blank and during interviews, no member of an organization can legally ask discriminatory questions. The two major rules of thumb to follow are: (1) Every question asked should be job-related. When developing questions, you should have a purpose for using the information. Only ask legal questions you plan to use in your selection process. (2) Any general question that you ask should be asked of all candidates.

WORK APPLICATION

1. Have you or anyone you know been asked for discriminatory information during the preemployment process? If yes, please explain the situation in language acceptable to all.

Figure 8–2 lists what you can (lawful information you can use to disqualify candidates) and cannot (prohibited information you cannot use to disqualify candidates) ask during the selection process. In all cases, the assumption is that the information asked for is not a bona fide occupational qualification (BFOQ) for the job. A **bona fide occupational qualification** *allows discrimination where it is reasonably necessary to normal operation of a particular organization.* In an example of a BFOQ upheld by its supreme court, the state of Alabama required all guards in male maximum-security correctional facilities to be male. People believing that this requirement was sexual discrimination took it to court. The supreme court upheld the male sex requirement on the grounds that 20 percent of the inmates were convicted of sex offenses, and this creates an excessive threat to the security of female guards.

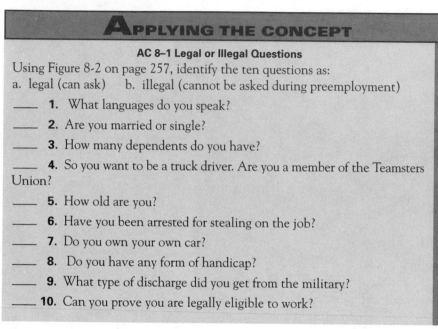

APPLYING THE CONCEPT

AC 8–1 Legal or Illegal Questions

Using Figure 8-2 on page 257, identify the ten questions as:
a. legal (can ask)   b. illegal (cannot be asked during preemployment)

_____ **1.** What languages do you speak?

_____ **2.** Are you married or single?

_____ **3.** How many dependents do you have?

_____ **4.** So you want to be a truck driver. Are you a member of the Teamsters Union?

_____ **5.** How old are you?

_____ **6.** Have you been arrested for stealing on the job?

_____ **7.** Do you own your own car?

_____ **8.** Do you have any form of handicap?

_____ **9.** What type of discharge did you get from the military?

_____ **10.** Can you prove you are legally eligible to work?

bona fide occupational qualification (BFOQ)
Allows discrimination where it is reasonably necessary to normal operation of a particular organization.

WORK APPLICATION

2. State your involvement with the human resources department in an organization you work or have worked for.

The Human Resources Department

Human resources is one of the four major functional departments in an organization. It is a staff department that advises and assists all the other departments in the organization.

In organizations large enough (usually about 100 or more employees) to have a separate human resources department, the department develops the human resources plans for the entire organization:

- It recruits employees so the line managers can select which employees to hire.

- It orients employees and trains many of them to do their jobs.

- It usually develops the performance appraisal system and forms used by managers throughout the organization.

- It determines compensation for employees.

- It is usually responsible for employee health and safety programs, works on labor relations, and is involved with the termination of employees. Employment records are kept in and by the human resources department, and it is often involved with legal matters.

Name

Can Ask: Current legal name and whether the candidate has ever worked under a different name.

Cannot Ask: Maiden name or whether the person has changed his or her name.

Address

Can Ask: Current residence and length of residence.

Cannot Ask: If the candidate owns or rents his or her home, unless it is a bona fide occupational qualification (BFOQ).

Age

Can Ask: If the candidate is between specific age groups, 21 to 70, to meet job specifications. If hired, can you furnish proof of age? For example, an employee must be 21 to serve alcoholic beverages.

Cannot Ask: How old are you? Or to see a birth certificate. Do not ask an older person how much longer he or she plans to work before retiring.

Sex

Can Ask: Only if sex is a BFOQ.

Cannot Ask: If it is not a BFOQ. To be sure not to violate sexual harassment laws, do not ask questions or make comments remotely considered flirtatious. Do not ask about sexual preferences.

Marital and Family Status

Can Ask: If the candidate can meet the work schedule or job and whether the candidate has activities, responsibilities, or commitments that may hinder meeting attendance requirements. The same question(s) should be asked of both sexes.

Cannot Ask: To select a marital status or any questions regarding children or other family issues.

National Origin, Citizenship, Race, or Color

Can Ask: If the candidate is legally eligible to work in the United States, and if this can be proven if hired.

Cannot Ask: To identify national origin, citizenship, race, or color (or that of parents and other relatives).

Language

Can Ask: To list languages the candidate speaks and/or writes fluently. The candidate may be asked if he or she speaks and/or writes a specific language if it is a BFOQ.

Cannot Ask: The language spoken off the job, or how the applicant learned the language.

Convictions

Can Ask: If the candidate has been convicted of a felony and other information if the felony is job-related.

Cannot Ask: If the candidate has ever been arrested. (An arrest does not prove guilt.) For information regarding a conviction that is not job-related.

Height and Weight

Can Ask: If the candidate meets or exceeds BFOQ height and/or weight requirements, and if it can be proven if hired.

Cannot Ask: The candidate's height or weight if it is not a BFOQ.

Religion

Can Ask: If the candidate is of a specific religion when it is a BFOQ. If the candidate can meet the work schedules or must be absent for religious reasons (holidays, etc.).

Cannot Ask: Religious preference, affiliations, or denominations.

Credit Ratings or Garnishments

Can Ask: If it is a BFOQ.

Cannot Ask: If it is not a BFOQ.

Education and Work Experience

Can Ask: For information that is job-related.

Cannot Ask: For information that is not job-related.

References

Can Ask: For names of people willing to provide references. For the names of people who suggested the candidate apply for the job.

Cannot Ask: For a reference from a religious leader.

Military

Can Ask: For information on education and experience gained that relates to the job.

Cannot Ask: Dates and conditions of discharge. Draft classification or other eligibility for military service. National Guard or reserve units of candidates. About experience in foreign armed services.

Organizations

Can Ask: To list membership in job-related organizations, such as union, professional, or trade associations.

Cannot Ask: To identify membership in any non-job-related organization that would indicate race, religion, and so on.

Disabilities

Can Ask: If the candidate has any disabilities that would prevent him or her from performing the specific job.

Cannot Ask: For information that is not job-related. Focus on abilities, not disabilities.

Figure 8-2
Preemployment Inquiries

HUMAN RESOURCES PLANNING

In this section you will learn about strategic human resources planning and job analysis. **Strategic human resources planning** *is the process of staffing the organization to meet its objectives.* The job of the human resources department is to provide the right kinds of people, in the right quantity, with the right skills, at the right time. Human resources plans are based on the organization's strategy.[3] If the strategy is growth, then employees will need to be hired. If the strategy is retrenchment, then there will be a layoff. Strategic human resources management has become increasingly important.[4]

Based on the organization's strategy, human resources managers analyze its current human resources based on its environment and sales forecast. The next step is to forecast specific human resources needs. The final step is to develop a plan to provide the employees necessary to meet the organization's objectives. For example, at Lands' End, a mail-order business, the firm's staffing needs increase during the Christmas holiday season. Over 2,000 seasonal and temporary workers are required to fill these needs. Staffing is done according to a plan formulated as early as January of that year.

Job Analysis

Strategic human resources planning determines the number of people and skills needed, but it does not specify how each job is performed. An important part of human resources planning is the review of information about the job.[5] Job design is the process of combining tasks that each employee is responsible for completing. In order to design jobs, they must be analyzed.[6] *Job analysis* is the process of determining what the position entails and the qualifications needed to staff the position. As the definition implies, job analysis is the basis for the job description and the job specifications.

The **job description** *identifies the tasks and responsibilities of a position.* In other words, it identifies what employees do to earn their compensation. The trend is to describe jobs more broadly in order to design enriched jobs.[7] Figure 8–3 shows a sample job description.

Realistic Job Preview. Part of the job analysis should be to develop a realistic job preview (RJP). The RJP provides the candidate with an accurate, objective understanding of the job.[8] Research indicates that employees who feel they were given accurate descriptions are more satisfied with the organization, believe the employer stands behind them and is trustworthy, and express a lower desire to change jobs than do those who feel they were not given an accurate job description.

Based on the job description, the second part of job analysis is to determine job specifications. **Job specifications** *identify the qualifications needed to staff a position.* The job specifications identify the types of people needed.[9, 10]

---

strategic human resources planning
The process of staffing the organization to meet its objectives.

2. Explain the difference between a job description and a job specification and why they are needed.

job description
Identifies the tasks and responsibilities of a position.

job specifications
Identify the qualifications needed to staff a position.

WORK APPLICATION

3. Complete a job analysis for a job you hold or held; write a simple job description and job specifications.

4. Were you given a realistic job preview? Explain.

DEPARTMENT: Plant Engineering

JOB TITLE: Lead Sheet Metal Specialist

JOB DESCRIPTION:

Responsible for the detailed direction, instruction, and leading of sheet metal department personnel in the construction and repair of a wide variety of sheet metal equipment. Also must perform similar related or more complex phases of the work most of the time. Receives verbal or written instructions from foreman as to sequence and type of jobs or special methods to be used. Allocates work to members of the group. Directs the layout, fabrication, assembly, and removal of sheet metal units according to drawing or sketches and generally accepted trade procedures. Obtains materials or supplies needed for specific jobs according to standard procedures. Trains new employees, as directed, regarding metalworking procedures and safe working practices. Checks all work performed by the group. Usually makes necessary contacts for the group with supervision or engineering personnel. May report irregularities to higher supervision but has no authority to hire, fire, or discipline other employees.

Figure 8-3
Job Description

Job analysis is an important part of human resources planning because it serves as a basis for attracting, developing, and retaining employees. For example, if you don't understand the job: How can you select employees to do the job? How can you train them to do the job? How can you evaluate their performance? How do you know how much to pay employees?

3. State the two parts of attracting employees and the difference between them.

ATTRACTING EMPLOYEES

After hiring needs have been determined and jobs analyzed, the human resources department generally recruits and line managers select people to fill positions.[11] In this section you will learn about recruiting, the selection process, and how to conduct an interview.

recruiting
The process of attracting qualified candidates to apply for job openings.

Recruiting

Recruiting *is the process of attracting qualified candidates to apply for job openings.* To fill an opening, possible candidates must first be made aware that the organization is seeking employees. They must then be persuaded to apply for the jobs.[12] Recruiting can be conducted internally and externally; Figure 8–4 lists possible recruiting sources.

Internal Recruiting. *Internal recruiting* involves filling job openings with current employees or people they know.[13] Promotion from within and employee referral are two common types of internal recruiting. Others include previous employees, and previous applicants who can be contacted.

Figure 8-4
Recruiting Sources

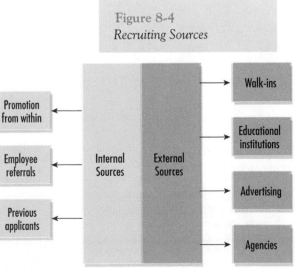

WORK APPLICATION

5. Identify the recruiting source used to hire you for one or more jobs.

APPLYING THE CONCEPT

AC 8–2 Recruiting Sources

Select the major recruiting source that should be used for each of the five job openings described.

Internal Sources
a. promotion from within
b. employee referrals

External Sources
c. walk-ins
d. educational institutions
e. advertising
f. agencies
g. executive recruiters

_____ 11. One of your workers was hurt on the job and will be out for one month. The person must be replaced.

_____ 12. One of the first-line supervisors is retiring in two months.

_____ 13. You need an engineer who has very specific qualifications. There are very few people who can do the job.

_____ 14. Your sales manager likes to hire young people without experience in order to train them to sell using a unique approach.

_____ 15. Your maintenance department needs a person to perform routine cleaning services.

- *Promotions from Within.* Many organizations post job openings on bulletin boards, in company newsletters, and so on. Current employees may apply or bid for the open positions.

- *Employee Referrals.* When job openings are posted internally, employees may be encouraged to refer friends and relatives for the positions. Generally, employees will refer only good candidates. However, the government has stated that the referral method is not acceptable when current employees are predominantly white or male since it tends to perpetuate the present composition of the work force, resulting in discrimination.

External Recruiting. The following are external recruiting sources:[14]

- *Walk-Ins.* Without actually being recruited, good candidates may come to the organization "cold" and ask for a job. However, professionals tend to send a résumé and cover letter asking for an interview.

- *Educational Institutions.* Recruiting takes place at high schools, vocational/technical schools, and colleges. Many schools offer career planning and placement services to aid the students and potential employers. Educational institutions are good places to recruit people without prior experience.

- *Agencies.* There are three major types of agencies: (1) *Temporary agencies*, like Kelly Services, provide part- or full-time help for limited periods. They are useful for replacing employees who will be out for a short period of time or for supplementing the regular work force during busy periods. (2) *Public agencies* are nationwide state employment services. They generally provide job candidates to employers at no, or very low, direct cost. (3) *Private employment agencies* are privately owned and charge a fee for their service. Agencies are good for recruiting people with prior experience. *Executive recruiters* are a type of private agency often referred to as "headhunters." They specialize in recruiting managers and/or those with specific high-level technical skills, like engineers and computer experts. They tend to charge the employer a large fee.

- *Advertising.* It is important to use the appropriate source to reach qualified candidates. A simple help wanted sign in the window is an advertisement. A newspaper is good for most positions, but professional and trade magazines may be more suitable for specific professional recruiting.

Technology is changing how organizations recruit and select employees.[15] A new form of advertising is available on the World Wide Web. Several Web sites provide job opportunities. Two examples include the Monster Board (http://www.monster.com), which introduced job fairs intended for particular localities and industries, and the Online Career Center (http://www. occ.com), which offers a cultural Diversity Virtual Job Fair intended for employers wanting to hire employees with diverse backgrounds.[16] The diversity site is important as it is a difficult selection decision to hire new employees who fit the culture or those who contribute to the work force's diversity.[17]

The Selection Process

Selection *is the process of choosing the most qualified applicant recruited for a job.* No set sequence is universally followed. Organizations may even use different selection methods for different jobs. Selection is important because bad hiring decisions can hang around to haunt the organization.[18] You will now learn about the application form, screening interviews, testing, background and reference checks, interviewing, and hiring.

Application Form. As part of the selection process, the recruited applicants may be asked to complete an application. Organizations may use different application forms for different jobs. For professional jobs, a résumé may replace the application form.

Organizations including the White House, Disneyland, and Ford now use computers to read/scan application forms and résumés. Before sending in a résumé, you may want to check to see if the organization uses computers. If it does, the human resources department can give you specific instructions to make sure your résumé information is scanned accurately.

The selection process can be thought of as a series of obstacles that the applicant must overcome to be offered the job. The first obstacle is typically the application. The data the applicant provides are compared to the job specifications. If they match, the applicant may progress to the next obstacle.

Screening Interview. Specialists in the human resources department often conduct screening interviews to select the top candidates who will continue on in the selection process. This especially helps save line managers' time when there are large numbers of job applicants. Organizations including Nike and Pricewaterhouse Coopers are using computers to conduct screening interviews.[19] For example, at Great Western Bank job candidates for a teller job sit before a computer, with a microphone, which asks them to make change, respond to tough customers, and sell products that customers don't ask for.

selection
The process of choosing the most qualified applicant recruited for a job.

Testing. Tests can be used to predict job success when they meet EEO guidelines for validity (people who score high on the test do well on the job and those who score low do not do well on the job) and reliability (if people take the same test on different days, they will get approximately the same score each time). Illegal tests can result in lawsuits. Some of the major types of tests include: *achievement* tests, *aptitude* tests, *personality* tests, *interest* tests, and *physical* exams.

Internal and external candidates for management positions are tested through assessment centers. **Assessment centers** *are places where job applicants undergo a series of tests, interviews, and simulated experiences to determine their managerial potential.* Candidates who perform well are selected for management positions.

Background and Reference Checks. Organizations should prevent poor hiring decisions and negligent hiring liability by instituting a reference-checking system to verify the information on a candidate's application form and/or résumé. Many applications contain false or erroneous material. For example, people have stated that they have earned college degrees when they have never even attended college.

Interviewing. The interview is the most heavily weighted selection criterion. A human resources manager for Xerox gives the résumé about 30 percent and the interview about 60 percent of the weight in the selection process. The interview is usually the final hurdle in the selection process. The interview gives the candidate a chance to learn about the job and organization. The interview also gives a manager a chance to learn things about candidates that can't be obtained from an application, test, or references, such as the candidate's ability to communicate, personality, appearance, and motivation. Because job interviewing is so important,[20] you will learn how to prepare for and conduct a job interview in this section.

Hiring. After obtaining information using the selection methods discussed, the manager compares the candidates without bias, and decides who is best suited for the job. Diversity should be considered when selecting a candidate. The candidate is contacted and offered the job. If the candidate does not accept the job, or accepts but leaves after a short period of time, the next best candidate is offered the job.

Scitor has a growth strategy; therefore, it is continually attracting employees. However, due to its reputation as an excellent company to work for, which was developed through its human resources practices, it does not have problems attracting well-qualified employees.

Selection Interviewing

After completing this chapter, you will know how to conduct a job interview. You can develop this skill in Skill-Building Exercise 8–1.

Types of Interviews and Questions. Figure 8–5 lists the types of interviews and questions.

---

assessment centers
Places where job applicants undergo a series of tests, interviews, and simulated experiences to determine their managerial potential.

WORK APPLICATION

6. Identify the selection methods used for a job you were offered. List each method from the selection process and state whether or not it was used. If a test was used, be sure to specify the type of test.

---

4. Describe the difference between hypothetical and probing questions.

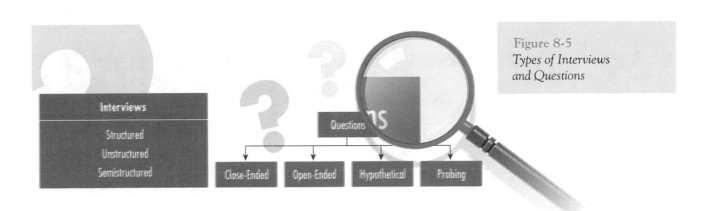

Figure 8-5
*Types of Interviews
and Questions*

Interviews. Three basic types of interviews are based on structure: (1) The *structured* interview has a list of prepared questions to ask all candidates. (2) The *unstructured* interview has no preplanned questions or sequence of topics. (3) The *semistructured* interview has a list of questions to ask, but the interviewer also asks unplanned questions. The semistructured interview is generally preferred because, although it helps ensure against discrimination in that the interviewer has a list of prepared questions to ask all candidates, it also allows the interviewer to ask each candidate questions relating to his or her own situation. The interviewer departs from the structure when appropriate. At the same time, using a standard set of questions makes it easier to compare candidates. The amount of structure you should use depends on your experience. The less experience you have, the more structure you need.

Questions. The questions you ask give you control over the interview; they allow you to get the information you need to make your decision. All questions should have a purpose, be job-related, and ask all candidates for the same information. You may use four types of questions during an interview: (1) The *closed-ended* question requires a limited response, often a yes or no answer, and is appropriate for dealing with fixed aspects of the job. "Do you have a class one license and can you produce it if hired?" (2) The *open-ended* question requires an unlimited response and is appropriate for determining abilities and motivation. "Why do you want to be a computer programmer for our company?" "What do you see as a major strength you can bring to our company?" (3) The *hypothetical* question requires the candidate to describe what he or she would do and say in a given situation;[21] it is appropriate in assessing capabilities. "What would the problem be if the machine made an XYZ sound?" (4) The *probing* question requires a clarification response and is appropriate for improving understanding. The probing question is not planned. It is used to clarify the candidate's response to an open-ended or hypothetical question. "What do you mean by 'it was tough'?" "What was the dollar increase in sales you achieved?"

**WORK
APPLICATION**

7. What types of job interviews have you experienced?
8. Identify the types of questions you were asked during a job interview. Write down some of the questions, identifying their types.

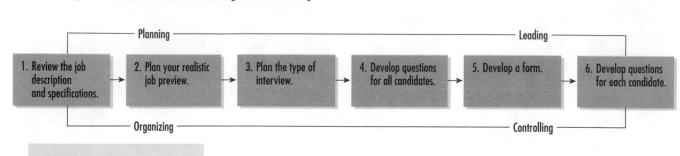

Model 8-1
Interview Preparation Steps

Preparing for the Interview. Completing the preparation steps will help you improve your interviewing skills. Model 8–1 lists the steps.

step 1. **Review the job description and specifications.** You cannot effectively match the candidate to the job if you do not thoroughly understand the job. Read and become familiar with the job description and job specifications. If they are outdated, or do not exist, conduct a job analysis.

step 2. **Plan your realistic job preview.** Candidates should understand what the job is and what they are expected to do. They should know the good and bad points of the job. Plan how you will present the realistic job preview using the job description. It often helps to give candidates a tour of the work area.

step 3. **Plan the type of interview.** What level of structure will you use? The interview should take place in a private, quiet place, without interruptions. It may be appropriate to begin the interview in an office and then tour the facilities while asking questions. Plan when the tour will take place and what questions will be asked. Take your form if you intend to ask several questions.

step 4. **Develop questions for all candidates.** Your questions should be job-related, nondiscriminatory, and asked of all candidates. Use the job description and specifications to develop questions that relate to each job task and responsibility.[22] Use a mixture of closed-ended, open-ended, and hypothetical questions. Don't be concerned about the order of questions; just write them out at this point.

step 5. **Develop a form.** Once you have completed your list of questions, determine the sequence. Start with the easy questions. One approach starts with closed-ended questions, moves on to open-ended questions, and then to hypothetical questions; use probing questions as needed. Another approach structures the interview around the job description and specifications; explain each and then ask questions relating to each responsibility.

Write out the questions in sequence, leaving space for checking off closed-ended responses, for making notes on the responses to open-ended and hypothetical questions, and for follow-up questions. Add information gained from probing questions where appropriate. You are guided through the interview as you record the candidate's responses on the form. Make a copy of the form for each candidate, and a few extras for future use when filling the same job, or as a reference when developing forms for other jobs.

step 6. **Develop questions for each candidate.** Review each candidate's application/résumé. You will most likely want to verify or clarify some of the information given during the interview. Examples include the following: "I noticed that you did not list any employment during 1995; were you unemployed?" "On the application you stated you had computer training; what computer were you trained to operate?" Be sure the individual questions are not discriminatory; for example, do not ask only women whether they can lift 50 pounds; ask all candidates, men or women, this question.

You can either add the individual questions to the standard form, writing them in where appropriate, or you can add a list at the end of the form.

Conducting the Interview. Following the steps listed will help you do a better job of interviewing candidates. Model 8–2 lists the interviewing steps.[23]

step 1. **Open the interview.** Develop a rapport. Put the candidate at ease by talking about some topic not related to the job. Maintain eye contact in a way that is comfortable for you and the candidate.

step 2. **Give your realistic job preview.** Be sure the candidate understands the job requirements. Answer any questions the candidate has about the job and the organization. If the job is not what the candidate expected, or wants to do, allow the candidate to disqualify himself or herself and close the interview at that point.

step 3. **Ask your questions.** Steps 2 and 3 can be combined if you like. To get the most out of a job interview, you must take notes on responses to your questions.[24] Tell the candidate that you have prepared a list of questions you will be asking, and that you plan to take notes.

During the interview, the candidate should do most of the talking. Give the candidate a chance to think and respond. If the candidate did not give you all the information you wanted, ask an unplanned probing question. However, if it is obvious that the candidate does not want to answer the question, don't force it. Go on to the next question or close the interview. End with a closing question such as, "I'm finished with my questions. Is there anything else you want to tell me about, or ask me?"

step 4. **Introduce top candidates to coworkers.** Introduce top candidates to people with whom they will be working to get a sense of their interpersonal skills and overall attitude. Introductions can also give you a sense if the person is a team player.

step 5. **Close the interview.** Do not lead candidates on. Be honest without making a decision during the interview. Thank candidates for their

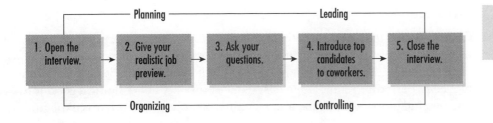

Model 8-2
Interviewing Steps

WORK APPLICATION

9. Using Model 8–2, identify the steps used or not used when you were interviewed for a job.

time, and tell them what the next step in the interview process is, if any. Tell candidates when you will contact them. For example, say, "Thank you for coming in for this interview. I will be interviewing over the next two days and will call you with my decision by Friday of this week." After the interview, be sure to jot down general impressions not covered by specific questions.

Selecting the Candidate. After all interviews are completed, compare each candidate's qualifications to the job specifications to determine who would be best for the job. Be sure to get the coworkers' impressions of each candidate.

Problems to Avoid. Avoid the following problems during the selection process:

* *Rushing.* Try not to be pressured into hiring "any" candidate. Find the best person available.[25]
* *Stereotyping.* Don't prejudge or leap to conclusions. Match the candidate to the job based on analysis rather than instinct.
* *"Like Me" Syndrome.* Don't look for a candidate who is your clone. People who are not like you may do an excellent job. Remember the benefits of diversity.
* *Halo and Horn Effect.* Do not judge a candidate on the basis of one or two favorable or unfavorable characteristics. Make the selection on the basis of the total qualifications of all candidates.
* *Premature Selection.* Don't make your selection based on the application/résumé or after interviewing a candidate who impressed you. Do not compare candidates after each interview. The order in which you interview applicants can influence you. Be open-minded during all interviews and make a choice only after you have finished all interviews. Compare each candidate on each job specification.

*skillbuilder

DEVELOPING EMPLOYEES

After employees have been recruited and selected (attracting), they must be oriented, trained, and evaluated (developing).

5. Discuss the difference between orientation and training and development of employees.

orientation
The process of introducing new employees to the organization and their jobs.

Orientation

Orientation *is the process of introducing new employees to the organization and their jobs.* Orientation is learning the ropes or the rules of the game. Some of the benefits of effective orientation include reduced time to get the employee to perform to standard levels, reduced anxiety about doing a good job and getting along with peers, and accurate perceptions of what is expected of the employee. Employees tend to stay on the job longer (reduced turnover) and have improved attitudes and performance when they go through orientation.

Orientation Programs. The time it takes and the content of orientation vary greatly from organization to organization. At Disney World, all new employees go through an 8-hour orientation followed by 40 hours of apprenticeship training. The purpose is to familiarize them with Disney's history, tradition, policies, expectations, and ways of doing things. Starbucks Coffee encourages employees to take pride in their work and to develop a sense of purpose, commitment, and enthusiasm for their job and the company.

Although orientation programs vary in formality and content, five important elements should be included; they are listed in Figure 8–6. Explain what your department does, how the new employee's job relates to other jobs in the department, and the interrelationship among departments. Be sure to clearly explain the new employee's job tasks and responsibilities and the standing plans that need to be followed. Provide a tour of the facilities and introduce the new employee to coworkers. Organizations that have developed innovative orientation programs based on these areas include System One, Southwest Airlines, Quad/Graphics, and Ernst & Young.[26]

> Organization and department functions.
> Job tasks and responsibilities.
> Standing plans.
> Tours.
> Introduction to coworkers.

Figure 8-6
Orientation Programs

WORK APPLICATION

10. Recall an orientation you experienced. Which parts of an orientation program did it include and exclude? Describe the entire orientation.

Training and Development

Employees will have to be taught how to perform a new job.[27] Orientation and training may, and often do, take place simultaneously. **Training** *is the process of acquiring the skills necessary to perform a job.* Training typically develops the technical skills of nonmanagers.[28] **Development** *is the ongoing education to improve skills for present and future jobs.* Development is less technical and aimed at developing human, communication, conceptual, and decision-making skills in managerial and professional employees.

Training and development are a good investment because they benefit individuals, their organizations, and the economy as a whole.[29] IBM, General Motors, Motorola, Texas Instruments, and Xerox invest heavily in training and development. However, overall, American organizations underinvest in employee development.[30]

Off- and On-the-Job Training. Employees can learn to perform their jobs off and/or on the job.

Off-the-Job Training. As the name implies, this training is conducted away from the work site, often in some sort of classroom setting. A common method is vestibule training. **Vestibule training** *develops skills in a simulated setting.* It is used when teaching job skills at the work site is impractical. For example, many large retail stores have training rooms where new employees learn how to run the cash registers and other equipment. The training is usually conducted by a training specialist. Most organizations conduct development programs off the job.

training
The process of acquiring the skills necessary to perform a job.

development
The ongoing education to improve skills for present and future jobs.

vestibule training
Develops skills in a simulated setting.

Model 8-3
*Job Instructional Training
Steps*

On-the-Job Training (OJT). This training is done at the work site with the resources the employee uses to perform the job. The manager, or an employee selected by the manager, usually conducts the training. Because of its proven record of success, job instructional training (JIT) is a popular method worldwide.

Job Instructional Training. JIT has four steps, presented in Model 8–3 and described here. Remember that things we know well seem very simple, but they are usually difficult for the new trainee.

6. List the steps in job instructional training.

step 1. **Preparation of the trainee.** Put the trainee at ease as you create interest in the job and encourage questions. Explain the quantity and quality requirements and their importance.

step 2. **Presentation of the task.** Perform the task yourself at a slow pace, explaining each step several times. Once the trainee seems to have the steps memorized, have him or her explain each step as you perform the job at a slow pace. For complex tasks with multiple steps, write them out and give a copy to the trainee.

step 3. **Performance of the task by the trainee.** Have the trainee perform the task at a slow pace, explaining each step. Correct any errors and be willing to help the trainee perform any difficult steps. Continue until the employee can proficiently perform the task.

step 4. **Follow-up.** Tell the trainee who to go to for help with any questions or problems.[31] Gradually leave the trainee alone. Begin by checking quality and quantity frequently, then decrease the amount of checking based on the trainee's skill level. Watch the trainee perform the task and be sure to correct any errors or faulty work procedures before they become a habit. Be sure to be patient and encouraging.

**WORK
APPLICATION**

11. Identify which steps of JIT your trainer used to train you for a present or past job. Was the training on or off the job?

*skillbuilder

The Training Cycle

Following the steps in the training cycle will help ensure that training is done in a systematic way. A discussion of the five steps of the systems training cycle, presented in Figure 8–7, follows.

step 1. **Conduct a needs assessment.** Before you begin training, you must determine your employees' training needs. Common needs assessment methods include observation, interviews, and questionnaires. These needs will differ depending on whether you are training new or existing employees. An assessment center may be used to determine training needs.

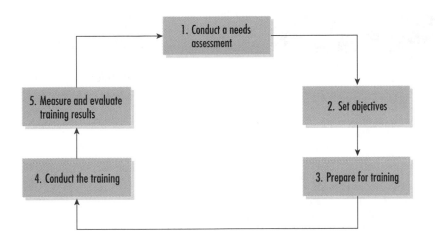

Figure 8-7
The Training Cycle

step 2. **Set objectives.** Any training program should have well-defined, performance-based objectives. As with all plans, you should begin by determining the end result you want to achieve. The criteria for your objectives should meet the criteria discussed in Chapter 4.

step 3. **Prepare for training.** Before conducting a training session, you should have written plans and all the necessary materials ready. If you ever had an instructor come to class obviously unprepared, you know why preparation before training is necessary for success. As many as 30 hours of preparation are needed for one hour of training.

An important part of preparation is selecting the training method. You have already learned about JIT. Figure 8–8 lists training methods. Whatever method you develop, break the task down into steps. What we do as part of our routine seems simple, but it may seem very complicated to the new employee. Write out each step and go through the steps to make sure they work.

step 4. **Conduct the training.** Be sure to have your written plan with you, as well as any other materials needed.

step 5. **Measure and evaluate training results.** Link training outcomes and business results.[32] During training and at the end of the program, you should measure and evaluate the results to determine whether or not the objectives were achieved. If they were, the training is over; if they were not, you either have to continue the training until objectives are met or take employees off the job if they cannot meet the standards. Revise and improve your written plans for future use.

Training Methods

Figure 8–8 lists training methods available, many of which can be used as part of JIT. The third column, skill development, lists the primary skill developed.[33] However, some of the technical methods can be combined. Technical skill also includes acquiring knowledge that can be tested.

When selecting a training method, keep the following statistics in mind: People learn 10 percent of what they read, 20 percent of what they

Method	Definition	Skill Developed
Written material	Manuals, books, and so on.	Technical
Lecture	Spoken word; class lectures.	Technical
Video	Television; class videos.	Technical
Question and answer	After another method(s) above, the trainer and/or trainees can ask questions about what they read, heard, and/or watched.	Technical
Discussion	A topic can be presented and discussed.	Technical
Programmed learning	A computer or book is used to present material, followed by a question or problem. The trainee is asked to select a response, then is given feedback on his or her response. Based on the material presented, programmed learning may possibly develop human and conceptual skills.	Technical
Demonstration	The trainer shows the trainee how to perform the task. This is step 2 of job instructional training. Demonstrations can also be used as part of developing human and decision-making skills.	Technical
Job rotation	Employees learn to perform multiple jobs.	Technical and conceptual
Projects	Special assignments, such as developing a new product or doing a special report, are given. Projects that require working with people and other departments may also develop human and conceptual skills.	Technical
Role playing	Trainees act out a possible job situation, such as handling a customer complaint, to develop skill at handling similar situations on the job.	Human and communication
Behavior modeling	It involves four steps: (1) The trainees observe how to perform the task correctly. This may be done via a live demonstration or a videotape. (2) Trainees role-play a situation using the observed skills. (3) Trainees receive feedback on how well they performed. (4) Trainees develop plans for using the new skills on the job. Behavior modeling is a feature of this book.	Human and communication
Cases	The trainee is presented with a situation and asked to diagnose and solve the problems involved. The trainee is usually asked to answer questions. There is a case at the end of each chapter in this book.	Conceptual and decision making
In-basket exercise	The trainee is given actual or simulated letters, memos, reports, telephone messages, and so forth that would typically be found in the in-basket of a person holding the job for which training is given. Trainees are asked what, if any, action they would take for each item, and to assign priorities to the material.	Conceptual and decision making
Management games	The trainees manage a simulated company. They make decisions in small teams and get the results back, usually on a quarterly basis, over a period of several game "years." Teams are in an "industry" with several competitors.	Conceptual and decision making
Interactive video	Trainees sit at a computer and respond as directed. The job interview at Great Western Bank uses interactive video. The bank could use the same technology to train tellers how to handle complaints, as well as testing them on it during the job interview.	Any of the three skills

Figure 8-8
Training Methods

hear, and 30 percent of what they see. People learn 50 percent of what they see and hear. They learn 70 percent of what they talk over with others. People learn 80 percent of what they use and do in real life. They learn 95 percent of what they teach someone else.

Managerial Use of Training Methods. Managers commonly use reading, lecture, video, question and answer, discussion, programmed learning, demonstration, job rotation, and projects to train employees how to perform their jobs. Managers do not commonly use role playing and behavior modeling. However, they are appropriate for managers who need to train employees how to handle human relations such as customer complaints. The manager can also teach human skills to employees by example.[34]

Management games, in-basket exercises, and cases are commonly used to train managers, not employees. Therefore, managers may be trained with these methods, but will probably not use these training methods with their employees.

APPLYING THE CONCEPT

AC 8–3 Training Methods

Select the most appropriate training method in the following situations.

a. written material	f. programmed learning	k. behavior modeling
b. lecture	g. demonstration	l. management games
c. video	h. job rotation	m. in-basket exercise
d. question and answer	i. projects	n. cases
e. discussion	j. role playing	

_____ 16. You have a large department with a high turnover rate. Employees must learn several rules and regulations in order to perform their jobs.

_____ 17. You occasionally have new employees whom you must teach to handle the typical daily problems they will face on the job.

_____ 18. Your boss has requested a special report.

_____ 19. You want to be sure that employees can cover for each other if one or more of them are absent.

_____ 20. You need to teach employees how to handle customer complaints.

Performance Appraisal

After you have hired and trained employees, you must evaluate how well they perform their jobs. **Performance appraisal** *is the ongoing process of evaluating employee performance.*

Types of Performance Appraisal. The two types of performance appraisal (PA) are developmental and evaluative. *Developmental performance appraisal* is used to make decisions and plans for performance improvements. *Evaluative performance appraisal* is used to make administrative decisions, including pay raises, transfers and promotions, and demotions and terminations. The evaluative PA focuses on the past, whereas the developmental PA focuses on the future. They are related because the developmental plans are always based on an evaluative PA. However, the primary purpose of PA should be to help employees to continuously improve their performance,[35] as it influences employee productivity and job satisfaction.[36]

When both the developmental and evaluative PA are conducted together, which they commonly are, the development is often less effective, especially when the employee disagrees with the evaluation. Most managers are not good at being both a judge and a coach. Therefore, separate meetings make the two uses clear and can help the manager be both a judge and a coach.

The Performance Appraisal Process. See Figure 8–9 for an illustration of the performance appraisal process. Note the connection between the organization's mission and objectives and the performance appraisal process.

performance appraisal
The ongoing process of evaluating employee performance.

7. Explain the two types of performance appraisal.

Figure 8-9
The Performance Appraisal Process

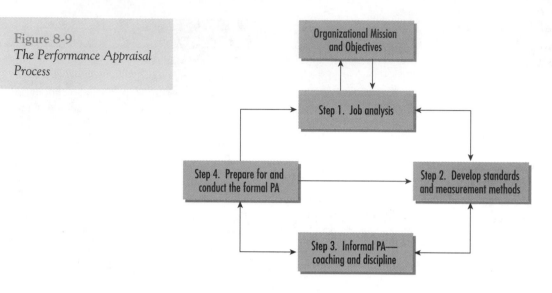

The feedback loop indicates the need for the PA to control human resources performance.[37] Based on the organization's mission and objectives (Chapter 4), employees' performance should be measured against the achievement of these goals.

 Job analysis. The job analysis includes determining the job description and job specification. The job description responsibilities should be ranked in order of importance.

 Develop standards and measurement methods. After determining what it takes to do the job, standards and methods for measuring performance can be developed. The next section discusses setting standards and describes several common performance appraisal methods.

 Informal performance appraisals—coaching and discipline. A performance appraisal should not just consist of the once-a-year-formal interview. As stated in its definition, PA is an ongoing process. Employees need regular informal feedback on their performance. Coaching involves giving praise for a job well done to maintain performance, or taking corrective action when standards are not met. The employee performing below standard may need daily or weekly coaching or discipline to meet standards. In Chapter 14, we will discuss coaching and discipline.

 Prepare for and conduct the formal performance appraisal. Follow the steps in Models 8–1 and 8–2.

Developing Performance Standards. As a manager, make sure that your employees know what the standards are. If you give an employee an average rather than a good rating, you should be able to clearly explain why. The employee should understand what needs to be done during the next performance period to get the higher rating. With clear standards and coaching, there shouldn't be any surprise disagreements over performance during the formal performance appraisal. In Chapter 14, you will learn how to set standards in the areas of quantity, quality, time, cost, and behavior.

You Get What You Reward. One of the most important things you should learn in this course is that people will do what they are rewarded for doing. People seek information concerning what activities are rewarded, and then seek to do (or at least pretend to do) those things, often to the exclusion of activities not rewarded. The extent to which this occurs depends on the attractiveness of the rewards offered.

For example, if a professor gives a class a reading list of several sources, but tells students (or they realize without being told) they will not discuss them in class or be tested on them, how many students will acquire and read them? Or, "A, B, and C from this chapter are important and I'll test you on them, but X, Y, and Z are not." Will students spend equal time studying both?

Measurement Methods. The formal performance appraisal is often conducted based on a standard form, usually rating scales or BARS, developed by the human resources department to measure employee performance. See Figure 8–10 for a list of the commonly used performance appraisal measurement methods on a continuum based on their use in administrative and developmental decisions. Below the listing of measurement methods is an explanation of each.

8. Explain the concept, "You get what you reward."

APPLYING THE CONCEPT

AC 8–4 Selecting Performance Appraisal Methods

Select the performance appraisal method that is most appropriate for the given situation, using Figure 8-10 on page 274.

a. critical incidents   d. ranking
b. rating scales   e. MBO
c. BARS   f. narrative

_____ 21. You started a small company with ten employees. You are overworked, but you want to develop one performance appraisal form you can use with all employees.

_____ 22. You have been promoted from a supervisory position to a middle management position. You have been asked to select your replacement.

_____ 23. Winnie is not performing up to standard. You decided to talk to her in order to improve her performance.

_____ 24. You want to create a system for developing each employee.

_____ 25. Your small business has grown to 50 employees. Employees have complained that the one form does not work well for different types of employee jobs. You have decided to hire a professional to develop a performance appraisal system that is more objective and job specific with PA forms for your various employee groups.

The Evaluative Performance Appraisal Interview

It is recommended that you plan before you act for performance appraisal interviews. Therefore, this section is separated into preparing for and conducting the PA interview. Because the evaluative interview is the basis for the development interview, it is completed first.

Preparing for an Evaluative Interview. When preparing for this interview, follow the steps in the evaluative performance appraisal process, Model 8–4.

Ranking		BARS	Rating Scales	MBO	Narrative		Critical Incidents
Administrative Decisions		Both		Mostly Developmental			Developmental Decisions

Explanation of performance appraisal measurement methods

The Critical Incidents File

The critical incidents file is a performance appraisal method in which the manager writes down positive and negative performance behavior of employees throughout the performance period. The critical incidents file is a form of documentation that is needed in this litigious environment.

The Rating Scale

The rating scale is a performance appraisal form on which the manager simply checks off the employee's level of performance. Some of the possible areas evaluated include quantity of work, quality of work, dependability, judgment, attitude, cooperation, and initiative.

Behaviorally Anchored Rating Scales (BARS)

BARS is a performance appraisal method combining rating and critical incidents. It is more objective and accurate than the two methods separately. Rather than having ratings of excellent, good, average, and so forth, the form has several statements that describe the employee's performance, from which the manager selects the one that best describes the employee's performance for that task. Standards are clear when good BARS are developed.

Ranking

Ranking is a performance appraisal method that is used to evaluate employee performance from best to worst. Under the ranking method, the manager compares an employee to another employee, rather than comparing each one to a standard measurement. An off-shoot of ranking is the forced

distribution method, which is similiar to grading on a curve. A predetermined percentage of employees are placed in performance categories: for example, excellent—5 percent, above average—15 percent, average—60 percent, below average—15 percent, and poor—5 percent.

Management by Objectives (MBO)

MBO is a process in which managers and their employees jointly set objectives for the employee, periodically evaluate the performance, and reward according to the results (review Chapter 4 for details).

The Narrative Method

The narrative method requires the manager to write a statement about the employee's performance. The system can vary. Managers may be allowed to write whatever they want, or they may be required to answer questions about employee's performance. The narrative is often combined with another method.

Which Performance Appraisal Method Is the Best?

Determining the best appraisal method depends upon the objectives of the system. A combination of the methods is usually superior to any one method. For developmental objectives, critical incidents and MBO work well. For administrative decisions, a ranking method based on rating scales or BARS works well. The real success of performance appraisal does not lie in the method or form used; it depends on the manager's human relations skills.

Figure 8-10
Performance Appraisal Measurement Methods with Their Decision Use

Conducting an Evaluative Interview. Encourage the employee to talk. The appraisal should be a give-and-take interview with both parties contributing on a 50–50 basis. The steps to follow when conducting the evaluative performance appraisal interview are also listed in Model 8–4.

Planning — Leading

Preparation for the PA Steps

| 1. Make an appointment. | 2. Have the employee perform a self-assessment. | 3. Assess performance. | 4. Identify strengths and areas for improvement. | 5. Predict employee reactions and plan how to handle them. |

Conducting the PA Steps

| 1. Open the interview. | 2. Go over the PA form. | 3. Agree on strengths and areas for improvement. | 4. Close the interview. |

Organizing — Controlling

Model 8-4
The Evaluative Performance Appraisal

The Developmental Performance Appraisal Interview

As with the evaluative interview, you should prepare for and conduct the developmental performance appraisal.

Preparing for a Developmental Interview. After the evaluation is completed, you should prepare for the developmental interview. To do this, follow the steps in Model 8–5.

Conducting the Developmental Interview. To do this, also follow the steps in Model 8–5.

Scitor has a formal orientation program. Employees are well trained to perform their present jobs, and the company is also committed to developing employees for future jobs as the industry changes quickly and the firm continues to grow. With its growth strategy, training is an ongoing necessity to achieve organizational objectives. Performance appraisal is very important at Scitor because it serves as the basis for making decisions on who gets promoted. Promotions continually become available with growth.

Model 8-5
The Developmental Performance Appraisal

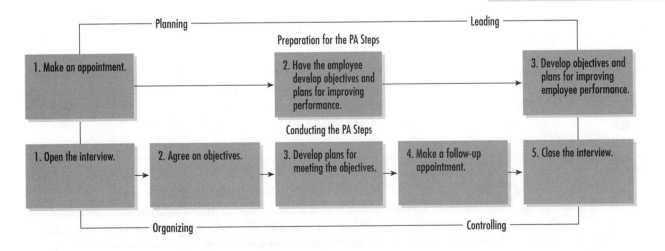

Planning — Leading

Preparation for the PA Steps

| 1. Make an appointment. | 2. Have the employee develop objectives and plans for improving performance. | 3. Develop objectives and plans for improving employee performance. |

Conducting the PA Steps

| 1. Open the interview. | 2. Agree on objectives. | 3. Develop plans for meeting the objectives. | 4. Make a follow-up appointment. | 5. Close the interview. |

Organizing — Controlling

RETAINING EMPLOYEES

After attracting and developing employees, an organization must have human resources systems to retain employees.[38] Employee turnover can reduce overall efficiency, profitability, and morale.[39] The cost of replacing a good employee ranges from half to several times a year's pay, depending on the job.[40] Thus, rather than focus on recruiting new workers, try to keep the ones you have.[41] Employees who believe they are being justly rewarded tend to stay.[42] Challenging work and good feedback also hold people.[43] Recall that Scitor's human resources systems are designed to retain employees; the company has a turnover rate of 2.1 percent, versus the industry average of 16.5 percent. In this section you will learn about compensation, health and safety, labor relations, and termination and outplacement.

Compensation

9. State the major components of compensation.

compensation
The total cost of pay and benefits to employees.

Compensation *is the total cost of pay and benefits to employees.* Compensation affects both attracting and retaining employees.[44] An important overall compensation decision is pay level. *Pay level* refers to the choice to be a high-, medium-, or low-paying organization. Scitor is a high-paying company, which results in its attracting and retaining excellent employees. Low-paying firms may save money on pay, but the savings can be lost to the high cost of turnover. We will cover pay and benefits separately.

Pay Systems. There are three general pay methods, and organizations can use all three. (1) *Wages* are paid on an hourly basis. (2) *Salary* is based on time—week, month, or year. A salary is paid regardless of the number of hours worked. (3) *Incentives* are pay for performance. Incentives include piece rate (pay based on production), commissions (pay based on sales), merit raises (the more productive workers get paid more), and bonuses. Two common types of bonus include stating a specific reward for reaching an objective and profit sharing in which employees get a part of the profits. The use of bonuses is on the increase.[45] Organizations including Hewlett Packard, Polaroid, and West Bend are creating innovative incentive pay systems. The trend is toward replacing wages with salaries and offering incentives to all employees.[46]

10. Describe the difference between the use of job analysis and job evaluation.

job evaluation
The process of determining the worth of each job relative to the other jobs within the organization.

Pay Determination. A difficult decision is how much to pay each employee. An external approach is to find out what other organizations pay for the same or similar jobs and set the pay based on the pay level decision. An internal approach is to use job evaluation. **Job evaluation** *is the process of determining the worth of each job relative to the other jobs within the organization.* Organizations commonly group jobs into pay grades. The higher the worth/grade of the job, the higher the pay. Both approaches are often used together.

A related controversial issue important to job evaluation is comparable worth. *Comparable worth* means that jobs that are distinctly different but with similar levels of ability, responsibility, skills, working conditions, etc., that make jobs of equal value, should have the same pay scale.

Benefits. *Benefits* are the part of compensation paid for by the employer that benefit employees, and often their families. Benefits are commonly noncash and are not merit-based.[47] Legally required benefits include *workers' compensation* to cover job-related injuries, *unemployment compensation* for when employees are laid off or terminated, and *Social Security* for retirement. Your employer matches the amount the government takes out of your pay for Social Security. Commonly offered optional benefits include health insurance; paid sick days, holidays, and vacations; and pension plans.[48] Optional benefits can be paid in full by employers, split between employee and employer, or paid completely by the employee. Other benefits less commonly offered include dental and life insurance, membership to fitness centers, membership in credit unions, and tuition reimbursement.

The benefits percentage of compensation has been increasing over the years, primarily due to the high cost of health insurance. The percentage varies with the level of job from one- to two-thirds of compensation, but it has been estimated that the average employee receives slightly over 40 percent of compensation from benefits.[49] Scitor is very generous, offering many optional benefits.

WORK APPLICATION

13. Identify the compensation package offered by your present or past employer.

Health and Safety

The Occupational Safety and Health Act (OSHA) of 1970 requires employers to pursue workplace safety. Employers must meet OSHA safety standards, maintain records of injuries and deaths due to workplace accidents, and submit to on-site inspections. The human resources department commonly has responsibility for ensuring the health and safety of employees.[50] It works closely with the other departments and often conducts new employee and ongoing training sessions, as well as maintaining health and safety records.[51] As a manager, you should know the safety rules, be sure your employees know them, and enforce them to prevent accidents.

Labor Relations

Labor relations *are the interactions between management and unionized employees.* Labor relations are also called union–management relations and industrial relations. There are many more organizations without unions than there are with unions. Therefore, not all organizations have labor relations as part of their human resources systems. The *union* is an organization that represents employees in collective bargaining with the employer. Unions are also a source of recruitment. The National Labor Relations Act (also known as the Wagner Act, after its sponsor) established the National Labor Relations Board (NLRB), which oversees labor relations by conducting unionization elections, hears unfair labor practice complaints, and issues injunctions against offending employers.

The Union-Organizing Process. There are typically five stages in forming a union, which Figure 8–11 lists.

labor relations
The interactions between management and unionized employees.

11. Explain why most organizations do not have labor relations.

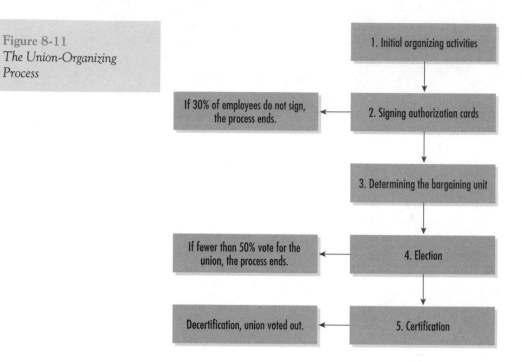

Figure 8-11
The Union-Organizing Process

1. Initial organizing activities

If 30% of employees do not sign, the process ends. ← 2. Signing authorization cards

3. Determining the bargaining unit

If fewer than 50% vote for the union, the process ends. ← 4. Election

Decertification, union voted out. ← 5. Certification

collective bargaining
The negotiation process resulting in a contract that covers employment conditions.

Collective Bargaining. **Collective bargaining** *is the negotiation process resulting in a contract that covers employment conditions.* The most common employment conditions covered in the contract include compensation, hours, and working conditions. But, the contract can include any issue that both sides agree to. Job security is a major bargaining issue for unions today.

To avoid a strike or lockout (refusing to let employees work) and to handle *grievances* by either side, collective bargainers sometimes agree to use neutral third parties, called mediators, from the Federal Mediation and Conciliation Service (FMCS). A *mediator* is a neutral party who helps management and labor settle their disagreements. In cases where management and labor are not willing to compromise but do not want to call a strike or lockout, they may call in an arbitrator. An *arbitrator* is different from a mediator in that the arbitrator makes a binding decision for management and labor. The arbitrator's decision must be followed. The services of an arbitrator are more commonly used to settle grievances than to deal with impasses in collective bargaining.

Termination and Outplacement

There are three primary reasons employees leave organizations: (1) Attrition results in some employees leaving for other jobs, electing to stop working for a period of time, or retiring. In any case, employees lost to attrition often need to be replaced. Employees who leave voluntarily are often interviewed to find out the reason for leaving. The *exit interview*, usually conducted by the human resources department, can help identify problem areas that lead to turnover. (2) Firing results in employees who break the rules and do not perform to standards being terminated.[52] In Chapter 14 you will learn how to handle problem employees. (3) Layoffs result in employees being let go. Layoffs usually occur because of economic and organizational problems and mergers and acquisitions. Apple, Boeing, General Dynamics, GM, IBM, McDonnell Douglas, and Sears laid off tens of thousands of employees during the 1990s to cut costs.

When companies have a layoff, they may offer outplacement services. *Outplacement services* help employees find new jobs. For example, when General Electric had a layoff of 900 employees, it set up a reemployment center to help employees find new jobs or to learn new skills. Because of Scitor's human resources practices, it has little difficulty in attracting and retaining employees. It has no labor relations, low termination, and has had no need for outplacement services.

CHAPTER SUMMARY AND GLOSSARY

The chapter summary is organized to answer the twelve learning objectives for Chapter 8.

1. List the four parts of the human resources management process.
The four parts of the human resources management process are (1) human resources planning, (2) attracting employees, (3) developing employees, and (4) retaining employees.

2. Explain the difference between a job description and a job specification and why they are needed.
The job description identifies what the employee does on the job, whereas the job specification identifies the qualifications needed to get the job. Job analysis is needed because it serves as the basis for attracting, developing, and retaining employees.

3. State the two parts of attracting employees and the difference between them.
The two parts of attracting employees are recruiting and selecting. Recruiting is the process of attracting qualified candidates to apply for job openings. Selecting is the process of choosing the most qualified applicant recruited for a job.

4. Describe the difference between hypothetical and probing questions.
A hypothetical question is planned; it requires the candidate to describe what he or she would do and say in a given situation. A probing question is not planned; it is used to clarify a response to an open-ended or a hypothetical question.

5. Discuss the difference between orientation and training and development of employees.

Orientation is the process of introducing new employees to the organizational culture and their jobs. Training and development is the process of acquiring the skills necessary to perform present and future jobs.

6. List the steps in job instructional training.

The steps in job instructional training are (1) prepare the learner, (2) present the task, (3) performance of the task by the trainee, and (4) follow-up.

7. Explain the two types of performance appraisal.

The two types of performance appraisal are developmental and evaluative. Developmental PA is used to make decisions and plan for performance improvements. Evaluative PA is used to make administrative decisions, including pay raises, transfers and promotions, and demotions and terminations.

8. Explain the concept, "You get what you reward."

People seek information concerning what activities are rewarded, and then seek to do (or at least pretend to do) those things, often to the exclusion of activities not rewarded.

9. State the major components of compensation.

The two components of compensation are pay and benefits.

10. Describe the difference between the use of job analysis and job evaluation.

A job analysis is used to determine what the job entails and the qualifications needed to staff the position. Job evaluation is used to determine how much to compensate employees for their jobs.

11. Explain why most organizations do not have labor relations.

Labor relations are the interactions between management and unionized employees. Because most organizations do not have unions, they do not have labor relations.

12. Define the following key terms (in order of appearance in the chapter):

Select one or more methods: (1) fill in the missing key terms from memory, (2) match the key terms from the end of the summary with their definitions below, or (3) copy the terms in order from the list at the beginning of the chapter.

The _____ consists of planning, attracting, developing, and retaining employees.

A _____ allows discrimination where it is reasonably necessary to normal operation of a particular organization.

_____ is the process of staffing the organization to meet its objectives.

The _____ identifies the tasks and responsibilities of a position.

_____ identify the qualifications needed to staff a position.

_____ is the process of attracting qualified candidates to apply for job openings.

_____ is the process of choosing the most qualified applicant recruited for a job.

_____ are places where job applicants undergo a series of tests, interviews, and simulated experiences to determine their managerial potential.

_____ is the process of introducing new employees to the organization and their jobs.

_____ is the process of acquiring the skills necessary to perform a job.

_____ is the ongoing education to improve skills for present and future jobs.

_____ develops skills in a simulated setting.

_____ is the ongoing process of evaluating employee performance.

_____ is the total cost of pay and benefits to employees.

_____ is the process of determining the worth of each job relative to other jobs within the organization.

_____ are the interactions between management and unionized employees.

_____ is the negotiation process resulting in a contract that covers employment conditions.

KEY TERMS

assessment centers 262
bona fide occupational qualification (BFOQ) 256
collective bargaining 278
compensation 276
development 267

human resources management process 254
job description 258
job evaluation 276
job specifications 258
labor relations 277
orientation 266

performance appraisal 271
recruiting 259
selection 261
strategic human resources planning 258
training 267
vestibule training 267

REVIEW AND DISCUSSION QUESTIONS

1. What is your opinion of allowing a bona fide occupational qualification?

2. What are the components of a job analysis?

3. What is your opinion of using promotion from within as an internal recruiting source?

4. Do you agree that the interview should be the primary criterion for selection?

5. What is the most common problem to avoid during interviewing?

6. If you work for a company with a human resources department, does this mean that, as a manager, you don't have to orient and train employees? Explain.

7. How does setting objectives affect measuring and evaluating training results in the training cycle?

8. How is compensation both an attracting and retaining part of the human resources process?

9. Why don't most employees realize how expensive benefits are and how much they contribute to compensation cost?

10. Are unions greedy because they expect more than they are worth, or is management greedy because it takes excessive salaries and gives too large a share of the profits to the owners?

11. What is the difference between a mediator and an arbitrator?

OBJECTIVE CASE

Cunningham Communication, Inc.

Andrea Cunningham started her own public relations (PR) firm in Santa Clara, California. Andrea developed a mission that gave the firm a competitive advantage because it keeps clients apprised of how they are perceived by the market. Cunningham keeps tabs on the financial community, the press, consultants, customers, and even employees within the firm. High-quality employees are critical to PR success. Client turnover is high at most PR agencies, and employee job-hopping is also common as PR representatives search for higher pay and new challenges.

Cunningham acquired some of Silicon Valley's best clients, including Borland International and Aldus Corporation software makers and Hewlett-Packard and Motorola. Andrea's Cunningham Communication revenues grew to over $3 million annually with 24 employees. However, Andrea made a common entrepreneurial error. She tried to make all the decisions herself without delegating authority. As a result, managers were constantly fighting, morale was very low, turnover of both clients and employees was very high, and Andrea faced the threat of losing money for the first time since she started the business.

Andrea came to the realization that she had to delegate authority if she was going to have a turnaround. She decided to develop a goal-driven system with a cooperative management program called *input teams*. Andrea set annual objectives for each team to develop the necessary plans and budgets to achieve the objectives. Every employee was a member of at least one team that met for five hours per week. Andrea also realized that her human resources practices had to support the Cunningham mission and new management system. Working with her human resources manager and others, they developed the following program.

To attract and retain employees, called associates, they developed a career path system. A career path is a sequence of job assignments that leads to more responsibility with raises and promotions.

The career path system was designed to develop associates to a level of competence that inspired the confidence of clients. New associates are oriented to the organizational culture, called the Cunningham Culture. They learn about the various departments, they are taught about the input teams, and they develop team skills and time-management skills. New associates attend Cunningham Communication Inc. University for a formal three-day training session.

The compensation system was also changed. All associates receive a set pay for the year and a bonus based on meeting objectives. Each associate determines his or her responsibilities, objectives, and pay. Andrea says that associates rarely request compensation that they are not worth. Frequent advisory sessions give associates feedback from their boss on how well they are meeting expectations. On occasion when associates have fallen short of their objectives, compensation has been withheld without complaint. To increase compensation, associates have to generate more revenue.

Within six months of implementing the changes, all but three members of the senior staff voluntarily terminated employment at Cunningham. Andrea was sad to see them go, but felt they were not right for the new management system. On the positive side, the company became profitable and continues to grow; the number of associates went from 24 to 59 under the new systems.

Select the best alternative for the following questions. Be sure you are able to explain your answers.

_____ 1. Which of the components of the human resources management process is not discussed in the case?

    a. human resources planning

    b. attracting

    c. developing

    d. retaining employees

OBJECTIVE CASE

(continued)

___ 2. Poor job analysis and poor realistic job previews were major reasons for the high turnover rate at Cunningham.

    a. true   b. false

___ 3. Cunningham's primary problem was in the area of

    a. attracting employees

    b. developing employees

    c. retaining employees

___ 4. Cunningham's primary recruiting source would have to be

    a. internal   b. external

___ 5. Cunningham training focuses more on

    a. technical skills

    b. human and conceptual skills

___ 6. Advisory sessions are a ___ tool.

    a. recruiting   d. orientation

    b. training   e. selection

    c. performance appraisal

___ 7. Cunningham's compensation system does not include

    a. wages   b. salary   c. incentives

___ 8. There are good labor relations at Cunningham.

    a. true   b. false

___ 9. Cunningham offers outplacement services.

    a. true   b. false

___ 10. Cunningham's primary changes to increase performance focused on

    a. globalization   d. quality and TQM

    b. diversity   e. participative management

    c. ethics

11. Are the human resources problems at Cunningham unique or are they common to other organizations?

12. Andrea went from one extreme of having total responsibility for running the business to letting the employees run the business. Would you have recommended a gradual move or an extreme change?

13. Would you allow associates to set their own pay?

14. What else would you recommend Cunningham do to attract, develop, and retain associates?

For current information on Cunningham Communication, use Internet address http://www.ccipr.com. For ideas on using the Internet, see Appendix B.

VIDEO CASE

Next Door Food Stores II

(8-1 14 Minutes)
Case Summary

This is a continuation of Next Door Food Stores I from Chapter 5. Next Door is a retail chain with unique opportunities to create a competitive advantage in the convenience store industry. This case illustrates how quality management decisions created a competitive edge. Day-to-day operational planning and implementation of human resources practices are illustrated.

VIDEO CASE (continued)

Students' Learning Objective

To better understand how job satisfaction and employee retention can be influenced by human resources functions and the need for cost containment.

Critical Thinking Questions

1. How can Next Door Food Store's human resources department help reduce employee turnover?

2. How can Next Door Food Store's human resources department help control the following personnel costs?

workers' compensation

medical benefits

BEHAVIOR MODEL VIDEO

Behavior Model Video 8–1 (8 minutes), Employment Interviewing, shows Craig conducting a job interview with Betsy, following the steps in Model 8–2. This video serves as a behavior model, which can be used prior to conducting Skill-Building Exercise 8–1, Selecting a Tennis Coach.

*skillbuilder

R

Skill-Building Exercise 8–1

Selecting a Tennis Coach

Preparing for Skill-Building Exercise 8–1

You are in your first year as athletic director at a local high school. While planning your human resources needs, you realize the tennis coach position will be open. You must staff the position. The compensation for the job is set in the budget. It is to be paid in one lump sum at the end of the season. It is competitive with the pay of other tennis coaches in the area.

Recruiting

Because you have no recruiting budget, you do some internal recruiting and contact some athletic directors in your area to spread the word about the opening. You recruit three candidates for the coaching position. Following is a brief listing of their qualifications.

Candidate A has been a history teacher at your school for ten years. This person was the tennis coach for two years. It's been five years since the teacher coached the team. You don't know why the candidate stopped coaching or how good a job was done. Candidate A never played competitive tennis. However, someone told you the candidate plays regularly and is pretty good. You guess the teacher is about 35 years old.

Candidate B works as a supervisor on the 11 P.M. to 7 A.M. shift for a local business. This candidate has never coached before. However, the person was a star player in high school and college. Candidate B still plays in local tournaments and you see the name in the paper now and then. You guess this candidate is about 25 years old.

Candidate C has been a basketball coach and physical education teacher at a nearby high school for the past five years. The person has a master's degree in physical education. You figure it will take the person 20 minutes to get to your school. Candidate C has never coached tennis, but did play on the high school team. The candidate plays tennis about once a week. You guess the person is about 45 years old.

Preparing for the Interviews

Follow the six interview preparation steps in Model 8–1. For step 1, there are no job descriptions and specifications. Because there are only three candidates, you have decided to interview them all, even if they do not meet your job specifications.

Conducting the Interviews

During the in-class part of this exercise you will conduct a job interview. Be sure to bring your preparation—written questions on a form—material for class use.

Doing Skill-Building Exercise 8–1 in Class

Objectives
To perform a job analysis and to develop skills in employment selection interviewing.

Preparation
You should have your form with a list of questions for candidates.

Experience
You will discuss your preparation. You will also conduct a job interview, be an interviewee, and observe an interview.

Procedure 1 (5–10 minutes)
Break into groups of five or six, pass your preparation materials around to the other members, and discuss them. You may make changes to improve your preparation. For example, you may want to add some good questions you did not think of.

Procedure 2 (3–5 minutes)
Break into groups of three; do not divide into the same groups used in procedure 1. Make one or two groups of two, if necessary. Each person selects one of the three candidates (A, B, or C) he or she will role-play during

the interview. Use your own name, but assume you have the person's qualifications; ad lib realistically.

Procedure 3 (25–75 minutes)
1-1. Interview 1 takes place. The person who chose A is the interviewer, B is the interviewee, and C is the observer. A conducts the interview using his or her interview materials, while B answers the questions. C observes quietly, and gives feedback on how well the interview went. (If there are only two in your group, B is also the observer.) You may not be able to ask all your questions in the allotted time (5 to 20 minutes). Keep the opening short and be sure to close when you are ready to or the time is up.

1-2. Integration (3–5 minutes). C gives his or her observation of the interview. All three group members discuss the interview and how it could be improved. Do not go on to the next interview until you are told to do so.

2-1. Interview 2 takes place. B is the interviewer, C is the interviewee, and A is the observer. Follow the guidelines for 1-1.

2-2. Integration. Follow the guidelines for 1-2.

3-1. Interview 3 takes place. C is the interviewer; A is the interviewee; and B is the observer. Groups of two join other triads as observers. Follow the guidelines for 1-1.

3-2. Integration. Follow the guidelines for 1-2.

Procedure 4 (2–4 minutes)
Individually select the candidate you would offer the job to. The instructor counts how many students would hire each candidate to determine the class selection.

Conclusion
The instructor may lead a class discussion and make concluding remarks.

Application (2–4 minutes)
What did I learn from this experience? How will I use this knowledge in the future?

Sharing
Volunteers give their answers to the application section.

BEHAVIOR MODEL VIDEO

Behavior Model Video 8–2 (4 1/2 minutes) shows Chris conducting a job instructional training session with Betsy, following the steps in Model 8–3. This video serves as a behavior model which can be used prior to conducting Skill-Building Exercise 8–2, Job Instructional Training.

*skillbuilder

R

Skill-Building Exercise 8–2

Job Instructional Training

Preparing for Skill-Building Exercise 8–2

For this exercise, you will prepare to conduct a training session using Model 8–3 by following the training cycle below:

Step 1. Conduct a Needs Assessment. Select a task you are familiar with that most people don't know how to do and that you can teach someone else to do in ten minutes (knitting, a job function, an athletic technique, how to play a game, conduct a magic trick, and so on).

Step 2. Set Objectives. Write down your objective(s) for the training session.

Step 3. Prepare for Training. Write out a description of your plan, following the four steps in the JIT model. Be sure to develop steps for presenting the operation. The "who" will be determined in class. The "when" and "where" will be in class. Be sure to bring the necessary material (knitting, ball, game, etc.) to class to conduct the training session.

Step 4. Conduct the Training. The training will be done in class. Be sure to bring all the materials you will need.

Step 5. Measure and Evaluate Results. This will be done in class. But make sure that your plan includes how you will measure and evaluate your training results.

Doing Skill-Building Exercise 8–2 in Class

Objective

To develop skills in designing and implementing training using the training cycle and job instructional training (JIT).

Preparation

You should have planned how to train someone to perform a task and have brought the necessary materials to conduct the training session.

Experience

You will give, receive, and observe JIT.

Procedure 1 (2–3 minutes)

Break into groups of three, preferably with people who are not familiar with the task you will be teaching. Make some groups of two, if necessary. Decide who will be the trainer (A), trainee (B), and observer (C) for the first training session. During the training session, the trainer teaches the trainee to perform the task while the observer makes notes on the integration sheet at the end of this exercise.

Procedure 2 (20–40 minutes)

1-1. *Training session 1 takes place.* Member A trains B to perform the task using JIT, as C observes and takes notes on the integration sheet.

1-2. *Integration.* When the training is over, or the time is up, observer C leads a group discussion on which JIT steps the trainer did and did not follow. Focus on how the trainer can improve his or her skills. Do not go on to the next training session until you are told to do so.

2-1. *Training session 2 takes place.* Member A is now the trainee; C becomes the trainer; and B becomes the observer.

2-2. *Integration.* Same as procedure 1-2; B leads the discussion. Do not go on to the next training until told to do so.

3-1. *Training session 3 takes place.* Each person plays the role he or she hasn't played yet; B trains C while A observes.

3-2. *Integration.* Same as procedure 1-2.

Conclusion
The instructor may lead a class discussion and/or make concluding remarks.

Application (2–4 minutes)
What did I learn from this experience? How will I use this knowledge in the future?

_____

_____

Sharing
Volunteers give their answers to the application section.

Integration Sheet
The observer gives feedback to the trainer on how well he or she performed each step of JIT. Focus on things done well and how to improve at each step. Refer to the text for the details of what should take place for each step.

Step 1. Preparation of the Trainee.

_____

_____

Step 2. Presentation of the Task.

_____

_____

Step 3. Performance of the Task by the Trainee.

_____

_____

Step 4. Follow-up.

_____

_____

9 Organizational Behavior: Power, Politics, Conflict, and Stress

Learning Objectives

After studying this chapter, you should be able to:

1. List the differences along the continuum for each of the big five personality traits (extraversion, agreeableness, neuroticism, conscientiousness, and openness to experience).

2. Explain the perception process and the two factors it is based on.

3. Describe the interrelationship among personality, perception, and attitude, and why they are important.

4. State what job satisfaction is and why it is important.

5. Define *power* and the difference between position and personal power.

6. Explain the difference among reward, legitimate, and referent power.

7. Discuss how power and politics are related.

8. Describe how money and politics have a similar use.

9. Explain what networking, reciprocity, and coalitions have in common.

10. List and define the five conflict management styles.

11. List the steps in the initiating conflict resolution model.

12. Explain the stress tug-of-war analogy.

13. Define the following **key terms** (in order of appearance in the chapter):

organizational behavior	coalition
win-win situation	conflict
personality	functional conflict
perception	initiating conflict resolution
attribution	model
attitudes	BCF model
Pygmalion effect	mediator
power	arbitrator
politics	stress
networking	stressors
reciprocity	

Skill Development

skillbuilder 1. You can develop your skill at using power and negotiation (Skill-Building Exercise 9–1). Power is a leadership management function. Power requires the use of interpersonal, informational, and decision-making management roles. The SCANS competencies of interpersonal skills and information, as well as basic, thinking, and personal qualities are developed through the exercise.

skillbuilder 2. You can develop your collaborative conflict management skills (Skill-Building Exercise 9–2). Conflict management is a leadership management function. Conflict management requires the use of interpersonal, informational, and decision-making management roles. The SCANS competencies of interpersonal skills and information, as well as basic, thinking, and personal qualities are developed through the exercise.

Legend has it that Ross Perot started his business career as a boy delivering newspapers in a Texarkana, Texas, ghetto and became a successful young salesperson for IBM by meeting his annual sales quota in the first month. According to Doron Levin, author of *Irreconcilable Differences: Ross Perot versus General Motors*, Perot's motives are money, attention, and power. His need for attention and power influenced his decision to spend millions of dollars running for the presidency of the United States, although he officially withdrew, and to later work to develop a third political party to compete with the Republican and Democratic parties.

Perot's power-based personality is illustrated in his motto, which he quotes from Winston Churchill, "Never give in. Never." When Perot decides to do something, he is convinced that he is right, and those who disagree with him become his enemies. He exerts power and politics and creates conflict and stress in others to get what he wants. He has been known to discredit competitors and use political arm-twisting to win business deals. However, Perot is supportive of employees who are loyal to him. People who have worked for him have stated that they are a bit afraid of him, in awe of him, sometimes angry with him, but they like working for him!

Perot started Electronic Data Systems, Inc. (EDS) and became a powerful self-made billionaire. EDS assists client organizations in the development of computer information systems designed to address and solve business problems. He went on to sell EDS to General Motors (GM) and became a member of GM's board of directors and a GM stockholder. Perot was very outspoken against GM management practices and was pressing for drastic changes. He was so powerfully intimidating and successful at building a political network that GM management decided to buy his GM stock at a premium price to get rid of him. He went on to recruit EDS employees away from GM when he created a competing company, Perot Systems. Although Ross Perot is basically an autocratic leader, he has always been against bureaucracy and hierarchy and for informal communication.

For current information on EDS, use Internet address **http://www.eds.com**. For ideas on using the Internet, see Appendix B.

Recall that human and communication skills is one of the three important management skills. Human skills are also known as interpersonal skills.[1] Management requires getting the job done through others. Thus, how well you relate to others determines your career success.[2] Interpersonal skills are especially an important part of the leadership management function. Therefore, in the leadership section, Chapters 9–13, you will learn about these concepts. To climb the corporate ladder, you will have to understand organizational behavior and to gain power, engage in politics, and manage your conflicts and stress. You will learn about these concepts in this chapter.

Have you ever wondered why people behave the way they do at work? This is what organizational behavior (OB) is all about. Behavior consists of what you say and do, or it is your actions. **Organizational behavior** *is the study of actions that affect performance in the workplace.* The *goal of OB* is to explain and predict actions and how they will affect performance. An important part of OB is creating a win-win situation. A **win-win situation** *occurs when the organization and the employees get what they want.* OB has three levels of focus: individual, group, and organizational. In this chapter you will learn about individual behavior, in the next chapter about group behavior, and you already learned about the organizational level in Chapter 7—organizational development.

Generally, the better you understand OB, the more effective you will be at working with others as a manager or worker. The foundations of individual behavior include personality, perception, and attitudes. However, these foundations are not observable. You can only observe actions and try to explain the behavior based on your understanding of the foundations. At the next level, you can try to predict people's actions in a given situation based on understanding their personalities, perceptions, and attitudes.

organizational behavior
The study of actions that affect performance in the workplace.

win-win situation
When the organization and employees get what they want.

To this end, the next three sections focus on the foundations of individual behavior.

PERSONALITY

Why are some people outgoing and others shy, loud and quiet, warm and cold, aggressive and passive? This list of behaviors is made up of individual traits. *Personality is a combination of traits that classifies individuals.* Understanding people's personalities is important because personality affects behavior, as well as perceptions and attitudes.[3] Knowing personalities helps you to explain and predict others' behavior and job performance.[4] Therefore, many organizations give personality tests to ensure a proper match between the worker and the job.[5] For example, an outgoing personality is generally a trait of successful sales reps and strong analytical traits are common for people who work in technical/computer jobs.

personality
A combination of traits that classifies individuals.

Personality is developed based on genetics and environmental factors. Your personality traits are influenced by genes you received before you were born.[6] Your family, friends, school, and work also influence your personality. There are many personality classification methods. Three widely recognized methods are the single trait, Jung personality types, and the big five personality traits.

Single Traits of Personality

Some of the single traits of personality include the locus of control, optimism, risk propensity, Machiavellianism, self-esteem, and self-efficacy. Because self-esteem and self-efficacy are based on perception, they will be discussed with perception.

Locus of Control. Locus of control lies on a continuum between external and internal belief over who has control over one's destiny. Personality traits are externalizers or internalizers. Externalizers believe that they have no control over their fate and that their behavior has little to do with their performance. Internalizers believe that they control their fate and that their behavior has a direct effect on their performance. Internalizers have been shown to have higher levels of performance.

Optimism. Optimism lies on a continuum between optimistic and pessimistic. Optimistic people believe that things will go well and they tend to be happy. Pessimistic people believe that things will not go well and they tend to be unhappy much of the time. Optimistic employees usually have higher levels of performance as their optimism often leads them to take action to meet objectives, whereas pessimists usually give up easily and say "I told you I/we could not do it."

Risk Propensity. *Risk propensity* lies on a continuum between risk taking and risk avoiding. Entrepreneurs are risk takers. Successful organizations are looking for managers who will take risks based on research. Organizations with risk-avoiding managers often go out of business because they do not keep up with the changes in their industry.

Machiavellianism. *Machiavellianism* is the degree to which people believe that ends can justify the means and use power to get what they want. The term comes from the sixteenth century renaissance philosopher, Niccolo Machiavelli. High Machs are generally considered effective in situations where bargaining and winning is important, such as in a variety of negotiation jobs (purchasing/labor) or as commissioned sales reps. However, high Machs are more concerned about meeting their needs than helping the organization. Thus, they tend to create win-lose situations, and may use unethical behavior to win, which can have a negative effect on the organization and other employees. Ross Perot has an internal locus of control; is an optimist, which leads to his motto, never give in, because he will succeed; is a risk taker; and is a high Mach.

Jung's Personality Types

Like the single traits of personality, Jung focused on one trait—introverted/extroverted. The introverted personality is characterized as shy, reserved, and withdrawn. The extroverted personality is outgoing, generally friendly, and may be dominant. However, unlike single traits, Jung extended introvert/extrovert to include four personality types based on sensing/intuition—processing information and thinking/feeling—making decisions.

Sensing personality types process information in a concrete logical analytic method, like established routines, usually finish tasks, accept details, and are good with precision work. *Intuition personality types* process information based on insight and hunch, dislike repetitive work, jump to conclusions, and are impatient with details and precision. Is your personality more of a sensing or intuition trait? *Thinking personality types* are analytical and look for logical relationships among the inputs of a situation. They do well at planning and technical work. *Feeling personality types* are conceptual, allowing personal values and experience into the decision-making process, and do well working with people. Is your personality more of a thinking or feeling trait? Do you prefer working with things or people?

Using Figure 9–1, determine your personality type. However, remember that personality is a combination of traits. You may not fit neatly into one of the four types. For example, there is a continuum of how logical vs. insightful people actually are. The same applies for thinking/feeling. Either selection (things/people) does not mean that you are not successful with the other. All four types may make good managers depending on the situation. Ross Perot is a sensing/thinking personality type. Myers and Briggs developed a more complex personality types matrix by adding introvert/extrovert and judging/perceiving to the Jung matrix to create a matrix with sixteen personality types.[7]

	Thinking	**Feeling**
Sensing	Sensing/Thinking A logical information processor and factual decision maker who does well working with things.	Sensing/Feeling A logical information processor and conceptual decision maker who does well working with people.
Intuition	Intuition/Thinking An insightful/hunch information processor and factual decision maker who does well working with things.	Intuition/Feeling An insightful/hunch information processor and conceptual decision maker who does well working with people.

Figure 9-1
Jung Personality Types

The Big Five Personality Traits

The big five personality traits is the most widely accepted way to classify personalities. The big five essentially combines five single traits into one set of dimensions of personality. It has also been published with slightly different descriptors.[8] The five dimensions of personality are:

Extraversion. Extraversion lies on a continuum between extrovert and introvert, as described by Jung. Do you like to meet new people? Extroverts do well in sales and often management.

Agreeableness. Agreeableness lies on a continuum between cooperation and competition. Do you like to cooperate or compete with your fellow workers/teammates? Organizations with work teams that cooperate with members and compete with external teams generally have higher levels of performance than when they compete internally.

Neuroticism. Neuroticism lies on a continuum between being emotionally stable and unstable. Stable refers to being calm, secure, and positive, whereas unstable is nervous, insecure, and negative. Do you generally behave with a positive or a negative attitude? Workers with a positive attitude generally perform better.

Conscientiousness. Conscientiousness lies on a continuum between responsible/dependable and irresponsible/undependable. It has also been polarized by being a planner and organized or not. Are you responsible and dependable or not? Responsible employees outperform nonresponsible ones.

Openness to Experience. Openness to experience lies on a continuum between being willing to try new things and not being willing. Do you like to try new experiences or stay with the routine? With the fast rate of change, employees who are open to learning new things are more productive to the organization. Ross Perot is generally an extrovert, competitive, positive, conscientious, and open to new experiences.

To review the personality traits, and to better understand your own personality, complete Self-Assessment Exercise 9–1.

1. List the differences along the continuum for each of the big five personality traits (extraversion, agreeableness, neuroticism, conscientiousness, and openness to experience).

WORK APPLICATION

1. Identify your present or past boss's personality using all 10 personality traits in Self-Assessment Exercise 9–1.

Self-Assessment Exercise 9–1

Personality Traits

For each personality trait identify on the continuum, by placing a check, the level that characterizes you. Be honest. Also, it would be a good idea to have people who know you well also complete the traits for you to see if your perception of your personality is the same as others'. Perception is our next topic.

Generally, there are no simple right traits from the individual perspective. However, from the organizational perspective, it is generally better to recruit and retain people with personality traits listed on the left-hand side of the continuums because people with these traits are more productive. Review your personality type; realize that you can change your personality. More details on changing your personality are in Exercise 9–1.

Single Traits of Personality

Locus of Control
I'm an internalizer   ____ ____ ____ / ____ ____ ____   I'm an externalizer

Optimism
I'm an optimist   ____ ____ ____ / ____ ____ ____   I'm a pessimist

Risk Propensity
I'm a risk taker   ____ ____ ____ / ____ ____ ____   I'm a risk avoider

Machiavellianism
I'm not a power user   ____ ____ ____ / ____ ____ ____   I'm a power user

Jung's Personality Types

I'm _____ sensing/thinking, _____ sensing/feeling, _____ intuition/thinking, _____ intuition/feeling

The Big Five Personality Traits

Extraversion
I'm an extrovert   ____ ____ ____ / ____ ____ ____   I'm an introvert

Agreeableness
I'm cooperative   ____ ____ ____ / ____ ____ ____   I'm competitive

Neuroticism
I'm positive   ____ ____ ____ / ____ ____ ____   I'm negative

Conscientiousness
I'm dependable   ____ ____ ____ / ____ ____ ____   I'm not dependable

Openness to experience
I try new things   ____ ____ ____ / ____ ____ ____   I avoid doing new things

PERCEPTION

Why do some people perceive Ross Perot (and others) as a nice guy while others can't stand him? Why do some employees view a decision made by a manager as fair while others do not?[9] Why do some people view Kodak film as a quality product while others do not?[10] Understanding perception is important because needs and perception are the starting point of behavior. People tend to treat people they perceive to be likable differently than people they perceive to be unlikable. Employees may work harder for a manager they perceive to be a good manager than one they don't like. If Kodak film is perceived to be a quality product, people may buy it, if not, they won't. Perception refers to a person's interpretation of reality. In reality, is Ross Perot a good guy/manager or a bad guy/manager? It is important to realize that perceptions, right or wrong, affect behavior and performance. In this section you will learn about the perception process and perception bias.

The Perception Process

Perception *is the process of selecting, organizing, and interpreting environmental information.* No two people experience anything exactly the same through this perception process. How people perceive things at work is based on individual and organizational factors.[11] How you select, organize, and interpret information is based on internal individual factors including your personality,[12] self-esteem,[13] attitudes, intelligence, needs, values, and so on. *Self-esteem, or self-concept, is your perception of yourself.* Recall that self-esteem is a personality trait; it lies on a continuum between positive and negative or high and low. Do you like yourself? Are you a valuable person/employee? Do you believe you are capable of doing new things well, or do you fear failure? Employers are recruiting employees with positive self-esteem[14] because it has a positive effect on performance.[15] For example, an employee who is open to experience and who has positive self-esteem will have a different perception of and performance on a new, delegated task than an employee who is not.

The second factor of the perception process is the information itself from the external environment. The more accurate the information that is received, the more closely the perception may be to reality. Inaccurate rumors cause perception problems in organizations. Continuing the previous example, if the manager delegates the task very poorly, the employee's perception of the task and performance may be different than if the delegation is performed well.

The Attribution Process. **Attribution** *is the process of determining the reason for behavior.* The process begins when people find out about behavior through direct observation or through other sources such as reading about the behavior or friends reporting it. When the reason for the behavior is determined, people usually want to know if the intent was situational or intentional. Situational refers to the behavior being accidental or basically out of

2. Explain the perception process and the two factors it is based on.

perception
The process of selecting, organizing, and interpreting environmental information.

attribution
The process of determining the reason for behavior.

the control of the individual. To determine intent, three variables are used: distinctiveness (the extent to which a person behaves in the same way in other situations), consensus (the extent to which others in the same situation behave the same way), and consistency (the extent to which a person behaves in the same way at different times). Based on intent, the reason for the behavior is determined. Lastly, behavior is often affected by the other person's behavior; a behavioral response is determined, which could be to do nothing. A manager's behavior will usually be different based on attribution being perceived as situational or intentional. This process is illustrated in Model 9–1.

For example, a manager, Eduardo, observes an employee, Pat, coming to work late. Eduardo thinks about Pat being late coming back from lunch, being the only one who is late, and being late with some consistency. Thus, Eduardo determines the intent of the late behavior as intentional and determines the reason for the behavior as not caring about being on time. The behavioral response of the manager is to discipline the employee. However, if this was the first time Pat was late, Eduardo may have determined the intent to be situational (car problem, traffic, etc.) and take no action to discipline Pat.

Attribution refers to determining the reasons for your behavior and that of others. However, as in the previous example, most people spend more time determining the reasons for others' behavior. When people determine the reasons for their own behavior they tend to take the credit for success as being intentional. Conversely, when they fail they tend to blame situational factors. They also tend to reverse the credit and blame when determining the reason for others' behavior. This is clearly a perception difference issue.

Bias in Perception

Some of the reasons why people perceive the same behavior differently include the bias of selectivity, frame of reference, stereotypes, and expectation.

Selectivity. *Selectivity* refers to screening information in favor of the desired outcome. People will sometimes make great efforts to find information that supports their point of view, yet ignore information that does not. In other words, people only hear what they want to hear. For example, a per-

WORK APPLICATION

2. Using Model 9–1, explain how you used the attribution process at work.

Model 9-1
The Attribution Process

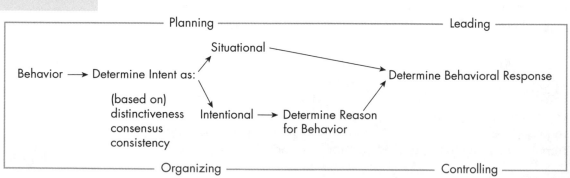

son could hear 10 good points about Ross Perot and only one bad point. However, they focus on the one negative point and conclude that he is not a good manager. A related bias is the *halo effect* in which people judge others on many tasks based on their perception of a single trait.

Frame of Reference. *Frame of reference* refers to seeing things from your own point of view. Employees often view management decisions differently than do managers.[16] Managers and employees commonly use the same data during contract negotiations; however, managers perceive that employees want more pay and are not willing to increase productivity, but employees perceive managers as greedy and not willing to share the wealth, which employees perceive that they create. One of the problems with labor negotiations is that it tends to create a win-lose situation. Thus, as a manager, don't be surprised that employees don't perceive things the way that you do. Remember that it is not your perception but the employees' perception that will influence their behavior and performance. Try to see things from the employees' perspective and create a win-win situation so that all parties get what they want.

Stereotypes. *Stereotyping* is the process of generalizing the behavior of a group to one individual. Stereotypes are made in terms of differences in race/nationality, religion, sex, age, and so forth. Stereotyping a person can lead to perception errors because not all "fill-in your own example" are "fill-in." Try not to negatively stereotype employees; get to know them as individuals.

Expectations. Read the phrase in the triangle below

Did you read the word "the" twice? Or, like most people, did you read what you expected, only one "the"? Many people, especially those who know each other well, often do not really listen to each other. They simply hear what they expect to hear.

Another type of expectation is the *"like me"* assumption that others perceive things as you do because they are similar to you. Remember to value diversity. Don't expect others to behave as you do, and don't judge others' behavior as wrong just because it is different from yours. All people are subject to these perception biases. Has anyone accused you of not hearing them for any of the biases?

ATTITUDES

Attitudes *are positive or negative evaluations of people, things, and situations.* Your personality self-esteem trait affects your attitudes.[17] Attitude is a major factor in determining performance.[18] Employers recruit employees with positive self-esteem and attitudes toward their careers and personal lives,

WORK APPLICATION

3. Give an example of when you and someone else experienced the same situation but perceived it differently. Which of the biases to perception seem to be the major reason for the difference in perception?

3. Describe the interrelationship among personality, perception, and attitude, and why they are important.

attitudes
Positive or negative evaluations of people, things, and situations.

because they are more likely to be loyal workers who can be relied on to accomplish their tasks.[19] J.W. Marriott, Jr., president of Marriott Corporation, stated, "We have found that our success depends more upon employee attitude than any other single factor." You can change your overall attitude to be more positive. See Exercise 9–1 for more details. Diversity training has changed attitudes by helping to eliminate negative stereotypes. In this section you will learn about how attitudes are formed and affect behavior, and how management attitudes affect performance and job satisfaction.

Attitude Formation

Attitude formations are based on perceptions.[20] Family, friends, teachers, coworkers, the mass media and so on affect your attitude formation. Before you signed up for this course, you may have read the course description and talked to students who have completed it to find out more about the course and thought about your interest in the course. Based on what you read and heard and your interest in the subject, you may have started this course with a positive or negative attitude. People generally find what they are looking for, so if you had a positive (negative) attitude coming into the course you probably like (dislike) it. However, attitudes can be changed. Has your attitude toward this course become more positive, negative, or remained the same? What were the primary factors that formed your present attitude toward this course?

Attitudes and Behavior

Attitudes often reflect feelings and affect behavior. People with positive attitudes toward a person, job, course, or event (also called a situation) often behave differently. Based on knowledge and feelings, people determine how to behave toward or in the situation. Avoiding situations is a sign of negative attitudes toward them. People generally are consistent with their attitudes and behavior, but not always. For example, have you, or anyone you know, ever had a negative attitude toward a person (dislike them), such as a coworker or boss, yet when you interact with that person your behavior does not reflect your attitude? People's attitudes toward you also affect your behavior. Do you behave differently with people who like you than with those who don't?

How Management Attitudes Affect Performance

J. Sterling Livingston developed the Pygmalion effect.[21] *The* **Pygmalion effect** *states that managers' attitudes and expectations of employees and how they treat them largely determine their performance.* Various studies have supported this theory. One example includes employees who were being trained as welders by the manager. The manager was given the names of employees who were intelligent and would do well. Actually, the trainees were selected

---

WORK APPLICATION

4. Give an example of how your attitude affected your behavior at work.

Pygmalion effect
Managers' attitudes and expectations of employees and how they treat them largely determine their performance.

at random. The only difference was the manager's expectations, which formed a positive attitude and influenced his behavior toward these trainees. The so-called intelligent trainees significantly outperformed the other trainees. Mara Collins started her own inner-city school, primarily for minority students of any ability. Her grade school students read Shakespeare, whereas many of their public school friends can barely read and write.

Unfortunately, some managers negatively stereotype their employees as having low ability or willingness to work. Their negative attitude leads to low expectations and not treating employees with respect. Their employees see and do as their managers expect. These managers' expectations lead to their *self-fulfilling prophecy* of low-performing employees.

In summary, the proper attitude is essential for a manager's effectiveness.[22] Managers need to understand the importance of their attitudes and how they affect worker attitudes, behavior, and performance.[23] Managers need to build and reinforce employees' organization-based self-esteem to encourage good performance.[24] Although others' attitudes can affect your behavior and performance, you are responsible for your own actions. Try to ignore negative comments and stay away from people with negative attitudes. As a manager, if you create win-win situations by expecting high performance and treating employees as capable and special, you will get the best performance from them.

Attitudes and Job Satisfaction

Job satisfaction is a person's attitude toward his or her job, and is generally measured along a continuum between satisfied (positive attitude) and dissatisfied (negative attitude) or high and low through OD survey (Chapter 7).

Job Satisfaction and Performance. Job satisfaction is important because if affects employee absenteeism and turnover.[25] Employees with optimistic personality traits[26] and positive self-esteem[27] tend to have greater job satisfaction. Satisfied employees tend to miss work less and stay with the organization longer. However, there has been a long debate over the expression that a happy worker is a productive worker. Do you know anyone who has high job satisfaction but low productivity and vice versa? However, overall, there is recent support that a positive relationship exists between job satisfaction and productivity.[28] Also, job satisfaction can affect satisfaction off the job[29] as people tend to take their jobs home with them, which affects their behavior.

Determinants of Job Satisfaction. Six major determinants of job satisfaction are presented in Self-Assessment Exercise 9–2. Complete it to find out the determinants of job satisfaction and your level of job satisfaction. You can have an overall high level of job satisfaction and not like some aspects of your job; this is common.

WORK APPLICATION

5. Recall a person (parent, friend, teacher, coach, boss) who really expected you to perform well or poorly, and treated you as if you would do well or poorly, which strongly affected your success or failure. Explain how the Pygmalion effect influenced your performance.

4. State what job satisfaction is and why it is important.

Self-Assessment Exercise 9–2

Job Satisfaction

Select a present or past job. For each of the following determinants of job satisfaction, identify your level of satisfaction by placing a check on the continuum.

Personality

I have a positive
self-esteem   ___ ___ ___/___ ___ ___   I have a negative
self-esteem

Work itself

I enjoy doing the tasks
I perform   ___ ___ ___/___ ___ ___   I *do not* enjoy doing
the tasks I perform

Compensation

I am fairly
compensated   ___ ___ ___/___ ___ ___   I am *not* fairly
compensated

Growth and upward mobility

I have the opportunity
to learn new things
and get better jobs   ___ ___ ___/___ ___ ___   I have *no* opportunity
to learn new things
and get better jobs

Coworkers

I like and enjoy
working with my
coworkers   ___ ___ ___/___ ___ ___   I *do not* like and enjoy
working with my
coworkers

Management

I believe that managers
are doing a good job   ___ ___ ___/___ ___ ___   I *do not* believe that
managers are doing a
good job

Overall Job Satisfaction

When determining overall job satisfaction for yourself, you cannot simply add up a score based on the above six determinants, because they are most likely of different importance to you. Thus, thinking about your job and the above factors, rate your overall satisfaction level with your job.

I am satisfied with my
job (high level of satisfaction)   _6_   _5_   _4_ / _3_   _2_   _1_   I am dissatisfied with my
job (low level of satisfaction)

Remember that job satisfaction is based on personality and perception; thus, it can be changed. See Exercise 9–1 for more details. If you work at being more positive by focusing on the good parts of your job, and spend less time thinking about and especially complaining to others about your job, you can have greater job satisfaction. People with negative attitudes often change jobs because they are not satisfied. They think that they will be more satisfied on another job. Unfortunately, they often find that the new job is no better than the old one. One exception is when the real cause of dissatisfaction is the job task performed. However, some people with truly negative personality types never find a job they are satisfied with no matter how many job changes they make.

Thus, remember to recruit and retain employees with positive attitudes. If you ask job candidates about their prior jobs and they make negative statements, cannot think of anything good to say, or hesitate, they may have a negative personality and job attitude. Improving your human relationship skills can help you to get along better with coworkers and managers and increase your job satisfaction, as well as increase your chances for growth and opportunity for advancement and higher compensation.

POWER

To be effective in an organization, you must understand how power is gained and used. You will study the importance of power in organizations, the bases of power, and how to increase your own power.

Organizational Power

Some people view power as the ability to make people do what they want them to do, or the ability to do something to people or for people. These definitions may be true, but they tend to give power a manipulative, negative connotation, as does Plato's saying, "Power corrupts and absolute power corrupts absolutely." For our purposes, having **power** *is the ability to influence others' behavior*. Ross Perot is considered a powerful person because of his ability to influence others' behavior.

Within an organization, power should be viewed in a positive sense. Without power, managers could not achieve organizational objectives. Leadership and power go hand in hand. Employees are not influenced without a reason, and the reason is often the power a manager has over them. You do not actually have to use power to influence others. Often it is the "perception" of power, rather than the actual power, that influences others.

Power starts at the top of the organization, and today top managers are giving more power to employees (*empowerment*).[30] Organizations, including AT&T, Corning, GE, and Motorola, have an office of the CEO with a team, rather than one autocratic leader. CEOs are pushing teamwork downward.[31]

5. Define *power* and the difference between position and personal power.

power
The ability to influence others' behavior.

There are two types of power: position and personal. *Position power* is derived from top management and is delegated down the chain of command. *Personal power* is derived from the follower based on the individual's behavior. Charismatic leaders have personal power.[32] Therefore, personal power can be gained or lost. It is best to have both position power and personal power. There is no universal acceptance of which source of power is more important. However, with the trend toward empowered teams, personal power is becoming more important than position power.[33]

Bases of Power and How to Increase Your Power

The seven bases of power, along with their sources, are presented in Figure 9–2 and each base of power is discussed along with how to increase it. You can build your power base, without taking power away from others. Generally, power is given to those who get results and have good human relations skills.

Coercive Power. The use of *coercive power* involves threats and/or punishment to influence compliance. Out of fear of reprimands, probation, suspension, or dismissal, employees often do as their boss requests. Other examples of coercive power include verbal abuse, humiliation, and ostracism. Group members may use coercive power to enforce norms. Coercive power is appropriate to use in maintaining discipline when enforcing rules. Ross Perot has been known to use coercive power to get what he wants.

Increasing Coercive Power. Generally, to have coercive position power you need to have a management job that enables you to gain and maintain the ability to hire, discipline, and fire your employees. However, some people can pressure others to do what they want without position authority.

Connection Power. *Connection power* is based on the user's relationship with influential people. You rely on the use of contacts or friends who can influence the person you are dealing with. The right connections can give power or at least the "perception" of having power. If people know you are friendly with people in power, they are more apt to do as you request.

When you are looking for a job or a promotion, connections can help. There is a lot of truth in the statement, "It's not what you know, it's who you know." Connection power can also help you get the resources you need and increased business.

Increasing Connection Power. To increase your connection power, expand your network of contacts with important managers who have power.

Figure 9-2 *Sources and Bases of Power*	Position Power						Personal Power
	Coercive	Connection	Reward	Legitimate	Referent	Information	Expert

Join the "in crowd" and the "right" clubs. Sports such as golf may help you meet influential people. When you want something, identify the people who can help you attain it, make alliances, and win them over to your side. Connections are developed through political networking, the topic of the next section. When Ross Perot entered politics, he realized how important connection power can be.

Reward Power. *Reward power* is based on the user's ability to influence others with something of value to them. It is based on transactional leadership. In a management position, use positive reinforcement with incentives such as praise, recognition, pay raises, and promotions to influence others' behavior. With peers, you can exchange favors as a reward, or give something of value to them. Let people know what's in it for them by creating a win-win situation. Employees at EDS get a variety of rewards for doing a good job.

Increasing Reward Power. Get a management position and gain and maintain control over evaluating your employees' performance and determining their raises and promotions. Find out what others value and try to reward them in that way. Using praise can help increase your power. Employees who feel they are appreciated rather than being used will give the manager more power.

Legitimate Power. *Legitimate power* is based on the user's position power given by the organization. Employees tend to feel that they ought to do what the boss says within the scope of the job.[34] Day-to-day manager-employee interactions at EDS and other organizations are based on legitimate power.

Increasing Legitimate Power. Get a management job and let people know the power you possess, and work at gaining people's "perception" that you do have power.

Referent Power. *Referent power* is based on the user's personal power relationship with others. It is based primarily on personality. For example, say "Will you please do it for me?" not "This is an order." The use of referent power is particularly appropriate for people with weak, or no, position power. Referent power is needed in self-managed teams because leadership should be shared.[35]

Increasing Referent Power. To gain referent power, develop your human relations skills. Remember that your boss's success depends on you. Gain his or her confidence in order to get more power; work at your relationship with your boss.

Information Power. *Information power* is based on data desired by others.[36] Managers rely on information from others. The information is usually related to the job, but not always. Some secretaries have more information and are more helpful answering questions than the managers they work for. An important part of the manager's job is to convey information. Employees often come to managers for information on what to do and how to do it.

6. Explain the difference among reward, legitimate, and referent power.

Increasing Information Power. Have information flow through you. Know what is going on in the organization. Provide service and information to other departments. Serve on committees because it gives you both information and a chance to increase connection power.

Expert Power. *Expert power* is based on the user's skill and knowledge. Being an expert makes other people depend on you. Employees with expert power are often promoted to management positions. The fewer people who possess an expertise, the more power the individual has. For example, basketball star Michael Jordan commanded multimillion dollar contracts. It's a supply and demand issue.

Managers are often, but not always, experts within their departments. Expert power is essential to people who have to work with employees from other departments and organizations. They have no direct position power to use, so being seen as an expert gives credibility and power. EDS gets its clients based on its expertise in setting up information computer systems needed by clients.

Increasing Expert Power. To become an expert, take all the training and educational programs your organization provides. Keep up with the latest technology. Volunteer to be the first to learn something new. Stay away from routine tasks in favor of more complex, hard-to-evaluate tasks. Project a positive image.

Why do some people want and seek power whereas others will not take it even if it's offered to them? McClelland's acquired needs theory of motivation (Chapter 12) states that the answer is based on one's need for power. You will determine your need for power in Self-Assessment Exercise 12–1. Do you want to influence others? Do you plan to follow the suggestions in the text to increase your power base?

WORK APPLICATION

6. Identify a present or past boss. Which power base does/did the boss use most often? Explain. Also, give at least one example of another power base you saw the boss use.

7. Which one or two suggestions for increasing your power base are the most relevant to you? Explain.

APPLYING THE CONCEPT

AC 9–1 Using Power

Identify the appropriate power to use in each situation.

a. coercive   c. reward or legitimate   e. information or expert
b. connection   d. referent

_____ 1. Bridget, one of your best workers, needs little direction from you. However, recently her performance level has dropped. You are quite sure Bridget has a personal problem affecting her work.

_____ 2. You want a new personal computer to help you do a better job. PCs are allocated by a committee, which is very political in nature.

_____ 3. One of your best workers, Jean, wants a promotion. Jean has talked to you about getting ahead and has asked you to help prepare her for when the opportunity comes.

_____ 4. John, one of your worst employees, has ignored one of your directives again.

_____ 5. Whitney, who needs some direction and encouragement from you to maintain production, is not working to standard today. As she does occasionally, she claims that she does not feel well but cannot afford to take time off. You have to get an important customer order shipped today.

ORGANIZATIONAL POLITICS

In this section, you will study the nature of politics, political behavior, and guidelines for developing political skills. Begin by determining your use of political behavior by completing Self-Assessment Exercise 9–3.

Self-Assessment Exercise 9–3

Use of Political Behavior

Select the response that best describes your actual or planned use of the following behavior on the job. Place the number 1–5 on the line before each statement.

(1) rarely   (2) seldom   (3) occasionally
(4) frequently   (5) usually

____ 1. I get along with everyone, even those considered to be difficult to get along with.

____ 2. I avoid giving my personal opinion on controversial issues, especially when I know others don't agree with them.

____ 3. I try to make people feel important by complimenting them.

____ 4. I compromise when working with others and avoid telling people they are wrong.

____ 5. I try to get to know the key managers and find out what is going on in all the organizational departments.

____ 6. I dress the same way as the people in power and take on the same interests (watch or play sports, join the same clubs, etc.).

____ 7. I purposely seek contacts and network with higher level managers so they will know who I am by name and face.

____ 8. I seek recognition and visibility for my accomplishments.

____ 9. I get others to help me to get what I want.

____ 10. I do favors for others and use their favors in return.

To determine your political behavior, add the ten numbers you selected as your answers. The number will range from 10 to 50. The higher your score, the more political behavior you use. Place your score here ____ and on the continuum below.

Nonpolitical 10——20——30——40——50 Political

The Nature of Organizational Politics

Political skills are a part of power.[37] **Politics** *is the process of gaining and using power.* Politics is a reality of organizational life.[38] Like power, politics often has a negative connotation due to people who abuse political power.[39] A positive way to view politics is to realize that it is simply a medium of exchange. Like money, politics in and of itself is neither good nor bad. It is simply a means of getting what we want. In our economy, money is the medium of exchange; in an organization, politics is the medium of exchange.

Managers cannot meet their objectives without the help of other people and departments over which they have no authority or position power. For example, Carmen, a production department manager, needs materials and supplies to make the product, but must rely on the purchasing department to acquire them. If Carmen does not have a good working relationship with purchasing, materials may not be there when needed. This is especially true for rush jobs.

7. Discuss how power and politics are related.

8. Describe how money and politics have a similar use.

politics
The process of gaining and using power.

The amount and importance of politics varies from organization to organization. However, larger organizations tend to be more political; and the higher the level of management, the more important politics becomes.[40] A survey of executives revealed that 20 percent of their time is spent on politics.[41]

Political Behavior

Networking, reciprocity, and coalitions are important political behaviors.

9. Explain what networking, reciprocity, and coalitions have in common.

networking
The process of developing relationships for the purpose of socializing and politicking.

Networking. **Networking** *is the process of developing relationships for the purpose of socializing and politicking.* Management activities and the time spent on each area have been studied and classified into four areas: traditional management, communication, human resources management, and networking. Of these four activities, networking has the most relative contribution to management success because it helps get the job done. Successful managers spend around twice as much time networking as average managers.[42]

reciprocity
Involves creating obligations and developing alliances and using them to accomplish objectives.

Reciprocity. Using **reciprocity** *involves creating obligations and developing alliances and using them to accomplish objectives.* When people do something for you, you incur an obligation that they may expect to be repaid. When you do something for people, you create a debt that you may be able to collect at a later date when you need a favor. You should work at developing a network of alliances that you can call on for help in meeting your objectives.[43]

coalition
A network of alliances that will help a manager achieve an objective.

Coalitions. A **coalition** *is a network of alliances that will help a manager achieve an objective.* Reciprocity is used to achieve ongoing objectives, whereas coalitions are developed for achieving a specific objective. For example, Pedro, a team member, has an idea for a new service to be offered by EDS. By himself, Pedro has no authority to offer a new service. A suggested procedure for building a coalition would be for Pedro to first go to his boss or bosses. Pedro would present the idea to his boss and get approval to get wider support. Pedro would then get peers and people at other levels as allies. It is important to align yourself with powerful people who can help.[44] Pedro may offer payoffs from the new service in return for support, time, money, and other resources that peers and others contribute. The focus is on telling others how they will benefit if the service is provided. With a coalition in place, Pedro would then go to the person with the power to approve the new service. A formal presentation is often required. When higher-level managers know that the lower levels are in favor of the idea, and it is a good one, approval is often given. If the service is approved, Pedro may be the team leader to offer it, and his coalition members may be on the team.

Guidelines for Developing Political Skills

If you want to climb the corporate ladder, you should develop your political skills. More specifically, review the ten statements in Self-Assessment Exercise 9–3 and the three political behaviors and consciously increase your use of these behaviors. Successfully implementing these behaviors results in increased political skills. However, if you don't agree with one of the political behaviors, don't use it; you don't have to use all of them to be successful. Learn what it takes in the organization where you work as you follow the guidelines in Figure 9–3.

Learn the Organizational Culture. Learn the cultural shared values and beliefs (Chapter 7) and how business and politics operate where you work. Learn to read between the lines. Use political behavior to promote yourself, but be sure to use methods that are considered appropriate[45] and ethical. Remember that there is always more than one way to get what you want, and the method you use determines your success.

Learn the Power Players. It is natural, especially for young people, to take a purely rational approach to a job without considering politics. But don't do this because many business decisions are very nonrational and are simply based on power and politics.[46] Your boss is a key player to you. By understanding powerful key players, you can tailor the presentation of your ideas and style to fit the needs of each individual. For example, some managers want to see detailed financial numbers and statistics, while others don't.

Don't Surprise Your Boss. If you want to get ahead, you should have a good working relationship with your boss. Get to know what your boss expects from you and do it. It's common to put off telling the boss bad news. But, if you are having a job problem, let your boss know early. If you are behind schedule to meet an important deadline and your boss finds out about it from others, it is embarrassing, especially if your boss finds out from his or her boss. And don't show your boss up in public. When developing a coalition, include your boss.

WORK APPLICATION

8. Give a job example of how networking, reciprocity, or a coalition was used to achieve an organizational objective.
9. Which one or two suggestions for developing political skills are the most relevant to you? Explain.

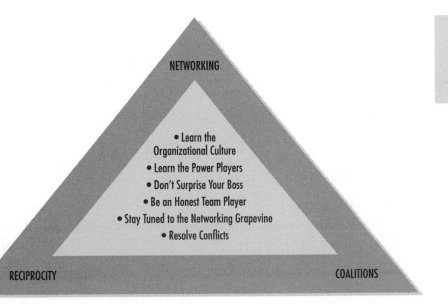

Figure 9-3
Political Behaviors and Guidelines for Developing Political Skills

NETWORKING

- Learn the Organizational Culture
- Learn the Power Players
- Don't Surprise Your Boss
- Be an Honest Team Player
- Stay Tuned to the Networking Grapevine
- Resolve Conflicts

RECIPROCITY

COALITIONS

Be an Honest Team Player. Some backstabbing gossips may get short-term benefits from their behavior, but in the long run they are generally unsuccessful because others gossip about them in return. In any organization, you must earn others' respect, confidence, and trust. Once caught in a lie, it's difficult to regain trust. There are very few, if any, jobs in which organizational objectives can be achieved without the support of a group/team. The trend is toward teamwork,[47] so if you are not a team player, work at it.

Stay Tuned to the Networking Grapevine. Find out what is going on through the grapevine.[48] The grapevine can help you to learn the organizational culture[49] and key players to include in your coalitions. Your grapevine should include a network of people within and outside your organization. Join trade or professional associations and attend meetings.

Resolve Conflicts. When climbing the corporate ladder, you may have to be careful not to get thrown off it. Following the preceding guidelines can help you avoid a political fight. However, if you are suddenly left out of the information loop, or if your coworkers or boss start treating you differently, find out why. Use your networking grapevine to find out if someone is trying to undermine you and why. You need to understand where your enemies are coming from, how they operate, who's behind them, and what weapons they might use. Confront individuals or groups suspected of instigating conflict.[50] If you did something to offend your adversary, an apology may clear the air. In any case, confront your adversary to resolve the conflict using the ideas in the next section.

APPLYING THE CONCEPT

AC 9–2 Political Behavior

Identify the behavior in each situation as effective or ineffective political behavior.

a. effective   b. ineffective

_____ **6.** Jill is taking golf lessons so she can join the Saturday golf group that includes some higher-level managers.

_____ **7.** Paul tells his boss's boss about mistakes his boss makes.

_____ **8.** Sally avoids socializing so that she can be more productive on the job.

_____ **9.** John sent a very positive performance report to three higher-level managers to whom he does not report. They did not request copies.

_____ **10.** Carlos has to drop off daily reports by noon. He brings them around 10:00 on Tuesday and Thursday so that he can run into some higher-level managers who meet at that time near the office where the report goes. On the other days, Carlos drops the report off around noon on his way to lunch.

MANAGING CONFLICT

conflict
Exists whenever people are in disagreement and opposition.

A **conflict** *exists whenever people are in disagreement and opposition.* Conflict is inevitable; you cannot avoid it.[51] Managers need strong conflict resolution and negotiation skills if they want to be successful.[52] How well you handle conflict affects your job satisfaction and success.[53]

In this section you will learn that conflict can be functional or dysfunctional, and five conflict management styles.

Conflict Can Be Dysfunctional or Functional

People often think of conflict as fighting and view it as disruptive. When conflict prevents the achievement of organizational objectives, it is negative or *dysfunctional conflict*. However, it can be postive. **Functional conflict** *exists when disagreement and opposition support the achievement of organizational objectives.* The question today is not whether conflict is negative or positive, but how to manage conflict to benefit the organization.

Too little or too much conflict is usually dysfunctional. If people are not willing to disagree and optimize, or if they fight too much without resolution, objectives may not be met and performance will be lower than optimal. A balance of conflict is functional to organizations because it optimizes performance outcomes. Challenging present methods and presenting innovative change causes conflict, but leads to improved performance. Figure 9 4 illustrates the effects conflict has on performance.

functional conflict
Exists when disagreement and opposition support the achievement of organizational objectives.

Conflict Management Styles

When you are in conflict, you have five conflict management styles to choose from. The five styles are based on two dimensions of concerns—concern for others' needs and concern for your own needs—which result in three types of behavior: passive, aggressive, and assertive. Each conflict behavior style results in a different combination of win-lose situations. The five styles, along with concern for needs and win-lose combinations, are presented in Figure 9–5 and discussed in the following section in order of passive, aggressive, and assertive behavior.

Avoiding Conflict Style. The *avoiding conflict style* user attempts to passively ignore the conflict rather than resolve it. When you avoid a conflict, you are being unassertive and uncooperative. People avoid the conflict by refusing to take a stance, escaping the conflict by mentally withdrawing, and by physically leaving. A lose-lose situation is created because the conflict is not resolved.

10. List and define the five conflict management styles.

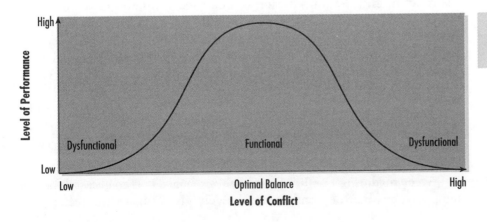

Figure 9-4
Conflict and Performance

Figure 9-5
Conflict Management Styles

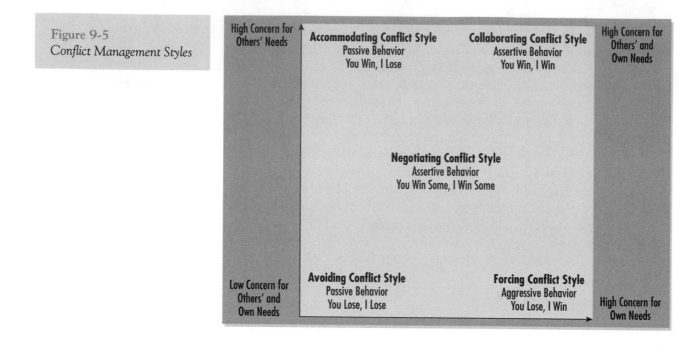

Advantages and Disadvantages of the Avoiding Conflict Style. The advantage of the avoiding style is that it may maintain relationships that would be hurt through conflict resolution. The disadvantage of this style is the fact that conflicts do not get resolved.[54] An overuse of this style leads to conflict within the individual. People tend to walk all over the avoider. Some managers allow employees to perform poorly without confronting them. Avoiding problems usually does not make them go away; the problems usually get worse. The longer you wait to confront others, the more difficult the confrontation usually is.[55]

Appropriate Use of the Avoiding Conflict Style. The avoiding style is appropriate to use when: (1) the conflict is trivial, (2) your stake in the issue is not high, (3) confrontation will damage an important relationship, (4) you don't have time to resolve the conflict, or (5) emotions are high. When you don't have time to resolve the conflict or people are emotional, you should confront the person(s) later. However, it is inappropriate to repeatedly avoid confrontation until you get so upset that you end up yelling at the other person(s). This passive-aggressive behavior tends to make the situation worse by hurting human relations. Often people do not realize they are doing something that bothers you (that you are in conflict) and, when approached properly, are willing to change. The proper approach is explained with the collaborating conflict style.

Accommodating Conflict Style. The *accommodating conflict style* user attempts to resolve the conflict by passively giving in to the other party.

When you use the accommodating style you are being unassertive but cooperative. You attempt to satisfy the other party, but neglect your own needs by letting others get their own way. A win-lose situation is created.

A common difference between the avoiding and accommodating styles is based on behavior. With the avoiding style you don't have to do anything you really don't want to do, but you do with the accommodating style. If you are talking to someone who makes a statement that you disagree with, you can say nothing to avoid a conflict. For example, you have to put up a display with someone and the person wants to do it a certain way. If you disagree and don't want to do it the other person's way but say nothing and put it up the other person's way, you have done something you really did not want to do.

Advantages and Disadvantages of the Accommodating Conflict Style. The advantage of the accommodating style is that relationships are maintained by doing things the other person's way. The disadvantage is that giving in may be counterproductive. The accommodated person may have a better solution, such as a better way to put up the display. An overuse of this style tends to lead to people taking advantage of the accommodator, and the type of relationship the accommodator tries to maintain is usually lost.

Appropriate Use of the Accommodating Conflict Style. The accommodating style is appropriate when (1) the person enjoys being a follower, (2) maintaining the relationship outweighs all other considerations, (3) the changes agreed to are not important to the accommodator, but are to the other party, (4) the time to resolve the conflict is limited, and (5) you have an autocratic boss who uses the forcing style.

Forcing Conflict Style. The *forcing conflict style* user attempts to resolve the conflict by using aggressive behavior to get his or her own way. When you use the forcing style you are uncooperative and aggressive; you do whatever it takes to satisfy your own needs at the expense of others. Forcers use authority, threaten, intimidate, and call for majority rule when they know they will win. Forcers commonly enjoy dealing with avoiders and accommodators. If you try to get others to change without being willing to change yourself, regardless of the means, then you use the forcing style. A win-lose situation is created.

Advantages and Disadvantages of the Forcing Style. The advantage of the forcing style is that better organizational decisions, rather than less effective, compromised decisions will be made when the forcer is correct. The disadvantage is that overuse of this style leads to hostility and resentment toward its user. Forcers tend to have poor human relations. However, some of them do not care about people.

Appropriate Use of the Forcing Style. Some managers commonly use their position power to force others to do things their way. The forcing style is appropriate to use when (1) unpopular action must be taken on important issues,[56] (2) commitment by others to proposed action is not crucial to its implementation (in other words, people will not resist doing what you want them to do), (3) maintaining relationships is not critical, and (4) the conflict resolution is urgent.

Negotiating Conflict Style. The *negotiating conflict style* user attempts to resolve the conflict through assertive give-and-take concessions. It is also called the *compromising style*. When you use the compromising approach you are moderate in assertiveness and cooperation. An I-win-part-I-lose-part situation is created through compromise.

Advantages and Disadvantages of the Negotiating Conflict Style. The advantage of the negotiating conflict style is that the conflict is resolved relatively quickly, and working relationships are maintained. The disadvantage is that the compromise often leads to counterproductive results such as suboptimum decisions. An overuse of this style leads to people playing games such as asking for twice as much as they need in order to get what they want. It is commonly used during collective bargaining.

Appropriate Use of the Negotiating Conflict Style. The negotiating conflict style is appropriate to use when (1) the issues are complex and critical and there is no simple and clear solution, (2) parties have about equal power and are interested in different solutions, (3) a solution will only be temporary, and (4) time is short.

Collaborating Conflict Style. The *collaborating conflict style* user assertively attempts to jointly resolve the conflict with the best solution agreeable to all parties. It is also called the *problem-solving style*. When you use the collaborating approach you are being assertive and cooperative. Although avoiders and accommodators are concerned about others' needs and forcers are concerned about their own needs, the collaborator is concerned about finding the best solution to the problem that is satisfactory to all parties. Unlike the forcer, the collaborator is willing to change if a better solution is presented.[57] While negotiating is often based on secret information, collaboration is based on open and honest communication. This is the only style that creates a true win-win situation.[58]

WORK APPLICATION

10. Select a present or past boss. Which conflict management style did the boss use most often? Explain through a typical example.

11. Which one of the five conflict management styles do you tend to use most often? Explain.

APPLYING THE CONCEPT

AC 9–3 Selecting Conflict Management Styles

Identify the most appropriate conflict management style as:

a. avoiding   c. forcing   e. collaborating
b. accommodating   d. negotiating

_____ 11. You have joined a committee in order to meet people. Your interest in what the committee does is low. While serving on the committee, you make a recommendation that is opposed by another member. You realize that you have the better idea. The other party is using a forcing style.

_____ 12. You are on a task force that has to select a new computer. The four alternatives will all do the job. It's the brand, price, and service that people disagree on.

_____ 13. You are a sales manager. Beth, one of your competent salespeople, is trying to close a big sale. The two of you are discussing the next sales call she will make. You disagree on the strategy to use to close the sale.

_____ 14. You're late and on your way to an important meeting. As you leave your office, at the other end of the work area you see Chris, one of your employees, goofing off instead of working.

_____ 15. You're over budget for labor this month. It's slow so you asked Kent, a part-time employee, to leave work early. Kent tells you he doesn't want to go because he needs the money.

A common difference between negotiating and collaborating is the solution. Continuing the putting up a display example: With negotiation, the two people may trade off by putting up one display one person's way and the next display the other person's way. This way they win and lose. With collaboration, the two people work together to develop one display method that they both like. It may be some form of both or simply one person's, if after an explanation, the other person really agrees that the method is better. The key to collaboration is agreeing that the solution is the best possible one.

Advantages and Disadvantages of the Collaborating Style. The advantage of the collaborating style is that it tends to lead to the best solution to the conflict using assertive behavior. The disadvantage is that the skill, effort, and time it takes to resolve the conflict are usually greater and longer than with the other styles. There are situations, mentioned under negotiation, where collaboration is difficult and when a forcer prevents its use. The collaborative style offers the most benefit to the individual, group, and organization.[59]

Appropriate Use of the Collaborating Conflict Style. The collaborating style is appropriate when (1) you are dealing with an important issue that requires an optimal solution; compromise would result in suboptimizing; (2) people are willing to place the group goal before self-interest; members will truly collaborate; (3) maintaining relationships is important; (4) time is available; and (5) it is a peer conflict.

The situational perspective states that there is no one best style for resolving all conflicts. A person's preferred style tends to meet his or her needs. Some people enjoy forcing, while others prefer to avoid conflict, and so forth. As with all management functions, success lies in one's ability to use the appropriate style to meet the situation.

Of the five styles, avoiding, accommodating, and forcing are generally the easiest to learn. If you have problems using the avoiding and accommodating styles, when appropriate, you need to work at giving in to others by saying or doing nothing or going along with others' way of doing things. If you have problems using the forcing style, Situational Management (Skill-Building Exercise 1–1) can help you to understand this style. The two most difficult styles to develop for most people are the negotiation and collaborating styles. Thus, these two styles are presented in the next section to teach you models that you can use during conflicts, and Skill-Building Exercises 9–1 and 9–2 develop your negotiation and collaboration conflict resolution skills.

*skillbuilder

THE NEGOTIATING AND COLLABORATING CONFLICT MANAGEMENT STYLES

In this section you will first learn how to negotiate and then how to use the collaborating method to initiate, respond to, and mediate a conflict resolution.

Negotiating

Negotiating is a process in which two or more parties are in conflict and attempt to come to an agreement. As stated, there are times when negotiations are appropriate, such as management-union collective bargaining, buying and selling goods and services, accepting a new job compensation offer, getting a raise—all without a fixed price/deal. If there is a set "take it or leave it" deal, there is no negotiation. For example, when one of Ross Perot's business facilities in California voted to organize a union, Perot shut down the facility rather than negotiate a contract agreement. Perot used the forcing conflict style, but when it did not work he did not use the negotiating style. Also, not all negotiations end with an agreement, especially sales. Using power and politics are tools of negotiation.

Create an "I Win Some, You Win Some" Situation. With negotiation there is often a zero sum game in which one party's gain is the other party's loss. For example, every dollar less that you pay for a car is your gain and the seller's loss. Therefore, you don't have a true collaboration win-win situation. Negotiating is about getting what you want. To get what you want you have to sell your ideas and convince the other party to give you what you want. However, negotiation should be viewed by all parties as I win some and you win some, rather than a win-lose situation, or all parties should believe they got a good deal. If union employees believe they lost and management won, employees may have job dissatisfaction, which could result in lower performance in the long run. If customers believe they got a bad deal, they will not give repeat business.

The Negotiation Process

The negotiation process has three and possibly four steps: plan, negotiations, possibly a postponement, and an agreement or no agreement. These steps are summarized in Model 9–2 and discussed in this section. Like the other models in this book, 9–2 is meant to give you step-by-step guidelines to follow. However, in making it apply to multiple types of negotiation, you may have to make slight adjustments.

Plan. Success or failure in negotiating is often based on preparation.[60] Be clear about what it is you are negotiating. Is it price, options, delivery time, sales quantity, or all four? Planning has four steps:

| step 1. | **Research the other party(s).** As discussed, know the key power players. Try to find out what the other parties want and what they will and will not be willing to give up before you negotiate. Find out, through your networking grapevine, their personality traits and negotiation style. The more you know about the other party, the better your chances are of reaching an agreement. If you have worked with the other party, such as your boss or a potential customer, what worked |

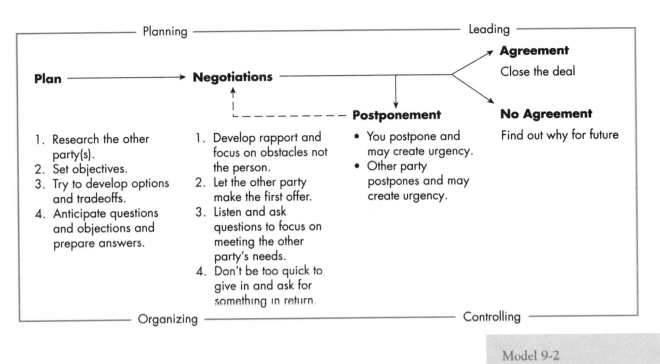

Model 9-2
The Negotiation Process

and did not work in the past? How can you use the past experience in your negotiation, such as to get a raise or make a sale?

step 2. **Set objectives.** Based on your research, what can you expect? Set a lower, target, and opening objective. In many negotiations the objective will be a price, but it could be working conditions, longer vacation, job security, and so on. (A) Set a specific lower limit and be willing to not come to an agreement unless you get it. (B) Set a target objective of what you believe is a fair deal. (C) Set an opening objective offer that is higher than you expect; you might get it. Remember that the other party is probably also setting three objectives, so don't view their opening offer as final. The key to successful negotiations is for all parties to get between their minimum and target objective. This creates an I win some you win some situation. Remember that it is helpful to decision making to have must and want criteria (Chapter 3) related to your objectives.

step 3. **Try to develop options and tradeoffs.** In purchasing and looking for a job, if you have multiple sellers and job offers you are in a stronger power position to get your target price. It is common practice to quote other offers and to ask if the other party can beat it.

If you have to give up something, or cannot get exactly what you want, be prepared to ask for something else in return. If you cannot get the size raise you want, maybe you can get more days off, more in your retirement account, a nicer office, an assistant, and so on. When Eastern Airlines was having financial difficulty, it asked employees to take a pay cut. Rather than simply accept a cut, they asked for a tradeoff and got company stock. Based on your research, what tradeoffs do you expect from the other party?

step 4. **Anticipate questions and objections and prepare answers.** The other party may want to know why you are selling something, looking for a job, how the product or service works, what are the features and benefits. You need to be prepared to answer the unasked question—what's in it for me? Don't focus on what you want but on how your deal will benefit the other party. Talk in "you" and "we" not "I" terms, unless you are telling others what you will do for them.

There is a good chance that you will be given objection—reasons why the negotiations will not result in agreement/sale. When a union asks for a raise, management typically says the organization can't afford it. However, the union has done its research and quotes the specific profits for a set period of time to overcome the objection. Unfortunately for you, not everyone will come out and tell you their real objections. Thus, you need to listen and ask questions to find out what is preventing the agreement.

You need to fully understand your product/deal and project a positive self-esteem that shows enthusiasm and confidence. If the other party does not trust you, and believes the deal is not a good one, you will not reach an agreement. Thus, during the selection process, you must convince the manager that you can do the job or that your product will benefit the customer. When you are in sales, you should have some statements prepared to close the sale, such as, Would you take the "white" one or the "blue" one?

Negotiations. After you have planned, you are now ready to negotiate the deal. Face-to-face negotiations are generally preferred because you can see the other person's nonverbal behavior (discussed in Chapter 11) and better understand objections. However, telephone and written negotiations work, too. Again, know the other party's preference.

step 1. **Develop rapport and focus on obstacles not the person.** Smile and call the other party by name as you greet them. A smile tells people you like them, are interested in them, and enjoy them.[61] Open with some small talk, like the weather. How much time to wait until you get down to business depends on the other party's style. Some people like to get right down to business, but others, like the Japanese, want to get to know you before discussing business. However, you want the other party to make the first offer, so don't wait too long or you may lose your chance.

Focusing on the obstacle not the person means to never attack the other's personality or put others down with negative statements like, "You are being unfair to ask for such a price cut." If you do so, the other party will become defensive, you may end up arguing, and it will be harder to reach an agreement. Make statements like, "You think my price is too high?" Not saying negative things about others includes competitors; you should just state your competitive advantage in a positive way. People look for four things: inclusion, control, safety, and respect. If most people perceive that you are trying to push them into something, threaten them in some way or belittle them, they will not trust you and will not make the agreement.

step 2. **Let the other party make the first offer.** You have the advantage if the other party offers you more than your target objective, and can close the agreement. For example, if you are expecting to be paid $25,000 a year (your target objective) and the other party offers you $30,000, are you going to reject it? On the other hand, if you are offered $20,000 you can realize that it may be low and work the compensation up. Ask questions like, "What is the salary range?" or "What do you expect to pay for such a fine product?"

When others pressure you to make the first offer with a common question like, "Give us your best price, and we'll tell you whether we'll take it," try asking them a question such as, "What do you expect to pay?" or "What is a reasonable price?" When this does not work, say something like, "Our usual/list price is XXX. However, if you make me a proposal, I'll see what I can do for you."

If things go well during steps 1 and 2, you may skip to closing the agreement. If you are not ready to agree proceed to the next step or two.

| step 3 ■ | **Listen and ask questions to focus on meeting the other party's needs.** Create opportunity for the other party to disclose reservations and objections. When you speak you give out information, but when you ask questions and listen you receive information that will help you to overcome the other party's objections. If you go on and on about the features you have to offer, without finding out what features the other party is really interested in, you may be killing the deal. Ask questions such as, "Is the price out of the ballpark?" "Is it fast enough for you?" "Is there any feature you wanted that is missing?" If the objection is a want criteria, such as two years of work experience and you have only one, play up the features they do want that you have and you may get an agreement.[62] If the objection is a must criteria you cannot meet, at least you found out and don't waste time chasing a deal that will not happen. However, be sure the objection is really a must criteria; what if the employer gets no applicants with two years' experience and you apply? They may offer you the job.

| step 4 ■ | **Don't be too quick to give in and ask for something in return.** Those who ask for more get more. Don't give up whatever it takes to get the agreement. If your competitive advantage is service and you quickly give in during negotiation for a lower price, you blow all the value in a minute. You want to satisfy the other party without giving up too much during the negotiation.[63] Remember not to go below your minimum objective, if it is realistic, and be prepared to walk away. When you are not getting what you want, having other planned options can help give you bargaining power. If you do walk away, you may be called back, and if not, you may be able to come back for the same low price, but not always. If the other party knows you are desperate or just weak and will accept a low agreement, they will likely take advantage of you. Have you ever seen a sign on a product saying "Must sell—need cash"? What type of price do you think they get? You also need to avoid being intimidated by comments such as, "Are you kidding me, that's too much" (in a loud voice). Many people will quickly drop the price, but don't.

However, when you are dealing with a complex deal like a management–union contract negotiation with tradeoffs, be willing to be the first to make a concession. The other party tends to feel obligated and then you can come back with a counter tradeoff that is larger than the one you gave up.

Avoid giving unilateral concessions. Recall your planned tradeoffs. If the other party asks for a lower price ask for a concession such as a large volume sale to get it, a longer delivery time, a less popular color, and so on. You need to send the message that you don't just give things away.[64]

Postponement. When there doesn't seem to be any progress, it may be wise to postpone the negotiations.

- *The other party is postponing and you may create urgency.* The other party says, "I'll get back to you." When you are not getting what you want, you may try to create urgency, for example, by saying, "This is on sale and it ends today." However, honesty is the best policy. The primary reason people will negotiate with you is that they trust and respect you. Establishing a relationship of trust is the necessary first step in closing a deal. Honesty and integrity are the most important assets a negotiator can possess.[65] If you do have other options, you can use them to create urgency, such as, "I have another job offer pending. When will you let me know if you want to offer me the job?"

If urgency does not apply, or does not work, and the other party says, "I'll think about it," say, "That's a good idea." Then at least review the major features the other party liked about your proposed deal and ask if it meets their needs. The other party may decide to come to an agreement/sale.[66] If not, and they don't tell you when they will get back to you, ask, "When can I expect to hear if I got the job?" Try to pin the other party down for a specific time and tell the person that if you don't hear from them by then, you will call them. If you are really interested, follow up with a letter (mail, E-mail, fax) of thanks for their time and again highlight your features they liked. If you forgot to include any during the negotiation, add them in the letter.

One thing to remember is that when the other party becomes resistant to making the agreement, the hard sell will not work. Take the pressure off[67] by asking something like (to a client) "Where do you want to go from here?" If you press for an answer, it may be no agreement; however, if you wait you may have a better chance. Try saying (to a boss), "Why don't we think about it and discuss it some more later" (pick an advantageous time to meet with your boss).

You also need to learn to read between the lines. Some people will not come right out and tell you no deal. For example, it is common for the Japanese to say something like, "It will be difficult to do business." Americans tend to perceive this to mean keep trying to close the deal, but the Japanese businessperson means stop trying, but will not say so directly because it is impolite.

- *You want to postpone and the other party may create urgency.* If you are not satisfied with the deal, or want to shop around, tell the other party you want to think about it. You may also need to check with your boss, or someone else, which simply may be for advice, before you can finalize the deal. If the other party is creating urgency, be sure it really is urgent. In many cases, you can get the same deal at a later date; don't be pressured into making a deal you are not satisfied with or may regret later. If you do want to postpone, give the other party a specific time that you will get back to them, and do so with more prepared negotiations or to simply tell them you cannot make an agreement.

Agreement. Once the agreement has been made, restate it and/or put it in writing when appropriate. It is common to follow up an agreement with a letter of thanks that restates the agreement to ensure the other party has not changed its mind regarding the agreement terms. Also, after the deal is made, stop selling it. Change the subject to a personal one and/or leave, depending on the other person's preferred negotiations. If they want a personal relationship, then stick around, if not, you should leave.

No Agreement. Rejection, refusal, and failure happen to us all, even the superstars. The difference between the also-rans and the superstars lies in how they respond to the failure.[68] The successful people keep trying and learn from their mistakes and continue to work hard; failures usually don't persevere. If you cannot come to an agreement, analyze the situation and try to determine where you went wrong so you can improve in the future. You may also ask the other party for advice, such as, "I realize I did not get the job, thanks for your time. Can you offer me any ideas for improving my résumé, interview skills, and other ideas to help me to get a XXX job?"

Initiating Collaborating Conflict Resolution

An initiator is the person who confronts the other person(s) to resolve the conflict. When initiating a conflict resolution using the collaborating style, use the following model: The **initiating conflict resolution model** *steps are to (1) plan a BCF statement that maintains ownership of the problem, (2) present your BCF statement and agree on the conflict, (3) ask for and/or give alternative conflict resolutions, and (4) make an agreement for change.* This is illustrated in Model 9–3.

✳ **skillbuilder**

11. List the steps in the initiating conflict resolution model.

initiating conflict resolution model
The steps are to: (1) plan a BCF statement that maintains ownership of the problem, (2) present your BCF statement and agree on the conflict, (3) ask for and/or give alternative resolutions, and (4) make an agreement for change.

Model 9-3
The Collaborating Conflict Style

Planning — Leading

Initiating Conflict Resolution	Responding to Conflict Resolution	Mediating Conflict Resolution
Step 1. Plan a BCF statement that maintains ownership of the problem.	Step 1. Listen to and paraphrase the conflict using the BCF model.	Step 1. Have each party state his or her complaint using the BCF model.
Step 2. Present your BCF statement and agree on the conflict.	Step 2. Agree with some aspect of the complaint.	Step 2. Agree on the conflict problem(s).
Step 3. Ask for, and/or give, alternative conflict resolutions.	Step 3. Ask for, and/or give, alternative conflict resolutions.	Step 3. Develop alternative conflict resolutions.
Step 4. Make an agreement for change.	Step 4. Make an agreement for change.	Step 4. Make an agreement for change.
		Step 5. Follow up to make sure the conflict is resolved.

Organizing — Controlling

step 1 ▪ **Plan a BCF statement that maintains ownership of the problem.** Planning is the beginning management function and starting point of initiating a conflict resolution. Let's begin by stating what "maintains ownership of the problem" means. Assume you don't smoke and someone who is smoking visits you. Is it you or the smoker who has a problem? The smoke bothers you, not the smoker. It's your problem. Open the confrontation with a request for the respondent to help you solve your problem. This approach reduces defensiveness and establishes an atmosphere of problem solving that will maintain the relationship.

The **BCF model** *describes a conflict in terms of behavior, consequences, and feelings.* When you do B (behavior), C (consequences) happens, and I feel F (feelings). An example of a BCF statement is: "When you smoke in my room (behavior), I have trouble breathing and become nauseous (consequence), and I feel uncomfortable and irritated (feeling)." You can vary the sequence and start with a feeling or consequence to fit the situation and to provide variety. For example, "I fear (feeling) that the advertisement is not going to work (behavior), and that we will lose money (consequences)."

When developing your opening BCF statement, be descriptive, not evaluative. Keep the opening statement short. The longer the statement, the longer it will take to resolve the conflict. People get defensive when kept waiting for their turn to talk. Avoid trying to determine who is to blame for something or who is right and wrong. Both parties are usually partly to blame or partly correct. Fixing blame or correctness only makes people defensive, which is counterproductive to conflict resolution. Timing is also important. If others are busy, see them later to discuss the conflict. In addition, don't confront a person on several unrelated issues at once.

After planning your BCF statement, you should practice saying it before confronting the other party. In addition, think of some possible alternatives you can offer to resolve the conflict. However, be sure your ideas show high concern for others rather than just for yourself. Try to put yourself in the other person's position. If you were the other person, would you like the ideas presented by the confronter? Create a win-win situation.[69]

 step 2 ▪ **Present your BCF statement and agree on the conflict.** After making your short planned BCF statement, let the other party respond. If the other party does not understand or avoids acknowledgment of the problem, persist. You cannot resolve a conflict if the other party will not even acknowledge its existence. Repeat your planned statement several times by explaining it in different terms until you get an acknowledgment or realize that it's hopeless. But don't give up too easily.

step 3 ▪ **Ask for, and/or give, alternative conflict resolutions.** Begin by asking the other party what can be done to resolve the conflict. If you agree, great; if not, offer your resolution. However, remember that you are collaborating not simply trying to change others. When the other party acknowledges the problem, but is not responsive to resolving it, appeal to common goals. Make the other party realize the benefits to him or her and the organization as well.

 step 4 ▪ **Make an agreement for change.** Try to come to an agreement on specific action you will both take to resolve the conflict. Clearly state, or better yet for complex change, write down the specific behavior changes necessary

---

BCF model
Describes a conflict in terms of behavior, consequences, and feelings.

WORK APPLICATION

12. Use the BCF model to describe a conflict you face or have faced.

by all parties to resolve the conflict. Again, remember that you are collaborating, not forcing.

Skill-Building Exercise 9–2 gives you the opportunity to develop your skill at initiating a conflict resolution.

✳skillbuilder

Responding to Conflict Resolution

As the responder, an initiator has confronted you. Here's how to handle the role of responder to a conflict. Most initiators do not follow the model. Therefore, the responder must take responsibility for successful conflict resolution by following the conflict resolution model steps: (1) Listen to and paraphrase the conflict using the BCF model. (2) Agree with some aspect of the complaint. (3) Ask for, and/or give, alternative conflict resolutions. (4) Make an agreement for change. The steps are also listed in Model 9–3.

Mediating Conflict Resolution

Frequently, conflicting parties cannot resolve their dispute alone. In these cases, a mediator should be used. A **mediator** *is a neutral third party who helps resolve a conflict.* In nonunionized organizations, managers are commonly the mediators. But some organizations have trained and designated employees as mediators. In unionized organizations, the mediator is usually a professional from outside the organization. However, a conflict resolution should be sought internally first.[70]

mediator
A neutral third party who helps resolve a conflict.

Before bringing the conflicting parties together, the mediator should decide whether to start with a joint meeting or to conduct individual meetings. If one employee comes to complain, but has not confronted the other party, or if there is a serious discrepancy in employee perceptions, meet one-on-one with each party before bringing them together. On the other hand, when both parties have a similar awareness of the problem and motivation to solve it, you can begin with a joint meeting when all parties are calm. The manager should be a mediator, not a judge. Get the employees to resolve the conflict, if possible.[71] Remain impartial, unless one party is violating company policies. Don't belittle the parties in conflict. Don't make comments such as, "I'm disappointed in you two" or "you're acting like babies."

When bringing conflicting parties together, follow the mediating conflict model steps: (1) Have each party state his or her complaint using the BCF model. (2) Agree on the conflict problem(s). (3) Develop alternative conflict resolutions. (4) Make an agreement for change. (5) Follow up to make sure the conflict is resolved. These steps are also listed in Model 9–3.

As a mediator, do not try to place the blame on any one party. If either party blames the other, make a statement such as, "We are here to resolve the conflict; placing blame is not productive." Focus on how the conflict is affecting their work. Discuss the issues by addressing specific behavior,

arbitrator
A neutral third party who makes a binding decision to resolve a conflict.

not personalities.[72] If a person says, "We cannot work together because of a personality conflict," ask him or her to state the specific behavior in question. The discussion should make the parties aware of their behavior and its consequences.[73]

If the conflict has not been resolved, an arbitrator may be used as a follow up.[74] An **arbitrator** *is a neutral third party who makes a binding decision to resolve a conflict.* The arbitrator is like a judge whose decision must be followed. However, the use of arbitration should be kept to a minimum because it is not a collaborative style. Arbitrators commonly use a negotiating style in which each party wins some and loses some. Mediation and then arbitration tend to be used in management–labor negotiations when collective bargaining breaks down and the contract deadline is near.

Dealing with different personality types, varying perceptions and attitudes, power, politics, and conflict can be very stressful. Therefore, in the next section you will study the causes and consequences of stress and how to manage it.

STRESS

stress
The body's reaction to environmental demands made on it.

People react to external environmental stimuli internally. **Stress** *is the body's reaction to environmental demands made on it.* Body reactions can be emotional and/or physical reactions to environmental activities and events.[75] Some organizations, including EDS, offer stress management programs to better enable employees to handle stress.

Stress Can Be Functional or Dysfunctional

Stress is functional when it helps improve performance by challenging and motivating people to meet objectives. People perform best under some pressure. When deadlines are approaching, adrenaline flows and people rise to the occasion with top-level performance. In order to meet deadlines, managers often have to apply some pressure to themselves and their employees.

However, too much stress, for the individual, results in irritability, headaches and other body tension, stomach problems (poor digestion, heartburn, and ulcers), diseases (weakened immune system; elevated blood sugar levels, blood pressure, and cholesterol levels; and heart problems)[76] and premature death. Mild signs of stress include an increased breathing rate and an excessive amount of perspiration.

stressors
Situations in which people feel overwhelmed by anxiety, tension, and pressure.

Situations in which too much stress exists are known as stressors. **Stressors** *are situations in which people feel overwhelmed by anxiety, tension, and pressure.* On the other hand, if the situation is stress-free, people usually perform at lower levels.

Stress that is constant, chronic, and severe can lead to burnout over a period of time. *Burnout* is the constant lack of interest and motivation to perform one's job due to stress. Burnout results in physical and/or emotional exhaustion and the more severe stomach problems and diseases listed above. From the organizational side, high stress results in employee job dissatisfaction, absenteeism, turnover, and lower levels of productivity.[77]

Stress, like perception, is an individual matter. In the same situation one person may be very comfortable and stress-free while another feels it is a stressor situation. In other words, abilities to handle pressure vary.

Causes of Stress

There are five common job stressors. Complete Self-Assessment Exercise 9–4 to determine your personality type as it relates to stress.

Self-Assessment Exercise 9–4

Stress Personality Type

Identify how frequently each item applies to you at work or school. Place the number 1–5 on the line before each statement.

(5) usually (4) often (3) occasionally
(2) seldom (1) rarely

____ 1. I enjoy competition and I work/play to win.

____ 2. I skip meals or eat fast when there is a lot of work to do.

____ 3. I'm in a hurry.

____ 4. I do more than one thing at a time.

____ 5. I'm aggravated and upset.

____ 6. I get irritated or anxious when I have to wait.

____ 7. I measure progress in terms of time and performance.

____ 8. I push myself to work to the point of getting tired.

____ 9. I work on days off.

____ 10. I set short deadlines for myself.

____ 11. I'm not satisfied with my accomplishments for very long.

____ 12. I try to outperform others.

____ 13. I get upset when my schedule has to be changed.

____ 14. I consistently try to get more done in less time.

____ 15. I take on more work when I already have plenty to do.

____ 16. I enjoy work/school more than other activities.

____ 17. I talk and walk fast.

____ 18. I set high standards for myself and work hard to meet them.

_____ 19. I'm considered a hard worker by others.

_____ 20. I work at a fast pace.

_____ Total. Add up the numbers (1–5) you have for all 20 items. Your score will range from 20 to 100. Place an X on the continuum that represents your score.

Type A   100–90–80–70–60–50–40–30–20   Type B

The number 5 (usually) represents Type A behavior, and the number 1 (rarely) represents Type B behavior. The higher your score the more characteristic you are of the Type A stress personality. The lower your score, the more characteristic you are of the Type B stress personality.

Personality Types. The degree to which stressors affect us is due, in part, to our personality type. The *Type A personality* is characterized as fast-moving, hard-driving, time-conscious, competitive, impatient, and preoccupied with work. The Type B personality is the opposite of Type A. People with Type A personalities have more stress than people with Type B personalities. If you have a high Type A personality, you could end up with some of the problems associated with stress.

Organizational Culture. The amount of cooperation, motivation, and morale affects stress levels. The more positive the organizational culture, the less stress there is. Organizations that push employees to high levels of performance create a stressful situation.[78]

Management Behavior. The better managers supervise their employees, the less stress there is. Calm, participative management styles are less stressful.[79] Workers with bad bosses are five times as likely to report stress-related lost sleep, headaches, and upset stomachs.[80]

Work Performed. Some types of work are more stressful than others. But part of the stress comes from the perception of the enjoyment of the work itself. People who have jobs in which they enjoy the work itself derive satisfaction and handle stress better than those who do not. In some cases, changing to a job with enjoyable work is a wise move that can lower or rid one of stressors.

Human Relations. When people do not get along, conflict exists which can be very stressful. Human relations is a very important factor in job satisfaction. People who don't really like the work performed but enjoy the people they work with can have job satisfaction. However, people who don't like the work or the people face a stressful situation, and they usually have high absenteeism and turnover.[81]

Signs of Stress. A few of the mild signs of stress include an increased breathing rate and an excessive amount of perspiration. When stress continues for a period of time, it tends to lead to disillusionment, irritableness, headaches and other body tension, the feeling of exhaustion, and stomach problems. When you continually feel pressured and fear that you will not meet deadlines or fail you are experiencing stress. People watch TV/movies, drink, take drugs, eat, or sleep more than usual to escape stress.

Stress Management

Stress management is the process of eliminating or reducing stress. You can better control stress by following a three-stage stress management plan: (1) identify stressors, (2) determine their causes and consequences, and (3) plan to eliminate or decrease the stress. There are six stress management techniques you can use:

Time Management. Generally, people with good time management skills experience less job stress. Refer to Chapter 5 for details on time management.

Relaxation. Relaxation is an excellent stress management technique. Get enough rest and sleep; have some fun and laugh. If you are a Type A personality, slow down and enjoy yourself. Have some enjoyable off-the-job interests. People without a balanced career and personal life commonly suffer burnout. Some of the things you can do to relax include socializing with friends, prayer, meditation, music, reading, TV, movies, hobbies, and so forth.

Relaxation Exercises. When you feel stress, you can perform some simple relaxation exercises. One of the most popular and simplest is deep breathing because it relaxes the entire body. If you feel tension in one muscle, you may do a specific relaxation exercise; or you may relax your entire body going from head to toe, or vice versa. Figure 9–6 lists relaxation exercises that you can do almost anywhere. Deep breathing can be done during and/or between the other exercises.

Deep Breathing. You simply take a slow deep breath, preferably through your nose, hold it for a few seconds (you may count to five), then let it out slowly, preferably through lightly closed lips. To breathe deeply you must inhale by expanding the stomach, not the chest. Breathe in without lifting your shoulders and/or expanding your chest. Think of your stomach as a balloon and slowly fill it then empty it. As you inhale, think and visualize breathing in healing energy that makes you feel better, more energetic, less pain, and so on that results from stress. As you exhale think and visualize breathing out the tension, pain, illness, and so on that stress you. This same positive thinking technique can also be used during the other relaxation exercises.

Energy. Stress depletes your energy. Even feeling pressured and worrying about a stressor to come depletes your energy without physically doing anything. Mental stress can be more exhausting than physical stress. Remember that air (breathing), relaxation (especially sleep), and nutrition are major sources of the energy you need to resist stress. Contrary to the belief of many, proper exercise also increases your energy level rather than depleting it.

Nutrition. Good health is essential to everyone's performance, and nutrition is a major factor in health. Underlying stress can lead to overeating

Muscles Relaxed	Exercise (Tighten muscles as much as you can without straining, and perform as many tightening-relaxing repetitions as needed to feel relaxed without straining.)
All	Take a deep breath, hold it for around 5 seconds, then let it out slowly. See the deep breathing discussion in the text for more specific details. Deep breathing may be performed during and/or between other relaxation exercises.
Forehead	Wrinkle your forehead by trying to make your eyebrows touch your hairline for 5 seconds. Relax.
Eyes, nose	Close your eyes tightly for 5 seconds. Relax.
Lips, cheeks, jaw	Draw the corners of your mouth back tightly (grimace) for 5 seconds. Relax.
Neck	Drop your chin to your chest, then slowly rotate your head without tilting it back. Relax.
Shoulders	Lift your shoulders up to your ears and tighten for 5 seconds. Relax.
Upper arms	Bend your elbows and tighten your upper arm muscles for 5 seconds. Relax.
Forearms	Extend your arms out against an invisible wall and push forward with your hands for 5 seconds. Relax.
Hands	Extend your arms in front of you; clench your fists tightly for 5 seconds. Relax.
Back	Lie on your back on the floor or bed and arch your back up off the floor, while keeping your shoulders and buttocks on the floor, and tighten for 5 seconds. Relax.
Stomach	Suck in and tighten your stomach muscles for 5 seconds. Relax. Repeating this exercise several times throughout the day can help reduce the size of your waistline.
Hips, buttocks	Tighten buttocks for 5 seconds. Relax.
Thighs	Press your thighs together and tighten them for 5 seconds. Relax.
Feet, ankles	Flex your feet with toes pointing up as far as you can and tighten for 5 seconds; then point your feet down and tighten for 5 seconds. Relax.
Toes	Curl your toes under and tighten for 5 seconds then wiggle them. Relax.

Figure 9-6
Relaxation Exercises

and compulsive dieting, and being overweight is stressful. When you eat, take your time and relax because rushing is stressful and can cause an upset stomach. Also, when people eat slower they tend to eat less. So don't eat at your work area/desk. Taking a break generates energy and makes you more productive.[82]

Breakfast is considered the most important meal of the day. Getting up and going to work without eating until lunch is stressful. A good breakfast increases your ability to resist stress, and a good breakfast may include eggs. Current empirical medical researchers report that eggs do not negatively increase cholesterol.[83]

Watch your intake of junk foods because they are stressful to your body. Consume fat (fried meat and vegetables including french fries and chips), sugar (pastry, candy, fruit drinks, soda—many cans of soda contain 10 teaspoons), caffeine (coffee, tea, soda), and salt (combined with the others and put on food from a shaker) in moderation. Eat more natural foods such as fruits and vegetables and drink their juice. Realize that poor nutrition and the use of overeating, smoking, alcohol, and drugs to reduce stress often create other stressful problems over a period of time.

Exercise. Physical exercise is an excellent way to improve health while releasing stress. Aerobic exercise, in which you increase the heart rate and maintain it for 20 to 30 minutes three or more days per week, is generally considered the best type of exercise. Exercises such as fast walking or jogging, biking, swimming, and aerobic dance/exercise fall into this category.

Before starting an exercise program, check with a doctor to make sure you are able to do so safely. Always remember that the objective is to relax and reduce stress. The no pain–no gain mentality applies to competitive athletes, not to stress management. Besides, if you don't enjoy exercising it may be because you are pushing yourself too hard, and if you do, you will most likely quit anyway.

Positive Thinking. People with an optimistic personality/attitude generally have less stress than pessimists. Once you start having doubts about your ability to do what you have to do, you become stressed. Make statements to yourself in the affirmative, such as "This is easy," or "I will do it." Repeat positive statements while doing deep breathing, but be realistic. Positive thinking will not guarantee that you will not get a stress headache, but many people have talked themselves into having headaches or other illnesses.

Don't Procrastinate or Be a Perfectionist. Procrastinating gives you more time to think about what you have to do and to get stressed before you start. You do a good quality job, but perfectionism stresses you as you perform rework.

Support Network. Talking to others in a support network can help reduce stress. Develop a network of family and friends you can go to for help with your problems. But don't continually lean on others to help you or use stress to get attention. Political reciprocity and coalitions can be used to help you and your network to reduce each other's stress.

WORK APPLICATION

13. Follow the stress management plan steps: (1) Identify your major stressors, (2) determine their causes and consequences, and (3) plan to eliminate or decrease the stress. Be sure to identify each step and the stress management techniques you will use.
14. At which of the six stress management techniques are you best and worst? What can you do to improve your stress management skills?

The Stress Tug-of-War

12. Explain the stress tug-of-war analogy.

Think of stress as a tug-of-war with you in the center, as illustrated in Figure 9–7. On your left are causes of stress (ropes) trying to pull you to the left to burnout. On your right are stress management techniques (ropes) you pull to keep you in the center. If the stress becomes too powerful it will pull you off center, to the left, and you lose as you suffer burnout. The stress tug-of-war is an ongoing game. On easy days you move to the right, and on overly tough days you move to the left. Your main objective is to stay in the center and avoid burnout.

APPLYING THE CONCEPT

AC 9–4 Stress Management Techniques

Identify each statement by the technique being used:
a. time management c. nutrition e. positive thinking
b. relaxation d. exercise f. support network

____ 16. "I've been repeating statements to myself to be more optimistic."
____ 17. "I've set up a schedule for myself."
____ 18. "I've been getting up earlier and eating breakfast."
____ 19. "I've been talking to my partner about my problems."
____ 20. "I've been praying."

Figure 9-7
The Stress Tug-of-War

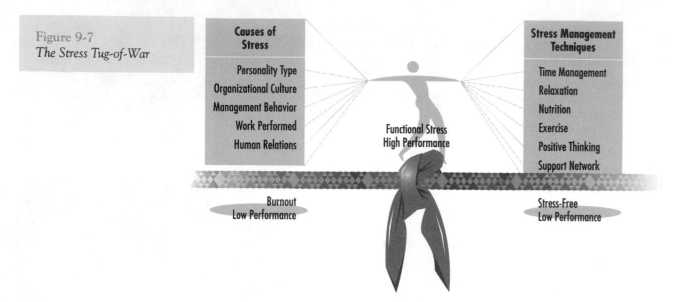

Causes of Stress	Stress Management Techniques
Personality Type	Time Management
Organizational Culture	Relaxation
Management Behavior	Nutrition
Work Performed	Exercise
Human Relations	Positive Thinking
	Support Network

Functional Stress
High Performance

Burnout
Low Performance

Stress-Free
Low Performance

Stress management does not require the use of all six techniques. Use the ones that work best for you. If you use stress management and experience permanent burnout, you should seriously consider getting out of the situation. Ask yourself two questions: "Is my long-term health important?" and "Is this situation worth hurting my health for?" If you answer yes and no, a change of situations/jobs is advisable. Drop the ropes and walk away to a new tug-of-war.

CHAPTER SUMMARY AND GLOSSARY

The chapter summary is organized to answer the nine learning objectives for Chapter 9.

1. List the differences along the continuum for each of the big five personality traits (extraversion, agreeableness, neuroticism, conscientiousness, and openness to experience).

Extraversion lies on a continuum between extrovert and introvert; agreeableness between cooperative and competitive; neuroticism between positive and negative attitude; conscientiousness between dependable and not dependable; and openness to experience between willingness to try and not to try new things.

2. Explain the perception process and the two factors it is based on.

Perception is the process of selecting, organizing, and interpreting environmental information. How you select, organize, and interpret information is based on internal individual factors including your personality and attitudes. The second factor of the perception process is the information itself from the external environment.

3. Describe the interrelationship among personality, perception, and attitude, and why they are important.

Personality affects perception and attitudes. Perception also affects attitudes, and attitudes also affect perception. Changing your perception of self-esteem and attitude adjustment changes single personality traits. Thus, all three are interrelated and are important because combined they directly affect behavior and performance.

4. State what job satisfaction is and why it is important.

Job satisfaction is a person's attitude toward his or her job. Job satisfaction is important because it has a direct relationship with absenteeism, turnover, and performance.

5. Define *power* and the difference between position and personal power.

Power is the ability to influence others' behavior. Position power is derived from top management and delegated down the chain of command, whereas personal power is derived from the followers based on the individual's behavior.

6. Explain the difference among reward, legitimate, and referent power.

The difference is based on how the person with power influences others. Reward power is based on the user's ability to influence others with something of value to them. Legitimate power is based on the user's position power given by the organization. Employees feel that they should be influenced. Referent power is based on the user's personal power relationship with others.

7. Discuss how power and politics are related.

Power is the ability to influence the behavior of others. Politics is the process of gaining and using power. Therefore, political skills are a part of power.

8. Describe how money and politics have a similar use.

Money and politics have a similar use because they are mediums of exchange. In our economy, money is the medium of exchange. In an organization, politics is the medium of exchange.

9. Explain what networking, reciprocity, and coalitions have in common.

Networking, reciprocity, and coalitions are all political behaviors. Networking is the process of developing relationships for the purpose of socializing and politicking. Reciprocity involves creating obligations and developing alliances and using them to accomplish objectives. Coalitions are a network of alliances that will help the person achieve an objective.

10. List and define the five conflict management styles.

(1) The *avoiding conflict style* user attempts to passively ignore the conflict rather than resolve it. (2) The *accommodating conflict style* user attempts to resolve the conflict by passively giving in to the other party. (3) The *forcing conflict style* user attempts to resolve the conflict by using aggressive behavior to get his or her own way. (4) The *negotiating conflict style* user attempts to resolve the conflict through assertive give-and-take concessions. (5) The *collaborating conflict style* user assertively attempts to resolve the conflict with the best solution agreeable to all parties.

11. List the steps in the initiating conflict resolution model.

The steps in the initiating conflict resolution model are: (1) plan a BCF statement that maintains ownership of the problem, (2) present your BCF statement and agree on the conflict, (3) ask for, and/or give, alternative conflict resolutions, and (4) make an agreement for change.

12. Explain the stress tug-of-war analogy.

Under the stress tug-of-war, you are in the center where stress is functional and performance is high. On your left are the causes of stress trying to pull you off center. On your right are the stress management techniques you use to keep you in the center. If the causes of stress pull you off center, you burn out and performance decreases. If there is an absence of stress, performance is also decreased.

13. Define the following key terms (in order of appearance in the chapter):

Select one or more methods: (1) fill in the missing key terms from memory, (2) match the key terms from the end of the summary with their definitions below, or (3) copy the key terms in order from the list at the beginning of the chapter.

_____ is the study of actions that affect performance in the workplace.

A _____ occurs when the organization and the employees get what they want.

_____ is a combination of traits that classifies individuals.

_____ is the process of selecting, organizing, and interpreting environmental information.

_____ is the process of determining the reason for behavior.

_____ are positive or negative evaluations of people, things, and situations.

The _____ states that managers' attitudes and expectations of employees and how they treat them largely determine their performance.

_____ is the ability to influence others' behavior.

_____ is the process of gaining and using power.

_____ is the process of developing relationships for the purpose of socializing and politicking.

_____ involves creating obligations and developing alliances and using them to accomplish objectives.

A _____ is a network of alliances that will help the person achieve an objective.

A _____ exists whenever people are in disagreement and opposition.

_____ exists when disagreement and opposition support the achievement of organizational objectives.

The _____ steps are: (1) plan a BCF statement that maintains ownership of the problem, (2) present your BCF statement and agree on the conflict, (3) ask for, and/or give, alternative conflict resolutions, and (4) make an agreement for change.

The _____ describes a conflict in terms of behavior, consequences, and feelings.

A _____ is a neutral third party who helps resolve a conflict.

An _____ is a neutral third party who makes a binding decision to resolve a conflict.

_____ is the body's reaction to environmental demands placed on it.

_____ are situations in which people feel overwhelmed by anxiety, tension, and pressure.

KEY TERMS

arbitrator 322
attitudes 297
attribution 295
BCF model 320
coalition 306
conflict 308
functional conflict 309

initiating conflict resolution model 319
mediator 321
networking 306
organizational behavior 290
perception 295
personality 291
politics 305

power 301
Pygmalion effect 298
reciprocity 306
stress 322
stressors 322
win-win situation 290

REVIEW AND DISCUSSION QUESTIONS

1. What are the big five personality traits?
2. What are the four biases in perception?
3. What are the determinants of job satisfaction? Are they of equal importance to everyone?
4. What are the seven bases of power?
5. Can management order the end of power and politics in the organization? If yes, should they?

6. Why should you learn the organizational culture and identify power players where you work?

7. How do you know when you are in conflict?

8. What is the difference between functional and dysfunctional conflict and how does each affect performance?

9. What is the primary reason for your conflicts?

10. What is meant by "maintain ownership of the problem"?

11. How is the BCF model used?

12. What is the difference between a mediator and an arbitrator?

13. What are the characteristics of a Type A personality?

14. What are the six stress management techniques?

OBJECTIVE CASE

Ohio Mutual Insurance Company

Ohio Mutual is a national insurance company. One of its locations is in Akron, Ohio.[84] At this facility, Debbie Townson is manager of the claims department. She is going to be promoted in one month. Debbie has been asked to select her replacement as manager of the claims department. She has narrowed down her selection to two finalists: Ted Shea and Libby Lee. Ted and Libby know they are competing for the promotion because Debbie told them that she will select one of them as the new manager on the day before she leaves for her new job. Their years of experience and quality and quantity of work are about the same. Following is some of the political behavior each has been using to help get the promotion.

Ted is good at sports and has been playing golf and tennis with some of the upper-level managers for over a year now. In the department, especially with Debbie, Ted drops names as he refers to conversations with managers all the time. When Ted does something for someone, he or she can expect to do a favor in return. Ted really wants this promotion, but he fears that with more women and minorities being promoted to management positions, Libby will get the job just because she is a woman and minority. To increase his chances of getting the job, Ted occasionally

reminds Debbie of past errors that Libby has made, and he makes negative remarks to everyone about her behind her back.

Libby has been going to night classes and company training programs in management to prepare herself for the promotion. Knowing that Debbie was an officer in a local chapter of a national insurance businesswomen's organization, Libby joined the club six months ago and now serves on a committee. At work, Libby talks regularly to Debbie about the women's organization. Libby makes an effort to know what is going on throughout the organization. She gets along well with everyone. Libby is very upbeat and goes out of her way to be nice to people and to compliment them.

Ted and Libby used to cooperate until they heard that they were competing for Debbie's management job. A few of Libby's friends have told her that Ted is talking negatively about her behind her back. One of Libby's friends has suggested that she talk about Ted to get even; another suggested talking to Ted and telling him to stop it; and a third suggested that Libby tell Debbie what he is doing. Libby is not sure what to do. Libby is too polite to talk negatively about Ted,

OBJECTIVE CASE

(continued)

and she really does not want to be a tattletale. In Libby's opinion, her only real option is to confront Ted about his behavior. However, her Asian cultural background and family upbringing have taught her to be cooperative. Just the thought of confronting anyone, especially Ted, makes her feel anxiety. Libby is stressed but has decided to wait and see if things get better.

Debbie is aware of the situation because one of her employees told her about Ted. She has observed both of them being uncooperative. At this point, Debbie is wondering if she should do anything. And if she does do something what she should do or how to handle the situation. After all, there are only two more weeks before she is promoted and leaves the department.

Select the best alternative to the following questions. Be sure you are able to explain your answers.

___ 1. Which employee has the following personality traits: high Machiavellianism, competitive, and pessimistic with the most negative attitude?

    a. Ted   b. Libby

___ 2. Debbie has ___ power.

    a. position   b. personal

___ 3. To be promoted, Ted has worked to develop a ___ power base. Refer to the opening statement about Ted.

    a. coercive   e. referent
    b. connection   f. information
    c. reward   g. expert
    d. legitimate

___ 4. To be promoted, Libby has worked to develop a ___ power base. Refer to the opening statement about Libby.

    a. coercive   c. reward
    b. connection   d. legitimate

    e. referent   g. expert
    f. information

___ 5. Debbie and Libby belong to the insurance professional association, which is ___ political behavior.

    a. networking   b. reciprocity
    c. coalitions

___ 6. ___ has conducted the most effective political behavior to identify "the power players" to get this promotion.

    a. Ted   b. Libby

___ 7. In Libby's conflict with Ted, she is using the ___ conflict management style.

    a. avoiding   d. negotiating
    b. accommodating   e. collaborating
    c. forcing

___ 8. In the conflict between Ted and Libby, ___ should maintain ownership of the problem.

    a. Ted   b. Libby

___ 9. Debbie is in the position to be the ___ of the conflict between Ted and Libby.

    a. initiator
    b. responder
    c. mediator

___ 10. Libby's primary cause of stress is

    a. personality type
    b. organizational culture
    c. management behavior
    d. work performed
    e. human relations

11. What action, if any, should Libby take? What would you do if you were in her situation?

12. What do you think of Ted's talking about Libby to discredit her? Is this ethical behavior?

13. What action, if any, should Debbie take to resolve the conflict?

OBJECTIVE CASE

(continued)

14. Should Libby's being an Asian woman affect the promotion decision? Should Ted's recent behavior affect the decision? In Debbie's situation, who would you select for your job?

15. Could Debbie have handled this promotion situation more effectively? In Debbie's situation, how would you have handled selecting your replacement?

*skillbuilder

Skill-Building Exercise 9–1

R

Car Dealer Negotiation[85]

Preparing for Skill-Building Exercise 9–1
You should have read and understood the negotiation process.

Doing Skill-Building Exercise 9–1 in Class

Objective
To develop your understanding of power and to build negotiation skills.

Experience
You will be the buyer or seller of a used car.

Procedure 1 (1–2 minutes)
Break up into groups of two and sit facing each other so that you cannot read each other's confidential sheet. Each group should be as far away from other groups as possible so that they cannot overhear each other's conversations. If there is an odd number of students in the class, one student will be an observer or work with the instructor. Decide who will be the buyer and who will be the seller of the used car.

Procedure 2 (1–2 minutes)
The instructor goes to each group and gives the buyer and seller their confidential sheets, which do not appear in this textbook.

Procedure 3 (5–6 minutes)
Buyers and sellers read their confidential sheets and jot down some plans (what will be your basic approach, what will you say) for the lunch meeting.

_____

_____

_____

Procedure 4 (3–7 minutes)
Negotiate the sale of the car. Try not to overhear your classmates' conversations. You do not have to buy or sell the car. After you make the sale, or agree not to sell, read your partner's confidential sheet and discuss the experience.

Integration (5–7 minutes)
Answer the following questions:

1. The appropriate type of plan for this situation was a ___ ?
   a. general single-use project plan.
   b. detailed standing-policy plan

2. The most relevant power base to help you successfully negotiate this car deal was ___ ?

    a. coercive   d. legitimate   g. expert

    b. connection   e. referent

    c. reward   f. information

3. Did this exercise create some stress (faster heart rate, perspiration; did you feel anxiety, tension, or pressure)?

    a. yes   b. no

4. Did you set a lower limit, target, and opening price? ___

    a. yes   b. no

5. Did you imply that you had other options and/or develop tradeoffs? ___

    a. yes   b. no

6. Did you anticipate questions and objections and prepare answers? ___

    a. yes   b. no

7. Did you develop rapport and focus on obstacles, not the person? ___

    a. yes   b. no

8. Did you let the other party make the first offer? ___

    a. yes   b. no

9. Did you listen and ask questions to focus on meeting the other party's needs? ___

    a. yes   b. no

10. Were you quick to settle for less than your target price and/or ask for something in return for giving concessions? ___

    a. yes   b. no

11. Was there a postponement in negotiations? ___

    a. yes   b. no

12. Did you reach a sales agreement?

    a. yes   b. no

    If yes, did you receive your ___ price?

    a. minimum

    b. target

    c. opening or more than expected

Conclusion

The instructor leads a class discussion or simply gives the answers to the integration questions and makes concluding remarks.

Application (2–4 minutes)

What did I learn from this experience? How will I use this knowledge in the future?

_____

_____

Sharing

Volunteers give their answers to the application section.

BEHAVIOR MODEL VIDEO

Behavior Model Video 9–1 (4½ minutes), Initiating Conflict Resolution, shows Alex initiating a conflict resolution over an advertising account with coworker Catherine. Alex follows the steps in Model 9–3. This video serves as a behavior model which can be used prior to conducting Skill-Building Exercise 9–2.

*skillbuilder

R

Skill-Building Exercise 9–2

Initiating Conflict Resolution

Preparing for Skill-Building Exercise 9–2

During class you will be given the opportunity to role-play a conflict you are facing, or have faced, in order to develop your conflict skills. Students and workers have reported that this exercise helped prepare them for a successful initiation of a conflict resolution with roommates and coworkers. Fill in the following information:

Other party(s) (You may use fictitious names) _____

_____

Describe the conflict situation: _____

_____

_____

List pertinent information about the other party (i.e., relationship to you, knowledge of the situation, age, background, etc.):

_____

_____

Identify the other party's possible reaction to your confrontation. (How receptive will he or she be to collaborating? What might he or she say or do during the discussion to resist change?)

_____

_____

_____

How will you overcome this resistance to change?

_____

_____

_____

Following the initiating conflict resolution model steps, write out your planned opening BCF statement that maintains ownership of the problem.

_____

_____

_____

Doing Skill-Building Exercise 9–2 in Class

Objective

To experience and develop skills in resolving a conflict.

Preparation

You should have completed the conflict information questions in the preparation for this exercise.

Experience

You will initiate, respond to, and observe a conflict role-play, and then evaluate the effectiveness of its resolution.

Video (4½ minutes)

Behavior Model Video 9–1, Initiating Conflict Resolution, may be shown.

Procedure 1 (2–3 minutes)

Break into as many groups of three as possible. If there are any people not in a triad, make one or two groups of two. Each member selects the number 1, 2, or 3. Number 1 will be the first to initiate a conflict role-play, then 2, followed by 3.

Procedure 2 (8–15 minutes)

A. Initiator number 1 tells or gives his or her information from the preparation to number 2 (the responder) to read. Once number 2 understands, role-play (see B). Number 3 is the observer.

B. Role-play the conflict resolution. Number 3, the observer, writes his or her observations on the feedback sheet at the end of this exercise.

C. Integration. When the role-play is over, the observer leads a discussion on the effectiveness of the conflict resolution. All three group members should discuss the effectiveness. Number 3 is not a lecturer. Do not go on to the next procedure until told to do so.

Procedure 3 (8–15 minutes)
Same as procedure 2, only number 2 is now the initiator, number 3 is the responder, and number 1 is the observer.

Procedure 4 (8–15 minutes)
Same as procedure 2, only number 3 is the initiator, number 1 is the responder, and number 2 is the observer.

Conclusion
The instructor leads a class discussion and/or makes concluding remarks.

Application (2–4 minutes)
What did I learn from this experience? How will I use this knowledge in the future?

_____

_____

Sharing
Volunteers give their answers to the application section.

Feedback Form
Try to have positive improvement comments for each step in initiating conflict resolution. Remember to be DESCRIPTIVE and SPECIFIC, and for all improvements have an alternative positive behavior (APB) (i.e., if you would have said/done . . . , it would have improved the conflict resolution by . . .).

Initiating Conflict Resolution Model Steps
Step 1. Plan a BCF statement that maintains ownership of the problem. (Did the initiator have a well-planned, effective BCF statement?)

_____

_____

Step 2. Present your BCF statement and agree on the conflict. (Did the initiator present the BCF statement effectively? Did the two agree on the conflict?)

_____

_____

Step 3. Ask for, and/or give, alternative conflict resolutions. (Who suggested alternative solutions? Was it done effectively?)

_____

_____

Step 4. Make an agreement for change. (Was there an agreement for change?)

_____

_____

BEHAVIOR MODEL VIDEO

Behavior Model Video 9–2 (6½ minutes), Mediating Conflict Resolution, Peter brings Alex and Catherine together to resolve their advertising account conflict. They follow the steps in Model 9–3. There is no Skill-Building Exercise to follow up this mediating conflict video.

Exercise 9–1

Improving Personality Traits

I G

Preparation for Exercise 9–1

You are not doing this exercise because you have a problem personality, but because we can all improve our personalities. In preparation for this exercise, write out the answers as follows.

Review Self-Assessment Exercise 9–1 and determine traits that would be worth improving to increase your job performance and satisfaction. Look especially at the left-hand side of the 9 continuums. Select the one trait that is most important for you to develop. After listing the trait, write a plan that will help you develop it. Below are a few examples. However, try not to simply copy one of them.

To develop a more *optimistic and positive attitude*, I will work at thinking and talking more positively.

- I will think and say positive things, such as I will do well on the test because I've worked hard; I will get the job done on time because I'm doing a good job; I will do well at that new task.

- I will be aware of what I think and say, and if I start to think or say something negative I will catch myself and stop the negative thought or statement and replace it with a positive one.

- I will tell my friends and/or coworkers of my working on being more positive, and ask them to tell me if I am being negative so I can be aware of my negativism and change.

- Zig Ziglar recommends that if you want to be more positive about your situation (work, school, family, relationship, etc.) you need to focus on the good side, not dwell on the negative. To do so, write out a list of everything you like about the situation, plus some positive affirmations such as I have a positive attitude; I enjoy my job; I like Fred. Every morning and evening, while looking in the mirror, read your list. Or you may record your list and play it. Do it for a month and you and others will see a changed positive personality.

To develop a more *extrovert* personality trait:

- I will say hi to people before they say hi to me.

- I will attend a party at which I don't know many people and I will approach people first to talk to them.

- I will go to class early (or stay after class) once a week and approach someone I don't know, or don't know well, and talk to them for a few minutes before (or after) class.

- The Zig Ziglar example also applies. A positive affirmation is, I enjoy meeting new people.

Place one trait and your plan to improve it below. You may repeat the process for more traits.

_____

_____

_____

_____

_____

Doing Exercise 9–1 in Class

Objective
To further develop your plan to improve your personality, and to help others improve their plans.

Preparation
You should have identified at least one trait and developed a plan to improve it.

Procedure 1 (1–2 minutes)
Break into groups of three. You may need a group(s) of two.

Procedure 2 (4–6 minutes)
One of the group members volunteers to go first. The first volunteer states the personality trait they want to work on and states the plan. The other group members give feedback on how to improve the plan. Try to give other plan ideas that can be helpful and/or provide some help. Using the examples above, you may volunteer to make the person aware of any negative comments they make or to take the person somewhere so they can meet new people. You can also make an agreement to ask each other how you are progressing at set class intervals. Don't change roles until told to do so.

Procedure 3 (4–6 minutes)
A second group member volunteers to go next. Follow the same procedure as above.

Procedure 4 (4–6 minutes)
The third group member goes last. Follow the same procedure as above.

Conclusion
The instructor may lead a class discussion and/or make concluding remarks.

Application (2–4 minutes)
What did I learn from this exercise? Will I really try to improve my personality?

_____

_____

10

Group and Team Development

Learning Objectives

After studying this chapter, you should be able to:

1. Describe the major differences between groups and teams.
2. State the group performance model.
3. List and explain the three dimensions of group types.
4. Define the three major roles played in groups.
5. Explain the differences between rules and norms.
6. Describe cohesiveness and why it is important to teams.
7. List the four major stages of group development and state the level of commitment and competence and the appropriate leadership style.
8. Explain the difference between a group manager and a team leader.
9. Discuss the three parts of meetings.
10. Define the following **key terms** (in order of appearance in the chapter):

group	group process
team	group process dimensions
group performance model	group roles
group structure dimensions	norms
group types	group cohesiveness
command groups	status
task groups	stages of group development
group composition	team leaders

skillbuilder

1. You can develop your skill at analyzing a group's development stage and selecting the appropriate leadership (Skill-Building Exercise 10–1).

Group skills are an important part of the leadership function of management. Group skills require interpersonal roles, particularly the leader and liaison roles; informational roles of monitor, disseminator, and spokesperson; and decisional roles of disturbance handler, resource allocator, and negotiator. The SCANS competencies of interpersonal skills, information, and systems are developed, and basic, thinking, and personal qualities are developed through the exercise.

ethodist Medical Center (MMC) of Oak Ridge, Tennessee, is a fully accredited, nonprofit organization that has grown into a 300-bed facility. MMC's primary goal is to deliver quality health care.

In the mid-1980s, the health care market became increasingly competitive. President and CEO Marshall Whisnant took action to improve performance. After a few failed attempts, he decided to take a systems approach to MMC. New initiatives included employee involvement, long-term thinking, pride in work quality, and an emphasis on teamwork to get the job done. With the help of consultants from QualPro, MMC launched "Quality Together."

Quality Together has four principles: (1) Quality assessment is to be performed by the employees doing the procedures by forming teams that use statistics to monitor work processes and make improvements on a continuous basis. (2) The number one rule is to satisfy customers, whether they are patients, physicians, corporate clients, or third-party payers. Measures of performance are customer-focused. (3) The focus of improving performance should be on making the overall customer satisfaction system and its processes function better, not on the management of employees or discrete events. (4) Top management focuses on the interrelationship of the entire system, and the other levels are responsible for reducing variation caused by special events and problems that deviate from the normal system.

To implement Quality Together value principles, QualPro consultants led MMC through four phases: (1) *Commitment.* A needs assessment was conducted to determine areas for improvement. The top management team went through team training. The team selected several process improvement projects. (2) *Initial Success.* Teams of managers and employees were formed to work on the projects selected in Phase 1. Team members were trained in teamwork, and QualPro consultants led the groups through applying an improvement process to their projects. The teams had great success at improving the processes of their projects. (3) *Implementation.* Many new teams were formed to focus on improving interdepartmental processes throughout the system. Members were trained in teamwork and building interdepartmental teams. (4) *Self-Sufficiency.* During the final phase, QualPro consultants trained MMC employees, called facilitators, to conduct the teamwork training, to train team leaders to run the team meeting, and to serve on teams as resource persons.

Managers developed teams within their own departments and kept informed on team progress by visiting team meetings. The managers provided support and resources to implement team recommendations. Managers were also encouraged to request interdepartmental project teams to improve specific process areas. Through this process, MMC implemented teams throughout the system, emphasizing the involvement of all employees. For current information on MMC, use Internet address **http://www.mmcoakridge.com**. For ideas on using the Internet, see Appendix B.

THE LESSON OF THE GEESE

When you see geese heading south for the winter flying in a "V" formation, you might be interested in knowing what scientists have discovered about why they fly that way.

1. As each bird flaps its wings, it creates an uplift for the bird following. By flying in a "V" formation, the flock adds 71 percent greater flying range than if each bird flew on its own.

   Lesson: People who share a common direction and sense of community can get where they are going quicker and easier because they are traveling on the thrust of one another.

2. Whenever a goose falls out of formation, it suddenly feels the drag and resistance of trying to go it alone and quickly gets back into formation to take advantage of the lifting power of the bird immediately in front.

   Lesson: There is strength and power and safety in numbers when traveling in the same direction as others with whom we share a common goal.

3. When the lead goose gets tired, he or she rotates back into formation and another goose flies point.

   Lesson: It pays to take turns doing the hard jobs.

4. The geese honk from behind to encourage those up front to keep up their speed.

Lesson: We all need to be remembered with active support and praise.

5. When a goose gets sick or is wounded and falls out, two geese fall out of formation and follow him or her down to help and protect. They stay with the downed goose until the crisis resolves, and then they launch out on their own with another formation to catch up with their group.

Lesson: We must stand by each other in times of need.

GROUPS AND TEAMS AND PERFORMANCE

Groups are the backbone of organizations because of the systems effect in which each group/department is affected by at least one other group and each department affects the performance of the total organization. Managers report spending most of their time in some form of group activity. Management performance depends on team performance, and leadership behavior affects team performance.[1] The better you understand groups and their performance, the more effective you will be as both a group member and leader. It is recommended that you have team experience.[2] Put it on your résumé to help you get a job.[3]

In this section you will study the differences between groups and teams, about factors that affect group performance, and how organizational context affects performance.

Groups and Teams

Although the terms *group* and *team* are used interchangeably, a distinction can be made.[4] Distinctions between groups and teams and their levels of autonomy are presented in Figure 10–1. To summarize the differences between groups and teams, they are defined as follows. A **group** *is two or more members with a clear leader who perform independent jobs with individual accountability, evaluation, and rewards.* A **team** *is a small number of members with shared leadership who perform interdependent jobs with both individual and group accountability, evaluation, and rewards.*

As shown in the bottom of Figure 10–1, groups and teams are on a continuum; it's not always easy to make a clear distinction. The terms *management-directed, semi-autonomous,* and *self-managed* (or directed)[5] are commonly used to differentiate along the continuum. Management-directed is clearly a group, self-directed is clearly a team, and semi-autonomous is between.

The U.S. Congress, workers on a traditional assembly line, and traditional sales forces are groups, not teams. Geese are more of a team than a group, although large numbers of them sometimes fly together. The teams at Methodist Medical Center (MMC) are closer to being a group than a team because they are problem-solving groups for an area rather than teams of workers actually getting the job done on a day-to-day basis.

The trend is toward teams[6] as AES, Cooper Industries, Hewlett Packard, Pitney Bowes, Nucor Steel, Goodyear Tire and Rubber, and the

1. Describe the major differences between groups and teams.

group
Two or more members with a clear leader who perform independent jobs with individual accountability, evaluation, and rewards.

team
A small number of members with shared leadership who perform interdependent jobs with both individual and group accountability, evaluation, and rewards.

Differences Between Groups and Teams

Characteristics	Group	Team
Size	Two or more; can be large.	Small number, often 5 to 12.
Leadership	One clear leader making decisions.	Shared leadership.
Jobs	Members perform one clear job; individual members do one independent part of a process (make one part of the product and pass it on to next person to do the next part).	Members share job responsibility by performing many interdependent tasks with complementary skills; the team completes an entire process (makes the entire product).
Accountability and Evaluation	Leader evaluates employees' individual performance.	Members evaluate each other's individual performance and group performance.
Rewards	Members are rewarded based on individual performance only.	Members are rewarded for both individual and group performance.
Objectives	Organizational.	Organizational and those set by the team.

Level of Autonomy

Group
Management-Directed   Semi-Autonomous   Team
                                                                        Self-Directed

Figure 10-1
Group versus Teams

2. State the group performance model.

group performance model
Group performance is a function of organizational context, group structure, group process, and group development stage.

Federal Way School District, just to name a few, have made tremendous performance improvements because of teams.[7] All teams are groups, but not all groups are teams. Therefore, when the term "group" is used, as it will be throughout this chapter, it can also include teams.

The Group Performance Model

The performance of groups is based on four major factors and can be listed as a formula. *In the* **group performance model,** *group performance is a function of organizational context, group structure, group process, and group development stage.* The group performance model is illustrated in Figure 10–2. The other three factors affecting group performance will be covered in detail in separate sections.

Organizational Context

A number of overall organizational and environmental factors affect how groups function and their level of performance. These organizational context factors have been discussed in prior chapters and are listed in Figure 10–2.

APPLYING THE CONCEPT

AC 10–1 Group or Team

Based on each statement, identify it as characteristic of:
a. group   b. team

_____ **1.** "My boss conducts my performance appraisals, and I get good ratings."

_____ **2.** "We don't have any departmental goal; we just do the best we can to accomplish the mission."

_____ **3.** "My compensation is based primarily on my department's performance."

_____ **4.** "I get the assembled product from Jean, I paint it and send it to Tony for packaging."

_____ **5.** "There are about 30 people in my department."

Group Performance	(f)	Organizational Context	Group Structure	Group Process	Group Development Stage
High to Low		Environment	Type	Roles	Orientation
		Mission	Size	Norms	Dissatisfaction
		Strategy	Composition	Cohesiveness	Resolution
		Culture	Leadership	Status	Production
		Structure	Objectives	Decision making	Termination
		Systems and Processes		Conflict resolution	

(f) = a function of

Figure 10-2
Group Performance Model

GROUP STRUCTURE

Group structure dimensions *include group type, size, composition, leadership, and objectives.* Each of these five components of group structure is described in this section.

group structure dimensions
Include group type, size, composition, leadership, and objectives.

3. List and explain the three dimensions of group types.

Group Types

Dimensions of group types include formal or informal, functional or cross functional, and command or task.

group types
Include formal or informal, functional or cross-functional, and command or task.

Formal or Informal Groups. *Formal groups,* such as departments and smaller subparts, are created by the organization as part of the formal structure; the groups generally have their own formal structure for conducting business. *Informal groups* are not created by the organization as part of the formal structure. They are spontaneously created when members join together voluntarily because of similar interests. People from any part of the organization who get together for breaks, lunch, and after work make up an informal group, which may be referred to as a *clique.* Throughout this text, the focus is on formal groups and teams.

Functional or Cross-Functional Groups. *Functional,* or vertical, *groups* have members who perform jobs within one limited area. Work units/departments make up a functional group. For example, the marketing, finance, operations, and human resources departments are functional groups. *Cross-functional,* or horizontal, *groups* have members from different areas and possibly different levels.[8] Generally, the higher the management level, the more cross-functional the responsibility.

Each manager in the organization serves as the link between each group. Ideally, all functional groups coordinate their activities through the aid of the managers who are responsible for linking the activities together. Rensis Likert calls this the *linking-pin role.* Figure 10–3 illustrates functional and cross-functional groups with managers acting as linking pins. The current trend is toward using more cross-functional groups to better coordinate the functional areas of the organization.[9]

Key:

Each manager serves as the linking pin between each group.

Figure 10-3
Functional and Cross-Functional Groups

command groups
Consist of managers and their employees.

task groups
Consist of employees selected to work on a specific objective.

Command or Task Groups. Command groups *consist of managers and their employees.* People are hired to be a part of a command group. Command groups are distinguished by department membership as being functional or cross-functional. In Figure 10–3, the president and the vice presidents are a cross-functional command group, whereas the vice presidents and their managers are functional command groups.

Task groups *consist of employees selected to work on a specific objective.* Task groups are usually called *committees.* There are two primary types of task groups: task forces and standing committees.[10]

A *task force,* or ad hoc committee, is a temporary group formed for a specific purpose. Project teams, using a matrix structure (Chapter 6), are a form of task group in which employees have a functional boss and work with cross-functional departments as needed.[11] In Figure 10–3, the purpose of the task force is to select three top candidates to present to the board of directors as potential replacements for the current president who will retire in six months. One employee from each of the functional areas, selected by their peers, serves on the task force.

A *standing committee* is a permanent group that works on continuing organizational issues. For example, the functional teams at MMC regularly meet to provide continuous improvement, and it always has a budget committee because it creates a new budget every year. Membership on standing committees is often rotated every year so that new ideas are brought to the group. For example, membership may be for three years, with one-third of the committee replaced every year.

Some organizations, including Dow, GE, Monsanto, Westinghouse, and Union Carbide have venture groups that develop new products and lines of business to enter. 3M has at least 24 venture groups developing new lines of business at one time, and six of its current divisions grew out of these venture groups. At MMC a cross-functional steering committee makes the decisions on projects over $500.

There are a couple of major differences between a command and task group. One difference is the membership. Command groups tend to be functional, whereas task groups are often cross-functional. Another difference is in who belongs to which type of group. Everyone in an organization belongs to a command group, but employees may work for an organization for many years without ever being a member of a cross-functional task group. Generally, the higher the level of management, the more variety and time is spent in task groups and their meetings.

Group Size

Is There an Ideal Group Size? There is no consensus on the ideal size for groups; some say three to nine, others say five or six to eight, and still others say up to twenty. The number varies depending on the purpose. Groups tend to be larger than teams. At Titeflex teams of six to ten people manufacture fluid and gas-holding systems. EDS has project teams of 8 to 12 members. Johnsonville Foods uses self-managed teams of around 12. Digital Equipment Corporation believes the ideal team size is 14 or 15.

If the group is too small, it limits ideas and creativity. It tends to be too cautious and the workload is not distributed over enough members. On the other hand, if a group is too large, it tends to be too slow and not everyone gets to participate. With 20 or more members, you have a group rather than a team because there are too many members to reach consensus on decisions, and members tend to form subgroups. In large groups, free-riding is a problem. *Free-riding* occurs when members rely on others to carry their share of the workload.

How Size Affects Leadership. Group size affects leadership, members, and the group's process of completing the job.[12] The appropriate leadership style may vary with group size.[13] The larger the size, the more formal or autocratic the leadership needs to be to provide direction. Managers tend to be more informal and participative when they have smaller teams. Group members are more tolerant and appreciative, at times, of autocratic leadership in large groups.[14] Larger groups tend to inhibit equal participation. Generally, participation is more equal in groups of around five. This is why teams are small in size. The larger the group, the greater need there is for formal structured plans, policies, procedures, and rules.

Leadership Implications. Usually, managers have no say in the size of their command groups. However, if you have a large department, you can

WORK APPLICATION

2. Identify task groups used in an organization you work or have worked for. Be sure to specify each group as a task force or standing committee.

take a larger group and break it into teams. As the chair of a committee, you may be able to select the group size. In doing so, keep the group size appropriate for the task and be sure to get the right group composition.

Group Composition

group composition
The mix of members' skills and abilities.

What Is Group Composition? **Group composition** *is the mix of members' skills and abilities.* Group and team performance, regardless of type and size, is affected by its composition. Without the right mix of skills and abilities, groups will not perform at high levels.

People with a high need for affiliation tend to make better team players than people with a high need for power, who work better in groups. Managers tend to have a high need for power and a low need for affiliation, which contributes to their use of groups and their resistance to changing to teams.

Leadership Implications. One of the most important group leadership functions is to attract, select, and retain the best people for the job. When selecting group or team members, be sure to include a diversity of members.[15] Diverse groups tend to outperform homogeneous groups. With teams you want members with complementary skills, rather than selecting people with the same skills. Cross-functional teams provide diversity and complementary skills.

Group Leadership and Objectives

Leadership. To a large extent, the leader provides and determines group structure. In Figure 10–1, you learned that the leadership style is different in groups and teams. Group performance is affected by the team leader.[16] Throughout this chapter you will learn more about group and team leadership.

Objectives. In Chapter 4 you learned the benefits of setting objectives; they apply to both individuals and groups.[17] In groups, the objective is commonly very broad—usually to fulfill the mission. However, teams develop their own objectives. One of the reasons teams tend to outperform groups is because they have their own objectives; groups do not. Objectives help to provide the structure required to identify organizational need to achieve the objective.[18]

Leadership Implications. Companies in the Forbes top 25 are focusing on developing team leadership and goal-setting skills.[19] As a manager, you need to provide the appropriate leadership style for the situation.[20] Part of leadership responsibility is to be sure the size and composition are appropriate for the situation. As a group or team leader, or as a member with leadership skills, be sure that the group or team has clear objectives.

MMC has groups in all three dimensions of group type. It has moved from groups to teams. The Quality Together program includes command

**WORK
APPLICATION**

3. Recall a present or past job. State the type of group/team you belonged to and describe its size, composition, leadership, and objectives.

and task groups of various sizes. MMC teams have leaders, but they share leadership responsibilities with members. When managers develop teams, they do consider composition and the teams develop their own objectives.

In summary, group structure dimensions include group type, size, composition, leadership, and objectives. See Figure 10–4 for a review of group structure dimensions.

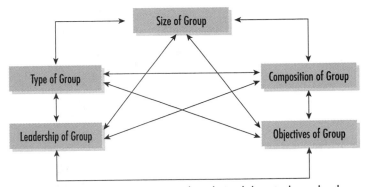

The arrows indicate the effect (or systems interrelationship) each dimension has on the others.

GROUP PROCESS

Group process *refers to the patterns of interactions that emerge as members perform their jobs.* Group process is also called *group dynamics* and the process can change over time. Team members need training in group process to be successful. Attention to group process improves the performance of groups.[21] Regardless of the type of groups you work in, your ability to understand group process and to develop these skills will affect your performance, the group's performance, and all members' job satisfaction.

Group process dimensions *include roles, norms, cohesiveness, status, decision making, and conflict resolution.* These components are presented in this section.

Group Roles

As a group works toward achieving its objectives, it has to perform certain functions. As functions are performed, people develop roles. *Job roles* are shared expectations of how group members will fulfill the requirements of their position. It is important that employees have clear roles so they know their responsibilities.[22] Job descriptions help to clarify functional roles. People often have multiple roles within the same position. For example, a professor may have the roles of teacher, researcher, writer, consultant, advisor, and committee member. Job roles vary greatly but group roles have just three classifications.

Classifying Group Roles. The three primary **group roles** *are task, maintenance, and self-interest.* In Chapter 1, you learned that when managers interact with employees, they can use task behavior or maintenance behavior; in addition, both behaviors or neither can be used to develop the four leadership styles.[23] These same two dimensions are performed by group members as they interact.

Group task roles are played when members do and say things that directly aid in the accomplishment of the group's objectives. Terms used to describe task roles include structuring, job-centered, production, task-oriented, and directive.

Figure 10-4
Group Structure Dimensions

group process
Refers to the patterns of interactions that emerge as members perform their jobs.

group process dimensions
Include roles, cohesiveness, status, decision making, and conflict resolution.

4. Define the three major roles played in groups.

group roles
Task, maintenance, and self-interest.

Group maintenance roles are played when members do and say things to develop and sustain the group process. Terms used to describe maintenance roles include consideration, employee-centered, relationship-oriented, and supportive.

Self-interest roles are played when members do and say things that help the individual but hurt the group. When group members put their own needs before those of the group, its performance suffers. For example, if a member supports an alternative solution rather than the best solution because he or she is only concerned about getting his or her own way, a self-interest is being met.

As a team member, watch for self-interest roles and hidden agendas as you learn to distinguish between a self-interest that benefits both the individual and the organization (a win-win situation) and one that benefits the individual and hurts the organization (a win-lose situation) as you strive to achieve objectives. It has been said that group performance can increase dramatically if its members are not concerned about who gets credit for the idea.

How Roles Affect Group Performance. To be effective, a group must have members who play task roles and maintenance roles, while minimizing self-interest roles. Groups that only have task performers may suffer performance problems because they do not deal with conflict effectively, and because the job will be boring if there is no maintenance. Its group process will hurt performance. On the other hand, groups that have a great time but do not have members playing task roles will not get the job done. Any group whose members are playing self-interest roles will not produce to its fullest potential.[24]

Leadership Implications. When in a group, the leader should be aware of the roles its members play.[25] If the members are not playing the task and/or maintenance roles required at a given time, the leader should play the role. If the group has a leader who does not provide the proper roles when the members do not, any group member can provide the necessary leadership. The leader should also make the group aware of the need to play these roles and the need to minimize self-interest roles. In the next major section, you will learn about group development and how the leader should use task and maintenance roles to help the group develop. Team

WORK APPLICATION

4. Recall a present or past job. Identify group/team members, including yourself, and state the primary role they played in the group.

APPLYING THE CONCEPT

AC 10–2 Roles

Identify each statement by the role it fulfills:

a. task   b. maintenance   c. self-interest

_____ **6.** "Wait. We can't make the decision because we haven't heard Rodney's idea yet."

_____ **7.** "I don't understand. Could you explain why we are doing this again?"

_____ **8.** "We tried that before you came to work here; it did not work. My idea is much better."

_____ **9.** "What does this have to do with the problem we are working on? We are getting sidetracked."

_____ **10.** "I like Ted's idea better than mine. Let's go with his idea instead of mine."

members at MMC and many other organizations get training to help them to understand group roles.

Group Norms

Command groups generally have policies, procedures, and rules to help provide the necessary guidelines for behavior, whereas task groups do not. However, standing plans cannot be complete enough to cover all situations. All groups tend to form their own unwritten norms about how things are done. **Norms** *are the group's shared expectations of its members' behavior.* Norms determine what should, ought, or must be done in order for the group to maintain consistent and desirable behavior.

How Norms Develop. Norms are developed spontaneously as the members interact through the group's routine. Each group member has cultural values and past experience. The group's beliefs, attitudes, and knowledge influence the type of norms developed. For example, the group decides, without ever actually talking about it and agreeing this would be a rule, what is an acceptable level of work. If the group members develop a shared expectation that this level is desirable, members will produce it. The use of certain words or jokes, like swearing and ethnic jokes, are considered acceptable or not. If a member swears or tells an ethnic joke, and members look at the person like he or she is strange or make comments against it, members will tend not to use these words or jokes. On the other hand, if everyone else jumps in with swearing or jokes, members will use these behaviors. Norms can change over time to meet the needs of the group. Diversity training tends to discourage ethnic jokes.

How Groups Enforce Norms. If a group member does not follow the norm, the other members try to enforce compliance. The common ways groups enforce norms include ridicule, ostracism, sabotage, and physical abuse. For example, if a member, Sal, produces more than the accepted level of performance, other members may kid or ridicule him. If Sal continues to break the norm, members could use physical abuse or ostracize him to enforce compliance with the norm. Members could also damage his work or take his tools or supplies to slow down his production.

Leadership Implications. Group norms can be positive, helping the group meet its objectives, or they can be negative, hindering the group from meeting its objectives. For example, if the company's production standard is 110 units per day, a group norm of 100 is a negative norm. However, if the standard were 90, it would be a positive norm. Leaders should be aware of their group's norms. They should work toward maintaining and developing positive norms and try to eliminate negative norms. Leaders should confront groups with negative norms and try to work out agreeable solutions to make them positive.

---

5. Explain the differences between rules and norms.

norms
The group's shared expectations of its members' behavior.

WORK APPLICATION

5. Recall a present or past job. Identify at least two group/team norms. Explain how you know they are norms and how the group enforces these norms.

6. Describe cohesiveness and why it is important to teams.

group cohesiveness
The extent to which members stick together.

Group Cohesiveness

The extent to which a group will abide by and enforce its norms depends on its degree of cohesiveness. **Group cohesiveness** *is the extent to which members stick together.* The more cohesive the group, the more it sticks together as a team. The more desirable group membership is, the more willing the members are to behave according to the group's norms. For example, in a highly cohesive group all members would produce about the same amount of work. However, in a moderate or low cohesive group, members could produce at different levels without the norm being enforced. Also, if some group members take drugs, and the group develops a norm of taking drugs together, cohesive members will sometimes behave in ways they really don't agree with to be accepted by the group.

Factors Influencing Cohesiveness. Six factors influence cohesiveness:

Objectives. The stronger the agreement and commitment made to the achievement of the group's objectives, the higher the cohesiveness of the group.

Size. Generally, the smaller the group, the higher the cohesiveness. Three to nine members seems to be a good group size for cohesiveness.

Homogeneity. Generally, the more similar the group members are, the higher the cohesiveness, but diverse groups usually make better decisions. People tend to be attracted to people who are similar to themselves.

Participation. Generally, the more equal the level of participation among group members, the higher the group's cohesiveness.[26]

Competition. The focus of the competition affects cohesiveness. If the group focuses on internal competition, its members will try to outdo each other, and low cohesiveness results. If the group focuses on external competition, its members tend to pull together as a team to beat its rivals.

Success. The more successful a group is at achieving its objectives, the more cohesive it tends to become. Success tends to breed cohesiveness, which in turn breeds more success. People want to be on a winning team.

How Cohesiveness Affects Group Performance. Many research studies have compared cohesive and noncohesive groups and concluded that cohesive groups tend to have a higher level of success at achieving their objectives with greater satisfaction. Cohesive group members tend to miss work less often, are more trusting and cooperative, and have less tension and hostility. Cohesiveness is associated with performance in the following ways:

- Groups with the highest level of productivity were highly cohesive and accepted management's level of productivity.

- Groups with the lowest levels of productivity were also highly cohesive, but rejected management's level of productivity; they set and enforced their own level below that of management. This can happen in organizations with unions that have the "us against them" attitude.

- Groups with intermediate levels of productivity were low cohesive groups, irrespective of their acceptance of management's level of productivity. The widest variance of individual group members' performance was among the groups with the lower cohesiveness. They tended to be more tolerant of nonconformity with group norms.

Leadership Implications. As a leader, you should strive to develop cohesive groups that accept a high level of productivity. The use of participation helps the group develop cohesiveness and builds agreement and commitment toward its objectives.[27] The use of coaching helps to encourage and develop cohesiveness. Some intragroup competition may be helpful, but leaders should focus primarily on intergroup competition. It helps to develop a cohesive winning team, which in turn motivates the group to higher levels of success. However, recall the many advantages of managing a diverse group, and meet the challenge of developing a cohesive diversified group.

Status within the Group

As group members interact, they develop respect for one another on numerous dimensions. The more respect, prestige, influence, and power a group member has, the higher his or her status within the group. *Status is the perceived ranking of one member relative to other members in the group.*

The Development of Status. Status is based on several factors, including member's performance, job title, wage or salary, seniority, knowledge or expertise, interpersonal skills, appearance, education, race, age, sex, and so on. Group status depends on the group's objectives, norms, and cohesiveness. Members who conform to the group's norms tend to have higher status than members who do not. A group is more willing to listen to and overlook a high-status member who breaks the norms. High-status members also have more influence on the development of the group's norms and the decisions made by the group. Lower-level members' ideas are often ignored, and they tend to copy high-status members' behavior and agree with their suggestions to be accepted.

How Status Affects Group Performance. The high-status members have a major impact on the group's performance. In a command group, the boss is usually the member with the highest status. The leader's ability to manage affects the group performance. In addition to the leader, high-status members of command groups also affect performance. If high-status members support positive norms and high productivity, chances are the group will, too.

WORK APPLICATION

6. Recall a present or past job. Identify the group/team's level of cohesiveness as high, medium, or low. Be sure to explain the level.

status
The perceived ranking of one member relative to other members in the group.

WORK APPLICATION

7. Recall a present or past job. List each member, including yourself, and identify each person's level of status within the group as high, medium, or low. Explain why each member has the level of status you assigned.

APPLYING THE CONCEPT

AC 10–3 Group Process

Identify each statement by a dimension of the group process:

a. roles   c. cohesiveness e. decision making
b. norms   d. status   f. conflict resolution

_____ **11.** "Although we do have occasional differences of opinion, we really get along well and enjoy working together."

_____ **12.** "When you need advice on how to do things, go see Shirley; she knows the ropes around here better than anyone."

_____ **13.** "I'd have to say that Carlos is the peacemaker around here. Every time there is a disagreement, he tries to get the members to work out the problem."

_____ **14.** "Kenady, you're late for the meeting. Everyone else was on time, so we started without you."

_____ **15.** "What does this have to do with solving the problem? We are getting sidetracked."

Another important factor influencing group performance is status congruence. *Status congruence* is the acceptance and satisfaction members receive from their group status. Members who are not satisfied with their status may not be active participants of the group. They may physically or mentally escape from the group and not perform to their full potential. Or they may cause group conflict as they fight for a higher status level.

Leadership Implications. To be effective, the leader needs to have high status within the command group. The leader should maintain good human relations with the group, particularly with the high-status informal leader(s), to be sure they endorse positive norms and objectives. In addition, the leader should be aware of conflicts that may be the result of lack of status congruence. Ideally, status should be about equal within the group.

Decision Making and Conflict Resolution

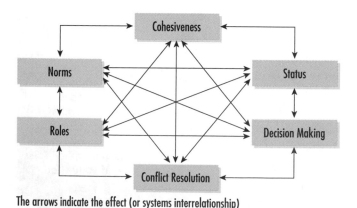

The arrows indicate the effect (or systems interrelationship) each dimension has on the others.

Figure 10-5
Group Process Dimensions

The decisions made by groups and teams have a direct effect on performance.[28] With groups, decision-making authority is held by the manager. However, with teams, decision-making authority is held by the members. Creative problem solving and decision making have already been covered in Chapter 3.

Conflict is common in groups and teams, and unresolved conflicts can have a negative effect on performance.[29] In the last chapter you developed your skills at resolving conflict.

The managers, team leaders, and team members at MMC were trained to develop their group process skills through organizational development (OD) interventions (Chapter 7). If you understand and develop group process skills, you will be a more effective group/team member and leader. Figure 10–5 summarizes the six dimensions of group process/dynamics.

GROUP DEVELOPMENT STAGES AND LEADERSHIP STYLES

All groups have unique organizational context, group structure, and group processes that change over a period of time. However, it is generally agreed that all groups go through the same stages as they grow from a collection of individuals to a smoothly operating and effective group or team.[30] *The stages of group development are orientation, dissatisfaction, resolution, production, and termination.*

Situational leadership can be applied to the stages of group development.[31] In other words, the appropriate leadership style changes with the level of group development. In this section, you will study the five stages of group development and the appropriate leadership style for each stage.

Stage 1. Orientation

The orientation stage, also known as the *forming* stage, is characterized by low development level (D1)—high commitment and low competence. When people first form a group, they tend to come to the group with a moderate to high commitment to the group.[32] However, because they have not worked together, they do not have the team competence to do the job.

During orientation, members have *group structure issues* over the leadership and objectives of the group. The size of the group and its composition are checked out. With regard to type of group, command groups are rarely started with all new members. This stage is more characteristic of task groups that have clear new beginnings. *Group process issues* include anxiety over how members will fit in (status), what will be required of them (roles and norms), what the group will be like (cohesiveness), how decisions will be made, and how members will get along (conflict). These group structure and group process issues must be resolved to progress to the next stage of group development.

Leadership Style. During the orientation stage, the appropriate leadership style is autocratic (high task/low maintenance). When a group first comes together, the leader needs to spend time helping the group clarify its objectives, providing clear expectations of members. The leader should also allow some time for group members to start to get to know one another.

Stage 2. Dissatisfaction

The dissatisfaction stage, also known as the *storming* stage, is characterized by moderate development level (D2)—lower commitment and some competence. As members work together for some time, they tend to become dissatisfied with the group.[33] Members start to question: Why am I a member? Is the group going to accomplish anything? Why don't other group

7. List the four major stages of group development and state the level of commitment and competence and the appropriate leadership style.

stages of group development
Orientation, dissatisfaction, resolution, production, and termination.

members do what is expected? and so forth. Often the task is more complex and difficult than anticipated; members become frustrated and have feelings of incompetence. However, the group does develop some competence to perform the task.

During the dissatisfaction stage, the group needs to work on resolving its group structure and process issues[34] before the group can progress to the next stage of development. Groups can get stuck in this stage of development and never progress to being satisfied with the group and learning to perform as a team.

Leadership Style. During the dissatisfaction stage, the appropriate leadership style is consultative (high task/high maintenance). When satisfaction drops, the leader needs to focus on playing the maintenance role to encourage members to continue to work toward the objectives. The leader should help the members meet their needs as they develop the appropriate group structure and process. At the same time, the leader needs to continue to provide the task behavior necessary to help the group develop its level of competence.

Stage 3. Resolution

The resolution stage, also called the *norming* stage, is characterized by high development level (D3)—variable commitment and high competence. With time, members often resolve the differences between initial expectations and realities in relation to the objectives, tasks, skills, and so forth. As members develop competence, they often become more satisfied with the group. Relationships develop that satisfy group members' affiliation needs.[35] Members learn to work together as they develop a group structure and process with acceptable leadership, norms, status, cohesiveness, and decision making. During periods of conflict or change, the group needs to resolve these issues.

Commitment can vary from time to time as the group interacts. If the group does not deal effectively with group process issues, the group may regress to stage 2 or plateau, fluctuating in commitment and competence. If the group is successful at developing a positive group structure and process, it will develop to the next stage.

Leadership Style. During the resolution stage, the appropriate leadership style is participative (low task/high maintenance). Once group members know what to do and how to do it, there is little need to provide task behavior.[36] The group needs the leader to play a maintenance role.

When commitment varies, it is usually due to some problem in the group's process, such as a conflict. The leader needs to focus on maintenance behavior to get the group through the issue(s) it faces. If the leader continues to provide task directives that are not needed, the group can become dissatisfied and regress or plateau at this level.

Stage 4. Production

The production stage, also called the *performing* stage, is characterized by outstanding development level (D4)—high commitment and high competence. At this stage commitment and competence do not fluctuate much. The group works as a team with high levels of satisfaction. The group maintains a positive group structure and process. The fact that members are very productive helps lead to positive feelings. The group structure and process may change with time, but the issues are resolved quickly and easily; members are open with each other.[37]

Leadership Style. During the production stage, the appropriate style is empowerment (low task/low maintenance). Groups that develop to this stage have members who play the appropriate task and maintenance roles; the leader does not need to play either role, unless there is a problem, because the group has effective shared leadership.

Stage 5. Termination

The termination stage, also called the *adjourning stage,* is not reached in command groups unless there is some drastic reorganization. However, task groups do terminate. During this stage, members experience feelings about leaving the group.

MMC has a variety of types of groups. Different groups make it to different levels of development. However, to help ensure that groups develop, MMC employees are trained to develop group process skills. Teams tend to develop to higher levels than groups. As a leader or member of a group/team, be aware of the group's development stage and use the appropriate leadership style to help it develop to the productivity level.

Changes in Group Development and Leadership Style. The two key variables identified through each stage of group development are work on the task (competence) and the socioemotional tone or morale (commitment). The two variables do not progress in the same manner. Competence tends to continue to increase through each of the first four stages, whereas commitment tends to start high in stage 1, drops in stage 2, then rises through stages 3 and 4. This pattern is illustrated in Figure 10–6, along with the appropriate leadership style for each stage of development at the bottom. In Skill-Building Exercise 10–1, Group Situational Management, you will develop your ability to identify group development stages and the appropriate leadership style for the group/team.

WORK APPLICATION

8. Recall a present or past job. Identify the group's stage of development and the leader's situational management style. Does the leader use the appropriate style? Explain what can be done to improve the group's structure and/or process.

*skillbuilder

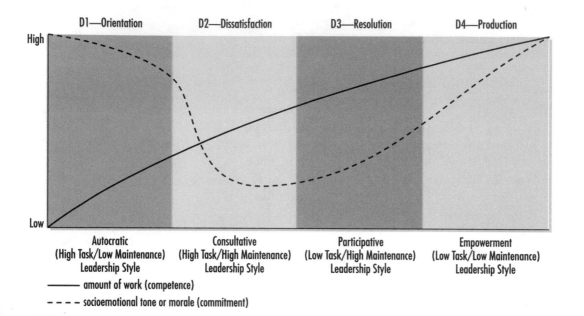

D1—Orientation	D2—Dissatisfaction	D3—Resolution	D4—Production
Autocratic (High Task/Low Maintenance) Leadership Style	Consultative (High Task/High Maintenance) Leadership Style	Participative (Low Task/High Maintenance) Leadership Style	Empowerment (Low Task/Low Maintenance) Leadership Style

———— amount of work (competence)

– – – – socioemotional tone or morale (commitment)

Figure 10-6
Group Development Stages and Leadership

8. Explain the difference between a group manager and a team leader.

DEVELOPING GROUPS INTO TEAMS

As shown in Figure 10–1, groups and teams are different. The trend is toward the empowerment of teams because teams are more productive than groups.[38] To turn groups into teams, first consider the size of the department/group. If you have 20 or more members, break the group into two or three teams. In this section you will learn about training, planning, organizing and staffing, leading, and controlling teams and the difference between a group manager and a team leader.

Training

If you expect a group to function as a team, members need training in group process skills so they can make decisions and handle conflict. A team-building program, as discussed in Chapter 7, is also very helpful in turning groups into teams. At MMC, management did not just place people into teams and expect them to be successful; they trained them to be successful.

The Management Functions

The management functions are handled differently in groups and teams.[39] In this section, you will learn how the job of the manager is changing.

Planning. Important parts of planning are setting objectives and decision making. To go from a group to a team, the manager must allow the members, along with the manager, to set objectives, develop plans, and make the decisions. The manager's role changes to focusing on involving members and making sure they know the objectives, accept them, and are committed to achieving them.[40]

Organizing and Staffing. The important parts of organizing and staffing as a team is for its members to participate in selecting, evaluating, and rewarding members. Jobs are more interchangeable and are assigned by the members as they perform dependent parts of the entire process.

Leading. In teams, leadership is shared. However, most teams do identify a specific person as the leader, but the leader shares this responsibility.[41] The leader does not focus on telling employees what to do and assigning individuals to do it. Effective team leaders are highly skilled in group process and team building. The leader focuses on developing group structure and process. Effective leaders work to bring the team to the development production level; they change leadership styles with the level of group development.

Controlling. To go from a group to a team, its members are responsible for monitoring progress, taking corrective action, and performing quality control.[42]

In summary, the roles of the group manager and team leader are different.[43] The group manager takes responsibility for performing the four functions of management. **Team leaders** *empower members to take responsibility for performing the management functions and focus on developing effective group structure, group process, and group development.* At MMC, in general, the role of managers has changed to team leader. In fact, in some teams managers are not even the official leader.

team leaders

Team leaders empower members to take responsibility for performing the management functions while focusing on developing effective group structure, group process, and group development.

MEETING LEADERSHIP SKILLS

It is common for teams to have daily meetings.[44] With the trend toward teams, meetings are taking up an increasing amount of time. Therefore, the need for meeting management skills is stronger than ever.[45] The success of meetings depends on the leader's skill at managing group process.[46] Common complaints about meetings are that there are too many of them, they are too long, and they are unproductive.[47] In this section, you will learn how to plan and conduct a meeting and how to handle problem group members.

Planning Meetings

The leaders' and members' preparation for the meeting have a direct effect on the meeting. Unprepared leaders tend to conduct unproductive meetings.[48] There are at least five areas where planning is needed: objectives, selecting participants and making assignments, the agenda, the time and place for the meeting, and leadership. A written copy of the plan should be sent to members prior to the meeting (see Figure 10–7).[49]

Objectives. Probably the single greatest mistake made by those who call meetings is that they often have no clear idea and purpose for the meeting.

Content

- **Time.** List date, place (if it changes), and time (both beginning and ending).

- **Objective.** State the objectives and/or purpose of the meeting. The objectives can be listed with agenda items, as shown below, rather than as a separate section. But be sure objectives are specific.

- **Participation and Assignments.** If all members have the same assignment, if any, list it. If different members have different assignments, list their names and assignments. Assignments may be listed as agenda items as shown below for Ted and Karen.

- **Agenda.** List each item to be covered in priority order with its approximate time limit. Accepting the minutes of the last meeting may be an agenda item.

Example

GOLD TEAM MEETING

November 22, 200X, Gold Room, 9:00 to 10:00 A.M.

Participation and Assignments

All members will attend and should have read the six computer brochures enclosed before the meeting. Be ready to discuss your preferences.

Agenda

1. Discussion and selection of two PCs to be presented to the team at a later date by PC representatives—45 minutes. (Note that this is the major objective; the actual selection takes place later.)
2. Ted will give the Venus project report—5 minutes.
3. Karen will present an idea for changing the product process slightly without discussion—5 minutes. Discussion will take place at the next meeting after you have given the idea some thought.

Figure 10-7
Meeting Plans

Before calling a meeting, you should clearly define its purpose and set objectives to be accomplished during the meeting.

Participants and Assignments. Before calling the meeting, you should decide who should attend the meeting. When too many members attend a meeting, the speed of completing the work will often slow down. Does the full group/team need to attend? Should some nongroup specialist be invited to provide input? On controversial issues, the leader may find it wiser to talk with the key members before the meeting to discuss the issue. Participants should know in advance what is expected of them at the meeting.[50] If any preparation is expected (read material, do some research, make a report, and so forth), they should have adequate advance notice.

Agenda. Before calling the meeting, you should identify the activities that will take place in order to achieve the objective. The agenda tells the members what is expected and how the meeting will progress.[51] Having a set time limit for each agenda item helps keep the group on target;[52] needless discussion and getting off the subject is common at meetings. When this happens, someone needs to speak up to get back on the topic. However, you need to be flexible and allow more time when really needed. Members may also submit agenda items to include. If you get agenda items that require action, they should have objectives.

Place agenda items in order of priority. Then, if the group does not have time to cover every item, the least important items will carry forward.

Date, Place, and Time. To determine which day(s) and time(s) of the week are best for meetings, get members' input. Members tend to be more alert early in the day. When members are close, it is better to have more frequent shorter meetings focusing on one or just a few items. However, when members have to travel, fewer longer meetings are needed. Be sure to select an adequate place for the meeting and plan for the physical comfort of the group.[53] Be sure seating provides eye contact for small discussion groups, and plan enough time so that the members do not have to rush. If reservations are needed for the meeting place, make them far enough in advance to get a proper meeting room.

Leadership. The leader should determine the appropriate leadership style for the meeting. Each agenda item may need to be handled differently. For example, some items may simply call for disseminating information, but others may require a discussion, vote, or a consensus; still other items require a simple quick report from a member, and so forth. An effective way to develop group members' ability is to rotate the role of the group moderator/leader for each meeting.

Technology. E-mail has cut the need for some meetings.[54] Also, with advances in technology, telephone conferences/meetings are becoming common. Videoconferences are also gaining popularity. These techniques save travel costs and time, and they may result in better and quicker decisions. Some of the companies using videoconferencing include Aetna, Arco, Boeing, Ford, IBM, TRW, and Xerox. The personal computer is said to be the most useful tool for running meetings since Robert's Rules of Order. The personal computer can be turned into a large-screen "intelligent chalkboard" that can dramatically change meeting results. Minutes (notes on what took place during a meeting) can be taken on the personal computer and a hard or E-mail copy can be distributed at the end of the meeting.

Conducting Meetings

9. Discuss the three parts of meetings.

The First Meeting. At the first meeting, the group is in the orientation stage. The leader should use the high-task role. However, the members should be given the opportunity to spend some time getting to know one another. Introductions set the stage for subsequent interactions. A simple technique is to start with introductions, then move on to the group's purpose, objectives, and members' job roles. Some time during or following this procedure, have a break that enables members to interact informally. If members find that their social needs will not be met, dissatisfaction may occur quickly.

The Three Parts of Meetings. Meetings should have the following three parts:

1. *Identify objectives.* Begin the meeting on time; waiting for late members penalizes the members who are on time and develops a norm for coming late. Begin by reviewing progress to date, the group's objectives, and the purpose/objective for the specific meeting. If minutes are recorded, they are usually approved at the beginning of the next meeting. For most meetings, it is recommended that a secretary be appointed to take minutes.

2. *Cover agenda items.* Be sure to cover agenda items in priority order. Try to keep to the approximate times, but be flexible. If the discussion is constructive and members need more time, give it to them; however, if the discussion is more of a destructive argument, move ahead.

3. *Summarize and review assignments.* End the meeting on time. The leader should summarize what took place during the meeting. Were the meeting's objectives achieved? Review all of the assignments given during the meeting. The secretary and/or leader should record all assignments. If there is no accountability and follow-up on assignments, members may not complete them.

Leadership. The team leader needs to focus on group structure, process, and development. As stated, the leadership style needed changes with the group's level of development. The leader must be sure to provide the appropriate task and/or maintenance behavior when it is needed.

Handling Problem Members

As members work together, personality types tend to emerge. Certain personality types can cause the group to be less efficient than possible. Some of the problem members you may have in your group are the following: silent, talker, wanderer, bored, and arguer.

Silent. To be fully effective, all group members should participate.[55] If members are silent, the group does not get the benefits of their input.

It is the leader's responsibility to encourage silent members to participate,[56] without being obvious or overdoing it. One technique the leader can use is the rotation method, in which all members take turns giving their input. This method is generally less threatening than directly calling on them. However, the rotation method is not appropriate all the time. To build up silent members' confidence, call on them with questions they can easily answer. If you are a silent type, try to participate more often. Know when to stand up for your views and be assertive; trust yourself,[57] and take risks.[58]

Talker. Talkers have something to say about everything. They like to dominate the discussion. However, if they do dominate, the other members do not get to participate. The talker can cause intragroup problems such as low cohesiveness and conflicts.

It is the leader's responsibility to slow talkers down, not to shut them up. Do not let them dominate the group.[59] The rotation technique is also effective with talkers because they have to wait their turn. When not using a rotation method, gently interrupt the talker and present your own ideas or call on other specific members to present their ideas. If you tend to be a talker, try to slow down. Give others a chance to talk and do things for themselves. Good leaders develop others' ability in these areas.

Wanderer. Wanderers distract the group from the agenda items, they tend to change the subject, and often like to complain.

The leader is responsible for keeping the group on track.[60] If the wanderer wants to socialize, cut it off. Be kind, thank the member for the contribution, then throw a question out to the group to get it back on track.

If you tend to be a wanderer, try to be aware of your behavior and stay on the subject at hand.

Bored. Your group may have one or more members who are not interested in the job. The bored person may be preoccupied with other issues and not pay attention or participate in the group meeting. The bored member may also feel superior.

Assign the bored member a task such as recording ideas on the board and recording the minutes. Call on bored members; bring them into the group. If you allow them to sit back, things may get worse and others may decide not to participate either. If you tend to be bored, try to find ways to help motivate yourself. Work at becoming more patient and in control of behavior that can have negative effects on other members.

Arguer. Like the talker, the arguer likes to be the center of attention. Arguers enjoy arguing for the sake of arguing, rather than helping the group. They turn things into a win-lose situation, and they cannot stand losing.

The leader should resolve conflict, but not in an argumentative way. Do not get into an argument with arguers; that is

---

APPLYING THE CONCEPT

AC 10–4 Group Problem People

Identify the problem type as:
a. silent b. talker c. wanderer d. bored e. arguer

_____ **16.** Charlie is always first or second to give his ideas. He is always elaborating on ideas. Because Charlie is so quick to respond, others sometimes make comments to him about it.

_____ **17.** One of the usual active group members is sitting back quietly today for the first time. The other members are doing all the discussing and volunteering for assignments.

_____ **18.** As the group is discussing a problem, Billy asks the group if they heard about the company owner and the mailroom clerk.

_____ **19.** Eunice is usually reluctant to give her ideas. When asked to explain her position, she often changes her answers to agree with others in the group.

_____ **20.** Dwayne enjoys challenging members' ideas. He likes getting his own way. When a group member does not agree with Dwayne, he makes wise comments about the member's prior mistakes.

WORK APPLICATION

10. Recall a meeting you attended. Did you receive an agenda prior to the meeting? How well did the leader conduct the meeting? Give ideas on how the meeting could have been improved. Did the group have any problem members? How well did the leader handle them?

exactly what they want to happen. If an argument starts, bring others into the discussion. If it is personal, cut it off. Personal attacks only hurt the group. Keep the discussion moving on target. If you tend to be an arguer, strive to convey your views in an assertive debate format, not as an aggressive argument. Listen to others' views and be willing to change if they have better ideas.[61]

Working with Group Members. Whenever you work in a group, do not embarrass, intimidate, or argue with any members, no matter how much they provoke you. If you do, the result will make martyrs of them and a bully of you to the group. If you have serious problem members who do not respond to the preceding techniques, confront them individually outside of the group. Get them to agree to work in a cooperative way.

CHAPTER SUMMARY AND GLOSSARY

This chapter summary is organized to answer the ten learning objectives for Chapter 10.

1. Describe the major differences between groups and teams.

The major differences are based on size, leadership, jobs, accountability and evaluation, rewards, and objectives. A group is two or more members with a clear leader who perform independent jobs with individual accountability, evaluation, and rewards. A team has a small number of members with shared leadership who perform interdependent jobs with both individual and group accountability, evaluation, and rewards.

2. State the group performance model.

Group performance is a function of organizational context, group structure, group process, and group development stage.

3. List and explain the three dimensions of group types.

The three group type dimensions are formal or informal, functional or cross-functional, and command or task. Formal groups are created as part of the organizational structure; informal groups are not. Functional group members come from one area, whereas cross-functional members come from different areas. Command groups include managers and their employees, whereas task groups include selected employees who work on a specific objective. A task force is temporary, whereas a standing committee is ongoing.

4. Define the three major roles played in groups.

Group task roles are played when members do and say things that directly aid in the accomplishment of the group's objectives. Group maintenance roles are played when members do and say things that develop and sustain the group process. Self-interest roles are played when members do and say things that help the individual but hurt the group.

5. Explain the differences between rules and norms.

Rules are formally established by management or by the group itself. Norms are the group's shared expectations of its members' behavior. Norms are not developed by management or agreed to by the groups; they develop as members interact.

6. Describe cohesiveness and why it is important to teams.

Group cohesiveness is the extent to which members stick together. Group cohesiveness is important because highly cohesive groups that accept management's level of productivity have a higher level of productivity than groups with low levels of cohesiveness.

7. List the four major stages of group development and state the level of commitment and competence and the appropriate leadership style.

Group development stages: (1) Orientation is characterized by low development level (D1)—high commitment and low competence and the appropriate leadership style is autocratic. (2) Dissatisfaction is characterized by moderate development level (D2)—lower commitment and some competence and the appropriate leadership style is consultative. (3) Resolution is characterized by high development level (D3)—variable commitment and high competence and the appropriate leadership style is participative. (4) Production is characterized by outstanding development level (D4)—high commitment and high competence and the appropriate leadership style is empowerment.

8. Explain the difference between a group manager and a team leader.

The group manager takes responsibility for performing the four functions of management. The team leader empowers the members to take responsibility for performing the management functions, and focuses on developing effective group structure, group process, and group development.

9. Discuss the three parts of meetings.

Meetings should begin with covering the objectives for the meeting. During the meeting, agenda items should be covered in priority order. The meeting should end with a summary of what took place and assignments to be completed for future meetings.

10. Define the following key terms (in order of appearance in the chapter):

Select one or more methods: (1) fill in the missing key terms from memory, (2) match the key terms from the end of the summary with their definitions below, or (3) copy the key terms in order from the list at the beginning of the chapter.

A _____ is two or more members with a clear leader who perform independent jobs with individual accountability, evaluation, and rewards.

A _____ is a small number of members with shared leadership who perform interdependent jobs with both individual and group accountability, evaluation, and rewards.

In the _____, group performance is a function of organizational context, group structure, group process, and group development stage.

_____ include group type, size, composition, leadership, and objectives.

_____ include formal or informal, functional or cross-functional, and command or task.

_____ consist of managers and their employees.

_____ consist of employees selected to work on a specific objective.

_____ is the mix of members' skills and abilities.

_____ refers to the patterns of interactions that emerge as members perform their jobs.

_____ include roles, norms, cohesiveness, status, decision making, and conflict resolution.

_____ include task, maintenance, and self-interest.

_____ are the group's shared expectations of its members' behavior.

_____ is the extent to which members stick together.

_____ is the perceived ranking of one member relative to other members in the group.

_____ are orientation, dissatisfaction, resolution, production, and termination.

_____ empower members to take responsibility for performing the management functions and focus on developing effective group structure, group process, and group development.

KEY TERMS

command groups   346
group   343
group cohesiveness   352
group composition   348
group performance model   344
group process   349

group process dimensions   349
group roles   349
group structure dimensions   345
group types   345
norms   351
stages of group development   355

status   353
task groups   346
team   343
team leaders   359

REVIEW AND DISCUSSION QUESTIONS

1. Which are usually larger, groups or teams?
2. Which level of management has the most influence over organizational context?

3. Is there an ideal group size?
4. Why is diversity important to group composition?
5. Why are objectives important to groups?

6. How do groups enforce norms?

7. Which type of group tends to terminate and which does not?

8. Does the level of commitment to the group continue to increase through all four stages of group development?

9. Are the four functions of management important to both groups and teams?

10. Why is it important to keep records of meeting assignments?

11. Describe the five types of problem members in meetings. How does each cause a problem to the group?

OBJECTIVE CASE

Fine Furniture

Saul Fine worked for the State of Vermont highway department. In his spare time, he made wood furniture, mostly tables and chairs, which he sold to a local furniture store. Saul got to the point of having many more orders than he could fill working only nights and weekends. Plus, he was tired of working so many hours. With 20 years of service to the state, he retired at age 42 with a small pension and opened Fine Furniture. Even working full time, he could not keep up with the demand for his furniture. Over a few years, as his business grew, he moved out of his basement into a shop and hired more employees. Saul has three separate areas or departments making furniture. Each department has seven or eight employees and a crew leader. All three departments make one standard size set and each department makes a few other different products as well. The crew leaders are Joel, Samantha, and Carl.

Saul was happy with the size of his operation, so he did not want to grow any more. However, he was not satisfied with the rate of productivity. Saul had very few meetings with his crew leaders, and they were not informed of each other's productivity rates. Crew leaders worked alongside the employees. The only real management responsibilities they had were staffing and leadership. Saul did the planning, organizing, and controlling for all three crews. Saul set up independent jobs and evaluated and rewarded employees on an individual basis. However, everyone was paid about the same wages. Crew leaders trained the other employees and helped them if they had problems. The three crew leaders were very good furniture makers and, as Fine Furniture expanded, Saul appointed them crew leaders without giving them any management training. Saul made the following observations about each crew.

Samantha's crew has the highest rate of productivity. Members help each other and get along well; they usually go on breaks and to lunch together. Samantha and all crew members seem to do about the same amount of work.

Joel's crew has the middle rate of productivity. Members seem to be split. Joel and three employees get along well and produce at about the same high rate. The other four members seem to be individual-oriented. One is very fast, one produces at about the same rate as the group of three, and the other two are slow. They just seem to take it slow and easy and Joel and the others do not say anything to them about their productivity level.

Carl's crew has the lowest productivity rate. All but one of the members seems to work at a slow, easy pace. Carl and the one fast worker get along well, but the two of them do not get along well with the rest of the crew members who seem to want the other members to slow down the production rate to their level.

OBJECTIVE CASE

(continued)

Saul called a meeting with Joel, Samantha, and Carl to discuss his observations and to discuss ways of increasing productivity throughout the company.

Select the best alternative to the following questions. Be sure you are able to explain your answers.

___ 1. At Fine Furniture, the three crews are primarily

    a. groups   b. teams

___ 2. Saul, Joel, Samantha, and Carl make up a ___ group/team.

    a. command

    b. task force

    c. standing committee

___ 3. Leadership has a ___ impact on crew productivity.

    a. major   b. minor

___ 4. ___'s crew has the most negative norms.

    a. Samantha   b. Joel   c. Carl

___ 5. Which leader's crew is not highly cohesive?

    a. Samantha   b. Joel   c. Carl

___ 6. Cohesiveness has a ___ effect on productivity.

    a. major   b. moderate   c. minor

___ 7. Which crew member has the lowest status within his or her crew?

    a. Samantha   b. Joel   c. Carl

___ 8. Samantha's crew appears to be at the ___ stage of development and the appropriate leadership style is ___ (select two answers).

    a. orientation   c. resolution

    b. dissatisfaction   d. production

    a. autocratic   c. participative

    b. consultative   d. empowerment

___ 9. Joel's crew appears to be at the ___ stage of development and the appropriate leadership style is ___ (select two answers).

    a. orientation   c. resolution

    b. dissatisfaction   d. production

    a. autocratic   c. participative

    b. consultative   d. empowerment

___ 10. Carl's crew appears to be at the ___ stage of development and the appropriate leadership style is ___ (select two answers).

    a. orientation   c. resolution

    b. dissatisfaction   d. production

    a. autocratic   c. participative

    b. consultative   d. empowerment

11. Do you think that promoting employees to supervisory positions without management training has had any effect on the present situation? Explain.

12. What would you recommend doing to increase productivity in each of the three crews?

VIDEO CASE

Valassis Communications
(10–1 12 Minutes)

Case Summary

George Valassis founded the business as a contract printing company in 1969, and in 1972 he changed the mission to solicit coupon advertising. Nearly three-quarters of American households use coupons, and a significant percentage of these coupons are printed by Valassis Communications. Valassis created free-standing inserts (FSIs), multi-page, multi-color coupon booklets that are placed in newspapers all across North America. Valassis has 3,000 customers, and each week Valassis prints 55 million free-standing coupon booklets, which appear in 400 newspapers across the country. Valassis is also expanding internationally as well. Valassis uses teams and has worked hard to develop a loyal group of employees and an excellent quality of work life.

Students' Learning Objective

To better understand how teams work in organizations, the team environment, and the important skills needed for high-performance work teams.

Critical Thinking Questions

1. Why would an organization such as Valassis use teams?

2. How would an organization such as Valassis create an environment to support effective team work?

Follow-up Question. What skills are necessary to become an effective team member? How can you develop those skills?

---

*skillbuilder

I G

Skill-Building Exercise 10–1

Group Situational Management

Preparing for Skill-Building Exercise 10–1
To determine your preferred group leadership style, complete Self-Assessment Exercise 10–1.

Self-Assessment Exercise 10–1

Determining Your Preferred Group Leadership Style

In the following situations, select the response that represents what you would actually do as the group's leader. Ignore the D and S lines; they will be used in class as part of Skill-Building Exercise 10–1.

1. Your group works well together; members are cohesive with positive norms. They maintain a fairly consistent level of production that is above the organizational average, as long as you continue to provide maintenance behavior. You have a new assignment for them. To accomplish it you would: D___

   a. Explain what needs to be done and tell them how to do it. Oversee them while they perform the task. S___

b. Tell the group how pleased you are with its past performance. Explain the new assignment, but let them decide how to accomplish it. Be available if they need help. S___

c. Tell the group what needs to be done. Encourage them to give input on how to do the job. Oversee task performance. S___

d. Explain to the group what needs to be done. S___

2. You have been promoted to a new supervisory position. The group appears to have little talent to do the job, but they do seem to care about the quality of the work they do. The last supervisor was terminated because of the department's low productivity level. To increase productivity you would: D___

a. Let the group know you are aware of its low production level, but let them decide how to improve it. S___

b. Spend most of your time overseeing group members as they perform their jobs. Train them as needed. S___

c. Explain to the group that you would like to work together to improve productivity. Work together as a team. S___

d. Tell the group how productivity can be improved. With their ideas, develop methods and make sure they are implemented. S___

3. Your department continues to be one of the top performers in the organization. The members work well as a team. In the past, you generally let them take care of the work on their own. You decide to: D___

a. Go around encouraging group members on a regular basis. S___

b. Define members' roles and spend more time overseeing performance. S___

c. Continue things the way they are; leave them alone. S___

d. Hold a meeting. Recommend ways to improve and get members' ideas as well. After agreeing on changes, oversee the group to make sure it implements the new ideas and does improve. S___

4. You have spent much of the past year training your employees. However, they do not need you to oversee production as much as you used to. Several group members no longer get along as well as they did in the past. You've played referee lately. You: D___

a. Have a group meeting to discuss ways to increase performance. Let the group decide what changes to make. Be supportive. S___

b. Continue things the way they are now. Supervise them closely and be the referee when needed. S___

c. Let the group alone to work things out for themselves. S___

d. Continue to supervise closely as needed, but spend more time playing maintenance roles; develop a team spirit. S___

5. Your department has been doing such a great job that it has increased in size. You are surprised at how fast the new members were integrated. The team continues to come up with ways to improve performance on its own. Due to the growth, your department will be moving to a new, larger location. You decide to: D___

a. Design the new layout and present it to the group to see if the members can improve upon it. S___

b. In essence become a group member and allow the group to design the new layout. S___

c. Design the new layout and put a copy on the bulletin board so employees know where to report for work after the move. S___

d. Hold a meeting to get employee ideas on the layout of the new location. After the meeting, think about their ideas and finalize the layout. S___

6. You are appointed to head a task group. Because of the death of a relative, you had to miss the first meeting. At the second meeting, the group seems to have developed objectives and some ground rules. Members have volunteered for assignments that have to be accomplished. You: D___

a. Take over as a strong leader. Change some ground rules and assignments. S___

b. Review what has been done so far, and keep things as they are. However, you take charge and provide clear direction from now on. S___

c. Take over the leadership but allow the group to make the decisions. Be supportive and encourage them. S___

d. Seeing that the group is doing so well, leave and do not attend any more meetings. S___

7. Your group was working at, or just below, standard. However, there has been a conflict within the group. As a result, production is behind schedule. You: D___

a. Tell the group how to resolve the conflict. Then closely supervise to make sure it does what you say and production increases. S___

b. Let the group work it out. S

c. Hold a meeting to work as a team to come up with a solution. Encourage the group members to work together. S___

d. Hold a meeting to present a way to resolve the conflict. Sell the members on its merits, include their input, and follow up. S___

8. The organization has allowed flextime. Two of your employees have asked if they could change work hours. You are concerned because all busy work hours need adequate coverage. The department is very cohesive with positive norms. You decide to: D___

a. Tell them things are going well; we'll keep things as they are now. S___

b. Hold a department meeting to get everyone's input, then reschedule their hours. S___

c. Hold a department meeting to get everyone's input; then reschedule their hours on a trial basis. Tell the group that if there is any drop in productivity, you will go back to the old schedule. S___

d. Tell them to hold a department meeting. If the department agrees to have at least three people on the job during the busy hours, they can make changes, giving you a copy of the new schedule. S___

9. You have arrived 10 minutes late for a department meeting. Your employees are discussing the latest assignment. This surprises you because, in the past, you had to provide clear direction and employees rarely would say anything. You: D___

a. Take control immediately and provide your usual direction. S___

b. Say nothing and just sit back. S___

c. Encourage the group to continue, but also provide direction. S___

d. Thank the group for starting without you, and encourage them to continue. Support their efforts. S___

10. Your department is consistently very productive. However, occasionally the members fool around and someone has an accident. There has never been a serious injury. You hear a noise and go to see what it was. From a distance you can see Sue sitting on the floor, laughing, with a ball made from company material in her hand. You: D___

a. Say and do nothing. After all, she's OK, and the department is very productive; you don't want to make waves. S___

b. Call the group together and ask for suggestions on how to keep accidents from recurring. Tell them you will be checking up on them to make sure the behavior does not continue. S___

c. Call the group together and discuss the situation. Encourage them to be more careful in the future. S___

d. Tell the group that's it; from now on you will be checking up on them regularly. Bring Sue to your office and discipline her. S___

11. You are at the first meeting of an ad hoc committee you are leading. Most of the members are second- and third-level managers from the marketing and financial areas; you are a supervisor from production. You decide to start by: D___

a. Working on developing relationships. Get everyone to feel as though they know each other before you talk about business. S___

b. Going over the group's purpose and the authority it has. Provide clear directives. S___

c. Asking the group to define its purpose. Because most of the members are higher-level managers, let them provide the leadership. S___

d. Start by providing both direction and encouragement. Give directives and thank people for their cooperation. S___

12. Your department has done a great job in the past. It is now getting a new computer, somewhat different from the old one. You have been trained to operate the computer, and you are expected to train your employees to operate it. To train them you: D___

a. Give the group instructions and work with them individually, providing direction and encouragement. S___

b. Get the group together to decide how they want to be instructed. Be very supportive of their efforts to learn. S___

c. Tell them it's a simple system. Give them a copy of the manual and have them study it on their own. S___

d. Give the group instructions. Then go around and supervise their work closely, giving additional instructions as needed. S___

Scoring. To determine your preferred group leadership style, circle the letter you selected as the alternative you chose in situations 1–12. The column headings indicate the style you selected.

	Autocratic (S1A)	Consultative (S2C)	Participative (S3P)	Empowerment (S4E)
1.	a	c	b	d
2.	b	d	c	a
3.	b	d	a	c
4.	b	d	a	c
5.	c	a	d	b
6.	a	b	c	d
7.	a	d	c	b
8.	a	c	b	d
9.	a	c	d	b
10.	d	b	c	a
11.	b	d	a	c
12.	d	a	b	c
Total	___	___	___	___

Add up the number of circled items per column. The total column should equal 12. The column with the highest number represents your preferred group leadership style. There is no one best style in all situations.

The more evenly distributed the numbers are between the four styles, the more flexible you are at leading groups. A total of 0 or 1 in any column may indicate a reluctance to use the style(s). You could have problems in situations calling for this style.

Is your preferred group leadership style the same as your preferred situational management style (Chapter 1)?

As discussed in the group development stages and leadership styles section of this chapter, first determine the level of development then use the appropriate leadership style. For a review and for use in the in-class part of this exercise, see Model 10–1.

Doing Skill-Building Exercise 10–1 in Class

Objectives
To help you understand the stages of group development and to use the appropriate group situational management style.

Preparation
You should understand the group development stages and have completed Self-Assessment Exercise 10–1.

Experience
You will discuss your selected management styles for the 12 preparation situations, and you will be given feedback on your accuracy in selecting the appropriate style to meet the situation.

Procedure 1 (3–10 minutes)
The instructor reviews Model 10–1 and explains how to apply it to situation 1. The instructor states the group's developmental stage, the leadership style of each of the four alternative actions, and the scoring

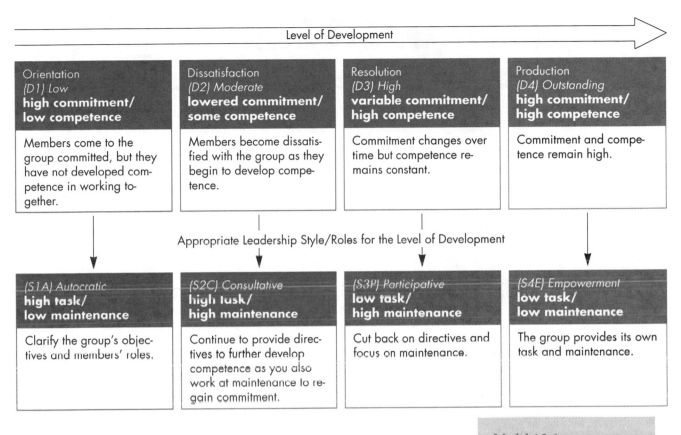

Level of Development

Orientation (D1) Low	Dissatisfaction (D2) Moderate	Resolution (D3) High	Production (D4) Outstanding
high commitment/ low competence	**lowered commitment/ some competence**	**variable commitment/ high competence**	**high commitment/ high competence**
Members come to the group committed, but they have not developed competence in working together.	Members become dissatisfied with the group as they begin to develop competence.	Commitment changes over time but competence remains constant.	Commitment and competence remain high.

Appropriate Leadership Style/Roles for the Level of Development

(S1A) Autocratic	(S2C) Consultative	(S3P) Participative	(S4E) Empowerment
high task/ low maintenance	**high task/ high maintenance**	**low task/ high maintenance**	**low task/ low maintenance**
Clarify the group's objectives and members' roles.	Continue to provide directives to further develop competence as you also work at maintenance to regain commitment.	Cut back on directives and focus on maintenance.	The group provides its own task and maintenance.

Model 10.1
Group Situational Management

for each alternative. Follow the three steps below as you try to select the most appropriate alternative action for each of the 12 situations.

Step 1. For each situation, determine the group's level of development. Place the number 1, 2, 3, or 4 on the D line.

Step 2. Identify each management style of all four alternatives A–D. Place the letters A, C, P, or E on the S lines.

Step 3. Select the appropriate management style for the group's level of development. Circle its letter, either a, b, c, or d.

Procedure 2
Option A (3–5 minutes). The instructor gives the class the recommended answers to situations 2–12, as in procedure 1, without any explanation.

Option B (15–45 minutes). Break into teams of two or three and go over the number of situations stated by the instructor. The instructor will go over the recommended answers as in Option A.

Conclusion
The instructor leads a class discussion and/or makes concluding remarks.

Application (2–4 minutes)
What did I learn from this experience? How will I use this knowledge in the future?

Sharing
Volunteers give their answers to the application section.

Exercise 10–1

Group Performance

Preparing for Exercise 10–1

Note: This exercise is designed for class groups that have worked together for some time. (Five or more hours of prior classwork are recommended.)

Answer the following questions as they apply to your class group/team.

1. Using Figure 10–1, would you classify your members as a group or a team? Why?

Group Structure

2. What type of group/team are you? [formal/informal, functional/cross-functional (by majors), command/task]

3. What is the size of your group/team? The size is (too large, too small, good).

4. What is the group/team composition?

5. Is there a clear leader? (Who is/are the leader[s])

6. Does your group/team have clear objectives?

7. List some ways in which group structure could be improved to increase group performance.

_____

_____

Group Process

8. List each group member, including yourself, and the major role(s) each plays.

 1. _____   4. _____
 2. _____   5. _____
 3. _____   6. _____

9. Identify at least three group norms. Are they positive or negative? How does the group enforce them?

10. How cohesive is your group (high, moderate, low)?

11. List each group member, including yourself, in order of status.

 1. _____   4. _____
 2. _____   5. _____
 3. _____   6. _____

12. How are decisions made in your group/team?

13. How is conflict resolved in your group/team?

14. List some ways in which group process could be improved to increase group performance.

_____

_____

Group Development Stage

15. At what stage of group development is your group/team? Explain.

16. List some ways in which your group/team can develop to a higher level of development to increase group performance.

_____

_____

Meetings

17. List some ways in which your meetings could be improved to increase group performance.

_____

_____

18. Does your group have any problem members? What can be done to make them more effective?

Doing Exercise 10–1 in Class

Note: This exercise is designed for groups that have worked together for some time. (Five or more hours are recommended.)

Objectives

To gain a better understanding of the group structure, process, development, and meetings and how they affect group performance, and to improve group performance.

Experience

You will discuss your group's performance and develop plans to improve it.

Preparation

You should have answered the 18 preparation questions.

Procedure (10–20 minutes)
Groups/teams get together to discuss their answers to the 18 preparation questions. Be sure to fully explain and discuss your answers. Try to come up with some specific ideas on how to improve your group's structure, process, development, and meetings.

Conclusion
The instructor leads a class discussion and/or makes concluding remarks.

Application (2–4 minutes)
What did I learn from this experience? How will I use this knowledge in the future?

_____

_____

Sharing
Volunteers give their answers to the application section.

11 Communicating

Learning Objectives

After studying this chapter, you should be able to:

1. Describe the three ways communication flows through organizations.

2. List the four steps in the communication process.

3. State the major advantages of oral over written communication, and the advantages of written over oral communication.

4. State the general guide to channel selection.

5. List the five steps in the face-to-face message-sending process.

6. Describe paraphrasing and state why it is used.

7. List and explain the three parts of the message-receiving process.

8. Define reflecting responses and state when it should be used.

9. Discuss what should and should not be done to calm an emotional person.

10. Define the following **key terms** (in order of appearance in the chapter):

communication
vertical communication
horizontal communication
grapevine
communication process
encoding
communication channels
decoding

nonverbal communication
message-sending process
feedback
paraphrasing
message-receiving
  process
reflecting responses
empathic listening

*skillbuilder 1. You can develop your skill at giving instructions (Skill-Building Exercise 11–1).

Giving instructions requires human and communication skills, and the mangement roles require communication skills.

Communication is a part of the leadership management function. The SCANS competencies of interpersonal skills and information require communication skills. In addition, the basic and personal qualities foundation skills are based on communication skills.

*skillbuilder 2. You can develop your situational communication skills (Skill-Building Exercise 11–2).

Skill-Building Exercise 11–2 develops your ability to know which of the four management styles is most appropriate to use with people outside your department in a given situation.

Delta Airlines made the decision to cap travel agents' commissions on ticket sales. Prior to the cap, the commission was based on 10 percent of the airfare. For example, if a flight cost $1,000, the commission was $100. However, the cap set an upper limit of $50 for domestic round-trip tickets and $25 for one-way tickets. Within a short time, other major airlines—including American, Northwest, United, and US-Air—also set the same commission cap. TWA set the cap and then removed it to try to get extra business from competitors. Most travel agents were notified about the cap through a fax message from the airline.

The commission caps hurt some travel agents more than others. The travel agents that target the business travel market were hurt the most because business travel is often a last minute decision and the traveler pays top price. Travel agents that target the leisure travel market were not hurt as much because travelers plan well in advance and prices are usually lower. In addition, leisure travel agents focus on selling travel packages, including hotel and car rentals, which pay a commission of 13 to 15 percent.

National news media gave coverage of the commission cap. The American Society of Travel Agents, the major trade association, responded in protest with full-page advertisements in major newspapers. The ads failed to communicate the travel agency community's stability. The media had given travel agents their best opportunity to describe what they do and how they make money, but they failed to take advantage of the opportunity.

Many of the travel agents never communicated with their clients to explain the commission cap and how it would affect the travel agents. Failure to communicate with clients is fairly common in the travel industry. Profitable midsize accounts that switch agencies usually do not hear from the old agent for three to six months, if ever.[1]

For current information on Delta Airlines, use Internet address **http://www.delta-air. com.** For ideas on using the Internet, see Appendix B.

At all organizational levels, at least 75 percent of each workday is consumed in communication. Seventy-five percent of what we hear, we hear imprecisely; and 75 percent of what we hear accurately, we forget within three weeks. Good communications skills are an important part of management practice.[2] Many jobs require good[3] or excellent[4] communication skills for individuals and teams.[5] In addition, many organizations[6] have recognized the importance of increasing communication with current employees to ensure good management–union relations and productivity.[7]

communication
The process of transmitting information and meaning.

Communication *is the process of transmitting information and meaning.* Two major types of communications occur: organizational and interpersonal. At the organizational level, communication takes place among organizations and among units/departments of an organization. At the interpersonal level, communication takes place among people. In this chapter you will learn about both major types of communications.

1. Describe the three ways communication flows through organizations.

ORGANIZATIONAL COMMUNICATION

Communication is one of the three major skills needed by managers (Chapter 1). The management roles (interpersonal, informational, and decisional) and management functions (planning, organizing, leading, and controlling) all require effective communication skills. The organizational mission, strategy, goals, and culture all must be communicated effectively. Lee Iacocca, former top executive credited with saving Chrysler from bankruptcy, said, "The most important thing I learned in school was how to communicate."[8]

Organizational communication needs to be enhanced[9] so that it can freely flow[10] formally in a vertical and horizontal direction and informally through the grapevine. Figure 11–1 illustrates organizational communication.

Figure 11-1
Organizational Communication

Vertical Communication

Vertical communication *is the flow of information both downward and upward through the organizational chain of command.* It is also called *formal communication* because it is recognized as officially sanctioned transmission of information and meaning.

vertical communication
The flow of information both downward and upward through the organizational chain of command.

Downward Communication. When top-level management makes decisions, policies, procedures, and so forth, they are often communicated down the chain of command to instruct employees. It is the process of higher-level managers telling those below them what to do and how to do it. The delegation process is a downward communication.

There should be official communication policies and procedures to ensure accurate and effective transmission of information. Many firms have computer information systems and an executive who oversees all aspects of information technology such as computing, office systems, and telecommunication. The current trend gives the title of chief information officer (CIO) to the executive.[11] You will learn more about information systems in Chapter 15.

Upward Communication. When employees send a message to their bosses, they are using upward communication. Managers learn about what is going on in the organization, and often about customers, through employees. Employees gain from upward communication as they discuss issues with their managers.[12] By listening, upper managers set a good example throughout the organization.

To help facilitate upward communication, many organizations, including Caterpillar Tractor, use an open-door policy that allows employees to feel at ease in going to managers. Connecticut Mutual Life Insurance offers free breakfasts and lunches to employees who sit with managers in a no-holds-barred question-and-answer session. Ford, Sears, and other organizations do periodic surveys to assess employees' attitudes and opinions. Ed Carlson of United Airlines coined the term *management by wandering around* (MBWA), which involves getting out of the office and talking frequently and informally with employees.

Horizontal Communication

horizontal communication
The flow of information between colleagues and peers.

Horizontal communication *is the flow of information between colleagues and peers.* It is formal communication, but it does not follow the chain of command because it is multidirectional.[13] Horizontal communication is needed to coordinate within a department, among team members,[14] and among different departments. Most employees spend more time communicating with peers than with managers. When the manager of the marketing department communicates with the manager of the production department, or other departments, horizontal communication takes place.

Organizations including Arco, Bell Laboratories, Reliance Insurance, and Shell use teleconferencing to link participants throughout the country and world. Managers hold meetings with people from different departments to coordinate their efforts and resolve conflicts between them.

WORK APPLICATION

1. Give an example of vertical (upward and downward), horizontal, and grapevine communication where you work or have worked.

Grapevine Communication

grapevine
The flow of information in any direction throughout the organization.

The **grapevine** *is the flow of information in any direction throughout the organization.* It is informal communication because it is not official or sanctioned by management. The grapevine, or rumor and gossip mill, can begin with anyone in the organization and can flow in any direction. Employees complain, talk about sports and news events, and whisper secrets about coworkers through the grapevine. With the trend toward downsizing, many employees hear of layoffs long before the pink slips are officially sent out.[15]

The methods for improving formal communication also apply to informal communication. If managers hear of incorrect information being passed along the grapevine, they can use formal and/or informal means to correct the situation.

Delta and other airlines officially communicated the commission cap to travel agents by fax. However, many agents first heard about the caps through the grapevine or media.

APPLYING THE CONCEPT

AC 11–1 Communication Flow

Identify the communication flow as:

a. vertical-downward   c. horizontal
b. vertical-upward   d. grapevine

____ **1.** "Hey, Carl, have you heard that Paul and Helen were caught. . . ?"

____ **2.** "Juanita, will you come here and hold this so I can get it straight, the way I do it for you all the time."

____ **3.** "Tom, here is the letter you asked me to type. Check it and I'll make changes."

____ **4.** "Robin, I have two new customers who want to set up charge accounts. Please rush the credit check so we can increase business."

____ **5.** "Ted, please take this letter to the mail room for me right now."

THE COMMUNICATION PROCESS AND COMMUNICATION BARRIERS

The **communication process** *consists of a sender who encodes a message and transmits it through a channel to a receiver who decodes it and may give feedback.* Figure 11–2 illustrates the communication process and explains each step with common communication barriers[16] at each stage.

1. The Sender Encodes the Message and Selects the Transmission Channel

Encoding the Message. The *sender* of the message is the person who initiates the communication. The *message* is the information and meaning

2. List the four steps in the communication process.

communication process
Consists of a sender who encodes a message and transmits it through a channel to a receiver who decodes it and may give feedback.

---

1. Encodes the message and selects the transmission channel.

2. Message transmitted through a channel.

3. Decodes the message and decides if feedback is needed.

Sender

Receiver

4. Feedback, response, or new message may be transmitted through a channel.

Figure 11-2
The Communication Process

The sender and receiver may continually change roles as they communicate.

encoding
The sender's process of putting the message into a form that the receiver will understand.

communicated. Communicators should have a clear objective for their messages.[17] **Encoding** *is the sender's process of putting the message into a form that the receiver will understand.* The sender should consider the receiver of the message, and determine the best way to encode the message to ensure transmitting information and meaning.[18]

Perception Communication Barriers. As messages are transmitted, receivers use their perception to translate the message so that it makes sense to them. *Semantics* and *jargon* can be communication barriers, because the same word often means different things to different people. For example, the term "wicked good" can be confusing to people not familiar with the term, who do not realize it does mean good.

Overcoming Perception Barriers. To overcome perception problems, you need to consider how the other person will most likely perceive the message and try to encode and transmit it appropriately. Thus, the choice of words is important. Be careful not to use jargon with people who are not familiar with the terminology, especially people from countries with different cultures.[19]

Information Overload Communication Barriers. People have a limit on the amount of information they can understand at any given time. Information overload commonly occurs for new employees during the first few days, because they are often presented with too much information to comprehend in that period of time. With the widespread use of computers and with so much information available, managers are often dazzled and don't know what to do with it all.

Overcoming Information Overload. To minimize information overload, send messages in a quantity that the receiver can understand. When sending a message, do not talk for too long without checking to be sure the receiver understands the message as you intended. If you talk for too long, the receiver can become bored or lose the thread of the message.

communication channels
The three channels are oral, nonverbal, and written.

Selecting the Transmission Channel. The message is transmitted through a channel. *The three primary* **communication channels** *are oral, nonverbal, and written.* The sender should determine the most appropriate channel to meet the needs of the situation; you will learn how in the next section.

Channel Selection Communication Barriers. Use of an inappropriate channel can result in missed communication. For example, if a manager catches an employee in the act of breaking a rule, the manager should use one-on-one, face-to-face communication. Another channel will not be as effective.

Overcoming Channel Selection Barriers. Before sending a message, give careful thought to selecting the most effective channel. In the next major section of this chapter, you will study the appropriate use of various channels.

2. The Sender Transmits the Message

After the sender encodes the message and selects the channel, he or she transmits the message through the channel to a receiver(s). The managers at Delta Airlines selected a written fax as the channel to inform travel agents of the commission cap.

Noise Communication Barriers. Noise factors during the transmission of a message can disturb or confuse the receiver. Noise is anything that interferes with message transmission. For example, a machine or people may make noise that makes it difficult to hear, the sender may not speak loud enough for the receiver to hear well, or a radio or TV may distract the receiver, causing message interpretation errors.

Overcoming Noise Barriers. To overcome noise you need to consider the physical surroundings before transmitting the message. Try to keep noise to a minimum. If possible, stop the noise or distraction or move to a quiet location.

3. The Receiver Decodes the Message and Decides if Feedback Is Needed

The person receiving the message decodes it. **Decoding** *is the receiver's process of translating the message into a meaningful form.* The receiver combines the message with other ideas and interprets the meaning of the message. The receiver decides if feedback, a response, or a new message is needed.[20] With oral communication, feedback is commonly given immediately. However, with written communication, it is often not necessary to reply. When Delta Airlines sent the fax stating the commission cap, they did not expect any feedback from the travel agents.

Trust and Credibility Communication Barriers. During communication, receivers take into account the trust they have in the senders, as well as their credibility. When receivers do not trust senders,[21] and when they do not believe senders know what they are talking about, receivers are reluctant to accept the message.[22]

Overcoming Trust and Credibility Barriers. To improve your trust level, be open and honest with people.[23] If people catch you in a lie, they may never trust you again. To gain and maintain credibility, get the facts straight before you communicate. Send clear, correct messages. Become an expert in your area.

Not Listening Barrier to Communication. People usually hear what the sender is saying, but often they do not listen to the message or understand what is being transmitted. Not listening is sometimes the result of not paying attention or noise distractions.

Overcoming Not Listening Barriers. One method to help ensure that people listen to your message involves questioning them and having them paraphrase the message back to you. When listening, you should follow the listening tips presented later in this chapter.

Emotional Barriers to Communication. Everyone has emotions, such as anger, hurt, fear, sorrow, happiness, and so on. Emotional people find it difficult to be objective and to listen.[24]

Overcoming Emotional Barriers. When communicating, you should remain calm and be careful not to make others emotional by your behavior. Later in this chapter you will learn how to calm an emotional employee.

decoding
The receiver's process of translating the message into a meaningful form.

WORK APPLICATION

2. Give an example of a message that was transmitted where you work or have worked. Be sure to illustrate the four steps in the communication process, state the channel, and identify if feedback was given.

3. Give two examples of different communication barriers you encountered at work. Explain how the barrier could have been overcome.

4. Feedback: A Response or a New Message May Be Transmitted

After the receiver decodes the message, feedback may be given to the sender.[25] You should realize that the role of sender and receiver can change during a communication exchange. Even though Delta did not want any feedback, many travel agents contacted Delta directly to complain about the commission cap, and the American Society of Travel Agents took out a full-page ad in several newspapers complaining about the cap.

Filtering Communication Barriers. Filtering is the process of altering or distorting information to project a more favorable image. For example, when people are asked to report progress toward objectives, they may stress the positive and deemphasize, or even leave out, the negative side or they may lie.

Overcoming Filtering Barriers. To help eliminate filtering, you should treat errors as a learning experience rather than as an opportunity to blame and criticize employees. You will learn about criticism later in this chapter. Using an open-door policy can create and support a two-way communication climate.

Summary. An example of the preceding stages of the communication process would be: (1) A professor (sender) prepares for a class and encodes by preparing a lecture. (2) The professor transmits the message orally through a lecture during class. (3) The students (receivers) decode the lecture (message) by listening and/or taking notes in a meaningful way. (4) Students usually have the option of asking questions (feedback) during or after class. See Figure 11–3 for a review of the communication barriers.

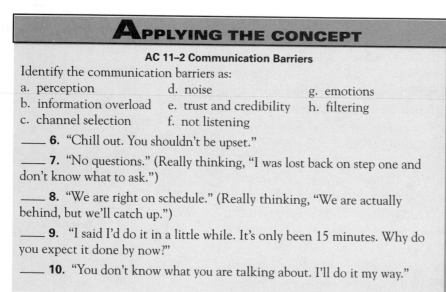

APPLYING THE CONCEPT

AC 11–2 Communication Barriers

Identify the communication barriers as:

a. perception   d. noise   g. emotions
b. information overload   e. trust and credibility   h. filtering
c. channel selection   f. not listening

_____ 6. "Chill out. You shouldn't be upset."

_____ 7. "No questions." (Really thinking, "I was lost back on step one and don't know what to ask.")

_____ 8. "We are right on schedule." (Really thinking, "We are actually behind, but we'll catch up.")

_____ 9. "I said I'd do it in a little while. It's only been 15 minutes. Why do you expect it done by now?"

_____ 10. "You don't know what you are talking about. I'll do it my way."

Figure 11-3
Major Communication Barriers

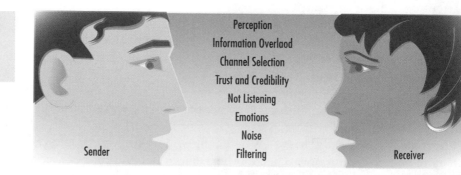

Perception
Information Overload
Channel Selection
Trust and Credibility
Not Listening
Emotions
Noise
Filtering

Sender   Receiver

MESSAGE TRANSMISSION CHANNELS

When encoding the message, the sender should give careful consideration to selecting the channel. Channels (the forms of the transmitted message) include oral, nonverbal, and written communications. Figure 11–4 lists the major channel sources. Applying the concepts at the end of this section gives you the opportunity to select the various channels for messages.

Oral Communication

The five most common media for oral communication are face-to-face, meetings, presentations, the telephone, and voice mail. The major advantage of oral over written communication is that it is usually easier and faster[26] and encourages feedback.[27] The disadvantages are that it is usually less accurate and provides no record.

Face-to-Face. Managers should communicate one-on-one, face-to-face with employees.[28] Sam Walton, founder and former head of Wal-Mart, relied on face-to-face communication to keep the firm growing. Top executives visit 6 to 12 stores each week.

Face-to-face communication is the appropriate channel for delegating tasks, coaching, disciplining, sharing information, answering questions, checking progress toward objectives, and developing and maintaining human relations. Managers also spend one-on-one, face-to-face time communicating with their bosses, colleagues, and peers.

Meetings. Meetings were discussed in Chapter 10. The manager's most common meeting is the brief, informal get-together with two or more employees. With the increased use of teams, more time is spent in meetings.

3. State the major advantages of oral over written communication, and the advantages of written over oral communication.

Figure 11-4
Message Transmission Channels

Oral Communication	Nonverbal Communication	Written Communication
Face-to-face	Setting	Memos
Meetings	Body language	Letters
Presentations	facial expressions	Reports
Telephone	vocal quality	computers (e-mail)
Voice mail	gestures	fax machines
	posture	Bulletin boards
	Posters (pictures)	Posters (words)
		Newsletters

Meetings are appropriate for coordinating employee activities, delegating a task to a group, and resolving employee conflicts.

Presentations. Many studies have shown that the single most important factor in career advancement and professional success is your communication skill, so polish your public speaking skills.[29] After all, every successful person is in the communication business.[30] Begin your speech with an attention-grabbing opener. It could be a quote, a joke, or an interesting story that will ignite interest in your topic.[31] Be sure your presentations have the following three parts: (1) Beginning—the presentation should begin with a purpose statement and an overview of the main points to be covered. (2) Middle—the presentation supports its purpose through a discussion of the main points in the detail necessary to get the message across. (3) End—the presentation should summarize the purpose, main points, and any action required of the audience.

The same basic presentation skills are used for one-on-one communications and for large audiences. Speaking skills are needed in virtually every job.[32] Thus, the need for presentation skills isn't limited to the times when you are asked to give a formal speech. Speaking is an essential part of working with employees and customers, negotiating, resolving conflicts, training, presenting products and reports, and running meetings.[33]

Telephone. The amount of time spent on the telephone varies greatly with the job. Before making a call, set an objective and write down what you plan to discuss. Use the paper to write notes during the call. When receiving a call, determine the purpose of the call and decide if you or another person should handle it. When receiving calls at inconvenient times, arrange for a callback. Conference calls (three or more people talking) are being used more frequently.

The telephone is the appropriate channel for quick exchanges of information and checking up on things.[34] It is especially useful for saving travel time. However, it is inappropriate for personal matters such as discipline.

Voice Mail. Voice mail is commonly used to replace written memos and to leave messages for people who don't answer the telephone. Voice mail memos are appropriate for sending short messages containing information not needed in written form. Voice mail is also ideal for leaving a message that does or does not require the receiver to call you back.

As the technology improves and the costs go down, *video conferencing* will be used more frequently.

Nonverbal Communication

nonverbal communication
Messages sent without words.

Every time you use oral, face-to-face communication, you also use nonverbal communication. **Nonverbal communication** *is messages sent without words.* Nonverbal communication includes the *setting* (physical surroundings) of the communication and *body language.* Psychologists claim that 56 percent of the impact of any piece of communication is dependent on body language.[35] Body language includes (1) facial expressions (eye contact and a wink or a smile, a frown, or a dirty look); (2) vocal quality (it does not refer to the "words" used but how they are said. For example, the message can be sent in a calm/excited/upset/slow/fast, soft/yelling quality to convey a message such as anger and disappointment or happiness and approval); (3) gestures (the use of body motion such as using hands, pointing and signaling, and nodding of the head); and (4) posture (sitting up straight or slouching, leaning back or forward, crossing arms and/or legs). The old adage, "Actions speak louder than words," holds true. For example, if a manager gives a stern look at an employee doing something wrong, it may be more powerful than words. Also, if Amy, a manager, tells employees to do a quality job but does not do a quality job herself and does not reward quality performance, employees will most likely ignore the verbal message.

To make nonverbal communication effective, you should be aware of your nonverbal communication and make sure it is consistent with your oral and/or written communication. Be aware of, or read, other people's nonverbal communication because it tells you their feelings and attitudes toward the communication and you as a person/manager. Arrange your office so that it is conducive to open communication. Generally, you should not sit behind your desk and have the other person in front of the desk. Sitting side-by-side creates a more open atmosphere. When talking to people, use nonverbal communication to convey openness to messages. Smile, face the person, and use eye contact comfortable for all; lean forward a bit and gesture frequently to convey that you are listening and are interested. Do not cross your arms or legs (signs of being closed to communication), and speak in a pleasant, calm tone of voice.

Written Communication

Probably nothing can reveal your weaknesses more clearly than poorly written communication. Organizations are recruiting employees with good writing skills.[36, 37] So you should learn how to write effectively. With the increasing use of E-mail, writing skills are becoming even more important. The major advantages of written over oral communication are that it is usually more accurate and provides a record. The major disadvantages are that it usually takes longer and hinders feedback.

A list of commonly used written communications includes:

1. *Memos*—commonly used to send intraorganizational messages.

2. *Letters/technology*—commonly used to communicate with people outside the organization. *Computers*—electronic mail (*E-mail*) is used to send memos and letters to save time and paper. *Fax machine*—also used to send memos and letters instantly. Note that E-mail and fax are not numbered because they are forms of using memos and letters.

3. *Reports*—used to convey information. Reports usually involve an evaluation, analysis, and/or recommendation to management or colleagues. Reports can also be sent by fax or as an attachment to E-mail.

4. *Bulletin board notices*—usually are a supplement to another form of communication.

5. *Posters (or signs)*—commonly used as reminders of important information, such as the mission statement, safety instructions, quality, clean-up before you leave, etc. Posters can also be nonverbal or graphic communication. An example is the "no" signs with a picture of what you are not supposed to do circled with a line through it.

6. *Newsletters*—used to convey general information to all employees.

Written communication is appropriate for sending general information; for saying thank you;[38] for messages requiring future action; for formal, official, or long-term messages (especially those containing facts and figures); and for messages that affect several people in a related way. Ford Motor Company has over 40,000 users on its global communication system, which indicates that E-mail can be highly preferable to phoning overseas.[39]

Writing Tips. Lack of organization is the number one writing problem.[40] Before you begin writing, set an objective for your communication. Keep the audience in mind. What do you want them to do? Make an outline, using letters and/or numbers, of the major points you want to get across. Now put the outline into written form. The first paragraph states the purpose of the communication. The middle paragraphs support the purpose of the communication: fact, figures, and so forth. The last paragraph summarizes the major points and clearly states the action, if any, to be taken by you and the receivers.

Write to communicate clearly, not to impress. Keep the message short and simple. Limit each paragraph to a single topic and an average of five sentences. Sentences should average 15 words. Vary paragraph and sentence length; however, a paragraph should not exceed half of a page. Write in the active voice (I recommend . . .) rather than the passive voice (it is recommended . . .).

Edit your work and rewrite where necessary.[41] Wait a while and edit your work again. To improve sentences and paragraphs, add to them to convey full meaning, cut out unnecessary words and phrases, and/or rearrange the words. Check your work with computer spelling and grammar checkers. Have others edit your work as well.

Combining Channels

Nonverbal communication is combined with oral communication. You can also combine oral, nonverbal, and written communication. Repetition is often needed to ensure that the message has been conveyed with mutual understanding of the meaning.[42] Using combined channels is appropriate when the message is important and you want to ensure that employees attend to and understand it. For example, managers sometimes send a memo, then follow up with a personal visit or telephone call to see if there are any questions. Managers often formally document a face-to-face meeting, particularly in a disciplinary situation.

Selecting the Message Transmission Channel

Before you send a message, be sure to select the most appropriate channel of transmission. Another consideration in selecting a channel is media richness.

Media richness refers to the amount of information and meaning conveyed through the channel. The more information and meaning, the "richer" the channel. Face-to-face is the richest channel because it allows full oral and nonverbal communication to be used. The telephone is less rich than face-to-face because most of the nonverbal cues are lost when you cannot see facial expressions and gestures. All forms of oral communication are richer than written communication because oral communication allows at least some nonverbal cues, which are lost with written messages.

A General Guide to Channel Selection. As a general guide, use rich oral channels for sending difficult and unusual messages, less rich written channels for transmitting simple and routine messages to several people, and combined channels for important messages that employees need to attend to and understand.

Delta selected the fax written communication channel to send the message of the commission cap. Many of the travel agents used a variety of channels to provide feedback to Delta. The American Society of Travel Agents elected written newspaper advertisements to give feedback to the airlines and to inform its members of the situation.

4. State the general guide to channel selection.

WORK APPLICATION

4. Give an example of an oral and a written message you received at work. Be sure to specify the channel of the oral and written message.

APPLYING THE CONCEPT

AC 11–3 Channel Selection

For each of the five communication situations, select the most appropriate channel for transmitting the message. If you would use combined media, place the letter of the second channel you would use at the end of the situation.

Oral communication	Written communication	
a. face-to-face	e. memo	h. bulletin board
b. meeting	f. letter	i. poster
c. presentation	g. report	j. newsletter
d. telephone		

____ **11.** You are waiting for an important letter to arrive by FedEx and you want to know if it is in the mail room yet. ____

____ **12.** Employees have been leaving the lights on in the stock room when no one is in it. You want them to shut the lights off. ____

____ **13.** José, Jamal, and Sam will be working as a team on a new project. You need to explain the project to them. ____

____ **14.** John has come in late for work again; you want this practice to stop. ____

____ **15.** You have exceeded your departmental goals and want your boss to know about it, because it should have a positive influence on your upcoming performance appraisal. ____

SENDING MESSAGES

Have you ever heard a manager say, "This isn't what I asked for"? When this happens, it is usually the manager's fault. A common complaint of secretaries is bosses who don't give clear instructions.[43] Managers often make incorrect assumptions and do not take 100 percent of the responsibility for ensuring that the message is transmitted with mutual understanding.

The second step in the communication process involves sending the message. Before you send a message, you should carefully select the channel and plan how you will send the message. Then, send the message using the message-sending process.

Planning the Message

Before sending a message, you should answer the following questions:

- *What?* What is the goal of the message?[44] What do you want the end result of the communication to be? Set an objective.[45]
- *Who?* Determine who should receive the message.
- *How?* With the receiver(s) in mind, plan how you will encode the message so that it will be understood. Select the appropriate media for the audience and situation. What will be said, done, written, etc.?
- *When?* When will the message be transmitted? Timing is important. For example, if it is going to take 15 minutes to transmit a message, don't approach an employee 5 minutes before quitting time. Wait until the next day. Make an appointment when appropriate.
- *Where?* Decide where the message will be transmitted (setting)— your office, his or her work place, etc. Remember to keep distractions to a minimum.

5. List the five steps in the face-to-face message-sending process.

message-sending process
(1) Develop rapport, (2) state your communication objective, (3) transmit your message, (4) check the receiver's understanding, and (5) get a commitment and follow up.

The Message-Sending Process

When sending a face-to-face message, follow the steps in *the* **message-sending process:** *(1) develop rapport, (2) state your communication objective, (3) transmit your message, (4) check the receiver's understanding, and (5) get a commitment and follow up.*

 Develop rapport. Put the receiver at ease. It is usually appropriate to begin communication with small talk related to the message. It helps prepare the employee to receive the message.

 State your communication objective. The common business communication objectives are to influence, inform, and express feelings. Objectives are also commonly combined. With the goal of influencing, it is helpful for the receiver to know the end result of the communication before covering all of the details.

step 3. **Transmit your message.** If the communication objective is to influence, tell the people what you want them to do, give instructions, and so forth. Be sure to set deadlines for completing tasks. If the objective is to inform, give the people the information. If the objective is to express feeling, do so.

 Check the receiver's understanding. The only time you may not want to check understanding is when the objective is to express feelings. When influencing and giving information, you should ask direct questions and/or use paraphrasing. Simply asking "Do you have any questions?" does not check understanding. After step 5, you will learn how to check understanding.

step 5. **Get a commitment and follow up.** When the goal of communication is to inform or express feelings, a commitment is not needed. However, when the goal of communication is to influence, get a commitment to the action. Managers should make sure that employees can do the task and have it done by a certain time or date. In situations in which employees do not intend to get the task done, it is better to find out when sending the message, rather than waiting until the deadline. When employees are reluctant to commit to the necessary action, managers can use persuasive power within their authority. When communicating to influence, follow up to ensure that the necessary action has been taken.[46]

Model 11–1 lists the five steps in the message-sending process.

Checking Understanding: Feedback

Feedback *is the process of verifying messages.* Questioning, paraphrasing, and allowing comments and suggestions are all forms of feedback that check understanding. Feedback motivates employees to achieve high levels of performance[47] and improves retention.[48]

Mutual understanding of the meaning of the message must exist for communication to take place. The best way to make sure communication has taken place is to get feedback from the receiver of the message through questioning and paraphrasing. **Paraphrasing** *is the process of having the receiver restate the message in his or her own words.*

The Common Approach to Getting Feedback on Messages and Why It Doesn't Work. The most common approach to getting feedback is to send the entire message, followed by asking "Do you have any questions?" Feedback usually does not follow because people tend not to ask questions. There are four good reasons why people do not ask questions:

1. *Receivers feel ignorant.* To ask a question, especially if no one else does, is often considered an admission of not paying attention or not being bright enough to understand the issue.

2. *Receivers are ignorant.* Sometimes people do not know enough about the message to know whether or not it is incomplete, incorrect, or subject to interpretation. There are no questions because what was said sounds right. The receiver does not understand the message, or does not know what to ask.

feedback
The process of verifying messages.

paraphrasing
The process of having the receiver restate the message in his or her own words.

Model 11-1
The Face-to-Face Message-Sending Process

3. *Receivers are reluctant to point out the sender's ignorance.* This commonly occurs when the sender is a manager and the receiver is an employee. Employees often fear that asking a question suggests that the manager has done a poor job of preparing and sending the message. Or it suggests that the manager is wrong. Regardless of the reason, it has the same end result. Generally, employees don't ask questions when they do not understand; students don't either.

4. *Receivers have cultural barriers.* In many Asian countries, for example, it is considered impolite to disagree with the boss, so the employee (receiver) would answer "yes" when asked by the manager (sender) if the message was understood.

After managers send a message and ask if there are questions, they then proceed to make another common error. They assume that if no questions are asked the communication is complete, and that mutual understanding of the message exists. In reality, the message is often misunderstood. When "this isn't what I asked for" happens, the task has to be done over again. The end result is often wasted time, materials, and effort.

The most common cause of messages not resulting in communication is the lack of getting feedback that ensures mutual understanding. The proper use of questioning and paraphrasing can help you ensure that your messages are communicated.

How to Get Feedback on Messages. You should use the following four guidelines when getting feedback on messages. They are appropriate for managers and nonmanagers.

- *Be open to feedback.* There are no dumb questions. When someone asks a question, you need to be responsive and patiently answer and explain things clearly. If people sense that you get upset if they ask questions, they will not ask. Instead, praise good questions.

- *Be aware of nonverbal communication.* Make sure that your nonverbal communication encourages feedback. For example, if you say "I encourage questions," but when people ask questions you look at them as though they are stupid, or you are impatient, people will learn not to ask questions. You must also read people's nonverbal communication. For example, if you are explaining a task to Larry and he has a puzzled look on his face, he is probably confused but may not be willing to say so. In such a case, you should stop and clarify things before going on.

- *Ask questions.* When you send messages, you should know whether or not the messages are understood before taking action.[49] That way, the action will not have to be changed or repeated. Because communicating is 100 percent the responsibility of message senders, you should ask questions to check understanding, rather than simply asking, "Do you have any questions?" Direct questions dealing with the specific information you have given will indicate if the receiver has been listening and whether or not he or she understands enough to give a direct reply. If the response is not accurate, you need to repeat the message, giving more examples or elaborating more. You can also ask indirect questions to obtain feedback. You can ask "how do you feel?" questions about the message. You can also ask "if you were me" questions, such as "If you were me, how would you explain how to do it?" Or you can ask third-party questions, such as "How will employees feel about this?" The response to indirect questions will tell you the receiver's attitude.

- *Use paraphrasing.* The most accurate indicator of understanding is paraphrasing. How you ask the receiver to paraphrase will affect his or her attitude. For example, saying "Joan, tell me what I just said so that I can be sure you will not make a mistake as usual," would probably result in defensive behavior on Joan's part. Joan would probably make a mistake. Two examples of proper requests for paraphrasing follow:

"Now tell me what you are going to do so that we will be sure that we are in agreement."

"Would you tell me what you are going to do so that I can be sure that I explained myself clearly?"

Notice that the second statement takes the pressure off the employee. The sender is asking for a check on his or her ability, not that of the employee. These types of requests for paraphrasing should result in a positive attitude toward the message and the sender. They show concern for the employee and for communicating effectively.

Delta Airlines' communication objective was to inform travel agents of its decision to cap their commissions. Delta selected the written fax to send the message. Delta did not check understanding because it knew the feedback would be negative. What type of feedback would you give to a person who told you that you will do the same work, but you will be paid less, possibly half as much, for doing it? The written fax was chosen because it does not often encourage a response.

RECEIVING MESSAGES

The third step in the communication process requires the receiver to decode the message and decide if feedback is needed. With oral communication, the key to successfully understanding the message is listening.

Listening Skills

Complete Self-Assessment Exercise 11–1 to determine how good a listener you are, then read the tips for improving listening skills in the message-receiving process.

Self-Assessment Exercise 11–1

Listening Skills

Select the response that best describes the frequency of your actual behavior. Place the letter A, U, F, O, or S on the line before each of the 15 statements.

A—almost always   U—usually   F—frequently

O—occasionally   S—seldom

_____ 1. I like to listen to people talk. I encourage others to talk by showing interest, smiling, nodding, and so forth.

_____ 2. I pay closer attention to people who are more similar to me than people who are different from me.

_____ 3. I evaluate people's words and nonverbal communication ability as they talk.

_____ 4. I avoid distractions; if it's noisy, I suggest moving to a quiet spot.

_____ 5. When people come to me and interrupt me when I'm doing something, I put what I was doing out of my mind and give them my complete attention.

_____ 6. When people are talking, I allow them time to finish. I do not interrupt, anticipate what they are going to say, or jump to conclusions.

_____ 7. I tune people out who do not agree with my views.

_____ 8. While the other person is talking, or professors are lecturing, my mind wanders to personal topics.

_____ 9. While the other person is talking, I pay close attention to the nonverbal communication to help me fully understand what he or she is trying to communicate.

_____ 10. I tune out and pretend I understand when the topic is difficult for me to understand.

_____ 11. When the other person is talking, I think about and prepare what I am going to say in reply.

_____ 12. When I think there is something missing or contradictory, I ask direct questions to get the person to explain the idea more fully.

_____ 13. When I don't understand something, I let the other person know I don't understand.

_____ 14. When listening to other people, I try to put myself in their position and see things from their perspective.

_____ 15. During conversations I repeat back to the other person what has been said in my own words to be sure I understand what has been said.

If people you talk to regularly answer these questions about you, would they have the same responses that you selected? To find out, have friends fill out the questions using "you" (your name) rather than "I." Then compare answers.

To determine your score, give yourself 5 points for each A, 4 for each U, 3 for each F, 2 for each O, and 1 for each S for statements 1, 4, 5, 6, 9, 12, 13, 14, and 15. Place the numbers on the line next to your response letter. For items 2, 3, 7, 8, 10, and 11 the score reverses: 5 points for each S, 4 for each O, 3 for each F, 2 for each U, and 1 for each A. Place these score numbers on the lines next to the response letters. Now add your total number of points. Your score should be between 15 and 75. Place your score on the continuum below. Generally, the higher your score, the better your listening skills.

Poor listener   Good listener

15–20–25–30–35–40–45–50–55–60–65–70–75

Listening is one of the most important skills in business.[50] Thus, you need to practice to develop active listening skills that encourage others to be more communicative.[51] It is important to let the sender know you received the message.[52] You learn when you listen, and listening clues you in to the other party's needs and desires.[53] This is why listening is so important in sales, negotiation, and conflict resolution. By using the message-receiving process, you can become a better listener.

The Message-Receiving Process

The **message-receiving process** *includes listening, analyzing, and checking understanding.* To improve your listening skills, spend one week focusing your attention on listening by concentrating on what other people say and the nonverbal communications they send when they speak. Notice if their verbal and nonverbal communications are consistent. Do the nonverbals reinforce the speaker's words or detract from them? Talk only when necessary so that you can listen and see what others are saying. If you apply the following tips, you will improve your listening skills. The tips are presented in the receiving-messages process; we should listen, analyze, then check understanding, which Figure 11-5 illustrates.

Listening. Listening is the process of giving the speaker your undivided attention. As the speaker sends the message, you should listen by:

- *Paying attention.* When people interrupt you to talk, stop what you are doing and give them your complete attention immediately. Quickly relax and clear your mind so that you are receptive to the speaker.[54] This will get you started correctly. If you miss the first few words, you may miss the message.

- *Avoiding distractions.* Keep your eyes on the speaker. Do not fiddle with pens, papers, or other distractions. For important messages, put your phone on "take a message." If you are in a noisy or distracting place, suggest moving to a quiet spot.

- *Staying tuned in.* While the other person is talking or the professor is lecturing, do not let your mind wander to personal topics.[55] If it does wander, gently bring it back. Do not tune out the speaker because you do not like something about the person or because you disagree with what is being said. If the topic is difficult, do not tune out; ask questions. Do not think about what you are going to say in reply, just listen. As you listen, mentally paraphrase the message to stay tuned in.[56]

- *Not assuming and interrupting.* Do not assume you know what the speaker is going to say, or listen to the beginning and jump to conclusions. Most listening mistakes are made when people hear the first few words of a sentence, finish it in their own minds, and miss the second half.[57] Listen to the entire message without interrupting the speaker.

7. List and explain the three parts of the message-receiving process.

message-receiving process
Includes listening, analyzing, and checking understanding.

Listening
Pay attention
Avoid distractions
Stay tuned in (mentally paraphrase)
Don't assume and interrupt
Watch nonverbals
Ask questions
Take notes (when appropriate)
Convey meaning

Analyzing
Think
Wait to evaluate until after listening

Checking Understanding
Paraphrase
Watch nonverbals

Figure 11-5
The Message-Receiving Process

- *Watching nonverbals*. Understand both the feelings and the content of the message. People sometimes say one thing and mean something else. So watch as you listen to be sure that the speaker's eyes, body, and face are sending the same message as the verbal message. If something seems out of sync, get it cleared up by asking questions.

- *Asking questions*. When you feel there is something missing, contradictory, or you just do not understand, ask direct questions to get the person to explain the idea more fully.

- *Taking notes (when appropriate)*. Part of listening is writing important things down so you can remember them later, and documenting them when necessary, especially when listening to instructions.[58] You should always have something to write with and on, such as a pen and a notebook or some index cards.

- *Conveying meaning*. The way to let the speaker know you are listening to the message is to use verbal clues, such as "you feel . . . ," "uh huh," "I see," "I understand." You should also use nonverbal communication, such as eye contact, appropriate facial expressions, nodding of the head, or leaning slightly forward in your chair to indicate you are interested and listening.

Analyzing. *Analyzing* is the process of thinking about, decoding, and evaluating the message. Poor listening is caused in part by the fact that people speak at an average rate of 120 words per minute, but they are capable of listening at a rate of 600 words per minute. The ability to comprehend words more than five times faster than the speaker can talk often results in wandering minds.[59] To analyze, as the speaker sends the message, you should be:

- *Thinking*. To help overcome the discrepancy in the speed between your ability to listen and people's rate of speaking, use the speed of your brain positively. Listen actively by mentally paraphrasing, organizing, summarizing, reviewing, interpreting, and critiquing often. These activities will help you to do an effective job of decoding the message.

- *Waiting to evaluate until after listening*. When people try to listen and evaluate what is said at the same time they tend to miss part or all of the message. You should just listen to the entire message, then come to your conclusions. When you evaluate the decision, base your conclusion on the facts presented rather than on stereotypes and generalities.

Checking Understanding. *Checking understanding* is the process of giving feedback. After you have listened to the message, or during if it's a long message, check your understanding of the message by:

- *Paraphrasing*. Begin speaking by giving feedback through paraphrasing the message back to the sender. When you can paraphrase the message correctly, you convey that you have listened and understood the other person. Now you are ready to offer your ideas, advice, solution, decision, or whatever the sender of the message is talking to you about.

- *Watching nonverbals.* As you speak, watch the other person's nonverbals. If the person does not seem to understand what you are talking about, clarify the message before finishing the conversation.

Do you talk more than you listen? To be sure your perception is correct, ask your boss, coworkers, and friends who will give you an honest answer. If you spend more time talking than listening, you are probably failing in your communications and boring people, too. Regardless of how much you listen, if you follow these guidelines, you will improve your conversation and become a person that people want to listen to instead of a person they feel they have to listen to. To become an active listener, take 100 percent of the responsibility for ensuring mutual understanding. Work to change your behavior to become a better listener. Review the 15 statements in Self-Assessment Exercise 11–1. Do items 1, 4, 5, 6, 9, 12, 13, 14, and 15. Do not do items 2, 3, 7, 8, 10, and 11. Effective listening requires responding to the message to ensure mutual understanding takes place.

**WORK
APPLICATION**

7. Refer back to Self-Assessment Exercise 11–1 and the listening tips. What is your weakest listening skill area? How will you improve your listening ability?

RESPONDING TO MESSAGES

The fourth, and last, step in the communication process involves responding to the message. However, not all messages require a response.

With oral communication, the sender often expects the receiver to respond to the message.[60] When the receiver does respond, the roles are reversed as the receiver now becomes the sender of a message. Roles can continue to change throughout the conversation. In this section you will study five response styles, how to deal with emotional people, and how to give and receive criticism.

Response Styles

As the sender transmits a message, how you as the receiver respond to the message directly affects the communication. The response should be appropriate for the situation. The five response styles appear in Figure 11–6. An example of each response style is shown for this employee message:

"You supervise me so closely that you disrupt my ability to do my job."

Advising. *Advising responses* provide evaluation, personal opinion, direction, or instructions. Employees often come to the manager for advice on how to do something or for the manager to make the decision.[61] Advising tends to close, limit, or direct the flow of communication away from the sender to the receiver.

Figure 11-6
Response Styles

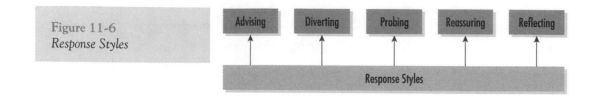

Appropriate Use of Advising Responses. Giving advice is appropriate when you are directly asked for it. However, quickly giving advice tends to build dependence. Managers need to develop their employees' ability to think things through and to make decisions. When asked for advice by employees who you believe don't really need it, ask questions such as, "What do you think is the best way to handle this situation?"

Example Advising Responses. Example manager's advising responses to the employee's message are: "You need my directions to do a good job; you lack experience." "I disagree. You need my instructions and for me to check your work." Note that in this situation advice was not asked for, but it was given anyway.

Diverting. *Diverting responses* switch the focus of the communication to a new message; it is commonly called changing the subject. Diverting responses tend to redirect, close, or limit the flow of communication. Diverting responses used during the early stages of receiving the message may cause the sender to feel that the message is not worth discussing, or that the other party's message is more important.

Appropriate Use of Diverting Responses. The diverting response is appropriate when either party is uncomfortable with the topic. Diverting responses may be helpful when used to share personal experiences or feelings that are similar to those of the sender but that change the topic.

Example Diverting Response. An example manager's diverting response to the employee's message is: "You've reminded me of a manager I once had who . . . ."

Probing. A *probing response* asks the sender to give more information about some aspect of the message. It can be useful to get a better understanding of the situation. When probing, "what" questions are preferred to "why" questions.

Appropriate Use of Probing Responses. Probing is appropriate during the early stages of the message to ensure that you fully understand the situation. After probing, the other response styles are often needed.

Example Probing Response. An example manager's probing response to the employee's message is: "What do I do to cause you to say this?" Not: "Why do you feel this way?"

Reassuring. A *reassuring response* is given to reduce the intensity of the emotions associated with the message. Essentially you're saying, "Don't worry; everything will be OK." "You can do it." You are pacifying the sender.

WORK APPLICATION

8. Recall two situations in which you received an oral message. State the message and your response to it. Be sure to identify your response style and use two different response styles.

Appropriate Use of Reassuring Responses. Reassuring is appropriate when the other person lacks confidence. Encouraging responses that give praise can help employees develop confidence.

Example Reassuring Responses. Example manager's reassuring responses to the employee's message are: "Don't worry, I will not do it for much longer." "Your work is improving, so I may be able to provide less direction soon."

Reflecting. **Reflecting responses** *paraphrase the message and communicate understanding and acceptance to the sender.* When reflecting, be sure NOT to use the senders' exact words or they may feel you are mimicking them, not understanding them, or not listening closely. Reflecting in your own words leads to the most effective communication and most effective human relations. Female managers are generally more likely than males to favor reflecting and probing responses over evaluative advising responses.[62]

Appropriate Use of Reflecting Responses. Reflecting responses should be used when coaching and counseling.[63] The sender can feel listened to, understood, and free to explore the topic in more depth. As the communication progresses, it is often appropriate to change to other response styles.

Example Reflecting Responses. Example manager's reflecting responses to the employee's message are: "My checking up on you annoys you?" "You don't think I need to check up on you, is this what you mean?" Note that these responses allow the employee to express feelings and direct the communication.

8. Define reflecting responses and state when they should be used.

reflecting responses
Paraphrase the message and communicate understanding and acceptance to the sender.

APPLYING THE CONCEPT

AC 11–4 Identifying Response Styles

Identify each of the six responses as:
a. advising   c. probing   e. reflecting
b. diverting   d. reassuring

Secretary: Boss, do you have a minute to talk?

Boss: Sure, what's up?

Secretary: Can you do something about all the swearing people do in the operations department? It carries through these thin walls into my work area. It's disgusting. I'm surprised you haven't done anything.

Boss:

____ **16.** "I didn't know anyone was swearing. I'll look into it."

____ **17.** "You don't have to listen to it. Just ignore the swearing."

____ **18.** "Are you feeling well today?"

____ **19.** "So you find this swearing offensive?"

____ **20.** "What specific swear words are they saying that offend you?"

Dealing with Emotional People

As a manager, an employee or customer may send you a message in an emotional state. Emotions tend to hurt communications,[64] but they can bring about new ideas and new ways of doing things. You should understand emotions and how to deal with them.

Understanding Feelings. You should realize that:

- Feelings are subjective; they tell us people's attitudes and needs.
- Feelings are usually disguised as factual statements. For example, when people are hot, they tend to say "It's hot in here" rather than "I feel

hot." When they are bored, they tend to say, "This topic is boring," rather than, "I'm feeling bored by this topic." Often, not everyone will be hot in the same environment or bored by the same material.

- And most important, feelings are neither right nor wrong.[65]

People cannot choose their feelings, or control them. However, they can control how they express feelings. For example, if Rachel, an employee, says "You *!!" (pick a swear word that would make you angry) to Louise, her manager, she will feel its impact. However, Louise can express her feelings in a calm manner, or she can yell, hit, give Rachel a dirty look, and so on. Managers should encourage people to express their feelings in a positive way, but they can't allow employees to go around yelling, swearing, or hitting others. You should avoid getting caught up in others' emotions. Staying calm when dealing with an emotional person works much better than getting emotional, too.

Calming the Emotional Employee. When an emotional employee comes to you, NEVER make put-down statements[66] such as, "You shouldn't be angry," "Don't be upset," "You're acting like a baby," "Just sit down and be quiet," or "I know how you feel." (No one knows how anyone else feels. Even people who experience the same thing at the same time don't feel the same.) These types of statements only make the feelings stronger. You may get employees to shut up and show them who is boss, but effective communication will not take place. The problem will still exist and your human relations with the employee will suffer because of it, as will your relations with others who see or hear about what you said and did. When the employee complains to peers, some peers will feel you were too hard or easy on the person. You lose either way.

Reflective Empathic Responding. **Empathic listening** *is the ability to understand and relate to another's situation and feelings.* The empathic responder deals with feelings, content, and the underlying meaning being expressed in the message. Empathy is needed to develop human relationships based on trust.[67] To calm emotional people, don't argue with them. Encourage them to express their feelings in a positive way. Empathically let them know that you understand how they feel.[68] People want to be listened to and understood; if you do not listen to and understand others they will avoid you. Do not agree or disagree with the feelings; simply identify them verbally. Paraphrase the feeling to the person. Use statements such as, "You were *hurt* when you didn't get the assignment." "You *resent* Charlie for not doing his share of the work; is that what you mean?" "You are *doubtful* that the job will be done on time; is that what you're saying?"

After you deal with emotions, you can proceed to work on content (solving problems). It may be wise to wait until a later time if emotions are very strong. You will find that just understanding others' feelings is often the solution rather than giving advice. Sometimes employees simply need to vent their emotions. A manager with strong listening skills may be just the solution employees need.

9. Discuss what should and should not be done to calm an emotional person.

empathic listening
The ability to understand and relate to another's situation and feelings.

WORK APPLICATION

9. Recall a situation in which a manager had to handle an emotional employee. Did the manager follow the guidelines for calming an emotional person? Did the manager use reflective empathic responses?

Criticism

Giving Criticism. Even when bosses ask, they usually don't want to hear personal criticism. In a meeting, if your boss asks you for feedback on how good a manager he or she is or how he or she can improve, it may sound like the ideal opportunity to unload your complaints, but don't criticize. In such a situation, the first rule of thumb is to never publicly criticize your boss, even if specifically asked to do so. You are better off airing criticism in private. Don't criticize your boss behind his or her back either; bosses often find out about it. Criticizing your boss could hurt your human relations and career.

An important part of the manager's job is to improve employee performance through criticism.[69] Chapter 14 will show you how to accomplish this task.

Getting Criticism. If you're asking for personal feedback, remember that you are asking to hear things that may surprise, upset, insult, or hurt your feelings. If you become defensive and emotional (and it is hard not to when you feel attacked) the person will stop giving feedback. The criticizer will probably tell others what happened, and others will not give you truthful feedback either. You should realize that criticism from your boss, peers, or employees is painful. People do not really enjoy being criticized, even when it is constructive. Keep the phrase "no pain, no gain" in mind when it comes to criticism. If you want to improve your performance, and your chances of having a successful career, seek honest feedback about how you can improve your performance. When you get criticism, whether you ask for it or not, view it as an opportunity to improve, stay calm (even when the other person is emotional), and don't get defensive. Use the feedback to improve your performance.[70]

WORK APPLICATION

10. How would you rate yourself on your ability to accept criticism without getting emotional and defensive? How could you improve your ability to accept criticism?

CHAPTER SUMMARY AND GLOSSARY

This chapter summary is organized to answer the ten learning objectives for Chapter 11.

1. Describe the three ways communication flows through organizations.

First, communication formally flows vertically downward and upward through the chain of command. Second, communication formally flows horizontally between colleagues and peers. Third, communication flows informally through the grapevine in any direction.

2. List the four steps in the communication process.

(1) The sender encodes the message and selects the transmission channel. (2) The sender transmits the message through a channel. (3) The receiver decodes the message and decides if feedback is needed. (4) The receiver may give feedback, make a response, or send a new message through a channel.

3. State the major advantages of oral over written communication, and the advantages of written over oral communication.

The major advantage of oral over written communication is that it is usually easier and faster and encourages feedback. The disadvantages are that it is usually less accurate and provides no record.

   The major advantages of written over oral communication is that it is usually more accurate and provides a record. The major disadvantages are that it usually takes longer and hinders feedback.

4. State the general guide to channel selection.

As a general guide, use rich oral channels for sending difficult and unusual messages, less rich written channels for transmitting simple and routine messages to several people, and combined channels for important messages that employees need to attend to and understand.

5. List the five steps in the face-to-face message-sending process.

The face-to-face message-sending process involves five steps: (1) Develop rapport. (2) State your communication objective. (3) Transmit your message. (4) Check the receiver's understanding. (5) Get a commitment and follow up.

6. Describe paraphrasing and state why it is used.

Paraphrasing is the process of having the receiver restate the message in his or her own words. The receiver uses paraphrasing to check understanding of the transmitted message. If the receiver can paraphrase the message accurately, communication has taken place. If not, communication is not complete.

7. List and explain the three parts of the message-receiving process.

The three parts of the message-receiving process are listening, analyzing, and checking understanding. Listening is the process of giving the speaker your undivided attention. Analyzing is the process of thinking about, decoding, and evaluating the message. Checking understanding is the process of giving feedback.

8. Define reflecting responses and state when they should be used.

Reflecting responses paraphrase the message and communicate the sender's understanding and acceptance. Reflecting responses are appropriate to use when coaching and counseling.

9. Discuss what should and should not be done to calm an emotional person.

To calm an emotional person, do not make statements that put the person down. Make reflective empathic responses that let the emotional person know that you understand how he or she feels. Paraphrase the feelings.

10. Define the following key terms (in order of appearance in the chapter):

Select one or more methods: (1) fill in the missing key terms from memory, (2) match the key terms from the end of the summary with their definitions below, or (3) copy the key terms in order from the list at the beginning of the chapter.

_____ is the process of transmitting information and meaning.

_____ is the flow of information both downward and upward through the organizational chain of command.

_____ is the flow of information between colleagues and peers.

The _____ is the flow of information in any direction throughout the organization.

The _____ consists of a sender who encodes a message and transmits the message through a channel and a receiver who decodes it and may give feedback.

_____ is the sender's process of putting the message into a form that the receiver will understand.

The three primary _____ are oral, nonverbal, and written.

_____ is the receiver's process of translating the message into a meaningful form.

_____ is messages sent without words.

The _____ includes: (1) develop rapport, (2) state your communication objective, (3) transmit your message, (4) check the receiver's understanding, and (5) get a commitment and follow up.

_____ is the process of verifying messages.

_____ is the process of having the receiver restate the message in his or her own words.

The _____ includes listening, analyzing, and checking understanding.

_____ paraphrase the message and communicate understanding and acceptance to the sender.

_____ is the ability to understand and relate to another's situation and feelings.

KEY TERMS

communication   378

communication channels   382

communication process   381

decoding   383

empathic listening   400

encoding   382

feedback   391

grapevine   380

horizontal communication   380

message-receiving process   395

message-sending process   390

nonverbal communication   386

paraphrasing   391

reflecting responses   399

vertical communication   379

REVIEW AND DISCUSSION QUESTIONS

1. What is the difference among vertical, horizontal, and grapevine communication?

2. What is the difference between encoding and decoding?

3. What does perception have to do with encoding and decoding?

4. What is filtering?

5. What is the difference between nonverbal setting and body language?

6. What is the difference between voice mail and E-mail?

7. What are the three parts of a written outline?

8. As an average, how many words should a sentence have and how many sentences should there be in a paragraph?

9. What is media richness?

10. What should be included in your plan to send a message?

11. What are the four ways to get feedback on messages?

12. Why should you listen, analyze, then check understanding?

13. Which response style do you use most often?

14. When calming an emotional employee, why shouldn't you make put-down statements to him or her?

OBJECTIVE CASE

Wal-Mart Stores

In the 1950s, Sam Walton visited discount stores throughout the United States to learn about this industry. Walton asked employees questions and wrote in his little notebook. In 1963, Sam opened his first Wal-Mart store. Before Sam retired, several hundred Wal-Mart stores had been opened, and the company established headquarters in Bentonville, Arkansas. Sam would visit all Wal-Mart stores at least once a year. He also continued to visit hundreds of competitors, looking for ideas to improve operations. Sam would simply walk through the store and talk to the employees, who are called associates, and customers. He continued to write in a notebook. Sam required all executives to visit stores. Sam wanted all employees involved in continuous improvements, so all managers ask associates what he or she can do to improve store operations. All employees have access to complete financial results to keep them focused on the bottom line.

Sam Walton died in April 1992. The same year, Wal-Mart became the largest retailer in the nation based on sales of $55 billion. Wal-Mart also owns Sam's Warehouse Club, SuperCenters, and Hypermarts.

Sam's son Rob, chairman of the board, and David Glass, CEO, manage Wal-Mart. However, Sam's original communication system is still used today, and management is committed to continuing it. When Glass is not personally visiting stores, he maintains communication through a six-channel satellite system. The communication goal is to link every store by voice and video to facilitate store-to-store and store-to-home office communications. The satellite also gathers store data for the master computers.

By satellite, Glass and other executives can talk via video to every store at the same time as often as they want to. They can also communicate with only a few stores. When associates come up with suggestions for improving operations, such as increasing sales or decreasing costs, the satellite system quickly transmits the information to all stores. The major advantage of the satellite is its use in merchandising, which follows the old saying: a picture is worth a thousand words. A buyer can go on video and make an announcement such as, "These are the new items for Department 12. Here is how you should display them." Associates can see how the merchandise is displayed and copy it.

In addition to store visits and the satellite system, a third major means of communication is the company magazine, *Wal-Mart World*, which is used as a combined channel to send some of the

OBJECTIVE CASE

(continued)

same messages. *Wal-Mart World* is also used to announce the names and show pictures of the winners of its various contests.

Select the best alternative to the following questions. Be sure you are able to explain your answers.

___ 1. When David Glass sends a message to all stores via satellite, he is using ____ communication.

    a. downward   c. horizontal

    b. upward   d. grapevine

___ 2. When store managers seek ideas from associates to improve operations, they are using ____ communication.

    a. downward   c. horizontal

    b. upward   d. grapevine

___ 3. When Wal-Mart executives and store managers walk around stores and talk to associates and customers, they are involved in ____ communication.

    a. formal   b. informal

___ 4. The biggest communication barrier to using the satellite to send messages is most likely

    a. perception   f. not listening

    b. information overload   g. emotions

    c. channel selection   h. filtering

    d. noise

    e. trust and credibility

___ 5. The satellite system itself is a(n) ____ of communication.

    a. encoding   c. channel

    b. decoding   d. feedback

___ 6. When used for merchandising, the Wal-Mart satellite relies most heavily on ____ communication.

    a. oral   b. nonverbal   c. written

___ 7. Wal-Mart places ____ emphasis on feedback.

    a. great   b. little

___ 8. At Wal-Mart, the ability to listen is considered

    a. very important

    b. important

    c. somewhat important

    d. not very important

___ 9. The most appropriate response for Wal-Mart executives to use when walking around and talking to associates and customers is

    a. advising   d. reassuring

    b. diverting   e. reflecting

    c. probing

___ 10. Wal-Mart ____ criticism.

    a. openly seeks   c. does not really want

    b. will listen to   d. avoids

11. What message do you think Wal-Mart executives send to associates when they visit stores?

12. What effect has the satellite had on formal communication?

13. What part would you say communication has played in Wal-Mart's success?

For current information on Wal-Mart, use Internet address http://www.wal-mart.com. For ideas on using the Internet, see Appendix B.

Skill-Building Exercise 11–1

Giving Instructions

Doing Skill-Building Exercise 11–1 in Class

Objective

To develop your ability to give and receive messages (communication skills).

Experience

You will plan, give, and receive instructions for the completion of a drawing of three objects.

Preparation

No preparation is necessary except reading and understanding the chapter. The instructor will provide the original drawings.

Procedure 1 (3–7 minutes)

Read all of Procedure 1 twice. The task is for the manager to give an employee instructions for completing a drawing of three objects. The objects must be drawn to scale and look like photocopies of the originals. You will have up to 15 minutes to complete the task.

The exercise has four separate parts or steps:

1. The manager plans.
2. The manager gives the instructions.
3. The employee does the drawing.
4. The results are evaluated.

Rules. The rules are numbered to correlate with the four parts of the exercise.

1. *Planning.* While planning, the manager may write out instructions for the employee, but may not do any drawing of any kind.

2. *Instructions.* While giving instructions, the manager may not show the original drawing to the employee. (The instructor will give it to you.) The instructions may be given orally and/or in writing, but no nonverbal hand gestures are allowed. The employee may take notes while the instructions are being given, but cannot do any drawing. The manager must give the instructions for all three objects before drawing begins.

3. *Drawing.* Once the employee begins the drawing, the manager should watch but no longer communicate in any way.

4. *Evaluation.* When the employee is finished or the time is up, the manager shows the employee the original drawing. Discuss how you did. Turn to the integration section and answer the questions. The manager writes the answers, not the employee. The employee will write when playing the manager role.

Procedure 2 (2–5 minutes)

Half of the class members will act as the manager first and give instructions. Managers move their chairs to one of the four walls (spread out). They should be facing the center of the room with their backs close to the wall.

Employees sit in the middle of the room until called on by a manager. When called on, the employee brings a chair to the manager. The employee sits facing the manager so that he or she cannot see any managers' drawing.

Procedure 3 (Up to 15 minutes for drawing and integration)

The instructor gives each manager a copy of the drawing, being careful not to let any employees see it. The manager plans the instructions. When a manager is ready, he or she calls an employee and gives the instructions. It is helpful to use the message-sending process. Be sure to follow the rules. The employee should do the drawing on an 8½" by 11" sheet of paper, not in this book. If you use written instructions, they may be on the reverse side of the page that the employee draws on or on a different paper. The employee has up to 15 minutes to complete the drawing and for integration (evaluation). When the drawing is finished, turn to the evaluation questions in the integration section.

Procedure 4 (up to 15 minutes)

The employees are now the managers and sit in the chairs facing the center of the room. New employees go to the center of the room until called for.

Follow Procedure 3 with a different drawing. Do not work with the same person (change partners).

Integration

Evaluating Questions. You may select more than one answer. The manager and employee discuss each question and the manager, not the employee, writes the answers.

1. The goal of communication was to:

   a. influence b. inform c. express feelings

2. The communication was:

   a. vertical-downward c. horizontal

   b. vertical-upward d. grapevine

3. The manager did an ____ job of encoding the message and the employee did an ____ job of decoding the message.

   a. effective b. ineffective

4. The manager transmitted the message through ____ communication channel(s):

   a. oral c. nonverbal

   b. written d. combined

5. The manager spent ____ time planning.

   a. too much b. too little c. the right amount of

Questions 6 to 10 relate to the steps in the message-sending process.

6. The manager developed rapport. (Step 1)

   a. true b. false

7. The manager stated the communication objective. (Step 2)

   a. true b. false

8. The manager transmitted the message (Step 3)

   a. effectively b. ineffectively

9. The manager checked understanding by using (Step 4)

   a. direct questions c. both

   b. paraphrasing d. neither

The amount of checking was:

   a. too frequent c. about right

   b. too infrequent

10. The manager got a commitment and followed up. (Step 5)

    a. true b. false

11. The employee did an ____ job of listening, an ____ job of analyzing, and an ____ job of checking understanding through the receiving-messages process.

    a. effective b. ineffective

12. The primary response style used by the employee was ____ and the two most appropriate response styles were ____ and ____ for this situation.

    a. advising c. probing e. reflecting

    b. diverting d. reassuring

13. The manager and/or employee got emotional.

    a. true b. false

14. When going over this integration, the manager was ____ and the employee was ____ to criticism that can help improve communication skills.

    a. open b. closed

15. Were the objects drawn to approximate scale (same size)? If not, why not?

16. Did you follow the rules? If not, why not?

17. If you could do this exercise over again, what would you do differently to improve communication?

_____

_____

Conclusion
The instructor leads a class discussion and/or makes concluding remarks.

Application (2–4 minutes)
What did I learn from this experience? How will I use this knowledge in the future?

_____

_____

_____

Sharing
Volunteers give their answers to the application section.

BEHAVIOR MODEL VIDEO

Behavior Model Video 11–1 (12 minutes), Situational Communications, shows two managers, Steve and Darius, meeting to discuss faulty parts. The video illustrates the four situational management styles, explained in Skill-Building Exercise 11–2.

Objective
To better understand the four situational communication styles.

Procedure 1 (10–20 minutes)
The instructor shows Video Module 11–1, Situational Communications. As you view each of the four scenes, identify the four communication styles being used by the manager. Write the letters and number of the style on the scene line.

Scene 1. _____ Autocratic (S1A)
Scene 2. _____ Consultative (S2C)
Scene 3. _____ Participative (S3P)
Scene 4. _____ Empowerment (S4E)

Option A. View all four scenes and identify the style used by the manager. Select the style that you would use in this situation. Are other styles also ap-

propriate? Which style would you not use (not appropriate) for this situation? Next to each style listed, write the letter A for appropriate or N for not appropriate. After everyone is done, the instructor leads a class discussion and/or gives the correct answers.

Option B. After each scene the class discusses the style used by the manager. The instructor states the correct answer after each of the four scenes.

Conclusion
The instructor leads a class discussion and/or makes concluding remarks.

Application (2–4 minutes)
What did I learn from this exercise? How will I use this knowledge in the future?

_____

_____

_____

Sharing
Volunteers give their answers to the application section.

---

*skillbuilder

I G

Skill-Building Exercise 11–2

Situational Communications

Preparing for Skill-Building Exercise 11–2
When you work with people outside your department, you have no authority to give them direct orders. You must use other means to achieve your goal. Situational communications is a model for conducting interpersonal communications with people outside your department or organization, or with peers and managers in higher levels of management than you. The situational communications model will teach you

how to analyze a given situation and select the most appropriate style of communication.

Through this skill-building exercise you will learn the interactive process system, situational communication styles, situational variables, and how to select the most appropriate communication style in a given situation. Begin by determining your preferred communication style by completing Self-Assessment Exercise 11–2.

Self-Assessment Exercise 11–2

Determining Your Preferred Communication Style

To determine your preferred communication style, select the alternative that most closely describes what you would do in each of the following 12 situations. Do not be concerned with trying to pick the correct answer; select the alternative that best describes what you would actually do. Circle the letter a, b, c, or d. Ignore all of the answer spaces for now. They will be explained later in this exercise, and will be used during the in-class part of this skill-building exercise.

____ 1. Wendy, a knowledgeable person from another department, comes to you, the engineering supervisor, and requests that you design a special product to her specifications. You would:

____ time   ____ information
____ acceptance   ____ capability
____ communication style

a. Control the conversation and tell Wendy what you will do for her. S ___

b. Ask Wendy to describe the product. Once you understand it, you would present your ideas. Let her know that you are concerned and want to help with your ideas. S ___

c. Respond to Wendy's request by conveying understanding and support. Help clarify what is to be done by you. Offer ideas, but do it her way. S ___

d. Find out what you need to know. Let Wendy know you will do it her way. S ___

____ 2. Your department has designed a product that is to be fabricated by Saul's department. Saul has been with the company longer than you have; he knows his department. Saul comes to you to change the product design. You decide to:

____ time   ____ information
____ acceptance   ____ capability
____ communication style

a. Listen to the change and why it would be beneficial. If you believe Saul's way is better, change it; if not, explain why the original design is superior. If necessary, insist that it be done your way. S ___

b. Tell Saul to fabricate it any way he wants. S ___

c. You are busy; tell Saul to do it your way. You don't have time to listen and argue with him. S ___

d. Be supportive; make changes together as a team. S ___

____ 3. Upper management has a decision to make. They call you to a meeting and tell you they need some information to solve a problem they describe to you. You:

____ time   ____ information
____ acceptance   ____ capability
____ communication style

a. Respond in a manner that conveys personal support and offer alternative ways to solve the problem. S ___

b. Just answer their questions. S ___

c. Explain how to solve the problem. S ___

d. Show your concern by explaining how to solve the problem and why it is an effective solution. S ___

_____ 4. You have a routine work order. The work order is to be placed verbally and completed in three days. Sue, the receiver, is very experienced and willing to be of service to you. You decide to:

_____ time   _____ information

_____ acceptance   _____ capability

_____ communication style

    a. Explain your needs, but let Sue make the order decision. S ___

    b. Tell Sue what you want and why you need it. S ___

    c. Decide together what to order. S ___

    d. Simply give Sue the order. S ___

_____ 5. Work orders from the staff department normally take three days; however, you have an emergency and need the job today. Your colleague Jim, the department supervisor, is knowledgeable and somewhat cooperative. You decide to:

_____ time   _____ information

_____ acceptance   _____ capability

_____ communication style

    a. Tell Jim that you need it by three o'clock and will return at that time to pick it up. S ___

    b. Explain the situation and how the organization will benefit by expediting the order. Volunteer to help in any way you can. S ___

    c. Explain the situation and ask Jim when the order will be ready. S ___

    d. Explain the situation and together come to a solution to your problem. S ___

_____ 6. Danielle, a peer with a record of high performance, has recently had a drop in productivity. Her problem is affecting your performance. You know Danielle has a family problem. You:

_____ time   _____ information

_____ acceptance   _____ capability

_____ communication style

    a. Discuss the problem; help Danielle realize that the problem is affecting her work and yours. Supportively discuss ways to improve the situation. S ___

    b. Tell the boss about it and let him decide what to do. S ___

    c. Tell Danielle to get back on the job. S ___

    d. Discuss the problem and tell Danielle how to solve the work situation; be supportive. S ___

_____ 7. You are a knowledgeable supervisor. You buy supplies from Peter regularly. He is an excellent salesperson and very knowledgeable about your situation. You are placing your weekly order. You decide to:

_____ time   _____ information

_____ acceptance   _____ capability

_____ communication style

    a. Explain what you want and why. Develop a supportive relationship. S ___

    b. Explain what you want and ask Peter to recommend products. S ___

    c. Give Peter the order. S ___

    d. Explain your situation and allow Peter to make the order. S ___

_____ 8. Jean, a knowledgeable person from another department, has asked you to perform a routine staff function to her specifications. You decide to:

_____ time   _____ information

_____ acceptance   _____ capability

_____ communication style

    a. Perform the task to her specifications without questioning her. S ___

    b. Tell her that you will do it the usual way. S ___

    c. Explain what you will do and why. S ___

    d. Show your willingness to help; offer alternative ways to do it. S ___

_____ 9. Tom, a salesperson, has requested an order for your department's services with a short delivery date. As usual, Tom claims it is a take-it-or-leave-it offer. He wants your decision now, or within a few minutes, because he is in the customer's office. Your action is to:

____ time   ____ information

____ acceptance   ____ capability

____ communication style

a. Convince Tom to work together to come up with a later date. S ___

b. Give Tom a yes or no answer. S ___

c. Explain your situation and let Tom decide if you should take the order. S ___

d. Offer an alternative delivery date. Work on your relationship; show your support. S ___

___ 10. As a time-and-motion expert, you have been called regarding a complaint about the standard time it takes to perform a job. As you analyze the entire job, you realize the one element of complaint should take longer, but other elements should take less time. The end result is a shorter total standard time for the job. You decide to:

____ time   ____ information

____ acceptance   ____ capability

____ communication style

a. Tell the operator and foreman that the total time must be decreased and why. S ___

b. Agree with the operator and increase the standard time. S ___

c. Explain your findings. Deal with the operator and/or foreman's concerns, but ensure compliance with your new standard. S ___

d. Together with the operator, develop a standard time. S ___

___ 11. You approve budget allocations for projects. Marie, who is very competent in developing budgets, has come to you with a proposed budget. You:

____ time   ____ information

____ acceptance   ____ capability

____ communication style

a. Review the budget, make revisions, and explain them in a supportive way. Deal with concerns, but insist on your changes. S ___

b. Review the proposal and suggest areas where changes may be needed. Make changes together, if needed. S ___

c. Review the proposed budget, make revisions, and explain them. S ___

d. Answer any questions or concerns Marie has and approve the budget as is. S ___

___ 12. You are a sales manager. A customer has offered you a contract for your product with a short delivery date. The offer is open for two days. The contract would be profitable for you and the organization. The cooperation of the production department is essential to meet the deadline. Tim, the production manager, and you do not get along very well because of your repeated request for quick delivery. Your action is to:

____ time   ____ information

____ acceptance   ____ capability

____ communication style

a. Contact Tim and try to work together to complete the contract. S ___

b. Accept the contract and convince Tim in a supportive way to meet the obligation. S ___

c. Contact Tim and explain the situation. Ask him if you and he should accept the contract, but let him decide. S ___

d. Accept the contract. Contact Tim and tell him to meet the obligation. If he resists, tell him you will go to his boss. S ___

To determine your preferred communication style, circle the letter you selected as the alternative in situations 1–12. The column headings indicate the style you selected.

	Autocratic (S1A)	Consultative (S2C)	Participative (S3P)	Empowerment (S4E)
1.	a	b	c	d
2.	c	a	d	b
3.	c	d	a	b
4.	d	b	c	a
5.	a	b	d	c
6.	c	d	a	b
7.	c	a	b	d
8.	b	c	d	a
9.	b	d	a	c
10.	a	c	d	b
11.	c	a	b	d
12.	d	b	a	c
Total				

Add up the number of circled items per column. The total column should equal 12. The column with the highest number represents your preferred communication style. There is no one best style in all situations. The more evenly distributed the numbers are between the four styles, the more flexible your communications. A total of 0 or 1 in any column may indicate a reluctance to use the style(s). You could have problems in situations calling for the use of this style.

The Interactive Process System
Communication has the following five dimensions, which are each on a continuum:

Initiation _____ Response

Initiation. The sender starts, or initiates, the communication. The sender may or may not expect a response to the initiated message.

Response. The receiver replies or takes action on the sender's message. In responding, the receiver can become an initiator. As two-way communication takes place, the role of initiator (sender) and responder (receiver) may change.

Presentation _____ Elicitation

Presentation. The sender's message is structured, directive, or informative. A response may not be needed, although action may be called for. ("We are meeting to develop next year's budget." "Please open the door.")

Elicitation. The sender invites a response to the message. Action may or may not be needed. ("How large a budget do we need?" "Do you think we should leave the door open?")

Closed _____ Open

Closed. The sender expects the receiver to follow the message. ("This is a new form to fill out and return with each order.")

Open. The sender is eliciting a response as a means of considering the receiver's input. ("Should we use this new form with each order?")

Rejection _____ Acceptance

Rejection. The receiver does not accept the sender's message. ("I will not fill out this new form for each order!")

Acceptance. Agreement with the sender's message. ("I will fill out the new form for each order.")

Strong _____ Mild

Strong. The sender will use force or power to have the message acted on as directed. ("Fill in the form or you're fired.")

Mild. The sender will not use force or power to have the message acted on as directed. ("Please fill in the form when you can.")

Situational Communication Styles
The interactive process can be used with situational management. For example, when using the autocratic

style, the sender initiates a closed, strong presentation, whereas the sender using the empowerment style initiates an open, mild elicitation. The mild to strong component can be used with any of the styles, but the strong messages tend to be used more often with the autocratic and consultative styles. Acceptance or rejection can come from any of the styles because, to a large extent, it is out of the sender's control.

Following is the interactive process as it is used with each of the four situational management styles.

The **Autocratic Communication Style (S1A)** demonstrates high task/low relationship behavior (HT-LR), initiating a closed presentation. The other party has little, if any, information and is low in capability.

- *Initiation/Response.* You initiate and control the communication with minimal, if any, response.

- *Presentation/Elicitation.* You make a presentation letting the other parties know they are expected to comply with your message; there is little, if any, elicitation.

- *Closed/Open.* You use a closed presentation; you will not consider the receiver's input.

The **Consultative Communication Style (S2C)** demonstrates high task/high relationship behavior (HT-HR), using a closed presentation for the task with an open elicitation for the relationship. The other party has moderate information and capability.

- *Initiation/Response.* You initiate the communication by letting the other party know that you want him or her to buy into your influence. You desire some response.

- *Presentation/Elicitation.* Both are used. You use elicitation to determine the goal of the communication. For example, you may ask questions to determine the situation and follow up with a presentation. When the communication goal is known, little task elicitation is needed. Relationship communication is elicited in order to determine the interest of the other party and acceptance of the message. The open elicitation should show your concern for the other party's point of view and motivate him or her to follow your influence.

- *Closed/Open.* You are closed to having the message accepted (task), but open to the person's feelings (relationship). Be empathetic.

The **Participative Communication Style (S3P)** demonstrates low task/high relationship behavior (LT-HR), responding with open elicitation, some initiation, and little presentation. The other party is high in information and capability.

- *Initiation/Response.* You respond with some initiation. You want to help the other party solve a problem or get him or her to help you solve one. You are helpful and convey personal support.

- *Presentation/Elicitation.* Elicitation can occur with little presentation. Your role is to elicit the other party's ideas on how to reach objectives.

- *Closed/Open.* Open communication is used. If you participate well, the other party will come to a solution you can accept. If not, you may have to reject the other party's message.

The **Empowerment Communication Style (S4E)** demonstrates low task/low relationship behavior (LT-LR), responding with the necessary open presentation. The other party is outstanding in information and capability.

- *Initiation/Response.* You respond to the other party with little, if any, initiation.

- *Presentation/Elicitation.* You present the other party with information, structure, and so forth.

- *Closed/Open.* Open—You convey that the other party is in charge; you will accept the message.

Situational Variables

When selecting the appropriate communication style, you should consider four variables: time, information, acceptance, and capability. Answering the questions related to each of the following variables can help you select the appropriate style for the situation. These same four variables appear in Model 4–2 (Chapter 4).

Time. Do I have enough time to use two-way communication—yes or no? When there is no time, the other three variables are not considered; the autocratic style is appropriate. When time is available, any of the other styles may be appropriate, depending on the other variables. Time is a relative term; in one situation a few minutes may be considered a short time period, whereas in another a month may be a short period of time.

Information. Do I have the necessary information to communicate my message, to make a decision, or to take action? When you have all the information you need, the autocratic style may be appropriate. When you have some of the information, the consultative style may be appropriate. When you have little information, the participative or laissez-faire style may be appropriate.

Acceptance. Will the other party accept my message without any input? If the receiver will accept the message, the autocratic style may be appropriate. If the receiver will be reluctant to accept it, the consultative style may be appropriate. If the receiver will reject the message, the participative or empowerment style may be appropriate to gain acceptance. There are situations where acceptance is critical to success, such as in the area of implementing changes.

Capability. Capability has two parts. (1) *Ability:* Does the other party have the experience or knowledge to participate in two-way communications? Will the receiver put the organization's goals ahead of personal needs or goals? (2) *Motivation:* Does the other party want to participate? When the other party is low in capability, the autocratic style may be appropriate; if he or she is moderate in capability, the consultative style may be appropriate; if he or she is high in capability, the participative style may be appropriate; if he or she is outstanding in capability, the empowerment style may be appropriate. In addition, capability levels can change from one task to another. For example, a professor may have outstanding capability in class-

room teaching but be low in capability for advising students.

Selecting Communication Styles

Successful managers rely on different communication styles according to the situation. There are three steps to follow when selecting the appropriate communication style in a given situation.

Step 1. Diagnose the Situation. Answer the questions for each of the four situation variables. In Self-Assessment Exercise 11–2, you were asked to select an alternative to 12 situations. You were told to ignore the other answer spaces. Now you will complete this part in Doing Skill-Building Exercise 11–2 in class by placing the style letters (S1A, S2C, S3P, S4E) on the lines provided for each of the 12 situations.

Step 2. Select the Appropriate Style for the Situation. After analyzing the four variables, you select the appropriate style for the situation. In some situations, where variables may have conflicting styles, you should select the style of the most important variable for the situation. For example, capability may be outstanding (C-4), but you have all the information needed (S1A). If the information is more important, use the autocratic style even though the capability is outstanding. When doing the in-class part of this skill-building exercise, place the letters (S1A, S2C, S3P, S4E) for the appropriate styles on the S ___ (style) lines.

Step 3. Implement the Appropriate Communication Style. During the in-class part of this exercise, you will identify one of the four communication styles for each alternative action; place the S1A, S2C, S3P, or S4E on the S ___ lines. Select the alternative a, b, c, or d that represents the appropriate communication for each of the 12 situations, and place it on the line before the number of the situation.

Model 11–2 summarizes the material in this preparation for the exercise. Use it to determine the appropriate communication style in situation 1 and during the in-class part of this exercise.

Step 1. Diagnose the Situation

Variables

Use of Management Style (S 1–4)

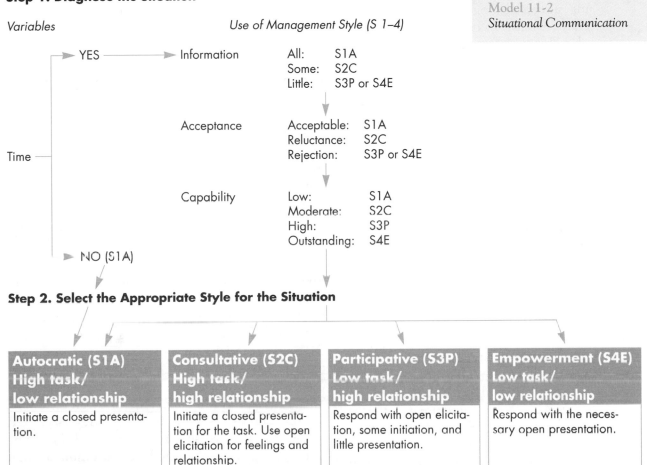

Step 2. Select the Appropriate Style for the Situation

Autocratic (S1A) High task/ low relationship	Consultative (S2C) High task/ high relationship	Participative (S3P) Low task/ high relationship	Empowerment (S4E) Low task/ low relationship
Initiate a closed presentation.	Initiate a closed presentation for the task. Use open elicitation for feelings and relationship.	Respond with open elicitation, some initiation, and little presentation.	Respond with the necessary open presentation.

Step 3. Use the Appropriate Communication Style for the Situation

Determining the Appropriate Communication Style for Situation 1

Step 1. Diagnose the Situation. Answer the four variable questions from the model, and place the letters on the following four variable lines.

_____ 1. Wendy, a knowledgeable person from another department, comes to you, the engineering supervisor, and requests that you design a special product to her specifications. You would:

_____ time   _____ information

_____ acceptance   _____ capability

_____ communication style

a. Control the conversation and tell Wendy what you will do for her. S _____

b. Ask Wendy to describe the product. Once you understand, you would present your ideas. Let her know that you are concerned and want to help with your ideas. S _____

c. Respond to Wendy's request by conveying understanding and support. Help clarify what is to be done by you. Offer ideas, but do it her way. S ___

d. Find out what you need to know. Let Wendy know you will do it her way. S ___

Step 2. Select the Appropriate Communication Style for the Situation. Review the four variables. If they are all consistent, select one style. If they are conflicting, select the most important variable as the style to use. Place its letters (S1A, S2C, S3P, or S4E) on the style line.

Step 3. Select the Appropriate Action. Review the four alternative actions. Identify the communication style for each, placing its letters on the S line, then check the appropriate match alternative.

Let's See How You Did. (1) *Time.* Time is available (or you have time); it can be any style. *Information.* You have little information, so you need to use a participative or empowerment style to find out what Wendy wants done: S3P or S4E. *Acceptance.* If you try to do it your way rather than Wendy's way, she will most likely reject it. You need to use a participative or empowerment style: S3P or S4E. *Capability.* Wendy is knowledgeable and has a high level of capability: S3P. (2) Reviewing the four variables, you see that there is a mixture of S3P and S4E. Since you are an engineer, it is appropriate to participate with Wendy to give her what she needs. Therefore, the choice is S3P. (3) Alternative a is S1A; this is the autocratic style, high task/low relationship. Alternative b is S2C; this is the consultative style, high task/high relationship. Alternative c is S3P; this is the participative style, low task/high relationship. Alternative d is S4E; this is empowerment style, low task/low relationship behavior. If you selected c as your action, you chose the most appropriate action for the situation. This was a three-point answer. If you selected d as your answer, this is also a good alternative; it scores two points. If you selected b, you get one point for overdirecting. If you selected a, you get zero points; this is too much directing and will most likely hurt communications.

The better you match your communication style to the situation, the more effective you will be at communicating. In the in-class part of this exercise, you will apply the model to the other 11 situations in Self-Assessment Exercise 11–2 to develop your ability to communicate as a situational communicator.

Doing Skill-Building Exercise 11–2 in Class
Objective
To develop your ability to communicate using the appropriate style for the situation.

Preparation
You should have completed the preparation for this exercise.

Experience
You will work at selecting the appropriate style for situations 2–12 in Self-Assessment Exercise 11–2. On the time line place Y (yes), on the information, acceptance, and capability lines place the letters S1A, S2C, S3P, or S4E that are appropriate for the situation. Based on your diagnoses, select the one style you would use by placing its letters S1A, S2C, S3P, or S4E on the communication style line. On the four S lines write the letters S1A, S2C, S3P, or S4E to identify each style being used. Place the letter a, b, c, d on the line before the number that represents the most appropriate communication style for the situation.

Procedure 1 (15–20 minutes)
Behavior Model Video 11–1 is shown to illustrate the four styles. Use the form on page 408 to record answers.

Procedure 2 (5–10 minutes)
The instructor reviews the situational communications model and explains how to apply it to determine the appropriate style for situation 2.

Procedure 3 (5–10 minutes)
Students working alone complete situation 3 of Self-Assessment Exercise 11–2 using the model. Then the instructor goes over the recommended answers.

Procedure 4 (20–50 minutes)

1. Break into groups of two or three. As a team, apply the model to situations 4 through 8. The in-

structor will go over the appropriate answers when all teams are done or the time is up.

2. Break into new groups of two or three and do situations 9 through 12. The instructor will go over the appropriate answers.

Conclusion

The instructor leads a class discussion and/or makes concluding remarks.

Application (2–4 minutes)

What did I learn from this experience? How will I use this knowledge in the future?

_____

_____

Sharing

Volunteers give their answers to the application section.

Motivating

Learning Objectives

After studying this chapter, you should be able to:

1. Illustrate the motivation process.

2. Explain the performance formula and how to use it.

3. Discuss the major similarity and difference among the four content motivation theories: hierarchy of needs, ERG, two-factor, and acquired needs.

4. Discuss the major similarity and difference among the three process motivation theories: equity, goal-setting, and expectancy.

5. Explain the four types of reinforcement: positive, avoidance, extinction, and punishment.

6. State the major difference among content, process, and reinforcement theories.

7. Explain the major difference between the Japanese and U.S. approach to motivating employees.

8. Define the following **key terms** (in order of appearance in the chapter):

motivation	acquired needs theory
motivation process	process motivation theories
performance formula	equity theory
content motivation theories	goal-setting theory
hierarchy of needs theory	expectancy theory
ERG theory	reinforcement theory
two-factor theory	giving praise model

Skill Development

*skillbuilder

1. You can improve your skill in giving motivational praise (Skill-Building Exercise 12–1).

   Giving praise is a leadership management function and an interpersonal management role of a leader. Giving praise requires human and communication management skills. The SCANS competencies of interpersonal skills are developed through Skill-Building Exercise 12–1.

Donna Brogle has enjoyed sewing since her childhood. Following her hobby, Donna worked as a seamstress for a major hospital. However, being married with four children, she preferred to be at home with her family. The hospital administrator decided to order new drapes and gave Donna the job. Gaining drapery experience at the hospital, Donna decided to quit working for the hospital and start her own business, "Draperies by Donna." She set goals for her business and found women in the process of retiring who gave her some help getting started. In 1989 Donna set up shop in her basement. She enjoyed the flexibility of setting her own schedule and working at home. Things went well until the recession hit in 1990–1991 and business dropped. As luck would have it, the hospital called her and asked her to come back as an employee to make drapes. Donna did not want to lose her independence, so she offered to work for the hospital as a vendor. They agreed that Donna would work at home and continue to run her business as well. After gaining more experience, and the economy turned around, the number of Donna's customers increased to the point where she no longer depended on the hospital as a customer.

Eventually, Donna's business thrived and she needed to hire some help. Now she is having a problem with her employee Susan.[1] Susan is often late for work, and even though she can do a good job, she does not regularly perform to expectations. Donna had a talk with Susan to determine the cause of the problem. Susan said the money is okay and she is treated fairly, but the job is boring. Susan complained that she didn't have any say about how to do her job and that Donna continually checked up on her. If you were in Donna's position, how would you motivate Susan? In this chapter you will learn specific motivation theories and techniques that can be used to motivate Susan and employees in all organizations.

Recall from Chapter 1 that Bonnie stated the importance of motivating employees and that having to deal with employee performance problems is the part she likes the least about being a manager. The more you can motivate employees, the less time you will have to spend dealing with performance problems.

MOTIVATION AND PERFORMANCE

In this section you will study what motivation is and why it is important, how motivation affects performance, and how managers affect employee motivation and performance. You will also get an overview of three major theories of motivation.

1. Illustrate the motivation process.

motivation
The willingness to achieve organizational objectives.

motivation process
Employees go from need to motive to behavior to consequence to satisfaction or dissatisfaction.

What Is Motivation and Why Is It Important?

What Is Motivation? Motivation is an inner desire to satisfy an unsatisfied need. From a business perspective, **motivation** *is the willingness to achieve organizational objectives.* People primarily do what they do to meet their needs or wants.

Through the **motivation process,** *employees go from need to motive to behavior to consequence to satisfaction or dissatisfaction.* For example, you are thirsty (need) and have a desire (motive) to get a drink. You get a drink (behavior) that quenches (consequence and satisfaction) your thirst. However, if you could not get a drink, or a drink of what you really wanted, you would be dissatisfied. Satisfaction is usually short-lived. Getting that drink satisfied you, but soon you will need another drink. For this reason, the motivation process has a feedback loop:

$$\text{Need} \rightarrow \text{Motive} \rightarrow \text{Behavior} \rightarrow \text{Consequence} \rightarrow \text{Satisfaction or Dissatisfaction}$$
$$\uparrow \qquad\qquad\qquad\qquad\qquad\qquad\qquad\qquad\qquad\qquad \downarrow$$
$$\longleftarrow \longleftarrow \text{Feedback} \longleftarrow \longleftarrow\longleftarrow$$

Some need or want motivates all behavior. However, needs and motives are complex; people don't always know what their needs are or why they do the things they do. Have you ever done something and not known why you did it? Understanding needs will help you understand behavior. You will gain a better understanding of why people do the things they do.

You cannot observe motives, but you can observe behavior and infer the person's motive. (This attribution process is explained in Chapter 9, Model 9–1.) However, it is not easy to know why people behave the way they do, because people do the same things for different reasons. Also, people often attempt to satisfy several needs at once.

Why Is Motivation Important? Motivation is the number one problem facing businesses today.[2] Managers have come to realize that a motivated and satisfied work force can contribute powerfully to the bottom-line profits.[3] Knowing how to motivate will help you eliminate or reduce these performance problems, such as those experienced by Susan in the opening case.

Motivation is important not only to small businesses such as Donna's but also to major corporations. Much of General Electric's success is attributed to CEO Jack Welch and his ability to motivate employees.[4] CEO David House took Bay Networks from its deathbed to healthy profits in a year and a half by teaching management skills classes that included motivating employees.[5] Giving immediate, frequent, and direct feedback leads to higher motivation and performance.[6] This correlation is true for both CEOs Welch and House.

Recall from Chapter 9 that job satisfaction leads to lower absenteeism and turnover and higher levels of performance. Generally, people who are satisfied with their jobs are more highly motivated. To motivate employees, you should make work fun. Developing an organizational culture that values making work fun fuels the most productive people and organizations in North America.[7] Companies that bring play and celebration into the workplace often have higher profits. One example is Southwest Airlines, which incorporates games and contests into its flying experience. [8] Offering incentives is a proven way of increasing motivation and productivity and adding the fun factor to a workplace.[9] Have you ever had a job that was fun? How did it affect your motivation?

The Role of Expectations in Motivation and Performance

The poor performance of employees can be inadvertently caused by managers themselves and not inadequacies such as poor skills, a lack of experience, and insufficient motivation.[10] Recall that the Pygmalion effect (Chapter 9) states that managers' attitudes toward expectations of and treatment of employees largely determine employees' motivation and performance. Managers need to have high expectations and treat employees as though they are high achievers to get the best from them.

Some managers try to motivate employees and instead end up making performance worse.[11] Part of the problem is that managers have a perception problem resulting from their frame of reference. Managers assume that everyone is like them and what will motivate them will motivate all employees, or they stereotype employees. Managers need to get to know their employees as individuals and motivate them in ways that will meet their unique and diverse needs.[12] You will learn how to motivate employees throughout this chapter.

2. Explain the performance formula and how to use it.

In addition to managers' expectations, employees' expectations also affect performance. Closely related to the Pygmalion effect is the *self-fulfilling prophecy*. Henry Ford said, if you believe you can, or you believe you can't; you are right. If you think you will be successful, you will be. If you think you will fail, you will, because you will fulfill your own expectations. You will live up to or down to your own expectations, so be positive, confident, and optimistic. Recall from Chapter 9 that you can change your personality to be more positive with a higher level of self-esteem. Refer back to Exercise 9–1, Improving Personality Traits. If you did not do this exercise, consider doing it now. If you did do the exercise, have you been working toward improving your personality traits?

APPLYING THE CONCEPT

AC 12–1 The Performance Formula

Identify the factor contributing to low performance in the following five situations.

a. ability   b. motivation   c. resources

____ **1.** Latoya went on a sales call. When she reached into her briefcase she realized that she did not have her product display book. Trying to explain the products without providing the customer with a visual look at the product resulted in a lost sale.

____ **2.** Frank does not produce as much as the other department members, because he does not put much effort into the job.

____ **3.** "I practice longer and harder than my track teammates, Heather and Linda. I don't understand why they beat me in the running races."

____ **4.** "I could get all *A*s in school if I wanted to. But I'd rather relax and have a good time."

____ **5.** The government would be more efficient if it cut down on waste.

---

performance formula
performance = ability × motivation × resources.

How Motivation Affects Performance

Generally, a motivated employee will try harder to do a good job than someone who is not motivated. However, performance is not simply based on motivation. Three interdependent factors determine the level of performance attained: ability, motivation, and resources. Stated as a **performance formula:** *performance = ability × motivation × resources*.

For maximum performance levels, all three factors must be high. If any factor is low or missing, the performance level will be adversely affected. As a manager, if you want to attain high levels of performance, you must be sure that you and your employees have the ability, motivation, and resources to meet objectives. When performance is not at the standard level or above, you must determine which performance factor needs to be improved, and improve it. In the opening case, Susan has the ability and resources, but lacks motivation. To increase Susan's performance, Donna needs to motivate her.

An Overview of Three Major Classifications of Motivation Theories

There is no single universally accepted theory of how to motivate people. In this chapter you will study three major classifications of motivation theories, plus subtheories, and how you can use them to motivate yourself and others. Figure 12–1 lists the major motivation theories. After studying all of the theories, you can select one theory to use, employ several theories in de-

Classification of Motivation Theories

1. **Content motivation theories** focus on identifying and understanding employees needs.

Specific Motivation Theory

a. **Hierarchy of needs theory** proposes that employees are motivated through five levels of needs: physiological, safety, social, esteem, and self-actualization.

b. **ERG theory** proposes that employees are motivated by three needs: existence, relatedness, and growth.

c. **Two-factor theory** proposes that employees are motivated by motivators (higher-level needs) rather than maintenance (lower-level needs) factors.

d. **Acquired needs theory** proposes that employees are motivated by their need for achievement, power, and affiliation.

2. **Process motivation theories** focus on understanding how employees choose behaviors to fulfill their needs.

a. **Equity theory** proposes that employees will be motivated when their perceived inputs equal outputs.

b. **Goal-setting theory** proposes that achievable but difficult goals motivate employees.

c. **Expectancy theory** proposes that employees are motivated when they believe they can accomplish the task and the rewards for doing so are worth the effort.

3. **Reinforcement theory** proposes that through the consequences for behavior employees will be motivated to behave in predetermined ways.

Type of reinforcement

a. **Positive reinforcement** proposes that offering attractive consequences (rewards) for desirable peformance encourages continued behavior.

b. **Aviodance reinforcement** proposes that offering negative consequences for poor performance encourages continued desirable behavior.

c. **Extinction** proposes that withholding reinforcement for an undesirable behavior reduces or eliminates that behavior.

d. **Punishment** proposes that providing and undesirable consequence (punishment) for an undesirable behavior prevents the behavior.

Figure 12-1
Major Motivation Theories

veloping your own theory, or apply the theory that best fits the specific situation. As each motivation theory and technique is presented, you will study how Donna can apply it to motivate Susan or others.

3. Discuss the major similarity and difference among the four content motivation theories: hierarchy of needs, ERG, two-factor, and acquired needs.

content motivation theories
Focus on identifying and understanding employees' needs.

hierarchy of needs theory
Proposes that employees are motivated through five levels of needs: physiological, safety, social, esteem, and self-actualization.

CONTENT MOTIVATION THEORIES

According to content motivation theorists, if you want to have satisfied employees you must meet their needs. When employees are asked to meet objectives they think, but usually do not ask, "What's in it for me?" The key to success for organizations is to meet the needs of employees and achieve organizational objectives. As you create a win-win situation, you need to sell the benefits that meet the employees' needs to the employees.[13]

The **content motivation theories** *focus on identifying and understanding employees' needs*. In this section, you will study four content motivation theories: hierarchy of needs theory, ERG theory, two-factor theory, and acquired needs theory, and how managers use them to motivate employees.

Hierarchy of Needs

The **hierarchy of needs theory** *proposes that employees are motivated through five levels of needs: physiological, safety, social, esteem, and self-actualization*. In the 1940s, Abraham Maslow developed this theory[14] based on four major assumptions: (1) Only unmet needs motivate. (2) People's needs are arranged in order of importance (hierarchy) going from basic to complex. (3) People will not be motivated to satisfy a higher-level need unless the lower-level need(s) has been at least minimally satisfied. (4) Maslow assumed that people have five classifications of needs, which are presented here in hierarchical order from lowest to highest level of need.

Physiological needs. These include people's primary or basic needs: air, food, shelter, sex, and relief from or avoidance of pain.

Safety needs. Once they satisfy their physiological needs, people are concerned with safety and security.

Social needs. After establishing safety, people look for love, friendship, acceptance, and affection.

Esteem needs. After they meet their social needs, people focus on ego, status, self-respect, recognition for accomplishments, and a feeling of self-confidence and prestige.

Self-actualization needs. The highest level of need is to develop one's full potential. To do so, people seek growth, achievement, and advancement.

Maslow did not take into consideration that a person can be at different levels of needs based on different aspects of their lives. Nor did he mention that people can revert back to lower-level needs. Also, our needs change, and needs often exist in combination. It is difficult to set up a motivation program to satisfy needs based on Maslow's hierarchy.

Motivating Employees with Hierarchy of Needs Theory. Today people realize that needs cannot be confined to a simple five-step hierarchy. Man-

WORK APPLICATION

1. On what level of hierarchy of needs are you at this time for a specific aspect of your life (professional or personal)? Be sure to specify the level by name and explain why you are at this level.

Self-Actualization Needs
Organizations meet these needs by providing employees with skills development, the chance to be creative, achievement and promotions, and the ability to have complete control over their jobs.

Esteem Needs
Organizations meet these needs through titles, the satisfaction of completing the job itself, merit pay raises, recognition, challenging tasks, participation in decision making, and opportunity for advancement.

Social Needs
Organizations meet these needs by providing employees with the opportunity to interact with others, to be accepted, and to have friends. Activities include parties, picnics, trips, and sports teams.

Safety Needs
Organizations meet these needs through safe working conditions, salary increases to meet inflation, job security, and fringe benefits (medical insurance/sick pay/pensions) that protect the physiological needs.

Physiological Needs
Organizations meet these needs through adequate salary, breaks, and safe working conditions.

Figure 12-2
How Managers Motivate with Hierarchy of Needs Theory

agers should meet employees' lower-level needs so that they will not dominate the employees' motivational process. Dr. Maslow stated that enlightened managers who truly understand that human resources are the organization's most valuable asset remain far from conventional practice. Most managers continue to focus on short-term and nonhuman aspects rather than work conditions leading to self-actualization. Dr. Maslow called for self-directed teams that meet self-actualization needs decades before they became popular in the 1990s.[15] Figure 12–2 lists ways in which managers attempt to meet these five needs.

ERG Theory

Figure 12–1 shows several motivation theories. ERG is a well-known simplification of the hierarchy of needs theory. *The* **ERG theory** *proposes that employees are motivated by three needs: existence, relatedness, and growth.* Clayton Alderfer reorganized Maslow's needs hierarchy into three needs: existence (physiological and safety needs), relatedness (social), and growth

ERG theory
Proposes that employees are motivated by three needs: existence, relatedness, and growth.

(esteem and self-actualization). Alderfer maintained the higher- and lower-order needs. He agreed with Maslow that unsatisfied needs motivate individuals, but disagreed that only one need level is active at one time.[16]

Motivating Employees with ERG Theory. To use ERG theory, you must determine which needs have been met, which needs have not been met or have been frustrated, and how to meet the unsatisfied needs. You need to satisfy employees' needs and achieve the organizational objectives. Donna observed Susan and took the time to talk to her to determine her needs. Susan's needs for existence and relatedness have been met; however, her need for growth has been frustrated. To motivate Susan, Donna must meet her need for growth. Donna should allow her to have more say in how she does her work and not check up on her as often, as long as Susan meets expected performance levels.

Two-Factor Theory

In the 1950s, Frederick Herzberg classified two sets of needs that he called *factors*.[17] Herzberg combined lower-level needs into one classification he called *maintenance* or *hygiene*, and higher-level needs into one classification he called *motivators*. The **two-factor theory** *proposes that employees are motivated by motivators rather than maintenance factors*. Maintenance factors are also called *extrinsic motivators*, because motivation comes from outside the job itself; they include pay, job security, and title; working conditions; fringe benefits; and relationships. Motivators are called *intrinsic motivators* because motivation comes from the work itself; they include achievement, recognition, challenge, and advancement.

two-factor theory
Proposes that employees are motivated by motivators rather than maintenance factors.

Herzberg and associates, based on research, disagreed with the traditional view that satisfaction and dissatisfaction were at opposite ends of one continuum. Two continuums exist: not dissatisfied with the environment (maintenance) to satisfied, and satisfied with the job itself (motivators) to not satisfied.

Employees are on a continuum from satisfied to not satisfied with their environment. Herzberg contended that providing maintenance factors will keep employees from being dissatisfied, but it will not make them satisfied or motivate them. In other words, maintenance factors will not satisfy or motivate employees; they will only keep them from being dissatisfied. For example, if employees are dissatisfied with their pay and they get a raise, they will no longer be dissatisfied with their pay. However, before long people get accustomed to the new standard of living and will become dissatisfied again. Employees will need another raise to not be dissatisfied again. The vicious cycle goes on. If you got a pay raise, would you be motivated and more productive? The current view of money as a motivator is that money matters more to some people than others and that it may motivate some employees. However, money does not necessarily motivate employees to work harder.[18] Recall (Chapter 9) that you can have overall job satisfaction without being satisfied with all determinants of job satisfaction, which include pay. Herzberg says that you must first ensure that maintenance factors are adequate. Once employees are no longer dissatisfied with their environment, they can be motivated through their jobs.

Employees are on a continuum from satisfied to not satisfied with the job itself. To motivate employees you need to make their jobs more interesting and challenging, give them more responsibility, provide them with the opportunity for growth, and offer them recognition for a job well done. A recent study supported Herzberg's theory and concluded that enhanced and sustained job performance is directly related to the intrinsic feelings that produce positive attitudes about the job.[19] Figure 12–3 illustrates the two-factor theory.

High	**Maintenance Factors**	Low
(extrinsic motivators—physiological, safety, and social needs—existence and relatedness needs) pay, benefits, job security, working conditions, company policies, human relations		
Not Dissatisfied	(with the Maintenance Factors)	Dissatisfied

Motivator Factors		
(intrinsic motivators—esteem and self-actualization needs—growth needs) work itself, recognition, achievement, increased responsibility, growth, advancement		
Satisfied (Motivated)	(with the Job Motivator Factors)	Not Satisfied (Not Motivated)

Figure 12-3
Two-Factor Theory

Motivating Employees with Two-Factor Theory. The best way to motivate employees is to ensure that they are not dissatisfied with maintenance factors, and then focus on motivating them. One successful way to motivate is to build challenge and opportunity for achievement into the job itself.[20] Entrepreneurs stated that to stay motivated they find new challenge inside the business.[21] Herzberg developed a method for increasing motivation—called *job enrichment*—which you studied in Chapter 6. The Job Characteristics Model (also in Chapter 6) has been shown to consistently predict outcomes such as internal work motivation, job involvement, and job satisfaction.[22]

In the opening case, Susan said she was not dissatisfied with maintenance factors. Since Susan said the job is boring, will a pay raise or better working conditions increase her level of satisfaction? If Donna is going to motivate Susan, she will have to focus on intrinsic job motivation, not maintenance. Donna needs to give Susan more input into how she does her job.

Acquired Needs Theory

The **acquired needs theory** *proposes that employees are motivated by their need for achievement, power, and affiliation.* Henry Murray developed the general needs theory.[23] It was adapted by John Atkinson,[24] and David McClelland developed a specific acquired needs theory.[22] McClelland does not have a classification for lower-level needs. His affiliation needs are the same as social and relatedness, and power and achievement are related to esteem, self-actualization, and growth.

Unlike Maslow, McClelland believed that needs are based on personality and are developed as people interact with the environment. All people possess the need for achievement, power, and affiliation, but to varying degrees. One of the three needs tends to be dominant in individuals and motivates

WORK APPLICATION

2. Recall a present or past job; were you dissatisfied or not dissatisfied with the maintenance factors? Were you satisfied or not satisfied with the motivators? Be sure to identify and explain your satisfaction with the specific maintenance and motivator factors.

acquired needs theory
Proposes that employees are motivated by their need for achievement, power, and affiliation.

their behavior. Before getting into the details of each need, complete Self-Assessment Exercise 12–1 to determine your dominant or primary need.

Self-Assessment Exercise 12–1

Acquired Needs

Identify each of the 15 statements according to how accurately it describes you. Place the number 1–5 on the line before each statement.

Like me   Somewhat like me   Not like me
5 ————— 4 ————— 3 ————— 2 ————— 1

_____ 1. I get enjoyment out of working hard.

_____ 2. I enjoy competing and winning.

_____ 3. I enjoy having lots of friends.

_____ 4. I enjoy a difficult challenge.

_____ 5. I enjoy being in a leadership role.

_____ 6. I want other people to like me.

_____ 7. I want to know how I am progressing as I complete tasks.

_____ 8. I confront people who do things I disagree with.

_____ 9. I enjoy frequent gathering with people such as at parties.

_____ 10. I enjoy setting and achieving realistic goals.

_____ 11. I try to influence other people to get my way.

_____ 12. I enjoy belonging to lots of groups/organizations.

_____ 13. I enjoy the satisfaction of completing a difficult task.

_____ 14. In a leaderless situation, I tend to step forward and take charge.

_____ 15. I enjoy working with others more than working alone.

To determine your primary need, place the number 1–5 that represents your score for each statement. Each statement/column represents a specific need.

Achievement	Power	Affiliation
___ 1.	___ 2.	___ 3.
___ 4.	___ 5.	___ 6.
___ 7.	___ 8.	___ 9.
___ 10.	___ 11.	___ 12.
___ 13.	___ 14.	___ 15.
Totals ___	___	___

Add up the total of each column, which should be between 5 and 25 points. The column with the highest score is your dominant or primary need.

The Need for Achievement (n Ach). People with a high n Ach tend to be characterized as wanting to take personal responsibility for solving problems. They are goal oriented and they set moderate, realistic, attainable goals. They seek a challenge, excellence, and individuality; take calculated, moderate risk; desire concrete feedback on their performance, and are willing to work hard. People with a high n Ach think about ways to do a better job, how to accomplish something unusual or important, and career progression. They perform well in nonroutine, challenging, and competitive situations, whereas people low in n Ach do not perform well in these situations.

McClelland's research showed that only about 10 percent of the U.S. population has a dominant need for achievement. Evidence of a correlation exists between high achievement need and high performance. People with a high n Ach tend to enjoy sales and entrepreneurial-type positions. Managers tend to have a high n Ach.

Motivating Employees with a High n Ach. Give them nonroutine, challenging tasks with clear, attainable objectives. Give them fast and frequent feedback on their performance.[26] Continually give them increased responsibility for doing new things. Keep out of their way.

The Need for Power (n Pow). People with a high need for power tend to be characterized as wanting to control the situation, wanting influence or control over others, enjoying competition in which they can win (they do not like to lose), and willing to confront others. People with high n Pow think about controlling a situation and others, and seek positions of authority and status. People with high n Pow tend to have a low need for affiliation. Managers tend to have a high n Pow. They understand that power is essential for successful management.

Motivating Employees with a High n Pow. Let them plan and control their jobs as much as possible. Try to include them in decision making, especially when the decision affects them. They tend to perform best alone rather than as team members. Try to assign them to a whole task rather than just a part of it.

In the opening case, Susan's primary need seems to be power. Susan wants more say on how to do her job and wants Donna to do less checking up on her. If Donna empowers Susan by giving her more job-related responsibility, it may satisfy Susan's needs, resulting in higher performance.

The Need for Affiliation (n Aff). People with a high n Aff tend to be characterized as seeking close relationships with others, wanting to be liked by others, enjoying lots of social activities, and seeking to belong. They join groups and organizations. People with a high n Aff think about friends and relationships. They tend to enjoy developing, helping, and teaching others. They tend to have a low n Pow. People with high n Aff seek jobs in teaching, social work, human resources management, and in other helping professions. They tend to avoid management because they like to be one of the group rather than its leader.

Motivating Employees with High n Aff. Be sure to let them work as part of a team. They derive satisfaction from the people they work with rather than the task itself. Give them lots of praise and recognition. Delegate responsibility for orienting and training new employees to them. They make great buddies and mentors.

Donna, from the opening case, like all people, has a need for achievement, power, and affiliation. Taking the risk to start her own business indicates her need for achievement and power; her motivation to work at home so she could be with her family came from her need for affiliation.

Figure 12–4 compares the four content theories of motivation.

WORK APPLICATION

3. Explain how your need for achievement, power, and/or affiliation has affected your behavior motivation, or that of someone you work or have worked with.

Hierarchy of Needs (Maslow)	ERG Theory (Alderfer)	Two-Factor Theory (Herzberg)	Acquired Needs Theory (McClelland)
Self-Actualization →	Growth →	Motivators →	Achievement and Power
Esteem →	Growth →	Motivators →	Achievement and Power
Social →	Relatedness →	Maintenance →	Affiliation
Safety →	Existence →	Maintenance →	Not classified
Physiological →	Existence →	Maintenance →	Not classified
Needs must be met in a hierarchical order.	Unmet needs can be at any level simultaneously.	Maintenance factors will not motivate employees.	Motivating needs are developed through experience.

Figure 12-4
A Comparison of Four Content Motivation Theories

4. Discuss the major similarity and difference among the three process motivation theories: equity, goal-setting, and expectancy.

process motivation theories
Focus on understanding how employees choose behavior to fulfill their needs.

equity theory
Proposes that employees are motivated when their perceived inputs equal outputs.

PROCESS MOTIVATION THEORIES

Process motivation theories *focus on understanding how employees choose behavior to fulfill their needs.* Process motivation theories are more complex than content motivation theories. Content motivation theories simply focus on identifying and understanding employees' needs. Process motivation theories go a step further to understand why employees have different needs, why their needs change, how and why they choose to try to satisfy needs in different ways, the mental process they go through as they understand situations, and how they evaluate their need satisfaction. In this section, you will study three process motivation theories: equity theory, goal-setting theory, and expectancy theory.

Equity Theory

Equity theory, primarily J. Stacy Adams' motivation theory, proposes that people are motivated to seek social equity in the rewards they receive (output) for their performance (input).[27] **Equity theory** *proposes that employees are motivated when their perceived inputs equal outputs.* Based on a knowledge of equity theory, you may be able to predict behavior.

According to equity theory, people compare their inputs (effort, experience, seniority, status, intelligence, and so forth) and outputs (praise, recognition, pay, benefits, promotions, increased status, supervisor's approval, etc.) to that of relevant others. A relevant other could be a coworker or group of employees from the same or different organizations, or even from a hypothetical situation. Notice that the definition says *perceived* and not actual inputs to outputs. Equity may actually exist. However, if employees believe there is inequity, they will change their behavior to create equity. Employees must perceive that they are being treated fairly,[28] relative to others.

Unfortunately, many employees tend to inflate their own efforts or performance when comparing themselves to others. They also tend to overestimate what others earn. Employees may be very satisfied and motivated until they find out that a relevant other is earning more for the same job or earning the same for doing less work. When employees perceive inequity, they are motivated to reduce it by reducing input or increasing output. A comparison with relevant others leads to three conclusions: The employee is underrewarded, overrewarded, or equitably rewarded.

Underrewarded. When employees perceive that they are underrewarded, they may try to reduce the inequity by increasing outputs (get a raise), reducing inputs (doing less work, absenteeism, long breaks, etc.), rationalizing (finding a logical explanation for inequity), changing others' inputs or outputs (get them to do more, or get less), leaving the situation (get transferred or leave for a better job), or changing the object of comparison (they make/get less than I do).

Overrewarded. Being overrewarded does not disturb most employees. However, research suggests that employees may reduce perceived inequity by increasing input (work harder or longer), reducing output (take a pay cut), rationalizing (I'm worth it), or trying to increase others' output (give them the same as me).

Equitably Rewarded. Inputs and outputs are perceived as being equal; motivation exists. Employees may believe that relevant others should have greater outputs when they have more experience, education, and so on.

Motivating with Equity Theory. Research supporting equity theory is mixed. One view of equity proposes that it is similar to Herzberg's maintenance factors. When employees are not dissatisfied they are not actively motivated, but maintenance factors do demotivate when employees are dissatisfied. Related to equity theory, when employees believe they are equitably rewarded they are not actively motivated. However, when employees believe they are underrewarded they are demotivated.

Using equity theory in practice can be difficult, because you don't know the employees' reference group and their view of inputs and outcomes. However, it does offer some useful general recommendations:

1. Managers should be aware that equity is based on perception, which may not be correct. Possibly, managers can create equity or inequity. Some managers have favorite subordinates who get special treatment; others don't.

2. Rewards should be equitable. When employees perceive that they are not treated fairly, morale and performance problems occur. Employees producing at the same level should be given equal rewards.

3. High performance should be rewarded, but employees must understand the inputs needed to attain certain outputs. When using incentive pay, there should be clear standards specifying the exact requirements to achieve the incentive. A manager should be able to objectively tell others why one person got a higher merit raise than another.

WORK APPLICATION

4. Give an example of how equity theory has affected your motivation or someone else's you work or have worked with. Be sure to specify if you were under-, over-, or equitably rewarded.

In the opening case, Susan said that she was equitably treated. Therefore, Donna does not need to be concerned about equity theory with Susan. However, it could be an issue with another employee.

Goal-Setting Theory

goal-setting theory
Proposes that achievable but difficult goals motivate employees.

Goal-setting theory is currently one of the most valid approaches to work motivation.[29] It complements Herzberg's[30] and McClelland's[31] theories as goals lead to higher levels of motivation and performance.[32] Goals provide challenge, thus, people with a high need for achievement set goals. *The* **goal-setting theory** *proposes that achievable but difficult goals motivate employees.* Chapter 4 presented setting objectives and management by objectives (MBO) in detail. Our behavior has a purpose, which is usually to fulfill a need. Goals give us a sense of purpose—why we are working to accomplish a given task. Setting objectives helps employees identify ways of meeting their needs, and the attainment of objectives is reinforcing in itself. According to Parkinson's Law, work expands to fill the time available for its completion. If you set difficult but achievable goals with quick deadlines, people will not take their time but will work hard to complete the task in the allotted time.

WORK APPLICATION

5. Give an example of how a goal(s) affected your motivation and performance, or someone else's you work or have worked with.

Using Goal-Setting to Motivate Employees. Lou Holtz, former coach of the University of Notre Dame national championship football team, stated that the three keys to success are a winning attitude, positive self-esteem, and setting a higher goal.[33] A winning attitude leads to positive self-esteem, which in turn motivates you to a higher level of goals, which in turn gives a more positive attitude and self-esteem. Every year each player had personal goals and the team set goals, which Coach Holtz wrote in his notebook. Lou said, "Of all my experiences in managing people, the power of goal setting is the most incredible." All good performance starts with clear goals.[34] When setting objectives, be sure that they are challenging, achievable, specific,[35] measurable, have a target date for accomplishment, and are jointly set when possible (see Chapter 4 for details). However, remember that setting goals is not enough. You need to formulate action plans (Chapter 5) to achieve the goals[36] and to measure progress.

Domino's Pizza used to have its well-known objective of free delivery in 30 minutes or less. However, due to delivery auto accidents resulting in lawsuits because employees placed too much emphasis on deadlines versus safety, the 30-minute time limit was dropped. However, quick delivery is still an important goal. In the opening case, Donna could use MBO to identify objectives that could motivate Susan.

Expectancy Theory

expectancy theory
Proposes that employees are motivated when they believe they can accomplish the task and the rewards for doing so are worth the effort.

Expectancy theory is based on Victor Vroom's formula: motivation = expectancy × valence.[37] *The* **expectancy theory** *proposes that employees are* *motivated when they believe they can accomplish the task and the rewards for doing so are worth the effort.* The theory is based on the following assumptions: (1) both internal (needs) and external (environment) factors affect behavior; (2) behavior is the individual's decision; (3) people have different needs, desires, and goals; and (4) people make behavior decisions based on their perception of the outcome.

Two important variables in Vroom's formula must be met for motivation to take place.

Expectancy. Expectancy refers to the person's perception of his or her ability (probability) to accomplish an objective. Generally, the higher one's expectancy, the better the chance for motivation. When employees do not believe that they can accomplish objectives, they will not be motivated to try. Also important is the perception of the relationship between performance and the outcome or reward, which is referred to as *instrumentality*. Generally, the higher one's expectancy of the outcome or reward, the better the chance for motivation. If employees will certainly get the reward, they probably will be motivated. When not sure of the reward, employees may not be motivated. For example, Dan believes he would be a good manager and wants to be promoted. However, Dan has an external locus of control (Chapter 9) and believes that working hard will not result in a promotion anyway. Therefore, he will not be motivated to work for the promotion.

Valence. Valence refers to the value a person places on the outcome or reward. Generally, the higher the value (importance) of the outcome or reward, the better the chance of motivation. For example, the supervisor, Jean, wants an employee, Sim, to work harder. Jean talks to Sim and tells him that working hard will result in a promotion. If Sim wants a promotion, he will probably be motivated. However, if Sim does not want the promotion, it will not motivate him.

Motivating with Expectancy Theory. Expectancy theory can accurately predict a person's work effort, satisfaction level, and performance,[38] but only if you plug the correct values into the formula. Therefore, this theory works in certain contexts but not in others. The following conditions should be implemented to make the theory result in motivation:

1. Clearly define objectives and the necessary doable performance needed to achieve them.

2. Tie performance to rewards. High performance should be rewarded. When one employee works harder to produce more than other employees and is not rewarded, he or she may slow down productivity (equity).

3. Be sure rewards have value to the employee. Managers should get to know employees as individuals.

4. Make sure your employees believe you will do what you say you will do. For example, employees must believe you will give them a merit raise if

WORK APPLICATION

6. Give an example of how expectancy theory has affected your motivation or someone else's you work or have worked with. Be sure to specify the expectancy and valence.

they work hard. And you must do as you say you will, so employees will believe you.

In the opening case, if Donna allows Susan to work independently, she may be motivated to perform to expectations, creating a win-win situation for both of them.

REINFORCEMENT THEORY

reinforcement theory
Proposes that through the consequences for behavior employees will be motivated to behave in predetermined ways.

B.F. Skinner, reinforcement motivation theorist, contended that to motivate employees managers do not need to identify and understand needs (content motivation theories) or to understand how employees choose behaviors to fulfill them (process motivation theories). Instead, managers need to understand the relationship between behaviors and their consequences and then arrange contingencies that reinforce desirable behaviors and discourage undesirable behaviors. *The **reinforcement theory** proposes that through the consequences for behavior employees will be motivated to behave in predetermined ways.* Reinforcement theory uses behavior modification (apply reinforcement theory to get employees to do what you want them to do) and operant conditioning (types and schedules of reinforcement). Skinner stated that behavior is learned through experiences of positive and negative consequences. Skinner proposes three components:[39]

Stimulus ⟶ Responding Behavior ⟶ Consequences of Behavior—
(legal speed limit)   (speed)   Reinforcement (police officer gives speeder a negative consequence—ticket/fine—to dis courage repeat performance).

Employees learn what is, and is not, desired behavior as a result of the consequences for specific behavior. The two important concepts used to modify behavior are the types of reinforcement and the schedules of reinforcement.

Types of Reinforcement

5. Explain the four types of reinforcement: positive, avoidance, extinction, and punishment.

The four types of reinforcement are: positive, avoidance, extinction, and punishment.

Positive Reinforcement. A method of encouraging continued behavior is to offer attractive consequences (rewards) for desirable performance. For example, an employee arrives on time for a meeting and is rewarded by the supervisor thanking him or her. The praise is used to reinforce punctuality. Other reinforcements include pay raises, promotions, time off, increased status, and so forth. Positive reinforcement is an excellent motivator for increasing productivity.[40] Charles Jeffress said that positive reinforcement is the guiding principle of his term as administrator of OSHA.[41] You can use positive incentives to motivate your team.[42] Giving recognition for a job well done is an effective, no-cost positive reinforcement,[43] because the power of talking to an employee one-on-one is profound.[44]

Avoidance Reinforcement. Avoidance is also called negative reinforcement. As with positive reinforcement, you are encouraging continued desirable behavior. The employee avoids the negative consequence. For example, an employee is punctual for a meeting to avoid the negative reinforcement, such as a reprimand. Standing plans, especially rules, are designed to get employees to avoid certain behavior. However, rules in and of themselves are not a punishment. Punishment is only given if the rule is broken.

Extinction. Rather than encouraging desirable behavior, extinction (and punishment) attempts to reduce or eliminate it by withholding reinforcement when the behavior occurs. For example, an employee who arrives late for a meeting is ignored rather than rewarded with praise. Or you withhold a reward of value, a pay raise, until the employee performs to set standards. From another perspective, managers who do not reward good performance can cause its extinction. In other words, if you ignore good employee performance, good performance may stop as employees think, "Why should I do a good job if I'm not rewarded in some way?"

Punishment. Punishment can be used to provide an undesirable consequence for undesirable behavior. For example, an employee who arrives late for a meeting is reprimanded.[45] Notice that with avoidance there is no actual punishment; it's the threat of punishment that controls behavior. Other methods of punishment include taking away privileges, probation, fining, demoting, firing, and so forth. Using punishment may reduce the undesirable behavior, but it may cause other undesirable behavior, such as poor morale, lower productivity, and acts of theft or sabotage. Punishment is the most controversial method and the least effective at motivating employees. Figure 12–5 illustrates the four types of reinforcement.

6. State the major difference among content, process, and reinforcement theories.

Figure 12-5
Types of Reinforcement

As a manager, you have a secretary who makes many errors when completing correspondence. Your objective, which you discussed with the secretary, is to decrease the error rate. You have four types of reinforcement that you can use with the secretary when you next review the work:

Employee Behavior	Type of Reinforcement	Manager Action (Consequence)	Employee Behavior Modification (Future)
Improved performance →	Positive →	Praise improvements →	Repeat quality work*
Improved performance →	Avoidance →	Do not give any reprimand →	Repeat quality work
Performance not improved →	Extinction →	Withhold praise/raise →	Do not repeat poor work
Performance not improved →	Punishment →	Discipline action, i.e., written warning →	Do not repeat poor work

*Assuming the employee improved performance, positive reinforcement is the best motivator.

Remember that employees will do what they are rewarded for doing. Within TQM, if managers say quality of production is important, but employees who do a quality job are not rewarded, and nothing happens to employees (extinction or punishment) who do not do a quality job, employees will not be motivated to do a quality job. If a professor tells students to read this book, but does not test students on the book (reward or punishment based on test performance)—test questions only come from lectures—what percentage of students do you think will read and study this book versus those that will simply take notes and study them for exams?

Schedule of Reinforcement

The second reinforcement consideration in controlling behavior is when to reinforce performance. The two major classifications are continuous and intermittent.

Continuous Reinforcement. With a continuous method, each and every desired behavior is reinforced. Examples of this method would be a machine with an automatic counter that lets the employee know, at any given moment, exactly how many units have been produced, piece rate of $1 for each unit produced, or a manager who comments on every customer report.

Intermittent Reinforcement. With intermittent reinforcement, the reward is given based on the passage of time or output. When the reward is based on the passage of time, it is called an *interval* schedule. When it is based on output, it is called a *ratio* schedule. Ratios are generally better motivators than intervals. When electing to use intermittent reinforcement, you have four alternatives:

1. Fixed interval schedule (giving a salary paycheck every week; breaks and meals at the same time every day).
2. Variable interval schedule (giving praise only now and then, a surprise inspection, a pop quiz).
3. Fixed ratio schedule (giving a piece rate or bonus after producing at a standard rate).
4. Variable ratio schedule (giving praise for excellent work, a lottery for employees who have not been absent for a set time).

Motivating with Reinforcement

Several organizations, including 3M, Frito-Lay, and B. F. Goodrich, have used reinforcement to increase productivity. Michigan Bell used reinforcement to achieve a 50 percent improvement in attendance and above-standard productivity and efficiency level. Emery Air Freight went from 30 to 90 percent of employees meeting standards after using reinforcement. Emery estimates that its reinforcement program has resulted in a $650,000 yearly savings.

WORK APPLICATION

7. Give a few examples of the types of reinforcement, and the schedules used, on a present or past job.

Generally, positive reinforcement is the best motivator. Continuous reinforcement is better for sustaining desired behavior; however, it is not always possible or practical. Some general guidelines include:

1. Make sure employees know exactly what is expected of them. Set clear objectives.[46]

2. Select appropriate rewards. A reward to one person could be considered a punishment by another. Know your employees' needs.

3. Select the appropriate reinforcement schedule.

4. Do not reward mediocre or poor performance.[47]

5. Look for the positive and give praise,[48] rather than focusing on the negative and criticizing. Make people feel good about themselves (Pygmalion effect).

6. Never go a day without giving praise.

7. Do things for your employees, instead of to them, and you will see productivity increases.

In the opening case, Susan has been performing below expectations. If Donna talks to Susan about changing her job to better meet Susan's needs, in an MBO format, this would be positive reinforcement. Scheduling of MBO meetings could be at a fixed interval, say once every week or two, to quickly review Susan's performance. If positive reinforcement doesn't change Susan's performance, Donna can use avoidance reinforcement. Based on her authority, Donna could tell Susan that if the next time performance is below a specific level, she will receive a specific punishment, such as withholding part of her pay. If Susan does not avoid this behavior, Donna must follow up and give the punishment reinforcement.

As a manager, try the positive first. Positive reinforcement is a true motivator because it creates a win-win situation by meeting both the employee's and the manager's/organization's needs. From the employees' perspective, avoidance and punishment create a lose-win situation. The organization/manager wins by forcing them to do something they really don't want to do, but may ultimately lose if the highly skilled and trained employee quits.

Reinforcement for Getting Employees to Come to Work and to Be on Time

The traditional method used to get employees to come to work and to be on time is avoidance and punishment. If employees miss a specific number of days, they don't get paid. If an employee is late, the time card indicates this, and the employee receives punishment. Many managers today use positive reinforcement by offering employees rewards for coming to work and being on time. For example, ADV Marketing Group offers prizes to all employees for showing up and being on time. Mediatech uses a variable ratio schedule by holding a cash lottery including only the employees who have attended on time up to the drawing.

A popular technique used by many organizations, which reduces the problem of being late for work, is *flextime*.[49] Flextime allows employees to determine when they start and end work, provided they work their full number of hours, with certain restrictions on working hours. A typical schedule permits employees to begin work between 6:00 and 9:00 A.M. and to complete their work day between 3:00 and 6:00 P.M. Flextime helps meet the goal of good human relations because it allows employees to schedule their time to accommodate their personal needs and job requirements.[50]

Giving Praise

In the 1940s, Lawrence Lindahl conducted a survey revealing that what employees want most from a job is full appreciation for work done. Similar studies have been performed over the years with little change in results. When was the last time your boss gave you a thank-you or some praise for a job well done? When was the last time your boss complained about your work? If you are a manager, when was the last time you praised or criticized your employees? What is the ratio of praise to criticism?

Giving praise develops positive self-esteem in employees and leads to better performance—the Pygmalion effect and self-fulfilling prophecy. Praise is a motivator (not maintenance), because it meets employees' needs for esteem/self-actualization, growth, and achievement. Giving praise creates a win-win situation. It is probably the most powerful, simplest, least costly, and yet most underused motivational technique.

giving praise model
(1) Tell the employee exactly what was done correctly; (2) Tell the employee why the behavior is important; (3) Stop for a moment of silence; (4) Encourage repeat performance.

Ken Blanchard and Spencer Johnson popularized giving praise through their best-selling book *The One-Minute Manager*.[51] They developed a technique that involves giving one-minute feedback of praise. Model 12–1, Giving Praise, shows an adaptation. *The steps in the* **giving praise model** *are: (1) Tell the employee exactly what was done correctly; (2) Tell the employee why the behavior is important; (3) Stop for a moment of silence; (4) Encourage repeat performance.* Blanchard calls it one-minute praise because it should not take more than one minute to give the praise. The employee need not say anything. The four steps are presented in Model 12–1 and discussed here.

Model 12-1
Giving Praise

| step 1. | **Tell the employee exactly what was done correctly.** When giving praise, look the person in the eye. Eye contact shows sincerity and concern. Be very specific and descriptive. General statements such as "You're a good worker" are not as effective. On the other hand, don't talk for too long, or the praise loses its effectiveness. |

Donna: "Susan, I just overheard you deal with that customer's complaint. You did an excellent job of keeping your cool; you were polite. That person came in angry and left happy."

| step 2. | **Tell the employee why the behavior is important.** Briefly state how the organization, and/or person, benefits from the action. Also, tell the employee how you feel about the behavior. Be specific and descriptive. |

Donna: "Without customers, we don't have a business. One dissatisfied customer can cause hundreds of dollars in lost sales. It really made me proud to see you handle that tough situation the way you did."

| step 3. | **Stop for a moment of silence.** Being silent is tough for many managers.[52] The rationale for the silence is to give the employee the chance to "feel" the impact of the praise. It's like "the pause that refreshes." When you are thirsty and take the first sip/gulp of a refreshing drink, it's not until you stop, and say "AH," that you feel the quench. |

Donna: (Silently counts to five.)

| step 4. | **Encourage repeat performance.** This reinforcement motivates the employee to continue the desired behavior. Blanchard recommends touching the employee. Touching has a powerful impact. However, he recommends it only if both parties feel comfortable. Others say don't touch employees; it could lead to a sexual harassment charge. |

Donna: "Thanks, Susan, keep up the good work" (while touching her on the shoulder, or shaking hands).

APPLYING THE CONCEPT

AC 12–2 Motivation Theories

Identify the theory behind each supervisor's statement on how to motivate employees.

a. hierarchy of needs	d. acquired needs	g. expectancy
b. ERG theory	e. equity	h. reinforcement
c. two-factor	f. goal-setting	

_____ **6.** "I motivate employees by making their jobs interesting and challenging."

_____ **7.** "I make sure I treat everyone fairly to motivate them."

_____ **8.** "I know Kate likes people, so I give her jobs in which she works with other employees."

_____ **9.** "Carl would yell in the halls because he knew it bothered me. So I decided to ignore his yelling, and he stopped."

_____ **10.** "I got to know all of my employees' values. Now I can offer rewards that will motivate them when they achieve attainable task performance."

_____ **11.** "Our company now offers good working conditions, salaries, and benefits, so we are working at developing the third need for socialization."

_____ **12.** "When my employees do a good job, I thank them using a four-step model."

_____ **13.** "I used to try to improve working conditions to motivate employees. But I stopped and now focus on giving employees more responsibility so they can grow and develop new skills."

_____ **14.** "I tell employees exactly what I want them to do, with a tough deadline that they can achieve."

_____ **15.** "I now realize that I tend to be an autocratic manager because it helps fill my needs. I will work at giving some of my employees more autonomy on how they do their jobs."

_____ **16.** "I used to try to meet needs in a five-step sequence. After I heard about this new technique, I now focus on three needs and realize that needs can be unmet at more than one level at a time."

As you can see, giving praise is easy and it doesn't cost a penny. Managers trained to give praise say it works wonders. It's a much better motivator than giving a raise or other monetary reward. One manager stated that an employee was taking his time stacking cans on a display. He gave the employee praise for stacking the cans so straight. The employee was so pleased with the praise that the display went up with about a 100 percent increase in productivity. Note that the manager looked for the positive and used positive reinforcement, rather than punishment. The manager could have given a reprimand comment such as, "Quit goofing off and get the display up faster." That statement would not have motivated the employee to increase productivity. All it would have done was hurt human relations and it could have ended in an argument. The cans were straight. The employee was not praised for the slow work pace. However, if the praise had not worked, the manager should have used another reinforcement method.[53]

*skillbuilder

In the opening case, Donna should give Susan praise for increasing performance to encourage her to continue this behavior. Praise is an effective positive reinforcement when used with a variable interval schedule. Sending written thank-you notes are also important.[54] A written note can follow a verbal praise.

PUTTING THE MOTIVATION THEORIES TOGETHER WITHIN THE MOTIVATION PROCESS

Motivation is important because it helps to explain why employees behave the way they do. At this point, you may be wondering: How do these theories fit together? Is one the best? Should I try to pick the correct theory for a given situation? The groups of theories are complementary; each group of theories refers to a different stage in the motivation process. Each group of theories answers a different question. Content motivation theories answer the question: What needs do employees have that should be met on the job? Process motivation theories answer the question: How do employees choose behavior to fulfill their needs? Reinforcement theory answers the question: What can managers do to get employees to behave in ways that meet the organizational objectives?

In the first section of this chapter you found that the motivation process went from need to motive to behavior to consequence to satisfaction or dissatisfaction. Now the motivation process becomes a little more complex by incorporating the motivation theories, or answers to the preceding questions, into the process. See Figure 12–6 for an illustration. Note that Step 4 loops back to Step 3 because, according to reinforcement theory, behavior is learned through consequences. Step 4 does not loop back to Steps 1 or 2 because reinforcement theory is not concerned with needs, motives, or satisfaction; it focuses on getting employees to behave in predetermined ways, through consequences provided by managers. Also note that Step 5 loops back to Step 1 because meeting needs is ongoing; meeting our needs is a never-ending process. Finally, be aware that, according to the two-factor theory, Step 5, satisfaction or dissatisfaction, is not on one continuum but on two separate continuums (satisfied to not satisfied or dissatisfied to not dissatisfied), based on the level of need being met (motivator or maintenance).

DO MOTIVATION THEORIES APPLY GLOBALLY?

When you expand the business to other countries, the diversity continues to increase in complexity. The motivation theories you have studied were developed largely in America. As organizations become *global*, managers must be aware of the cultural limitation to theory generalizations. In 1980 it was recognized that motivational concerns vary globally.[55] A survey revealed distinct differences among U.S. salespeople and Japanese and Korean salespeople, but not among salespeople in the two Asian countries.[56] An example from NAFTA countries includes a U.S. firm in Mexico that gave workers a raise to motivate them to work more hours. The raise actually motivated the employees to work less hours because they could now make enough money to live and enjoy life (one of their primary values) in less time, so why should they work more hours? In Sweden there is a very high tax rate on overtime pay that makes it very difficult to motivate employees to work more hours based on money.

Intrinsic motivation of higher-level needs tends to be more relevant to developed countries than to Third World countries in which most people are on a lower level of hierarchy of need than those in developed countries. The term *self-actualization* is not translatable in the Chinese language. Even in developed countries, the level of needs focus varies. In the United States, people tend to be motivated by higher-level needs of self-actualization (do your own thing) and esteem; in Greece and Japan security is more important, but in Sweden, Norway, and Denmark, people are more concerned with social needs. McClelland's acquired need for achievement is more predominant in the United States. *Achievement* is difficult to translate into most other languages. Therefore, acquired achievement need has limited use outside of the United States and Canada unless managers are willing to train employees to acquire the need for achievement.

Expectancy theory holds up fairly well cross-culturally, because it is flexible. It allows for the possibility that there may be differences in expectations and valences across cultures. For example, societal acceptance may be of higher value than individual recognition in collective societies.[57]

Individual versus Collective Cultures and Motivation. One major cultural difference is in the focus on individualistic versus group approaches to business.[58] Individualistic societies (the United States, Canada, Great

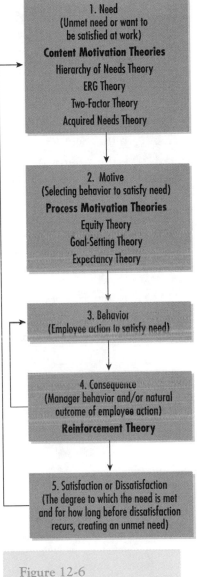

Figure 12-6
The Motivation Process with the Motivation Theories

7. Explain the major difference between the Japanese and U.S. approach to motivating employees.

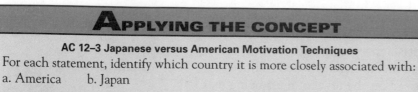

APPLYING THE CONCEPT

AC 12–3 Japanese versus American Motivation Techniques

For each statement, identify which country it is more closely associated with:
a. America   b. Japan

___ **17.** Tends to focus on motivating groups versus individuals.

___ **18.** Would be the country where you would tend to get the best results with acquired needs theory.

___ **19.** Is the country in which managers provide the greater job security.

___ **20.** Is the country where managers develop a system of giving pins/stars/etc. as a symbol of achievement of high performance.

Britain, Australia) tend to value self-accomplishment. Collective societies (Japan, Mexico, Singapore, Venezuela, Pakistan) tend to value group accomplishment and loyalty. Cultural differences suggest that self-actualization, achievement, and esteem needs tend to be met from group membership in Japan and from individualism in the United States.

The late Dr. W. Edwards Deming, often credited with making Japan a world business leader, said that America must change from an individualistic society to a collective society if it is to survive in the global economy. He was pessimistic that U.S. businesses would make the changes he thought are necessary to compete.[59] However, U.S. businesses have been moving toward the use of more *teams and participative management*.

CHAPTER SUMMARY AND GLOSSARY

The chapter summary is organized to answer the eight learning objectives for Chapter 12.

1. Illustrate the motivation process.

Employees go through the five-step process to meet their needs. Note that this is a circular process because needs recur.

Need → Motive → Behavior → Consequence → Satisfaction or Dissatisfaction
← Feedback ←

2. Explain the performance formula and how to use it.

The performance formula proposes that performance is based on ability, motivation, and resources. If any of these three components are low, performance will be negatively affected. When a performance problem occurs, managers need to determine which component of the performance formula is the reason for the performance level and take appropriate action to correct the problem.

3. Discuss the major similarity and difference among the four content motivation theories: hierarchy of needs, ERG, two-factor, and acquired needs.

The similarity between the four content motivation theories is their focus on identifying and understanding employees' needs. The theories identify similar needs, but are different in the way they classify the needs. Hierarchy of needs theory includes physiological, safety, social, esteem, and self-actualization needs. ERG theory includes existence, relatedness, and growth needs. Two-factor theory includes motivators and maintenance factors. Acquired needs theory includes achievement, power, and affiliation needs. (See Figures 12–1 and 12–4 for a comparison of the four content theories of motivation.)

4. Discuss the major similarity and difference among the three process motivation theories: equity, goal-setting, and expectancy.

The similarity among the three process motivation theories is their focus on understanding how employees choose behaviors to fulfill their needs. However, they are very different in how they perceive employees are motivated. Equity theory proposes that employees are motivated when their perceived inputs equal outputs. Goal-setting theory proposes that achievable but difficult goals motivate employees. Expectancy theory proposes that employees are motivated when they believe they can accomplish the task and the rewards for doing so are worth the effort.

5. Explain the four types of reinforcement: positive, avoidance, extinction, and punishment.

With positive reinforcement you provide the employee with a reward consequence for performing the desired behavior. With avoidance reinforcement you encourage employees to perform the desired behavior in order to avoid a negative consequence. With extinction reinforcement you withhold a positive consequence to get the employee to stop performing undesirable behavior. With punishment reinforcement you give the employee a negative consequence to get him or her to stop performing undesirable behavior.

6. State the major difference among content, process, and reinforcement theories.

Content motivation theories focus on identifying and understanding employees' needs. Process motivation goes a step further to understand how employees choose behavior to fulfill their needs. Reinforcement theory is not concerned about employees' needs; it focuses on getting employees to do what managers want them to do through the consequences provided by managers for their behavior. The use of rewards is the means of motivating employees.

7. Explain the major difference between the Japanese and U.S. approach to motivating employees.

The Japanese tend to focus their motivational systems on a group basis, whereas the Americans tend to focus their motivational systems on an individual basis.

8. Define the following key terms (in order of appearance in the chapter).

Select one or more methods: (1) fill in the missing key terms from memory, (2) match the key terms from the end of the summary with their definitions below, or (3) copy the key terms in order from the list at the beginning of the chapter.

_____ is the willingness to achieve organizational objectives.

Through the _____, employees go from need to motive to behavior to consequence to satisfaction or dissatisfaction.

In the _____ performance = ability × motivation × resources.

_____ focus on identifying and understanding employee needs.

The _____ proposes that employees are motivated through five levels of needs: physiological, safety, social, esteem, and self-actualization.

_____ proposes that employees are motivated by three needs: existence, relatedness, and growth.

_____ proposes that employees are motivated by motivators rather than maintenance factors.

_____ proposes that employees are motivated by their need for achievement, power, and affiliation.

_____ focus on understanding how employees choose behavior to fulfill their needs.

_____ proposes that employees are motivated when their perceived inputs equal outputs.

_____ proposes that achievable but difficult goals motivate employees.

_____ proposes that employees are motivated when they believe they can accomplish the task and the rewards for doing so are worth the effort.

_____ proposes that through the consequences for behavior employees will be motivated to behave in predetermined ways.

The steps in the _____ are as follows: (1) Tell the employee exactly what was done correctly. (2) Tell the employee why the behavior is important. (3) Stop for a moment of silence. (4) Encourage repeat performance.

KEY TERMS

acquired needs theory   427

content motivation theories   424

equity theory   430

ERG theory   425

expectancy theory   432

giving praise model   438

goal-setting theory   432

hierarchy of needs theory   424

motivation   420

motivation process   420

performance formula   422

process motivation theories   430

reinforcement theory   434

two-factor theory   426

REVIEW AND DISCUSSION QUESTIONS

1. What is motivation and why is it important to know how to motivate employees?

2. Do you agree that managers' attitudes and expectations affect employee motivation and performance? Explain your answer.

3. Do you agree with the performance formula? Will you use it on the job?

4. Do people really have diverse needs?

5. Which of the four content motivation theories do you prefer? Why?

6. Which of the three process motivation theories do you prefer? Why?

7. What reinforcement methods have been used to get you to go to work and to be on time?

8. Reinforcement theory is unethical because it is used to manipulate employees. Do you agree with this statement? Explain your answer.

9. Which motivation theory do you feel is the best? Explain why.

10. What is your motivation theory? What are the major methods, techniques, etc., you plan to use on the job as a manager to increase motivation and performance?

11. Do you agree with Deming's statement that Americans need to change to a group approach to compete in a global economy?

OBJECTIVE CASE

Friedman's Microwave Ovens

The following conversation took place between Art Friedman and Bob Lussier. In 1970, Art Friedman implemented a new business technique. At that time his business was called Friedman's Appliances and it employed 15 workers in Oakland, California. Friedman's is an actual business that uses the technique you will read about.

Bob: What is the reason for your success in business?

Art: My business technique.

Bob: What is it? How did you implement it?

Art: I called my 15 employees together and told them, "From now on I want you to feel as though the company is ours, not mine. We are all bosses. From now on you decide what you're worth and tell the accountant to put it in your pay envelope. You decide which days and hours you work and when to take time off. We will have an open petty cash system that will allow anyone to go into the box and borrow money when they need it."

Bob: You're kidding, right?

Art: No, it's true. I really do these things.

Bob: Did anyone ask for a raise?

Art: Yes, several people did. Charlie asked for and received a $100-a-week raise.

Bob: Did he and the others increase their productivity to earn their raises?

Art: Yes, they all did.

Bob: How could you run an appliance store with employees coming and going as they pleased?

Art: The employees made up schedules that were satisfactory to everyone. We had no problems of under- or overstaffing.

Bob: Did anyone steal from the petty cash box?

Art: No.

Bob: Would this technique work in any business?

Art: It did work, it still works, and it will always work!

In 1976, Art Friedman changed his strategy. Art's present business is Friedman's Microwave Ovens. It is a franchise operation, which still utilizes his technique of making everyone a boss. In its first three years, Art's business grew from one store in Oakland to 20 stores, which sold over 15,000 microwaves. In 1988 Art had over 100 stores nationwide. Friedman's now sells around 125,000 microwaves per year.

OBJECTIVE CASE
(continued)

Select the best alternative for the following questions. Be sure to be able to give an explanation to support your answers.

_____ 1. Art's techniques focus on motivation and performance.

    a. true   b. false

_____ 2. Art focused on which factor in the performance formula?

    a. ability b. motivation c. resources

_____ 3. Art's employees appear to be on which needs level for their job?

    a. physiological   d. esteem

    b. safety   e. self-actualization

    c. social

_____ 4. Art is focusing on which level of ERG needs?

    a. existence b. relatedness c. growth

_____ 5. Art's technique has less emphasis on meeting which need?

    a. achievement b. power c. affiliation

_____ 6. Herzberg would say Art is using

    a. maintenance b. motivators

_____ 7. Vroom would agree that Art uses expectancy motivation theory.

    a. true   b. false

_____ 8. Adams would say Art has

    a. equitable rewards

    b. underrewards

    c. overrewards

_____ 9. Art uses goal-setting theory.

    a. true   b. false

_____ 10. Art uses which types of reinforcement?

    a. positive   c. extinction

    b. avoidance   d. punishment

11. Do you know of any organizations that use Art's or any other unusual techniques? If yes, what is the organization's name? What does it do?

12. Could Art's technique work in all organizations? Explain your answer.

13. In a position of authority, would you use Art's technique? Explain your answer.

For current information on Friedman's Microwave Ovens, use Internet address http://www.friedmansmicrowave.com.

BEHAVIOR MODEL VIDEO

Behavior Model Video 12–1 (4½ minutes), Giving Praise, shows a bank branch manager, Laura, giving praise to Kelly, a teller, for successfully handling an angry customer. Laura follows the steps in Model 12–1. This video serves as a behavior model, which can be used prior to conducting Skill-Building Exercise 12–1.

Skill-Building Exercise 12–1

R

Giving Praise

Preparing for Skill-Building Exercise 12–1
Think of a job situation in which you did something well, deserving of praise and recognition. For example, you may have saved the company some money, you may have turned a dissatisfied customer into a happy one, and so on. If you have never worked or done something well, interview someone who has. Put yourself in a management position and write out the praise you would give to an employee for doing what you did.

Briefly describe the situation:

_____

_____

_____

Step 1. Tell the employee exactly what was done correctly.

_____

_____

_____

Step 2. Tell the employee why the behavior is important.

_____

_____

_____

Step 3. Stop for a moment of silence. (Count to five silently.)

Step 4. Encourage repeat performance.

_____

_____

_____

Doing Skill-Building Exercise 12–1 in Class
Objective
To develop your skill at giving praise.

Preparation
You should have completed the preparation for this exercise by rating the 12 job factors prior to class.

Experience
You will give and receive praise.

Video (5–10 minutes)
Behavior Model Video 12–1, Giving Praise, may be shown to illustrate how to give praise.

Procedure (12–17 minutes)
Break into groups of four to six. One at a time, give the praise.

1. Explain the situation.
2. Select a group member to receive the praise.
3. Give the praise. (Talk; don't read it off the paper.) Try to select the position you would use if you were actually giving the praise on the job (both standing, both sitting, etc.).
4. Integration. The group gives the giver of praise feedback on how he or she did:
   Step 1. Was the praise very specific and descriptive? Did the giver look the employee in the eye?
   Step 2. Was the importance of the behavior clearly stated?
   Step 3. Did the giver stop for a moment of silence?
   Step 4. Did the giver encourage repeat performance? Did the giver of praise touch the receiver (optional)?

Did the praise take less than one minute? Was the praise sincere?

Conclusion
The instructor leads a class discussion and/or makes concluding remarks.

Application (2–4 minutes)
What did I learn from this experience? How will I use this knowledge in the future?

_____

_____

Sharing
Volunteers give their answers to the application section.

Exercise 12–1

G

Job Motivators and Maintenance Factors

Preparing for Exercise 12–1 (Self-Assessment)

Self-Assessment Exercise 12–2

What Motivates You?

Following are 12 job factors that contribute to job satisfaction. Rate each according to how important it is to you by placing the number 1–5 on the line before each factor.

Very important	Somewhat important	Not important
5 ——— 4 ———	3 ——— 2 ———	1

_____ 1. An interesting job I enjoy doing.

_____ 2. A good boss that treats people fairly.

_____ 3. Getting praise and other recognition and appreciation for the work that I do.

_____ 4. A satisfying personal life at the job.

_____ 5. The opportunity for advancement.

_____ 6. A prestigious or status job.

_____ 7. Job responsibility that gives me freedom to do things my way.

_____ 8. Good working conditions (safe environment, nice office, cafeteria, etc.).

_____ 9. The opportunity to learn new things.

_____ 10. Sensible company rules, regulations, procedures, and policies.

_____ 11. A job I can do well and succeed at.

_____ 12. Job security.

Place the numbers 1–5 that represent your answers below.

Motivating Factors Score	Maintenance Factors Score
1. ___	2. ___
3. ___	4. ___
5. ___	6. ___
7. ___	8. ___
9. ___	10. ___
11. ___	12. ___
___ Total points	___

Add each column vertically. Did you select motivators or maintenance factors as being more important to you?

Doing Exercise 12–1 in Class
Objectives
To help you better understand how job factors affect motivation. To help you realize that people are motivated by different factors. What motivates you may turn someone else off.

Preparation
You should have completed the preparation for this exercise.

Experience
You will discuss the importance of job factors.

Procedure 1 (8–20 minutes)
Break into groups of four to six and discuss job factors selected by group members in the preparation for this exercise. Come to a consensus on the three factors that are most important to the group. They can be either motivators or maintenance factors. If the group mentions other job factors not listed, such as pay, you may add them.

Procedure 2 (3–6 minutes)
A representative from each group goes to the board and writes its group's three most important job factors.

Conclusion
The instructor leads a class discussion and/or makes concluding remarks.

Application (2–4 minutes)
What did I learn from this experience? How will I use this knowledge in the future?

_____

_____

Sharing
Volunteers give their answers to the application section.

13

Leading

Learning Objectives

After studying this chapter, you should be able to:

1. State the difference among trait, behavioral, and situational leadership theorists.

2. Explain why the terms *management* and *leadership* are not interchangeable.

3. Describe leadership trait theory and, according to Ghiselli, the most important leadership trait.

4. Discuss the major similarity and difference between two-dimensional leadership styles and the Leadership Grid.

5. Identify the management levels that are the focus of charismatic, transformational, transactional, and symbolic leadership.

6. State the primary difference between the contingency leadership model and the other situational leadership models.

7. Discuss the major criticism shared by the leadership continuum model and the path-goal leadership model.

8. Describe the major characteristic shared by the normative leadership model and the situational leadership model.

9. Define the following **key terms** (in order of appearance in the chapter):

leadership

leadership trait theorists

behavioral leadership
   theorists

leadership style

two-dimensional
   leadership styles

leadership grid model

charismatic leadership

transformational leadership

transactional leadership

symbolic leadership

situational leadership theorists

contingency leadership model

leadership continuum model

path-goal model

normative leadership model

situational leadership model

substitutes for leadership

complaint

*skillbuilder

1. You can develop your ability to select the appropriate leadership style for a given situation using the situational leadership model (Skill-Building Exercise 13–1).

Leadership skill is one of the four functions of management and requires human and communication and often decision-making skills. Leadership requires interpersonal management roles of leader and liaison; informational roles of monitor, disseminator, and spokesperson; and decisional roles of disturbance handler and negotiator. The SCANS competencies of interpersonal skills and information are developed, as well as basic and thinking skills and personal qualities foundation skills, through the exercises.

*skillbuilder

2. You can develop your skill to better handle complaints (Skill-Building Exercise 13–2).

Handling complaints takes human and communication skills and is an important part of the decisional roles: the disturbance-handler and negotiator roles and possibly the resource-allocator role, depending on the complaint. The SCANS skill competencies of using resources, interpersonal, information, and systems, as well as the basic, thinking, and personal qualities foundation skills are also developed.

Liz Claiborne worked in the clothing industry and developed a reputation as a top-notch women's fashion designer. In the 1970s, as the number of career women increased, Liz saw a gap between the casual slacks and jeans look and the boardroom-career suit with bow tie look. She believed that women wanted clothing that would give them style, quality, fit, and value. A huge market existed for relaxed yet functional and coordinated separates that career women could mix and match.

In January 1976, Liz and her husband Arthur Ortenberg started Liz Claiborne Inc. with $50,000 of savings and $200,000 from family and friends. After only one year, sales reached $200 million. People in the fashion industry referred to Liz as a "visionary" and "the great pathfinder." After only 11 years, Liz Claiborne was included in the Fortune 500 largest company list. Liz Claiborne was one of the youngest companies, and only one of two companies started by a woman to make the Fortune 500. Liz Claiborne grew to become the largest women's apparel company in the world, and it does not own any manufacturing facilities, nor does it have a sales force on the road. Claiborne outsources manufacturing to independent suppliers overseas. Liz built the business into a $2 billion-plus fashion empire before turning over the leadership position to Jerome Chazen.

Liz Claiborne grew to become the top-selling women's clothing label for two important reasons. First, Liz and her employees really listen to their customers and design the clothing to fit their lifestyles and build a whole wardrobe around what they want. Liz Claiborne offers customer value. There are 150 specialists who visit stores, talk to customers, and give seminars to salespeople. Retailers say

that Liz Claiborne responds to the customer better than any other apparel company. This is especially important in the global marketplace where women in different countries have very different preferences. Liz Claiborne entered the continental European market in the 1980s.

Second, the company's success resulted from Liz's leadership. Liz wanted employees to feel as though they are a part of the company. She wanted employees with team spirit. Therefore, Liz spent part of each work day with the teams of designers. Liz did not do the designs herself; she worked with the teams to develop their design skills. Liz delegated responsibility to the teams and rewarded their success. Through her coaching leadership style, Liz built positive relationships with employees.

For current information on Liz Claiborne, use Internet address **http://www.lizclaiborne.com**. For ideas on using the Internet, see Appendix B.

---

1. State the difference among trait, behavioral, and situational leadership theorists.

LEADERSHIP AND TRAIT THEORY

In this section, you will study leadership and its importance in organizations, the difference between leadership and management, and leadership trait theory.

Leadership

leadership
The process of influencing employees to work toward the achievement of organizational objectives.

Leadership *is the process of influencing employees to work toward the achievement of organizational objectives.* Leadership is one of the most talked-about, researched, and written-about management topics. Ralph Stogdill's well-known *Handbook of Leadership* contains over 3,000 references on the topic, and Bass's revision of it contains well over 5,000 publications on leadership.[1] Survey results have revealed that academicians and practitioners alike agree that leadership is the most important topic of all within the realm of organizational behavior/human relations.[2] The major reason for employee failure is poor leadership.[3] To succeed in the global arena, leadership is imperative.[4] Thus, organizations have placed increased importance on leadership training and development.[5] A current trend is to focus on team leadership[6] as organizations realize that an effective senior leadership team is essential for success.[7] Thus, human resources managers are taking a greater role in leadership skill development.[8]

Leadership and Management Are Not the Same

People tend to use the terms *manager* and *leader* interchangeably. However, managers and leaders differ. Leading is one of the four management functions (planning, organizing, leading, and controlling). Management is broader in scope than leadership; leading is only one of the management functions.[9] A manager can have this position without being a true leader. There are managers—you may know of some—who are not leaders because they do not have the ability to influence others. There are also good leaders who are not managers. The informal leader, an employee group member, is a case in point. You may have worked in a situation where one of your peers had more influence in the department than the manager. Managers need to change from being the boss to being the leader.[10] Everyone has the potential to become an effective leader.[11] You can develop your leadership skills by applying the principles in this chapter. Liz Claiborne is both an effective manager and leader.

Leadership Trait Theory

An organized approach to studying leadership began in the early 1900s. Over the years, the trait, behavioral, and contingency paradigms of leadership have contributed to the development of an understanding of leadership.[12] Thus, in this section you will learn about trait theory, and in the next two sections about behavioral and contingency leadership theories.

The early studies were based on the assumption that leaders are born, not made. Researchers wanted to identify a set of characteristics or traits that distinguished leaders from followers or effective from ineffective leaders. **Leadership trait theorists** *attempt to determine a list of distinctive characteristics accounting for leadership effectiveness.* Researchers analyzed physical and psychological traits, or qualities, such as appearance, aggressiveness, self-reliance, persuasiveness, and dominance in an effort to identify a set of traits that all successful leaders possessed. The list of traits would be a prerequisite for promotion of candidates to leadership positions. Only candidates possessing all the identified traits were to be given leadership positions.

Inconclusive Findings. In 70 years, over 300 trait studies were conducted.[13] However, no one compiled a universal list of traits that all successful leaders possess. In all cases, there were exceptions. For example, several lists identified successful leaders as being tall. However, Napoleon was short. On the other hand, some organizations came up with a list of traits and found people who possessed them all, only to find that these people were not successful leaders. In addition, some people were successful in one leadership position but not in another. People also questioned whether traits like assertiveness and self-confidence were developed before or after one became a leader. Peter Drucker says there is no such thing as "leadership qualities or a leadership personality."[14] Indeed, if leaders were simply born and

---

2. Explain why the terms *management* and *leadership* are not interchangeable.

3. Describe leadership trait theory and, according to Ghiselli, the most important leadership trait.

leadership trait theorists
Attempt to determine a list of distinctive characteristics accounting for leadership effectiveness.

not made (in other words, if leadership skills could not be developed), there would be no need for courses in management.

The Ghiselli Study. Edwin Ghiselli conducted probably the most widely publicized trait theory study. He studied over 300 managers from 90 different businesses in the United States and published his results in 1971.[15] He concluded that certain traits are important to effective leadership, though not all of them are necessary for success. Ghiselli identified the following six traits, in order of importance, as being significant traits for effective leadership: (1) *Supervisory ability*. Getting the job done through others. Basically, the ability to perform the four functions of management you are studying in this course. (2) *Need for occupational achievement*. Seeking responsibility. The motivation to work hard to succeed. (3) *Intelligence*. The ability to use good judgment, reasoning, and thinking capacity. (4) *Decisiveness*. The ability to solve problems and make decisions competently. (5) *Self-assurance*. Viewing oneself as capable of coping with problems. Behaving in a manner that shows others that you have self-esteem. (6) *Initiative*. Self-starting in getting the job done with a minimum of supervision from one's boss. Liz Claiborne has demonstrated supervisory ability, and probably all of the other traits as well.

Current Use of Trait Theory. Even though it is generally agreed that no universal set of leadership traits or qualities exists, people continue to study and write about leadership traits. For example, in Chapter 1 you completed Self-Assessment Exercise 1–1, which answered the question, What are the most important traits for success as a manager? They included integrity, industriousness, and ability to get along with people.

Personality Traits. Recall (Chapter 9) that your personality is made up of traits. It is personality, and other types of traits, that researchers were trying to identify. Thus, personality is an important part of trait theory, because organizations today continue to select managers with identified personality traits.[16] Recall (Chapter 8) that some organizations give personality tests as part of the selection process. To be an effective leader, you must first be yourself and be aware of who you are as a leader.[17] You get to know yourself better through the self-assessment exercises throughout this book. Your personality traits affect your leadership style; however, you can change your personality for the better (Exercise 9–1) and still be yourself.

Ethics and Spirituality in the Workplace. Recall the importance of business ethics (Chapter 2). A leader's ethical behavior is strongly based on personal values,[18] which are also based on personality. Leading by example is important today.[19] Related to ethics and values is spirituality. People are questioning, "Why am I here?"[20] They are looking for meaning in life at work. Organizations are offering programs to help employees find this meaning by engaging consulting firms such as Spirit at Work.[21]

WORK APPLICATION

1. Of Ghiselli's six traits, explain which ones your present/past boss does and does not possess.

Evangelist Billy Graham said that the four main character traits that are personal qualities of leadership are: (1) *Integrity*—being the same on the inside as you claim to be on the outside. (2) *Personal security*—knowing and accepting who you are, why you are here, and where you are going. (3) *Sense of priority*—"You should love the Lord your God with all your heart, all your soul, and all your strength. Seek God's Kingdom first, and all these other things will be added unto you." (4) *Vision*—a determination to do God's will.[22] Zig Ziglar, world famous motivational speaker and best-selling author who trains people to be successful,[23] and Peter Lowe, who conducts Success seminars all over the world,[24] also teach that proper emphasis on the spiritual aspects of life is extremely important to success. Research has shown that people who attend church regularly make more money, have better health, are happier with their jobs and family life, and have a much lower divorce rate. "In short, they get more of the things that money can buy and all of the things that money can't buy."[25]

BEHAVIORAL LEADERSHIP THEORIES

By the late 1940s, most of the leadership research had changed from analyzing trait theory to focusing on what the leader did. In the continuing quest to find the best leadership style in all situations, researchers attempted to identify the differences in the behavior of the effective leaders versus the ineffective leaders. The focus on what leaders do and how they behave provides an insight into the relationship between leaders and their followers.[26] **Behavioral leadership theorists** *attempt to determine distinctive styles used by effective leaders.* Recall that Douglas McGregor, a behavioral theorist, developed Theory X and Theory Y. Complete Self-Assessment Exercise 13–1 to determine your leadership behavior according to Theory X and Theory Y.

behavioral leadership theorists
Attempt to determine distinctive styles used by effective leaders.

Self-Assessment Exercise 13–1

McGregor Theory X and Theory Y Behavior

For each of the following ten statements, place the letter (U, F, O, S) that best describes what you would do as a manager on the line preceding the statement. There are no right or wrong answers.

Usually (U)   Frequently (F)
Occasionally (O)   Seldom (S)

____ 1. I would set the objectives for my department alone, rather than include employees' input.

____ 2. I would allow employees to develop their own plans, rather than develop them myself.

_____ 3. I would delegate several tasks I enjoy doing to employees, rather than do them myself.

_____ 4. I would allow employees to make decisions to solve problems, rather than make them myself.

_____ 5. I would recruit and select new employees alone, rather than include employees' input.

_____ 6. I would orient and train new employees myself, rather than have employees do it.

_____ 7. I would tell employees only what they need to know, rather than give them access to anything they want to know.

_____ 8. I would spend time praising and recognizing my employees' work efforts, rather than just give criticism.

_____ 9. I would set several controls for employees to ensure that objectives are met, rather than allow employees to set their own controls.

_____ 10. I would frequently observe my employees to ensure that they are working and meeting deadlines, rather than leave them alone.

To better understand your own behavior toward employees, score your answers. For items 1, 5, 6, 7, 9, and 10, give yourself one point for each usually (U) answer; two points for each frequently (F) answer; three points for each occasionally (O) answer; and four points for each seldom (S) answer. For items 2, 3, 4, and 8, give yourself one point for each seldom (S) answer; two points for each occasionally (O) answer; three points for each frequently (F) answer; and four points for each usually (U) answer. Total all points. Your score should be between 10 and 40. Place your score here _____. Theory X and Theory Y are on opposite ends of a continuum. Some people's behavior falls somewhere between the two extremes. Place a checkmark on the continuum that represents your score.

Theory X 10——20——30——40 Theory Y
Behavior   Behavior
(More Autocratic)   (More Participative)

The lower your score (10), the stronger the Theory X behavior, and the higher your score (40), the stronger the Theory Y behavior. A score of 20–30 could be considered balanced between the two theories. Your score may not be an accurate measure of how you would behave in an actual job. However, it should help you to understand your own behavior toward your employees.

In this section you will study the basic leadership styles, two-dimensional leadership styles, The Leadership Grid, and contemporary perspectives on behavior leadership.

Basic Leadership Styles

leadership style
The combination of traits, skills, and behaviors managers use to interact with employees.

Leadership style _is the combination of traits, skills, and behaviors managers use to interact with employees._ Note that behavioral theorists focus on the leaders' behavior. However, leaders' behaviors are also based on their traits and skills.

In the 1930s, before behavioral theory became popular, research was conducted on the leadership style of the manager. The studies identified three basic leadership styles: (1) _Autocratic:_ The leader makes the decisions, tells employees what to do, and closely supervises employees—similar to Theory X behavior. (2) _Democratic:_ The leader encourages employee participation in decisions, works with employees to determine what to do, and does not closely supervise employees—similar to Theory Y behavior. (3) _Laissez-_

Faire: The leader takes a leave-the-employees-alone approach, allowing them to make the decisions, decide what to do, and does not follow up. The Iowa studies contributed to the behavioral movement and led to an era of behavioral rather than trait research.

Liz Claiborne used the democratic style as she worked with the design teams rather than making the designs for them or leaving them alone. However, Liz Claiborne also used the laissez-faire leadership style when she left design teams alone to make decisions.

Two-Dimensional Leadership Styles

Two-dimensional leadership styles *are based on job structure and employee consideration, which result in four possible leadership styles.* The two dimensions are structuring (job-centered) and consideration (employee-centered).

Structuring and Consideration Styles. In 1945, the Personnel Research Board of Ohio State University, under the principal direction of Ralph Stogdill, began a study to determine effective leadership styles. In the attempt to measure leadership styles, they developed an instrument known as the Leader Behavior Description Questionnaire (LBDQ). Respondents to the questionnaire perceived their leader's behavior toward them on two distinct dimensions:

1. *Initiating structure.* The extent to which the leader takes charge to plan, organize, lead, and control as the employee performs the task. It focuses on getting the job done.

2. *Consideration.* The extent to which the leader communicates to develop trust, friendship, support, and respect. It focuses on developing relationships with employees.

Job-Centered and Employee-Centered Styles. At approximately the same time the Ohio State studies began, the University of Michigan's Survey Research Center began leadership studies under the principal direction of Rensis Likert. Their research identified the same two dimensions or styles of leadership behavior. However, they called the two styles *job-centered* (the same as initiating structure) and *employee-centered* (the same as consideration).

Using Two-Dimensional Leadership Styles. When interacting with employees, the manager can focus on getting the job done through directing (initiating structure, job-centered behavior) and/or developing supportive relationships (consideration, employee-centered behavior). Combinations of the two dimensions of leadership result in four leadership styles, which Figure 13–1 illustrates. The Ohio State and University of Michigan Leadership Models differ because UM placed the two dimensions at opposite ends of the same continuum. OSU considered the two dimensions independent of one another.

---

4. Discuss the major similarity and difference between two-dimensional leadership styles and the Leadership Grid.

two-dimensional leadership styles
Based on job structure and employee consideration, which result in four possible leadership styles.

WORK APPLICATION

2. Recall a present or past boss. Which of the four leadership styles, based on the two-dimensional leadership style, did your boss use most often? Describe the behavior of your boss.

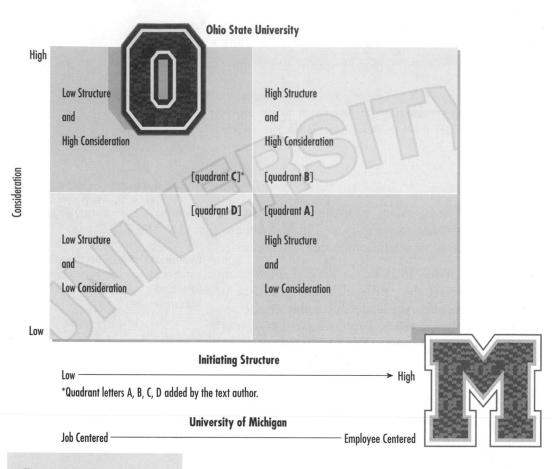

Ohio State University

Consideration

High

Low Structure
and
High Consideration

[quadrant **C**]*

High Structure
and
High Consideration

[quadrant **B**]

[quadrant **D**]

[quadrant **A**]

Low Structure
and
Low Consideration

High Structure
and
Low Consideration

Low

Initiating Structure

Low ——————————————————————→ High

*Quadrant letters A, B, C, D added by the text author.

University of Michigan

Job Centered ————————————————— Employee Centered

Figure 13-1
*The Ohio State and
University of Michigan
Two-Dimensional
Leadership Styles*

With the design teams, Liz Claiborne tended to use a high structure (job-centered) and high consideration (employee-centered) leadership style. However, sometimes she left the design teams alone, using low structure (job-centered) and low consideration (employee-centered).

The Leadership Grid®

Robert Blake and Jane Mouton developed the Managerial Grid[27] which later became the Leadership Grid,[28] with Anne Adams McCanse replacing Mouton. The Leadership Grid is based on the same two leadership dimensions, which they called "concern for production" and "concern for people." *The* **leadership grid model** *identifies the ideal leadership style as having a high concern for both production and people.* They use a questionnaire to measure the concern for both people and production on a scale from 1 to 9. Therefore, the grid has 81 possible combinations of concern for production and people. Figure 13–2 is an adaptation of the Leadership Grid. However, they identify five major styles:

leadership grid model
Identifies the ideal leadership style as having a high concern for both production and people.

(1, 1)   *The impoverished leader* has low concern for both production and people. The leader does the minimum required to remain employed in the position.

(9, 1)   *The authority-compliance leader* has a high concern for production and a low concern for people. The leader focuses on getting the job done as people are treated like machines.

(1, 9)   *The country club leader* has a high concern for people and a low concern for production. The leader strives to maintain a friendly atmosphere without regard for production.

(5, 5)   *The middle of the road leader* has balanced, medium concern for both production and people. The leader strives to maintain minimal satisfactory performance and morale.

(9, 9)   *The team leader* has a high concern for both production and people. This leader strives for maximum performance and employee satis-faction. According to the behavioral theorists, the team leadership style is the most appropriate style to use in all situations. However, researchers have found this belief to be a myth.[29] The trend toward teams has resulted in a call for leaders to have a balanced directive and supportive style.[30] Liz Claiborne most likely changed management styles, but commonly used the team leader style.

Figure 13-2
Blake, Mouton, and
McCanse Leadership Grid

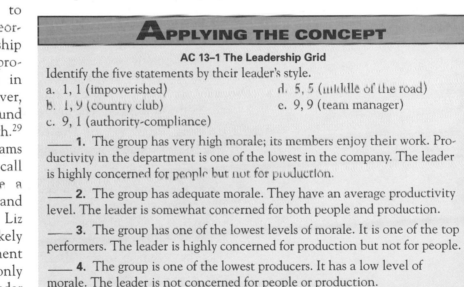

APPLYING THE CONCEPT

AC 13–1 The Leadership Grid

Identify the five statements by their leader's style.

a. 1, 1 (impoverished)   d. 5, 5 (middle of the road)
b. 1, 9 (country club)   e. 9, 9 (team manager)
c. 9, 1 (authority-compliance)

____ **1.** The group has very high morale; its members enjoy their work. Productivity in the department is one of the lowest in the company. The leader is highly concerned for people but not for production.

____ **2.** The group has adequate morale. They have an average productivity level. The leader is somewhat concerned for both people and production.

____ **3.** The group has one of the lowest levels of morale. It is one of the top performers. The leader is highly concerned for production but not for people.

____ **4.** The group is one of the lowest producers. It has a low level of morale. The leader is not concerned for people or production.

____ **5.** The group is one of the top performers. They have high morale. The leader is highly concerned for both people and production.

Contemporary Perspectives

Current researchers focus on top-notch managers who exhibit certain behaviors that make them outstanding despite the possibility of wide variations in individual leadership styles.[31] Some of the current behavioral researchers focus on charismatic, transformational, transactional, and symbolic leadership.

Charismatic Leadership. **Charismatic leadership** *is based on a leadership style that inspires loyalty, enthusiasm, and high levels of performance.* The term *charismatic* has been applied to many leaders including Pope John Paul II and Mother Teresa (Catholic Church leaders), Martin Luther King, Jr.

**WORK
APPLICATION**

3. Recall a present or past boss. Which of the five leadership grid styles did your boss use most often? Describe the behavior of your boss.

charismatic leadership
Based on a leadership style that inspires loyalty, enthusiasm, and high levels of performance.

5. Identify the management levels that are the focus of charismatic, transformational, transactional, and symbolic leadership.

(civil rights leader), Michael Jordan (basketball), Mary Kay Ashe (Mary Kay Cosmetics), Liz Claiborne (Liz Claiborne), Lee Iacocca (Chrysler), and Bill Gates (Microsoft). Charismatic leaders have an idealized goal or vision, have a strong personal commitment to that goal, communicate the goal to others, display self-confidence, and are viewed as being able to make the radical changes needed to reach the goal.[32] The followers in turn trust the leaders' beliefs, adopt those beliefs themselves, feel affection for the leaders, obey the leaders, and develop an emotional involvement with the goal, which leads to higher levels of performance.[33] Researchers have recommended that top-level managers should attempt to develop the charismatic roles of leadership as part of organizational culture.[34]

transformational leadership
Based on change, innovation, and entrepreneurship as the manager continually takes the organization through three acts.

Transformational Leadership. **Transformational leadership** *is based on change, innovation, and entrepreneurship as the manager continually takes the organization through three acts.* Although all leaders can be transformational leaders, the primary focus is on top-level managers, CEOs of large organizations who are considered to be charismatic leaders. Transformational leaders perform, or take the organization through, three acts on an ongoing basis:[35, 36]

Act 1. Recognizing the need for revitalization. The transformational leader recognizes the need to change the organization to keep up with the rapid changes in the environment and to keep ahead of the global competition, which is becoming more competitive all the time.

Act 2. Creating a new vision. The transformational leader visualizes the changed organization and motivates people to make it become a reality.

Act 3. Institutionalizing change. The transformational leader guides people as they make the vision become a reality. Recent studies found that transformational leadership had a positive effect on organizations.[37, 38] Liz Claiborne was a successful transformational leader because she continually scanned the environment and made the necessary changes to stay ahead of the competition.

transactional leadership
Based on leadership style and exchange.

Transactional Leadership. Transformational leadership has been contrasted with transactional leadership.[39] **Transactional leadership** *is based on leadership style and exchange.* The exchange is based on the principle of "you do this work for me and I'll give this reward to you." The manager may engage in both task and consideration leadership behavior with employees during the exchange. Transactional leadership focuses more on middle and first-line management. However, top level managers usually approve of monetary rewards used by the lower-level managers in exchanges.

symbolic leadership
Based on establishing and maintaining a strong organizational culture.

Symbolic Leadership. **Symbolic leadership** *is based on establishing and maintaining a strong organizational culture* (Chapter 7). Employees learn the culture (shared values, beliefs, and assumptions of how they should behave in the organization) through leadership.[40] Liz Claiborne took a team approach to leadership in designing women's clothing. She emphasized sharing ideas and open communication when working with design teams. Employees throughout the organization recognized and adopted these values. Symbolic leadership starts with top management and should flow down to middle and first-line managers.

SITUATIONAL LEADERSHIP THEORIES

Both the trait and behavioral leadership theories were attempts to find the best leadership style in all situations. In the late 1960s, it became apparent that one leadership style is not appropriate in all situations. A recent study showed no relationship between leadership style and financial performance.[41] The trend toward teams has also shown that leadership styles vary from one group to another.[42]

Situational leadership theorists *attempt to determine the appropriate leadership style for various situations.* In this section you will study some of the most popular situational or contingency leadership theories, including contingency leadership theory, leadership continuum, path-goal theory, normative leadership theory, and situational leadership. You will also learn about leadership substitutes and neutralizers.

Contingency Leadership Model

In 1951, Fred E. Fiedler began to develop the first situational leadership theory—"Contingency Theory of Leader Effectiveness."[13] Fiedler believed that one's leadership style reflects one's personality (trait theory oriented) and remains basically constant. Leaders do not change styles. *The* **contingency leadership model** *is used to determine if one's leadership style is task- or relationship-oriented and if the situation matches the leader's style.*

Leadership Style. The first major factor is to determine one's leadership style as being task- or relationship-oriented. To do so, the leader fills in the Least Preferred Coworker (LPC) scales. The LPC essentially answers the question, Are you more task-oriented or relationship-oriented in working with others? The two leadership styles are *task* and *relationship*. Note that unlike two-dimensional leadership, there are only two, not four leadership styles.

Situational Favorableness. After determining your leadership style, you determine the situational favorableness. Situation favorableness refers to the degree a situation enables the leader to exert influence over the followers. The three variables, in order of importance, are:

1. *Leader-member relations.* Is the relationship good or poor? Do the followers trust, respect, accept, and have confidence in the leader? Is it a friendly, tension-free situation? Leaders with good relations have more influence. The better the relations, the more favorable the situation.

2. *Task structure.* Is the task structured or unstructured? Do employees perform repetitive, routine, unambiguous, standard tasks that are easily

WORK APPLICATION

4. Recall the top manager from an organization you work or have worked for. Would you call this CEO a charismatic transformational leader? Why or why not?

situational leadership theorists
Attempt to determine the appropriate leadership style for various situations.

6. State the primary difference between the contingency leadership model and the other situational leadership models.

contingency leadership model
Used to determine if one's leadership style is task- or relationship-oriented and if the situation matches the leader's style.

understood? Leaders in a structured situation have more influence. The more repetitive the jobs, the more favorable the situation.

3. *Position power.* Is position power strong or weak? Does the leader have the power to assign work, reward and punish, hire and fire, and give raises and promotions? The leader with position power has more influence. The more power, the more favorable the situation.

Determining the Appropriate Leadership Style. To determine whether task or relationship leadership is appropriate, the user answers the three questions pertaining to situational favorableness, using the Fiedler contingency theory model. Figure 13–3 shows an adapted model. The user starts with question 1 and follows the decision tree to *good* or *poor* depending on the relations. The user then answers question 2. When answering question 3, the user ends up in one of eight possible situations.

Liz Claiborne had *good* relations with design teams, the task is *nonrepetitive,* and Liz had *strong* position power as CEO. This is *Situation 3,* in which the appropriate leadership style is *task.* If Liz's preferred style were task, Fiedler would say do nothing. However, if Liz's preferred style was relationship, Fiedler would suggest that Liz change the situation to meet her preferred leadership style.

One of the major criticisms of Fiedler concerns his view that leaders should change their style rather than the situation.[44] The other situational writers suggest changing leadership styles, not the situation. More recently, Fiedler has written about the leader knowing when to lead and when to stand back.[45]

Leadership Continuum Model

Robert Tannenbaum and Warren Schmidt stated that leadership behavior occurs on a continuum from boss-centered to employee-centered leadership. Their model focuses on who makes the decisions. They identify seven ma-

	1. Are leader and follower relations good or poor?	2. Is the task repetitive or nonrepetitive?	3. Is the leader's power strong or weak?	Situation	Appropriate Style for Situation
		repetitive	strong	1	Task
	good		weak	2	Task
		nonrepetitive	strong	3	Task
Start			weak	4	Relationship
		repetitive	strong	5	Relationship
	poor		weak	6	Relationship
		nonrepetitive	strong	7	Relationship
			weak	8	Task

If the manager's preferred leadership style matches the situation, the manager does nothing. If the preferred leadership style does not match the situation, the manager changes the situation to match his or her preferred leadership style.

Figure 13-3
Fiedler Contingency Leadership Model

jor styles from which the leader can choose. Figure 13–4, an adaptation of their model, lists the seven styles.[46] The **leadership continuum model** *is used to determine which of seven styles to select based on one's use of boss-centered versus employee-centered leadership.*

Before selecting one of the seven leadership styles, the leader must consider the following three factors or variables:

The Manager. The leader's preferred style, based on experience, expectation, values, background, knowledge, feeling of security, and confidence in the subordinates is considered in selecting a leadership style.

The Subordinates. The subordinates' preferred style for the leader, based on experience, expectation, and so on is considered in selecting a leadership style. Generally, the more willing and able the subordinates are to participate, the more freedom of participation should be used, and vice versa.

The Situation. The environmental considerations, such as the organization's size, structure, climate, goals, and technology, are considered in selecting a leadership style. Upper-level managers also influence leadership styles. For example, if a middle manager uses an autocratic leadership style, the supervisor may tend to use it, too. The time available is also another consideration.

leadership continuum model
Used to determine which of seven styles to select based on one's use of boss-centered versus employee-centered leadership.

WORK APPLICATION

6. Using the leadership continuum model, identify your boss's most commonly used leadership style by number. Would you say this is the most appropriate leadership style based on the manager, subordinates, and situation? Explain.

Figure 13-4
Tannenbaum and Schmidt's Leadership Continuum Model

Autocratic Style

Participative Style

1. Leader makes decision and announces it to employees individually or in a group without discussion. (It could also be in writing.)	2. Leader makes decision and sells it to employees through a presentation of why it's a good idea. (It could also be in writing.)	3. Leader presents ideas and invites employee questions.	4. Leader presents tentative decision subject to change.	5. Leader presents problem, gets suggested solutions, and makes the decision.	6. Leader defines limits and asks the employees to make a decision.	7. Leader permits employees to make ongoing decisions within defined limits.

APPLYING THE CONCEPT

AC 13–3 Leadership Continuum

Using Figure 13–4, match the five statements with their style.

a. 1   b. 2   c. 3   d. 4   e. 5   f. 6   g. 7

_____ **11.** "Chuck, I selected you to be transferred to the new department, but you don't have to go if you don't want to."

_____ **12.** "Sam, go clean off the tables right away."

_____ **13.** "From now on, this is the way it will be done. Does anyone have any question about the procedure?"

_____ **14.** "These are the two weeks we can go on vacation. You select one."

_____ **15.** "I'd like your ideas on how to stop the bottleneck on the production line. But I have the final say on the solution we implement."

In a follow-up to their original 1973 article, Tannenbaum and Schmidt recommended that the leader become a group member when allowing the group to make decisions; that the leader clearly state the style (subordinate's authority) being used; that the leader should not try to trick the followers into thinking they made a decision that was actually made by the leader; and that it's not the number of decisions the followers make, but rather, their significance that counts.[47]

Even though the continuum leadership model was very popular, one of the major criticisms concerns the fact that the three factors to consider when selecting a leadership style are very subjective. In other words, determining which style to use when is difficult. Although Liz Claiborne changed leadership styles to meet the needs of the situation, she tended to make greater use of the participative styles.

Path-Goal Model

path-goal model
Used to determine employee objectives and to clarify how to achieve them using one of four styles.

Robert House developed the path-goal leadership model.[48] *The* **path-goal model** *is used to determine employee objectives and to clarify how to achieve them using one of four styles.* It focuses on how leaders influence employees' perceptions of their goals and the paths they follow toward goal attainment. As shown in Figure 13–5 (an adaptation of the model), the model uses the sit-

Situational Factors (determine)	Leadership Styles (affect)	Goal Achievement

Subordinate
    authoritarianism
    locus of control
    ability
Environment
    task structure
    formal authority
    work group
	Directive
	Supportive
	Participative
	Achievement-oriented
		Performance
		Satisfaction

Figure 13-5
*House Path-Goal
Leadership Model*

uational factors to determine the leadership style that affects goal achievement through performance and satisfaction.

Situational Factors. *Subordinate* situational characteristics include: (1) authoritarianism—the degree to which employees defer to and want to be told what to do and how to do the job; (2) locus of control—the extent to which employees believe they control goal achievement (internal) or if goal achievement is controlled by others (external); and (3) ability—the extent of employee ability to perform tasks to achieve goals. *Environment* situational factors include: (1) task structure—the extent of repetitiveness of the job; (2) formal authority—the extent of the leader's power; and (3) work group—the extent to which coworkers contribute to job satisfaction.

Leadership Styles. Based on the situational factors, the leader can select the most appropriate leadership style by following these general guidelines:

1. *Directive.* The leader provides high structure. Directive leadership is appropriate when the subordinates want authority leadership, have external locus of control, and their ability is low. Directive leadership is also appropriate when the environmental task is complex or ambiguous, formal authority is strong, and the work group provides job satisfaction.

2. *Supportive.* The leader provides high consideration. Supportive leadership is appropriate when the subordinates do not want autocratic leadership, have internal locus of control, and their ability is high. Supportive leadership is also appropriate when the environmental tasks are simple, formal authority is weak, and the work group does not provide job satisfaction.

3. *Participative.* The leader includes employee input into decision making. Participative leadership is appropriate when subordinates want to be involved, have internal locus of control, and their ability is high. Participative leadership is also appropriate when the environmental task is complex, authority is either strong or weak, and job satisfaction from coworkers is either high or low.

WORK APPLICATION

7. Identify your boss's most commonly used path-goal leadership style (directive, supportive, participative, achievement-oriented). Would you say this is the most appropriate leadership style based on the situational factors? Explain.

4. *Achievement-Oriented.* The leader sets difficult but achievable goals, expects subordinates to perform at their highest level, and rewards them for doing so. In essence, the leader provides both high structure and high consideration. Achievement-oriented leadership is appropriate when subordinates are open to autocratic leadership, have external locus of control, and their ability is high. Achievement-oriented leadership is also appropriate when the environmental task is simple, authority is strong, and job satisfaction from coworkers is either high or low.

Although path-goal theory is more complex and specific than the leadership continuum, it also has been criticized because it is difficult to know which style to use when. As you can see, many situations occur in which the six situational factors are exactly as presented in the guidelines. Judgment calls are needed to select the appropriate style. Liz Claiborne tended to use the participative leadership style most often with her design teams.

Normative Leadership Model

Victor Vroom and Philip Yetton attempted to bridge the gap between leadership theory and managerial practice by developing a model.[49] *The* **normative leadership model** *is a decision tree that enables the user to select one of five leadership styles appropriate for the situation.* Vroom and Arthur Jago expanded it to four models.[50] The four models are based on two factors: individual versus group decisions and time-driven versus development-driven decisions.

Leadership Styles. Vroom and Yetton identified five leadership styles. Two are autocratic (AI and AII), two are consultative (CI and CII), and one is group-oriented (GII).

AI. The leader makes the decision alone using available information.

AII. The leader gets information from subordinates but makes the decision alone. Subordinates may or may not be told what the problem is. They are not asked for input into the decision.

CI. The leader meets individually with subordinates, explains the situation, and gets information and ideas on how to solve the problem. The leader makes the final decision alone. The leader may or may not use the subordinates' input.

CII. The leader meets with subordinates as a group, explains the situation, and gets information and ideas on how to solve the problem. The leader makes the decision alone after the meeting. Leaders may or may not use the subordinates' input.

GII. The leader meets with the subordinates as a group, explains the situation, and the decision is made by the group with the help, but not with the over-influence, of the leader.

Determining the Appropriate Leadership Style. To determine the appropriate style for a specific situation, you answer eight questions, some of

8. Describe the major characteristic shared by the normative leadership model and the situational leadership model.

normative leadership model
A decision tree that enables the user to select one of five leadership styles appropriate for the situation.

which may be skipped based on prior answers. The questions are sequential and are presented in a decision-tree format similar to the Fiedler model in which you end up with the best style to use.

Vroom and Yetton's model is popular in the academic community because it is based on research.[51] However, the model is not as popular with managers because they find it cumbersome to select from four models and to pull out the model and follow an eight-question decision tree every time they have to make a decision.

Liz Claiborne changed leadership styles, but tended to use the GII group approach to leadership and decision making.

WORK APPLICATION

8. Identify your boss's most commonly used normative leadership decision-making style (AI, AII, CI, CII, GII). Would you say this is the most appropriate leadership style? Explain.

Situational Leadership Model

Paul Hersey and Ken Blanchard developed the situational leadership model.[52] *The **situational leadership model** is used to select one of four leadership styles that match the employees' maturity level in a given situation.* For the most part, situational leadership takes the two-dimensional leadership styles of the Ohio State model (four quadrants, see Figure 13–1), and gives names to the four leadership styles:

situational leadership model
Used to select one of four leadership styles that match the employees' maturity level in a given situation.

Telling (lower right quadrant A—high structure, low consideration)

Selling (upper right quadrant B—high structure, high consideration)

Participating (upper left quadrant C—high consideration, low structure)

Delegating (lower left quadrant D—low consideration, low structure)

Hersey and Blanchard went beyond the behavioral theory by developing a model that tells the leader which style to use in a given situation. To determine the leadership style, the leader determines the followers' maturity level. Maturity level does not mean how grown up the employees act. Maturity means the level of employee development (based on competence and commitment)

APPLYING THE CONCEPT

AC 13–4 Situational Leadership

For each of the following situations, identify the maturity level of the employees and the appropriate leadership style, by quadrant in Figure 13–6, for you to use as the manager to get the job done.

a. Low Maturity (M1) of employee. The manager should use the *telling* style (high structure/low consideration).
b. Low to Moderate Maturity (M2) of employee. The manager should use the *selling* style (high structure/high consideration).
c. Moderate to High Maturity (M3) of employee. The manager should use the *participating* style (low structure/low consideration).
d. High Maturity (M4) of employee. The manager should use the *delegating* style (low structure/low consideration).

_____ **16.** Mary Ann has never done a report before, but you know she can do it with a minimum of help from you.

_____ **17.** You told John to fill the customer order to your specifications. However, he deliberately ignored your directions. The customer returned the order to you with a complaint.

_____ **18.** Tina is an enthusiastic employee. You have decided to expand her job responsibilities to include a difficult task, which she has never done before.

_____ **19.** Part of Pete's job, which he has done properly many times, is to take out the trash in your office when it's full. It is full now.

_____ **20.** Carl usually does an excellent job and gets along well with his coworkers. For the past two days you have noticed a drop in the quality of his work and saw him arguing with coworkers. You want Carl to return to his usual level of performance.

or readiness to do the job (based on ability and willingness). If the leadership style is:

Low (M1), the leader uses a telling style.

Moderate to low (M2), the leader uses a selling style.

Moderate to high (M3), the leader uses the participating style.

High (M4), the leader uses a delegating style.

Figure 13–6 shows an adaptation of their model. Situational leadership is also different from The Leadership Grid, because the grid recommends always using the team leader style, which is similar to the selling style. Hersey agrees that every manager should be highly concerned with both production and people. However, the problem the grid followers fell into was drawing behavioral conclusions from a model based on attitudes. Situational leadership extends this approach into a behavioral dimension. Considering preferred values and attitudes, the leader's question becomes: "How do I behave?"[53] or being concerned for both production and people, "Which leadership style do I use when?"

Situational management, in Skill-Building Exercise 1–1, is an adaptation of Hersey and Blanchard's situational leadership. Skill-Building Exercises 3–2, Situational Decision Making, 10–1, Group Situational Management, and 11–2, Situational Communications, are adapted from Hersey and Blanchard and Vroom and Yetton. Situational leadership has also been modified by others.[54]

Managers tend to like situational leadership because it is simple to use on the job. However, it lacks research and consistency in its instruments and model.[55] Liz Claiborne changed styles, but tended to use the participative leadership style.

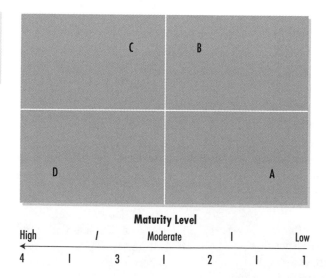

Figure 13-6

Hersey and Blanchard Situational Leadership Model

Hersey does not call situational leadership a theory, but rather he calls it a model. The difference is that a theory is something that you construct to analyze or understand a given event, whereas a model is something that is practical and applicable and that can be used on the job.[56] Every chapter of this book presents models that you can use on the job to improve your performance. Hersey uses a baseball metaphor to explain how his model helps managers: "You can't give me the way to hit a home run every time at bat, but you can help me to increase my batting average."[57] In other words, this book cannot teach you all the details of how to lead in every situation, but the models can help you to increase your leadership and management success.

Leadership Substitutes Theory

The leadership theories presented assume that some leadership style will be effective in each situation. Steven Kerr and John Jermier argued that certain situational variables prevent leaders from affecting subordinates' attitudes and behaviors.[58] **Substitutes for leadership** *are three characteristics that replace the need for a leader.* The three characteristics of the task, subordinates, or organization can also have the effect of counteracting or neutralizing the effect of leadership behavior.[59]

The following may substitute for or neutralize leadership by providing direction and/or support rather than a leader:

1. *Characteristics of subordinates.* Ability, knowledge, experience, training. Need for independence. Professional orientation. Indifference toward organizational rewards.

2. *Characteristics of task.* Clarity and routine. Invariant methodology. Provision of own feedback concerning accomplishment. Intrinsic satisfaction.

3. *Characteristics of the organization.* Formalization (explicit plans, goals, and areas of responsibility). Inflexibility (rigid, unbending rules and procedures). Highly specified and active advisory and staff functions. Closely knit, cohesive work groups. Organizational rewards not within the leader's control. Spatial distance between superior and subordinates.

A study of nursing work indicated that the staff nurses' education, the cohesion of the nurses, and work technology substituted for the head nurse's leadership behavior in determining the staff nurses' performance.[60] In other words, a leader providing direction and support was not necessary. Research has also shown that substitutes for leadership affect perception and stress.[61]

Although Liz Claiborne provided strong leadership when she was with the design groups, there were multiple design groups and Liz did not try to manage them. Primarily the groups provided the leadership substitutes.

substitutes for leadership
Three characteristics that replace the need for a leader.

> **WORK APPLICATION**
>
> 10. Identify your present or past boss. Could the characteristics of subordinates, task, or organization substitute for this leader? In other words, is your boss necessary? Explain.

PUTTING THE LEADERSHIP THEORIES TOGETHER

So far in this chapter you have studied three approaches to classifying leadership theories (trait, behavioral, situational) with seven behavioral leadership theories; plus, you studied situational management in Chapter 1. Figure 13–7 puts all of these leadership theories together. This figure should help you to better understand the similarities and differences between these theories. The models use the two dimensions of leadership; therefore, the boxed theories indicate the four possible leadership styles. Different authors use different names to indicate the same two dimensions, therefore directive and supportive behavior are used to represent the other terms.

Figure 13-7
Putting the Leadership Theories Together

	Two-Dimensional Leadership Styles			
	H$^+$D*/L^{++}S**	HD/HS	LD/HS	LD/LS
I. Trait Leadership	X	X	X	X
II. Behavioral Leadership				
Basic Leadership Styles	Autocratic	Democratic		Laissez-faire
Two-Dimensional [quadrant]	A	B	C	D
Leadership Grid	9,1 Authority	9,9 Team; moderate D&S 5,5 Middle road	1,9 Country	1,1 Impoverished
Charismatic Leadership	X	X	X	X
Transformational Leadership	X	X	X	X
Transactional Leadership	X	X	X	X
Symbolic Leadership	X	X	X	X
III. Situational Leadership				
Contingency Leadership	Task		Relationship	
Leadership Continuum	1	2 & 3	4 & 5	6 & 7
Path-Goal	Directive	Achievement	Supportive	
			Participative	
Normative Leadership	AI & AII	CI & CII		GII
Situational Leadership	Telling	Selling	Participating	Delegating
Situational Management	Autocratic	Consultative	Participative	Empowerment
Leadership Substitutes	X	X	X	X

$^+$ High $^{++}$ Low * Directive ** Supportive
X no two-dimensional leadership style used with this theory.

HANDLING COMPLAINTS

No matter how hard you try to do a good job, leading to satisfy all employees' and customers' needs, complaints will arise. *A **complaint** occurs when someone is not satisfied with a situation and seeks change.* Many employees complain at work but do not take the complaint to a manager who can resolve it. Handling complaints requires strong leadership skills. It is advisable to use an open-door policy that allows employees to feel free to come to you with a complaint. It is much better to get complaints out in the open and try to resolve them than to have employees complaining to everyone else about you. In this section you will learn how to handle complaints; Skill-Building Exercise 13–2 will help you develop this skill.

The Employee Complaint-Handling Model

When employees come to you with a complaint, try not to take it personally as a reflection on you or your leadership ability. Even the best leaders have to deal with complaints. Do not become defensive and try to talk the employee out of the complaint. You can use the complaint-handling model to help you resolve complaints when employees come to you. The *complaint-handling model* involves (1) listening to the complaint and paraphrasing it; (2) having the complainer recommend a solution; (3) scheduling time to get all the facts and/or make a decision; (4) developing a plan; and (5) implementing the plan and following up. A discussion of each step follows

step 1. **Listen to the complaint and paraphrase it.** This is a very important step. Listen to the full story without interruptions and paraphrase it (repeat it back to the complainer in your own words) to ensure accuracy. Listening and paraphrasing are necessary because if you cannot accurately state the complaint, you cannot resolve it. Paraphrasing is very important because employees often do not know how to state their complaint accurately. They often talk about one issue when something else is causing the problem. Your paraphrasing helps them see the difference and adjust accordingly. As the manager, it's your job to determine the true cause of the complaint.

When listening to the complaint, distinguish facts from opinions. There will be times when employees think they know the facts, when in reality they do not. For example, a more experienced employee may have heard that a less experienced worker earns the same wages. The experienced employee may complain. When the manager states the facts—that the experienced worker is paid more (it may be best not to state the specific amount)—the complaint may be dropped immediately.

It is also helpful to identify the person's feelings about the complaint and to determine the employee's motives for the complaint.

step 2. **Have the complainer recommend a solution.** After you have paraphrased the complaint and the employee has agreed with the paraphrasing, you should ask the complainer to recommend a solution. The complainer may

complaint
Occurs when someone is not satisfied with a situation and seeks change.

*skillbuilder

know a good solution you may not think of. Requesting a solution does not mean that you have to implement it. In some cases, the recommended solution may not solve the problem. Moreover, the solution may not be fair to others. Some recommendations may not be possible. In such cases, you should let the employee know that the solution is not possible and explain why.

step 3 ■ **Schedule time to get all the facts and/or make a decision.** Since employee complaints often involve other people, you may find it necessary to check records or to talk to others. It is often helpful to talk to your boss or your peers, who may have dealt with a similar complaint; they may be able to offer you some good advice on how best to resolve it. Even when you have all the facts, it is usually advisable to take some time to weigh them and make a decision.

Schedule a specific period of time. In many cases, it does not have to be long. Generally, the faster a complaint is resolved, the fewer the negative side effects. A poor management approach to complaints is to simply say, "I'll get back to you on this," without specifying a time period. This frustrates the employee. Some managers are purposely vague because they have no intention of getting back to the employee. They hope the employee will forget about the complaint or give it up. This tactic may get the employee to stop complaining, but it may also cause productivity and turnover problems.

step 4 ■ **Develop a plan.** After getting all the necessary facts and advice from others, you should develop a plan. The plan may be developed by simply using the complainer's recommended solution. However, when you do not agree with the complainer's solution, explain why, and either work with the employee to find an alternative or present your own plan. The level of the employee's participation in planning should be based on his or her capability level.

In cases where you decide not to take any action to resolve the complaint, you should clearly explain why you chose not to do so. State that if employees are not satisfied, they can appeal the decision to another level. The complainer should be told how to appeal the decision. In a nonunion organization, the usual step is to go to the manager's boss. In a union organization, the first step usually is to go to the union steward, who often accompanies the employee during the meeting with the supervisor.

step 5 ■ **Implement the plan and follow up.** It is important to make sure that the plan is implemented through follow-up methods. It may be appropriate to set a follow-up meeting. It is also advisable to make written documentation of all meetings and actions taken by you and others.

See Model 13–1 for a review of the five steps just discussed.

Model 13-1
The Employee Complaint Model

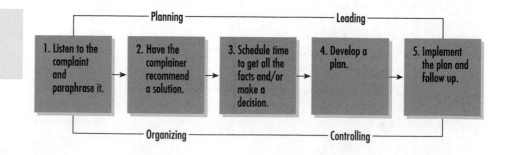

The Customer Complaint-Handling Model

Handling a customer complaint is somewhat different from handling an employee complaint when it involves something you and/or your organization did wrong. Successfully handling customer complaints is critical, because customer satisfaction is the major goal of many organizations today. The steps for handling customer complaints are outlined below and in Model 13–2.

| step 1. | **Admit the mistake and apologize.** As with the employee complaint model, you should listen to the complaint and paraphrase it to ensure that you are hearing the customer correctly. You should then admit that a mistake was made and apologize. For example, "We are sorry the technician got dirt on your car carpet. I'm sorry it happened."

| step 2. | **Agree on a solution.** Tell the customer what you are going to do about the problem. Continuing the example, "I'll have the technician go out and clean it right now." Or ask what the customer recommends you do about it. Asking, "How would you like us to handle the situation?" can often lead to more satisfied customers through better handling of the customer complaint and cost savings. Customers consistently recommend solutions that cost far less than what you might initially do.[62]

| step 3. | **Implement the solution quickly.** As with all plans, they are useless unless they are implemented. Quick implementation has a direct effect on customer satisfaction. Continuing the example, if the technician immediately goes out and cleans the carpet, the customer will most likely be happy and will be a repeat customer. However, if the customer has to wait for a half an hour for a solution to the problem, he or she will not be a satisfied customer and may never do business with you again.

| step 4. | **Prevent future complaints.** Take quick corrective action so that the mistake will not happen again, or will at least be minimized. Continuing the example, the manager should talk to the technician about the dirty carpet. You will learn how to coach and discipline employees in the next chapter.

See Model 13–2 for a review of the steps just discussed.

WORK APPLICATION

13. Identify a complaint you brought to a manager. State the complaint and identify which steps in the complaint-handling model the manager did or did not follow. If you have never complained, interview someone who has.

Model 13-2
The Customer Complaint Model

CHAPTER SUMMARY AND GLOSSARY

The chapter summary is organized to answer the nine learning objectives for Chapter 13.

1. State the difference among trait, behavioral, and situational leadership theorists.

Trait theorists try to find a list of distinctive characteristics accounting for leadership effectiveness. Behavioral theorists try to determine distinctive styles used by effective leaders and tend to seek the one best leadership style in all situations. Situational theorists try to find the appropriate style for various situations and believe the best leadership style varies from situation to situation.

2. Explain why the terms *management* and *leadership* are not interchangeable.

Management is broader in scope and includes planning, organizing, leading, and controlling. Leadership is the process of influencing employees to work toward the achievement of organizational objectives. A person who is a poor leader can be a manager and a person can be a good leader without being a manager.

3. Describe leadership trait theory and, according to Ghiselli, the most important leadership trait.

Leadership trait theory assumes that distinctive characteristics account for leadership effectiveness. According to Ghiselli, supervisory ability is the most important leadership trait. Supervisory ability is the ability to perform the four management functions of planning, organizing, leading, and controlling.

4. Discuss the major similarity and difference between two-dimensional leadership styles and the Leadership Grid.

Both theories use the same two dimensions of leadership, but they use different names for the dimensions. The major difference is that two-dimensional leadership theory has four major leadership styles (high structure/low consideration, high structure/high consideration, low structure/high consideration, low structure/low consideration), whereas the Leadership Grid has five leadership styles (1, 1 impoverished; 9, 1 authority-compliance; 1, 9 country club; 5, 5 middle of the road; and 9, 9 team).

5. Identify the management levels that are the focus of charismatic, transformational, transactional, and symbolic leadership.

Charismatic and transformational leadership focus on top-level management. Transactional leadership focuses on middle and first-line management. Symbolic leadership starts with top management and should flow down to middle and first-line management.

6. State the primary difference between the contingency leadership model and the other situational leadership models.

The contingency leadership model recommends changing the situation not the leadership style. The other situational leadership models recommend changing the leadership style not the situation.

7. Discuss the major criticism shared by the leadership continuum model and the path-goal leadership model.

The leadership continuum model and path-goal model are subjective, making which leadership style to use when difficult or unclear.

8. Describe the major characteristic shared by the normative leadership model and the situational leadership model.

The major characteristic shared by situational leadership and normative leadership theory is that they both provide one clear leadership style to use in a given situation.

9. Define the following key terms (in order of appearance in the chapter).

Select one or more methods: (1) fill in the missing key terms from memory, (2) match the key terms from the end of the summary with their definitions below, or (3) copy the key terms in order from the list at the beginning of the chapter.

_____ is the process of influencing employees to work toward the achievement of organizational objectives.

_____ attempt to determine a list of distinctive characteristics that account for leadership effectiveness.

_____ attempt to determine distinctive styles used by effective leaders.

_____ is the combination of traits, skills, and behaviors managers use to interact with employees.

_____ are based on job structure and employee consideration, which result in four possible leadership styles.

The _____ identifies the ideal leadership style as having a high concern for both production and people.

_____ is based on a leadership style that inspires loyalty, enthusiasm, and high levels of performance.

_____ is based on change, innovation, and entrepreneurship as the manager continually takes the organization through three acts.

_____ is based on leadership style and exchange.

_____ is based on establishing and maintaining a strong organizational culture.

_____ attempt to determine the appropriate leadership style for various situations.

The _____ is used to determine if one's leadership style is task- or relationship-oriented and if the situation matches the leader's style.

The _____ is used to determine which one of seven styles to select based on one's use of boss-centered versus employee-centered leadership.

The _____ is used to determine employee objectives and then to clarify how to achieve them using one of four styles.

The _____ is a decision tree that enables the user to select one of five leadership styles appropriate for the situation.

The _____ is used to select one of four leadership styles that matches the employees' maturity level in a given situation.

_____ are aspects of the task, subordinates, or organization that replace the need for a leader.

A _____ occurs when someone is not satisfied with a situation and seeks change.

KEY TERMS

behavioral leadership theorists   455
charismatic leadership   460
complaint   471
contingency leadership model   461
leadership   452
leadership continuum model   463

leadership grid model   458
leadership style   456
leadership trait theorists   453
normative leadership model   466
path-goal model   464
situational leadership model   467

situational leadership theorists   461
substitutes for leadership   469
symbolic leadership   460
transactional leadership   460
transformational leadership   460
two-dimensional leadership styles   457

REVIEW AND DISCUSSION QUESTIONS

1. What is leadership and why is it important?

2. What traits do you think are important to leaders?

3. Based on Self-Assessment Exercise 13–1, is your behavior more Theory X or Y?

4. What are the three parts of leadership style?

5. What are the two dimensions of leadership and the four possible leadership styles?

6. What are the five leadership grid leadership styles?

7. What is the difference between transformational and transactional leadership?

8. What are the two leadership styles of the contingency leadership model?

9. What are the two dimensions at the ends of the leadership continuum model?

10. What are the four leadership styles of the path-goal leadership model?

11. What are the five leadership styles of the normative leadership model?

12. What are the four leadership styles of the situational leadership model?

13. What are the three substitutes for leadership?

14. Do you believe men and women lead differently?

OBJECTIVE CASE

Wilson Sporting Goods

The Humboldt, Tennessee, facility was considered to be one of the least efficient plants within the Wilson Sporting Goods corporation. The facility produces golf balls and consistently lost money year after year. Major problems in the following areas caused Humboldt's lack of profitability: productivity, quality, cost, safety, morale, and housekeeping. The management and employee attitude toward each other was, "It's us against them." The plant manager Al Scott wanted to change the situation by solving these problems. He wanted Humboldt to make the best golf balls and have the most efficient production facilities in the world. With this vision in mind, Al developed the following mission statement: "Our mission is to be recognized . . . as the premier manufacturer of golf balls." To achieve the mission, Al developed the following five guiding philosophies, or what he wanted to become shared values: employee involvement, total quality management, continuous improvement, lowest total manufacturing cost, and just-in-time manufacturing.

Al held meetings with groups of employees to tell them about the vision, mission, and values he wanted them to share. He asked everyone to radically change their way of doing business. Al stressed the need to change from the old dictator management style to the new employee involvement style. Employees were referred to as associates and empowered to find new solutions to old problems. Managers were trained in employee involvement and developed skills to include employees in decision making. The leadership style did change at Humboldt, and in turn employee loyalty, morale, enthusiasm, and level of performance increased.

To solve Humboldt's problems, Al instituted a voluntary employee participation program called Team Wilson. Humboldt developed teams of associates to participate in problem solving in the areas of productivity, quality, cost, safety, morale, and housekeeping. To ensure team success, Humboldt gave all associates on teams training similar to that given to managers at the beginning of the change in process.

Within a few years 66 percent of associates had formed voluntary teams, which dramatically changed the Humboldt facility. Each team represented a specific area of the plant. The teams created their own unique logo, T-shirt, and posters to hang in the plant. Wilson holds several cookouts, picnics, and parties each year to show its appreciation to all associates. To recognize team accomplishments, Humboldt chooses three Team Wilson teams each quarter for awards.

Some team accomplishments include an increase in market share from 2 to 17 percent, an increase in inventory turns from 6.5 to 85, two-thirds reduction in inventory, reduction of manufacturing losses caused by scrap and rework by 67 percent, and an increase in productivity by 121 percent. The Humboldt plant produces over 1 billion golf balls each year, and the volume is growing. *Industry Week* magazine named it one of the "Best Plants in America."

Select the best alternative to the following questions. Be sure you are able to explain your answers.

_____ 1. Al Scott called for a change in basic management style from ____ to ____ .

    a. democratic to laissez-faire

    b. autocratic to laissez-faire

    c. laissez-faire to democratic

    d. autocratic to democratic

_____ 2. Based on two-dimensional leadership (Figure 13–1) and situational leadership (Figure 13–6), within the Team Wilson teams, the team leader primarily uses the ____ leadership style.

    a. telling—high structure/low consideration

    b. selling—high structure/high consideration

OBJECTIVE CASE

(continued)

c. participating—low structure/
   high consideration

d. delegating—low structure/
   low consideration

___ 3. Al Scott ___ be considered a charismatic leader.

   a. should   b. should not

___ 4. Al Scott should be considered a ___ leader.

   a. transformational   b. transactional

___ 5. Al Scott ___ focus on symbolic leadership at the Humboldt plant.

   a. did   b. did not

___ 6. Based on the original situation at Humboldt before Al made changes, determine Al's situation and the appropriate style using Figure 13–3.

   a. 1, task   e. 5, relationship

   b. 2, task   f. 6, relationship

   c. 3, task   g. 7, relationship

   d. 4, relationship   h. 8, task

___ 7. Based on the continuum model, Figure 13–4, the leadership style used was ___ .

   a. 1 b. 2 c. 3 d. 4 e. 5 f. 6 g. 7

___ 8. The management style at Humboldt was changed to the ___ path-goal leadership style.

   a. directive   c. participative

   b. supportive   d. achievement-oriented

___ 9. The normative leadership style used by the teams is ___ .

   a. AI b. AII c. CI d. CII e. GII

___ 10. Al ___ create substitutes for leadership at the Humboldt plant.

   a. did   b. did not

11. What role did leadership play in the improvements at Wilson's Humboldt plant?

12. Would the methods used by Al Scott work at an organization you work or have worked for? Explain your answer.

For current information about Wilson Sporting Goods, use Internet address http://www.wilsonsports.com.

VIDEO CASE

Sunshine Cleaning Systems I
(13–1, 12 Minutes)

Case Summary

Sunshine Cleaning Systems is a privately held company dedicated to providing the very highest quality cleaning service to a wide range of clients. Sunshine earns $10 million in sales per year and employs 1,000 people. Sunshine's clients include the Orlando Arena—home of the Orlando Magic, Fort Lauderdale Airports, and the Smithsonian Institute. The company was founded in 1976 by former baseball player and baseball coach Larry Calufetti who leads by coaching. You will see how Larry coaches his employees in similar ways to how he coached his athletes.

VIDEO CASE (Continued)

Students' Learning Objective

To understand characteristics of an effective coach, the results of coaching, and the environment and practices necessary for creating an organizational culture that is consistent with a coaching leadership style.

Critical Thinking Questions

1. How does coaching differ from managing?
2. What are the characteristics of a coaching leadership style at Sunshine?

---

*skillbuilder

I **G**

Skill-Building Exercise 13–1

The Situational Leadership Model

Preparing for Skill-Building Exercise 13–1

Think of a leadership situation, preferably from a present or past job. Describe the situation in enough detail so that others can understand it and determine the maturity level of the employees. Write the situation information below. If you have trouble thinking of a situation, refer back to Chapter 1, Skill-Building Exercise 1–1, Situational Management, for 12 examples.

_____

_____

_____

_____

For your situation, determine the maturity level of the follower(s) and select the situational leadership style appropriate for the situation (M1, low telling; M2, moderate to low selling; M3, moderate to high participating; M4, high delegating).

Doing Skill-Building Exercise 13–1 in Class

Objective

To develop your skill at determining the appropriate leadership style to use in a given situation.

Preparation

You should have a written leadership situation for others to analyze.

Experience

You may present your leadership situation to others for them to determine the appropriate leadership style, and you will hear others' leadership situations for you to determine the appropriate leadership style.

Procedure (10–50 minutes)

Option A. One at a time, volunteers or those selected by the instructor come to the front of the class and present their situation. After the statement, the class may ask questions to clarify the situation. The class members take a minute to determine the appropriate leadership style (telling, selling, participating, or delegating) for the situation. The student or instructor asks the class how many selected each of the four styles. The student may or may not tell the class the style he or she selected. The instructor may lead a class discussion of the most appropriate leadership style for the situation.

Option B. Break into groups of five or six. One at a time, present your situation to the group. Each group member determines the style he or she would use. Then the group members share styles and discuss the most appropriate. It is not necessary to reach a consensus.

Option C. Same as option B, but the group selects one example to be presented to the entire class using the option A format. The members of the group do not vote for the most appropriate style.

Conclusion
The instructor may lead a class discussion and/or make concluding remarks.

Application (2–4 minutes)
What did I learn from this experience? How will I apply this knowledge in the future?

_____

_____

_____

Sharing
Volunteers give their answers to the integration and/or application section.

BEHAVIOR MODEL VIDEO

Behavior Model Video 13–1 (7 minutes), Handling Complaints, has been made for Chapter 13. The video illustrates a manager, Cassandra, handling a complaint from Andrew about being passed over for a promotion. Cassandra follows the steps described in Model 13–1.

---

*skillbuilder

R

Skill-Building Exercise 13–2

Handling Complaints

Preparing for Skill-Building Exercise 13–2
During class you will be given the opportunity to role-play handling a complaint. Select a complaint. It may be one you brought to a manager, one that was brought to you, one you heard about, or one you made up. Fill in the information below for the person who will role-play bringing you a complaint to resolve. Explain the situation and complaint. List pertinent information about the other party that will help him or her play the role of the complainer (relationship with manager, knowledge, years of service, background, age, values, etc.). Review Model 13–1 and think about what you will say and do when you handle this complaint.

_____

_____

_____

COMPLAINT OBSERVER FORM
During the role-play, observe the handling of the complaint. Determine whether the manager followed the steps below during the exercise and how well. Try to have a positive and an improvement comment for each step in the complaint model. Be specific and descriptive. For all improvement comments, have an alternative positive behavior (APB). What could have been done or said that was not?

Step 1. How well did the manager listen? Was the manager open to the complaint? Did the manager try to talk the employee out of the complaint? Was the manager defensive? Did the supervisor get the full story without interruptions? Did the manager paraphrase the complaint?

Positive: _____

_____

Improvement: _____

_____

Step 2. Did the manager have the complainer recommend a solution? How well did the supervisor react to the solution? If the solution could not be used, did the supervisor explain why?

Positive: _____

_____

Improvement: _____

Step 3. Did the manager schedule time to get all the facts and/or make a decision? Was it a specific date? Was it a reasonable length of time?

Positive: _____

_____

Improvement: _____

_____

Step 4. Did the manager and employee develop a plan?

Positive: _____

_____

Improvement: _____

Step 5. Implement the plan and follow up. (This step will not be appropriate for the in-class exercise.)

Positive: _____

_____

Improvement: _____

_____

Doing Skill-Building Exercise 13–2 in Class
Objective
To experience and develop skills in resolving complaints.

Preparation
You should be prepared to handle a complaint.

Experience
You will initiate, respond to, and observe a complaint role-play. Then you will evaluate the effectiveness of its resolution.

Procedure 1 (2–3 minutes)
Break into as many groups of three as possible. If there are any people not in a triad, make one or two groups of two. Each member selects a number 1, 2, or 3. Number 1 will be the first to initiate a complaint role-play, then 2, followed by 3.

Procedure 2 (5–12 minutes)

A. Number 1 (the manager) tells Number 2 (the complainer) his or her complaint information from the preparation for this exercise. Once Number 2 understands, role-play (Procedure B). Number 3 is the observer.

B. Role-play the complaint. Put yourself in this person's situation and ad-lib. Number 3, the observer, writes his or her observations on the complaint observer form found on the previous page.

C. Integration. When the role-play is over, the observer leads a discussion on the effectiveness of the conflict resolution. All three people should discuss the effectiveness; Number 3 is not a lecturer. Do not go on until told to do so.

Procedure 3 (5–12 minutes)
Same as Procedure 2, only Number 2 is now the manager, Number 3 is now the complainer, and Number 1 is the observer.

Procedure 4 (5–12 minutes)
Same as Procedure 2, only Number 3 is the manager; Number 1 is the complainer; and Number 2 is the observer. Groups of two may join other groups as observers.

Conclusion
The instructor leads a class discussion and/or makes concluding remarks.

Application (2–4 minutes)
What did I learn from this experience? How will I use this knowledge in the future?

_____

_____

Sharing
Volunteers give their answers to the application section.

14

Control Systems: Financial and Human

Learning Objectives

After studying this chapter, you should be able to:

1. List the four stages of the systems process and describe the type of control used at each stage.

2. Describe the appropriate feedback process among the functional areas/departments.

3. List the four steps in the control systems process.

4. Describe the difference among the three control frequencies.

5. Explain the difference between line-item versus program budgets, static versus flexible budgets, and incremental versus zero-based budgets.

6. Explain how the *capital expenditures budget* is different from the expense budget.

7. List the three primary financial statements and what is presented in each of them.

8. Explain the importance of positive motivational feedback in coaching.

9. Explain the manager's role in counseling and the role of the employee assistance program staff.

10. State how to measure productivity and list the three ways to increase it.

11. Define the following **key terms** (in order of appearance in the chapter):

controlling	operating budgets
preliminary control	capital expenditures
concurrent control	budget
rework control	financial statements
damage control	coaching
control systems process	management by walking
standards	around
critical success factors	management counseling
control frequency	employee assistance program
management audit	discipline
budget	productivity

Skill Development

*skillbuilder 1. You should improve your skill at developing a control system for an organization/department (Skill-Building Exercise 14–1).

*skillbuilder 2. You can develop your skill at coaching employees to improve performance (Skill-Building Exercise 14–2).

*skillbuilder 3. You can develop your skill at disciplining an employee (Skill-Building Exercise 14–3).

Ensuring human resources performance is a controlling management function. It requires human relations and communications skills. The management roles of interpersonal leader, informational monitor, and decisional are needed for effective performance control. The SCANS competencies of resources, interpersonal skills, information, and systems, as well as basic and thinking skills and personal qualities, are developed through each of these exercises.

odern Control, Inc. (MOCON®) is an international company with headquarters in Minneapolis, Minnesota. Its shares are traded on the NASDAQ Stock Market under the symbol MOCON.

MOCON is a leading developer, manufacturer, and marketer of high technology instrumentation designed to test packages and packaging materials, films, and pharmaceutical products. The company employs several patented technologies to measure permeation of various gases, to gauge thickness and weight variation during production of materials, and to test for leakage in quality control applications. MOCON testing instrumentation is used in research laboratories, production environments, and quality control applications in the food, plastics, medical, and pharmaceutical industries.

MOCON has three major lines of business: (1) Permeation products address the needs of film converters and food packagers working on new or better packaging material.

> (2) Packaging products are used to test for leaks in finished food and snack packages. (3) Weighing and sorting systems serve pharmaceutical capsule and tablet manufacturers.
>
> In other words, MOCON is in the business of helping other companies control their operations. However, like all organizations, the management function of controlling is critical to MOCON's success.[1]
>
> For current information on MOCON, use Internet address **http://www.mocon.com**. For ideas on using the Internet, see Appendix B.

1. List the four stages of the systems process and describe the type of control used at each stage.

controlling
The process of establishing and implementing mechanisms to ensure that objectives are achieved.

preliminary control
Designed to anticipate and prevent possible problems.

ORGANIZATIONAL AND FUNCTIONAL AREA CONTROL SYSTEMS

As defined in Chapter 1, **controlling** *is the process of establishing and implementing mechanisms to ensure that objectives are achieved.* In this section you will learn about controlling the organizational system and its functional areas.

Organizational Systems Control

An important part of determining performance is measuring and controlling it.[2, 3] With multiple types of organizations and stakeholders, there is no universally accepted performance measure or control system; the controls must fit the situation. However, within the controlling section of this chapter, the focus will be on integrating various controls through the systems approach. In Chapter 2, you learned about the systems process which is now expanded to include types of controls at each stage. Figure 14–1 illustrates the systems process with types of controls.

Top managers use control systems to guide and effect changes in the organizations they lead.[4] Controlling starts at the top of the organization with long-range strategic planning and flows down the organization to the day-to-day operations.[5] At the different stages of the systems process, the four different types of controls are needed as explained next.

Preliminary Control (Inputs). **Preliminary control** *is designed to anticipate and prevent possible problems.* A major difference between successful and unsuccessful managers is their ability to anticipate and prevent problems, rather than solving problems after they occur.

Planning and organizing are the keys to preliminary control, which is also called *feedforward control.* The organization's mission and objectives guide the use of all organizational resources. Standing plans are designed to control employee behavior in recurring situations to prevent problems, and contingency plans tell employees what to do if problems occur.

A common preliminary control is preventive maintenance. Many production departments and transportation companies/departments routinely tune up their machines and engines to prevent breakdowns that would

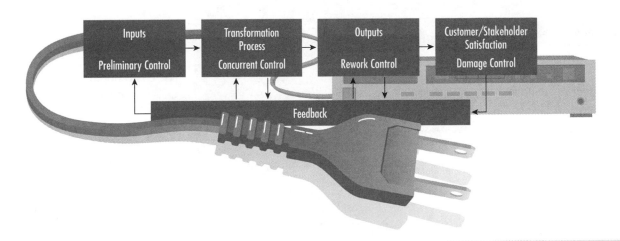

Figure 14-1
*The Systems Process with
Types of Controls*

cause problems later. Another important preliminary control is purchasing only quality inputs from other organizations to prevent product problems. For example, if Johnson & Johnson buys a MOCON weighing and sorting system for its Tylenol products and it does not work properly, it will have an adverse effect on J&J's transformation process and outputs.

Concurrent Control (Transformation Process). **Concurrent** control *is action taken as inputs are transformed into outputs to ensure that standards are met.* The key to success is quality control. MOCON tests instruments to be sold to customers as the products are being made to make sure they meet quality standards. It is more economical to reject faulty input parts than to wait and find out that the finished output does not work properly. Employees spend time checking quality during the transformation process, and managers spend time overseeing employees as they work.[6]

Rework Control (Outputs). **Rework** control *is action taken to fix an output.* Rework is necessary when preliminary and concurrent controls have failed. Most organizations inspect the final output before it is sold to the customer or sent as an input to other departments within the organization. Sometimes rework is not cost effective or possible, and outputs have to be accepted as is, discarded, or sold for salvage, which can be costly. For example, if MOCON has a bad year and loses money (outputs), it is too late; it cannot change the past. However, past performance can be used to improve preliminary controls for the next year.

Damage Control (Customer/Stakeholder Satisfaction). **Damage** control *is action taken to minimize negative impacts on customers/stakeholders due to faulty outputs.* When a faulty output gets to the customer, damage control is needed. Warranties, a form of damage control, require refunding the purchase price, fixing the product or reperforming the service (a form of rework), or replacing the product with a new one. In the last chapter, you learned how to handle customer complaints, which is a controlling technique.

concurrent control
Action taken as inputs are transformed into outputs to ensure that standards are met.

rework control
Action taken to fix an output.

damage control
Action taken to minimize negative impacts on customers/stakeholders due to faulty outputs.

WORK APPLICATION

2. Continuing your answer from work application 1, give an example of preliminary, concurrent, rework, and damage control for the organization you work or have worked for.

Feedback. An important part of the systems process is the feedback loop, particularly from the customer and other stakeholders. The only way to continually increase customer satisfaction is to use feedback from the customer to continually improve the products. Restaurant and hotel/motel evaluation cards are examples of feedback. Also, the "How's My Driving?" signs on trucks are another example of companies interested in using feedback controls.

Within the organization, the outputs should give feedback to the transformation process and inputs. The transformation process should give feedback to the inputs for continuous improvement throughout the systems process.[7]

Focus on Preliminary and Concurrent Types of Controls. Why is it that so many managers cannot find the time to use preliminary and concurrent controls, but they always find time to use rework and damage controls? Remember that focusing on the first two cuts down on the use of the last two.

Relying on rework control is not effective because it is more costly to do things twice than to do it right the first time by using effective preliminary and concurrent controls. Using rework to control performance means wasted resources, unpredictable delivery schedules, and extra inventory as safety stock. This approach is particularly problematic with services, such as manicures and haircuts and auto repairs, which are delivered as they are produced. The best solution is to prevent poor quality from ever happening in the first place. Doing so creates a win-win situation by minimizing warranty cost and maximizing customer satisfaction.

Functional Area/Department Control Systems

Although in most organizations the operations department is the only functional area that actually transforms the inputs into the outputs of goods and services (which are called *products*) that are sold to customers, all functional departments use the systems process. Figure 14–2 illustrates how this is done; it will be explained with each functional area in the following section. Note that damage control with the customer is primarily the function of the marketing department. The other department outputs stay within the organization and go to stakeholders, not the customer; therefore, internal damage control is necessary when outputs are faulty.

Recall from Chapters 1 and 6 that firms are commonly organized into four major functional departments: operations, marketing, human resources, and finance. Information is a fifth major functional area that may be a

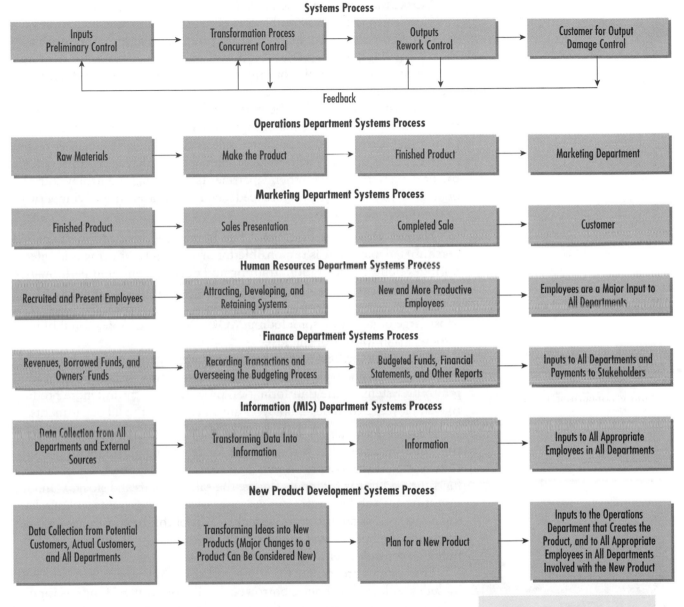

Systems Process

| Inputs
Preliminary Control | → | Transformation Process
Concurrent Control | → | Outputs
Rework Control | → | Customer for Output
Damage Control |

Feedback

Operations Department Systems Process

| Raw Materials | → | Make the Product | → | Finished Product | → | Marketing Department |

Marketing Department Systems Process

| Finished Product | → | Sales Presentation | → | Completed Sale | → | Customer |

Human Resources Department Systems Process

| Recruited and Present Employees | → | Attracting, Developing, and Retaining Systems | → | New and More Productive Employees | → | Employees are a Major Input to All Departments |

Finance Department Systems Process

| Revenues, Borrowed Funds, and Owners' Funds | → | Recording Transactions and Overseeing the Budgeting Process | → | Budgeted Funds, Financial Statements, and Other Reports | → | Inputs to All Departments and Payments to Stakeholders |

Information (MIS) Department Systems Process

| Data Collection from All Departments and External Sources | → | Transforming Data Into Information | → | Information | → | Inputs to All Appropriate Employees in All Departments |

New Product Development Systems Process

| Data Collection from Potential Customers, Actual Customers, and All Departments | → | Transforming Ideas into New Products (Major Changes to a Product Can Be Considered New) | → | Plan for a New Product | → | Inputs to the Operations Department that Creates the Product, and to All Appropriate Employees in All Departments Involved with the New Product |

Figure 14-2
Systems Processes for Functional Areas/Departments

standalone department or may fall under the finance functional area. Organizations have other departments as well, but you will only study the five key functional areas.

Operations Function. The operations, also called production and manufacturing, department is the functional area that is responsible for actually making the goods or performing the service. Figure 14–1 illustrates the operations process. In Chapter 15, you will learn more about the operations process and controls. MOCON describes itself as a leading developer and manufacturer of technology instrumentation.

Marketing Function. The marketing, including sales, department is the functional area that is responsible for selling the products. The four key areas (called the *four Ps*) of marketing are pricing, promoting (personal selling, advertising), placing (sales locations), and product attributes (features, packaging, brands, installation, instructions). Marketing also determines the target market for the products.

The systems process for the marketing department generally includes the finished product as the major input, the sales presentation as the transformation process, and the completed sale as the output. The marketing department deals primarily with the customer and uses damage control outside the organization, whereas other departments use damage control within the organization. Marketing provides feedback from customers and competitors to the other departments.

Human Resources Function. The human resources, formerly called personnel, department is responsible for attracting (recruiting and selecting), developing (orientation, training and development, and performance appraisal), and retaining (compensation, health and safety, and labor relations) employees. For details on human resources processes, see Chapter 8. Most large organizations, including MOCON, have a professional human resources staff to control employees.

The systems process for the human resources department generally includes recruited and present employees as inputs; attracting, developing, and retaining systems as the transformation process; and new and more productive employees as outputs. Employees are a major input to all departments.

Finance Function. The finance, including accounting, department is the functional area that is responsible for recording all financial transactions (primarily paying for inputs and the sale of outputs), for obtaining funds needed to pay for inputs (loans, the sale of bonds and stocks), and for investing any surplus funds (various forms of savings accounts and purchasing assets such as other company stocks). Part of this responsibility includes preparing the budgets and financial statements. You will learn more about financial controls later in this chapter.

The systems process for the finance/accounting department generally includes collected revenues, borrowed funds, and owners' funds as inputs. The transformation process includes recording transactions and overseeing the budgeting process. Outputs include budgets, financial statements, and other reports (such as tax returns, employee tax withholding, and annual reports). Its primary customers are the other departments through their budgets and payments to stakeholders such as employee paychecks, and payments to suppliers and lenders for their inputs.

Information Function. The management information systems (MIS) department is responsible for controlling information in a central location and for networks. MIS departments generally are responsible for the computers of the entire organization. You will learn more about controlling information in Chapter 15.

WORK APPLICATION

3. Continuing work application questions 1 and 2, using Figure 14–2, illustrate the systems process for a department you work or have worked for within the organization. Be sure to give examples of preliminary, concurrent, rework, and damage controls for your department.

The MIS department collects data from all departments and external sources as its inputs. *Data* includes unorganized facts and figures. The data is transformed into information. *Information* is data organized in a meaningful way to assist employees and managers in making decisions. MOCON has a sophisticated MIS department and most information is available to all employees. Its products provide data and information to other companies.

New Product Development Crossfunctions. Not all organizations have new product development departments or teams. Therefore, it is not listed as one of the four major functional departments. However, it is an important function in many firms and is usually located within either the marketing or operations department. As illustrated in Figure 14–2, ideas for major improvements or totally new products should come from external sources, especially potential customers, and from all areas of the firm that will be involved with the new product. For example, the Ford Motor Company Sigma Project for the Taurus changes the new model to appeal to new and existing customers by having the marketing function collect data. The operations team members give input into the practical aspects of producing the new Taurus. The finance team members give input into the cost and the effects on pricing of the car. The final plan for the production of the Taurus goes to the operations department. The marketing department plans how to promote and sell the new Taurus. The finance department works on the cost and budget for the Taurus and keeps records (information) on performance. The human resources department may need to make personnel changes or attract creative engineers to the company.

The Feedback Process within and among Functional Areas/Departments. Within each department, each employee also uses the systems process to transform inputs into outputs. Other department members may receive their outputs rather than other departments. For example, on a production line making the Taurus, each person works on one part of the car. When the work is completed, that person's output moves down the line to become the next person's input, and so on until the Taurus is completed. Each employee should also be using preliminary, concurrent, rework, and damage controls.

Throughout the systems process, feedback should be circulated among all the functional areas/departments to improve organizational performance in the input, transformation, and output processes while continually increasing customer satisfaction. Figure 14–3 illustrates the effective feedback process among the functional departments. Note that operations, marketing, finance, and human resources provide feedback to each other and to the information department. To be effective, feedback should be given to all departments, not just to the information department for dissemination to the other departments.

WORK APPLICATION

4. Continuing work application questions 1 through 3, illustrate the systems process you personally use within your department. Be sure to give an example of preliminary, concurrent, rework, and damage control you personally use.

2. Describe the appropriate feedback process among the functional areas/departments.

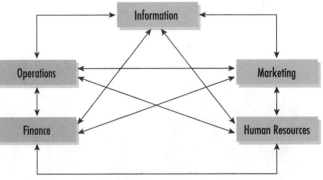

The arrows represent the flow of feedback throughout the systems process

Figure 14-3
The Feedback Process among Functional Areas/Departments

3. List the four steps in the control systems process.

ESTABLISHING CONTROL SYSTEMS

In this section you will study the four steps in the control systems process and ten specific control methods that can be used during the process.

The Control Systems Process

The **control systems process** *steps are (1) set objectives and standards, (2) measure performance, (3) compare performance to standards, and (4) correct or reinforce.* See Model 14–1 for an illustration of the control process. The same control systems process steps should be followed on an organizational level and within each functional area.

control systems process
(1) Set objectives and standards. (2) Measure performance. (3) Compare performance to standards. (4) Correct or reinforce.

 Set objectives and standards. Planning and controlling are inseparable. Part of planning should be to develop controls. Setting objectives (Chapter 4) is the starting point for both planning and controlling.[8] Setting objectives and standards is part of the input process, and they are preliminary controls.

Objectives, in a sense, are standards. However, additional standards are also used to measure whether you are meeting the objectives.[9, 10]

For standards to be complete, they should cover five major areas. **Standards** *measure performance levels in the areas of quantity, quality, time, cost, and behavior.* Incomplete standards usually lead to negative results. For example, if employees are only given high quantity standards with a fast time limit, they will tend to focus only on how many products are produced and may ignore quality.[11] Employees respond to what is measured,[12] so the development of balanced standards is a key management function that drives business success.

standards
Measure performance levels in the areas of quantity, quality, time, cost, and behavior.

- *Quantity.* How many units should employees produce to earn their pay? Some examples of quantity standards include the number of words a secretary should type, the number of loans a loan officer must make, and the number of classes a professor must teach. It is relatively easy to measure performance with quantitative standards.

Model 14-1
The Control Systems Process

- *Quality.* How well must a job be done? How many errors are acceptable? In any situation, you should set quality standards and follow through to make sure employees meet them.[13] If you don't, employees may not produce quality work.[14] Some examples of quality standards include the number of typing errors a secretary may make; the number or percentage of delinquent loans a loan officer may make; and the acceptable number or percentage of poor student evaluations a professor may get. Quality standards are often difficult to establish and measure. For example, how does an educational supervisor determine how "good" the teachers are? It's not easy, but quality must be measured and evaluated.[15]

- *Time.* When should the task be completed? Or how fast? When assigning a task, it is important to specify a time period. Deadlines are one form of a time-based standard. Performance may also be measured against a specific time period. Examples include how many words per minute a secretary types; how many loans a loan officer makes per month; and how many courses a professor teaches per semester or year.

- *Cost.* How much should it cost to do the job? How sophisticated a cost system should an organization have? The answers to these questions depend on the situation.[16] Some production departments use cost-accounting methods to ensure accuracy, whereas other departments have a set budget. Some examples of cost standards include: a secretary's typing cost may be reflected in a salary limit; a loan officer's cost may include an expense account to entertain customers, as well as the cost of an office, secretarial help, and so on. Cost could also be determined on the basis of delinquent loan losses only. The professor's cost may include a salary limit and an overhead cost.

- *Behavior.* What should employees do and not do? Standing plans, especially rules, help control or limit behavior. In addition, there may be specific things to do and say to customers. For example, a secretary may be expected to answer the telephone with a specific greeting. A loan officer may be expected to process a loan in a certain manner. A professor may be expected not to date current students. In many of the chapters you have learned about controlling behavior, reinforcement motivation theory being one example. Later in this chapter you will learn about coaching, counseling, and disciplining employees to control behavior.

In the previous paragraphs we discussed standards in terms of each of the five areas separately. Now we will set standards for the secretary, loan officer, and professor that combine all five areas, as effective standards should. The secretary's standard may be to type 50 words (quantity) per minute (time) with two errors or less (quality) at a maximum salary of $12.00 per hour (cost) and to answer the telephone with a specific greeting (behavior). The loan officer's standard may be to make $100,000 (quantity) in loans per quarter (time) with delinquency not to exceed $5,000 (quality and cost) while following procedures (behavior). The professor's standard is to teach 24 semester hours (quantity) per year (time), with an acceptable department chair performance evaluation (quality) at a salary of less than $50,000 (cost) without dating current students (behavior). Each of these jobs would have additional standards as well.

WORK APPLICATION

5. Give an example of a standard from an organization you work or have worked for that has the five characteristics of a complete standard.

critical success factors
The limited number of areas in which satisfactory results will ensure successful performance to achieve the objective/standard.

WORK APPLICATION

6. Give an example of the critical success factors for a job you have/had. Be sure to place them in priority order (first most important) and to explain why they are critical.

| step 2. | **Measure performance.** By measuring its performance, an organization knows if it is successful, and to what level, and how to improve success.[17] If you don't measure performance, how do you know if the organization's mission and objectives are being met? An important consideration in the control process is what to measure and how frequently to measure it.[18] What to measure and its frequency are inputs and require preliminary controls.

After setting objectives, but possibly while setting standards, the next step is to identify the critical success factors (CSFs). **Critical success factors** *are the limited number of areas in which satisfactory results will ensure successful performance to achieve the objective/standard.* In other words, you cannot control everything, so the organization, department/team, and individual should identify the few most important things to control.[19] For example, at the organizational level in supermarkets (including Edwards, Food Mart, Kroger, Safeway, and Stop & Shop), maintaining the right product mix in each local store, having the products on the shelves, having them advertised effectively to pull shoppers into the store, and having them priced correctly (since profit margins are low in this industry) are the critical success factors. At the departmental and employee level, these CSFs must be implemented and monitored.

How often should you measure performance and what methods of control should you use? It depends on the situation. There are three primary measures of performance based on frequency of use: constant, periodic, and occasional. You will learn how to measure performance through ten specific control methods you can use to control CSFs, once we finish the control process.

| step 3. | **Compare performance to standards.** After determining what, when, and how frequently performance is to be measured, you must follow up by comparing the actual results to the objective or standard in order to know if you are on schedule to achieve (or have achieved) the objective/standard.[20] This step is relatively easy if you have performed the first two steps correctly. This comparison determines the type of control, if any, needed in step 4. The productivity section of this chapter focuses on measuring and comparing productivity rates to standards.

A performance or variance report, such as the one shown in Figure 14–4, is commonly used to measure and evaluate performance.[21] Performance reports usually show standards, actual performance, and deviations from standards. In Figure 14–4, the results, although under production and over cost, are good because they are both under one percent deviation from standard (standard divided by deviation). When variances are significant, they should be explained. This will be covered in more detail under the exception principle of occasional control methods later in this section.

Figure 14-4
Operations Performance Report, January 2000

Outputs and Inputs	Standard/Budget	Actual	Variance
Units produced (outputs)	10,000	9,992	−8
Production cost (inputs)			
Labor, including overtime	$ 70,000	$ 68,895	$+105
Materials	95,500	95,763	−263
Supplies	4,750	4,700	+50
Totals	$170,250	$170,358	−108

step **4.**   **Correct or reinforce.** During the transformation process, concurrent controls are used to correct performance to meet standards.[22] MOCON focuses on preliminary and concurrent controls internally, as do the products it sells to customers.

When performance is complete and it is too late to take corrective action to meet the standard, the corrective action is to: (1) analyze why the standard was not met; (2) use the information to develop preliminary control; (3) feed back the preliminary control to take the corrective action necessary to meet the objective/standard next time. When performance affects others, also use damage control.

When the objective/standard has been met, there is no need for corrective action. However, do not be like most managers and end the control process here. Reinforce the behavior through rewarding employees for a job well done with techniques such as praise (Chapter 12). Letting employees know that they are meeting, or have met, objectives/standards and that you appreciate their efforts motivates them to higher levels of performance through continuous improvements.

Resistance to Control. When establishing control systems, especially the standards, it is important to consider employee reactions to them and their possible resistance to the changes. Managing change methods (Chapter 7) should be used when establishing control systems. Allowing employees to be involved in establishing the control system is very helpful at overcoming resistance to control.[23]

Control Frequency and Methods

There are ten specific methods you can use to measure and control performance. These ten methods fall into three categories of control frequency. **Control frequency** is: *constant, periodic, and occasional.*

Constant Controls. *Constant controls* are in continuous use and include self-control, clan control, and standing plans.

- *Self-Control.* If managers are not watching or somehow monitoring performance, will employees do the job? In any job, there is an element of self-control. The real issue is the degree of self-control employees are given versus imposed control by managers (such as standing plans). Too much or too little imposed control can cause problems (Situational management, Chapter 1).

- *Clan Control.* Clan, or group, *control* is a form of human resources control in which the organization relies heavily on its culture and norms to ensure specific behavior. Organizations that use teams tend to rely on clan control. Refer back to Chapter 10 for details on group control. Self- and clan control are used in all phases of the systems process with the four types of controls.

- *Standing Plans.* Policies, procedures, and rules are developed to influence employees' behavior in recurring predictable situations

WORK APPLICATION

7. Identify a situation in which corrective action was needed to meet an objective/standard. Describe the corrective action taken to meet the objective/standard.

4. Describe the difference among the three control frequencies.

control frequency
Constant, periodic, and occasional.

(Chapter 5). When standards are developed, they are similar to standing plans that are in constant use. When standing plans and standards are developed, they are preliminary controls. When standing plans and standards are implemented, they become concurrent, rework, or damage controls.

Periodic Controls. *Periodic controls* are used on a regular fixed basis, such as once per hour or day, every week, or at the end of the month, quarter, or year. Period controls include regular reports, budgets, and audits.

- *Regular Reports.* Regular reports can be oral or written. Regularly scheduled daily, weekly, and monthly meetings with one or more employees to discuss progress and any problems are common in all organizations. Regular written reports are commonly used. For example, at MOCON the sales manager may get a weekly sales report. A vice president may get a monthly income statement. The information (MIS) department is commonly responsible for periodic reports. Regular reports are designed as preliminary control. But, the report itself is used as a concurrent, rework, or damage control depending on the situation.

- *Budgets.* Budgets are one of the most widely used control tools. You will learn budgeting details in the next section of this chapter. When preparing a new budget, it is a preliminary control. As the year progresses, it becomes a concurrent control. At year end, it is reworked for the next year. A budget may also require damage control if significant changes such as overspending take place for some reason.

- *Audits.* There are two major types of audits: internal and external accounting and management. Part of the accounting function is to maintain records of the organization's transactions and assets. Most large organizations, including MOCON, have an *internal auditing* person or entire department that checks periodically to make sure the assets are reported accurately and to keep theft levels at a minimum. In addition to performing internal audits, many organizations hire outside accountants to verify the organization's financial statements through an *external accounting audit* firm, usually a certified public accounting (CPA) firm. Lastly, the **management audit** *analyzes the organization's planning, organizing, leading, and controlling functions for improvements.* The analysis focuses on the past, present, and future. The management audit can be conducted both internally and externally.

management audit
Analyzes the organization's planning, organizing, leading, and controlling functions for improvements.

Audits may also be occasional controls when used sporadically; for example, auditors may make unannounced visits at irregular intervals. The audit is designed as a preliminary control, but it is used to ensure accurate records and to control theft.

Occasional Controls. *Occasional controls* are used on a sporadic basis when needed. They include observation, exception principle, special reports, and project controls. Unlike periodic controls, they do not involve set time intervals.

- *Observation.* Managers personally watch and talk to employees as they perform their jobs. Observation is also done by video camera and electronic devices. Observation can be used with any of the four types of control. Management by walking around (MBWA) is a specific method of personal observation that increases performance.[24] MBWA is a coaching technique that will be explained later.

- *Exception Principle.* In this instance, control is left up to the employees unless problems occur, in which case employees go to the manager for help. Corrective action is taken to get the performance back on schedule. However, people are often reluctant to ask for help or to report that they are not performing up to standard until it is too late to take corrective action. Therefore, it is important for the manager and employees to agree on what constitutes an exception. The exception principle is designed as a preliminary control, but can be used with any of the other three types of controls.

- *Special Reports.* When problems or opportunities are identified, management often requests a special report to be compiled by one employee, a committee within the department/organization, or outside consultants who specialize in that area. These reports vary in content and nature but are often designed to identify the cause of a problem as well as a solution, or an opportunity and a way to take advantage of it.

- *Project Controls.* With nonrecurring or unique projects, the project manager needs to develop a control system to ensure the project is completed on time. Because planning and controlling are so closely linked, planning tools, such as Gantt charts and PERT networks (Chapter 5), are also project control methods. Project controls are designed as a preliminary control, but can be used with any of the other three types of controls.

APPLYING THE CONCEPT

AC 14–2 Frequency and Methods of Control

Identify the one primary method of control.

Constant	*Periodic*	*Occasional*
a. Self	d. Regular reports	g. Observation
b. Clan	e. Budgets	h. Exception principle
c. Standing plans	f. Audits	i. Special reports
		j. Project

_____ **6.** The boss asked an employee to meet to explain why the task is behind schedule.

_____ **7.** Signs are posted stating that helmets must be worn throughout the factory.

_____ **8.** The manager's desk is facing the employees.

_____ **9.** The secretary is working alone today since the boss is out of the office.

_____ **10.** The manager got the monthly operations performance report.

WORK APPLICATION

8. Give an example of a constant, a periodic, and an occasional control method used by an organization you work or have worked for. Identify each by name and explain why it is classified as such.

Figure 14-5
Types and Frequency and Methods of Control

Types of Control	Frequency and Methods of Control		
Preliminary (input)	*Constant Controls*	*Periodic Controls*	*Occasional Controls*
Concurrent (transformation process)	Self	Regular Reports	Observation
Rework (output)	Clan	Budgets	Exception Principle
Damage (customer satisfaction)	Standing Plans	Audits	Special Reports
			Project

For a review of the systems process with its four types of controls and the methods of control categorized by frequency, see Figure 14–5. The types and frequency and methods of control are listed separately because all four types of control may be used with any method. Recall how a budget changes its type of control over time, and that more than one control method can be used at once. You need to be aware of the stage of the systems process you are working in and the type of control used in that stage (Figure 14–1) and then select the appropriate method(s) for the type of control.

In Skill-Building Exercise 14–1, you will be asked to develop a control system for Bolton Employment Agency using the four steps of the control systems process.

*skillbuilder

FINANCIAL CONTROL

If you want to succeed in business, you must be able to work with budgets and financial statements to make important decisions. In this section you will learn about budgeting and financial statements. Important trends in budgeting include managers being required to develop tighter budgets[25] to cut costs,[26] and to use computerized spreadsheet programs such as Lotus 1-2-3 and Microsoft Excel.[27] Accounting is referred to as the language of business and is the primary measure of business success. Financial statements are used for proper planning and control,[28] since managers must focus on the bottom line,[29] and use financial statements to evaluate performance.[30]

Budgeting

budget
Planned quantitative allocation of resources for specific activities.

Preparing and following a well thought out budget for a business will ensure smoother financial management.[31] A **budget** *is a planned quantitative allocation of resources for specific activities*. Notice that the definition of *budget* does not include money. This is because all types of resources can be allocated. For example, in Figure 14–4 units of output were budgeted. Human resources, machines, time, space, and so on can also be budgeted. However, for our purposes, when we use the term *budgeting* in this chapter, we are referring to the narrower, more commonly used financial budget.

The Master Budgeting Process. The *master budgeting process steps* are to develop the (1) revenue and expenditure operating budgets, (2) capital expenditures budget, and (3) financial budgeted cash flow, income statement, and balance sheet. The three steps are illustrated with their substeps in Figure 14–6. Notice the feedback loop that takes into account possible revisions in a prior budget due to other budget developments.

The budget usually covers a one-year period, broken down by month, and the finance *controller* is responsible for the budgeting process that results in a *master budget* for the entire organization. In other words, it is the end result of the budgeting process. Although it is common for organizations to follow the three steps in the master budget process, the details of how each separate budget is actually developed do vary from organization to organization.

Each department submits its proposed budget to the controller/committee for approval. However, during the budgeting process, the use of power and politics is common, and the negotiating conflict management style (Chapter 9) is typically used to resolve expected conflicts that exist when allocating scarce resources. The controller/committee may negotiate recommended revisions with department managers and/or use its position power to require revisions.

Operating Budgets

The operating budgets include the revenue and expense budgets. You must first determine how much money you have, or will have, before you can plan how you are going to spend it. Therefore, the first step in the master budgeting process is to determine the revenue then the expenditure budgets.

Revenue Budgets. A *revenue budget* is the forecast of total income for the year. Although sales is the most common form of revenue, many organizations, including MOCON, have revenue from investments. Nonprofit organizations often get income from fees, donations, grants, and fundraisers. The revenue budget projects and adds all sources of income, such as sales for each product and/or location, together. The marketing/sales department commonly provides the revenue figures for the entire firm.

The revenue budget is primarily based on the sales forecast (Chapter 5). In a sense, the sales forecast revenue budget is the most important budget, because the other budgets are based on it.

Expense Budgets. An *expense budget* is the forecast of total operating spending for the year. It is common for each functional area/department manager to have an expenditure budget. Many managers fear budgets because they have weak math or accounting skills. In reality, budgeting requires planning skills rather than math and accounting skills. Using a computer makes the job even easier.[32] Through the systems effect, all department budgets affect the others; therefore, managers need to share information. For example, the operations department needs the sales forecast to determine how much it will produce, and the human resources department needs to determine organizationwide employee needs to develop its budget. Next, you will learn more about expenditure budgets.

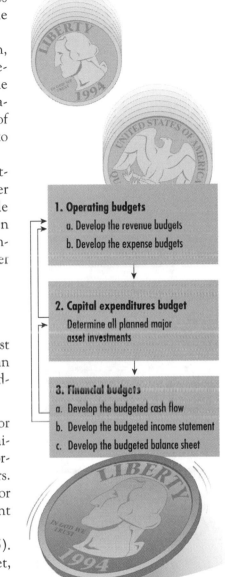

1. Operating budgets
   a. Develop the revenue budgets
   b. Develop the expense budgets

2. Capital expenditures budget
   Determine all planned major asset investments

3. Financial budgets
   a. Develop the budgeted cash flow
   b. Develop the budgeted income statement
   c. Develop the budgeted balance sheet

Figure 14-6
*The Master Budgeting
Process Steps*

operating budgets
Include the revenue and expense budgets.

5. Explain the difference between line-item versus program budgets, static versus flexible budgets, and incremental versus zero-based budgets.

Expense Budget Alternatives

Before expense budget alternatives are presented you should know about two important types of cost that are important to expenditure budgets. *Fixed costs* remain unchanged in total amount over a wide range of activities. For example, the cost of rent is the same regardless of how often the facility is actually used. *Variable costs* change in total amount as activity increases. For example, the cost of sales catalogs and mailing will increase with the number printed and mailed.

Line-Item versus Program Budgets. When projecting expenses, the format generally takes one of two forms, or it can combine them. A *line-item budget* identifies the major expenses of the department/organization, and is the most commonly used form. With the functional organizational structure (Chapter 6), each department is a cost center with its own line-item budget; these budgets are combined to form the expense budget for the master budget.

A *program budget* identifies the expenses of specific organizational activities or units. See Figure 14–7 for a combined line-item and program budget. The first column lists the "ten line items" and the last column lists the total expense for each line item. Thus, a line-item budget would only have columns 1 and 8. Columns 2–7 list the "six program budgets" for the school and the cost of each program. A simple program budget would also only have two columns. The six programs would be listed in the first column and only the total cost of the program would appear in the second column, or a separate budget for each program area would be created using the ten line-item categories with just program total costs listed. Those budgets would then be integrated into the combined line-item and program budget shown in Figure 14–7.

Static versus Flexible Budgets. A *static budget* has only one set of expenses, whereas a *flexible budget* has a series of expenses for a range of activities. The static budget is appropriate in a stable environment in which there

Figure 14-7
City of Milford School System Combined Line-Item and Program Budget for the Fiscal Year Ending June 30

Combined Line-Item and Program Budget

	Primary Educa.	Second. Educa.	Student Enrich.	Adult Educa.	Athletics	Comm. Service	Total
				Adopted Budget 2000–01			
Teachers' salaries	$392,000	$490,000	$58,000	$32,000	$ 6,000	$ 2,000	**$ 980,000**
Administrative salaries	65,000	40,000	6,000	3,000	4,000	2,000	**120,000**
Clerical salaries	34,000	28,000	4,000	2,500	1,000	500	**70,000**
Maintenance salaries	40,000	30,000	1,500	500	6,500	1,500	**80,000**
School supplies	38,000	43,000	3,000	4,000	1,000	1,000	**90,000**
Utilities	18,000	12,000	3,000	1,000	3,500	500	**38,000**
Maintenance supplies	8,000	6,000	700	500	4,500	300	**20,000**
Other facilities expenses	8,000	6,300	500	500	12,000	700	**28,000**
Miscellaneous expenses	1,000	1,700	300	12,000	6,000	3,000	**24,000**
Transportation	51,000	72,000	13,000	2,000	8,500	3,500	**150,000**
Total	**$655,000**	**$729,000**	**$90,000**	**$58,000**	**$53,000**	**$15,000**	**$1,600,000**

is little change in demand for the product. The Milford School System budget is a static budget. A flexible budget is appropriate in a turbulent environment in which demand for the product changes over a range of activities with variable cost.[33]

Incremental versus Zero-Based Budgets. Incremental and zero-based budgets do not change the presentation of the funds like the line-item versus program and static versus flexible budgets do. Their focus is on how the budgeted figures are derived based on their justification.

With *incremental budgeting*, past funds are allocated with only new expenses being justified and approved. With *zero-based budgeting* (ZBB) all funds must be justified each year. ZBB assumes that the previous year's budget should not be the base on which to rework the budget for the next year. The zero-base focus is on the mission and objectives and the determination of what it will cost to achieve them. ZBB is especially appropriate in turbulent environments in which some departmental activities/products are increasing dramatically but others are decreasing. Departments with decreasing activity should not simply be given their prior-year budget; it should be cut.

Activity-Based Cost Accounting (ABC). *Activity-based cost accounting is the process of allocating the costs of providing a good and/or service based on tasks performed and resources used.* ABC is a relatively new method and is not widely used like the other expense budget alternatives you learned about. However, it is particularly useful for organizations that offer a variety of goods and/or services with a wide diversity of tasks and resources used. For example, a hospital offers a wide variety of operations. Some operations may be simple procedures using few resources and taking little time, such as a tonsillectomy, which takes about an hour. Other operations may be very difficult procedures using many resources and taking a lot of time, such as a heart transplant, which takes about eight hours. What should the cost of one operation be versus the others? In our example, a simple "eight-times" method would not be accurate. If you determine that it costs $1,000 to perform the tonsillectomy, then to simply charge $8,000 to perform the heart transplant would not be accurate, because it does not reflect the difficulty factor and special resources used.

Capital Expenditures Budget

The second step in developing the master budget is to develop the capital expenditures budget. *The **capital expenditures budget** includes all planned major asset investments.* Major assets are owned by the organization and last for, and are paid for, over several years. The major assets budgeted for may include land, new buildings, whole new product lines or projects, or acquiring an existing company. On a lower level, other decisions include whether to replace existing assets such as machinery with new ones, to buy or lease assets, to make components yourself or to buy them through outsourcing, or to rework defective outputs or to sell or scrap them. In every case, the

WORK APPLICATION

9. Identify the major source of revenue(s) and expenses where you work or have worked. State which budget alternatives (line-item vs. program, static vs. flexible, and incremental vs. zero-based) are used at this organization. If you are not sure, call or talk to your present or past boss and find out.

6. Explain how the *capital expenditures budget* is different from the expense budget.

capital expenditures budget
Includes all planned major asset investments.

WORK APPLICATION

10. Identify the major capital asset expenditures your present or past organization invested in.

objective is to earn a satisfactory return on the invested funds. Raising the money to buy the capital asset is an important finance function.

It is true that controlling expenses is important. However, focusing on controlling costs of products that are decreasing in customer value and sales will only postpone business failure. There seems to be a strong link between capital budgets and long-term success of new product development.[34] Capital expenditure budgeting is the most important budget because it is based on developing ways to bring in additional revenues through new and improved products and projects that will create customer value. MOCON and other companies continually work to develop new products and plan to take advantage of opportunities.

Financial Statements and Budgets

The third step in the master budgeting process is to prepare financial budgets. In other words, before the year begins, the controller forecasts what each statement will be at year end. The financial statements are used by the internal managers of the firm, as well as external suppliers, creditors, and investors who make decisions to conduct business with the firm through evaluating a company's performance, growth rate, and consistency.[35] You will first learn about the three primary financial statements and then return to budgeting.

7. List the three primary financial statements and what is presented in each of them.

financial statements
Include the income statement, balance sheet, and cash flow statement.

The three primary **financial statements** *are the income statement, balance sheet, and cash flow statement.* They are presented in the order in which they appear in annual reports.

The Income Statement. The *income statement* presents revenues and expenses and the profit or loss for the stated time period. The income statement primarily covers one year. However, monthly and quarterly income statements are also developed to measure interim performance and to use concurrent control when necessary. Figure 14–8 is MOCON's abbreviated income statement.[36]

The two primary ways to increase net income are to (1) increase revenues and (2) decrease expenses. A combination of the two expedites income increases. The capital expenditure budget focuses on increasing revenues, whereas the expense budget can be used to focus on decreasing costs. As a manager, you have a fiscal responsibility to increase profits for your company.[37] In recent years there has also been an emphasis on cutting costs.[38]

An important thing you should understand is that profit is not the same as cash.[39] In fact, a company can be earning a profit and still need to borrow cash to pay its bills, because it is not collecting the cash for its sales. Cash does not appear on the income statement as revenue. Cash appears on the balance sheet and cash flow statement.

The Balance Sheet. The *balance sheet* presents the assets and liabilities and owners' equity. Assets are owned by the organization. Liabilities are its debts owed to others. Owners'/stockholders' equity is the assets minus the liabilities, or the share of assets owned. It is called a balance sheet because

	Income Statement
Revenue	$6,670,819
[sales − cost of goods sold = gross profit]	
Expenses	$4,817,842
[selling + administrative + R&D + taxes]	
Net Income (or Net Loss)	$1,852,977
[revenue − expenses]	
	Balance Sheet
Assets	$13,128,371
[current—cash / accounts receivables— +	
inventories + property and equipment]	
Liabilities and Stockholder's Equity	
Liabilities	$1,614,324
[current—accounts payable / accrued expenses	
estimated product warranties— +	
long term—mortgages / notes / bonds]	
Stockholder's Equity	$11,514,047
	$13,128,371

Figure 14-8
MOCON *Financial Statements*

the total of the assets always equals the total of the liabilities plus owners' equity for a particular point in time. Figure 14–8 includes MOCON's balance statement.

The operating budgets project the current assets and liabilities. The capital expenditure budget affects the major assets, commonly called property/plant and equipment, and the long-term liabilities. The long-term liabilities are the payments for the major assets made over several years, such as mortgages payable and bonds payable.

Cash Flow Statement. The *cash flow statement* presents the cash receipts and payments for the stated time period. It commonly has two sections: operating and financial activities. Checks are considered cash. Cash flow statements typically cover one year. However, monthly and quarterly statements are also developed to measure interim performance and to use concurrent control when necessary. The operating budgets and capital expenditures budget affect the cash flow statement as cash revenue is received and cash expenses and expenditures are paid.

Financial Budgets. The financial budgets are prepared last because the operating and capital expenditure budget figures are needed to prepare them. The cash flow budget is the first financial statement prepared because it is needed to prepare the other two. The income statement budget is prepared second because it is needed to prepare the balance sheet. If the budgeted financial statements do not meet expectations, the capital expenditures budget and/or operating budgets may need to be revised. Hence the need for the feedback loop in the master budget process in Figure 14–6. Revisions are common when a net loss is projected.

WORK APPLICATION

11. Does the company you work or have worked for make its financial statements available to the public? If it does, get a copy and review it. Also, does the organization develop operating, capital expenditures, and financial budgets? If it does, try to get copies for review. If you are not sure, call or talk to your present or past boss and find out.

Each statement is commonly budgeted for the year with each month and quarter presented. The difference between the budget, also called pro forma, statement and actual statements is that the term *budget* or *pro forma* is placed before each statement's name. One reports past results and the other projects future results. Budgets are preliminary control and actual statements are rework control.

HUMAN CONTROLS

In this section you will learn how to coach, counsel, and discipline employees to maintain and increase their performance.

Coaching

coaching
The process of giving motivational feedback to maintain and improve performance.

Coaching *is the process of giving motivational feedback to maintain and improve performance.* Employees who are given more immediate, frequent, and direct feedback perform at higher levels than those who are not.[40] Many people who hear the word coaching immediately think of athletes. If you have ever had a good coach, think about the behavior used that helped to maintain and improve your performance and that of other team members. The next time you watch a sporting event, keep an eye on the coaches and learn some techniques. Before reading on, recall the best and worst boss or coach you ever had.

Employees are the key to productivity increases.[41] Coaching is an important management skill[42] that is used to improve employee performance and is used by thriving organizations,[43] because you can get the best results from each employee.[44] Lou Holtz continually set higher standards for each of his football players through his coaching skills while at the University of Arkansas and later at Notre Dame.[45] Training is an important part of coaching, as coaching is continuous training. Zig Ziglar said that the only thing worse than training employees and losing them, is not training them and keeping them.[46] Coaching should be used to confront employees.[47]

8. Explain the importance of positive motivational feedback in coaching.

The Importance of Positive Feedback in Coaching. As implied in the definition of coaching, feedback is the central part of coaching, and it should be motivational. In other words, you should give more positive than negative feedback. Providing employees with positive feedback will create an abundance of enthusiasm and energy within an organization. It is important to cheer people on with an immediate response to excellent work.[48] Have you ever noticed that when athletes are performing and make good plays the coach and team members cheer them on? The same technique motivates people in the workplace; try it!

Unfortunately, many managers spend more time giving negative criticism than praise. Negative managers take the attitude, "Why should I thank employees for doing their job?" The answer is simple: it motivates employees to maintain and improve performance. Managers who only criticize employees tend to *demotivate* them. Demotivated employees tend to avoid critical bosses, play it safe and do the minimum, focus on not making errors, and cover up any errors so they don't get criticized. When they see the boss coming their way they think, "What did I do this time?"

Did your best boss or coach give you more positive feedback than your worst boss or coach? Did the feedback affect your motivation on the job and the selection between the best and worst boss or coach? Remember the Pygmalion effect; the giving praise model (Chapter 12) is a coaching technique that you should use daily.

Determining Corrective Coaching Action. Ability and motivation have a direct effect on performance.[49] When an employee is not performing to potential, even when acceptable standards are being met, the first step is to determine the reason why using the performance formula: Performance = Ability × Motivation × Resources (Chapter 12). When ability is holding back performance, training is needed. When motivation is lacking, motivational techniques, such as giving praise, may help. Talk to the employee to try to determine why motivation is lacking, and develop a plan together.[50] If motivation does not work, you may have to use discipline, which will be discussed later. When resources are lacking, work to obtain them. Management by walking around is an effective way to increase performance in the resource area, and the coaching model is effective in dealing with ability and motivation problems—these are the next two topics.

Management by Walking Around

Management by walking around (MBWA) *has three major activities: listening, teaching, and facilitating.*[51]

Listening. To find out what is going on, managers must do a lot more listening than talking, and be open to feedback. Learn to talk last, not first. Open with a simple question like, "How is it going?" Then use the communication skills from Chapter 11.

Teaching. Teaching does not mean telling employees what to do: this is training (Chapter 8). It means helping them to do a better job by solving their own problems. Use coaching statements such as, "What do you think should be done?"

Facilitating. *Facilitating* means taking action to help employees get their jobs done. The focus is primarily on improving the system to increase performance. When listening, find out what's getting in the way or slowing employees down. The manager's job is to run interference, to remove the stumbling blocks for the employees to improve the system.

Employees who tell the manager what's going on should be told what will be done about a given problem, if anything, and when. Managers who listen but don't facilitate through corrective action will find that employees will stop talking. The result is that the manager will lose the most valuable source of input for improving the system.

management by walking around (MBWA)
The three major activities are listening, teaching, and facilitating.

The Coaching Model

Coaching should be viewed as a way to provide ongoing feedback to employees about their job performance.[52] However, ask managers what they tend to put off doing and they'll likely say advising weak employees that they must improve their performance or risk losing their jobs.[53] These managers are hesitating to confront employees, even to the point of jarred nerves and sleepless nights.[54] Procrastinators hope that the employees will turn around on their own, only to find that the situation gets worse, often until it is too late.[55] Part of the problem is that managers don't know how to coach or are not good at coaching. Thus, Model 14–2 presents a four-step coaching model. Behavior Model Video 14–1 shows a manager using the coaching model. Managers at MOCON use coaching to improve performance.

The four steps in the coaching model are presented here and summarized in Model 14–2. They are illustrated in Behavior Model Video 14–1, Coaching.

WORK APPLICATION

12. How would you rate your present or past boss's coaching ability? Explain your answer using critical incidents.

step 1. **Describe current performance.** Using specific examples, describe the current behavior that needs to be changed.[56] Tell the employees exactly what they are not doing as well as they can. Notice the positive; don't tell them only what they are doing wrong.

For example, don't say, "You are picking up the box wrong." Say, "Billie, there is a more effective way of picking the box up off the floor than bending at the waist."

step 2. **Describe desired performance.** Tell the employees exactly what the desired performance is in detail.[57] If performance is *ability* related, demonstrate the appropriate way. If the employees know the proper way, it is *motivational*, and demonstration is not needed. Just describe desired performance as you ask the employees to state why the performance is important.

For example: *Ability*—"If you squat down and pick up the box using your legs instead of your back, it is easier and there is less chance of injuring yourself. Let me demonstrate for you." *Motivation*—"Why should you squat and use your legs rather than your back to pick up boxes?"

step 3. **Get a commitment to the change.** When dealing with an *ability* performance issue, it is not necessary to get employees to verbally commit to the change if they seem willing to make it. However, if employees defend their way, and you're sure it's not as effective, explain why your proposed way is better. If you cannot get the employees to understand and agree, get a verbal commitment. This step is also important for *motivation* performance issues, because if the employees are not willing to commit to the change, they will most likely not make the change.[58]

For example: *Ability*—In the box example, the employee will most likely be willing to do it correctly, so skip the step. *Motivation*—"Will you squat rather than use your back from now on?"

step 4. **Follow up.** Remember, some employees (those with low and moderate capability for self-control) do what managers *inspect*

Model 14-2
Coaching Model

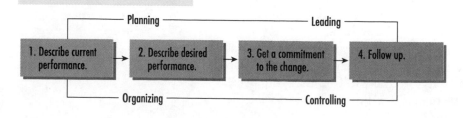

(imposed control), not what they *expect*. You should follow up to ensure that employees are behaving as desired.[59]

When dealing with an *ability* performance issue, and the person was receptive and you skipped step 3, say nothing. However, watch to be sure it is done correctly in the future. Coach again, if necessary. For a *motivation* problem, make a statement that you will follow up and that there are possible consequences for repeat performance.

For example: *Ability*—say nothing, but observe. *Motivation*—"Billie, picking up boxes with your back is dangerous; if I catch you doing it again, I will take disciplinary action."

*skillbuilder

Counseling

When coaching, you are fine-tuning performance; with counseling and disciplining, you are dealing with a problem employee who is not performing to standards, or is violating standing plans. Organizations realize the need to help employees with people problems.[60] A growing number of employers are using performance improvement counseling[61] as they train managers to counsel employees.[62]

Types of Problem Employees. There are four types of problem employees: (1) Employees who do not have the *ability* to meet the job performance standards. This is an unfortunate situation, but after training such employees and realizing they cannot do a good job, they should be dismissed.[63] Many employees are hired on a trial basis; this is the time to say, "Sorry, but you have to go." (2) Employees who do not have the *motivation* to meet job performance standards often need discipline. (3) Employees who intentionally *violate standing plans*. As a manager, it is your job to enforce the rules through disciplinary action. (4) Employees with *problems*. These employees may have the ability but have a problem that affects job performance. The problem may not be related to the job. It is common for personal problems, such as child care and relationship/marital problems, to affect job performance.[64] Employees with problems should be counseled before they are disciplined.

Counseling is presented next, and how to deal with motivation and intentional violation of standing plans is discussed later in this section. But first, Figure 14–9 lists some problem employees you may encounter. In reviewing the figure, you can see that it is not always easy to distinguish between the types of problem employees. Therefore, it is often advisable to start with coaching/counseling and change to discipline if the problem persists.

The late employee	The employee with a family problem
The absent employee	The insubordinate employee
The dishonest employee	The employee who steals
The violent or destructive employee	The sexual or racial harasser
The alcoholic or drug user	The safely violator
The nonconformist	The sick employee
The employee who's often socializing or doing personal work	

Figure 14-9
Problem Employees

Management Counseling. As mentioned, the first thing a manager should do with a person experiencing a personal problem is to attempt to help the employee solve the problem. This is usually done through counseling, which is a form of coaching.

9. Explain the manager's role in counseling and the role of the employee assistance program staff.

management counseling
The process of giving employees feedback so they realize that a problem is affecting their job performance, and referring employees with problems to the employee assistance program.

employee assistance program (EAP)
Consists of a staff of people who help employees get professional assistance in solving their problems.

When most people hear the term *counseling*, they think of psychological counseling or psychotherapy. That type of sophisticated help should not be attempted by noncounseling professionals such as a manager. Instead, **management counseling** *is the process of giving employees feedback so they realize that a problem is affecting their job performance, and referring employees with problems to the employee assistance program.*

Most managers do not like to hear the details of personal problems. This is not a requirement. Instead, the manager's role is to help employees realize that they have problems and that those problems affect their work. The manager is getting the employee back on track.

The manager should not give advice on how to solve personal problems such as relationship difficulty. When professional help is needed, the manager should refer the employee to the human resources department for professional help through the employee assistance program.[65] *The* **employee assistance program (EAP)** *consists of a staff of people who help employees get professional assistance in solving their problems.* There has been an increase in the number of EAPs offered at companies, because they improve retention and productivity.[66] EAPs are also offering a wider range of services to meet the needs of a diverse workforce.[67] MOCON, like most large businesses, has an EAP to help solve employees' personal problems.

To make the referral, a manager could say something like, "Are you aware of our employee assistance program? Would you like me to set up an appointment with Jean in the human resources department to help you get professional assistance?"

However, if job performance does not return to standard, discipline is appropriate because it often makes the employee realize the seriousness of his or her problem and the importance of maintaining job performance. Some time off from work, with or without pay depending on the situation, often helps the employee deal with the problem.

A manager's first obligation is to the organization's performance rather than to individual employees.[68] Not taking action with problem employees because you feel uncomfortable confronting them, because you feel sorry for their problem situation, or because you like the employee does not help you or the employee. Taking action is important because problem employees negatively affect their own productivity, as well as cause more work for managers and other employees. Problem employees lower employee morale as others resent them for not pulling their own weight. Recall, from coaching, the need to take quick action with problem employees.

Disciplining

Coaching, which includes counseling, should generally be the first step in dealing with a problem employee. However, an employee may be unwilling or unable to change or a rule may be broken. In such cases, discipline is necessary.

WORK APPLICATION

13. Identify a problem employee you observed on the job. Describe how the person affected the department's performance.

Discipline *is corrective action to get employees to meet standards and standing plans.* The major objective of discipline is to change behavior. Secondary objectives may be to (1) let employees know that action will be taken when standing plans or performance requirements are not met and (2) when challenged, to maintain authority.

The human resources department handles many of the disciplinary details and provides written discipline guidelines. Written policy procedures usually outline grounds for specific sanctions and dismissal based on the violation.[69] Common offenses include theft, sexual or racial harassment, verbal or substance abuse, and safety violations. You will learn some discipline guidelines and about progressive discipline.

Discipline Guidelines. Figure 14–10 lists eight guidelines for effective discipline.

Progressive Discipline. Many organizations have a series of more severe disciplinary actions. The progressive disciplinary steps are (1) oral warning, (2) written warning, (3) suspension, and (4) dismissal.[70] For minor violations, such as being late for work, all four steps are commonly followed. However, for more important violations, such as stealing, steps may be skipped. Be sure to document each step.

The Discipline Model

The steps in the discipline model should be followed each time an employee must be disciplined. What will change is the discussion based on the level of progression in discipline and the discipline given.

The five steps in the discipline model are presented here and summarized in Model 14–3. They are also illustrated in Behavior Model Video 14–2, Discipline.

step 1. **Refer to past feedback.** Begin the interview by refreshing the employee's memory. If the employee has been coached/counseled about the behavior, or if he or she has clearly broken a known rule, state that.

For example: *Prior coaching*—"Billie, remember my telling you about the proper way to lift boxes with your legs?" *Rule violation*—"Billie, you know the safety rule about lifting boxes with your legs."

APPLYING THE CONCEPT

AC 14–3 Guidelines for Effective Discipline

Identify which guideline is being followed, or not being followed, in the following statements. Use the guidelines in Figure 14–10 as the answers. Place the letters A–H of the guideline on the line before its statement.

____ **11.** "The boss must have been upset to yell that loudly."

____ **12.** "It's not fair. The manager comes back from break late all the time; why can't I?"

____ **13.** "When I leave the place a mess, the manager reprimands me. When Chris does it, nothing is ever said."

____ **14.** "The boss gave me a verbal warning for smoking in a restricted area and placed a note in my file."

____ **15.** "I want you to come into my office so that we can discuss this matter."

discipline
Corrective action to get employees to meet standards and standing plans.

a. Clearly communicate the standards and standing plans to all employees.
b. Be sure that the punishment fits the crime.
c. Follow the standing plans yourself.
d. Take consistent, impartial action when the rules are broken.
e. Discipline immediately, but stay calm and get all the necessary facts before you discipline.
f. Discipline in private.
g. Document discipline.
h. When the discipline is over, resume normal relations with the employee.

Figure 14-10
Guidelines for Effective Discipline

Model 14-3
The Discipline Model

 step 2. **Ask why the undesired behavior was used.** As in the guideline, you are giving the employee a chance to explain the behavior as part of getting all the necessary facts before you discipline. If you used prior coaching and the employee committed to changing the behavior, ask why the behavior did not change. If the behavior had changed, discipline would not be needed. Again, be sure to describe specific critical incidents to support your contention that behavior has not changed at all or has not changed enough to be at standard.

For example: *Prior coaching*—"Two days ago you told me that you would use your legs, rather than your back, to lift boxes. Why are you still using your back?" *Rule violation*—"Why are you breaking the safety rule and using your back, rather than your legs, to lift the box?"

step 3. **Give the discipline.** If there is no good reason for the undesirable behavior, give the discipline. The discipline will vary with the stage in the discipline progression.

For example: *Prior coaching*—"Because you have not changed your behavior, I'm giving you an oral warning." *Rule violation*—"Because you have violated a safety rule, I'm giving you an oral warning."

step 4. **Get a commitment to change and develop a plan.** Try to get a commitment to change. If the employee will not commit, make note of the fact in the critical incidents file or use the procedures for a written warning. A plan for change may have been developed in the past. If it has, the manager may try to get the employee to commit to it again. Develop a new plan, if necessary. A statement such as, "Your previous attempt has not worked; there must be a better way," is often helpful. With a personal problem, offer professional help again.

For example: *Prior coaching or rule violation*— "Will you lift with your legs from now on?" "Is there a way to get you to remember to use your legs instead of your back when you lift?"

step 5. **Summarize and state the follow up.** Summarize the discipline and state the follow-up disciplinary action to be taken. Part of follow up is to document the discipline. At the written warning and suspension stage, get the employee's signature. If necessary, take the next step in the discipline model until dismissal.

For example: *Prior coaching or rule violation*—"So you agree to use your legs instead of your back when you lift. If I catch you again, you will be given a written warning, which is followed by a suspension and dismissal if necessary."

*skillbuilder

PRODUCTIVITY

10. State how to measure productivity and list the three ways to increase it.

Employees would like to get paid more. However, if they are paid more without producing any more, the common approach is to raise product prices to offset the wage cost to maintain profits. In simple terms, this combined effect causes inflation. The only real way we can increase our standard of living is to increase productivity.[71] As a manager, you should understand how to measure and increase productivity, and to do so in the functional areas.

The long-term productivity trend appears to show that efficiency is improving.[72] Recall that managers have a major impact on employee productivity through the Pygmalion effect. Effective human resource management, more so than technology, is the key to increasing productivity.[73] Human resource practices increased productivity at several organizations including ConAgra[74] and MOCON. Some of the specific reported practices that improved productivity include counseling,[75] job design,[76] work teams,[77] flexible schedules,[78] telecommuting,[79] and incentives.[80]

Measuring Productivity

The U.S. government measures productivity rate on a macro level for various industries. Measuring productivity can be complex when determining cost, but it doesn't have to be. This section will outline a simple, yet realistic, approach for you to use on the job. The approach focuses on measuring productivity on the micro company level.

Productivity *is a performance measure relating outputs to inputs.* In other words, productivity is measured by dividing the outputs by the inputs. For example, a trucking company wants to measure productivity on a delivery. The truck traveled 1,000 miles and used 100 gallons of gas. Its productivity was 10 miles to the gallon:

productivity
A performance measure relating outputs to inputs.

$$\frac{\text{output: 1,000 miles traveled}}{\text{inputs: 100 gallons of gas}} = \text{productivity: 10 mpg}$$

The inputs selected can be in a variety of forms. In the preceding example, the inputs were gallons of gas. Inputs could also be labor hours, machine hours, number of workers, the cost of labor, and so on.

Another fairly simple example, following a four-step process, involves measuring the productivity of an accounts payable department. (1) Select a base period of time, such as an hour, day, week, month, quarter, or year. This example uses a week. (2) Determine how many bills were sent out during that period of time (outputs): 800—Check the records. (3) Determine the cost of sending out the bills (inputs). Determining cost can become complicated if you use overhead, depreciation, and so forth. In this instance, calculate cost based on direct labor charges for three employees who are each paid $7 per hour. They all worked 40 hours during the week, or a total of 120 hours. The total cost is $7 per hour times 120 hours, or $840. (4) Divide the number of output bills by the input costs to determine the productivity rate of .95 (800 ÷ $840 = .95).

The performance of .95 can be stated differently. It is usually stated as a ratio (in this case, .95:1), or as a percentage (95 percent). It can also be stated as a labor cost per unit. To determine the *labor cost per unit*, you reverse the process and divide the input by the output. In this case, it cost $1.05 to send out each bill ($840 ÷ 800).

Calculating Productivity Percentage Changes. The .95 productivity rate is set as the base standard. In the next week, the accounting department sent out 800 bills, but due to machine problems, concurrent corrective action of having employees work overtime was needed to meet the standard output at an additional cost of $100. The productivity rate went down to .85 (800 ÷$940). The labor cost per unit went up to $1.175 ($940 ÷ 800). To determine the percentage change, use this formula:

Current productivity rate	85
− Base standard productivity rate	95
= Change	10

Change ÷ base productivity rate (10 ÷ 95) = .1053 or there was a 10.53 percent decrease in productivity

Note that it is not necessary to use the decimal for .95 and .85, and when the base current productivity rate is less than the standard you have a decrease in productivity, but it is not necessary to use a negative number.

Production versus Productivity. It is important to calculate productivity rather than just production output, because it is possible to increase production but decrease productivity. For example, if the accounts payable department sends out 850 bills (production) but it takes 10 hours of overtime (which cost time-and-a-half at $10.50 per hour × 10 hours = $105), productivity has decreased to .90 (850 ÷ 945) from .95. In other words, if you only measure output production and it increases, you can be fooled into thinking you are doing a better job, when in reality you are doing a worse job.

Increasing Productivity

There are three ways to increase productivity:

- Increase the value of the outputs but maintain the value of the inputs (↑O ↔ I)
- Maintain the value of the outputs but decrease the value of the inputs (↑O ↓I)
- Increase the value of the outputs but decrease the value of the inputs (↑O ↓I)

Productivity Comparisons. Productivity measures are more meaningful when they are compared to other productivity rates. For example, you can

✱skillbuilder

compare your department's productivity to that of other organizations and/or departments. This is done in Skill-Building Exercise 14–1. Most important, you should compare your productivity during one period to your productivity in other periods. This comparison will enable you to identify increases or decreases in productivity over time. A productivity rate can also be set as the standard, and you can compare your productivity to the standard on an ongoing basis. This is done in Applying the Concept 14–4.

Productivity has been referred to as a state of mind because everyone should be constantly thinking of ways to increase it. As a manager, you should be working with your employees to measure productivity and continually work to increase it to provide customer value. Productivity comparisons should be made in the functional areas, which is our next topic.

APPLYING THE CONCEPT

AC 14–4 Measuring Productivity

The standard monthly productivity rate in your department is:

$$\frac{\text{outputs: 6,000 units}}{\text{inputs: \$9,000 cost}} = .67$$

For the first five months of the year, calculate the current productivity rate and show it as a ratio and percentage. Also, calculate the percentage productivity change, compared to the standard, stating if it was an increase or decrease.

16. January: outputs 5,900, inputs $9,000 ___ ratio, ___ %, ___ % change ↑ ↓

17. February: outputs 6,200, inputs $9,000 ___ ratio, ___ %, ___ % change ↑ ↓

18. March: outputs 6,000, inputs $9,300 ___ ratio, ___ %, ___ % change ↑ ↓

19. April: outputs 6,300, inputs $9,000 ___ ratio, ___ %, ___ % change ↑ ↓

20. May: outputs 6,300, inputs $8,800 ___ ratio, ___ %, ___ % change ↑ ↓

Productivity Measures in the Functional Areas

The basic concepts of productivity measurement can be applied to all functional areas in the organization. All productivity measures are indications of how well the organization is managed. See Figure 14–11 for a list of ratios in the functional areas. Although the ratios are separated by function, due to the systems effect, they are interrelated.

Information and Financial Productivity Measures. The role of the information (MIS) department is to take input data and transform it into output information that can be used by organization members. Therefore, the individual numbers are data that are transformed through math to provide information, which is listed in the last column in Figure 14–11.

The numbers used to calculate the financial ratios are taken from the income statement and balance sheet. As indicated in Figure 14–11, ratios

WORK APPLICATION

15. Does a company you work or have worked for calculate financial ratios? If you are not sure, call or talk to your present or past boss and find out. If it does, identify which ones it calculates and give the ratios. If it does not calculate ratios, or you cannot get them, but it does provide financial statements, calculate them yourself.

AREA

Finance	Ratio	Calculation	Information
Profitability	Gross profit margin	$\dfrac{Sales - COGS}{Sales}$	Shows efficiency of operations and product pricing.
	Net profit margin	$\dfrac{Net\ profit/income}{Sales}$	Shows product profitability.
	Return on investment	$\dfrac{Net\ profit/income}{Total\ assets}$	Shows return on total capital expenditures, or assets' ability to generate profit.
Liquidity	Current ratio	$\dfrac{Current\ assets}{Current\ liabilities}$	Shows ability to pay short-term debt.
	Quick ratio	$\dfrac{Current\ assets - inventory}{Current\ liabilities}$	Shows stronger measure of bill-paying ability because inventory may be slow to sell for cash.
Leverage	Debt to equity	$\dfrac{Total\ liabilities}{Owners'\ equity}$	Shows proportion of the assets owned by the organization. The higher the ratio, the more solvent the firm and the easier to get credit/funds.
Operations	Inventory turnover	$\dfrac{Cost\ of\ goods\ sold}{Average\ inventory}$	Shows efficiency in controlling investment in inventory. The larger the number the better because products are sold faster.
Marketing	Market share	$\dfrac{Company\ sales}{Total\ industry\ sales}$	Shows the organization's competitive position. The larger the better because it is outselling competitors.
	Sales to presentation	$\dfrac{Sales\ completed}{Sales\ presentations\ made}$	Shows how many presentations it takes to make one sale. The lower the better because less time is spent making nonproductive presentations.
Human Resources	Absenteeism	$\dfrac{No.\ of\ absent\ employees}{Total\ no.\ of\ employees}$	Shows the ratio / percentage of employees not at work for a given time period.
	Turnover	$\dfrac{No.\ of\ employees\ leaving}{Total\ no.\ of\ employees}$	Shows ratio / percentage of employees that must be replaced for a given period, usually one year.
	Work force composition	$\dfrac{No.\ of\ a\ specific\ group}{Total\ no.\ of\ employees}$	Shows ratio / percentage of women, Hispanics, African-Americans, and so on.

Figure 14-11
Functional Area Ratios

are easy to calculate and to understand and they are commonly used in the control system as the means of measurement.

Although the financial ratios indicate performance, they do not measure the performance of the finance department itself. For example, the profitability ratios are based heavily on sales, which is a marketing function. However, the performance of the other departments is affected by how well the finance department does its job. For example, the finance department controls the budget, which helps the other departments. Also, the marketing department sells the products on credit, but it is the finance department that collects the payments and pays for the purchases made throughout the organization.

Marketing and Operations Productivity Measures. The marketing and operations areas of an organization are similar to the heart and lungs of the body. The key to business success is for these two areas, with the aid of the others, to continually increase customer value. If the marketing and operations areas do not work well and together, the entire organization will not function properly and may go bankrupt. The financial profitability ratios of gross profit margin and net profit margin are also considered marketing ratios because they are based on sales.

APPLYING THE CONCEPT

AC 14–5 MOCON Financial Ratios

Using the figures from MOCON's income statement and balance sheet, Figure 14–8, and the numbers below that do not appear in Figure 14–8 but are taken from the complete statements of MOCON, calculate the following ratios using the calculations in Figure 14–11.

Income Statement
Sales = $10,612,752
Cost of Goods Sold = $3,941,933
Average Inventory = $1,733,766

Balance Sheet
Current assets = $9,843,115
Current liabilities = $1,585,324

____ % **21.** Net profit margin. (Profitability ratios are commonly reported as percentages.)

_____

____ % **22.** Return on investment.

_____

____ :1 **23.** Current ratio. (Liquidity ratios are commonly reported as a ratio compared to one.)

_____

____ :1 **24.** Debt to equity. (Leverage ratios are commonly reported as ratios.)

_____

____ **25.** Inventory turnover. (Operations ratios are reported as the number of times per year.)

_____

How would you say MOCON is doing financially based on these ratios?

_____

The operations function does not have a separate section in Figure 14–11 because it tends to use the basic productivity measure, which is more focused on input-output relations than other departments. However, the operations inventory turnover financial ratio is primarily the operations department's responsibility. However, it is dependent on the marketing department for its sales forecast, which it uses as the basis for its production budget. If sales forecasts are too optimistic, operations will produce too much product, which will sit in inventory, which decreases the turnover rate. You will learn more about controlling operations and quality in Chapter 15.

Human Resources Productivity Measures. The numbers for calculating the human resource ratios shown in Figure 14–11 do not come from the financial statements. The numbers for these calculations, which are commonly reported as percentages, are computed by the human resources or information (MIS) departments.

WORK APPLICATION

16. Describe how performance is measured in a functional department you work or have worked for. Is it measured as production or productivity? Explain. As the manager, how would you measure and increase productivity?

CHAPTER SUMMARY AND GLOSSARY

The chapter summary is organized to answer the eleven learning objectives for Chapter 14.

1. List the four stages of the systems process and describe the type of control used at each stage.

The first stage of the systems process is inputs. Preliminary control is designed to anticipate and prevent possible input problems. The second stage is the transformation process. Concurrent control is action taken as inputs are transformed into outputs to ensure that standards are met. The third stage is outputs. Rework control is action taken to fix an output. The fourth stage is customer/stakeholder satisfaction. Damage control is action taken to minimize negative impacts on customers/stakeholders due to faulty outputs. During the four stages feedback is used to improve upon the process to continually increase customer satisfaction.

2. Describe the appropriate feedback process among the functional areas/departments.

Throughout the systems process, feedback is circulated among all the functional areas to improve organizational performance in the input, transformation, and output processes and to continually increase customer satisfaction.

3. List the four steps in the control systems process.

The control systems process steps are: (1) set objectives and standards; (2) measure performance; (3) compare performance to standards; and (4) correct or reinforce, with a feedback loop for continuous improvement.

4. Describe the difference among the three control frequencies.

Constant controls are in continuous use. Periodic controls are used on a regular, fixed basis such as once a day or week. Occasional controls are used on a sporadic basis when needed.

5. Explain the difference between line-item versus program budgets, static versus flexible budgets, and incremental versus zero-based budgets.

The line-item budget identifies the major expenses of the organization/department, whereas the program budget identifies the expenses of specific organizational activities or units. A static budget has only one set of expenses, whereas a flexible budget has a series of expenses for a range of activities. With incremental budgeting, past funds are allocated with only new expenses being justified and approved. With zero-based budgeting, all funds must be justified each year.

6. Explain how the *capital expenditures budget* is different from the expense budget.

The capital expenditures budget includes all planned major asset investments. It consists of funds allocated for investments in major assets that will last, and be paid for, over several years. The expense budget contains funds allocated to pay for operating cost during the budgeting year. With expense budgets, the focus is on cost control. With capital expenditures, the focus is on the more important role of developing ways to bring in additional revenues through new and improved products and projects that will create customer value.

7. List the three primary financial statements and what is presented in each of them.

The income statement presents revenue and expenses and the profit or loss for the stated time period. The balance sheet presents assets, liabilities, and owners' equity. The cash flow statement presents the cash receipts and payments for the stated time period.

8. Explain the importance of positive motivational feedback in coaching.

The objective of coaching is to improve performance. Positive feedback, such as giving praise, is used to motivate employees to maintain and improve their performance.

9. Explain the manager's role in counseling and the role of the employee assistance program staff.

The manager's role in counseling is to give employees feedback so they realize that a problem is affecting their job performance, and to refer employees with problems to the employee assistance program. The role of the employee assistance program staff is to help employees get professional help to solve their problems.

10. State how to measure productivity and list the three ways to increase it.

Productivity is measured by dividing the outputs by the inputs. Productivity is increased by (1) increasing the value of the outputs while maintaining the value of the inputs, (2) maintaining the value of the outputs while decreasing the value of the inputs, and (3) increasing the value of the outputs while decreasing the value of the inputs.

11. Define the following key terms (in order of appearance in the chapter):

Select one or more methods: (1) fill in the missing key terms from memory, (2) match the key terms from the end of the summary with their definitions below, or (3) copy the key terms in order from the list at the beginning of the chapter.

_____ is the process of establishing and implementing mechanisms to ensure that objectives are achieved.

_____ is designed to anticipate and prevent possible problems.

_____ is action taken as inputs are transformed into outputs to ensure standards are met.

_____ is action taken to fix an output.

_____ is action taken to minimize negative impacts on customers/ stakeholders due to faulty outputs.

The _____ steps include: (1) set objectives and standards; (2) measure performance; (3) compare performance to standards; and (4) correct or reinforce.

_____ measure performance levels in the areas of quantity, quality, time, cost, and behavior.

_____ are the limited number of areas in which satisfactory results will ensure successful performance to achieve the objective/standard.

_____ includes constant, periodic, and occasional.

The _____ analyzes the organization's planning, organizing, leading, and controlling functions for improvements.

A _____ is a planned quantitative allocation of resources for specific activities.

The _____ include the revenue and expense budgets.

The _____ includes all planned major asset investments.

The three primary _____ are the income statement, balance sheet, and cash flow statement.

_____ is the process of giving motivational feedback to maintain and improve performance.

_____ has three major activities: listening, teaching, and facilitating.

_____ is the process of giving employees feedback so they realize that a problem is affecting their job performance, and referring employees with problems to the employee assistance program.

The _____ consists of a staff of people who help employees get professional assistance in solving their problems.

_____ is corrective action to get employees to meet standards and standing plans.

_____ is a performance measure relating outputs to inputs.

KEY TERMS

budget   496
capital expenditures budget   499
coaching   502
concurrent control   485
control frequency   493
controlling   484
control systems process   490

critical success factors   492
damage control   485
discipline   507
employee assistance program   506
financial statements   500
management audit   494
management by walking around   503

management counseling   506
operating budgets   497
preliminary control   484
productivity   509
rework control   485
standards   490

REVIEW AND DISCUSSION QUESTIONS

1. Why is damage control important?

2. Why should you focus on preliminary and concurrent types of control rather than rework and damage control?

3. Who are the primary customers/stakeholders for the outputs of the operations, marketing, human resources, finance, and information functional areas/departments?

4. What are the five areas of performance that standards measure?

5. Why is measuring performance important to an organization?

6. What is shown in a performance report?

7. What is the role of reinforcement in the control systems process?

8. What are the three constant control methods, the three periodic control methods, and the four occasional control methods?

9. What are the three steps in the master budgeting process?

10. Why is the capital expenditures budget the most important budget?

11. What is the difference between financial statements and financial budgets?

12. What is the objective of coaching?

13. How do managers commonly demotivate employees?

14. What is the performance formula and how is it used with coaching?

15. What are the three activities of management by walking around and what is the role of facilitating?

16. What is the difference among coaching, counseling, and disciplining?

17. Which of the eight discipline guidelines is most relevant to you personally? Explain.

18. Why should you measure productivity rather than just production?

19. What are some of the major ratio measures in the functional areas of finance, marketing, and human resources?

OBJECTIVE CASE

Rodriguez Clothes Manufacturing

Carmen Rodriguez started his small business about 15 years ago in the Garment District in New York City. Carmen employs around 50 people. One of Rodriguez's teams presently makes quality shirts for men's clothing stores. The five teams at Rodriguez work in one big room in which all clothes are made.

Carmen works in his separate office and spends his time on marketing, finance, and human resources management. He does not spend much time with the manufacturing employees. Team leader responsibility is to keep team production records and the hours worked, to train the members, and to help them when there is a problem. Team leaders do not get involved with discipline or other problems.

Before Carmen came up with a new way to increase the workers' speed, employees made around 48 shirts per eight-hour day. Unlike some competitors, Carmen does not want to run a sweatshop, so he pays employees a salary rather than a low piece rate for actual work performed. However, if employees don't produce an average of 48 shirts, they lose their jobs. Carmen's employees have a higher rate of job satisfaction than the competitors', and Rodriguez has a quality reputation.

With all the competition, Carmen is not making much money. Carmen wanted to get employees to produce more shirts. Carmen thought about buying new machines as a capital expenditure, but he really does not have the money or the desire, because his present machines are working fine. Carmen has also considered changing to piece-rate pay. However, he figured that if he pays employees more to produce more it will have an offsetting effect, which will not benefit him much. He also feared that if he went to

OBJECTIVE CASE

(continued)

piece-rate pay he would have quality problems, which he did not want to risk. Carmen prides himself on being ethical and socially responsible to all stakeholders.

Carmen came up with the idea of setting a new quota in addition to the 48-shirt standard. Employees could leave work early once they met the new 53-shirt quota. Carmen figured he was not pushing his employees too hard and that they could get out of work around a half-hour early each day.

Carmen met with the employees in the shirt team and told them, "I want to try a new idea, which I think is fair to everyone, for the next two weeks. If you produce 53 shirts you can go home for the day and get your full pay. I figure you can get out around 4:30 instead of 5 o'clock without having to rush your work. The same level of quality is required and will be checked as usual. You can continue to produce 48 shirts and work the full eight hours." They discussed the new system and they all liked the idea of working less hours for the same pay. If it did not work, they would go back to the old system.

After the first week, on the following Monday, Carmen got his weekly production reports, which state the number of units made by each worker and the hours each employee worked, from each team. Carmen got around to reading them after closing time, as usual. He went right to the shirt team report to see how the new system was working. Carmen was happy to see that everyone was producing 53 shirts and getting out around 4:30. However, on Friday, Maria made 53 shirts but left at 2:30. Carmen did not understand how this was possible. He decided to talk to Maria to see what was going on.

On Tuesday morning Carmen visited Maria at work and asked her how it was possible to get out at 2:30. Maria said, "All I did was adjust my machine and place this new gadget on it to speed it up. Plus I developed a new procedural sequence in which I make the shirt. Watch how much

faster I can sew now; especially placing buttons on is so much faster." Carmen watched her make a shirt in amazement. He did not know what to say. Carmen told her to keep up the good work and went back to his office.

As Carmen walked back to his office he wondered to himself: "Should I continue to let her leave that early? Do the other workers think it's fair for Maria to get out so much earlier than they do? This is only a two-week trial that is subject to changes that are fair to everyone. What is the fair thing to do?"

Select the best alternative to the following questions. Be sure you are able to explain your answers.

_____ **1.** Carmen's allowing employees to go home early when they finished their work was a _____ control.

    a. preliminary   c. rework

    b. concurrent   d. damage

_____ **2.** The primary customer for the operations products is the _____.

    a. customer   b. marketing   c. finance

_____ **3.** Carmen did not make the new standard clear in the area of _____.

    a. quantity   d. cost

    b. quality   e. behavior

    c. time

_____ **4.** The primary control method Carmen used in letting employees leave when they met the quota/standard was _____.

Constant	Periodic	Occasional
a. self-	d. regular	g. observation
b. clan	reports	h. exception
c. standing	e. budgets	principle
plans	f. audits	i. special
		reports
		j. project

OBJECTIVE CASE

(continued)

_____ 5. In this case, Carmen is focusing on ___.

a. operating budgets
b. capital expenditures
c. financial budgets
d. productivity

_____ 6. Carmen's new leave-early control system has a meaningful direct effect on ___ financial statement(s).

a. the income statement
b. the balance sheet
c. the cash flow
d. none of these

_____ 7. From coaching, which part of the performance formula is the primary reason for Maria's increase in productivity?

a. ability
b. motivation
c. resources

_____ 8. Carmen's new control focuses on increasing

a. production
b. productivity

_____ 9. Carmen's new control technique focuses on

a. Increasing the value of the outputs and maintaining the value of the inputs.

b. Maintaining the value of the outputs and decreasing the value of the inputs.

c. Increasing the value of the outputs and decreasing the value of the inputs.

_____ 10. Carmen's new control technique has the greatest potential to affect the ___ ratio because it measures the manufacturing department's performance.

a. profitability
b. liquidity
c. leverage
d. operations
e. marketing
f. human resource

11. Did Carmen Rodriguez follow the four steps in the control systems process in this case? Explain your answer listing the steps he did and/or did not follow.

12. Calculate the production/productivity increase percentage change from before and after the new control method was introduced.

13. Is there any potential problem with Maria adjusting her machine?

14. Should Carmen keep the control system the way it is now and continue to let Maria leave two hours earlier than the other employees? If not, what should he do?

15. Is there any potential threat to employees with the increased production/productivity? Explain.

VIDEO CASE

Sunshine Cleaning Systems II
(14–1 13 Minutes)

Case Summary

This is a continuation of the video from the last chapter. Sunshine Cleaning Systems is a privately held company dedicated to providing the very highest quality cleaning service to a wide range of clients. Sunshine earns $10 million in sales per year and employs 1,000 people. The company was founded in 1976 by former baseball player and baseball coach Larry Calufetti who leads by coaching. You will see how Sunshine controls four regional offices, hundreds of employees, and hundreds of customers with differing needs to ensure quality and consistency.

Students' Learning Objective

To understand the elements necessary to establish an effective control system and the effects that ability, motivation, and resources have on performance.

Critical Thinking Questions

1. What types of effective control systems could Sunshine develop to enable it to provide cost-effective quality service?

2. How could Sunshine control quality through an inspection process?

---

*skillbuilder

I **G**

Skill-Building Exercise 14-1

Bolton Control System

Preparing for Skill-Building Exercise 14-1

Marie Bolton owns and operates the Bolton Clerical Employment Agency. As the name indicates, her agency focuses on providing clerical employees to its business clients. They have a file of clerical employees looking for jobs, or better jobs. When employers place job orders with the agency, the agency recruiter tries to find a person who fits the job specifications. The agency sends possible candidates to the employer. The employment agencies charge the employer a fee only when one of their referred candidates is hired by the company. The fee is based on the employee's first-year salary. The average fee paid by employers is $1,000.

Each agency recruiter gets 35 percent of the fee charged as a salary. Pay is 100 percent commission. Refunds are made if the person placed does not stay on the job for three months.

Marie has two employees called recruiters. With only two employees, Marie is also a full-time recruiter. She does the management functions in addition to recruiting.

Marie has no formal control methods because her two recruiters are very competent professionals who are paid only by commission; she places minimal restriction on them. Marie is somewhat satisfied with the way her business is operating. However, through a professional association she found out that her business is not doing as well as the average employment agency. Being competitive by nature, Marie does not want to be below average.

Marie has asked you to set up a control system to help her improve her agency's performance. She has provided you with the following performance report comparing her agency figures to those of the average agency. The professional association forecasts that revenues for next year will not increase for the industry.

Performance Information Report for Last Year		
	Bolton	Average
Placement Revenue (refunds deducted, not taxes)	$230,000	$250,000
Recruiter commissions paid	$80,500	$87,500
Refunds	$8,000	$10,000
Number of placements	230	250
Number of company interviews	*	1,000
Number of full-time recruiters (including owners who recruit)	3	3
*Bolton does not keep records of the number of candidates it sends to companies for interviews.		

Identify the systems process for Bolton by identifying its primary:

Inputs	Transformation Process	Outputs	Customers/ Stakeholders

Identify major types of control for each stage of the systems process:

Preliminary	Concurrent	Rework	Damage

To set up a control system for Bolton, follow the steps in the control systems process.

Step 1. Set Objectives and Standards
Marie's objective is to earn $250,000 in revenue for the next year, which is the industry average. Establish standards for the year that will enable Marie to reach her objective.

Quantity of interviews and placements per recruiter: ____ ____

Calculate the number of additional interviews needed to meet the standard per recruiter ____ and the percentage increase ____ %.

Quality. Dollar value and number of acceptable refunds per recruiter: $ ____ ____

Time. State the time period in which the quantity and quality standards should be met: ____

Cost. State the cost based on commissions per recruiter: $ ____

Behavior. Identify any new behavior employees should change to help them meet the standards.

_____

_____

Step 2. Measure Performance
What are the critical success factors for employment agencies? Have you identified the critical success factors within your standards? If not, rework them.

How often should Marie measure performance and what methods of control should she use?

Time frequency to measure performance: _____

Quantity of interviews and placements per recruiter for time period: ____ ____

Specific control methods to use: _____

_____

Step 3. Compare Performance to Standards
How should Marie compare her agency performance to her new standards? _____

_____

_____

Step 4. Correct or Reinforce
What type of corrective action should Marie take if standards are not being met, or reinforcement if they are? _____

_____

_____

Assume that Bolton does exactly meet the standard.

1. Calculate the rate of productivity for Bolton's past performance and for the new performance standard (average agency). ____ ____ Is there a change in productivity? ___ yes ___ no If yes, did it increase or decrease by what percentage? _____ Base the inputs on recruiter commissions only.

2. Calculate the past commission per employee and the new commission per employee (average agency). ____ ____ What percentage of a pay increase do recruiters get ___ ?

3. Do profits increase with the new standards being met? _____

_____

How do you think the employees will react to your proposed control system? Do you think they will resist the control? Why or why not?

_____

_____

Doing Skill-Building Exercise 14–1 in Class
Objective
To improve your skill at developing a control system for an organization/department.

Preparation and Experience
You should have developed a control system for Bolton Clerical Employment Agency in the preparation section of this exercise. In class you may work in a group to develop the control system.

Procedure (15–50 minutes)
Option A. The instructor goes over a possible control system for Bolton.

Option B. The instructor calls on one or more students to present their control system to the class.

Option C. Break into groups of four to six and develop the best control system for Bolton. Have one member be the spokesperson and write down the group's answers and report them to the class. The instructor will give you a set time, such as 10 to 15 minutes, for developing the control system.

Conclusion
The instructor may lead a class discussion and/or make concluding remarks about the exercise.

Application (2–4 minutes)
What did I learn from this exercise? How will I use this knowledge in the future?

_____

Sharing
Volunteers give their answers to the application sections.

BEHAVIOR MODEL VIDEO

Behavior Model Video 14–1 (3½ minutes), Coaching, shows Sarah coaching Dan. Dan is an Internet Web page designer who is not meeting deadlines. Sarah follows the Steps in Model 14–2. This video serves as a behavior model which can be used prior to conducting Skill-Building Exercise 14–2, Coaching, below.

---

*skillbuilder

R

Skill-Building Exercise 14–2

Coaching

Preparing for Skill-Building Exercise 14–2
You should have read and understand the text material on coaching. You may also view Behavior Model Video 14–1, which illustrates how to conduct a coaching session using the coaching model.

Doing Skill-Building Exercise 14–2 in Class
Objective
To develop your skill at improving performance through coaching.

Experience
You will coach, be coached, and be observed coaching using Model 14–2.

Procedure 1 (2–4 minutes)
Break into groups of three. Make some groups of two, if necessary. Each member selects one of the following three situations in which to be the manager, and a different one in which to be the employee. In each situation, the employee knows the standing plans; he or

she is not motivated to follow them. You will take turns coaching and being coached.

Three Problem Employee Situations

1. Employee 1 is a clerical worker. The person uses files, as do the other ten employees in the department. The employees all know that they are supposed to return the files when they are finished so that others can find them when they need them. Employees should have only one file out at a time. The supervisor notices that Employee 1 has five files on the desk, and another employee is looking for one of them. The supervisor thinks that Employee 1 will complain about the heavy workload as an excuse for having more than one file out at a time.

2. Employee 2 is a server in an ice cream shop. The employee knows that the tables should be cleaned up quickly after customers leave so that new customers do not have to sit at dirty tables. It's a busy night. The supervisor finds dirty dishes on two of this employee's occupied tables. Employee 2 is socializing with some friends at one of the tables. Employees are supposed to be friendly; Employee 2 will probably use this as an excuse for the dirty tables.

3. Employee 3 is an auto technician. All employees at the garage where this person works know that they are supposed to put a paper mat on the floor of each car so that the carpets don't get dirty. When the service supervisor got into a car Employee 3 repaired, the car did not have a mat and there was grease on the carpet. Employee 3 does excellent work and will probably make reference to this fact when coached.

Procedure 2 (3–7 minutes)

Prepare for coaching to improve performance. Below, each group member writes an outline of what he or she will say when coaching Employee 1, 2, or 3, following the steps below:

1. Describe current performance. _____
   _____

2. Describe the desired behavior. (Don't forget to have the employee state why it is important.)
   _____
   _____

3. Get a commitment to the change. _____
   _____

4. Follow up. _____
   _____

Procedure 3 (5–8 minutes)

a. Role-playing. The manager of Employee 1, the clerical worker, coaches him or her as planned. (Use the actual name of the group member playing Employee 1.) Talk—do not read your written plan. Employee 1, put yourself in the worker's position. You work hard; there is a lot of pressure to work fast. It's easier when you have more than one file. Refer to the workload while being coached. Both the manager and the employee will have to ad lib.

The person not playing a role is the observer. He or she makes notes on the observer form below. Try to make positive comments and point out areas for improvement. Give the manager alternative suggestions for what he or she could have said to improve the coaching session.

OBSERVER FORM

1. How well did the manager describe current behavior?
   _____
   _____

2. How well did the manager describe desired behavior? Did the employee state why the behavior is important?
   _____
   _____

3. How successful was the manager at getting a commitment to the change? Do you think the employee would change?_____
   _____

4. How well did the manager describe how he or she was going to follow up to ensure that the employee performed the desired behavior? _____
   _____

b. Feedback. The observer leads a discussion of how well the manager coached the employee. (This should be a discussion, not a lecture.) Focus on what the manager did well and how the manager could improve. The employee should also give feedback on how he or she felt and what might have been more effective in getting him or her to change. Do not go on to the next interview until you are told to do so. If you finish early, wait for the others to finish.

Procedure 4 (5–8 minutes)
Same as procedure 3, but change roles so that Employee 2, the server, is coached. Employee 2 should make a comment about the importance of talking to customers to make them feel welcome. The job is not much fun if you can't talk to your friends.

Procedure 5 (5–8 minutes)
Same as procedure 3, but change roles so that Employee 3, the auto technician, is coached. Employee 3 should comment on the excellent work he or she does.

Conclusion
The instructor leads a class discussion and/or makes concluding remarks.

Application (2–4 minutes)
What did I learn from this experience? How will I use this knowledge in the future?

_____

_____

Sharing
Volunteers give their answers to the application section.

BEHAVIOR MODEL VIDEO

Behavior Model Video 14–2, (5 minutes)

In Discipline, Dan continues to miss deadlines so Sarah disciplines him following the steps in Model 14–3 on pages 507–508. This video serves as a behavior model which can be used prior to conducting Skill-Building Exercise 14–3, Disciplining, below.

---

*Skillbuilder

Skill-Building Exercise 14–3

R

Disciplining

Preparing for Skill-Building Exercise 14–3
You should have read and understand the text material on disciplining. You may also view Behavior Model Video 14–2, which illustrates how to conduct a discipline session using the discipline model.

Doing Skill-Building Exercise 14–3 in Class
Objective
To develop your ability to discipline an employee.

Experience
You will discipline, be disciplined, and observe a discipline session using Model 14–3. This is a follow-up exercise to Skill-Building Exercise 14–2.

Procedure 1 (2–4 minutes)
Break into groups of three. Make some groups of two, if necessary. Each member selects one of the three situations from Skill-Building Exercise 14–2. Decide who will discipline Employee 1, the clerical worker; Employee 2, the ice cream shop server; and Employee 3, the auto technician. Also select a different group member to play the employee being disciplined.

Procedure 2 (3–7 minutes)
Prepare for the discipline session. Write a basic outline of what you will say to Employee 1, 2, or 3; follow the steps in the discipline model below.

1. Refer to past feedback. (Assume that you have discussed the situation before, using the coaching model.)_____

_____

2. Ask why the undesired behavior was used. (The employee should make up an excuse for not changing.)

_____

_____

3. Give the discipline. (Assume that an oral warning is appropriate.) _____

_____

4. Get a commitment to change and develop a plan.

_____

_____

5. Summarize and state the follow up.

_____

_____

Procedure 3 (5–8 minutes)

a. Role-play. The manager of Employee 1, the clerical worker, disciplines him or her as planned. (Use the actual name of the person playing the employee.) Talk—do not read your written plan. Employee 1, put yourself in the worker's position. You work hard; there is a lot of pressure to work fast. It's easier when you have more than one file. Both the manager and employee will need to ad lib.

The person not playing a role is the observer. He or she makes notes on the observer form below. For each of the following steps, try to make a statement about the positive aspects of the discipline and a statement about how the manager could have improved. Give alternative things the manager could have said to improve the discipline session. Remember, the objective is to change behavior.

OBSERVER FORM

1. How well did the manager refer to past feedback?

_____

_____

2. How well did the manager ask why the undesired behavior was used? _____

_____

3. How well did the manager give the discipline?

_____

_____

4. Did the manager get a commitment to change? Do you think the employee will change his or her behavior? _____

_____

5. How well did the manager summarize and state the follow up? How effective will the follow up be?

_____

_____

b. Feedback. The observer leads a discussion of how well the manager disciplined the employee. The employee should also give feedback on how he or she felt and what might have been more effective in getting him or her to change. Do not go on to the next interview until you are told to do so. If you finish early, wait until the others finish or the time is up.

Procedure 4 (5–8 minutes)

Same as procedure 3, but change roles so that Employee 2, the ice cream server, is disciplined. Employee 2, put yourself in the worker's position. You enjoy talking to your friends, and you're supposed to be friendly to the customers.

Procedure 5 (5–8 minutes)

Same as procedure 3, but change roles so that Employee 3, the auto technician, is disciplined. Employee 3, put yourself in the worker's position. You are an excellent technician. Sometimes you forget to put the mat on the floor.

Conclusion

The instructor leads a class discussion and makes concluding remarks.

Application (2–4 minutes)

What did I learn from this experience? How will I use this knowledge in the future?

_____

_____

Sharing

Volunteers give their answers to the application section.

15

Operations, Quality, Technology, and Information Control Systems

Learning Objectives

After completing this chapter, you should be able to:

1. Describe time-based competition and state why it is important.

2. Explain the difference among the three tangibilities of products, the three levels of customer involvement, the four flexibilities of operations processes, and the three intensities of resources.

3. Discuss what is meant by "quality is a virtue of design."

4. Explain product, process, cellular, and fixed-position types of facility layouts in terms of their customer involvement and flexibility.

5. Describe priority scheduling and list its three priorities.

6. Explain the difference among inventory control, just-in-time (JIT) inventory, and materials requirement planning (MRP).

7. Explain how statistical process control (SPC) charts and the exception principle are used in quality control.

8. Describe the three primary types of information systems and their relationship.

9. List the components of an information network.

10. Define the following **key terms** (in order of appearance in the chapter):

time-based competition	materials requirement
operations	planning (MRP)
product	quality control
customer involvement	International Standards
operations flexibility	Organization (ISO)
technology	statistical process control
facility layout	(SPC)
capacity	information
routing	types of information
priority scheduling	systems
inventory	computer networks
inventory control	information networks
just-in-time (JIT) inventory	

Skill Development

*skillbuilder

1. You can develop your skill at determining the economic order quantity (Skill-Building Exercise 15–1).

   Ordering the economic quantity of materials and supplies is a controlling management function that is based on mathematical technical skill. Doing so requires the decisional management role, which is based on the informational role. The SCAN competencies of resources, information, and systems, as well as basic and thinking foundation skills, are developed through this exercise.

PepsiCo designated 1997 as the year of reinventing PepsiCo to position it for long-term growth. PepsiCo made the strategic decision to get out of the restaurant business to better focus on its packaged goods businesses. Pizza Hut, Kentucky Fried Chicken, and Taco Bell were combined into a $10-billion company called Tricon Global Restaurants that spun off (sold) to its shareholders. Today PepsiCo consists of Pepsi-Cola beverages and Frito-Lay snacks, with annual global sales of over $21 billion, about 50 percent from each division, with a sales force of 63,000. Frito-Lay is by far the world leader in snack food sales and Pepsi-Cola is a strong second to Coca-Cola. In this chapter we will focus on the Frito-Lay division. Americans continue to eat more than 20 pounds of salty snacks a year.

PepsiCo is focusing on its consumers and customers. Its consumers are the people who eat and drink its products, whereas its customers are the companies (supermarkets, convenience stores, restaurants, and other businesses) that sell PepsiCo products to the consumers. PepsiCo's philosophy of success is that they have to give both groups exactly what they want, when and where they want it.

Strategy implementation and control are very important. To control, PepsiCo measures its marketplace performance as carefully as its financial performance. It evaluates product quality, service, value, brand image, and employee performance to make consumers and customers happy. The company's sales people/drivers were one of the first to use hand-held computers to transmit sales and inventory data back to headquarters.

A few reasons why Frito-Lay is so successful include aggressive marketing, an extensive distribution system, operating discipline to control consistent quality, and new product innovations. In 1997, WOW fat-free snacks, made with Olean, and Doritos 3Ds, a three-dimensional tortilla chip, were introduced. The Cracker Jack brand was also acquired from Borden to diversify Frito-Lay's core salty snacks.

Frito-Lay forecasts enormous global growth opportunities over many years. To this end, product packaging has been changed to create a similar look and feel for international consumers. The company is investing heavily for success to compete more effectively, manufacture more efficiently, distribute more widely, and promote more aggressively. Throughout this chapter you will learn more about Frito-Lay.[1]

For current information on Frito-Lay, use Internet address **http://www.fritolay.com**. For ideas on using the Internet, see Appendix B.

---

1. Describe time-based competition and state why it is important.

TIME-BASED COMPETITION AND OPERATIONS

Before we get into the details of the chapter, you should understand time-based competition and operations.

Time-Based Competition

time-based competition
Strategies to increase the speed of going from creativity to delivery.

Time-based competition *refers to strategies to increase the speed of going from creativity to delivery.* The organization that can take a creative idea, turn it into an innovation (a new product or process, Chapter 3), sell it, and deliver it to continually increase customer value has a first-mover competitive advantage (Chapter 4).

> **WORK APPLICATION**
>
> 1. Is your present or past organization concerned about time-based competition? If yes, what functional areas are primarily responsible for speed?

With globalization, the speed of competition has increased. You should remember that it is people, rather than machinery, who are the force behind operations.[2] Speed, efficiency, and cost control are the common goals of savvy companies,[3] such as Frito-Lay. Through time-based competition, 3M reduced its new product development time from two years to two months, Motorola cut its production lead time for cellular phones from several weeks to four hours, and Johnson and Johnson has the top-selling contact lens largely due to its rapid and reliable delivery of disposable contacts. Levi Strauss reduced its reorder cycle time from nine weeks to four days, resulting in lower costs, fewer stockouts, and higher flexibility.[4] Because the mission of all organizations revolves around providing products, the operations department is the primary focus of speed.[5]

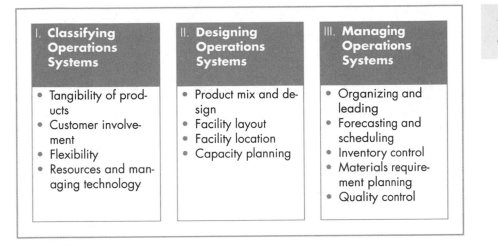

Figure 15-1
Operations

I. **Classifying Operations Systems**	II. **Designing Operations Systems**	III. **Managing Operations Systems**
• Tangibility of products • Customer involvement • Flexibility • Resources and managing technology	• Product mix and design • Facility layout • Facility location • Capacity planning	• Organizing and leading • Forecasting and scheduling • Inventory control • Materials requirement planning • Quality control

Operations

Operations *is the function in which resource inputs are transformed into product outputs. A* **product** *is a good, a service, or a combination of the two.* Figure 15-1 lists the three major functions of managing operations, which are discussed in this chapter.

operations
The function in which resource inputs are transformed into product outputs.
product
A good, a service, or a combination of the two.

CLASSIFYING OPERATIONS SYSTEMS

Operations can be classified by the tangibility of products, customer involvement, flexibility, and resources and managing technology used.

Tangibility of Products

Tangibility of products refers to whether they are tangible, intangible, or mixed.

Tangible Products. *Tangible products* include goods such as Frito-Lay snack foods, Gateway 2000 computers, and this textbook.

Intangible Products. *Intangible products* include services, such as a hair cut, dry cleaning, or legal advice.

Mixed Products. *Mixed products* include both tangible and intangible qualities, for example, TWA airplanes are tangible, but the airline flight is an intangible service. Today, many organizations focus on products, not just goods. For example, major appliance retail stores, like Sears Brand Central, not only sell major appliances but also offer extended warranties and service what they sell.

2. Explain the difference among the three tangibilities of products, the three levels of customer involvement, the four flexibilities of operations processes, and the three intensities of resources.

Customer Involvement

customer involvement
Operations are make to stock, make to order, or assemble to order.

Customer involvement *refers to whether operations are make to stock, make to order, or assemble to order.*

Make to Stock (MTS). *Make-to-stock* operations produce products in anticipation of demand with a common design and price. Therefore, there is a low level of customer involvement. Most products that you see in retail stores, including Frito-Lay's, are from make-to-stock operations. Most services cannot be make to stock, such as a hair cut. However, some can, such as scheduled transportation such as airline flights and train and bus trips.

Make to Order (MTO). *Make-to-order* operations are only produced after receipt of an order from a specific customer. Therefore, there is a high level of customer involvement. Many services, such as auto repair, tailoring, development of an accounting system, a legal criminal defense, and medical services have to be make to order. Some goods are also make to order, such as custom clothes and drapes and a family portrait.

Assemble to Order (ATO). *Assemble-to-order* operations produce a standard product with some customized features. Some goods can only be produced after the receipt of an order, or to stock with different features. However, services can only be assembled to order after receipt of an order. Therefore, there is a moderate level of customer involvement. Relatively expensive goods, such as automobiles, mainframe computer systems, and furniture, are commonly assembled to order. McDonald's primarily makes its hamburgers and other products make to stock, whereas Burger King emphasizes "have it your way" with assemble to order by offering a standard burger with customized toppings.

Service can also be assemble to order. For example, standard training consulting packages and accounting and legal services can be customized to fit the needs of an organization.

Flexibility

operations flexibility
Products are produced continuously, repetitively, in batches, or individually.

Operations flexibility *refers to whether the products are produced continuously, repetitively, in batches, or individually.* Flexibility of operations is based on product volume and variety.[6] *Volume* refers to how many units of one product are produced, and *variety* refers to how many different products the operation produces. The four operations are presented in order by least to most flexible.

Continuous Process Operations (CPO). *Continuous process operations* produce outputs that

APPLYING THE CONCEPT

AC 15–1 Customer Level of Involvement

Identify each product by its level of customer involvement.

a. make to stock   b. assemble to order   c. make to order

_____ **1.** A haircut by Pierre.

_____ **2.** A soft drink in a can by 7-UP.

_____ **3.** Coffee ice cream in a sugar cone by Friendly's Ice Cream.

are not in discrete units, such as gas and oil, electricity, chemicals, and pulp. They tend to produce goods rather than services. Continuous process operations have no, or very little, variety and high volume, making them the least flexible operations systems. Therefore, they are used with *make-to-stock goods* operations.

Repetitive Process Operations (RPO). *Repetitive process operations* produce outputs in an assembly-line-type structure. Operations employees and equipment are quite specialized in function and location. Each unit of output follows the same path through labor and equipment. All kinds of consumer and industrial goods, such as automobiles and tableware, are repetitive process operations outputs. Some services can also be assembly-line oriented, such as an automatic car wash or dog grooming service. Repetitive process operations have some variety and a high volume of similar units. Therefore, they are primarily used with *make-to-stock or assemble-to-order goods* operations. Frito-Lay snacks can be produced on a repetitive process operations system.

Batch Process Operations (BPO). *Batch process operations* produce different outputs with the same resources. When both the volume and variety of products are moderate, flexibility is needed. Organizations often cannot justify the investment required to dedicate labor or equipment to a single product, so they have multiple uses. For example, a wood furniture maker could use the same people and machines to make dining room tables and chairs, desks, and bedroom dressers. Most of Frito-Lay's snacks are fried, so the same fryer can be used at different times to fry a variety of snacks. A few services, such as cleaning services who have business accounts, can also use *batch process operations.* Batch process operations have moderate variety and volume of similar units. Therefore, they are primarily used with *make-to-stock or assemble-to-order goods* operations.

Batch process operations require more controls than continuous process and repetitive process operations in coordinating the inputs, the transformation process, and the inventory of finished outputs. You have to be sure not to sell all of one product or have too much of it in stock.

Individual Process Operations (IPO). *Individual process operations* produce outputs to customer specifications. They have high variety and low volume. Therefore, they are *make-to-order goods and service* operations. Refer back to make-to-order examples of goods and services that are individual process operations. Individual process operations are the most flexible operations system. In manufacturing operations, the term for individual process operations is *job shop.* Because the large majority of retailers and service organizations use individual process operations, they do not usually classify their type of flexibility like manufacturers do.

As with batch process operations, individual process operations require more controls than continuous process and repetitive process operations in coordinating the inputs and the transformation process. You want to try to maintain an even flow of business.

Project Process Operations (PPO). *Project process operations* are another area of process that does not fit the more popular flexibility by volume and variety. Project process operations produce low-volume outputs that require a relatively long period of time to complete. Project process operations are commonly completed by sending the resources to the customer's site, rather than completing the project at the seller's facilities. Project process operations are used in the construction industry for building. Consulting services often blend individual process with project process operations, as the client gives the consultant a project to complete. The work may be divided between the two sites.

APPLYING THE CONCEPT

AC 15–2 Flexibility of Operations

Identify each product by the operations system that would produce it.

a. CPO   b. RPO   c. BPO   d. IPO   e. PPO

_____ **4.** A Whirlpool refrigerator.

_____ **5.** A swimming pool sold and installed by Teddy Bear Pools.

_____ **6.** The asphalt for a driveway delivered by Juan's Asphalt Company.

_____ **7.** Packages of Trident gum.

Resources and Managing Technology

technology
The process used in transforming inputs into outputs.

Operations is the function in which inputs are transformed into product outputs, but **technology** *is the process used to transform inputs into outputs*. Important decisions include the use of labor and capital intensity to make the product, how the customer will be served, and how the manufacturing or service technology will be managed.

Capital-Intensive Operations. In *capital-intensive operations*, machines do most of the work. Manufacturing companies that use the continuous and repetitive operations processes (such as oil, automobile, and steel companies) are capital-intensive because they invest large sums in the machines that make the goods. These companies tend to use high levels of technology that is often developed by other companies, such as Modern Controls products. Manufacturing firms are generally more capital-intensive than service organizations. Frito-Lay snacks are produced by capital-intensive repetitive operations process machines.

Labor-Intensive Operations. In *labor-intensive operations*, human resources does most of the work. Organizations that use the individual operations process tend to be labor-intensive. Retail and service organizations are generally less capital-intensive than manufacturing firms, and they tend to use lower levels of technology, but not always. Education and consulting, as well as personal services such as hair cutting, auto repair, accounting, and legal services, tend to be very labor-intensive.

Balanced-Intensity. Manufacturing firms use a balance of labor and capital in batch and individual operations processes because it takes skilled workers to use the flexible machines. Many large retailers have a balance of capital (because of the high cost of rent at malls or buying a store in a good location) and labor (they have a lot of employees). Frito-Lay snack distribution is labor-intensive with 41,000 delivery people, but it is also capital-intensive with more than 900 tractor trailers and a smaller truck for each delivery person.

Serving Customers. Customers can be served by people, machines, or both. Most Frito-Lay snacks are sold to retailers who hire cashiers. However, the company also sells snacks in vending machines. Candy, cigarettes, and food are also sold in machines. Some small banks service their customers only by personal tellers, whereas large banks tend to use both tellers and automatic teller machines. If you call to get information about movies and a variety of other things, you will probably get a recorded message. Also, where is the customer served—his or her home or office or the business's. Today, some banks send a loan officer to your home or office to take a mortgage loan application; others will do it over the phone. Some banks will let you make transactions, such as transferring funds between accounts and paying bills, over the phone or by computer.

Managing Manufacturing Technology. Two important areas of manufacturing technology used in organizations are (1) *automation*, the process of designing work to be performed by machine and (2) *computer-assisted manufacturing*, the process of using computers to design or manufacture goods. Computer-assisted manufacturing includes *computer-aided design (CAD)*,[7] *computer-aided manufacturing (CAM)*, and *computer-integrated manufacturing (CIM)*. CAD uses computers to design parts and complete goods and to simulate performance so that a prototype does not need to be constructed. Auto makers use it to speed up car designs, GE used it to change the design of circuit breakers, and Benneton uses CAD to design new styles and products. CAD is usually combined with CAM to ensure that the design is coordinated with its production. CAM is especially useful with individual operations processes when reorders come in, because it can quickly produce the desired product, prepare labels and copies of orders, and deliver it.[8]

CIM links CAD and CAM together, and all manufacturing activities are controlled by computer. With CIM, the computer can access the company's information systems and adjust machine placements and settings automatically to enhance both the complexity and flexibility of scheduling. Robots perform functions ordinarily thought to be only appropriate for human beings and are commonly used in CIM. Computer-integrated manufacturing is a powerful and complex management control system that is relatively expensive, and therefore is more commonly used with high-volume continuous and repetitive operations processes.[9]

Managing Service Technology. Manufacturers create the innovative products, such as computer hardware and software, that are commonly used by service firms to make them competitive. For example, VISA customers' credit card transactions are recorded and billed electronically. Hotels use technology to accept and record room reservations. Health care providers use technology to manage patient records, dispatch ambulances, and monitor patient vital signs.[10]

Combining Classification Methods. Figure 15–2 combines the four classification methods. Notice that the focus on the left is on manufacturing goods; the focus on the right is on providing services; and in the middle the focus is on integrating the two. However, it is not always easy to make a clear classification between closely related operations as processes should be seen as being part of a continuum, as they are in Figure 15–2. For example, with tangibility of products it's difficult to determine the mix cutoff or the exact balance of capital and labor intensity resources. There is some overlap in flexibility between processes. The trend today, with the fast-changing environment, is toward more flexible operations systems. Some organizations are designing repetitive process operations that try to gain the benefits of batch process operations.[11]

Some organizations have more than one type of operation within the same system. For example, Frito-Lay could use repetitive process operations for its best-selling items and batch process operations for its lower-selling items. It could also use individual process operations to make snacks for customers by placing them in bags with the customer's name on it, such as Safeway or Edwards food stores.

WORK APPLICATION

2. Using Figure 15–2, identify the operation system where you work or have worked based on tangibility, customer involvement, flexibility, and resources. Be sure to classify the operations by using the names below the continuum lines.

Figure 15-2
Classifying Operations Systems

Tangibility of Product

Tangible ←———————————————————————→ Intangible

Goods   Mixed Products   Services

Customer Involvement Level

Low ←———————————————————————→ High

Make-to-Stock (MTS)   Assemble-to-Order (ATO)   Make-to-Order (MTO)

Flexibility

Inflexible—high volume, low variety ←—————→ High variety, low volume—Flexible

| Continuous Process Operations | Repetitive Process Operations | Batch Process Operations | Individual Process Operations |

Resources

Developers and users of technology   Users of technology
Higher level of technology   Lower level of technology
commonly used   commonly used

Capital intensive ←————— Balanced —————→ Labor intensive

DESIGNING OPERATIONS SYSTEMS

With the classification of the operation system, the operations that will take inputs and transform them into product outputs must be designed. In a changing environment, the operation systems must be continually redesigned in the interrelated areas of product mix and design, facility layout, facility location, and capacity planning.

Product Mix and Design

Product Mix. Based on the organization's mission and objectives, top-level managers select the product mix. The *product mix* includes the number of product lines, the number of products within each line offered, and the mixture of goods and services within each line. With existing products, the product mix is set but can be changed.[12] For example, computer clone manufacturers (such as Dell and Gateway) used to focus on goods, but over the years they have increased their service. Frito-Lay's product lines include a variety of flavors in various sizes and packaging.

Product Design. *Product design* refers to new or improved product development. Large manufacturing companies generally have engineers who design products and a separate operations department that produces the products. Today, successful companies, including Hewlett-Packard, integrate design and manufacturing rather than treat them as separate steps in product development.

Quality Is a Virtue of Design. *Quality is a virtue of design* means that if products are designed with cross-functional team input to provide customer value, there will be fewer operations problems, the product will be easier to sell, and it will be less costly to service the product. Therefore, it is important for all functional areas to work together on the design of new products.[13]

The Need to Balance Time-Based Competition and Design. The answer to speeding up the process is not to rush through the design. For example, GM's Pontiac Fiero sports car lacked virtue of design. One design error was that the trunk contained a small spare tire. When a driver got a flat tire and put on the spare, the regular tire would not fit into the trunk, and with a small two-seat sports car interior, there was really no room for the tire. In addition, some of the engines caught on fire and there were all kinds of small problems that ran up the service costs. Because of these problems, the cars were hard to sell. The Fiero had one of the worst records for repeat buyers. Pontiac eventually discontinued the Fiero.

Facility Layout

Facilities are the physical resources used in the operations process. The building, machines, furniture, and so on are part of the facility. *Layout* refers

---

WORK APPLICATION

3. List the product mix for an organization you work or have worked for. Be sure to identify the number of major product lines, the number of products within the one major line offered, and the mixture of goods and services within the one major line.

3. Discuss what is meant by "quality is a virtue of design."

4. Explain product, process, cellular, and fixed-position types of facility layouts in terms of their customer involvement and flexibility.

facility layout
Whether operations use product, process, cellular, or fixed-position layouts.

to the spatial arrangement of operations units relative to each other. **Facility layout** *refers to whether operations use product, process, cellular, or fixed-position layouts.* The facility layout selected is based on the classification of operations system and the product design. An important consideration in layout is the flow of the product through its transformation.[14]

Product Layout. *Product layout* uses make-to-stock and/or assemble-to-order customer involvement, repetitive process or continuous process operations flexibility, and tends to be more capital-intensive.

Organizations with high volume and low variety have to decide what the sequence of assembly line flow will be. Frito-Lay makes snacks and IBM produces PCs on a product layout. American, Southwest, TWA, and the other airlines provide a service using product layout. Air travelers go to the check-in area, to the boarding area, and on the plane; when they arrive, passengers get off the plane, go to the luggage pickup area, and to ground transportation.

Process Layout. *Process, or functional, layout* uses make-to-order customer involvement, individual operations process flexibility, and tends to be labor-intensive or balanced.

Organizations with high variability and lower volume with products/customers that will have different needs and use only some processes/functions have to decide how they should be arranged. Most offices are set up functionally with assigned areas/departments, such as human resources and finance. Retail stores use process layouts so customers can go to departments to find what they need. Upscale restaurants make each meal to order and arrange the kitchen away from the dining area. The operations are arranged so cooks can move about in adequate work space to process numerous meals at the same time. In a health care facility, the patient is sent to the function(s) necessary to treat the patient, such as x-ray, laboratories, internal medicine, pharmacy, and so on. Many hospitals also bring functions to the patient (patient-centered care) to take the emphasis off confusing building layouts.

Cellular Layout. *Cellular layout* uses make-to-stock and/or assemble-to-order batch operations process, and tends to have balanced capital and labor intensity.

Organizations with moderate variability and volume products must decide how to *group technology* so that all the activities involved in creation of the product are located near one another. Grouping technology into cells provides some of the efficiencies of both product and process layouts. Multiple cells make it easy for employees with different skills to work together to deliver the final product. Self-managed teams (Chapter 10) are commonly used with each cell. Edy's Ice Cream uses cells with self-managed teams to make its various flavors in batches.

Flexible manufacturing systems group technology to take advantage of a product layout without creating a batch environment by using automated technology to produce both high-volume and high-variety products.[15] However, they still produce in batches. For example, Mazda's Japan Ujina plant can build up to eight different car models on a single assembly line. Most U.S. assembly lines, which can be an entire facility, make only one model. However, recall the control issues of batch process operations.

Fixed-Position Layout. Fixed-position layout uses make-to-order and/or assemble-to-order project process operations and tends to have balanced capital and labor intensity.

Organizations with low-volume products that take a relatively long period of time to complete each unit must determine the sequence of steps of workers who come to the product during its construction. Most contractors construct buildings, Boeing makes planes, and Newport News makes ships using fixed-position layout.

Figure 15–3 summarizes and compares the four types of layouts with their level of customer involvement and types of flexibility of operations process and provides an illustration of each systems process.

Facility Location

Location is the physical geographic site of facilities. The facility location must be based on the classification of operating systems, its product mix, layout requirements, and capacity planning.[16] Some of the major factors that are considered when making the location decision include the following.

Cost. Cost includes the cost of the land and facility (or rent); the expenses of human resources to staff it; and operating expenses such as utilities, taxes, and insurance.

Near Inputs, Customers, and/or Competitors. Some locations need to be near inputs. For example, General Mills and Pillsbury are both located in Minneapolis to get easy access to grains from Midwest farmers for processing into flour and other products to be sold to retail stores. On the other hand, some locations need to be easy to get to for customers. For example, retail stores are commonly located in malls in major suburbs. Fast food restaurants are commonly located on major thoroughfares. Some businesses want to locate away from competitors to be convenient to customers, whereas others want to be close to competitors. For example, Joe's Burger is at a distance, but McDonald's and Burger King are often located across from each other.

Transportation. For manufacturers, this includes access to air, rail, truck, and water transportation to get inputs and to deliver product outputs. For retailers, this includes getting merchandise delivered for sale, and

Figure 15-3
Facilities Layout

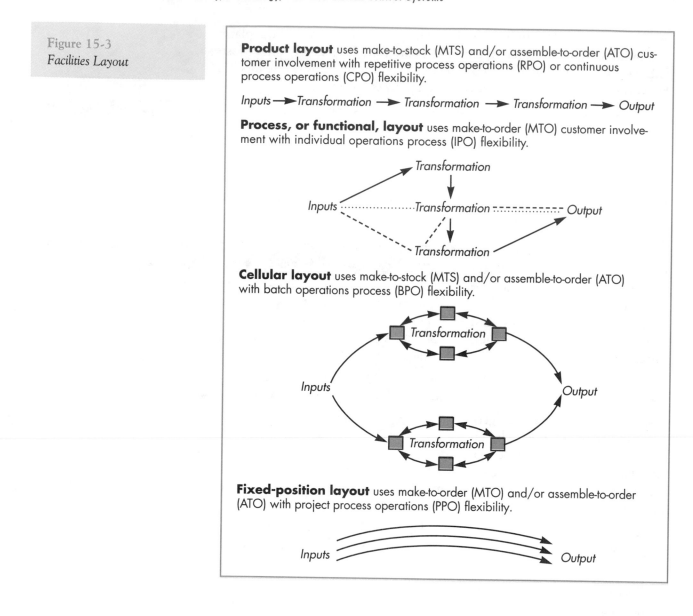

Product layout uses make-to-stock (MTS) and/or assemble-to-order (ATO) customer involvement with repetitive process operations (RPO) or continuous process operations (CPO) flexibility.

Inputs ➛ *Transformation* ➛ *Transformation* ➛ *Transformation* ➛ *Output*

Process, or functional, layout uses make-to-order (MTO) customer involvement with individual operations process (IPO) flexibility.

Transformation

Inputs · · · · · *Transformation* - - - - - *Output*

Transformation

Cellular layout uses make-to-stock (MTS) and/or assemble-to-order (ATO) with batch operations process (BPO) flexibility.

Transformation

Inputs *Output*

Transformation

Fixed-position layout uses make-to-order (MTO) and/or assemble-to-order (ATO) with project process operations (PPO) flexibility.

Inputs *Output*

whether employees and customers can easily get to the location. Parking has been one of the problems that has caused the failure of many downtown businesses. Many of these businesses have relocated to malls.

Access to Human Resources. Certain types of skilled labor can be more easily found in certain locations. For example, high-tech firms tend to go to the technology highway, Route 128 in the Boston area and Silicon Valley in California.

Community Interest. To gain jobs, many communities have offered economic incentives, such as cheap land and low taxes, to attract businesses to their area. Such incentives were considered in the foreign automobile companies' decision to locate plants in the Southern states.

Quality of Life Issues. The quality of local schools, the availability of recreational and cultural facilities, crime rates, and an overall community environment that will contribute to the firm's ability to attract and retain high-caliber employees, especially managers, are given some consideration in the location decision. Frito-Lay is headquartered in Dallas, Texas, whereas its parent PepsiCo is based in Purchase, New York.

Number of Facilities. Another important consideration is the number of facilities. Frito-Lay has increased its facilities to 42 over the years to make and deliver its products to customers all over the United States. In the other direction, many companies have downsized and closed facilities. For example, GE decided that it did not need six facilities to make circuit breakers. So, it invested heavily in capital intensity to automate one plant and closed the other five.

Capacity Planning

Another part of the facility decision is capacity and planning. **Capacity** is *the amount of products an organization can produce.* Should a facility be built to produce 2,000 or 5,000 units per day? How many checkouts/teller stations should a supermarket/bank have? Should a restaurant have 50 or 100 tables? How many rooms should a hotel build? How many beds should an intensive care unit of a hospital have?[17] Computerized mathematical models can be used to make these decisions.[18]

In most cases, capacity planning is made under uncertainty or at least a high risk (Chapter 3) because it usually requires a large capital investment, and the decision is made based on a long-term sales forecast (Chapter 5).

Under Capacity. If the organization selects to build a facility to produce 2,000 units per day, and the demand is 5,000 per day, it will lose sales, revenues, and profits. Modulate Corporation incorrectly forecasted capacity needs and at a high cost moved its head office six times in seven years.

Excess Capacity. Excess capacity is common in businesses with fluctuation demand such as restaurants. It is not unusual to have twice as many people going out on a Friday or Saturday night than on the other nights of the week, or for a hotel to be overbooked during peak season and underbooked during off season. Excess capacity can be expensive as assets must be paid for even though they are not being used.

Optimizing Capacity. It is necessary for many organizations to optimize capacity.[19] Ideally, organizations with fluctuating demand should maximize revenue by turning away some business during peak periods but not having too much excess capacity during the slow periods. For example, a restaurant that could fill 80 to 100 tables on a good weekend night but only 30 during the week should probably have 50 to 60 tables to maximize capacity. Hotels do the same.

Another way to optimize capacity is by offering products that are used at different times. For example, McDonald's started out selling only lunch

capacity
The amount of products an organization can produce.

WORK APPLICATION

5. Does the organization you work or have worked for have under, excess, or optimal capacity utilization? Explain your answer.

and dinner so its restaurants were idle during the morning, so they began to offer breakfast. Dunkin' Donuts was busiest during the morning, so it offered soup and sandwiches on a croissant to increase afternoon business.

After capacity is set, there are some scheduling techniques that can be used to adjust capacity to help optimize it. This topic, however, falls under managing operations systems, which is our next section.

MANAGING OPERATIONS SYSTEMS

After the operations systems have been designed, they must be managed. In this section you will study organizing and leading, forecasting and scheduling, inventory control, and materials requirement planning in operations.

Organizing and Leading

The principles of organization—authority, delegation, and especially organizational design and job design (Chapter 6)—are used with operations systems and control. The leadership theories (Chapter 13) as well as all the functional areas can be used in operations.

Operations and Departmentalization. A one-location firm that uses functional departmentalization will have one operations department. A firm that uses product departmentalization will have at least one operations department per business line. Frito-Lay is one of PepsiCo's business lines with its own operations departments at each of its 42 facilities. With decentralized product departmentalization, it is common for leadership to be shared.

Facility Layouts and Job Designs. With a product layout organizational structure, which is based on repetitive process operations, the job design used is commonly job simplification. With a process layout organizational structure, which is based on individual process operations, the job design used is commonly job expansion. With a cellular layout organizational structure, which is based on batch process operations, the job design is commonly work teams. With a fixed-position layout, which is based on project process operations, job simplification, job expansion, and/or work teams can be used as the various inputs come to the site to perform the transformation part of the output. With a cellular layout using teams, leadership is often shared at lower levels more than with the other layouts.

Planning: Forecasting and Scheduling

As with all plans, operations managers must plan to answer the questions who, what, when, where, and how.[20] The first step in planning operations is to determine the planning horizon. The *planning horizon* is based on how long it takes to get the inputs and to transform them into outputs. A contractor of major buildings may have a planning horizon of a year. A retail store manager may have a monthly time frame. A restaurant manager may only need to plan operations a few days ahead. Three important parts of planning are forecasting sales demand, scheduling operations to meet demand, and adjusting capacity to meet operations demand.

Forecasting. Forecasting operations to transform inputs into outputs is based on the sales forecast, which is a marketing function. For details on *qualitative* and *quantitative sales forecasting techniques* refer back to Chapter 5.

Scheduling. *Scheduling* is the process of listing activities that must be performed to accomplish an objective; activities are listed in sequence with the time needed to complete each one (Chapter 5). Scheduling answers the planning questions: Who (which employees) will make which products? What specific products will be produced? When will they be produced? Where will they be produced? And how will products be produced and how many of each? An important part of scheduling is routing.[21] **Routing** *is the path and sequence of transformations a product takes to become an output.* Routing is illustrated for each of the four facility layouts in Figure 15–3. Notice that with process and cellular layouts, routing is more complex. Routing is interrelated with priority scheduling, so it is discussed further there.

Three popular scheduling tools are the *Gantt chart*, *PERT*, and the *planning sheet*; for details on these techniques refer back to Chapter 5.

Priority Scheduling. **Priority scheduling** *is the continuing evaluation and reordering of the sequence in which products will be produced.* Priority scheduling depends on the layout used.[22] Three simple prioritization methods are used to schedule operations:

- *First Come-First Served.* Jobs are scheduled in the order they are received. This is common in service organizations.
- *Earliest Due Date.* The job with the earliest promised delivery date is scheduled first.
- *Shortest Operating Time.* Jobs that take the least time are scheduled first.
- *Combination.* Many organizations use a combination of the three methods.

Scheduling to Adjust Capacity. When comparing the forecast and schedule to the capacity, adjustments in capacity can be made to coordinate operations and demand in the following ways:

- *Fluctuating Demand.* When operations vary, a few things can be done to smooth capacity and demand. You should stagger work shifts so that there are more resources during busy times. For example, a restaurant will have more customers and will need more employees on a weekend night and it will need to order more food. You can offer incentives to get people to use the product during

routing
The path and sequence of transformations a product takes to become an output.

5. Describe priority scheduling and list its three priorities.

priority scheduling
The continuing evaluation and reordering of the sequence in which products will be produced.

WORK APPLICATION

6. Identify which priority scheduling method(s) the organization you work or have worked for uses.

low-demand periods. Examples are lower-priced luncheon and early bird specials, or off-season rates at resorts. You can use appointments for haircuts and reservations for dinner to help prevent long waiting lines that can result in lost sales.

- *Limited Resources and Economies of Scale.* To get the most out of your resources, you can limit the number of products and outsource part of the operations process. If demand increases temporarily, you can have employees work overtime. If the demand increase will be permanent, add a shift. Hospitals and many manufacturers are open 24 hours a day with three shifts.

- *Demand Exceeds Capacity.* If the business is at the point where demand exceeds capacity and the other methods are not effective, managers can decide to stay with the present facility or expand. Expansion can often take place within the existing facility or a new facility can be occupied. The new facility can be in addition to or in place of the old one. Opening multiple locations is a common strategy for organizations, such as McDonald's.

Classifying the operations system, designing it, and scheduling are all preliminary control methods. Inventory control, however, our next topic, uses preliminary, concurrent, rework, and damage control.

Inventory Control

Inventory *is the stock of materials held for future use.* Inventory is an idle resource. Controlling inventory, also called *materials control,* is an important responsibility of the operations manager because in many organizations materials (which include purchasing, moving, storing, insuring, and controlling) are the single major cost item. Clearly, the decisions that determine control of materials through operations are among the most important.[23]

Inventory Control. **Inventory control** *is the process of managing raw materials, work-in-process, finished goods, and in-transit goods.* Figure 15–4 illustrates inventory control within the systems process, and each type of inventory is explained here.

- *Raw Materials.* Raw materials are input material that has been received but has not been transformed in any way by the operations department, such as eggs at a restaurant or steel at an auto maker. Important preliminary controls in manufacturing, including food preparation, are the *purchasing* of raw materials and *scheduling* to have them delivered to your facility when needed.

- *Work-in-Process.* Work-in-process is material that has had some transformation, but is not yet an output, such as an egg that is being cooked or a car on the assembly line. Concurrent controls are used to ensure that products meet standards before they become finished goods.

6. Explain the difference among inventory control, just-in-time (JIT) inventory, and materials requirement planning (MRP).

inventory
The stock of materials held for future use.

inventory control
The process of managing raw materials, work-in-process, finished goods, and in-transit goods.

Figure 15-4
Inventory Control within the Systems Process

- *Finished Goods.* Finished goods are transformed outputs that have not yet been delivered to customers, such as the cooked eggs sitting on the plate waiting to be served to the customer or a car sitting at the factory waiting to be shipped to a dealer. Rework control may be needed, such as if the eggs get cold while waiting for the server, they may be reheated; or if the car cannot be driven off the assembly line, it will be fixed.

- *In-Transit (Pipeline) Goods.* In-transit goods are finished goods being delivered to the customer, such as the server walking to the table with the eggs or the truck delivering the cars to the dealer. Damage control may be needed. For example, if the server drops the eggs on the way to the table, the order will be redone; or if the car is damaged in delivery, it may need to be returned or fixed at the dealer at the manufacturer's expense. Deliverers of products commonly have insurance to cover the cost of damaged and lost goods.

Retailing and Services Inventory. The classifications of raw materials and work-in-process are used in manufacturing of goods, including food preparation, but they are not used by retailers and services.

Retail inventory control, including *purchasing*, consists almost exclusively of finished goods for resale as is. However, many, but not all, retailers do have in-transit inventory, such as the Home Shopping Network, catalog seller L.L. Bean, and major furniture and appliance stores.

Most service organizations do not have inventory control purchasing of finished goods. Services deal only with the finished goods inventory they create by providing the service. However, some services have in-transit inventory; accounting statements and legal documents are commonly delivered to the client.

just-in-time (JIT) inventory
A method that has necessary parts and raw materials delivered shortly before they are needed.

Just-In-Time (JIT) Inventory. The objective of inventory control is to have the correct amount of all four types of inventory available at the time they are needed and where they are needed, while minimizing the total cost. To accomplish this objective, many organizations now use JIT.[24] **Just-in-time (JIT) inventory** *is a method that has necessary parts and raw materials delivered shortly before they are needed.* The time frame varies among industries. For example, many auto repair shops, including Midas Muffler, keep a small inventory of low-cost, commonly used parts in stock. However, for more costly, less commonly used parts, they call the auto parts stores that typically will deliver the part in 20 to 30 minutes. For manufacturers *shortly* commonly means having parts and raw materials delivered 24 to 48 hours before they are needed. Depending on the size of the store, Frito-Lay commonly makes frequent deliveries to keep the shelves stocked so that little or no backroom storage is needed. For FedEx and UPS, same-day and overnight delivery make JIT easier to control.

JIT does, however, require a close working relationship between the organization and its suppliers to coordinate schedules. It is important to schedule enough, but not too much, lead time. Johnson Control and Chrysler successfully use JIT. Johnson makes seats and delivers them 75 miles to Chrysler so they arrive two hours before they are needed.

**WORK
APPLICATION**

7. Identify the type of inventory and how it is controlled where you work or have worked.

Materials Requirement Planning (MRP)

materials requirement planning (MRP)
A system that integrates operations and inventory control with complex ordering and scheduling.

Materials requirement planning (MRP) *is a system that integrates operations and inventory control with complex ordering and scheduling.* MRP develops a system to order raw materials and components in the right quantity and to have them arrive shortly before scheduled transformation into outputs, while having appropriate work-in-process ready as needed. JIT is part of inventory control, which is part of MRP.[25]

MRP is commonly used by companies that have different delivery systems and lead times. Companies including Boise-Cascade, Lockheed, Texas Instruments, and Westinghouse use MRP because they need hundreds of parts in vastly different quantities with arrival times that vary from hours to months. Coordinating and controlling such a complex system is virtually impossible for any manager. However, MRP uses computer software to manage the system fairly easily.[26]

Economic Order Quantity (EOQ). EOQ is a mathematical model that determines the optimal quantity to order when placing each reorder. The more often you reorder, the higher the ordering cost, but if you order less often, your holding cost goes up.[27] So you use EOQ to optimize ordering and holding cost, without running out of stock.

EOQ is a part of MRP. However, many organizations, especially small businesses, don't need MRP. Therefore, EOQ can be easily determined using a calculator as follows:

$$EOQ = \sqrt{\frac{2RS}{H}} = \frac{2(5,000)(25)}{2} = 5,000 \times 25 = 125,000 \times 2 = \frac{250,000}{2}$$

$$= 125,000 \sqrt{} = 353.55$$

EOQ	= optimal quantity to reorder	354
R	= total required over planning horizon (usually one year)	5,000
S	= cost of preparing one order (or setup)	$25.00
H	= cost of holding one unit for the planning horizon	$ 2.00

QUALITY CONTROL

Quality control is one of the functions of managing operations systems. However, because quality is such an important issue, it has been covered throughout the text and is covered in a separate section now as we compare quality control to TQM, present statistical quality control, and state contributions made by quality gurus.

TQM and Quality Control Are Different

TQM was discussed in Chapters 2 and 7. To quickly review, the four major TQM principles are: (1) Focus on delivering customer value.[28] (2) Continually improve systems and processes.[29] (3) Focus on managing processes rather than people.[30] (4) Use teams to continually improve.[31] A few of the differences between TQM and quality control are as follows:

- TQM is much broader in scope because part of its core value is to make it everyone in the organization's job to improve quality. Under quality control, the operations department is solely responsible. So, quality control is only one part of TQM.

- With TQM, quality is determined by customers[32] through the comparison of actual use to requirements to determine value, or purchasing benefits. With quality control, quality is determined by the standards set for quality acceptability.

- With TQM, the focus is not on acceptance or rejection of the product. With quality control, if products don't meet quality requirements, corrective action is needed to make them acceptable or they are rejected.

Quality Control. **Quality control** *is the process of ensuring that all four types of inventory meet standards.* As you can tell by the definition, quality control and inventory control overlap. In Figure 15–4, the top row shows the systems process steps, the middle row shows the four inventory stages, and the bottom row shows the four types of quality control. The eggs at a restaurant and the steel at an auto maker are quality control examples

quality control
The process of ensuring that all four types of inventory meet standards.

1. Put people before things.
2. Always be nice—no matter how busy you are.
3. Take your time with people.
4. Be polite: say please, thank you, and you're welcome.
5. Don't discriminate with your service (treat everyone well).
6. Avoid jargon.

Figure 15-5
Six Rules of Customer Human Relations

International Standards Organization (ISO)
Certifies organizations that meet set quality standards.

placed with each of the four types of inventory. Quality control is just as important for goods as it is for services.[33] The scrambled eggs can be considered a service and the car as a good.

Quality assurance means that you must "build in" quality; you cannot "inspect it in." Recall, from Chapter 14, that the quality focus should be on preliminary and concurrent control, not rework and damage control. Also, recall that quality is a virtue of design. This is the quality assurance approach.

Customer Quality Control. We have been focusing on creating customer value throughout this entire book. Figure 15–5 lists six rules that help ensure quality customer service. If you follow these rules, you will increase your chances of developing effective human relations skills. When reading the rules, remember that everyone you deal with is a customer.

International Standards Organization (ISO). *The **ISO** certifies organizations that meet set quality standards.* Both manufacturing and services sectors are applying for ISO certification to improve their management systems and operational control.[34] The original ISO standards focused on quality assurance but have changed to quality management.[35] JIT and TQM are part of ISO 9000 certification,[36] as organizations must document policies that address quality management, continuous improvement, and customer satisfaction.[37] The implementation of ISO 9000 greatly improved the efficiency of the Department of Agriculture's Meat Grading and Certification Branch.[38] The number of ISO-certified organizations will continue to grow as major companies, including GM and Ford, require their suppliers to be certified.

As an offshoot of ISO 9000, an SA (Social Accountability) 8000 workplace code on social accountability was developed by the Council on Economic Priority Accreditation Agency in New York. SA 8000 standards take into account Geneva Accord–based International Labor Organization principles, United Nations' human-rights treaties, and input from international businesses. Avon Products' Suffern, New York, plant is the first factory certified as meeting social accountability standards. Avon plans to have all of its plants certified and to ask all its international suppliers to seek SA 8000 certification, too.[39]

Another offshoot of ISO 9000 is ISO 14000. It is a standard for efficient environmental management programs from a particular facility. The ISO 14000 certification process is not considered to be a solution to environmental issues as compared to an integrated regulatory-compliance program.[40]

7. Explain how statistical process control (SPC) charts and the exception principle are used in quality control.

Statistical Quality Control

Statistical quality control is a management science technique that uses a variety of statistical tests based on probability to improve quality through decision making. Statistics improve the probability of identifying and eliminating quality problems. The most common test is statistical process control, which is a standard TQM technique.[41]

Statistical process control (SPC) *aids in determining if quality is within the acceptable standard range.* It is called a process control because quality is measured and corrected during the transformation process as a *concurrent control.* SPC is used to monitor operations and to minimize variances in the quality of products. McDonald's goes to great lengths to ensure that the quality of its Big Mac is the same all over the country.

Following are the four steps to implement SPC, followed by an example that is illustrated in Figure 15–6.

statistical process control (SPC)
Aids in determining if quality is within the acceptable standard range.

| step 1. | **Set the desired quality standard and a range.** The range includes the highest (upper control limit, UCL) and the lowest (lower control limit, LCL) level of acceptable quality, with the desired standard in the middle called the *mean*, which is an average. The narrower the range, the higher the quality consistency between products. |

| step 2. | **Determine the frequency of measuring performance and the sampling technique.** *Sampling technique* refers to how many products will be inspected; the range is from 0 to 100 percent. There are statistical models to help determine the percentage.[42] As a general rule, the more critical it is to stay within quality range, the more frequent the measures and the larger the sample inspected. |

| step 3. | **Measure performance and plot it on the chart.** You statistically analyze the variance in performance from each sample mean to the desired mean. |

| step 4. | **Use the exception principle and do nothing if performance is within range, but take corrective action if it is out of control limits.** |

Example. Frito-Lay is very concerned about quality and uses SPC. However, for illustrative purposes, here is a hypothetical example. Lay's potato chips come in a one-pound bag, as shown in Figure 15–6.

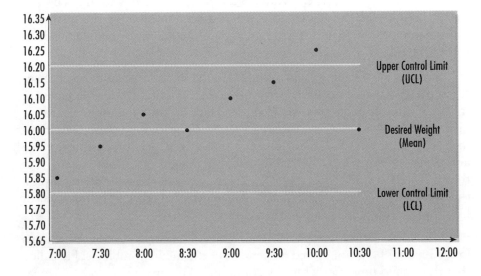

Figure 15-6
Statistical Process Control Chart by Ounces and Time of Day

(1) The desired quality, as measured by weight, is 16 ounces. However, weighing every bag on a very accurate scale is too costly. It is cheaper to give away a few extra chips or give a few people less chips than it is to make every bag weigh exactly one pound. So, you have an acceptable range of say .40 ounces; this gives you a high of 16.20 and a low of 15.80 ounces. If measured on a cheaper scale, both bags would legally weigh 16 ounces.

(2 & 3) Take five bags every one-half hour, and get the average (mean) weight, and plot it on Figure 15–6 with an asterisk.

(4) If the machine produces bags with more or less weight, it is *out of control* and production is stopped to correct the problem. Notice that this happened at 10:00, but at 10:30 weight was back within standard range.

Companies, including Modern Control, make machines that automatically produce statistical process control charts as frequently as per unit. With computerized statistical process control charts, all employees have to do is look at the chart to know when corrective action is needed.

Service Organizations. Service organizations also use statistical process control. An SPC system was created to help a credit company achieve timeliness goals for its car loans and to monitor setting up accounts for customer groups. The SPC method helped the loan-processing department in dispatching labor assignments and speeding up other operating procedures that caused delay. SPC also led to increased labor productivity and better response times and minimized the duration of poor service.[43]

WORK APPLICATION

8. Explain quality control in an organization where you work or have worked.

Quality Guru Contributions

Walter A. Shewhart. The beginning of the quality revolution goes back to May 16, 1924, when Walter Shewhart wrote a memo to his boss at Bell Labs stating that he wanted to use statistics to improve the quality of Bell telephones. Shewhart started the focus on concurrent control by delegating the role of inspector to the employees.

W. Edwards Deming. W. Edwards Deming went to Japan to teach quality in the 1950s and is credited with being instrumental in turning Japanese industry into an economic world power. The highest Japanese award for quality is the Deming Prize. Deming said that improving quality will automatically improve productivity. Deming called for a focus on customer value and continuous improvement. He called managers' attention to the fact that most quality problems, up to 90 percent, are not the fault of employees; the system is to blame. Refer back to Chapter 7, Figure 7–6, for a list of Deming's world-famous 14 points to improve quality.

Joseph M. Juran. Joseph M. Juran stated that 20 percent of the reasons for being out of control caused 80 percent of the quality problems. He called this the *Pareto principle*, which is commonly known as the *"80–20" rule*.

When performance is out of control, you first look at the usual "vital few" reasons (20 percent) and most of the time (80 percent) you have a standing-plan solution. Did you ever notice how manufacturers commonly have a place in the product manual that says, "If you have a problem try 1, 2, 3, 4"?

Armand V. Feigenbaum. Armand V. Feigenbaum made his world mark in the 1950s by publishing "total quality control" material, which is now more commonly called TQM. He focused on improving quality as an important way to lower costs. Feigenbaum worked to fight the myth that maintaining quality is expensive. In fact, he said that investing in quality improvement pays better dividends than any other investment a company can make. Hence, the emphasis on quality in capital budgeting.

Philip B. Crosby. Philip B. Crosby popularized the concepts "quality is free," "do it right the first time," and "zero defects" in the late 1970s. Crosby believed that it is possible to measure the cost of poor quality, and it is necessary to measure it to combat the notion that quality is expensive. He advocates that quality is not only free, it's easy.

Genichi Taguchi. Genichi Taguchi advocated that quality must be designed into each product. Hence, the emphasis on quality as a virtue of design.

Steven Kerr. Although not a TQM guru, Steven Kerr contributed indirectly to TQM by popularizing the idea that "you get what you reward." In other words, if you want people to do a quality job, you have to develop a system that really rewards employees for doing a quality job.

WORK APPLICATION

9. Are any of the gurus' quality contributions used where you work or have worked? Explain how.

TECHNOLOGY AND INFORMATION SYSTEMS

As discussed so far, information plays an important part in operations and quality control. In this section, you will learn about information and technology, the information systems (IS) process, computer hardware and software, functional area IS, types of IS, and integrating IS.

Important Terms. Data includes unorganized facts and figures. **Information** *is data organized in a meaningful way to assist employees in doing their jobs and making decisions.*

information
Data organized in a meaningful way to assist employees in doing their jobs and making decisions.

Information and Technology

The fast rate of change brought about by technology, and especially "information" technology, will not slow down. Technological advances occur virtually every day. Manufacturers who make the best use of information technology to meet their customers' needs stand the best chance of beating their competition.[44]

Time-based competition depends on information. Failure to keep up with innovative change can threaten a firm's competitive position and possibly even its survival.[45] Wal-Mart passed Sears and Kmart to become the leading retailer, as well as the low-cost leader, primarily based on information technology. Frito-Lay was one of the first to give its drivers hand-held computers to transmit sales back to headquarters.

The Information Age. In the information age, the computer is used as a tool that helps managers use information as an important organizational resource. Computer literacy is an important technical skill.[46] The first suggestion for boosting your job value is to conquer the computer.[47] Information systems have changed the way we do business and the way we manage organizations.

Information and the Management Skills and Functions. With the information age, you must be able to use and manage information to be successful. How you use information affects your management skills. Using information and the computer are technical skills. Information is also part of communications skills that affect human relations. Conceptual skills require information, which aids in decision making. Effective implementation of the management functions of planning, organizing, leading, and controlling all require the use of information.

Controlling Information Overload. The information age and the Internet have brought us to the point of information overload. Organizations are developing IS based on critical success factors (CSF)[48] to help with this problem. Here is a simple personal guide to controlling information overload. As you come upon data and information, ask yourself these two questions about its relevance: "Will this information help me to meet my objectives? Does the information affect my critical success factors?" If you answer yes, use the information; if not, use *information dump* and be aware of it for future reference, file it, or discard it. A good filing system is a time management technique (Chapter 5) that is critical to controlling information.

The Information Systems Process

Figure 15–7 illustrates the information systems process. Notice that the information department is placed in the center to show its staff role in getting data from the external and internal environments (Chapter 2) and converting it into information that can be used by all the organizational departments. Information is also sent to external stakeholders. Improving the internal and external linkage is an important current management issue for IS.[49]

Because most information departments are computerized, the computer devices are listed for each subsystem to illustrate how the computer transforms data into information. All people in an organization also continually transform data into information without the use of computers, although many do use computers as well.

Hardware and Software

Hardware. *Hardware* is the basic physical components of a computer. The computer input, storage, processor, and output devices listed in Figure

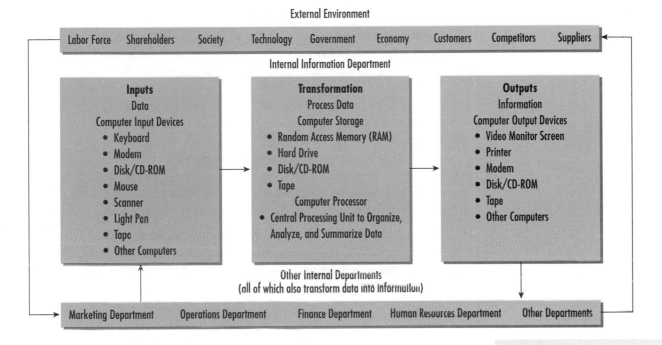

External Environment

| Labor Force | Shareholders | Society | Technology | Government | Economy | Customers | Competitors | Suppliers |

Internal Information Department

Inputs
Data
Computer Input Devices
- Keyboard
- Modem
- Disk/CD-ROM
- Mouse
- Scanner
- Light Pen
- Tape
- Other Computers

Transformation
Process Data
Computer Storage
- Random Access Memory (RAM)
- Hard Drive
- Disk/CD-ROM
- Tape
Computer Processor
- Central Processing Unit to Organize, Analyze, and Summarize Data

Outputs
Information
Computer Output Devices
- Video Monitor Screen
- Printer
- Modem
- Disk/CD-ROM
- Tape
- Other Computers

Other Internal Departments
(all of which also transform data into Information)

| Marketing Department | Operations Department | Finance Department | Human Resources Department | Other Departments |

Figure 15-7
The Information Systems Process

15-7 are all hardware. All three types of computers—mainframes, minicomputers, and microcomputers, better known as personal computers or PCs—require hardware.

Software. Software is a computer program, or set of commands, that instructs hardware to perform various operations, such as reading, analyzing, processing, and storing data. All computer hardware needs software to make it run. A variety of software has been developed for various functional areas in business, such as CAD/CAM for operations. Many organizations have computer programmers who develop software to meet specific needs.

Four popular software programs commonly used in IS include: *databases*, which permit the user to organize and manipulate primarily numerical data in interconnected ways, such as customer accounts; *word-processing*, which allows creating and editing written material; *spreadsheets*, which permit arranging numbers or words in a matrix of rows and columns and performs mathematical calculations; *graphics*, which allows drawing of graphs, charts, and other illustrations. Software makers now offer these products independently and in combined packages.

APPLYING THE CONCEPT

AC 15–4 Software Selection

Identify the most appropriate software to use for each task as being:
a. CAD   b. database   c. word-processing   d. spreadsheet   e. graphics

_____ **12.** You need to develop a budget for your department for next year.

_____ **13.** You work in accounts receivable and want to keep track of who owes you how much.

_____ **14.** You want to tell your boss your company's market share as compared to your competitor's.

_____ **15.** You want to develop a better mouse trap.

_____ **16.** You need to send a response to a customer's E-mail.

Functional Area Information Systems

All departments also get data and convert it into information and send data and information to other departments and external stakeholders, as the arrows directly to and from the external environment to the other departments illustrate in Figure 15–7. In the box listing the functional departments, there are no lines to illustrate that a free flow of data and information exists among all departments. All departments in organizations, including Frito-Lay, also have information systems they use for internal use.

As you read about each functional area, remember that it is common for each to have its own computer hardware, and many have their own special software programs. Remember that each area gives and receives data and information from the information department on an ongoing basis.

Finance. The processing of accounting data is commonly the first area to be computerized. Determining profit performance is computerized for speed and accuracy. Subsystems of accounting include accounts payable and receivable, job costing, payroll, sales and invoices, inventory control, and financial reports.

Accounting gets data from all departments, and IS provides managers in other departments with control information such as cost accounting and budgets. Accounting also sends information in the form of annual reports to external shareholders, pays taxes to the government, collects money from customers, pays suppliers, and so on.

Operations. In this chapter you have learned how organizations use computerized CAD, CAM, and CIM for designing, scheduling, and operations control; MRP for inventory control; and SPC for quality control to improve performance. Operations needs to get data in the form of a sales forecast from marketing in order to schedule production. Operations develops and uses technology with input and output to and from external sources.

Marketing. Marketing is responsible for the four *Ps* of selecting the *products*, the *price* to charge, the *place* where they will be sold, and the *promotion* used to sell the product. Frito-Lay has very strong marketing. Marketing needs to be in constant contact with its potential customers to gather data and to forecast sales that affect all departments.

The most important part of marketing is selling the products. Marketing information such as ads, brochures, and reports is produced on computer desktop publishing work stations. Many sales presentations today are created by a sales rep with the aid of high-quality computerized multimedia sources, and some video presentations replace a salesperson altogether.

Human Resources. The human resources department needs to communicate with the external labor force to recruit new employees. It also gets data from all departments to retain employees and to calculate absenteeism and turnover rates. The selection, development, and rewarding processes are based on information from both internal and external sources. The human resources department keeps benefits records and works with external insurance companies to control cost. It may also need to complete EEO, OSHA, and workers' compensation reports and may need to work with labor relations with both internal employees and external labor unions. The human resources department commonly keeps a file of data and information on each employee, which can be in paper and/or computerized form.

Types of Information Systems

The three primary **types of information systems** are transaction processing, management information, and decision support.

Transaction Processing Systems (TPS). Transaction processing systems are used to handle routine and recurring business matters. Most organizations, including Frito-Lay, use transaction processing systems to record accounting transactions, such as accounts receivable and payable and payroll. Most large retail organizations use scanners to record marketing sales transactions at the checkout counter. Banks process checks and deposits and record credit card transactions. Stockbrokers buy and sell stock for clients. Airlines and travel agents make flight reservations.

Management Information Systems (MIS). MIS transform data into the information managers need from the database to do their work. Managers' work usually consists of running their units/departments, and the information is commonly used for making routine (Chapter 3) decisions. For example, Frito-Lay's operations managers need to know the sales forecast to schedule routine production. Figure 15–7, the Information Systems Process, is an example of an MIS.

Executive Information Systems (EIS). Executive information systems are a form of MIS used by top-level managers. Executive information systems place greater emphasis on integrating external data and information with internal information in the critical success factors,[50] which are often industry-specific. In other words, executive information systems focus more on strategy development and revision, whereas MIS focus more on strategy implementation.

Decision Support Systems (DSS). Decision support systems use a manager's insights in an interactive computer-based process to assist in making nonroutine (Chapter 3) decisions. They use decision rules, decision models, and comprehensive databases.

Decision support systems are more flexible than MIS. However, the DSS interact with the MIS by applying specific mathematical operations to the information available in the MIS. These math tools allow managers to evaluate the possible effects of alternative decisions. For example, capital budgeting decisions (Chapter 14) can be done with DSS. Also, linear programming, queuing theory, and probability theory (Chapter 3) can be done with decision support systems.

WORK APPLICATION

11. Explain the information system used within the functional department you work or have worked for.

8. Describe the three primary types of information systems and their relationship.

types of information systems
Transaction processing, management information, and decision support

Frito-Lay was the first in its business to use decision support systems to help it make marketing decisions. Managers can estimate the effects a specific price discount promotional offer (such as a $1.49 bag of Lay's chips being sold for $1.25, 99 cents, and so on) will have on sales, and make the decision to discount or not, and how much to discount. Today, with the decision support systems, Frito-Lay managers know in days, rather than months, how a discounting promotion is affecting sales. They can also spot a competitor's challenge before it does too much damage.

Artificial Intelligence (AI). Artificial intelligence is the attempt to create computers that simulate human decision processes. AI is a form of decision support system that incorporates qualitative as well as quantitative information. It allows the user to inject intuition (fuzzy logic) into the simulation model provided by the computer. AI is being used in robotics and in designing expert systems.

APPLYING THE CONCEPT

AC 15–5 Types of Information Systems

Identify the type of IS as:

a. TP   b. MIS   c. EIS   d. DSS   e. expert systems

____ **17.** A manager wants to know if an important order has been shipped yet.

____ **18.** A manager wants to determine how many checkout counters to have in a new store.

____ **19.** A small business owner/manager wants to use an accounting software program.

____ **20.** A manager intuitively knows how to schedule customers. A top manager wants to help others do a good job of scheduling, too.

Expert Systems. Expert systems imitate the thought processes of a human being. They build on series of rules ("if-then" scenarios) to move from a set of data to a decision. Boeing uses an expert system called CASE (connector assembly specification expert). CASE produces assembly procedures for each of the 5,000 electrical connectors on its airplanes. It now takes the computer a few minutes to get a computer printout for a specific connector, rather than about 45 minutes of searching through 20,000 pages of printed material.

Summary. Transaction processing systems are used to record routine repetitive transactions. MIS, which also include transaction processing system totals, are used by managers to make routine decisions. Executive information systems are a form of MIS, but are used for strategic decisions, whereas MIS is used for strategy implementation. Decision support systems, using MIS, are used by managers to make nonroutine decisions. Artificial intelligence and expert systems are extended forms of DSS used when making specific routine decisions.

Integrating Information Systems

Database Management. With computers, each department can tie its data and information together, and the information department can tie all departments' data together and provide them with information through database management. *Databases* integrate department IS data and information in one central database. A database is created to reduce the duplication of information, effort, and cost and to provide controlled access to this information by employees in all departments. Figure 15–7 illustrates database management, which focuses primarily on MIS, including transaction processing system totals.

The trend today is to integrate the functional area IS. For example, at Taco Bell, orders are placed (marketing—sales) and sent to be filled (operations) by computer. The system is also used to collect the money (finance) to keep track of inventory (operations), and to reorder food and supplies. The IS also records which employee is using the system (human resources). If an employee has more sales than money received (finance), action can be taken. Hospitals are also integrating IS to facilitate their financial, patient, and administrative support functions to better serve patients.

Professional Help with Integrating Information Systems. Big computer companies including IBM, Unisys, and Hewlett-Packard sell fully developed and integrated information systems. EDS (Chapter 9) will take basic equipment and write custom software for an organization's IS needs. Some firms hire experienced managers to set up and run their IS; they are commonly given the title of chief information officer (CIO). Organizations are now getting professional help in setting up integrated IS using networks, which is covered in the next section.

INFORMATION NETWORKS AND TECHNOLOGY

The Age of the Information Network Is Here

Computer networks *connect independent computers so that they can function in interrelated ways.* Networks are commonly described as computers communicating or talking with each other. Networks are a way of integrating information systems. As shown in Figure 15–7, one computer's data can become another computer's input, and a third computer can be an output source of the information. For example, you could get an E-mail (input), use the E-mail data (process), and send your E-mail to someone else (output).

Lou Gerstner of IBM and Bill Gates of Microsoft agree that network-centric computing is the wave of the future. New information system skills will need to be assimilated, with network management, systems integration, and remote systems management representing future needs.[51]

Information networks *connect all employees from headquarters and remote facilities to each other, to suppliers and customers, and into databases.* Figure 15–8 illustrates the information network, and its components are discussed next.

9. List the components of an information network.

computer networks
Connect independent computers so that they can function in interrelated ways.

information networks
Connect all employees from headquarters and remote facilities to each other, to suppliers and customers, and into databases.

Figure 15-8
Information Network

Connecting All Employees

Internal computer networks are changing the way companies—and their employees—do business. With internal computer networks, employees in an organization have direct access to each other and to the information they need to do their work. All employees can do their jobs in a more informed and efficient manner by using the shared database and by having direct contact with others. Lotus uses its own Notes groupware to link its programmers around the world so they have instantaneous access to each other's work.

Local-Area Networks (LAN). Local-area networks directly link everyone via computers within one facility. In Figure 15–8, headquarters and each remote facility would use a LAN.

Wide-Area Networks (WAN). Wide-area networks link employees in different facilities via computers using telephone lines or long-range communications devices. In Figure 15–8, headquarters and each remote facility would be connected by a WAN, as well as each remote facility to the others.

The Virtual Office and Telecommunications

With information networks it is no longer necessary to have all employees in one facility. Within the *virtual office*, people who are spread out in remote locations work as though they were in one place using wide-area networks.[52]

The virtual office is made possible by telecommunications (machines linked by telephone) technology networks of telephones, centralized voice mail, E-mail, fax machines, and teleconferencing (also called videoconferencing, people can see and talk to each other from different locations). Sam Walton used teleconferencing for Saturday meetings with employees.

Telecommuters. With a virtual office, *telecommuters* transmit and receive required data and information to and from other employees and locations. Salespeople who have to travel and stay overnight have portable virtual offices they use on the road.

Telecommuters' remote location is commonly their home. Telecommuters only go to the central office at set intervals, such as once a week, and/or for special purposes. Telecommuting saves on expenses for office space, commuting, clothing, and going out to lunch when all employees work in one place.[53] With the dropping cost of a virtual office (equipment costs less than $3,000), telecommuting will continue to increase in the future.[54] However, to be successful, telecommuters need to have clear standing plans with lots of communication to guide their performance.[55]

Note that in Figure 15–8 telecommuters are in a sense a remote facility; that is why they are in the same box. The figure represents any organization. It could be a bank with a headquarters, often called the main branch, and any number of remote facility branches. It may also have telecommuters who are connected to everyone else in the information system.

Customers and Suppliers

Customers. Information networks facilitate faster response to customers' problems and needs. When a customer calls, or a salesperson reports a customer problem, networks allow a single employee to get the information, or person, who can help solve the problem.

Some situations, such as banking at home by computer, use a computer network to link customer and business. You can pay your bills by electronically transferring money from your account into the company's account. However, note that customers are often not connected by computer in the information network, as in the following example.

At Hewlett-Packard, when a customer calls with a technical problem, the call is routed to one of four engineering hubs around the world, depending on the time of day. This way customers have 24-hour access to technical support. The employee places data about the problem and customer into the system. All four hubs have access to information on how the problem was solved. When other customers with the same or similar problems call, employees have the information to solve that customer's problem. In a sense, they use the Pareto principle.

Suppliers. Through networks, companies can place orders for materials and supplies instantly via E-mail. Computerized material requirements planning also helps companies to know when and how much to order. Ford has a WAN that links its 15,000 dealers around the world so that it can supply dealers with the cars and trucks they want more quickly. The same WAN connects about 120,000 of Ford's computers around the world to Web sites. Ford's WAN is expected to save the company billions of dollars during the next few years.[56]

Customers and Suppliers. Manufacturing operations often use a *value-added network* (VAN) to link operations with their external customers and suppliers. The value-added network system allows for instant transfer of information about current inventories and will automatically place an order for new goods for shipment from operations to retailers when products are low. It helps keep retail inventories at a minimum level and results in cost saving through just-in-time inventories. Value-added networks are controlled through *electronic data interchange (EDI)*, such as the scanners cashiers use to ring up your sale at retail stores.

Databases

Online Services and the Internet. Networks are commonly used to tap into databases such as online services that may provide access to the Internet and its World Wide Web. The Internet is blurring roles in the supply chain and giving smaller suppliers the chance to work with large manufacturers on an even footing,[57] since the Internet is used to connect suppliers and customers to companies. The Internet is driving PC sales as consumers cited Internet access as the number-one reason for buying new PCs.[58] With AOL acquiring Netscape, AOL will be a major competitor with Microsoft's browser. Recall from Chapter 7 that IBM acquired Lotus primarily to get its Notes "groupware." IBM chairman Lou Gerstner promised heavy investment in its Lotus Notes line software that integrates Internet features.[59]

Other Databases. Although the Internet is used by business and for doing business, some businesses make greater use of other databases. For example, many businesses contact a database to check on the credit rating of a customer or supplier, or to find out whether a customer has adequate credit to cover the cost of the current purchase.

WORK APPLICATION

12. Explain how an organization you work or have worked for uses network telecommunications.

CHAPTER SUMMARY AND GLOSSARY

The chapter summary is organized to answer the ten learning objectives for Chapter 15.

1. Describe time-based competition and state why it is important.
Time-based competition refers to strategies to increase the speed of going from creativity to delivery. It is important because speed gives the organization a first-mover competitive advantage.

2. Explain the difference among the three tangibilities of products, the three levels of customer involvement, the four flexibilities of operations processes, and the three intensities of resources.
A product can be a tangible good, intangible service, or a combination of both. The three levels of customer involvement refer to whether the operation makes-to-stock with a standard product, makes-to-order with customer-specific products, or assembles-to-order with a standard product

with some customized features. Flexibility refers to whether the products are produced continually in nondiscrete units, repetitively on an assembly line for one product, in batches with the same resources used for multiple products, or individually to customer specifications. Intensity of resources refers to capital in which machines do most of the work, labor in which human resources do most of the work, or a balance of the two.

3. **Discuss what is meant by "quality is a virtue of design."**
"Quality is a virtue of design" means that if products are designed with cross-functional team input to provide customer value, there will be fewer operations problems, the product will be easier to sell, and it will be less costly to service the product. Therefore, it is important for cross-functional teams to work together on the design of new products.

4. **Explain product, process, cellular, and fixed-position types of facility layouts in terms of their customer involvement and flexibility.**
Product layout uses make-to-stock and/or assemble-to-order customer involvement with repetitive or continuous process operations flexibility. Process layout uses make-to-order customer involvement with individual operations process flexibility. Cellular layout uses make-to-stock and/or assemble-to-order with batch operations process flexibility. Fixed-position layout uses make-to-order and/or assemble-to-order with project process operations flexibility.

5. **Describe priority scheduling and list its three priorities.**
Priority scheduling is the continuous evaluation and reordering of the sequence in which products will be produced. Its three priorities are first come-first served, earliest due date, and shortest operating time; a combination of these may be used.

6. **Explain the relationship among inventory control, just-in-time (JIT) inventory, and materials requirement planning (MRP).**
Inventory control is the process of managing raw materials, work-in-process, finished goods, and in-transit goods. JIT is an inventory control method that has necessary parts and raw materials delivered shortly before they are needed. MRP is a system that integrates operations and inventory control. JIT is part of inventory control and both are part of MRP.

7. **Explain how statistical process control (SPC) charts and the exception principle are used in quality control.**
The statistical process control chart is used to graph actual performance to see if it is within the standard range. According to the exception principle, if performance is within standard range, do nothing; if performance is out of control range, take corrective action.

8. **Describe the three primary types of information systems and their relationship.**
Transaction process systems (TPS) are used to record routine repetitive transactions. Management information systems (MIS) are used by managers

to perform their work and to make routine decisions. Decision support systems (DSS) are used by managers to make nonroutine decisions. TPS is related to MIS because its totals are included in the MIS. DSS is related to MIS, which includes TPS totals, because it uses MIS databases.

9. List the components of an information network.

The components of an information network include connecting all employees from headquarters and remote locations to each other, to suppliers and customers, and into databases.

10. Define the following key terms (in order of appearance in the chapter):

Select one or more methods: (1) fill in the missing key terms from memory, (2) match the key terms from the end of the summary with their definitions below, or (3) copy the key terms in order from the list at the beginning of the chapter.

_____ refers to strategies to increase the speed of going from creativity to delivery.

_____ is the function in which resource inputs are transformed into product outputs.

A _____ is a good, service, or a combination of the two.

_____ refers to whether operations are make to stock, make to order, or assemble to order.

_____ refers to whether the products are produced continuously, repetitively, in batches, or individually.

_____ is the process used in transforming inputs into outputs.

_____ refers to whether operations use product, process, cellular, or fixed-position layout.

_____ is the amount of products an organization can produce.

_____ is the path and sequence of transformations a product takes to become an output.

_____ is the continuing evaluation and reordering of the sequence in which products will be produced.

_____ is the stock of materials held for future use.

_____ is the process of managing raw materials, work-in-process, finished goods, and in-transit goods.

_____ is a method that has necessary parts and raw materials delivered shortly before they are needed.

_____ is a system that integrates operations and inventory control with complex ordering and scheduling.

_____ is the process of ensuring that the four types of inventory meet standards.

The _____ certifies organizations that meet set quality standards.

_____ aids in determining if quality is within the acceptable standard range.

_____ is data organized in a meaningful way to assist employees in doing their jobs and making decisions.

_____ include transaction processing, management information, and decision support.

_____ connect independent computers so that they can function in interrelated ways.

_____ connect all employees from headquarters and remote locations to each other, to suppliers and customers, and into databases.

KEY TERMS

capacity   539

computer networks   555

customer involvement   530

facility layout   536

information   549

information networks   555

International Standards Organization
   (ISO)   546

inventory   542

inventory control   542

just-in-time (JIT) inventory   544

materials requirement planning
   (MRP)   544

operations   529

operations flexibility   530

priority scheduling   541

product   529

quality control   545

routing   541

statistical process control
   (SPC)   547

technology   532

time-based competition   528

types of information systems   553

REVIEW AND DISCUSSION QUESTIONS

1. What does the operations department do?

2. Which level of customer involvement is the highest? Why?

3. Which type of process operations is the most and least flexible?

4. Which type of process operations is most commonly used by retailers and service organizations?

5. Are most services more capital- or labor-intensive than manufacturers?

6. Why is it important to balance time-based competition and design?

7. Which two facility layouts are the most flexible and which two are the least flexible?

8. Why is capacity planning so important?

9. Why is sales forecasting important to operations?

10. What are the four types of inventories?

11. What does materials requirement planning integrate?

12. What is the relationship between inventory and quality control?

13. What are the six rules of customer relations?

14. What is the relationship between information and the management function?

15. What are the two questions you should ask yourself when dealing with information overload?

16. What takes place during the information systems process?

17. What is the difference among hardware, software, and groupware?

18. What is the function of database management?

19. What is the difference between a computer network and an information network?

OBJECTIVE CASE

Gitano

Haim and Isaac Dabah once successfully owned and managed Gitano Group, Inc. Haim headed the marketing area and created the high-fashion ads that established Gitano's young, slick, and sassy image. Haim's strategy was to sell Gitano, Gloria Vanderbilt, and Regatta Sport brands through department stores. Gitano focused on customers who shunned high-priced designers like Calvin Klein but who wanted the glitz of a label on their clothes at a moderate price. Gitano clothes sold at a high profit margin in department stores. However, when Haim changed strategies and also began to sell clothes to discount retail stores, including Wal-Mart, profit margins dropped. Wal-Mart bargains hard with suppliers.

Isaac managed the operations area. He acquired operations facilities in Mississippi, Guatemala, and Jamaica. Isaac had no experience or much skill at designing operations and controlling them. For example, the Jamaica plant wasted five times the industry average, or a full 20 percent of its materials. Rather than rework jeans that had been dyed the wrong colors, employees simply threw them away. There were no controls in any of the plants to determine where clothes were in the production process. Several thousand dollars' worth of inventory disappeared somehow. Isaac did not do any sales forecasting; he simply had manufacturing facilities run at full capacity so they had large inventories ready to ship when orders came in. Despite large inventories, it often took weeks or even months to ship orders, and they sometimes shipped the wrong merchandise, which wasted more time. Although Gitano's operations were managed poorly, surprisingly, quality of products was not a real problem.

Despite operations problems, Gitano did well through the 1980s. In fact, in 1989, it sold around $600 million worth of clothes with a net profit of $31 million. However, when the recession of the early 1990s hit, Gitano was caught without any strategic plans. During the recession, many prior customers stopped buying Gitano clothes. Isaac was years too late at cutting back production and he continued to produce at full capacity. Gitano got to the point of having at least three years' worth of most products on hand in finished inventory.

Because Isaac was running at full capacity without forecasting demand, Gitano had far too many outdated clothes and not enough of some newer styles. Gitano regularly substituted products to fill orders. Many of the stores did not realize that they were not getting the actual clothes they ordered. However, Wal-Mart ordered its vendors to begin tagging merchandise with bar codes. Wal-Mart could easily compare every pair of jeans against what it had actually ordered. Haim convinced Wal-Mart that it was developing a bar-coding system while it continued to substitute orders.

With at least three years of back inventory, Haim decided that the best way to get rid of it was to open Gitano's own retail stores. In four years it opened around 100 stores, but the stores did not help much. As new inventory came in, it was placed on top of the old merchandise. Eventually, stores were so backlogged that everything was marked down below cost in an attempt to get rid of it. At the urging of their bankers, the Dabah brothers hired Robert Gregory to run the business. Gregory was formerly the president and chief operating officer of VF Corporation, the maker of Lee jeans. His first priority was to establish a badly needed control system and to downsize operations. The attempt, however, was too little too late.

While Wal-Mart was unhappily waiting for Gitano to bar code its products, the Dabah brothers pleaded guilty to a scheme to avoid import quotas and agreed to pay $2 million in fines in December

OBJECTIVE CASE

(continued)

1993. Wal-Mart pulled its Gitano account, saying it would not do business with a company that engaged in unethical and socially irresponsible behavior. A few months later, Gitano announced it was filing for Chapter 11 bankruptcy protection and selling its assets to Fruit of the Loom, Inc., for $100 million.

How was Gitano able to make millions of dollars with no strategic plan, no forecasting, no budgets, and no control systems? Robert Gregory gave an assessment of the rise and fall of Gitano. He stated that back in the 1980s you could be successful with good marketing of high-profit margin products that covered the cost of poor management planning and control systems, but not in today's highly competitive global market.

Select the best alternative for the following questions. Be sure you are able to explain your answers.

_____ **1.** Gitano's level of customer involvement was

    a. make-to-stock   c. assemble-to-order

    b. make-to-order

_____ **2.** Gitano's flexibility of operations was

    a. continuous process

    b. repetitive process

    c. batch process

    d. individual process

_____ **3.** Gitano's operations resources were

    a. capital-intensive

    b. labor-intensive   c. balanced

_____ **4.** Product mix was important to Gitano's success.

    a. true   b. false

_____ **5.** Gitano's facility layout was

    a. product b. process c. cellular d. fixed

_____ **6.** Gitano's facility location selections were most likely based on

    a. cost   e. community interest

    b. proximity   f. quality of life

    c. transportation

    d. access to human resources

_____ **7.** Gitano was _____ at priority scheduling and scheduling to adjust operations capacity.

    a. effective   b. ineffective

_____ **8.** Using statistical quality control would have led to major improvement in solving Gitano's problems.

    a. true   b. false

_____ **9.** Gitano seemed to have _____ coordination and sharing of information among different departments.

    a. little   b. some   c. great

_____ **10.** The best way that Gitano could have controlled its operations problems would have been to have developed a type of _____ network.

    a. local-area   d. value-added

    b. wide-area   e. database

    c. virtual office

11. Describe Gitano's primary operations transformation process.

12. What was Gitano's approach to capacity planning and how could it be improved?

13. What was Gitano's approach to scheduling to adjust capacity and how could it be improved?

14. What was Gitano's approach to inventory control and how could it be improved?

15. What type(s) of information systems and networks would you recommend Gitano use?

Skill-Building Exercise 15–1

Economic Order Quantity

Preparing for Skill-Building Exercise 15–1
Calculate the EOQ for each of the four following situations:

___ 1. R = 2,000, S = $15.00, H = $5.00
___ 2. H = $10.00, R = 7,500, S = $40.00
___ 3. R = 500, H = $15.00, S = $35.00
___ 4. S = $50.00, H = $25.00, R = 19,000

Doing Skill-Building Exercise 15–1 in Class

Objective
To develop your skill at calculating EOQ.

Preparation
You should have calculated EOQ for the four situations in the preparation section.

Procedure 1 (10–20 minutes)
Option A. The instructor goes over the correct EOQ answers in class.

Option B. The instructor has students come to the front of the class and go over the EOQ answers.

Conclusion
The instructor leads a class discussion and/or makes concluding remarks.

Application (2–4 minutes)
What did I learn from this experience? How will I use this knowledge in the future?

_____

_____

Sharing
Volunteers give their answers to the application section.

Exercise 15–1

G

Implementing the Management Functions

Preparation for Exercise 15–1
You should have studied planning, organizing and staffing, leading, and controlling.

Doing Exercise 15–1 in Class

Objective
To develop skill at implementing the management functions.

Preparation
The preparation is to have studied the prior chapters covering the management functions.

Experience
During the in-class exercise, you will be either a member of Production Company that produces a product to make a profit or a customer and supplier who buys the product and sells materials. Your organization will compete against other class groups to earn the most profit. Your group will have to bid on how many products it will make and how much inventory to buy. Turn to the Production Company Contracts with Customers and Suppliers and Profit or Loss Statement to get an idea of bidding and purchasing supplies agreements you will make during the exercise.

**Production Company Contracts with Customer and Supplier and Profit or Loss Statement
(To be filled out by customer/supplier with Production Company)**

Customer Contract

Bid: number of products Production Company contracts to build during the period.
   The customer will not buy any products above the bid amount.   _____ *

Agreed price per product that meets inspection: $25,000.
   Number of products accepted ____ × $25,000 = $ _____

Agreed penalty charge of $30,000 for each product not delivered on time.
   Number not produced ____ × $30,000 =   – $ _____

Check paid by customer to Production Company. $ _____
   Fine for unethically making products before or after time period;
   if caught deduct $100,000 from amount of check to be paid to customer.

Supplier Contract

Number of raw material paper purchased ____ × $10,000 = $ _____ *

Raw material of unused paper cannot be used for other jobs. However, the
   supplier agrees to buy it back at a penalty.
      Number of returned unfolded papers ____ × $8,000 =   – $ _____

All work-in-progress cannot be sold after the contract period, nor returned to
   the supplier at a penalty fee. However, the supplier will buy it as scrap.
      Number of folded papers ____ × $5,000 =   – $ _____

Cost of Goods Sold (CGS) Check given to supplier from Production Company. $ _____

Profit or Loss Job Statement

Revenue (amount of check received from customer) $ _____

Cost of Goods Sold (variable cost, check given to supplier)   – _____

Gross Profit $ _____

Expenses (fixed cost for the period including labor, overhead, etc.)   – $ __250,000.__

Profit or Loss Before Taxes $ _____

Taxes (If you have a profit, multiply 25% tax rate times profit)   – $ _____

Net Income or Loss $ _____

*Filled out prior to production. All other lines filled-out after production period.

Procedure 1 (3–4 minutes)

Break into as many groups of five as possible while still having at least half as many students as the number of teams. The students in the groups are members of Production Company and will produce the product described below. This is not an ongoing product that is sold; it is a one-time order from one customer. All other students will be customers and suppliers. At least one student must be assigned to each group as its customer and/or supplier; if necessary, customer/suppliers may have more than one group. Teams should spread out as much as possible. Suppliers are given stacks of paper to sell to the groups. Customers/suppliers should sit close to their Production Company team and listen and observe. However, they may not communicate in any way with the team.

Procedure 2 (10 minutes)

Suppliers give each Production Company team ten free papers for planning purposes. Using the contract with customer and supplier (and profit or loss statement) sheet accompanying this exercise, each production team must plan its bid on how many products it will make during the ten-minute time period of the contract, and how much raw materials paper it will buy. In doing so, the team must plan how it will produce the products, as well as organize and staff, lead, and control its operations.

Steps for Making the Product

1. Fold the paper in half; unfold. Then fold it in half in the other direction; unfold.

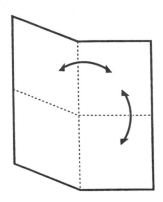

2. Turn the paper over. Fold the paper in half diagonally; unfold. Then fold it in half diagonally in the other direction.

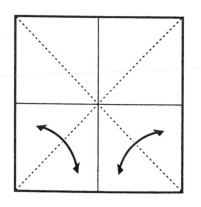

3. Fold each corner toward the middle.

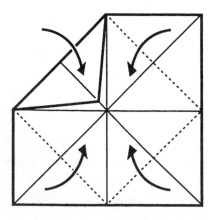

4. Turn the paper over. Fold each corner toward the middle.

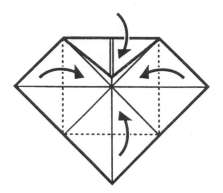

5. Fold it in half; unfold. Then fold it in half in the other direction; unfold.

6. Stick your thumbs and index fingers under flaps on undersides.

7. Be sure the paper looks like it is supposed to and that it folds easily in both directions. If it does, it should pass inspection by your team and the

customer. If not, fix it so that it does or scrap it at a cost of $7,000 each. Remember that you have exactly ten minutes of production time for the period.

Procedure 3 (3–6 minutes)

The customer/supplier goes to the Production Company and takes back the ten papers. If they are not used, they are placed with good sheets; if they are folded, they are discarded. On the contract sheet the customer writes in the bid and the supplier sells (gives) the paper and writes in the dollar amount of raw material purchased. Teams may not start manufacturing products until told to do so. Beginning work is unethical behavior, and if caught, a $100,000 fine will be imposed by the customer. Customers, watch your Production Company team members. If you catch them in unethical behavior, you save money.

Procedure 4 (10 minutes)
Production teams have ten minutes to make the product. The instructor will announce when there are two

minutes left, one minute left, 30 seconds left, 15 seconds left, and time to stop. When told to stop, all team members must stop. To finish the product is unethical behavior. All team members caught working after they are told to stop will be fined $100,000 by the customer.

Procedure 5 (8–10 minutes)
The customer/supplier goes to the Production Company and inspects the goods and buys the ones that pass inspection (look like they are supposed to and open and close in both directions). The supplier buys back any raw and work-in-process goods. Fill in the lines to determine the revenue, cost of goods sold, and profit or loss statement. The customer/supplier records the team's bid, actual number produced, number of papers bought, and profit or loss statement for all teams to see. With all comparative information recorded, the team with the greatest net income is the winner. However, every team that makes a profit also wins.

Integration (12–20 minutes)
Option A. Individually, everyone answers the following questions to identify how your team implemented the management functions, followed by the instructor going over the answers.

Option B. As a team, answer the following questions, followed by the instructor going over the answers.

Option C. The instructor goes over the answers to the following questions as individuals answer them.

Planning Skills (Chapters 3–5)

1. What were the important decisions that needed to be made to be successful in this exercise?____

   _____

2. The decisions in this exercise were ____ programmed ____ unprogrammed and the condition was ____ certainty ____ risk ____ uncertainty.

3. Our major decisions were made by ____ one individual ____ the group.

4. Our bid ____ was ____ was not the team objective, and our team ____ exactly made the bid or

____ did not produce enough ____ could have done more.

5. What was Production Company's basic mission or goal?_____

_____

6. As an environmental analysis, what were your team's strengths and weaknesses? How did your team stack up against the competition?

7. Our Production Company developed ____ strategic ____ operational plans.

8. The appropriate plans were ____ standing ____ single-use.

9. Forecasting in the area of ____ sales ____ operations was important in this exercise.

10. Time management ____ was ____ was not important in this exercise.

Organizing Skills (Chapters 6–8)

11. Our team members ____ developed a chain of command ____ were all basically equal.

12. Our team had ____ line ____ line and staff positions.

13. Jobs were ____ simplified (each person did one part of making each product) ____ job expansion (each person made an entire product). _____ was our fastest production worker.

14. Our group ____ was ____ was not a work team.

15. Managing change and innovation ____ were ____ were not very important in this exercise.

16. There ____ was ____ was not diversity within our team.

17. During this exercise the most relevant human resources process was ____ human resources planning ____ attracting employees ____ developing employees ____ retaining employees.

Leading Skills (Chapters 9–13)

18. Communications flowed ____ vertically ____ horizontally ____ grapevine.

19. Our team primarily used ____ oral ____ nonverbal ____ written communication.

20. Our team was ____ effective ____ ineffective at sending, receiving (listening to each other), and responding to messages.

21. Overall, our team members ____ were ____ were not motivated to win.

22. Being in competition ____ did ____ did not meet any member's need for power. In other words, were the people with a high need for power pushing more to win, and were they upset if they lost?

23. The most relevant process motivation theory in this exercise was ____ equity ____ goal-setting ____ expectancy theory.

24. The type of reinforcement used was ____ positive ____ avoidance ____ extinction ____ punishment.

25. Our team focused more on ____ task ____ relationship behavior.

26. Our team's primary leadership style was ____ autocratic ____ consultative ____ participative ____ empowerment.

27. Members were primarily influenced by ____ one member ____ a few members ____ shared leadership. However, I'd say our primary leader was _____.

28. We were a ____ group ____ team.

29. We had the following group types: ____ formal ____ informal; ____ functional ____ cross-functional; ____ command ____ task.

30. We made ____ effective ____ ineffective decisions, and we were ____ effective ____ ineffective at resolving conflict.

31. Our team progressed to the following stage of group development: ____ orientation ____ dissatisfaction ____ resolution ____ production ____ termination.

32. I'd say the most powerful group member was _____.

33. I'd say the person displaying the most effective political behavior was _____.

34. I'd say the person most effective at handling conflict in our team was _____.

35. Overall, our team found this exercise to be ____ stressful ____ nonstressful.

Controlling Skills (Chapters 14–15)

36. Our team's systems process was _____.

37. The preliminary, concurrent, rework, and damage controls our team used were: _____

_____

38. This exercise focused primarily on the ____ finance ____ marketing ____ operations ____ human resources functional area.

39. During this exercise, our team followed the steps in the control systems process (check all that apply): ____ set objectives and standards ____ measure performance ____ compare performance to the standard ____ correct, future correct, reinforce.

40. We had standards in the areas of (check all that apply): ____ quantity ____ quality ____ time ____ cost ____ behavior.

41. Our team used the following control methods (check all that apply): ____ constant ____ periodic ____ occasional.

42. The type of budget we developed was (check all that apply): ____ revenue ____ expense ____ capital expenditure.

43. Our expense budget was primarily ____ line-item ____ program; ____ static ____ flexible; ____ incremental ____ zero-based.

44. Our team developed the following financial statements (check all that apply): ____ income ____ balance sheet ____ cash flow.

45. Our team's level of productivity or cost per unit was _____ (outputs [number of products sold] divided by inputs [cost of goods sold plus expenses of $250,000]).

46. Our team focused more on ____ imposed control ____ self-control.

47. Our team ____ did ____ did not use coaching.

48. Our team ____ did ____ did not use discipline.

49. This exercise ____ was ____ was not a time-based competition.

50. Our team product is classified as ____ tangible ____ intangible; ____ make-to-stock ____ make-to-order ____ assemble-to-order; ____ continuous ____ repetitive ____ batch ____ individual process operations; operations were ____ capital-intensive ____ labor-intensive.

51. Our team facility layout for this exercise was ____ product ____ process ____ cellular ____ fixed-position.

52. Our inventory control resulted in ____ no ____ few ____ many raw material returns; ____ no ____ few ____ many work-in-process sold for scrap; ____ no ____ few ____ many finished goods rejected for sale. Overall, our materials requirement planning was ____ effective ____ ineffective and our quality control was ____ effective ____ ineffective.

53. Information ____ was ____ was not very important in this exercise.

54. The type of computer information system that would be most helpful in this exercise is ____ transaction processing ____ management information systems ____ decision support systems.

55. The information network in this exercise included (check all that apply): ____ connecting all employees ____ customers ____ suppliers ____ databases.

Procedure 6 (15–18 minutes)
Procedures 3–5 may be repeated one or more times. However, the customers/suppliers should change roles with team members.

Conclusion

The instructor may lead a class discussion and/or make concluding remarks.

Application (2–4 minutes)

What did I learn from this exercise? How will I use this knowledge in the future?

_____

_____

_____

VIDEO CASE

Wainwright Industries
(15–1 14½ Minutes)

Case Summary

Wainwright is a family-owned supplier to the automotive and aerospace industries. It decided to upgrade its quality to remain competitive. To move the company forward, Wainwright used the Baldridge Award criteria as guides to quality improvements and used TQM techniques. Through its efforts, Wainwright improved quality, lowered costs, improved safety, and increased profits. It subsequently won the Baldridge Quality Award in the Small Business classification.

Students' Learning Objective

To understand the concept of TQM including continuous improvement and employee empowerment.

Critical Thinking Questions

1. What should a manufacturing company such as Wainwright do to improve its quality?

2. What could a company such as Wainwright do to increase employee involvement in a continuous improvement process?

Appendix B: How to Research Case Material Using the Internet

Until the mid-1990s, finding information regarding a company that was being discussed in a case study was difficult. Today, conducting research to find company material is a whole new science. Going anywhere without hearing about the Internet is virtually impossible.

A major advantage of the Internet online data search is that the number of sources available to you is dramatically increased. Also, home access to the Net reduces the need to visit a physical library and enables you to remain in the comfort of your home or dormitory room.

Access to the Internet

Your college or university will provide you with access to the Internet on campus, often in the library and computer labs. Librarians and computer lab instructors often provide Internet training for groups and individuals. You may also be able to access the Internet through the college from your dorm or home. Off campus, the simplest way to gain access to the Internet is to sign up for an Internet provider such as America Online (AOL) or the Microsoft Network (MSN). These service providers charge a monthly fee for unlimited access to the Internet. Assuming you have gained access to the Net, the next question is, "How do I get information about the company in the case?" You may go directly to the Web site of the case company, access databases, and use search engines using key topics or words.

Going Directly to the Company's Web Site

A Web site is a location on the Net that a company has set up to disperse information about itself. Information can be gathered by accessing the World Wide Web through your service provider. Pages of company information from financial data to corporate strategies are provided. Current information can usually be found in the press release sections of most large companies' Web sites.

At the ends of the *opening* and *closing* cases of each chapter are the Web site addresses of companies that had Web addresses when the book was published. Other sites may now be available. Simply type in the case company address to access its information. For instance, Nike has an elaborate Web site that can be accessed by typing in *http://www.nike.com*.

Limitation of Company Web Sites and the Need to Cite at Least Two Other Sources

A limitation of company Web sites is that the information is provided by the company; therefore, it may be biased and not indicative of what other sources are writing about the company. You should also realize that researching only one journal, magazine, or newspaper (no matter which one) is not enough information to validate the findings of a company's Web site. In other words, simply using a company's Web site is not enough. You also need to use at least two, and preferably more, written sources of information.

Finding Sources of Company Information on the Internet

Databases such as *marketguide.com* and *hoovers.com* are designed to give investors or researchers information about companies. Through your college library, you may also be able to access Infotrack SearchBank, or other databases, that contain articles from several hundred journals, magazines, and newspapers by using key topic or word searches.

Additionally, search engines such as Lycos, Excite, and Yahoo can be accessed to search a desired topic or company. These types of databases may give you the ability to gain access to complete articles about the company you are researching. The information can be as current as today's issue of whichever source you are searching.

Referencing Internet Material

Finding information on the Internet does not allow you to bypass proper bibliographic procedures. Referencing material found on the Net is not as straightforward as citing books, journals, and magazines. Databases on the Net can be found anywhere in cyberspace. Material is only acceptable if you can specifically document its origins as if you were writing a traditional reference. You must write:

- The author's name
- Title of the article
- Name of publication
- Date and page numbers

Your instructor will provide you with more details on his or her expectations of how to use Internet material.

Source: Dr. David C. Kimbal, Associate Professor of Management, Elms College, Chicopee, Massachusetts.

Endnotes

Chapter 1

1. Information about the GAP taken from its 1997 Annual Report.

2. J. Gunther, "Staying Ahead of the Curve." *Risk Management* (April 1998), Vol. 45, No. 4, pp. 80–84.

3. T. Petzinger, Jr., "The Front Lines: Radical Work by Guru of Leadership Takes 30 Years to Flower." *The Wall Street Journal*, April 25, 1997, p. B1.

4. H. Lancaster, "Managing Your Career: What Do You Hate About Work? (Hint: It May Not Be Your Job)." *The Wall Street Journal*, November 4, 1997, p. B1.

5. D.J. Collis and C.A. Montgomery, "Creating Corporate Advantage." *Harvard Business Review* (May/June 1998), Vol. 76, No. 3, pp. 71–84.

6. S. Trussler, "The Rules of the Game." *Journal of Business Strategy* (January/February 1998), Vol. 19, No. 1, pp. 16–20.

7. "Information Management Resources, Inc. Acquires Lyon Consultants, S.A." PR Newswire, May 15, 1998, p. 515.

8. S. Trussler, "The Rules of the Game." *Journal of Business Strategy* (January/February 1998), Vol. 19, No. 1, pp. 16–20.

9. D.J. Collis and C.A. Montgomery, "Creating Corporate Advantage." *Harvard Business Review* (May/June 1998), Vol. 76, No. 3, pp. 71–84.

10. P.M. Buhler, "Managers: Out With the Old and in With the New—Skills That Is." *Supervision* (June 1998), Vol. 59, No. 6, pp. 22–25.

11. *The Wall Street Journal*, November 14, 1980, p. 33.

12. K. Tyler, "Mentoring Programs Link Employees and Experienced Execs." *HRMagazine* (April 1998), Vol. 43, No. 5, pp. 98–104.

13. A. Reinhardt, "Mr. House Finds His Fixer-upper." *Business Week* (February 2, 1998), No. 3563, pp. 66–69.

14. R. Katz, "Skills of an Effective Administrator." *Harvard Business Review*, September/October 1974, pp. 90–102.

15. L.J. Bassi and M.E. Van Buren, "The 1998 ASTD State of the Industry Report." *Training and Development* (January 1998), Vol. 52, No. 1, pp. 21–44.

16. J. Gunther, "Staying Ahead of the Curve." *Risk Management* (April 1998), Vol. 45, No. 4, pp. 80–84.

17. H. Lancaster, "Managing Your Career: What Do You Hate About Work? (Hint: It May Not Be Your Job)." *The Wall Street Journal*, November 4, 1997, p. B1

18. J. Gunther, "Staying Ahead of the Curve." *Risk Management* (April 1998), Vol. 45, No. 4, pp. 80–84.

19. S. Trussler, "The Rules of the Game." *Journal of Business Strategy* (January/February 1998), Vol. 19, No. 1, pp. 16–20.

20. E. Ghiselli, *Explorations in Management Talent* (Santa Monica, CA: Goodyear Publishing, 1971).

21. P.M. Buhler, "Managers: Out With the Old and in With the New—Skills That Is." *Supervision* (June 1998), Vol. 59, No. 6, pp. 22–25.

22. R.E. Thaler-Carter, "In-house Recruiters Fill a Specialized Niche." *HR Magazine* (April 1998), Vol. 43, No. 5, pp. 72–78.

23. D.J. Collis and C.A. Montgomery, "Creating Corporate Advantage." *Harvard Business Review* (May/June 1998), Vol. 76, No. 3, pp. 71–84.

24. R.E. Thaler-Carter, "In-house Recruiters Fill a Specialized Niche." *HR Magazine* (April 1998), Vol. 43, No. 5, pp. 72–78.

25. P. Bissonette, *NewsLetter* (Wayzata, MN: Learning Strategies Corporation, February 1995), p. 1.

26. P.M. Buhler, "Managers: Out With the Old and in With the New—Skills That Is." *Supervision* (June 1998), Vol. 59, No. 6, pp. 22–25.

27. L. Kurke and H. Aldrich, "Mintzberg Was Right! A Replication and Extension of *The Nature of Managerial Work*." *Management Science* (1983), Vol. 29, pp. 975–984.

28. C. Avert and A. Al, "Managerial Work: The Influence of Hierarchical Level and Functional Specialty." *Academy of Management Journal* (1983), Vol. 26. pp. 170–177.

29. C. Hales, "What Do Managers Do? A Critical Review of the Evidence." *Journal of Management Studies* (1986), Vol. 23, pp. 88–115.

30. H. Mintzberg, *The Nature of Managerial Work* (New York: Harper & Row, 1973).

31. C. Bartlett and S. Ghosal, "The Myth of the General Manager." *California Management Review* (Fall 1997), Vol. 40, No. 1, pp. 92–117.

32. P.M. Buhler, "Managers: Out With the Old and in With the New—Skills That Is." *Supervision* (June 1998), Vol. 59, No. 6, pp. 22–25.

33. C. Bartlett and S. Ghosal, "The Myth of the General Manager." *California Management Review* (Fall 1997), Vol. 40, No. 1, pp. 92–117.

34. J. Chang, "Cytec's Restructuring Success Setting Path for Other Players." *Chemical Market Reporter* (February 9, 1998), Vol. 253, No. 6, pp. 1–3.

35. P.M. Buhler, "Managers: Out With the Old and in With the New—Skills That Is." *Supervision* (June 1998), Vol. 59, No. 6, pp. 22–25.

36. J. Gunther, "Staying Ahead of the Curve." *Risk Management* (April 1998), Vol. 45, No. 4, pp. 80–84.

37. P.M. Buhler, "Managers: Out With the Old and in With the New—Skills That Is." *Supervision* (June 1998), Vol. 59, No. 6, pp. 22–25.

38. N. Karagozoglu and M. Lindell, "Internationalization of Small and Medium-sized Technology-based Firms: An Exploratory Study." *Journal of Small Business Management* (January 1998), Vol. 36, No. 1, pp. 44–60.

39. J. Paolillo, "The Manager's Self-Assessment of Managerial Roles; Small vs. Large Firms." *American Journal of Small Business*, January/March 1984, pp. 61–62

40. M. Mangelsdorf, "Big vs. Small." INC., May 1989, p. 22.

41. Entrepreneur of the Year, CNBC, November 17, 1996.

42. Ibid.

43. "Bill Gates Admitted," *The Wall Street Journal*, March 4, 1996, p. 1.

44. J.R. Schermerhorn, Jr., Ohio University, "Situational Leadership: Conversations with Paul Hersey." *Mid-American Journal of Business* (1998), Vol. 12, No. 2, pp. 5–11.

Appendix A

1. F.W. Taylor, *Principles of Scientific Management* (New York: Harper and Brothers, 1911).

2. H. Fayol, *General and Industrial Management*, translated by J.A. Conbrough (Geneva: International Management Institute, 1929).

3. F. Roethlisberger and W. Dickson, *Management and the Worker* (Boston: Harvard University Press, 1939).

4. A. Maslow, *Motivation and Personality*, 2nd ed. (New York: Harper & Row, 1970).

5. D. McGregor, *The Human Side of Enterprise* (New York: McGraw-Hill, 1960).

6. R. Ackoff, *Creating the Corporate Future* (New York: Wiley, 1981).

7. H. Koontz, "The Management Theory Jungle Revisited." *Academy of Management Review* (April 1980), Vol. 5, p. 175.

8. D. Katz and R. Khan, *The Social Psychology of Organizations,* 2nd ed. (New York: Wiley, 1978).

9. E.L. Trist and K.W. Bamforth, "Some Social and Psychological Consequences of the Wall Method of Coal Getting." *Human Relations* (1951), Vol. 4, pp. 3–38. F.E. Emery and E.L. Trist, *Socio-Technical Systems, Vol. 2 of Management Science: Methods and Techniques* (London: Pergamon, 1960).

10. T. Burns and G. Stalker, *The Management of Innovation* (London: Tavistock, 1961).

Chapter 2

1. Material throughout Chapter 2 is taken from the Federal Express Information Packet available to anyone upon request by calling (901) 395–3460.

2. D. Pyke, "Strategies for Global Sourcing." *The Financial Times*, February 20, 1998, pp. FTS3–5.

3. C.K. Bart, "Mission Matters." *CA Magazine* (March 1998), Vol. 131, No. 2, pp. 31–34.

4. B.K. Boyd and E.R. Elliott, "A Measurement Model of Strategic Planning." *Strategic Management Journal* (February 1998), Vol. 19, No. 2, pp. 181–200.

5. "Dr. W.E. Deming 1988/89 Winner of Dow Jones Award." *ESB*, Spring 1989, p. 3.

6. D. Pyke, "Strategies for Global Sourcing." *The Financial Times*, February 20, 1998, pp. FTS3–5.

7. C.K. Bart, "Mission Matters." *CA Magazine* (March 1998), Vol. 131, No. 2, pp. 31–34.

8. R. Ackoff, *Creating the Corporate Future* (New York: Wiley, 1981).

9. C.K. Bart, "Mission Matters." *CA Magazine* (March 1998), Vol. 131, No. 2, pp. 31–34.

10. D.J. Collis and C.A. Montgomery, "Creating Corporate Advantage." *Harvard Business Review* (May/June 1998), Vol. 76, No. 3, pp. 71–84.

11. R.W. Grubbstrom and J. Olhager, "Productivity and Flexibility: Fundamental Relations Between Two Major Properties and Performance Measures of the Production System." *International Journal of Production Economics* (October 15, 1997), Vol. 52, No. 1–2, pp. 73–83.

12. D.J. Collis and C.A. Montgomery, "Creating Corporate Advantage." *Harvard Business Review* (May/June 1998), Vol. 76, No. 3, pp. 71–84.

13. Ibid.

14. M.S. Spencer and L.K. Duclos, "TQM Stresses MIS: The Ache of Continuous Change." *Mid-American Journal of Business* (Spring 1998), Vol. 13, No. 1, pp. 59–65.

15. S.F. Ferris, R. Quint, and R. Sant, "Financial Theory and Practice in the Application of TQM: The Case of IBM Rochester." *Journal of Managerial Issues* (Spring 1998), Vol. 10, No. 1, pp. 13–30.

16. D. McAbe and A. Wilkinson, "The Rise and Fall of TQM: The Vision, Meaning and Operation of Change." (Total Quality Management), *Industrial Relations Journal* (March 1998), Vol. 29, No. 1, pp. 18–30.

17. D.J. Collis and C.A. Montgomery, "Creating Corporate Advantage." *Harvard Business Review* (May/June 1998), Vol. 76, No. 3, pp. 71–84.

18. D. Pyke, "Strategies for Global Sourcing." *The Financial Times*, February 20, 1998, pp. FTS3–5.

19. V. O'Connell, "Corporate Focus—Changing Tastes Dent Campbell's Canned-Soup Sales." *The Wall Street Journal*, April 28, 1998, pp. B1 and B6.

20. "What Goes Around Comes Around," News from ... Curtis [no year listed], Vol. 8, No. 1.

21. B.K. Boyd and E.R. Elliott, "A Measurement Model of Strategic Planning." *Strategic Management Journal* (February 1998), Vol. 19, No. 2, pp. 181–200.

22. D.J. Collis and C.A. Montgomery, "Creating Corporate Advantage." *Harvard Business Review* (May/June 1998), Vol. 76, No. 3, pp. 71–84.

23. D. Pyke, "Strategies for Global Sourcing." *The Financial Times*, February 20, 1998, pp. FTS3–5.

24. M. Imai, "Will America's Corporate Theme Song Be 'Just In Time?'" (Production Management), *The Journal for Quality and Participation* (March/April 1998), Vol. 21, No. 2, pp. 26–39.

25. "GM is Heading . . ." *The Wall Street Journal*, June 19, 1998, p. A1.

26. M.A. Berry and D.A. Rondinelli, "Proactive Corporate Environment Management: A New Industrial Revolution." *The Academy of Management Executive* (May 1998), Vol. 12, No. 2, pp. 38–51.

27. B. Bowonder, "Competitive and Technology Management Strategy: A Case Study of TELCO." *International Journal of Technology Management* (June/July 1998), Vol. 15, No. 6–7, pp. 646–681.

28. N. Gross, "Leapfrogging a Few Links." *Business Week* (June 22, 1998), No. 3583, pp. 140–142.

29. G. Steinmetz, "The Euro Designer's Art is Sure to Have Wide Currency." *The Wall Street Journal*, July 7, 1998, p. B1.

30. T. Peters, *Thriving on Chaos: Handbook for a Management Revolution* (New York: Knopf, 1987).

31. J. Birkinshaw, N. Hood, and S. Jonsson, "Building Firm-specific Advantages in Multinational Corporations: The Role of Subsidiary Initiative." *Strategic Management Journal* (March 1998), Vol. 19, No. 3, pp. 221–242.

32. D. Parkhurst, "To Succeed in the Global Arena, Leadership is a Must." *Nation's Cities Weekly* (May 25, 1998), Vol. 2, No. 21, pp. 6–7.

33. "Kodak Agreed . . ." *The Wall Street Journal*, March 24, 1998, p. A1.

34. "Fortune's Global 500." *Fortune* (July 26, 1993), Vol. 128, No. 2, p. 226.

35. M. Hordes, J.A. Clancy, and J. Baddaley, "A Primer for Global Start-ups." *The Academy of Management Executive* (May 1995), Vol. 9, No. 2, pp. 7–11.

36. R.N. Lussier, R. Baeder, and J. Corman, "Measuring Global Practices: Global Strategic Planning Through Company Situational Analysis," *Business Horizons* (October 1994), Vol. 37, No. 5, pp. 56–63.

37. J. Birkinshaw, N. Hood, and S. Jonsson, "Building Firm-specific Advantages in Multinational Corporations: The Role of Subsidiary Initiative." *Strategic Management Journal* (March 1998), Vol. 19, No. 3, pp. 221–242.

38. T. Kamm, "Continental Shift—Au Revoir, Malaise: Europe's Economies Are Back in Business." *The Wall Street Journal*, April 9, 1998, p. A1.

39. J. Birkinshaw, N. Hood, and S. Jonsson, "Building Firm-specific Advantages in Multinational Corporations: The Role of Subsidiary Initiative." *Strategic Management Journal* (March 1998), Vol. 19, No. 3, pp. 221–242.

40. "Business Bulletin—A Special Background Report on Trends in Industry and Finance." *The Wall Street Journal*, June 25, 1998, p. A1.

41. D. Pyke, "Strategies for Global Sourcing." *The Financial Times*, February 20, 1998, pp. FTS3–5.

42. D. Parkhurst, "To Succeed in the Global Arena, Leadership is a Must." *Nation's Cities Weekly* (May 25, 1998), Vol. 2, No. 21, pp. 6–7.

43. "Satisfying Customers . . ." *The Wall Street Journal*, January 9, 1997, p. A1.

44. "UPS Raises its Profile in New Zealand with Joint Venture." *Journal of Commerce and Commercial* (May 4, 1998), Vol. 416, No. 29212, pp. 3C–4C.

45. R.N. Lussier, R. Baeder, and J. Corman, "Measuring Global Practices: Global Strategic Planning Through Company Situational Analysis," *Business Horizons* (October 1994), Vol. 37, No. 5, pp. 56–63.

46. P. Drucker, "The New World According to Drucker." *Business Month* (May 1989), Vol. 133, No. 5, pp. 50–56.

47. J. Corman, R.N. Lussier, and R. Baeder, "Global Strategies for the Future: Large vs. Small Business." *Journal of Business Strategies* (Fall 1991), Vol. 8, No. 2, pp. 86–93.

48. N. Karagozoglu and M. Lindell, "Internationalization of Small and Medium-sized Technology-based Firms: An Exploratory Study." *Journal of Small Business Management* (January 1998), Vol. 36, No. 1, pp. 44–60.

49. R. Calori and B. Dufour, "Management European Style." *Academy of Management Executive*, February 1998, pp. 61–71.

50. R. Tierney, "Diversity." *World Trade* (December 1993), Vol. 6, No. 11, pp. 22–25.

51. "Putting on a Japanese Face." *International Business* (February 1994), Vol. 7, No. 2, p. 90.

52. B. Dufour, "Dealing with Diversity: Management Education in Europe." *Selections* (Winter 1994), Vol. 10, No. 2, pp. 7–15.

53. M. Johnson, "Doing le Business." *Management Training*, February 1992, pp. 62–65.

54. "Global Companies Reexamine Corporate Culture." *Personnel Journal* (August 1994), Vol. 73, No. 8, p. S12.

55. A. Brien, "Professional Ethics and the Culture of Trust." *Journal of Business Ethics* (March 1998), Vol. 17, No. 4, pp. 391–410.

56. E.M. Epstein, "Business Ethics and Corporate Social Policy: Reflections on an Intellectual Journey, 1964–1996, and Beyond." *Business and Society* (March 1998), Vol. 37, No. 1, pp. 7–40.

57. "The Machinists Union." *The Wall Street Journal*, April 28, 1998, p. A1.

58. R. Sharpe, "What's a Secretary to do When the Boss Asks Her to Lie?" *The Wall Street Journal*, February 3, 1998, p. B1.

59. "Ben and Jerry Speak at Success 1998 in Hartford, CT." June 11, 1998.

60. "The 1990s May Tame the Savage M.B.A." *The Wall Street Journal*, June 14, 1991, p. B1.

61. "High-Tech Interviews." *The Wall Street Journal*, March 22, 1994, p. 1.

62. P. Primeaux and J. Stieber, "Profit Maximization." *Journal of Business Ethics* (April 1994), Vol. 13, No. 4, pp. 287–294.

63. R. Guthrie, "The Ethics of Telework." *Information Systems Management* (Fall 1997), Vol. 14, No. 4, pp. 29–33.

64. B. Castro, "Business Ethics: Know Ourselves." *Business Ethics Quarterly* (April 1994), Vol. 4, No. 2, p. 181.

65. E.M. Epstein, "Business Ethics and Corporate Social Policy: Reflections on an Intellectual Journey, 1964–1996, and Beyond." *Business and Society* (March 1998), Vol. 37, No. 1, pp. 7–40.

66. B. Ettore, "How's Your Report Card? Why Shouldn't "No Guts, No Glory" Apply in the Corporate Suite?" *Management Review* (March 1998), Vol. 87, No. 3, pp. 1–2.

67. M. Barrier, "Doing the Right Thing." *Nation's Business* (March 1998), Vol. 86, No. 3, pp. 32–38.

68. M.A. Berry and D.A. Rondinelli, "Proactive Corporate Environment Management: A New Industrial Revolution." *The Academy of Management Executive* (May 1998), Vol. 12, No. 2, pp. 38–51.

69. R.B. Reich, "The New Meaning of Corporate Social Responsibility." *California Management Review* (Winter 1998), Vol. 40, No. 2, pp. 8–18.

70. L. Kalb, "Ben & Jerry Tell Their Tale of Ice Cream Success, Social Responsibility." *Knight-Ridder/Tribune Business News*, May 20, 1998, p. OKRB981400D3.

71. R. Simerly, "Corporate Social Performance and Firms' Financial Performance." *Psychological Reports* (December 1994), Vol. 75, No. 3, pp. 1091–1114.

72. W. Davidson, D. Worrell, and C. Lee, "Stock Market Reactions to Announced Corporate Illegalities." *Journal of Business Ethics* (December 1994), Vol. 13, No. 12, pp. 979–988.

73. R. Gildea, "Consumer Survey Confirms Corporate Social Action Affects Buying Decisions." *Public Relations Quarterly* (Winter 1994), Vol. 39, No. 4, pp. 20–21.

74. M. Forte and B.T. Lamont, "The Bottom Line Effects of Greening." *The Academy of Management Executive* (February 1998), Vol. 12, No. 1, pp. 89–91.

75. R.B. Reich, "The New Meaning of Corporate Social Responsibility." *California Management Review* (Winter 1998), Vol. 40, No. 2, pp. 8–18.

76. M. Forte and B.T. Lamont, "The Bottom Line Effects of Greening." *The Academy of Management Executive* (February 1998), Vol. 12, No. 1, pp. 89–91.

77. M. Hammer and J. Champy, "Re-Engineering Authors Reconsider Re-Engineering." *The Wall Street Journal*, January 17, 1995, p. B1.

78. S. Shellenburg, "Work and Family." *The Wall Street Journal*, February 1, 1995, p. B1.

79. M. Hammer and J. Champy, "Re-Engineering Authors Reconsider Re-Engineering." *The Wall Street Journal*, January 17, 1995, p. B1.

80. M. Hammer and J. Champy, "Managers Beware: You're Not Ready For Tomorrow's Job." *The Wall Street Journal*, January 24, 1995, p. B1.

81. "Profits Tied to Revamps Can Prove to be Costly Down the Road." *The Wall Street Journal*, April 6, 1995, p. 1.

82. J. Martin, "Remember the Merging '80s?" *America* (December 31, 1994), Vol. 171, No. 20, pp. 6–8.

83. "The Boom in the Temporary Help Business." *The Wall Street Journal*, April 11, 1995, p. A1.

84. "Business and Finance—Smoking Costs the . . ." *The Wall Street Journal*, March 25, 1998, p. A1.

Chapter 3

1. Information provided by Coca-Cola Company, *Financial Topics, Facts, Figures and Features*, and *1997 Annual Report*

2. H. Lancaster, "Managing Your Career." *The Wall Street Journal*, January 3, 1995, p. B1.

3. J.R. Katzenbach, "The Irony of Senior Leadership Teams." *The Journal for Quality and Participation* (May/June 1998), Vol. 21, No. 3, pp. 8–16.

4. W. Cottringer, "The Pain of Problem Solving." *Security Management* (March 1998), Vol. 42, No. 3, pp. 25–28.

5. H. Einhorn and R. Hogarth, "Decision-Making: Going Forward in Reverse." *Harvard Business Review*, January/February 1987, p. 66.

6. W. Cottringer, "The Pain of Problem Solving." *Security Management* (March 1998), Vol. 42, No. 3, pp. 25–28.

7. P.R. Berthon, L.F. Pitt, and M.H. Morris, "The Impact of Individual and Organizational Factors on Problem Perception Theory and Empirical Evidence from the Marketing-Technical Dyad." *Journal of Business Research* (May 1998), Vol. 42, No. 1, pp. 25–39.

8. J.R. Katzenbach, "The Irony of Senior Leadership Teams." *The Journal for Quality and Participation* (May/June 1998), Vol. 21, No. 3, pp. 8–16.

9. P.R. Berthon, L.F. Pitt, and M.H. Morris, "The Impact of Individual and Organizational Factors on Problem Perception Theory and Empirical Evidence from the Marketing-Technical Dyad." *Journal of Business Research* (May 1998), Vol. 42, No. 1, pp. 25–39.

10. E. McFadzean and T. Nelson, "Facilitating Problem-Solving Groups: A Conceptual Model." *Leadership and Organization Development Journal* (January/February 1998), Vol. 19, No. 1, pp. 6–14.

11. V. Papadakis, S. Lioukas, and D. Chambers, "Strategic Decision-Making Processes: The Role of Management and Context." *Strategic*

Management Journal (February 1998), Vol. 19, No. 2, pp. 115–148.

12. Ibid.

13. D. Budescu, R. Suleiman, and A. Rapoport, "Positional Order and Group Size Effects in Resource Dilemmas With Uncertainty." *Organizational Behavior & Human Decision Process* (March 1995), Vol. 61, No. 3, pp. 225–239.

14. E. McFadzean and T. Nelson, "Facilitating Problem-Solving Groups: A Conceptual Model." *Leadership and Organization Development Journal* (January/February 1998), Vol. 19, No. 1, pp. 6–14.

15. J.P. Muczyk and R.P. Steel, "Leadership Style and the Turnaround Executive." *Business Horizons* (March/April 1998), Vol. 41, No. 2, pp. 39–47.

16. E. McFadzean and T. Nelson, "Facilitating Problem-Solving Groups: A Conceptual Model." *Leadership and Organization Development Journal* (January/February 1998), Vol. 19, No. 1, pp. 6–14.

17. "What Gets Measured Gets Done—If Your Company Posts the Right Kinds of Numbers. Which is Why Scoreboards are Back—With a Twist." *INC.* (June 1998), Vol. 20, No. 8, pp. 80–81.

18. A. O'Leary-Kelly, J. Martocchio, and D. Frink, "The Art of Decision Making." *Academy of Management Journal* (October 1994), Vol. 37, No. 5, pp. 1285–1292.

19. H. Klean and J. Kim, "A Field Study of the Influence of Situational Constraints, Leader-Member Exchange, and Goal Commitment on Performance." *Academy of Management Journal* (February 1998), Vol. 41, No. 1, pp. 88–96.

20. C. Carlsson and R. Fuller, "Multiple Criteria Decision-Making: The Case for Interdependence." *Computers & Operations Research* (March 1995), Vol. 22, No. 3, pp. 251–261.

21. G. Rawlinson, "Driving Innovation With a Different Way of Thinking." *Materials World* (April 1998), Vol. 6, No. 4, pp. 207–210.

22. B. Morris and P. Waldman, "The Death of Premier." *The Wall Street Journal*, March 10, 1989, p. B14.

23. G.S. Wood, "Making Meetings Productive and Fun: How to Transform Board Meetings Into Creative, Energizing, Problem-Solving Sessions." *Association Management* (January 1998), Vol. 50, No. 1, pp. 48–52.

24. L. Mozzi, "Creativity Commandments." *The Journal for Quality and Participation* (May/June 1998), Vol. 21, No. 3, pp. 60–63.

25. S. Greco, "Where Great Ideas Come From." *INC.* (April 1998), Vol. 20, No. 5, pp. 76–83.

26. Ibid.

27. E. Diehl and J. Sterman, "Effects of Feedback Complexity on Dynamic Decision Making." *Organizational Behavior & Human Decision Processes* (May 1995), Vol. 62, No. 2, pp. 198–216.

28. S. Highhouse and K. Bottrill, "The Influence of Social (miss) Information on Memory for Behavior in an Employment Interview." *Organizational Behavior & Human Decision Process* (May 1995), Vol. 62, No. 2, pp. 220–230.

29. A. Kuhberger, "The Framing of Decision: A New Look at Old Problems." *Organizational Behavior & Human Decision Processes* (May 1995), Vol. 62, No. 2, pp. 230–241.

30. G. Rawlinson, "Driving Innovation With a Different Way of Thinking." *Materials World* (April 1998), Vol. 6, No. 4, pp. 207–210.

31. L. Mozzi, "Creativity Commandments." *The Journal for Quality and Participation* (May/June 1998), Vol. 21, No. 3, pp. 60–63.

32. G.S. Wood, "Making Meetings Productive and Fun: How to Transform Board Meetings Into Creative, Energizing, Problem-Solving Sessions." *Association Management* (January 1998), Vol. 50, No. 1, pp. 48–52.

33. M. Santosus, "Information Micromanagement." *CIO* (April 15, 1998), Vol. 11, No. 13, pp. 22B–23B.

34. S. Greco, "Where Great Ideas Come From." *INC.* (April 1998), Vol. 20, No. 5, pp. 76–83.

35. G. Kay, "Effective Meetings Through Electronic Brainstorming." *Management Quarterly* (Winter 1994), Vol. 35, No. 4, pp. 15–27.

36. R.L. Edgeman and J. Williams, "Select Leaders Using a Quality Management Process." *Quality Progress* (February 1998), Vol. 31, No. 2, pp. 78–83.

37. M. Wolfe, "A Theoretical Justification for Japanese Nemawashi/Rngi Group Decision Making and an Implementation." *Decision Support Systems* (April 1992), Vol. 8, No. 2, pp. 125–140.

38. T. Shin, "Using Delphi for a Long–range Technology Forecasting, and Assessing Directions of Future R&D Activities: The Korean Exercise." *Technological Forecasting & Social Change* (May/June 1998), Vol. 58, No. 1–2, pp. 125–155.

39. R.L. Edgeman and J. Williams, "Select Leaders Using a Quality Management Process." *Quality Progress* (February 1998), Vol. 31, No. 2, pp. 78–83.

40. C. Neck and C. Manz, "From Groupthink to Teamthink: Toward the Creation of Constructive Thought Patterns in Self-Managing Teams." *Human Relations* (August 1994), Vol. 47, No. 8, pp. 929–954.

41. A. Kuhberger, "The Framing of Decision: A New Look at Old Problems." *Organizational Behavior & Human Decision Processes* (May 1995), Vol. 62, No. 2, pp. 230–241.

42. C. Heath and R. Gonzalez, "Interaction With Others Increases Decision Confidence But Not Decision Quality: Evidence Against Information Collection Views of Interactive Decision-Making." *Organizational Behavior & Human Decision Processes* (March 1995), Vol. 61, No. 3, pp. 305–327.

43. V. Papadakis, S. Lioukas, and D. Chambers, "Strategic Decision-Making Processes: The Role of Management and Context." *Strategic Management Journal* (February 1998), Vol. 19, No. 2, pp. 115–148.

44. J.R. Katzenbach, "The Irony of Senior Leadership Teams." *The Journal for Quality and Participation* (May/June 1998), Vol. 21, No. 3, pp. 8–16.

45. W. Cottringer, "The Pain of Problem Solving." *Security Management* (March 1998), Vol. 42, No. 3, pp. 25–28.

46. "What Gets Measured Gets Done—If Your Company Posts the Right Kinds of Numbers. Which is Why Scoreboards are Back—With a Twist." *INC.* (June 1998), Vol. 20, No. 8, pp. 80–81.

47. N.Z. Dering, "Leadership in Quality Organizations." *The Journal for Quality and Participation* (January/February 1998), Vol. 21, No. 1, pp. 32–36.

48. J.R. Schermerhorn, Jr., Ohio University, "Situational Leadership: Conversations with Paul Hersey." *Mid-American Journal of Business* (1998), Vol. 12, No. 2, pp. 5–11.

Chapter 4

1. The information on Peter Clark came from a personal interview with the author. Information on Pennzoil and Jiffy Lube International was taken from the 1997 annual report.

2. A. Swasy, "Diaper's Failure Shows How Poor Plans, Unexpected Woes Can Kill New Products." *The Wall Street Journal*, October 9, 1990, p. B1.

3. L. Lee, "A Company Failing From Too Much Success." *The Wall Street Journal*, March 17, 1995, p. B1.

4. A. Campbell and M. Alexander, "What's Wrong With Strategy?" *Harvard Business Review* (November/December1997), Vol. 75, No. 6, pp. 42–50.

5. Christopher K. Bart, "Mission Matters." *CA Magazine* (March 1998), Vol. 131, No. 2, pp. 31–34.

6. B.K. Boyd and E.R. Elliott, "A Measurement Model of Strategic Planning." *Strategic*

Management Journal (February 1998), Vol. 19, No. 2, pp. 181–200.

7. J.W. Lea, "Vision Statements Must be Practical, not Pie-in-the-Sky." *Washington Business Journal* (May 22, 1998), Vol. 17, No. 2, pp. 48–49.

8. B.K. Boyd and E.R. Elliott, "A Measurement Model of Strategic Planning." *Strategic Management Journal* (February 1998), Vol. 19, No. 2, pp. 181–200.

9. D.J. Collis and C.A. Montgomery, "Creating Corporate Advantage." *Harvard Business Review* (May/June 1998), Vol. 76, No. 3, pp. 71–84.

10. A. Campbell and M. Alexander, "What's Wrong With Strategy?" *Harvard Business Review* (November/December1997), Vol. 75, No. 6, pp. 42–50.

11. S. Baker and K. Baker, "The 1998 Strategist's Guide to Software." *Journal of Business Strategy* (January/February 1998), Vol. 19, No. 1, pp. 39–52.

12. D.J. Collis and C.A. Montgomery, "Creating Corporate Advantage." *Harvard Business Review* (May/June 1998), Vol. 76, No. 3, pp. 71–84.

13. O. Gadiesh and J.L. Gilbert, "Profit Pools: A Fresh Look at Strategy." *Harvard Business Review* (May/June 1998), Vol. 76, No. 3, pp. 139–148.

14. M. Porter, "How Competitive Forces Shape Strategy." *Harvard Business Review* (March/April 1979), Vol. 57, No. 2, pp. 137–145.

15. D. Pyke, "Strategies for Global Sourcing." *The Financial Times*, February 20, 1998, pp. FTS3–5.

16. Ibid.

17. D.J. Collis and C.A. Montgomery, "Creating Corporate Advantage." *Harvard Business Review* (May/June 1998), Vol. 76, No. 3, pp. 71–84.

18. B.K. Boyd and E.R. Elliott, "A Measurement Model of Strategic Planning." *Strategic Management Journal* (February 1998), Vol. 19, No. 2, pp. 181–200.

19. C. Wheal, "So, Here's the Plan." *The Guardian*, March 4, 1998, pp. S25–27.

20. J. Berry, "Getting Naked With Wal-Mart: Inside the SWOT Papers." *Brandweek*, March 8, 1993, pp. 12–13.

21. B.K. Boyd and E.R. Elliott, "A Measurement Model of Strategic Planning." *Strategic Management Journal* (February 1998), Vol. 19, No. 2, pp. 181–200.

22. M.A. Berry and D.A. Rondinelli, "Proactive Corporate Environment Management: A New Industrial Revolution." *The Academy of Management Executive* (May 1998), Vol. 12, No. 2, pp. 38–51.

23. D.J. Collis and C.A. Montgomery, "Creating Corporate Advantage." *Harvard Business Review* (May/June 1998), Vol. 76, No. 3, pp. 71–84.

24. J. Pfeffer, "Producing Sustainable Competitive Advantage Through the Effective Management of People." *The Academy of Management Executive* (February 1995), Vol. 9, No. 1, pp. 55–68.

25. D.J. Collis and C.A. Montgomery, "Creating Corporate Advantage." *Harvard Business Review* (May/June 1998), Vol. 76, No. 3, pp. 71–84.

26. L. Mann, D. Samson, and D. Dow, "A Field Experiment on the Effects of Benchmarking and Goal Setting on Company Sales Performance." *Journal of Management* (January/February 1998), Vol. 24, No. 1, pp. 73–97.

27. H. Klean and J. Kim, "A Field Study of the Influence of Situational Constraints, Leader-Member Exchange, and Goal Commitment on Performance." *Academy of Management Journal* (February 1998), Vol. 41, No. 1, pp. 88–96.

28. B.K. Boyd and E.R. Elliott, "A Measurement Model of Strategic Planning." *Strategic Management Journal* (February 1998), Vol. 19, No. 2, pp. 181–200.

29. J.W. Lea, "Vision Statements Must be Practical, not Pie-in-the-Sky." *Washington Business Journal* (May 22, 1998), Vol. 17, No. 2, pp. 48–49.

30. H. Lancaster, "Managing Your Career." *The Wall Street Journal*, October 14, 1997, p. B1.

31. "Career Resolutions." *The Wall Street Journal*, December 30, 1997, p. 1.

32. N. Deogun, "Pop Culture." *The Wall Street Journal*, May 8, 1997, p. 1

33. H. Klean and J. Kim, "A Field Study of the Influence of Situational Constraints, Leader-Member Exchange, and Goal Commitment on Performance." *Academy of Management Journal* (February 1998), Vol. 41, No. 1, pp. 88–96.

34. B.K. Boyd and E.R. Elliott, "A Measurement Model of Strategic Planning." *Strategic Management Journal* (February 1998), Vol. 19, No. 2, pp. 181–200.

35. H. Klean and J. Kim, "A Field Study of the Influence of Situational Constraints, Leader-Member Exchange, and Goal Commitment on Performance." *Academy of Management Journal* (February 1998), Vol. 41, No. 1, pp. 88–96.

36. Ibid.

37. Ibid.

38. Ibid.

39. R. Rodgers and J. Hunter, "The Discard of Study Evidence by Literature Reviewers." *Journal of Applied Behavioral Science* (September 1994), Vol. 30, No. 3, pp. 329–346.

40. "James River Said." *The Wall Street Journal*, March 30, 1995, p. 1.

41. D. Pyke, "Strategies for Global Sourcing." *The Financial Times*, February 20, 1998, pp. FTS3–5.

42. "Pennzoil's Board." *The Wall Street Journal*, July 2, 1997, p. 1.

43. "Mergers and Acquisitions." *The Wall Street Journal*, January 2, 1998, p. 1.

44. "BankAmerica Has Agreed." *The Wall Street Journal*, April 13, 1998, p. 1.

45. "Pennzoil Plans." *The Wall Street Journal*, April 16, 1998, p. 1.

46. D. Pyke, "Strategies for Global Sourcing." *The Financial Times*, February 20, 1998, pp. FTS3–5.

47. D.J. Collis and C.A. Montgomery, "Creating Corporate Advantage." *Harvard Business Review* (May/June 1998), Vol. 76, No. 3, pp. 71–84.

48. "Maytag Agreed to Sell." *The Wall Street Journal*, May 31, 1995, p. 1.

49. "Seagram Will Sell." *The Wall Street Journal*, May 22, 1998, p. 1.

50. M. Sonfield and R.N. Lussier, "The Entrepreneurial Strategy Matrix: A Model for New and Ongoing Ventures." *Business Horizons* (May/June 1997), Vol. 40, pp. 73–77.

51. M. Porter, *Competitive Strategy: Techniques for Analyzing Industries and Competitors* (New York: The Free Press, 1980), p. 15.

52. "Roberto Goizueta in His Own Words." *The Wall Street Journal*, October 20, 1997, p. B1.

53. S. Trussler, "The Rules of the Game." *Journal of Business Strategy* (January/February 1998), Vol. 19, No. 1, pp. 16–20.

54. T. Petzinger, "The Front Line." *The Wall Street Journal*, January 30, 1998, p. B1.

55. S. Capparell, "The Front Line." *The Wall Street Journal*, August 29, 1997, p. B1.

56. V. Saran, "The Role of Life Cycles and Forecast Horizons in a Forecasting System: Reebok's Perspective." *Journal of Business Forecasting* (Spring 1998), Vol. 17, No. 1, pp. 23–25.

57. O. Gadiesh and J.L. Gilbert, "Profit Pools: A Fresh Look at Strategy." *Harvard Business Review* (May/June 1998), Vol. 76, No. 3, pp. 139–148.

58. R. Agarwal, "Evolutionary Trends of Industry Variables." *International Journal of Industrial Organization* (July 1998), Vol. 16, No. 4, pp. 511–526.

59. L.M. Birou, S.E. Fawcett, and G.M. Magnan, "The Product Life Cycle: A Tool for Functional Strategic Alignment." *International Journal of Purchasing and Materials Management* (Spring 1998), Vol. 34, No. 2, pp. 37–52.

60. A. Campbell and M. Alexander, "What's Wrong With Strategy?" *Harvard Business Review* (November/December1997), Vol. 75, No. 6, pp. 42–50.

61. "Mattel Agreed." *The Wall Street Journal*, June 16, 1998, p. 1.

Chapter 5

1. This case is based on an actual consultant, but the name and other information is changed to provide confidentiality for the consultant.
2. B.K. Boyd and E.R. Elliott, "A Measurement Model of Strategic Planning." *Strategic Management Journal* (February 1998), Vol. 19, No. 2, pp. 181–200.
3. C. Wheal, "So, Here's the Plan." *The Guardian*, March 4, 1998, pp. S25–27.
4. H. Lancaster, "Managing Your Career: What Do You Hate About Work? (Hint: It May Not Be Your Job)." *Wall Street Journal*, November 4, 1997, p. B1.
5. V. Papadakis, S. Lioukas, and D. Chambers, "Strategic Decision-Making Processes: The Role of Management and Context." *Strategic Management Journal* (February 1998), Vol. 19, No. 2, pp. 115–148.
6. J.H. Harris and L.A. Arendt, "Stress Reduction and the Small Business: Increasing Employee and Customer Satisfaction." *SAM Advanced Management Journal* (Winter 1998), Vol. 63, No. 1, pp. 27–35.
7. T. Pollock, "Attitudes That Can Help You Get Ahead: A Personal File of Stimulating Ideas, Little-known Facts and Daily Problem Solvers." *Supervision* (February 1998), Vol. 59, No. 2, pp. 24–27.
8. Ibid.
9. J.H. Harris and L.A. Arendt, "Stress Reduction and the Small Business: Increasing Employee and Customer Satisfaction." *SAM Advanced Management Journal* (Winter 1998), Vol. 63, No. 1, pp. 27–35.
10. G. Anthes, "Contingency Planning When Disaster Strikes." *Computerworld* (January 19, 1998), Vol. 32, No. 3, pp. 80–83.
11. M. Minehan, "Changing Conditions in Emerging Markets." *HRMagazine* (January 1998), Vol. 43, No. 1, pp. 160–161.
12. G. Anthes, "Contingency Planning When Disaster Strikes." *Computerworld* (January 19, 1998), Vol. 32, No. 3, pp. 80–83.
13. Ibid.
14. B. Lamons, "'Just Do it' Managers Must Start Planning Ahead." (Advertising to Business), *Marketing News* (February 2, 1998), Vol. 32, No. 3, pp. 10–11.
15. D. Pyke, "Strategies for Global Sourcing." *The Financial Times*, February 20, 1998, pp. FTS3–5.
16. A. Rutigliano, "Cloudy With a Change of Leads." *Sales & Marketing Management* (August 1994), Vol. 146, No. 8, p. 6.

17. T. Modis, "Life's Ups and Downs." *The Guardian*, January 12, 1995, p. S7.
18. S. Kalin, "Reading Between the Lines." *CIO* (April 1, 1998), Vol. 11, No. 12, pp. S42–47.
19. C. Mui and L. Downes, "Destroy Your Value Chain—Before Someone Else Does," *CIO* (June 15, 1998), Vol. 11, No. 15, pp. S68–73.
20. S. Rupley, "Era of the Low-Cost PC." *PC Magazine* (July 1998), Vol. 17, No. 17, pp. 28–29.
21. "Motorola Won." *The Wall Street Journal*, January 31, 1997, p. 1
22. N. Deogun, "Pop Culture." *The Wall Street Journal*, May 8, 1997, p. 1.
23. R. Gordon, "A Role for the Forecasting Function." *Journal of Business Forecasting* (Winter 1997), Vol. 16, No. 4, pp. 3–8.
24. W. Keenan, "Number Racket: Are Your Salespeople Contributing to the Effort to Predict Tomorrow's Business Results?" *Sales & Marketing Management* (May 1995), Vol. 147, No. 5, pp. 64–71.
25. R. Gordon, "A Role for the Forecasting Function." *Journal of Business Forecasting* (Winter 1997), Vol. 16, No. 4, pp. 3–8.
26. Ibid.
27. B. Peck, "Tools for Teams Addressing Total Customer Satisfaction, *Industrial Engineering* (January 1995), Vol. 27, No. 1, pp. 30–33.
28. M. Vandenbosch and M. Pearce, "Retail Sales Force Scheduling Based on Store Traffic Forecasting." *Journal of Retailing* (Spring 1998), Vol. 74, No. 1, pp. 61–88.
29. "Balancing People, Places and Times." (IT Tools Aid Health Care Scheduling) (Technology Information), *Health Management Technology* (June 1998), Vol. 19, No. 7, pp. 26–32.
30. H. Lancaster, "Managing Your Career: What Do You Hate About Work? (Hint: It May Not Be Your Job)." *Wall Street Journal*, November 4, 1997, p. B1.
31. B. Lamons, "'Just Do it' Managers Must Start Planning Ahead." (Advertising to Business), *Marketing News* (February 2, 1998), Vol. 32, No. 3, pp. 10–11.
32. C. Li and Y. Wu, "Minimal Cost Project Networks: The Cut Set Parallel Difference Method," *Omega* (July 1994), Vol. 22, No. 4, pp. 401–408.
33. B. Lamons, "'Just Do it' Managers Must Start Planning Ahead." (Advertising to Business), *Marketing News* (February 2, 1998), Vol. 32, No. 3, pp. 10–11.
34. "Cycle-Time Reduction: A Minute Saved is a Minute Earned." *Industrial Engineering* (March 1994), Vol. 26, No. 3, pp. 19–21.

35. R. Laliberte, "Simplify Your Life." *Success* (April 1998), Vol. 45, No. 4, pp. 56–62.
36. A. Feldman, "We'll Make You Scary." *Forbes* (February 14, 1994), Vol. 153, No. 4, p. 96.
37. R. Wartzman, "Billable Hours." *The Wall Street Journal*, March 14, 1995 p. 1.
38. B. Parks, "7 Time-Management Sanity Savers." *Instructor* (January/February 1998), Vol. 107, No. 5, pp. 46–47.
39. J. Laabs, "Executives on Hold." *Personnel Journal* (January 1994), Vol. 11, No. 1, pp. 18–20.
40. B. Parks, "7 Time-Management Sanity Savers." *Instructor* (January/February 1998), Vol. 107, No. 5, pp. 46–47.
41. R. Wartzman, "Billable Hours." *The Wall Street Journal*, March 14, 1995 p. 1.
42. R. Laliberte, "Simplify Your Life." *Success* (April 1998), Vol. 45, No. 4, pp. 56–62.
43. B. Lamons, "'Just Do it' Managers Must Start Planning Ahead." (Advertising to Business), *Marketing News* (February 2, 1998), Vol. 32, No. 3, pp. 10–11.
44. Ibid.
45. T. Norvell, "From Goal-setting to Goal-getting: With a Little Help From Your Coach." *Journal of Property Management* (January/February 1998), Vol. 63, No. 1, pp. 14–16.
46. B. Lamons, "'Just Do it' Managers Must Start Planning Ahead." (Advertising to Business), *Marketing News* (February 2, 1998), Vol. 32, No. 3, pp. 10–11.
47. S. Covey, "First Things First." *Success* (April 1994), Vol. 41, No. 3, pp. 8A–8D.
48. B. Parks, "7 Time-Management Sanity Savers." *Instructor* (January/February 1998), Vol. 107, No. 5, pp. 46–47.
49. Ibid.

Chapter 6

1. L. Gulick, "Notes on the Theory of Organization." *International Journal of Public Administration* (February–April 1998), Vol. 21, No. 2–4, pp. 445–90.
2. B. Gill, "Flextime Benefits Employees and Employers." *American Printer* (February 1998), Vol. 220, No. 5, pp. 70–71.
3. D.R. Dalton, C.M. Daily, A.E. Ellstrand, and J.L. Johnson, "Meta-analytic Reviews of Board Composition, Leadership Structure, and Financial Performance." *Strategic Management Journal* (March 1998), Vol. 19, No. 3, pp. 269–291.
4. G. van Merode, M. Oosten, O.J. Vrieze, et al., "Optimization of the Structure of the Clinical Laboratory." *European Journal of*

Operational Research (March 1, 1998), Vol. 105, No. 2, pp. 308–317.

5. J. Chang, "Cytec's Restructuring Success Setting Path for Other Players." *Chemical Market Reporter* (February 9, 1998), Vol. 253, No. 6, pp. 1–3.

6. D. McAbe and A. Wilkinson, "The Rise and Fall of TQM: The Vision, Meaning and Operation of Change." (Total Quality Management), *Industrial Relations Journal* (March 1998), Vol. 29, No. 1, pp. 18–30.

7. L. Gulick, "Notes on the Theory of Organization." *International Journal of Public Administration* (February–April 1998), Vol. 21, No. 2–4, pp. 445–90.

8. P. Lawrence and J. Lorsch, *Organization and Environment* (Burr Ridge, IL: Irwin, 1967).

9. J.R. Katzenbach, "The Irony of Senior Leadership Teams." *The Journal for Quality and Participation* (May/June 1998), Vol. 21, No. 3, pp. 8–16.

10. M.J. Cronin, "Ford's Intranet Success." *Fortune* (March 30, 1998), Vol. 137, No. 6, pp. 158–159.

11. L. Gulick, "Notes on the Theory of Organization." *International Journal of Public Administration* (February–April 1998), Vol. 21, No. 2–4, pp. 445–90.

12. D.J. Collis and C.A. Montgomery, "Creating Corporate Advantage." *Harvard Business Review* (May/June 1998), Vol. 76, No. 3, pp. 71–84.

13. L. Urwick, "Organization as a Technical Problem." *International Journal of Public Administration*, Vol. 21, No. 2–4, pp. 491–505.

14. J. Mooney, "The Principles of Organization." *International Journal of Public Administration*, Vol. 21, No. 2–4, pp. 535–545.

15. T. Petzinger, Jr., "The Front Lines—A Creative Staff Finds New Strength In Its Differences." *The Wall Street Journal*, April 11, 1998, p. B1.

16. J. Mooney, "The Principles of Organization." *International Journal of Public Administration*, Vol. 21, No. 2–4, pp. 535–545.

17. G. Gabriet, "Delegating Do's and Don'ts." *Working Women* (May 1998), Vol. 23, No. 5, pp. S15–16.

18. G. Hodgson, "Competence and Contract in the Theory of the Firm." *Journal of Economic Behavior & Organization* (April 1, 1998), Vol. 35, No. 2, pp. 179–182.

19. B. Gill, "Flextime Benefits Employees and Employers." *American Printer* (February 1998), Vol. 220, No. 5, pp. 70–71.

20. L. Gulick, "Notes on the Theory of Organization." *International Journal of Public Administration* (February–April 1998), Vol. 21, No. 2–4, pp. 445–90.

21. B. Gill, "Flextime Benefits Employees and Employers." *American Printer* (February 1998), Vol. 220, No. 5, pp. 70–71.

22. J. Mooney, "The Principles of Organization." *International Journal of Public Administration*, Vol. 21, No. 2–4, pp. 535–545.

23. L. Urwick, "Organization as a Technical Problem." *International Journal of Public Administration*, Vol. 21, No. 2–4, pp. 491–505.

24. J. Mooney, "The Principles of Organization." *International Journal of Public Administration*, Vol. 21, No. 2–4, pp. 535–545.

25. L.E. Greiner, "Evolution and Revolution as Organizations Grow." *Harvard Business Review* (May/June 1998), Vol. 76, No. 3, pp. 55–64.

26. O. Tukel and W. Rom, "Analysis of the Characteristics of Projects in Diverse Industries." *Journal of Operations Management* (March 1998), Vol. 16, No. 1, pp. 43–63.

27. M. Halasz, "NIH: Deconstruction of a Grand Synthesis?" *Administration & Society* (March 1997), Vol. 29, No. 1, pp. 97–113.

28. "Motorola Plans." *The Wall Street Journal*, March 31, 1998, p. 1.

29. O. Tukel and W. Rom, "Analysis of the Characteristics of Projects in Diverse Industries." *Journal of Operations Management* (March 1998), Vol. 16, No. 1, pp. 43–63.

30. C. Bartlett and S. Ghosal, "The Myth of the General Manager." *California Management Review* (Fall 1997), Vol. 40, No. 1, pp. 92–117.

31. M. West and M. Patterson, "Profitable Personnel." *People Management* (January 1998), Vol. 4, No. 1, pp. 28–32.

32. Ibid.

33. T. Barkin and M. Horn, "The Labor Lever Strategy." *Airline Business* (January 1998), Vol. 14, No. 1, pp. 46–50.

34. M.A. Verespej, "Lessons from the Best: Focus on People, Communicate, and Have Common Goals." *Industry Week* (February 16, 1998), Vol. 247, No. 4, pp. 28–34.

35. D. Edds, "Improving Performance With Self-directed Work Teams." *School Planning and Management* (March 1998), Vol. 37, No. 3, pp. 38–41.

36. M.A. Verespej, "Lessons from the Best: Focus on People, Communicate, and Have Common Goals." *Industry Week* (February 16, 1998), Vol. 247, No. 4, pp. 28–34.

37. D. Edds, "Improving Performance With Self-directed Work Teams." *School Planning and Management* (March 1998), Vol. 37, No. 3, pp. 38–41.

38. J.R. Rentsch and R.P. Steel, "Testing the Durability of Job Characteristics as Predictors of Absenteeism Over a Six–year Period." *Personnel Psychology* (Spring 1998), Vol. 51, No. 1, pp. 165–191.

39. R. Hackman and G. Oldham, *Work Redesign* (Reading, MA: Addison-Wesley, 1980).

40. C. Bartlett and S. Ghosal, "The Myth of the General Manager." *California Management Review* (Fall 1997), Vol. 40, No. 1, pp. 92–117.

41. T. Pollock, "Attitudes That Can Help You Get Ahead: A Personal File of Stimulating Ideas, Little-known Facts and Daily Problem Solvers." *Supervision* (February 1998), Vol. 59, No. 2, pp. 24–27.

42. T. Norvell, "From Goal-setting to Goal-getting: With a Little Help From Your Coach." *Journal of Property Management* (January/February 1998), Vol. 63, No. 1, pp. 14–16.

43. B. Parks, "7 Time-Management Sanity Savers." *Instructor* (January/February 1998), Vol. 107, No. 5, pp. 46–47.

44. L. Urwick, "Organization as a Technical Problem." *International Journal of Public Administration*, Vol. 21, No. 2–4, pp. 491–505.

45. This section and Skill-Building Exercise 6–1 are adapted from Harbridge House Training Materials (Boston).

46. J. Zoltak, "Making Sure Customers Get Satisfaction Discussed at Stadium Managers Seminar." *Amusement Business* (February 16, 1998), Vol. 110, No. 7, pp. 4–5.

47. B. Lamons, "'Just Do it' Managers Must Start Planning Ahead." (Advertising to Business), *Marketing News* (February 2, 1998), Vol. 32, No. 3, pp. 10–11.

48. "One of These Days." *The Wall Street Journal*, March 10, 1998, p. 1,

49. J. Zoltak, "Making Sure Customers Get Satisfaction Discussed at Stadium Managers Seminar." *Amusement Business* (February 16, 1998), Vol. 110, No. 7, pp. 4–5.

50. G. Adler, "When Your Star Performer Can't Manage." *Harvard Business Review* (July/August 1997), Vol. 75, No. 4, pp. 22–27.

51. R. Laliberte, "Simplify Your Life." *Success* (April 1998), Vol. 45, No. 4, pp. 56–62.

52. "Former ASAE Leaders Share Tips." (Time Management: American Society of Association Executives) (Leader to Leader) (Column), *Association Management* (January 1998), Vol. 50, No. 1, pp. 23–24.

53. L.E. Greiner, "Evolution and Revolution as Organizations Grow." *Harvard Business Review* (May/June 1998), Vol. 76, No. 3, pp. 55–64.

54. B. Bernard, "Delegating Duties the Right Way." *Nation's Business* (April 1998), Vol. 86, No. 4, pp. 10–11.

55. J. Mooney, "The Principles of Organization." *International Journal of*

Public Administration, Vol. 21, No. 2–4, pp. 535–545.

56. G. Adler, "When Your Star Performer Can't Manage." *Harvard Business Review* (July/August 1997), Vol. 75, No. 4, pp. 22–27.

57. T. Pollock, "Attitudes That Can Help You Get Ahead: A Personal File of Stimulating Ideas, Little-known Facts and Daily Problem Solvers." *Supervision* (February 1998), Vol. 59, No. 2, pp. 24–27.

58. G. Gabriet, "Delegating Do's and Don'ts." *Working Women* (May 1998), Vol. 23, No. 5, pp. S15–16.

59. T. Pollock, "Attitudes That Can Help You Get Ahead: A Personal File of Stimulating Ideas, Little-known Facts and Daily Problem Solvers." *Supervision* (February 1998), Vol. 59, No. 2, pp. 24–27.

60. T. Pollock, "Attitudes That Can Help You Get Ahead: A Personal File of Stimulating Ideas, Little-known Facts and Daily Problem Solvers." *Supervision* (February 1998), Vol. 59, No. 2, pp. 24–27.

61. G. Adler, "When Your Star Performer Can't Manage." *Harvard Business Review* (July/August 1997), Vol. 75, No. 4, pp. 22–27.

Chapter 7

1. Information for the opening case comes from *IBM Annual Report* 1997 and *The Wall Street Journal*, June 7, 1995, pp. B1 and B6, and June 12, 1995, pp. A3 and A4. Because the IBM acquisition of Lotus took place as the text chapter was being written, possible issues and options for the companies rather than actual events are presented throughout the chapter, as given in most chapters.

2. R. Hall, "Myth #4: Executive Order = Front-line Action." *Bank Marketing* (March 1998), Vol. 30, No. 3, pp. 48–49.

3. M. Orgland and G. Von Krogh, "Initiating, Managing and Sustaining Corporate Transformation: A Case Study." *European Management Journal* (February 1998), Vol. 16, No. 1, pp. 31–39.

4. M.L. Millenson, "3 Forces for Change: Money, Technology, and the Spirit of the Times Will Force Your Hand on Computer Systems That Measure Quality." *Hospitals and Health Networks* (February 20, 1998), Vol. 72, No. 4, pp. 44–26.

5. B. Bowonder, "Competitive and Technology Management Strategy: A Case Study of TELCO." *International Journal of Technology Management* (June/July 1998), Vol. 15, No. 6–7, pp. 646–681.

6. S. Greengard, "How Technology Will Change the Workplace." *Workforce* (January 1998), Vol. 77, No. 1, pp. 78–83.

7. "Get a Lawyer." *The Wall Street Journal*, June 30, 1998, p. A1.

8. L. Eisaguirre, "Welcome to the '90s, Boss." *Colorado Business Magazine* (March 1998), Vol. 25, No. 3, pp. 20–23.

9. "Get a Lawyer." *The Wall Street Journal*, June 30, 1998, p. A1.

10. R. Hall, "Myth #4: Executive Order = Front-line Action." *Bank Marketing* (March 1998), Vol. 30, No. 3, pp. 48–49.

11. Larry Reynolds, "Understand Employees' Resistance to Change." *HR Focus* (June 1994), Vol. 71, No. 6, p. 17.

12. John Mariotti, "The Challenge of Change." *Industry Week* (April 6, 1998), Vol. 247, No. 7, pp. 140–141.

13. Larry Reynolds, "Understand Employees' Resistance to Change." *HR Focus* (June 1994), Vol. 71, No. 6, p. 17.

14. John Mariotti, "The Challenge of Change." *Industry Week* (April 6, 1998), Vol. 247, No. 7, pp. 140–141.

15. L. Eisaguirre, "Welcome to the '90s, Boss." *Colorado Business Magazine* (March 1998), Vol. 25, No. 3, pp. 20–23.

16. M. Orgland and G. Von Krogh, "Initiating, Managing and Sustaining Corporate Transformation: A Case Study." *European Management Journal* (February 1998), Vol. 16, No. 1, pp. 31–39.

17. R. Ganzel, "Putting out the Welcome Mat." *Training* (March 1998), Vol. 35, No. 3, pp. 54–61.

18. K. Hultman, *The Path of Least Resistance* (Austin, Tex.: Learning Concepts, 1979).

19. R. Ganzel, "Putting out the Welcome Mat." *Training* (March 1998), Vol. 35, No. 3, pp. 54–61.

20. H. Lancaster, "Managing Your Career: To Avoid a Job Failure, Learn the Culture of a Company First." *The Wall Street Journal*, July 14, 1998, p. B1.

21. J.A. Parnell, "Improving the Fit Between Organizations and Employees." *SAM Advanced Management Journal* (Winter 1998), Vol. 63, No. 1, pp. 35–43.

22. E. Schein, *Organizational Culture and Leadership* (San Francisco: Josey-Bass, 1985).

23. T.N. Gilmore, G.P. Sheer, and M. Useem, "Side Effects of Corporate Cultural Transformations." *Journal of Applied Behavioral Science* (June 1997), Vol. 33, No. 2, pp. 174–190.

24. L.E. Greiner, "Evolution and Revolution as Organizations Grow." *Harvard Business Review* (May/June 1998), Vol. 76, No. 3, pp. 55–64.

25. M.A. Berry and D.A. Rondinelli, "Proactive Corporate Environment Management: A New Industrial Revolution." *The Academy of Management Executive* (May 1998), Vol. 12, No. 2, pp. 38–51.

26. "On Trends in Industry and Finance—Cultural Clashes After Combinations Spur a New Brand of Due Diligence." *The Wall Street Journal*, March 5, 1998, p. A1.

27. S. Greengard, "How Technology Will Change the Workplace." *Workforce* (January 1998), Vol. 77, No. 1, pp. 78–83.

28. C. Weyrich, "The Meaning of Innovation." *Electronic News (1991)* (February 16, 1998), Vol. 44, No. 2206, pp. 8–10.

29. A.L. Frohman, "Building a Culture for Innovation." *Research-Technology Management* (March/April 1998), Vol. 41, No. 2, pp. 9–13.

30. R. Ganzel, "Putting out the Welcome Mat." *Training* (March 1998), Vol. 35, No. 3, pp. 54–61.

31. C. Weyrich, "The Meaning of Innovation." *Electronic News (1991)* (February 16, 1998), Vol. 44, No. 2206, pp. 8–10.

32. A.L. Frohman, "Building a Culture for Innovation." *Research-Technology Management* (March/April 1998), Vol. 41, No. 2, pp. 9–13.

33. Ibid.

34. S.F. Ferris, R. Quint, and R. Sant, "Financial Theory and Practice in the Application of TQM: The Case of IBM Rochester." *Journal of Managerial Issues* (Spring 1998), Vol. 10, No. 1, pp. 13–30.

35. M.S. Spencer and L.K. Duclos, "TQM Stresses MIS: The Ache of Continuous Change." *Mid-American Journal of Business* (Spring 1998), Vol. 13, No. 1, pp. 59–65.

36. D. McAbe and A. Wilkinson, "The Rise and Fall of TQM: The Vision, Meaning and Operation of Change." (Total Quality Management), *Industrial Relations Journal* (March 1998), Vol. 29, No. 1, pp. 18–30.

37. D. Elmuti and T. AlDiab, "Improving Quality and Organizational Effectiveness Go Hand in Hand Through Deming's Management System." *Journal of Business Strategies* (Spring 1995), Vol. 12, No. 1, pp. 86–98.

38. A. Klein, R. Masi, and K. Weidner, "Organization Culture, Distribution and Amount of Control and Perceptions of Quality: An Empirical Study of Linkages." *Group & Organization Management* (June 1995), Vol. 20, No. 2, pp. 122–149.

39. B. Schneider, S.S. White, and M.C. Paul, "Linking Service Climate and Customer Perceptions of Service Quality: Test of a Causal Model." *Journal of Applied Psychology* (April 1998), Vol. 83, No. 2, pp. 150–164.

40. W. Hines, "The Stop and Start of Total Quality Management." *Quality Progress* (February 1998), Vol. 31, No. 2, pp. 61–65.

41. H. Rogers, "A Look at the Rosemount Plant." *Quality Progress* (April 1998), Vol. 31, No. 4, pp. 60–65.

42. D. McAbe and A. Wilkinson, "The Rise and Fall of TQM: The Vision, Meaning and Operation of Change." (Total Quality Management), *Industrial Relations Journal* (March 1998), Vol. 29, No. 1, pp. 18–30.

43. S. Trussler, "The Rules of the Game." *Journal of Business Strategy* (January/February 1998), Vol. 19, No. 1, pp. 16–20.

44. C.A. Bartlett and S. Ghosal, "Beyond Strategic Planning to Organization Learning: Lifeblood of the Individualized Corporation." *Strategy & Leadership* (January/February 1998), Vol. 26, No. 1, pp. 34–40.

45. Y. Altman and P. Iles, "Learning, Leadership, Teams: Corporate Learning and Organizational Change." *Journal of Management Development* (January 1998), Vol. 17, No. 1, pp. 44–56.

46. D.J. Collis and C.A. Montgomery, "Creating Corporate Advantage." *Harvard Business Review* (May/June 1998), Vol. 76, No. 3, pp. 71–84.

47. K. Starkey, "What Can We Learn from the Learning Organization?" *Human Relations* (April 1998), Vol. 51, No. 4, pp. 531–547.

48. C.A. Bartlett and S. Ghosal, "Beyond Strategic Planning to Organization Learning: Lifeblood of the Individualized Corporation." *Strategy & Leadership* (January/February 1998), Vol. 26, No. 1, pp. 34–40.

49. D. Nye, "Affirmative Action and the Stigma of Incompetence." *The Academy of Management Executive* (February 1998), Vol. 12, No. 1, pp. 88–90.

50. M. Frost, "Old-fashioned Career Fairs Gain Favor Online." *HRMagazine* (April 1998), Vol. 43, No. 5, pp. 31–45.

51. T. Petzinger, Jr., "The Front Lines—A Creative Staff Finds New Strength In Its Differences." *The Wall Street Journal*, April 11, 1998, p. B1.

52. S.M. Nkomo, "Diversity in Organizations: New Perspectives for a Changing Workplace." *Administrative Science Quarterly* (March 1998), Vol. 43, No. 1, pp. 189–192.

53. D. Nigro, "Diversity Initiatives." *Meetings and Conventions* (May 1998), Vol. 33, No. 6, pp. 73–77.

54. R.T. Barker, G.H. Gilbreath, and W.S. Stone, "The Interdisciplinary Needs of Organizations: Are New Employees Adequately Equipped?" *Journal of Management Development* (February/March 1998), Vol. 17, No. 2–3, pp. 214–233.

55. "Competitive Advantage Through Managing Diversity," *Franchising World* (January/February 1994), Vol. 26, No. 1, p. 35.

56. R. Pomerleau, "A Desideratum for Managing the Diverse Workplace," *Review of Public Personnel Administration* (Winter 1994), Vol. 14, No. 1, pp. 85–100.

57. J. Rodgers, "Implementing a Diversity Strategy." *LIMRA's Market Facts* (May/June 1993), Vol. 12, No. 3, pp. 26–29.

58. "Sex Still Shapes Sharing of Chores." *The Wall Street Journal*, December 11, 1991, p. B1.

59. "Three Decades After the Equal Pay Act, Women's Wages Remain Far From Parity." *The Wall Street Journal*, June 9, 1993, p. B1.

60. N. Adler, "Women Managers in a Global Economy." *Training & Development* (April 1994), Vol. 48, No. 4, pp. 22–25.

61. "Women Hold." *The Wall Street Journal*, July 10, 1990, p. B1.

62. M. Loder and J. Rosner, *Workforce America!* (Burr Ridge, IL: Business One–Irwin, 1991).

63. K. Tyler, "Mentoring Programs Link Employees and Experienced Execs." *HRMagazine* (April 1998), Vol. 43, No. 5, pp. 98–104.

64. J.A. Parnell, "Improving the Fit Between Organizations and Employees." *SAM Advanced Management Journal* (Winter 1998), Vol. 63, No. 1, pp. 35–43.

65. K. Tyler, "Mentoring Programs Link Employees and Experienced Execs." *HRMagazine* (April 1998), Vol. 43, No. 5, pp. 98–104.

66. M. Orgland and G. Von Krogh, "Initiating, Managing and Sustaining Corporate Transformation: A Case Study." *European Management Journal* (February 1998), Vol. 16, No. 1, pp. 31–39.

67. R. Hall, "Myth #4: Executive Order = Front-line Action." *Bank Marketing* (March 1998), Vol. 30, No. 3, pp. 48–49.

68. "A Larger Percentage . . ." *The Wall Street Journal*, May 26, 1998, p. A1.

69. B. Goldberg and J. Sifonis, "Keep On Keepin' On." *Journal of Business Strategy* (July/August 1994), Vol. 15, No. 4, pp. 23–25.

70. F. Kemske, "HR 2008: A Forecast Based on our Exclusive Study." *Workforce* (January 1998), Vol. 77, No. 1, pp. 46–58.

71. B. Fishel, "A New Perspective: How to Get the Real Story From Attitude Surveys." *Training* (February 1998), Vol. 35, No. 2, pp. 90–95.

72. R. Blake and J. Mouton, *The Managerial Grid III: Key to Leadership Excellence* (Houston: Gulf Publishing, 1985).

73. "Charmed Forces—Army's 'Baby Generals' Take a Crash Course in Sensitivity Training." *The Wall Street Journal*, January 19, 1998, p. A1.

74. T. Norvell, "From Goal-setting to Goal-getting: With a Little Help From Your Coach." *Journal of Property Management* (January/February 1998), Vol. 63, No. 1, pp. 14–16.

75. B. Fishel, "A New Perspective: How to Get the Real Story From Attitude Surveys." *Training* (February 1998), Vol. 35, No. 2, pp. 90–95.

Chapter 8

1. J. Meade, "Identifying Criteria for Success Helps in Making Effective Hiring Decisions." *HRMagazine* (April 1998), Vol. 43, No. 5, pp. 49–51.

2. "Equal Opportunity Pays." *The Wall Street Journal*, May 4, 1993, p. 1.

3. C.A. Bartlett and S. Ghosal, "Beyond Strategic Planning to Organization Learning: Lifeblood of the Individualized Corporation." *Strategy & Leadership* (January/February 1998), Vol. 26, No. 1, pp. 34–40.

4. F. Kemske, "HR 2008: A Forecast Based on our Exclusive Study." *Workforce* (January 1998), Vol. 77, No. 1, pp. 46–58.

5. J. Meade, "Identifying Criteria for Success Helps in Making Effective Hiring Decisions." *HRMagazine* (April 1998), Vol. 43, No. 5, pp. 49–51.

6. M. West and M. Patterson, "Profitable Personnel." *People Management* (January 1998), Vol. 4, No. 1, pp. 28–32.

7. J.H. Harris and L.A. Arendt, "Stress Reduction and the Small Business: Increasing Employee and Customer Satisfaction." *SAM Advanced Management Journal* (Winter 1998), Vol. 63, No. 1, pp. 27–35.

8. R.D. Bretz, Jr. and T.A. Judge, "Realistic Job Previews: A Test of the Adverse Self-selection Hypothesis." *Journal of Applied Psychology* (April 1998), Vol. 83, No. 2, pp. 330–338.

9. J.A. Parnell, "Improving the Fit Between Organizations and Employees." *SAM Advanced Management Journal* (Winter 1998), Vol. 63, No. 1, pp. 35–43.

10. O. Behling, "Employee Selection: Will Intelligence and Conscientiousness do the Job?" *The Academy of Management Executive* (February 1998), Vol. 12, No. 1, pp. 77–87.

11. D. Nye, "Affirmative Action and the Stigma of Incompetence." *The Academy of Management Executive* (February 1998), Vol. 12, No. 1, pp. 88–90.

12. K. Luthans, "Using HRM to Compete in the 21st Century." *Management Quarterly* (Winter 1998), Vol. 38, No. 4, pp. 17–23.

13. R.E. Thaler-Carter, "In-house Recruiters Fill a Specialized Niche." *HR Magazine* (April 1998), Vol. 43, No. 5, pp. 72–78.

14. G.N. Powell, "Reinforcing and Extending Today's Organizations: The Simultaneous Pursuit of Person–Organization Fit and Diversity." *Organizational Dynamics* (Winter 1998), Vol. 26, No. 3, pp. 50–62.

15. L. Thornburg, "Computer-assisted Interviewing Shortens Hiring Cycle."

HRMagazine (February 1998), Vol. 43, No. 2, pp. 73–79.

16. M. Frost, "Old-fashioned Career Fairs Gain Favor Online." *HRMagazine* (April 1998), Vol. 43, No. 5, pp. 31–45.

17. G.N. Powell, "Reinforcing and Extending Today's Organizations: The Simultaneous Pursuit of Person–Organization Fit and Diversity." *Organizational Dynamics* (Winter 1998), Vol. 26, No. 3, pp. 50–62.

18. J.R. Waddell, "Looking for Mr./Ms. Right." *Supervision* (February 1998), Vol. 59, No. 2, pp. 16–19.

19. L. Thornburg, "Computer-assisted Interviewing Shortens Hiring Cycle." *HRMagazine* (February 1998), Vol. 43, No. 2, pp. 73–79.

20. "Interview With Bruce Rohde, CEO of ConAgra, Inc. HR as Major Source of Competitive Advantage." *Human Resources Management* (Spring 1998), Vol. 37, No. 1, pp. 85–89.

21. J.R. Waddell, "Looking for Mr./Ms. Right." *Supervision* (February 1998), Vol. 59, No. 2, pp. 16–19.

22. J. Meade, "Identifying Criteria for Success Helps in Making Effective Hiring Decisions." *HRMagazine* (April 1998), Vol. 43, No. 5, pp. 49–51.

23. Adapted from R. Lussier, "Selecting Qualified Candidates Through Effective Job Interviewing," *Clinical Laboratory Management Review* (July/August 1995), Vol. 9, No. 4, pp. 257–275.

24. "Less Instinct More Analysis." *Industry Week*, July 17, 1995, pp. 11–12.

25. C.A. Bartlett and S. Ghosal, "Beyond Strategic Planning to Organization Learning: Lifeblood of the Individualized Corporation." *Strategy & Leadership* (January/February 1998), Vol. 26, No. 1, pp. 34–40.

26. R. Ganzel, "Putting out the Welcome Mat." *Training* (March 1998), Vol. 35, No. 3, pp. 54–61.

27. J.H. Harris and L.A. Arendt, "Stress Reduction and the Small Business: Increasing Employee and Customer Satisfaction." *SAM Advanced Management Journal* (Winter 1998), Vol. 63, No. 1, pp. 27–35.

28. M. West and M. Patterson, "Profitable Personnel." *People Management* (January 1998), Vol. 4, No. 1, pp. 28–32.

29. F. Kemske, "HR 2008: A Forecast Based on our Exclusive Study." *Workforce* (January 1998), Vol. 77, No. 1, pp. 46–58.

30. K. Luthans, "Using HRM to Compete in the 21st Century." *Management Quarterly* (Winter 1998), Vol. 38, No. 4, pp. 17–23.

31. N. Chase, "Managers Make Training Stick." *Quality* (April 1998), Vol. 37, No. 4, pp. 188–189.

32. "Intellectual Capital." *The Wall Street Journal*, December 11, 1997, pp. A1.

33. A. Mumford, "Choosing Development Methods." *Organizations & People* (May 1998), Vol. 5, No. 2, pp. 32–39.

34. "Interview With Bruce Rohde, CEO of ConAgra, Inc. HR as Major Source of Competitive Advantage." *Human Resources Management* (Spring 1998), Vol. 37, No. 1, pp. 85–89.

35. K. Luthans, "Using HRM to Compete in the 21st Century." *Management Quarterly* (Winter 1998), Vol. 38, No. 4, pp. 17–23.

36. F. Kniggendorf, "Helping Supervisors Define Standards of Performance." *Human Resource Focus* (February 1998), Vol. 75, No. 2, pp. 13–14.

37. "Multi-rater Feedback and Performance Evaluation Programs Do Not Mix." *Supervision*, March 1998, Vol. 59, No. 3, pp. 25–26.

38. C.A. Bartlett and S. Ghosal, "Beyond Strategic Planning to Organization Learning: Lifeblood of the Individualized Corporation." *Strategy & Leadership* (January/February 1998), Vol. 26, No. 1, pp. 34–40.

39. P.M. Buhler, "Meeting the Challenge of Retaining Employees." *Supervision* (April 1998), Vol. 59, No. 4, pp. 24–26.

40. S. Shellenbarger, "Work and Family." *The Wall Street Journal*, November 19, 1997, p. B1.

41. "Work Week: A Special News Report About Life On the Job—and Trends Taking Shape There." *The Wall Street Journal*, June 2, 1998, p. A1.

42. "A Larger Percentage . . ." *The Wall Street Journal*, May 26, 1998, p. A1.

43. "Work Week: A Special News Report About Life On the Job—and Trends Taking Shape There." *The Wall Street Journal*, June 2, 1998, p. A1.

44. F. Hansen, "Currents in Compensation and Benefits." *Compensation and Benefits Review* (May/June 1998), Vol. 30, No. 3, pp. 6–16.

45. "A Larger Percentage . . ." *The Wall Street Journal*, May 26, 1998, p. A1.

46. "Whose Rolodex Is it?" *The Wall Street Journal*, January 6, 1998, p. A1.

47. J. Case, "HR Learns How to Open the Books." *HR Magazine*, May 1998, Vol. 43, No. 6, pp. 71–79.

48. F. Hansen, "Currents in Compensation and Benefits." *Compensation and Benefits Review* (May/June 1998), Vol. 30, No. 3, pp. 6–16.

49. U.S. Chamber of Commerce, *Employee Benefits 1991* (Washington, D.C.: U.S. Government Printing Office, 1992).

50. S. Kapp, "Why Job Safety Analyses Work." *Safety & Health* (April 1998), Vol. 157, No. 4, pp. 54–58.

51. "Highway-Building Surge Could Mean More Deaths in Mining and Road Materials." *The Wall Street Journal*, June 2, 1998, p. A1.

52. C. Hymowitz, "Managing Your Career: Managers Struggle To Find a Way to Let Someone Go." *The Wall Street Journal*, July 28, 1998, p. B1.

Chapter 9

1. P.M. Buhler, "Managers: Out With the Old and in With the New—Skills That Is." *Supervision* (June 1998), Vol. 59, No. 6, pp. 22–25.

2. J. Gunther, "Staying Ahead of the Curve." *Risk Management* (April 1998), Vol. 45, No. 4, pp. 80–84.

3. S.H. Chiang and M. Gort, "Personality Attributes and Optimal Hierarchical Compensation Gradients." *Journal of Economic Behavior & Organization* (January 1998), Vol. 33, No. 2, pp. 227–241.

4. D.F. Caldwell and J.M. Burger, "Personality Characteristics of Job Applicants and Success in Screening Interviews." *Personnel Psychology* (Spring 1998), Vol. 51, No. 1, pp. 119–137.

5. A. Marie–Ryan, R.E. Ployhart, and L.A. Friedel, "Using Personality Testing to Reduce Adverse Impact: A Cautionary Note." *Journal of Applied Psychology* (April 1998), Vol. 83, No. 2, pp. 298–308.

6. J.M. Nash, "The Personality Genes." *Time* (April 27, 1998), Vol. 151, No. 16, pp. 60–62.

7. I. Briggs and P. Meyer, *Introduction to Type*, 5th ed. (Palo Alto, CA: Consulting Psychologists Press, 1993).

8. D.F. Caldwell and J.M. Burger, "Personality Characteristics of Job Applicants and Success in Screening Interviews." *Personnel Psychology* (Spring 1998), Vol. 51, No. 1, pp. 119–137.

9. D.M. Mansour-Cole and S.G. Scott, "Hearing it Through the Grapevine: The Influence of Source, Leader-relations, and Legitimacy on Survivors' Fairness Perceptions." *Personnel Psychology* (Spring 1998), Vol. 51, No. 1, pp. 25–55.

10. J. Curtis, "The Perception Question." *Marketing*, February 12, 1998, pp. 24–26.

11. P.R. Berthon, L.F. Pitt, and M.H. Morris, "The Impact of Individual and Organizational Factors on Problem Perception Theory and Empirical Evidence from the Marketing-Technical Dyad." *Journal of Business Research* (May 1998), Vol. 42, No. 1, pp. 25–39.

12. S.H. Chiang and M. Gort, "Personality Attributes and Optimal Hierarchical

Compensation Gradients." *Journal of Economic Behavior & Organization* (January 1998), Vol. 33, No. 2, pp. 227–241.

13. D.G. Gardner and J.L. Pierce, "Self-esteem and Self-efficacy Within the Organizational Context: An Empirical Examination." *Group and Organization Management* (March 1998), Vol. 23, No. 1, pp. 48–71.

14. F. Vinci, "Having a Positive Attitude—A Job Seeker's Most Important Asset." *LI Business News* (January 12, 1998), No. 2, pp. 38–39.

15. D.G. Gardner and J.L. Pierce, "Self-esteem and Self-efficacy Within the Organizational Context: An Empirical Examination." *Group and Organization Management* (March 1998), Vol. 23, No. 1, pp. 48–71.

16. S.K. DelVecchio, "The Salesperson's Operating Freedom: A Matter of Perception." *Industrial Marketing Management* (January 1998), Vol. 27, No. 1, pp. 31–41.

17. D.G. Gardner and J.L. Pierce, "Self-esteem and Self-efficacy Within the Organizational Context: An Empirical Examination." *Group and Organization Management* (March 1998), Vol. 23, No. 1, pp. 48–71.

18. M.A. Tietjen and R.M. Myers, "Motivation and Job Satisfaction." *Management Decision* (May/June 1998), Vol. 36, No. 3–4, pp. 226–232.

19. F. Vinci, "Having a Positive Attitude—A Job Seeker's Most Important Asset." *LI Business News* (January 12, 1998), No. 2, pp. 38–39.

20. J. Kim, J.S. Lim, and M. Bhargava, "The Role of Affect in Attitude Formation: A Classical Conditioning Approach." *Journal of the Academy of Marketing Science* (Spring 1998), Vol. 26, No. 2, pp. 143–153.

21. J.S. Livingston, "Pygmalion in Management." *Harvard Business Review on Human Relations* (New York: Harper & Row, 1979), p. 81.

22. T. Pollock, "Attitudes That Can Help You Get Ahead: A Personal File of Stimulating Ideas, Little-known Facts and Daily Problem Solvers." *Supervision* (February 1998), Vol. 59, No. 2, pp. 24–27.

23. M.A. Tietjen and R.M. Myers, "Motivation and Job Satisfaction." *Management Decision* (May/June 1998), Vol. 36, No. 3–4, pp. 226–232.

24. D.G. Gardner and J.L. Pierce, "Self-esteem and Self-efficacy Within the Organizational Context: An Empirical Examination." *Group and Organization Management* (March 1998), Vol. 23, No. 1, pp. 48–71.

25. N. Christiansen, P. Villanova, and S. Maculae, "Political Influence Compatibility: Fitting the Person to the Climate." *Journal of Organizational Behavior* (November 1997), Vol. 18, No. 6, pp. 709–31.

26. "An Optimistic Attitude About Life May Spur People to Love Their Jobs." *The Wall Street Journal*, p. C3.

27. D.G. Gardner and J.L. Pierce, "Self-esteem and Self-efficacy Within the Organizational Context: An Empirical Examination." *Group and Organization Management* (March 1998), Vol. 23, No. 1, pp. 48–71.

28. "C. Orts, "Relationships Between Satisfaction, Attitudes, and Performance: An Organizational Analysis." *Journal of Applied Psychology*, December, 1992, pp. 963–974.

29. K.S. Markel and M.R. Frone, "Job Characteristics, Work–School Conflict, and School Outcomes Among Adolescents: Testing a Structural Model." *Journal of Applied Psychology* (April 1998), Vol. 83, No. 2, pp. 277–288.

30. L. Eisaguirre, "Welcome to the '90s, Boss." *Colorado Business Magazine* (March 1998), Vol. 25, No. 3, pp. 20–23.

31. P.M. Buhler, "Managers: Out With the Old and in With the New—Skills That Is." *Supervision* (June 1998), Vol. 59, No. 6, pp. 22–25.

32. W.L. Gardner and B.J. Avolio, "The Charismatic Relationship: A Dramaturical Perspective." *Academy of Management Review* (January 1998), Vol. 23, No. 1, pp. 32–59.

33. E. Thomas Belu, "Acting From the Center: Your Response to Today's Leadership Challenges Must be Grounded in Personal Values." *Management Review* (March 1998), Vol. 87, No. 3, pp. 51–56.

34. D.M. Mansour-Cole and S.G. Scott, "Hearing it Through the Grapevine: The Influence of Source, Leader-relations, and Legitimacy on Survivors' Fairness Perceptions." *Personnel Psychology* (Spring 1998), Vol. 51, No. 1, pp. 25–55.

35. P.M. Buhler, "Managers: Out With the Old and in With the New—Skills That Is." *Supervision* (June 1998), Vol. 59, No. 6, pp. 22–25.

36. S.K. Goodman, "Business Politics for the Records Manager and Archivist." *Records Management Quarterly* (January 1998), Vol. 32, No. 1, pp. 19–33.

37. P. Wilson, "The Effects of Politics and Federal Executives." *Journal of Management* (Spring 1995), Vol. 21, pp. 101–118.

38. G.L. Lilien and A. Rangaswamy, "Powerful Marketing Starts With Model: Today's Software Lets Even Non-techies drum up sophisticated plans." *Business Marketing* (May 1998), Vol. 83, No. 5, pp. 6–7.

39. M. Clarke, "Can Specialists be General Managers? Developing Paradoxical Thinking in Middle Managers." *Journal of Management*

Development (February/March 1998), Vol. 17, No. 2–3, pp. 191–207.

40. R. Berner, "Saks's New Boss Is An Acquisitive Politician." *The Wall Street Journal*, July 7, 1998, p. B1.

41. "Executives Point the Finger at Major Time Wasters," *Personnel Journal* (August 1994), Vol. 73, p. 16.

42. S. Robbins and D. De Cenzo, *Fundamentals of Management* (Englewood Cliffs, NJ: Prentice Hall, 1995), pp. 10–11.

43. S.K. Goodman, "Business Politics for the Records Manager and Archivist." *Records Management Quarterly* (January 1998), Vol. 32, No. 1, pp. 19–33.

44. Ibid.

45. H. Lancaster, "How to Make Sure You Get Noticed But Not Seem Pushy." *Wall Street Journal*, February 24, 1998, p. B1.

46. M. Clarke, "Can Specialists be General Managers? Developing Paradoxical Thinking in Middle Managers." *Journal of Management Development* (February/March 1998), Vol. 17, No. 2–3, pp. 191–207.

47. P.M. Buhler, "Managers: Out With the Old and in With the New—Skills That Is." *Supervision* (June 1998), Vol. 59, No. 6, pp. 22–25.

48. D.M. Mansour-Cole and S.G. Scott, "Hearing it Through the Grapevine: The Influence of Source, Leader-relations, and Legitimacy on Survivors' Fairness Perceptions." *Personnel Psychology* (Spring 1998), Vol. 51, No. 1, pp. 25–55.

49. N. Christiansen, P. Villanova, and S. Maculae, "Political Influence Compatibility: Fitting the Person to the Climate." *Journal of Organizational Behavior* (November 1997), Vol. 18, No. 6, pp. 709–31.

50. Ibid.

51. B. Parks, "Got a Conflict with a Colleague? Here's How to Resolve it Now!" *Instructor* (April 1998), Vol. 107, No. 7, pp. 74–75.

52. T. Norvell, "From Goal-setting to Goalgetting: With a Little Help From Your Coach." *Journal of Property Management* (January/February 1998), Vol. 63, No. 1, pp. 14–16.

53. M. Barrier, "Putting A Lid On Conflicts." *Nation's Business* (April 1998), Vol. 86, No. 4, pp. 34–36.

54. Ibid.

55. C. Hymowitz, "Managing Your Career: Managers Struggle To Find a Way to Let Someone Go." *The Wall Street Journal*, July 28, 1998, p. B1.

56. B. Parks, "Got a Conflict with a Colleague? Here's How to Resolve it Now!" *Instructor* (April 1998), Vol. 107, No. 7, pp. 74–75.

57. B. Parks, "Got a Conflict with a Colleague? Here's How to Resolve it Now!" *Instructor* (April 1998), Vol. 107, No. 7, pp. 74–75.
58. K.O. Wilburn, "Employment Disputes: Solving Them Out of Court." *Management Review* (March 1998), Vol. 87, No. 3, p. 17–22.
59. B. Parks, "Got a Conflict with a Colleague? Here's How to Resolve it Now!" *Instructor* (April 1998), Vol. 107, No. 7, pp. 74–75.
60. P. Lowe, "9 Secrets of Superstar Salespeople." *Success Yearbook* (Tampa, FL: Peter Lowe International, 1998), pp. 38–39.
61. Ibid.
62. T. Hanks, "Four Sales Objections: And How to Handle Them." *Success Yearbook* (Tampa, FL: Peter Lowe International), pp. 58–59.
63. S. Lorge, "The Best Way to Negotiate." *Sales and Marketing Management* (March 1998), Vol. 150, No. 3, pp. 92–93.
64. Ibid.
65. P. Lowe, "9 Secrets of Superstar Salespeople." *Success Yearbook* (Tampa, FL: Peter Lowe International, 1998), pp. 38–39.
66. T. Hanks, "Four Sales Objections: And How to Handle Them." *Success Yearbook* (Tampa, FL: Peter Lowe International), pp. 58–59.
67. Ibid.
68. P. Lowe, "9 Secrets of Superstar Salespeople." *Success Yearbook* (Tampa, FL: Peter Lowe International, 1998), pp. 38–39.
69. K.O. Wilburn, "Employment Disputes: Solving Them Out of Court." *Management Review* (March 1998), Vol. 87, No. 3, p. 17–22.
70. Ibid.
71. B. Parks, "Got a Conflict with a Colleague? Here's How to Resolve it Now!" *Instructor* (April 1998), Vol. 107, No. 7, pp. 74–75.
72. Ibid.
73. M. Barrier, "Putting A Lid On Conflicts." *Nation's Business* (April 1998), Vol. 86, No. 4, pp. 34–36.
74. K.O. Wilburn, "Employment Disputes: Solving Them Out of Court." *Management Review* (March 1998), Vol. 87, No. 3, p. 17–22.
75. L.R. Ember, "Surviving Stress." *Chemical & Engineering News* (May 25, 1998), Vol. 76, No. 21, pp. 12–25.
76. Ibid.
77. J.H. Harris and L.A. Arendt, "Stress Reduction and the Small Business: Increasing Employee and Customer Satisfaction." *SAM Advanced Management Journal* (Winter 1998), Vol. 63, No. 1, pp. 27–35.
78. Ibid.
79. Ibid.
80. "Lousier Bosses." *The Wall Street Journal,* April 4, 1995, p. 1.

81. J.H. Harris and L.A. Arendt, "Stress Reduction and the Small Business: Increasing Employee and Customer Satisfaction." *SAM Advanced Management Journal* (Winter 1998), Vol. 63, No. 1, pp. 27–35.
82. "Table for One? The Hottest Plate to Eat Lunch These Days: Your Desk." *Wall Street Journal,* October 14, 1997, p. 1.
83. Reported in *The Wall Street Journal*, date unknown.
84. This is not an actual company.
85. The Car Dealer Negotiation confidential information is from A.G. Woodside, Tulane University. The Car Dealer Game is part of a paper, "Bargaining Behavior in Personal Selling and Buying Exchanges," presented at the 1980 Eighth Annual Conference of the Association for Business Simulation and Experiential Learning (ABSEL). It is used with Dr. Woodside's permission.

Chapter 10

1. "Team Accountability Needs to be Clear." (The Blanchard Management Report), *Manage* (February 1998), Vol. 49, No. 2, pp. 4–6.
2. E. McFadzean and T. Nelson, "Facilitating Problem-Solving Groups: A Conceptual Model." *Leadership and Organization Development Journal* (January/February 1998), Vol. 19, No. 1, pp. 6–14.
3. R.T. Barker, G.H. Gilbreath, and W.S. Stone, "The Interdisciplinary Needs of Organizations: Are New Employees Adequately Equipped?" *Journal of Management Development* (February/March 1998), Vol. 17, No. 2–3, pp. 214–233.
4. J. Katzenback and D. Smith, "The Discipline of Teams." *Harvard Business Review* (March/April 1993), Vol. 70, No. 2, pp. 111–120.
5. D. Edds, "Improving Performance With Self-directed Work Teams." *School Planning and Management* (March 1998), Vol. 37, No. 3, pp. 38–41.
6. M.A. Verespej, "Lessons from the Best: Focus on People, Communicate, and Have Common Goals." *Industry Week* (February 16, 1998), Vol. 247, No. 4, pp. 28–34.
7. D. Edds, "Improving Performance With Self-directed Work Teams." *School Planning and Management* (March 1998), Vol. 37, No. 3, pp. 38–41.
8. R. Lynch and T. Gerdes, "How to Form that Perfect Team Mold." *The Journal for Quality and Participation* (May/June 1998), Vol. 21, No. 3, pp. 46–47.
9. R.T. Barker, G.H. Gilbreath, and W.S. Stone, "The Interdisciplinary Needs of Organizations: Are New Employees Adequately Equipped?" *Journal of Management Development* (February/March 1998), Vol. 17, No. 2–3, pp. 214–233.
10. A.L. Frohman, "Building a Culture for Innovation." *Research-Technology Management* (March/April 1998), Vol. 41, No. 2, pp. 9–13.

11. R. Lynch and T. Gerdes, "How to Form that Perfect Team Mold." *The Journal for Quality and Participation* (May/June 1998), Vol. 21, No. 3, pp. 46–47.
12. A. Mejia, R. Shirazi, R. Beech, and D. Balmer, "Planning Midwifery Services to Deliver Continuity of Care." *Journal of the Operational Research Society* (January 1998), Vol. 49, No. 1, pp. 33–42.
13. N.Z. Dering, "Leadership in Quality Organizations." *The Journal for Quality and Participation* (January/February 1998), Vol. 21, No. 1, pp. 32–36.
14. J.P. Muczyk and R.P. Steel, "Leadership Style and the Turnaround Executive." *Business Horizons* (March/April 1998), Vol. 41, No. 2, pp. 39–47.
15. R.T. Barker, G.H. Gilbreath, and W.S. Stone, "The Interdisciplinary Needs of Organizations: Are New Employees Adequately Equipped?" *Journal of Management Development* (February/March 1998), Vol. 17, No. 2–3, pp. 214–233.
16. "Team Accountability Needs to be Clear." (The Blanchard Management Report), *Manage* (February 1998), Vol. 49, No. 2, pp. 4–6.
17. M.A. Verespej, "Lessons from the Best: Focus on People, Communicate, and Have Common Goals." *Industry Week* (February 16, 1998), Vol. 247, No. 4, pp. 28–34.
18. K.E. Hultman, "The 10 Commandments of Team Leadership." *Training & Development* (February 1998), Vol. 52, No. 2, pp. 12–14.
19. "West Point Pointers." *The Wall Street Journal,* June 22, 1995, p. 1.
20. P.M. Buhler, "Managers: Out With the Old and in With the New—Skills That Is." *Supervision* (June 1998), Vol. 59, No. 6, pp. 22–25.
21. K.E. Hultman, "The 10 Commandments of Team Leadership." *Training & Development* (February 1998), Vol. 52, No. 2, pp. 12–14.
22. "Team Accountability Needs to be Clear." (The Blanchard Management Report), *Manage* (February 1998), Vol. 49, No. 2, pp. 4–6.
23. J.R. Schermerhorn, Jr., Ohio University, "Situational Leadership: Conversations with Paul Hersey." *Mid-American Journal of Business* (1998), Vol. 12, No. 2, pp. 5–11.
24. K.E. Hultman, "The 10 Commandments of Team Leadership." *Training & Development* (February 1998), Vol. 52, No. 2, pp. 12–14.
25. "Communicating Well in the Office: Returning Your Telephone Calls and Messages." *Executive Advantage,* February 1998, p. 3.
26. S. Gassman, "Connection Before Content." *The Journal for Quality and Participation* (January/February 1998), Vol. 21, No. 1, pp. 56–57.

27. R. Tomlinson, "The Six Principles for Effective OR—Their Relevance in the 90's." *Journal of the Operational Research Society* (April 1998), Vol. 49, No. 4, pp. 403–408.

28. G.S. Wood, "Making Meetings Productive and Fun: How to Transform Board Meetings Into Creative, Energizing, Problem-Solving Sessions." *Association Management* (January 1998), Vol. 50, No. 1, pp. 48–52.

29. K.E. Hultman, "The 10 Commandments of Team Leadership." *Training & Development* (February 1998), Vol. 52, No. 2, pp. 12–14.

30. C. Robie, "Team Ghostbusters." *Strategy & Leadership* (January/February 1997), Vol. 25, No. 1, pp. 44–45.

31. D. Carew, E. Carew, and K. Blanchard, "Group Development and Situational Leadership." *Training and Development Journal,* June 1986, p. 48.

32. C. Robie, "Team Ghostbusters." *Strategy & Leadership* (January/February 1997), Vol. 25, No. 1, pp. 44–45.

33. Ibid.

34. K.E. Hultman, "The 10 Commandments of Team Leadership." *Training & Development* (February 1998), Vol. 52, No. 2, pp. 12–14.

35. R. Tomlinson, "The Six Principles for Effective OR—Their Relevance in the 90's." *Journal of the Operational Research Society* (April 1998), Vol. 49, No. 4, pp. 403–408.

36. L. Mozzi, "Creativity Commandments." *The Journal for Quality and Participation* (May/June 1998), Vol. 21, No. 3, pp. 60–63.

37. Ibid.

38. T. Peters, "When Muddling Through Can Be the Best Strategy." *Washington Business Journal,* January 27, 1995, pp. 19–20.

39. P.M. Buhler, "Managers: Out With the Old and in With the New—Skills That Is." *Supervision* (June 1998), Vol. 59, No. 6, pp. 22–25.

40. "Communicating Well in the Office: Returning Your Telephone Calls and Messages." *Executive Advantage,* February 1998, p. 3.

41. P.M. Buhler, "Managers: Out With the Old and in With the New—Skills That Is." *Supervision* (June 1998), Vol. 59, No. 6, pp. 22–25.

42. D. Edds, "Improving Performance With Self-directed Work Teams." *School Planning and Management* (March 1998), Vol. 37, No. 3, pp. 38–41.

43. N.Z. Dering, "Leadership in Quality Organizations." *The Journal for Quality and Participation* (January/February 1998), Vol. 21, No. 1, pp. 32–36.

44. A.L. Frohman, "Building a Culture for Innovation." *Research-Technology Management* (March/April 1998), Vol. 41, No. 2, pp. 9–13.

45. H. Lancaster, "Managing Your Career." *The Wall Street Journal,* May 26, 1998, p. B1.

46. R. Levasseur, "People Skills: What Every Professional Should Know About Designing and Managing Meetings." *Interface* (March/April 1992), Vol. 22, No. 2, pp. 11–14.

47. H. Lancaster, "Managing Your Career." *The Wall Street Journal,* May 26, 1998, p. B1.

48. E. McFadzean and T. Nelson, "Facilitating Problem-Solving Groups: A Conceptual Model." *Leadership and Organization Development Journal* (January/February 1998), Vol. 19, No. 1, pp. 6–14.

49. H. Lancaster, "Managing Your Career." *The Wall Street Journal,* May 26, 1998, p. B1.

50. G.S. Wood, "Making Meetings Productive and Fun: How to Transform Board Meetings Into Creative, Energizing, Problem-Solving Sessions." *Association Management* (January 1998), Vol. 50, No. 1, pp. 48–52.

51. T. Willumsen, "Conducting Effective Meetings With Your Investment Advisors." *Employee Benefits Journal* (June 1998), Vol. 23, No. 2, pp. 25–29.

52. R. Laliberte, "Simplify Your Life." *Success* (April 1998), Vol. 45, No. 4, pp. 56–62.

53. H. Lancaster, "Managing Your Career." *The Wall Street Journal,* May 26, 1998, p. B1.

54. "An Added Joy of E-Mail: Fewer Face-to-Face Meetings." *The Wall Street Journal,* July 14, 1998, p. A1.

55. "Team Accountability Needs to be Clear." (The Blanchard Management Report), *Manage* (February 1998), Vol. 49, No. 2, pp. 4–6.

56. H. Lancaster, "Managing Your Career." *The Wall Street Journal,* May 26, 1998, p. B1.

57. L. Mozzi, "Creativity Commandments." *The Journal for Quality and Participation* (May/June 1998), Vol. 21, No. 3, pp. 60–63.

58. H. Lancaster, "Managing Your Career." *The Wall Street Journal,* May 26, 1998, p. B1.

59. Ibid.

60. R. Laliberte, "Simplify Your Life." *Success* (April 1998), Vol. 45, No. 4, pp. 56–62.

61. L. Mozzi, "Creativity Commandments." *The Journal for Quality and Participation* (May/June 1998), Vol. 21, No. 3, pp. 60–63.

Chapter 11

1. W. Nichols, "What We Have Here . . . (Poor Communications Following Airlines' Decision to Cap Travel Agents' Commission)." *Travel Weekly,* July 3, 1995, pp. 22–23.

2. N.L. Reinsch Jr. and A.N. Shelby, "What Communications Abilities Do Practitioners Need? Evidence From MBA Students." *Business Communication Quarterly* (December 1997), Vol. 60, No. 4, pp. 7–30.

3. R.E. Thaler-Carter, "In-house Recruiters Fill a Specialized Niche." *HR Magazine* (April 1998), Vol. 43, No. 5, pp. 72–78.

4. J. Gunther, "Staying Ahead of the Curve." *Risk Management* (April 1998), Vol. 45, No. 4, pp. 80–84.

5. "Team Accountability Needs to be Clear." (The Blanchard Management Report), *Manage* (February 1998), Vol. 49, No. 2, pp. 4–6.

6. R.T. Barker, G.H. Gilbreath, and W.S. Stone, "The Interdisciplinary Needs of Organizations: Are New Employees Adequately Equipped?" *Journal of Management Development* (February/March 1998), Vol. 17, No. 2–3, pp. 214–233.

7. T. Barkin and M. Horn, "The Labor Lever Strategy." *Airline Business* (January 1998), Vol. 14, No. 1, pp. 46–50.

8. S. Shellenbarger, "Work and Family." *The Wall Street Journal,* November 19, 1997, p. B1.

9. "Multi-rater Feedback and Performance Evaluation Programs Do Not Mix." *Supervision* (March 1998), Vol. 59, No. 3, pp. 25–26.

10. L. Iacocca, *Iacocca* (New York: Bantam Books, 1985), p. 15.

11. C.F. Matusicky, "Building and Effective Corporate Compliance Program." *Healthcare Financial Management* (April 1998), Vol. 52, No. 4, pp. 77–81.

12. D.K. Lindo, "Are You Coaching the 'Bad News Bearers'?" *Supervision* (June 1998), Vol. 59, No. 6, pp. 3–5.

13. "The CIO's Seat Grows But Remains Difficult to Define." *The Wall Street Journal,* September 21, 1995, p. 1.

14. D.K. Lindo, "Are You Coaching the 'Bad News Bearers'?" *Supervision* (June 1998), Vol. 59, No. 6, pp. 3–5.

15. M.A. Verespej, "Lessons from the Best: Focus on People, Communicate, and Have Common Goals." *Industry Week* (February 16, 1998), Vol. 247, No. 4, pp. 28–34.

16. R. Lynch and T. Gerdes, "How to Form that Perfect Team Mold." *The Journal for Quality and Participation* (May/June 1998), Vol. 21, No. 3, pp. 46–47.

17. D.M. Mansour-Cole and S.G. Scott, "Hearing it Through the Grapevine: The Influence of Source, Leader-relations, and Legitimacy on Survivors' Fairness Perceptions." *Personnel Psychology* (Spring 1998), Vol. 51, No. 1, pp. 25–55.

18. M. Messmer, "Improving Your Listening Skills." *Management Accounting (USA)* (March 1998), Vol. 79, No. 9, pp. 14–15.

19. Ibid.

20. D.W. Farrant, "Take the Worry Out of Confronting." *Supervision* (March 1998), Vol. 59, No. 3, pp. 5–8.

21. N.L. Reinsch Jr. and A.N. Shelby, "What Communications Abilities Do Practitioners Need? Evidence From MBA Students." *Business*

Communication Quarterly (December 1997), Vol. 60, No. 4, pp. 7–30.

22. S.E. Moss and M.J. Martinko, "The Effects of Performance Attributions and Outcome Dependence on Leader Feedback Behavior Following Poor Subordinate Performance." *Journal of Organizational Behavior* (May 1998), Vol. 19, No. 3, pp. 269–275.

23. Q. Burger, "Why Should They Believe Us?" *Communication World* (January/February 1995), Vol. 12, No. 1, pp. 49–52.

24. H. Lawrence and A. Wiswell, "Feedback Is a Two-Way Street." *Training & Development* (July 1995), Vol. 49, No. 7, pp. 49–52.

25. L. King, "The Business of Communication." *Success Yearbook* (Tampa, FL: Peter Lowe International, 1998), p. 27.

26. M. Messmer, "Improving Your Listening Skills." *Management Accounting (USA)* (March 1998), Vol. 79, No. 9, pp. 14–15.

27. C. Robie, "Team Ghostbusters." *Strategy & Leadership* (January/February 1997), Vol. 25, No. 1, pp. 44–45.

28. "Communicating Well in the Office: Returning Your Telephone Calls and Messages." *Executive Advantage*, February 1998, p. 3.

29. D.K. Lindo, "Are You Coaching the 'Bad News Bearers'?" *Supervision* (June 1998), Vol. 59, No. 6, pp. 3–5.

30. S. Shellenbarger, "Work and Family." *The Wall Street Journal*, November 19, 1997, p. B1.

31. P. Lowe, "How to Boost Your Market Value." *Success Yearbook* (Tampa, FL: Peter Lowe International, 1998), pp. 22–23.

32. L. King, "The Business of Communication." *Success Yearbook* (Tampa, FL: Peter Lowe International, 1998), p. 27.

33. P. Lowe, "Keys to Irresistible Public Speaking." *Success Yearbook* (Tampa, FL: Peter Lowe International, 1998), pp. 28–29.

34. R.T. Barker, G.H. Gilbreath, and W.S. Stone, "The Interdisciplinary Needs of Organizations: Are New Employees Adequately Equipped?" *Journal of Management Development* (February/March 1998), Vol. 17, No. 2–3, pp. 214–233.

35. P. Lowe, "How to Boost Your Market Value." *Success Yearbook* (Tampa, FL: Peter Lowe International, 1998), pp. 22–23.

36. "Communicating Well in the Office: Returning Your Telephone Calls and Messages." *Executive Advantage*, February 1998, p. 3.

37. S. Gracie, "Body of Evidence." *The Guardian*, March 12, 1998, pp. T4–6.

38. R.T. Barker, G.H. Gilbreath, and W.S. Stone, "The Interdisciplinary Needs of Organizations: Are New Employees Adequately Equipped?" *Journal of Management Development* (February/March 1998), Vol. 17, No. 2–3, pp. 214–233.

39. T. Pollock, "Attitudes That Can Help You Get Ahead: A Personal File of Stimulating Ideas, Little-known Facts and Daily Problem Solvers." *Supervision* (February 1998), Vol. 59, No. 2, pp. 24–27.

40. "Communicating Well in the Office: Returning Your Telephone Calls and Messages." *Executive Advantage*, February1998, p. 3.

41. "E-Mail Etiquette," *The Wall Street Journal*, October 12, 1995, p. 1.

42. G. Blake, "It Is Recommended That You Write Clearly." *The Wall Street Journal*, April 2, 1995, p. 14.

43. P. Lowe, "How to Boost Your Market Value." *Success Yearbook* (Tampa, FL: Peter Lowe International, 1998), pp. 22–23.

44. "A Special Background Report on Trends in Industry and Finance." *The Wall Street Journal*, October 30, 1997, p. A1.

45. "The Machinists Union." *The Wall Street Journal*, April 28, 1998, p. A1.

46. "Sensible California: Suddenly, America's Weirdest State is Sending Messages Worth Hearing." *The Economist* (June 6, 1998), Vol. 347, No. 8071, pp. 21–22.

47. M. Messmer, "Improving Your Listening Skills." *Management Accounting (USA)* (March 1998), Vol. 79, No. 9, pp. 14–15.

48. "Multi-rater Feedback and Performance Evaluation Programs Do Not Mix." *Supervision* (March 1998), Vol. 59, No. 3, pp. 25–26.

49. "Communicating Well in the Office: Returning Your Telephone Calls and Messages." *Executive Advantage*, February, 1998, p. 3.

50. "Work Week: A Special News Report About Life On the Job—and Trends Taking Shape There." *The Wall Street Journal*, June 2, 1998, p. A1.

51. S.E. Moss and M.J. Martinko, "The Effects of Performance Attributions and Outcome Dependence on Leader Feedback Behavior Following Poor Subordinate Performance." *Journal of Organizational Behavior* (May 1998), Vol. 19, No. 3, pp. 269–275.

52. D.W. Farrant, "Take the Worry Out of Confronting." *Supervision* (March 1998), Vol. 59, No. 3, pp. 5–8.

53. M. Messmer, "Improving Your Listening Skills." *Management Accounting (USA)* (March 1998), Vol. 79, No. 9, pp. 14–15.

54. D.W. Farrant, "Take the Worry Out of Confronting." *Supervision* (March 1998), Vol. 59, No. 3, pp. 5–8.

55. D. Baily, "Are You Listening." *Chemist & Druggist* (January 31, 1998), Vol. 249, No. 6122, pp. S14–S16.

56. "Communicating Well in the Office: Returning Your Telephone Calls and Messages." *Executive Advantage*, February 1998, p. 3.

57. P. Lowe, "9 Secrets of Superstar Salespeople." *Success Yearbook* (Tampa, FL: Peter Lowe International, 1998), pp. 38–39.

58. M. Messmer, "Improving Your Listening Skills." *Management Accounting (USA)* (March 1998), Vol. 79, No. 9, pp. 14–15.

59. Ibid.

60. D. Baily, "Are You Listening." *Chemist & Druggist* (January 31, 1998), Vol. 249, No. 6122, pp. S14–S16.

61. M. Messmer, "Improving Your Listening Skills." *Management Accounting (USA)* (March 1998), Vol. 79, No. 9, pp. 14–15.

62. Ibid.

63. Ibid.

64. "Communicating Well in the Office: Returning Your Telephone Calls and Messages." *Executive Advantage*, February 1998, p. 3.

65. L. Bowes-Sperry, J.F. Veiga, and J.N. Yanouzas, "An Analysis of Managerial Helping Responses Based on Social Role Theory." *Group & Organization Management* (December 1997), Vol. 22, No. 4, pp. 445–460.

66. Ibid.

67. Ibid.

68. M. Messmer, "Improving Your Listening Skills." *Management Accounting (USA)* (March 1998), Vol. 79, No. 9, pp. 14–15.

69. D. Baily, "Are You Listening." *Chemist & Druggist* (January 31, 1998), Vol. 249, No. 6122, pp. S14–S16.

70. B. Yeargrin, "Know Your Employee's Emotional Temperament." *Boating Industry* (January 1998), Vol. 61, No. 1, pp. 47–49.

71. D.W. Farrant, "Take the Worry Out of Confronting." *Supervision* (March 1998), Vol. 59, No. 3, pp. 5–8.

72. L. Bowes-Sperry, J.F. Veiga, and J.N. Yanouzas, "An Analysis of Managerial Helping Responses Based on Social Role Theory." *Group & Organization Management* (December 1997), Vol. 22, No. 4, pp. 445–460.

73. B. Yeargrin, "Know Your Employee's Emotional Temperament." *Boating Industry* (January 1998), Vol. 61, No. 1, pp. 47–49.

74. P. Lowe, "9 Secrets of Superstar Salespeople." *Success Yearbook* (Tampa, FL: Peter Lowe International, 1998), pp. 38–39.

Chapter 12

1. Donna Brogle is the owner of Drapery Designs by Donna, but she does not have an employee named Susan. However, this motivation problem is common, and throughout the chapter you will learn how to motivate using Susan as an example.

2. T. Van Tassel, "Productivity Dilemmas." *Executive Excellence* (April 1994), Vol. 11, No. 4, pp. 16–17.

3. (General Electric's success attributed to CEO Jack Welch's Charisma and Micromanagement)

(Editorial) (Brief Article), "Management 101: Motivation Matters." *Business Week* (June 8, 1998), No. 3581, pp. 130–131.

4. A. Reinhardt, "Mr. House Finds His Fixer-upper." *Business Week* (February 2, 1998), No. 3563, pp. 66–69.

5. S.E. Moss and M.J. Martinko, "The Effects of Performance Attributions and Outcome Dependence on Leader Feedback Behavior Following Poor Subordinate Performance." *Journal of Organizational Behavior* (May 1998), Vol. 19, No. 3, pp. 269–275.

6. P. Lowe, "Maximized Management." *Success Yearbook* (Tampa, FL: Peter Lowe International, 1998), pp. 16–17.

7. "Work Hard, Play Hard: Employers use Fun to Boost Morale." *The Wall Street Journal*, August 11, 1998, p. A1.

8. P. Lowe, "Maximized Management." *Success Yearbook* (Tampa, FL: Peter Lowe International, 1998), pp. 16–17.

9. J.F. Manzoni and J.L. Barsoux, "The Set up to-Fail Syndrome." *Harvard Business Review* (March/April 1998), Vol. 76, No. 2, pp. 101–114.

10. J.F. Manzoni and J.L. Barsoux, "The Set-up-to-Fail Syndrome." *Harvard Business Review* (March/April 1998), Vol. 76, No. 2, pp. 101–114.

11. C. Miller, "The Achilles Syndrome: When High Potential Employees Choose to Withdraw." *Supervision* (March 1998), Vol. 59, No. 3, pp. 3–5.

12. P. Lowe, "Maximized Management." *Success Yearbook* (Tampa, FL: Peter Lowe International, 1998), pp. 16–17.

13. A. Maslow, "A Theory of Human Motivation." *Psychological Review* (1943), Vol. 50, pp. 370–96, and *Motivation and Personality* (New York: Harper & Row, 1954).

14. T. Petzinger, Jr., "The Front Line: Radical Work by Guru of Leadership Takes 30 Years to Flower." *The Wall Street Journal*, April 25, 1997, p. B1.

15. C. Alderfer, "An Empirical Test of a New Theory of Human Needs." *Organizational Behavior and Human Performance*, April 1969, pp. 142–175, and *Existence, Relatedness, and Growth* (New York: Free Press, 1972).

16. F. Herzberg, "One More Time: How Do You Motivate Employees?" *Harvard Business Review*, January/February 1968, pp. 53–62.

17. A. Kohn, "Challenging Behaviorist Dogma: Myths About Money and Motivation." *Compensation and Review Benefits Review* (March/April 1998), Vol. 30, No. 2, pp. 27–33.

18. M.A. Tietjen and R.M. Myers, "Motivation and Job Satisfaction." *Management Decision* (May/June 1998), Vol. 36, No. 3–4, pp. 226–232.

19. "Work Week: A Special News Report About Life On the Job—and Trends Taking Shape There." *The Wall Street Journal*, June 2, 1998, p. A1.

20. "How Entrepreneurs Stay Motivated." (CEO Survey Results)(Brief Article), *INC.* (March 1998), Vol. 20, No. 3, pp. 94–95.

21. J.R. Rentsch and R.P. Steel, "Testing the Durability of Job Characteristics as Predictors of Absenteeism Over a Six–year Period." *Personnel Psychology* (Spring 1998), Vol. 51, No. 1, pp. 165–191.

22. H. Murray, *Explorations in Personality* (New York: Oxford Press, 1938).

23. J. Atkinson, *An Introduction to Motivation* (New York: Van Nostrand Reinhold, 1964).

24. D. McClelland, *The Achieving Society* (New York: Van Nostrand Reinhold, 1961), and D. McClelland and D.H. Burnham, "Power Is the Great Motivator." *Harvard Business Review*, March/April 1978, p. 103.

25. S.E. Moss and M.J. Martinko, "The Effects of Performance Attributions and Outcome Dependence on Leader Feedback Behavior Following Poor Subordinate Performance." *Journal of Organizational Behavior* (May 1998), Vol. 19, No. 3, pp. 269–275.

26. J.S. Adams, "Toward an Understanding of Inequity." *Journal of Abnormal and Social Psychology* (1963), Vol. 67, pp. 422–36.

27. C.C. Chen, J.R. Meindl, and H. Hui, "Deciding on Equity or Parity: A Test of Situational, Cultural, and Individual Factors," *Journal of Organizational Behavior* (March 1998), Vol. 19, No. 2, pp. 115–130.

28. H. Klean and J. Kim, "A Field Study of the Influence of Situational Constraints, Leader-Member Exchange, and Goal Commitment on Performance." *Academy of Management Journal* (February 1998), Vol. 41, No. 1, pp. 88–96.

29. M.A. Tietjen and R.M. Myers, "Motivation and Job Satisfaction." *Management Decision* (May/June 1998), Vol. 36, No. 3–4, pp. 226–232.

30. J.M. Phillips and S.M. Gully, "Role of Goal Orientation, Ability, Need for Achievement, and Locus of Control in the Self-efficacy and Goal-setting Process." *Journal of Applied Psychology* (October 1997), Vol. 82, No. 5, pp. 792–803.

31. L. Mann, D. Samson, and D. Dow, "A Field Experiment on the Effects of Benchmarking and Goal Setting on Company Sales Performance." *Journal of Management* (January/February 1998), Vol. 24, No. 1, pp. 73–97.

32. Lou Holtz, "Setting a Higher Standard." *Success Yearbook* (Tampa, FL: Peter Lowe International, 1998), p. 74.

33. K. Blanchard, "Three Secrets of the One-minute Manager." *The CPA Journal* (April 1992), Vol. 62, No. 4, pp. 76–78.

34. H. Klean and J. Kim, "A Field Study of the Influence of Situational Constraints, Leader-Member Exchange, and Goal Commitment on Performance." *Academy of Management Journal* (February 1998), Vol. 41, No. 1, pp. 88–96.

35. T. Norvell, "From Goal-setting to Goal-getting: With a Little Help From Your Coach." *Journal of Property Management* (January/February 1998), Vol. 63, No. 1, pp. 14–16.

36. V. Vroom, *Work and Motivation* (New York: John Wiley & Sons, 1964).

37. D. Ilgen, D. Nebeker, and R. Pritchard, "Expectancy Theory Measures: An Empirical Comparison in an Experimental Simulation." *Organizational Behavior and Human Performance* (1981), Vol. 28, pp. 189–223.

38. B.F. Skinner, *Beyond Freedom and Dignity* (New York: Alfred A. Knopf, 1971).

39. C.B. Kedjidjian, "OSHA's New Boss: Charles Jeffress Expects Greater Cooperation as He Enforces The Law." *Safety & Health* (March 1998), Vol. 157, No. 3, pp. 24–26.

40. P. Lowe, "Maximized Management." *Success Yearbook* (Tampa, FL: Peter Lowe International, 1998), pp. 16–17.

41. T. Petzinger, Jr., "The Front Line: Radical Work by Guru of Leadership Takes 30 Years to Flower." *The Wall Street Journal*, April 25, 1997, p. B1.

42. S. Shellenbarger, "Work and Family." *The Wall Street Journal*, November 19, 1997, p. B1.

43. K. Blanchard, "Three Secrets of the One-minute Manager." *The CPA Journal* (April 1992), Vol. 62, No. 4, pp. 76–78.

44. Ibid.

45. P. Lowe, "Maximized Management." *Success Yearbook* (Tampa, FL: Peter Lowe International, 1998), pp. 16–17.

46. G. Adler, "When Your Star Performer Can't Manage." *Harvard Business Review* (July/August 1997), Vol. 75, No. 4, pp. 22–27.

47. B. Gill, "Flextime Benefits Employees and Employers." *American Printer* (February 1998), Vol. 220, No. 5, pp. 70–71.

48. S. Shellenbarger, "Work and Family." *The Wall Street Journal*, November 19, 1997, p. B1.

49. K. Blanchard and S. Johnson, *The One–Minute Manager* (New York: Wm. Morrow & Co., 1982).

50. This statement is based on R. Lussier's consulting experience.

51. This paragraph is based on R. Lussier's consulting experience.

52. "Communicating Well in the Office: Returning Your Telephone Calls and Messages." *Executive Advantage*, February 1998, p. 3.

53. G. Hofstede, "Motivation, Leadership, and Organizations: Do American Theories Apply Abroad?" *Organizational Dynamics*, Summer 1980, p. 55.

54. A. Dubinsky, M. Kotabe, C. Un Lim, and R. Michaels, "Differences in Motivational Perceptions Among U.S., Japanese, and Korean Sales Personnel, "*Journal of Business Research* (June 1994), Vol. 30, No. 2, pp. 175–185.

55. N.J. Alder, *International Dimensions of Organizational Behavior* (Boston: Kent, 1986).

56. C.C. Chen, J.R. Meindl, and H. Hui, "Deciding on Equity or Parity: A Test of Situational, Cultural, and Individual Factors, *Journal of Organizational Behavior* (March 1998), Vol. 19, No. 2, pp. 115–130.

57. "Deming's Demons." *The Wall Street Journal,* June 4, 1990, pp. R39, 41.

Chapter 13

1. B. Bass, *Stogdill's Handbook of Leadership*, rev. ed. (New York: Free Press, 1981), and F.R. Manfred and Kets des Vries, "The Leadership Mystique." *The Academy of Management Executive* (August 1994), Vol. 8, No. 3, pp. 73–92.

2. J. Meindle and S. Ehrlich, "The Romance of Leadership and the Evaluation of Performance." *Academy of Management Journal,* March 1987, p. 92.

3. F. Pacetta and R. Gittines, "Fire Them UP!" *Success* (May 1994), Vol. 41, No. 4, pp. 16A–16D.

4. D. Parkhurst, "To Succeed in the Global Arena, Leadership is a Must." *Nation's Cities Weekly* (May 25, 1998), Vol. 2, No. 21, pp. 6–7.

5. A. Thomson, C. Mabey, and J. Storey, "The Determinants of Management Development: Choice or Circumstance?" *International Studies of Management & Organization* (Spring 1998), Vol. 28, No. 1, pp. 91–114.

6. K.E. Hultman, "The 10 Commandments of Team Leadership." *Training & Development* (February 1998), Vol. 52, No. 2, pp. 12–14.

7. J.R. Katzenbach, "The Irony of Senior Leadership Teams." *The Journal for Quality and Participation* (May/June 1998), Vol. 21, No. 3, pp. 8–16.

8. "Interview With Bruce Rohde, CEO of ConAgra, Inc. HR as Major Source of Competitive Advantage." *Human Resources Management* (Spring 1998), Vol. 37, No. 1, pp. 85–89.

9. P.M. Buhler, "Managers: Out With the Old and in With the New—Skills That Is." *Supervision* (June 1998), Vol. 59, No. 6, pp. 22–25.

10. T. Pollock, "Attitudes That Can Help You Get Ahead: A Personal File of Stimulating Ideas, Little-known Facts and Daily Problem Solvers." *Supervision* (February 1998), Vol. 59, No. 2, pp. 24–27.

11. G. Capowski, "Revving up to Lead." *HR Focus* (January 1998), Vol. 75, No. 1, pp. 1–4.

12. R.J. House and R.N. Aditya, "The Social Scientific Study of Leadership: Quo Vadis?" *Journal of Management* (May/June 1997), Vol. 23, No. 3, pp. 409–474.

13. B. Bass, *Stogdill's Handbook of Leadership*, rev. ed. (New York: Free Press, 1981).

14. P. Drucker, ""Leadership: More Doing Than Dash." *The Wall Street Journal,* January 6, 1988, p. 24.

15. E. Ghiselli, *Explorations in Management Talent* (San Monica, CA: Goodyear, 1971).

16. L. Pratch and J. Jacobowitz, "Integrative Capacity and the Evaluation of Leadership: A Multimethod Assessment Approach." *Journal of Applied Behavioral Science* (June 1998), Vol. 34, No. 2, pp. 180–202.

17. K. Boyers, "Why Am I Here?" *Association Management* (March 1998), Vol. 50, No. 3, pp. 63–66.

18. E.T. Behr, "Acting From the Center: Your Response to Today's Leadership Challenges Must be Grounded in Personal Values." *Management Review* (March 1998), Vol. 87, No. 3, pp. 51–56.

19. P. Lowe, "Maximized Management." *Success Yearbook* (Tampa, FL: Peter Lowe International, 1998), pp. 16–17.

20. K. Boyers, "Why Am I Here?" *Association Management* (March 1998), Vol. 50, No. 3, pp. 63–66.

21. For more information on Spirit at Work, contact Dr. Judi Neal at the University of New Haven, CT 06516, 1–800–342–5814, or judineal@charger.newhaven.edu.

22. B. Graham, "Leadership & Spirituality." *Success Yearbook* (Tampa, FL: Peter Lowe International, 1998), p. 54.

23. Z. Ziglar, "Formula for Complete Success." *Success Yearbook* (Tampa, FL: Peter Lowe International, 1998), pp. 30 and 105.

24. P. Lowe, "The Fifth Level of Life." *Success Yearbook* (Tampa, FL: Peter Lowe International, 1998), pp. 91–93.

25. Z. Ziglar, "Formula for Complete Success." *Success Yearbook* (Tampa, FL: Peter Lowe International, 1998), pp. 30 and 105.

26. N.Z. Dering, "Leadership in Quality Organizations." *The Journal for Quality and Participation* (January/February 1998), Vol. 21, No. 1, pp. 32–36.

27. R. Blake and J. Mouton, *The Managerial Grid III: Key to Leadership Excellence* (Houston: Gulf Publishing, 1985).

28. R. Blake and A.A. McCanse, *Leadership Dilemmas—Grid Solutions* (Houston: Gulf Publishing, 1991).

29. P. Nystrom, "Managers and the Hi-HI Leader Myth." *Academy of Management Journal* (June 1978), Vol. 21, No. 3, pp. 325–331.

30. R. Trevelyan, "The Boundary of Leadership: Getting it Right and Having it All." *Business Strategy Review* (Spring 1998), Vol. 9, No. 1, pp. 37–45.

31. J. Komaki, "Emergence of the Operant Model of Effective Supervision or How an Operant Conditioner Got Hooked on Leadership." *Leadership & Organizational Development Journal* (August 1994), Vol. 15, No. 5, pp. 27–32.

32. J.R. Baum, E.A. Locke, and S.A. Kirkpatrick, "A Longitudinal Study of the Relation of Vision and Vision Communication to Venture Growth in Entrepreneurial Firms." *Journal of Applied Psychology* (February 1998), Vol. 83, No. 1, pp. 43–55.

33. W.L. Gardner and B.J. Avolio, "The Charismatic Relationship: A Dramaturical Perspective." *Academy of Management Review* (January 1998), Vol. 23, No. 1, pp. 32–59.

34. F.R. Manfred and K. des Vries, "The Leadership Mystique." *The Academy of Management Executive* (August 1994), Vol. 8, No. 3, pp. 73–93.

35. N. Tichy and M.A. Devanna, *The Transformational Leader* (New York: John Wiley & Sons, 1986).

36. G. Capowski, "Revving up to Lead." *HR Focus* (January 1998), Vol. 75, No. 1, pp. 1–4.

37. J.J. Sosik, B.J. Avolio, and S.S. Kahai, "Effects of Leadership Style and Anonymity on Group Potency and Effectiveness in a Group Decision Support System Environment." *Journal of Applied Psychology* (February 1997), Vol. 82, No. 1, pp. 89–104.

38. J.J. Sosik, "Effects of Transformational Leadership and Anonymity on Idea Generation in Computer-Mediated Groups." *Group & Organization Management* (December 1997), Vol. 22, No. 4, pp. 460–488.

39. J.J. Sosik, B.J. Avolio, and S.S. Kahai, "Effects of Leadership Style and Anonymity on Group Potency and Effectiveness in a Group Decision Support System Environment." *Journal of Applied Psychology* (February 1997), Vol. 82, No. 1, pp. 89–104.

40. R.J. House and R.N. Aditya, "The Social Scientific Study of Leadership: Quo Vadis?" *Journal of Management* (May/June 1997), Vol. 23, No. 3, pp. 409–474.

41. D.R. Dalton, C.M. Daily, A.E. Ellstrand, and J.L. Johnson, "Meta-analytic Reviews of Board Composition, Leadership Structure, and Financial Performance." *Strategic Management Journal* (March 1998), Vol. 19, No. 3, pp. 269–291.

42. N.Z. Dering, "Leadership in Quality Organizations." *The Journal for Quality and Participation* (January/February 1998), Vol. 21, No. 1, pp. 32–36.

43. F. Fiedler, *A Theory of Leadership Effectiveness* (New York: McGraw-Hill, 1967).

44. J.R. Schermerhorn, Jr., Ohio University, "Situational Leadership: Conversations with Paul Hersey." *Mid-American Journal of Business* (1998), Vol. 12, No. 2, pp. 5–11.

45. F. Fiedler, "When to Lead, When to Stand Back." *Psychology Today*, February 1988, pp. 26–27.

46. R. Tannenbaum and W. Schmidt, "How to Choose a Leadership Pattern." *Harvard Business Review*, May/June 1973, p. 166.

47. R. Tannenbaum and W. Schmidt, excerpts from "How to Choose a Leadership Pattern," *Harvard Business Review*, July/August 1986, p. 129.

48. R. House, "A Path Goal Theory of Leader Effectiveness," *Administrative Science Quarterly* (1971), Vol. 16, No. 2, pp. 321–329.

49. V. Vroom and P. Yetton, *Leadership and Decision Making* (Pittsburgh: University of Pittsburgh Press, 1973).

50. V. Vroom and A. Jago, *The New Leadership: Managing Partipation in Organizations* (Englewood Cliffs, NJ: Prentice Hall, 1987).

51. V. Vroom, "Can Leaders Learn to Lead?" *Organizational Dynamics*, Winter 1976, pp. 17–28.

52. P. Hersey and K. Blanchard, *Management of Organizational Behavior: Utilizing Human Resources*, 4th ed. (Englewood Cliffs, NJ: Prentice Hall, 1982).

53. J.R. Schermerhorn, Jr., Ohio University, "Situational Leadership: Conversations with Paul Hersey." *Mid-American Journal of Business* (1998), Vol. 12, No. 2, pp. 5–11.

54. O. M. Irgens, "Situational Leadership: A Modification of Hersey and Blanchard's Model." *Leadership & Organizational Development Journal*, 1995, Vol. 16, No. 2, pp. 36–40.

55. C. Graeff, "The Situational Leadership Theory: A Critical Review." *Academy of Management Review*, August 8, 1983, pp. 285, 290.

56. J.R. Schermerhorn, Jr., Ohio University, "Situational Leadership: Conversations with Paul Hersey." *Mid-American Journal of Business* (1998), Vol. 12, No. 2, pp. 5–11.

57. Ibid.

58. S. Kerr and J. Jermier, "Substitutes for Leadership: The Meaning and Measurement." *Organizational Behavior and Human Performance* (1978), Vol. 22, pp. 375–403.

59. S. Kerr, J. Jermier, and R. Gordon, "Substitutes for Leadership." *Supervision* (July 1994), Vol. 55, No. 7, pp. 17–20.

60. J.E. Sheridan, D.J. Vredenburgh, and M.A. Abelson, "Contextual Model of Leadership Influence in Hospital Units." *Academy of Management Journal* (1984), Vol. 27, No. 1, pp. 57–78.

61. R.S. Lapidus, J.A. Roberts, and L.B. Chonko, "Stressors, Leadership Substitutes, and Relations With Supervision Among Industrial Salespeople." *Industrial Marketing Management* (May 1997), Vol. 26, No. 3, pp. 255–270.

62. S. Gruner, "Can We Reduce the Cost of Handling Customers' Complaints?" *INC.* (December 1997), Vol. 19, No. 18, pp. 148–149.

Chapter 14

1. P.M. Buhler, "Managers: Out With the Old and in With the New—Skills That Is." *Supervision* (June 1998), Vol. 59, No. 6, pp. 22–25.

2. M.L. Millenson, "3 Forces for Change: Money, Technology, and the Spirit of the Times Will Force Your Hand on Computer Systems That Measure Quality." *Hospitals and Health Networks* (February 20, 1998), Vol. 72, No. 4, pp. 44–26.

3. D.J. Campbell, K.M. Campbell, and H.B. Chia, "Merit Pay, Performance Appraisal, and Individual Motivation: An Analysis and Alternative." *Human Resources Management* (Summer 1998), Vol. 37, No. 2, pp. 131–147.

4. R. Simmons, "How New Top Managers Use Control Systems as Levers of Strategic Renewal." *Strategic Management Journal* (March 1994), Vol. 15, No. 3, pp. 169–189.

5. S. Baraldi, "Management Control Systems in NPOs: An Italian Survey." *Financial Accountability & Management* (May 1998), Vol. 14, No. 2, pp. 141–165.

6. J. Zoltak, "Making Sure Customers Get Satisfaction Discussed at Stadium Managers Seminar." *Amusement Business* (February 16, 1998), Vol. 110, No. 7, pp. 4–5.

7. J. Zigon, "Team Performance Measurement." *The Journal for Quality and Participation* (May/June 1998), Vol. 21, No. 3, pp. 48–56.

8. F. Kniggendorf, "Helping Supervisors Define Standards of Performance." *Human Resource Focus* (February 1998), Vol. 75, No. 2, pp. 13–14.

9. "What Gets Measured Gets Done—If Your Company Posts the Right Kinds of Numbers. Which is Why Scoreboards are Back—With a Twist." *INC.* (June 1998), Vol. 20, No. 8, pp. 80–81.

10. J. Zigon, "Team Performance Measurement." *The Journal for Quality and Participation* (May/June 1998), Vol. 21, No. 3, pp. 48–56.

11. M.L. Millenson, "3 Forces for Change: Money, Technology, and the Spirit of the Times Will Force Your Hand on Computer Systems That Measure Quality." *Hospitals and Health Networks* (February 20, 1998), Vol. 72, No. 4, pp. 44–26.

12. "What Gets Measured Gets Done—If Your Company Posts the Right Kinds of Numbers. Which is Why Scoreboards are Back—With a Twist." *INC.* (June 1998), Vol. 20, No. 8, pp. 80–81.

13. W.K. Lindenmann, "Setting Minimum Standards For Measuring Public Relations Effectiveness." *Public Relations Review* (Winter 1997), Vol. 23, No. 1, pp. 391–409.

14. P. Lowe, "Maximized Management." *Success Yearbook* (Tampa, FL: Peter Lowe International, 1998), pp. 16–17.

15. M.L. Millenson, "3 Forces for Change: Money, Technology, and the Spirit of the Times Will Force Your Hand on Computer Systems That Measure Quality." *Hospitals and Health Networks* (February 20, 1998), Vol. 72, No. 4, pp. 44–26.

16. J. Talbott, L. Brack, and L. John, "Variance Analysis in a Service Business." *Planning Review (A Publication of the Planning Forum)* (May/June 1998), Vol. 16, No. 3, pp. 36–41.

17. W.K. Lindenmann, "Setting Minimum Standards For Measuring Public Relations Effectiveness." *Public Relations Review* (Winter 1997), Vol. 23, No. 1, pp. 391–409.

18. "What Gets Measured Gets Done—If Your Company Posts the Right Kinds of Numbers. Which is Why Scoreboards are Back—With a Twist." *INC.* (June 1998), Vol. 20, No. 8, pp. 80–81.

19. C.L. Kemper, "Global Training's Critical Success Factors." *Training and Development* (February 1998), Vol. 52, No. 2, pp. 35–38.

20. D.J. Campbell, K.M. Campbell, and H.B. Chia, "Merit Pay, Performance Appraisal, and Individual Motivation: An Analysis and Alternative." *Human Resources Management* (Summer 1998), Vol. 37, No. 2, pp. 131–147.

21. J. Talbott, L. Brack, and L. John, "Variance Analysis in a Service Business." *Planning Review (A Publication of the Planning Forum)* (May/June 1998), Vol. 16, No. 3, pp. 36–41.

22. J. Zoltak, "Making Sure Customers Get Satisfaction Discussed at Stadium Managers Seminar." *Amusement Business* (February 16, 1998), Vol. 110, No. 7, pp. 4–5.

23. F. Kniggendorf, "Helping Supervisors Define Standards of Performance." *Human Resource Focus* (February 1998), Vol. 75, No. 2, pp. 13–14.

24. P. Lowe, "Maximized Management." *Success Yearbook* (Tampa, FL: Peter Lowe International, 1998), pp. 16–17.

25. M.L. Millenson, "3 Forces for Change: Money, Technology, and the Spirit of the Times Will Force Your Hand on Computer Systems

That Measure Quality." *Hospitals and Health Networks* (February 20, 1998), Vol. 72, No. 4, pp. 44–26.

26. J.P. Muczyk and R.P. Steel, "Leadership Style and the Turnaround Executive." *Business Horizons* (March/April 1998), Vol. 41, No. 2, pp. 39–47.

27. J. Talbott, L. Brack, and L. John, "Variance Analysis in a Service Business." *Planning Review (A Publication of the Planning Forum)* (May/June 1998), Vol. 16, No. 3, pp. 36–41.

28. R.F. Outcalt and P.M. Johnson, "The Myth of the 'Bottom Line'." *Boating Industry* (June 1998), Vol. 61, No. 6, pp. 50–53.

29. P. Lowe, "Maximized Management." *Success Yearbook* (Tampa, FL: Peter Lowe International, 1998), pp. 16–17.

30. I. Kilpatrick, "If It Isn't Read, It Isn't Right." *CA Magazine* (March 1998), Vol. 13, No. 2, pp. 33–36.

31. C. Brown, "The Bottom Line on Budgets." *Black Enterprise* (November 1995), Vol. 26, No. 4, pp. 40–41.

32. J. Talbott, L. Brack, and L. John, "Variance Analysis in a Service Business." *Planning Review (A Publication of the Planning Forum)* (May/June 1998), Vol. 16, No. 3, pp. 36–41.

33. Ibid.

34. C.W. Neale, "Successful New Product Development: A Capital Budgeting Perspective." *Journal of Marketing Management* (May 1994), Vol. 10, No. 4, pp. 283–297.

35. I. Kilpatrick, "If It Isn't Read, It Isn't Right." *CA Magazine* (March 1998), Vol. 13, No. 2, pp. 33–36.

36. Financial statement information is taken form the Modern Control, 1994 report to include actual figures rather than to reflect MOLON current financial position, which would always be outdated when published in a textbook.

37. P. Lowe, "Maximized Management." *Success Yearbook* (Tampa, FL: Peter Lowe International, 1998), pp. 16–17.

38. J.P. Muczyk and R.P. Steel, "Leadership Style and the Turnaround Executive." *Business Horizons* (March/April 1998), Vol. 41, No. 2, pp. 39–47.

39. R.F. Outcalt and P.M. Johnson, "The Myth of the 'Bottom Line'." *Boating Industry* (June 1998), Vol. 61, No. 6, pp. 50–53.

40. K. Blanchard and S. Bowles, "Get Gung Ho: To Create Boundless Enthusiasm, Catch Your Employees in the Act of Doing Something Right." *Success* (May 1998), Vol. 45, No. 5, pp. 30–32.

41. T. Pollock, "Attitudes That Can Help You Get Ahead: A Personal File of Stimulating Ideas, Little-known Facts and Daily Problem Solvers." *Supervision* (February 1998), Vol. 59, No. 2, pp. 24–27.

42. J.O. Burdett, "Forty Things Every Manager Should Know About Coaching." *Journal of Management and Development* (February/March 1998), Vol. 17, No. 2–3, pp. 142–153.

43. B.E. Ellig, "Employment and Employability." *Human Resource Management* (Summer 1998), Vol. 37, No. 2, pp. 173–176.

44. Lou Holtz, "Setting a Higher Standard." *Success Yearbook* (Tampa, FL: Peter Lowe International, 1998), p. 74.

45. P. Lowe, "Maximized Management." *Success Yearbook* (Tampa, FL: Peter Lowe International, 1998), pp. 16–17.

46. D.W. Farrant, "Take the Worry Out of Confronting." *Supervision* (March 1998), Vol. 59, No. 3, pp. 5–8.

47. S.E. Moss and M.J. Martinko, "The Effects of Performance Attributions and Outcome Dependence on Leader Feedback Behavior Following Poor Subordinate Performance." *Journal of Organizational Behavior* (May 1998), Vol. 19, No. 3, pp. 269–275.

48. K. Blanchard and S. Bowles, "Get Gung Ho: To Create Boundless Enthusiasm, Catch Your Employees in the Act of Doing Something Right." *Success* (May 1998), Vol. 45, No. 5, pp. 30–32.

49. S.E. Moss and M.J. Martinko, "The Effects of Performance Attributions and Outcome Dependence on Leader Feedback Behavior Following Poor Subordinate Performance." *Journal of Organizational Behavior* (May 1998), Vol. 19, No. 3, pp. 269–275.

50. T. Norvell, "From Goal-setting to Goal-getting: With a Little Help From Your Coach." *Journal of Property Management* (January/February 1998), Vol. 63, No. 1, pp. 14–16.

51. T. Peters and N. Austin, *A Passion for Excellence* (New York: Random House, 1985), pp. 378–392.

52. K.R. Phillips, "The Achilles' Heel of Coaching." *Training and Development* (March 1998), Vol. 52, No. 3, pp. 41–46.

53. C. Hymowitz, "Managing Your Career: Managers Struggle To Find a Way to Let Someone Go." *The Wall Street Journal*, July 28, 1998, p. B1.

54. D.W. Farrant, "Take the Worry Out of Confronting." *Supervision* (March 1998), Vol. 59, No. 3, pp. 5–8.

55. C. Hymowitz, "Managing Your Career: Managers Struggle To Find a Way to Let Someone Go." *The Wall Street Journal*, July 28, 1998, p. B1.

56. Ibid.

57. K.R. Phillips, "The Achilles' Heel of Coaching." *Training and Development* (March 1998), Vol. 52, No. 3, pp. 41–46.

58. Ibid.

59. C. Hymowitz, "Managing Your Career: Managers Struggle To Find a Way to Let Someone Go." *The Wall Street Journal*, July 28, 1998, p. B1.

60. L. Bowes-Sperry, J.F. Veiga, and J.N. Yanouzas, "An Analysis of Managerial Helping Responses Based on Social Role Theory." *Group & Organization Management* (December 1997), Vol. 22, No. 4, pp. 445–4

61. A. Thorlakson, "Performance Improvement Counseling." *Canadian Manager* (Winter 1997), Vol. 22, No. 4, pp. 16–18.

62. B.E. Ellig, "Employment and Employability." *Human Resource Management* (Summer 1998), Vol. 37, No. 2, pp. 173–176.

63. A.R. Trellis, "People Power." *Builder* (January 1998), Vol. 21, No. 1, pp. 302–303.

64. A. Thorlakson, "Performance Improvement Counseling." *Canadian Manager* (Winter 1997), Vol. 22, No. 4, pp. 16–18.

65. C. Hymowitz, "Managing Your Career: Managers Struggle To Find a Way to Let Someone Go." *The Wall Street Journal*, July 28, 1998, p. B1.

66. R. Reynes, "Programs That Aid Troubled Workers." *Nation's Business* (June 1998), Vol. 86, No. 6, pp. 73–75.

67. G.S. Cohen, L.H. Gard, and W.R. Heffernan, "Employee Assistance Programs: A Preventive, Cost-effective Benefit." *Journal of Health Care Finance* (Spring 1998), Vol. 24, No. 3, pp. 45–54.

68. C. Hymowitz, "Managing Your Career: Managers Struggle To Find a Way to Let Someone Go." *The Wall Street Journal*, July 28, 1998, p. B1.

69. T. Pollock, "Attitudes That Can Help You Get Ahead: A Personal File of Stimulating Ideas, Little-known Facts and Daily Problem Solvers." *Supervision* (February 1998), Vol. 59, No. 2, pp. 24–27.

70. R.D. Ramsey, "Guidelines for the Progressive Discipline of Employees." *Supervision* (February 1998), Vol. 59, No. 2, pp. 10–13.

71. B. Ely, "Productivity and Inflation." *Journal of Commerce and Commercial* (June 4, 1998), Vol. 416, No. 29234, pp. 7A–8A.

72. "Labor Productivity Fell." *The Wall Street Journal*, August 12, 1998, pp. A1–A2.

73. M. West and M. Patterson, "Profitable Personnel." *People Management* (January 1998), Vol. 4, No. 1, pp. 28–32.

74. "Interview With Bruce Rohde, CEO of ConAgra, Inc. HR as Major Source of Competitive Advantage." *Human Resources Management* (Spring 1998), Vol. 37, No. 1, pp. 85–89.

75. C. Miller, "The Achilles Syndrome: When High Potential Employees Choose to

Withdraw." *Supervision* (March 1998), Vol. 59, No. 3, pp. 3–5.

76. M. West and M. Patterson, "Profitable Personnel." *People Management* (January 1998), Vol. 4, No. 1, pp. 28–32.

77. "Team Accountability Needs to be Clear." (The Blanchard Management Report), *Manage* (February 1998), Vol. 49, No. 2, pp. 4–6.

78. B. Gill, "Flextime Benefits Employees and Employers." *American Printer* (February 1998), Vol. 220, No. 5, pp. 70–71.

79. M. Apgar IV, "The Alternative Workplace: Changing Where and How People Work." *Harvard Business Review* (May/June 1998), Vol. 76, No. 3, pp. 121–137.

80. T. Barkin and M. Horn, "The Labor Lever Strategy." *Airline Business* (January 1998), Vol. 14, No. 1, pp. 46–50.

Chapter 15

1. Information taken from PepsiCo's 1997 Annual Report.

2. R.W. Schmenner, "Operations Management." *Business Horizons* (May/June 1998), Vol. 41, No. 3, pp. 3–5.

3. N. Gross, "Leapfrogging a Few Links." *Business Week* (June 22, 1998), No. 3583, pp. 140–142.

4. J. Jayaram and S.K. Vickery, "Supply-based Strategies, Human Resource Initiatives, Procurement Lead-time, and Firm Performance." *International Journal of Purchasing and Materials Management* (Winter 1998), Vol. 34, No. 1, pp. 12–24.

5. J. Jayaram and S.K. Vickery, "Supply-based Strategies, Human Resource Initiatives, Procurement Lead-time, and Firm Performance." *International Journal of Purchasing and Materials Management* (Winter 1998), Vol. 34, No. 1, pp. 12–24.

6. R.W. Grubbstrom and J. Olhager, "Productivity and Flexibility: Fundamental Relations Between Two Major Properties and Performance Measures of the Production System." *International Journal of Production Economics* (October 15, 1997), Vol. 52, No. 1–2, pp. 73–83.

7. M. Larson, "CAD to CMM: It's All in the Translation." *Quality* (June 1998), Vol. 37, No. 6, pp. 30–35.

8. "From Screen to Machine: Profitability by Design." *Textile World* (May 1998), Vol. 148, No. 5, pp. 58–67.

9. G. Wilson, "Changing the Process of Production." *Industrial Management* (January/February 1995), Vol. 37, No. 1, pp. 1–3.

10. G. Nairn, "Issues of Life and Death." *The Financial Times*, April 1, 1998, pp. FTS9–10.

11. R.W. Grubbstrom and J. Olhager, "Productivity and Flexibility: Fundamental Relations Between Two Major Properties and Performance Measures of the Production System." *International Journal of Production Economics* (October 15, 1997), Vol. 52, No. 1–2, pp. 73–83.

12. P. Eriksson and K. Rosanen, "The Bitter and the Sweet: Evolving Constellations of Product Mix Management in a Confectionery Company." (Faze Confectionery), *European Journal of Marketing* (March/April 1998), Vol. 32, No. 2, pp. 279–305.

13. J. Jayaram and S. Ahire, "Impact of Operations Management Practices on Quality and Time-based Performance." *International Journal of Quality and Reliability Management* (February/March 1998), Vol. 15, No. 2–3, pp. 192–205.

14. W.C. Chiang and C. Chiang, "Intelligent Local Search Strategies for Solving Facility Layout Problems with the Quadratic Assignment Problem Formulation." *European Journal of Operational Research* (April 16, 1998), Vol. 106, No. 2–3, pp. 457–489.

15. R.W. Grubbstrom and J. Olhager, "Productivity and Flexibility: Fundamental Relations Between Two Major Properties and Performance Measures of the Production System." *International Journal of Production Economics* (October 15, 1997), Vol. 52, No. 1–2, pp. 73–83.

16. Z. Drezner, G.O. Wesolowsky, and T. Drezner, "On the Logit Approach to Competitive Facility Location." *Journal of Regional Science* (May 1998), Vol. 38, No. 2, pp. 331–328.

17. J.C. Ridge, S.K. Jones, M.S. Nielsen, and A.K. Shahani, "Capacity Planning for Intensive Care Units." *European Journal of Operational Research* (March 1, 1998), Vol. 105, No. 2, pp. 346–356.

18. A. Gunasekaran, S.K. Goyal, T. Martikainen, and P. Yli-Olli, "Production Capacity Planning and Control in Multi-stage Manufacturing." *Journal of Operational Research Society* (June 1998), Vol. 49, No. 6, pp. 625–635.

19. Ibid.

20. B. Lamons, "'Just Do it' Managers Must Start Planning Ahead." (Advertising to Business), *Marketing News* (February 2, 1998), Vol. 32, No. 3, pp. 10–11.

21. "Balancing People, Places and Times." (IT Tools Aid Health Care Scheduling)(Technology Information), *Health Management Technology* (June 1998), Vol. 19, No. 7, pp. 26–32.

22. B. Lamons, "'Just Do it' Managers Must Start Planning Ahead." (Advertising to Business), *Marketing News* (February 2, 1998), Vol. 32, No. 3, pp. 10–11.

23. J. Jayaram and S. Ahire, "Impact of Operations Management Practices on Quality and Time-based Performance." *International Journal of Quality and Reliability Management* (February/March 1998), Vol. 15, No. 2–3, pp. 192–205.

24. M. Imai, "Will America's Corporate Theme Song Be 'Just In Time?'" (Production Management), *The Journal for Quality and Participation* (March/April 1998), Vol. 21, No. 2, pp. 26–39.

25. R. Germain and C. Droge, "The Context, Organizational Design, and Performance of JIT Buying Versus Non-JIT Buying Firms." *International Journal of Purchasing and Materials Management* (Spring 1998), Vol. 34, No. 2, pp. 12–19.

26. P.E. Spedding, "Revisiting Time-phased Order Points in the Health Care Industry." *IIE Solutions* (February 1998), Vol. 30, No. 2, pp. 22–25.

27. F. Fazel, K.P. Fischer, and E.W. Gilbert, "JIT Purchasing vs. EOQ with a Price Discount: An Analytical Comparison of Inventory Costs." (Comparison of Economic Order Quantity Model and Just-In-Time Techniques), *International Journal of Production Economics* (January 5, 1998), Vol. 54, No. 1, pp. 101–110.

28. B. Schneider, S.S. White, and M.C. Paul, "Linking Service Climate and Customer Perceptions of Service Quality: Test of a Causal Model." *Journal of Applied Psychology* (April 1998), Vol. 83, No. 2, pp. 150–164.

29. M.S. Spencer and L.K. Duclos, "TQM Stresses MIS: The Ache of Continuous Change." *Mid-American Journal of Business* (Spring 1998), Vol. 13, No. 1, pp. 59–65.

30. S.F. Ferris, R. Quint, and R. Sant, "Financial Theory and Practice in the Application of TQM: The Case of IBM Rochester." *Journal of Managerial Issues* (Spring 1998), Vol. 10, No. 1, pp. 13–30.

31. D. McAbe and A. Wilkinson, "The Rise and Fall of TQM: The Vision, Meaning and Operation of Change." (Total Quality Management), *Industrial Relations Journal* (March 1998), Vol. 29, No. 1, pp. 18–30.

32. B. Schneider, S.S. White, and M.C. Paul, "Linking Service Climate and Customer Perceptions of Service Quality: Test of a Causal Model." *Journal of Applied Psychology* (April 1998), Vol. 83, No. 2, pp. 150–164.

33. T.Y. Lee, "The Development of ISO 9000 Certification and the Future of Quality Management." *International Journal of Quality & Reliability Management* (February/March 1998), Vol. 15, No. 2–3, pp. 162–178.

34. Ibid.

35. R. Mullin, "A New Charge for Management Adrift Copy of the Revised ISO 9000." *Chemical*

Week (May 20, 1998), Vol. 160, No. 19, pp. 56–57.

36. B.E. Withers, M. Ebrahimpour, and N. Hikmet, "An Exploration of the Impact of TQM and JIT on ISO 9000 Registered Companies." *International Journal of Production Economics* (November 20, 1997), Vol. 53, No. 2, pp. 208–217.

37. R. Mullin, "A New Charge for Management Adrift Copy of the Revised ISO 9000." *Chemical Week* (May 20, 1998), Vol. 160, No. 19, pp. 56–57.

38. S. Daniels, "Department of Agriculture Uses ISO 9000 to Monitor Quality of Meat Products." (International Standards Organization), *Quality Progress* (June 1998), Vol. 31, No. 6, pp. 16–18.

39. "A Workplace Code." *The Wall Street Journal*, July 21, 1998, p. A1.

40. R. Swanekamp, "Does ISO 14000 Add Value?" *Power* (April 1998), Vol. 142, No. 2, pp. 31–14.

41. N. Chase, "Managers Make Training Stick." *Quality* (April 1998), Vol. 37, No. 4, pp. 188–189.

42. R. Fink and T. Margavio, "Economic Models for Single Sample Acceptance Sampling Plans." *Decision Sciences* (July/August 1994), Vol. 25, No. 4, pp. 625–654.

43. J. Mehring, "Achieving Multiple Timelines Goals for Auto Loans." *Interfaces* (July/August 1995), Vol. 25, No. 4, pp. 81–92.

44. S. Trussler, "The Rules of the Game." *Journal of Business Strategy* (January/February 1998), Vol. 19, No. 1, pp. 16–20.

45. "Former ASAE Leaders Share Tips." (Time Management: American Society of Association Executives) (Leader to Leader Column), *Association Management* (January 1998), Vol. 50, No. 1, pp. 23–24.

46. L.J. Bassi and M.E. Van Buren, "The 1998 ASTD State of the Industry Report." *Training and Development* (January 1998), Vol. 52, No. 1, pp. 21–44.

47. P. Lowe, "How to Boost Your Market Value." *Success Yearbook* (Tampa, FL: Peter Lowe International, 1998), pp. 22–23.

48. P.C. Chu, "Conceiving Strategic Systems." *Journal of Systems Management* (July/August 1995), Vol. 46, No. 4, pp. 36–42.

49. Ibid.

50. Ibid.

51. C. Babcock, "New World Demands New Skills." *Computerworld*, November 27, 1995, pp. 126–127.

52. T.L. Greenbaum, "Avoiding a 'Virtual' Disaster." *HR Focus* (February 1998), Vol. 75, No. 2, pp. 11–13.

53. M. Apgar IV, "The Alternative Workplace: Changing Where and How People Work." *Harvard Business Review* (May/June 1998), Vol. 76, No. 3, pp. 121–137.

54. "Telecommuting Grows." (US Telecommuters 1990 and 1997)(Industry Trend or Event)(Illustration), *Computerworld* (June 22, 1998), Vol. 32, No. 25, pp. 63–64.

55. K. Hildebrand, "Managing Telecommuters." *Colorado Business Magazine* (March 1998), Vol. 25, No. 3, pp. 48–50.

56. M.J. Cronin, "Ford's Intranet Success." *Fortune* (March 30, 1998), Vol. 137, No. 6, pp. 158–159.

57. N. Gross, "Leapfrogging a Few Links." *Business Week* (June 22, 1998), No. 3583, pp. 140–142.

58. S. Rupley, "Era of the Low-Cost PC." *PC Magazine* (July 1998), Vol. 17, No. 17, pp. 28–29.

59. "IBM's Chairman Promised." *The Wall Street Journal*, January 23, 1996, p. 1.

Internet Index

Company Index

Name Index

Subject Index